Praise for a previous edition

'Written by a team of authors working across both academia and government, *Behavioral Insights for Public Policy* examines how psychology can be applied to a range of public policy areas. The reader addresses a wide variety of concepts and cases from the origins of policy, as well as major findings from behavioural economics and nudge theory. It also presents applications of behavioural insights into health, wealth and finance, the consumer, energy and the environment, education, and the workplace, as well as public engagement.'

Journal of Consumer Policy

Psychology and Behavioral Economics

Psychology and Behavioral Economics offers an expert introduction to how psychology can be applied to a range of public policy areas. It examines the impact of psychological research for public policymaking in economic, financial, and consumer sectors; in education, healthcare, and the workplace; for energy and the environment; and in communications.

Your energy bills show you how much you use compared to the average household in your area. Your doctor sends you a text message reminder when your appointment is coming up. Your bank gives you three choices for how much to pay off on your credit card each month. Wherever you look, there has been a rapid increase in the importance we place on understanding real human behaviors in everyday decisions, and these behavioral insights are now regularly used to influence everything from how companies recruit employees through to large-scale public policy and government regulation. But what is the actual evidence behind these tactics, and how did psychology become such a major player in economics? Answering these questions and more, this team of authors, working across both academia and government, present this fully revised and updated reworking of *Behavioral Insights for Public Policy*.

This update covers everything from how policy was historically developed, to major research in human behavior and social psychology, to key moments that brought behavioral sciences to the forefront of public policy. Featuring over 100 empirical examples of how behavioral insights are being used to address some of the most critical challenges faced globally, the book covers key topics such as evidence-based policy, a brief history of behavioral and decision sciences, behavioral economics, and policy evaluation, all illustrated throughout with lively case studies.

Including end-of-chapter questions, a glossary, and key concept boxes to aid retention, as well as a new chapter revealing the work of the Canadian government's behavioral insights unit, this is the perfect textbook for students of psychology, economics, public health, education, and organizational sciences, as well as for public policy professionals looking for fresh insight into the underlying theory and practical applications in a range of public policy areas.

Kai Ruggeri is Assistant Professor in the Department of Health Policy and Management, Mailman School of Public Health at Columbia University, USA. He also founded the Policy Research Group at the University of Cambridge, UK, which is now part of the Centre for Business Research in the Judge Business School. His research focuses on population-level behaviors and how to better use these in public policy to reduce economic inequality and improve population well-being.

Psychology and Behavioral Economics

Applications for Public Policy

Second Edition

Edited by Kai Ruggeri

Routledge
Taylor & Francis Group
LONDON AND NEW YORK

Second edition published 2022
by Routledge
2 Park Square, Milton Park, Abingdon, Oxon, OX14 4RN

and by Routledge
605 Third Avenue, New York, NY 10158

Routledge is an imprint of the Taylor & Francis Group, an informa business

First edition published by Routledge 2019

British Library Cataloguing-in-Publication Data
A catalogue record for this book is available from the British Library

Library of Congress Cataloging-in-Publication Data
Names: Ruggeri, Kai, editor.
Title: Psychology and behavioral economics : applications for public policy / edited by Kai Ruggeri.
Other titles: Behavioral insights for public policy.
Description: Second edition. | Abingdon, Oxon ; New York, NY : Routledge, 2022. | Earlier edition published in 2019 as: Behavioral insights for public policy : concepts and cases. | Includes bibliographical references and index.
Identifiers: LCCN 2021014489 (print) | LCCN 2021014490 (ebook) | ISBN 9781032005409 (paperback) | ISBN 9781032021058 (hardback) | ISBN 9781003181873 (ebook)
Subjects: LCSH: Policy sciences – Psychological aspects. | Economics – Psychological aspects. | Political planning – Psychological aspects. | Psychology, Applied.
Classification: LCC H97 .P7745 2022 (print) | LCC H97 (ebook) | DDC 320.6 – dc23
LC record available at https://lccn.loc.gov/2021014489
LC ebook record available at https://lccn.loc.gov/2021014490

ISBN: 978-1-032-02105-8 (hbk)
ISBN: 978-1-032-00540-9 (pbk)
ISBN: 978-1-003-18187-3 (ebk)

DOI: 10.4324/9781003181873

Typeset in Minion Pro
by Apex CoVantage, LLC

With this work, we seek to support, train, and inspire the next generation of behavioral researchers, policymakers, and professionals. This is critical because not every person in the world is so fortunate to have individuals that enable them to choose their own path in life. For how they made it possible for one person, the following pages are dedicated to Mary Anne Forbes, who pushes you to be the absolute truest version of yourself in your youth, and to Joan M Ruggeri, a consigliere, backstop, financial guru, and role model for every major adult decision. If anyone wondered if always-rational, financially savvy, retirement-savings-ready, and – critically – loving family icons truly exist, I assure you, she does.

Contents

Figures

Tables

Boxes

Contributors

Jascha Achterberg University of Cambridge, UK

Thomas Lind Andersen Svendborg Municipality, Denmark

Amel Benzerga Sciences Po, France, and Kantar Health

Jana B. Berkessel University of Cologne, Germany

Philipe M. Bujold Center for Behavior and the Environment, Rare

Filippo Cavassini Organisation for Economic Cooperation and Development, France

Alessia Cottone University of Nottingham, UK

Clair Davison University of St Andrews, UK

Emir Demić University of Belgrade, Serbia

Julia Dhar Boston Consulting Group, USA

Hamish Evans RAND Europe, UK

Tomas Folke Columbia University, USA

Maja Friedemann University of Oxford, UK

Matteo M. Galizzi London School of Economics, UK

Shannon P. Gibson Oxford Brookes University, UK

Johanna Graeber Kiel University, Germany

Elizabeth Hardy Behavioral Insights and Experimentation Team, Privy Council, Government of Canada

Marlene Hecht Humboldt University of Berlin, Germany

Renata Hlavová Masaryk University, Czech Republic

Johanna Emilia Immonen University of Helsinki, Finland

Jon M. Jachimowicz Harvard University, USA

Hannes Jarke University of Cambridge, UK

Ondřej Kácha Masaryk University, Czech Republic

Ralitsa Karakasheva University of Nottingham, UK

Haris Khan Behavioral Insights and Experimentation Team, Privy Council, Government of Canada

Jakub M. Krawiec SWPS University of Social Sciences and Humanities, Poland

Marvin Kunz University of Groningen, The Netherlands

Wing Yi Lam University of Kent, UK

Matthew Lee Columbia University, USA

Yuna S. M. Lee Columbia University, USA

Mary MacLennan London School of Economics, UK

Fadi Makki Nudge Lebanon, Lebanon

Silvana Mareva University of Cambridge, UK

Mafalda Fontinha Mascarenhas University of Lisbon, Portugal, and ISPA University Institute, Portugal

Sara Morales Izquierdo University of Warwick, UK, and Basque Center on Cognition, Brain and Language, Spain

Faisal Naru Organisation for Economic Cooperation and Development, France

Olatz Ojinaga-Alfageme Birkbeck, University of London, UK

Meera Paleja Behavioral Insights and Experimentation Team, Privy Council, Government of Canada

Francesca Papa Organisation for Economic Co-operation and Development, France

Alessandro F. Paul Leiden University, The Netherlands

Dafina Petrova University of Granada, Spain

Nejc Plohl University of Maribor, Slovenia

Sahana K. Quail University of Oxford, UK

Carly D. Robinson Harvard University, USA

Enrico Rubaltelli University of Padova, Italy

Kai Ruggeri Columbia University, USA, and University of Cambridge, UK

Rachel C. Shelton Columbia University, USA

Kamilla Knutsen Steinnes University of Oslo, Norway, and Oslo Metropolitan University, Norway

Julia P. Stuhlreyer University Medical Center Hamburg-Eppendorf, Germany

Felicia Sundström Uppsala University, Sweden

Felice L. Tavera University of Cologne, Germany

Markus R. Tünte University of Vienna, Austria

Jay Van Bavel New York University, USA

Sander van der Linden University of Cambridge, UK

Bojana Većkalov University of Amsterdam, The Netherlands

Sanne Verra Columbia University, USA, and Utrecht University, The Netherlands

Ashley Whillans Harvard Business School, USA

Manou Willems Maastricht University, The Netherlands

Aleksandra Yosifova New Bulgarian University, Bulgaria

Zorana Zupan University of Belgrade, Serbia

About this book

The following textbook has been compiled to assist in the teaching and learning of behavioral science, particularly its history, critical theories and findings, and applications to many areas of public policy. It was compiled in line with the tone and style of many of the pioneering works in the subject, not to imitate, but to pay homage to the influential contributions made by those cited throughout the volume. To expand coverage, salient features are presented in text and visuals, but further study of original writings on each case is strongly encouraged, as well as attempts at replication of any insights or arguments presented.

Contributors to the volume range from early career researchers still involved in academic study through to globally recognized, established authors. This has been done to ensure that material is relevant for those who wish to utilize the content as well as engaging for those who may not have studied it before. This is to match the importance of the topic, as it has become increasingly influential in how policies are made given the critical mass now accumulated in the subject. That mass is what made this volume valuable to those who chose to engage in writing it.

The timing of this volume is both early in the life of the field yet concurrent with major recent applications of behavioral insights in national and international policies, regulations, and laws. These have been influenced by psychologists interested in economics, economists interested in behavior, and community leaders interested in innovative policies for better population outcomes. As such, this book has been compiled and produced to educate, engage, and inspire the next wave of behavioral scientists and as a teaching reference for those responsible for their development, as well as for those interested in directly applying evidence to the development and application of policy.

Should any errors be found, the editor welcomes recommended corrections be sent to kai.ruggeri@columbia.edu for resolution in future volumes.

Foreword

In Michael Lewis' best-selling book *Moneyball*, he describes how the Oakland Athletics baseball team made a risky – and revolutionary – move away from the ancient traditions of the sport. Instead of relying on the well-honed intuitions of professional baseball scouts to evaluate talent and draft players, the team management decided to rely on quantitative assessments of players. They determined what predicted individual success and team success on the field by crunching the numbers. In many cases, this put them in conflict with their own scouts and coaching staff. In the end, this approach marked a radical transition for the team and, indeed, for the entire sport.

By relying on hard data (and often overruling the eyes and ears of their scouting staff), the Athletics were able to draft and trade for unsung gems. They built a team that far exceeded expectations (as well as the meager payroll provided by ownership). Eventually, other teams started catching on. And, with the publication of *Moneyball*, other sports and industries began to retool their thinking. They shifted aggressively away from the tradition of intuitive decisions and toward a scientific approach that mirrored the traditions in the behavioral sciences.

In many ways, public policy has mirrored the approach of professional baseball. It has relied on politicians, their advisors, and practitioners to guide hugely consequential decisions. This book marks the same radical departure from that tradition as the Oakland Athletics. Ruggeri and colleagues rely on the science of psychology and behavioral economics to rethink public policy across a range of issues. Drawing on over 100 different empirical examples, they reveal how a data-driven approach can offer critical insights into the development and application of policy.

In many cases, the data line up with your intuitions. But having the intuition and knowing it is correct are two entirely different things. In other cases, the data shed surprising – and even radical – new insights into what might work. As we try to address some of the most critical challenges facing humanity, from the current global pandemic to the specter of catastrophic climate change, it will be indispensable to do it with our eyes open and clearly on the relevant facts. This is why *Psychology and Behavioral Economics* should be required reading for anyone from psychology, economics, and social science, with an interest in developing policy. It is long past time to leave our intuitions behind and leverage the growing toolbox of behavioral science to help us repair the social, political, and economic problems in society.

Prof. Jay Van Bavel,
New York University

Acknowledgments

The editor and authors wish to acknowledge a number of colleagues and institutions for their support in completing this second edition. First, we specifically thank a number of authors who contributed to the first edition, from which this volume was built, including Joe J. Gladstone, Andrijana Radukić, and David Rosenthal.

We also thank the UKRI-ESRC Research for Healthcare in Conflict-MENA, as well as Hannah Pütz, Gerhard Prinz, Andrijana Radukic', William McClanahan, Bhaven Sampat, Brian Head, Michael Howlett, Mari Louise Berge, Nastja Tomat, Keying Wang, Annalisa Robbiani, Matija Franklin, Amel Benzerga, Kamilla Knutsen Steinnes, Gerhard Prinz, Nejc Plohl, Felicia Sundström, Ludvig Bjørndal, Richard Griffith, Julia Stuhlreyer, Felicia Huppert, Dave Nussbaum, Frederick W. Thielen, Amiran Gelashvili, Filippo Cavassini, Faisal Naru, Alessandra Luna Navarro, and Abby Scott. We would further like to thank Luisa Braun for her concept and the initial draft of the cover design.

Editorial note

Since the 2000s, behavioral sciences – and really, all empirical sciences – have had to confront concerns about the replicability, transparency, and accessibility of research in their disciplines. Whether this related to long-standing, seminal theories and frameworks or just everyday studies, scientific conclusions have been scrutinized for lacking clarity in methods, for ambiguous and changing goalposts regarding findings and hypotheses, and for making grand claims based on limited data. Much of this has been discussed in the context of the so-called "replication crisis."

Whether or not you view these concerns as a crisis, there is little doubt that ever-increasing standards for science are a good thing. This is especially true for studies with immediate relevance for applications to the real world, such as policy, medicine, justice, and education. In this second edition of the book, we introduce over 200 cases of behavioral science in action. To the extent possible, we emphasize those studies that were tested in the real world with large samples and reproducible methods. For those that have been influential but concerns exist about the original methods, we try to include constructive warnings about how far to generalize the conclusions. We try to always emphasize the learning aspects alongside important limitations or opportunities to add to the robustness of the insights, particularly if sample sizes are small, effects are not particularly meaningful, concerns exist about the reliability, or the overall study power is not sufficient for broad generalization.

In some cases, fundamental theories originate from studies that predate these standards by decades, when the mass accumulation of data was not possible for behavioral researchers. Again, we aim to present these studies for teaching and instructional purposes, but the reader should always maintain a critical eye for limitations or opportunities to add to the robustness of those findings. Many of the authors of this book not only share this view but are directly contributing to attempts to replicate and reevaluate a number of these findings.[1] On top of investing ourselves into moving the field forward through those efforts, we also hope that raising this point will encourage readers to promote the best methodological practices if they aim to test or implement these concepts in their own work.

We also note that there are genuine and legitimate concerns about the use of psychological research to "change behaviors," irrespective of consent or individual autonomy. Certain approaches can appear unethical, particularly where it implies individuals or institutions empower themselves to determine what choices should be made by others. Wherever possible, we have aimed to present information without giving these impressions, and certainly we strongly endorse rigid ethical oversight, transparency, humility, and rigor in all work related to behavioral applications to policy. If any writing in this volume implies otherwise, we can assure readers it is merely a matter of sentence structure; we do not endorse any argument that implies misdirection or coercion, nor that behavioral policy implies a level of perfection in determining what choice is best for everyone. Instead, we refer you to the Golden Rule presented in Chapter 13.

Note

1 See Ruggeri, K., Alí, S., Berge, M. L., Bertoldo, G., Bjørndal, L. D., Cortijos-Bernabeu, A., . . . Folke, T. (2020). Replicating patterns of Prospect Theory for decision under risk. *Nature Human Behaviour, 4*(6), 622–633; Ruggeri, K., Većkalov, B., Bojanić, L., Andersen, T. L., Ashcroft-Jones, S., Ayacaxli, N., . . . & Folke, T. (2021). The general fault in our fault lines. *Nature Human Behaviour*, 1–11.

1 Psychology and policy

Kai Ruggeri, Kamilla Knutsen Steinnes,
Maja Friedemann, and Fadi Makki

Chapter summary

To reach desirable outcomes within a population, we regularly rely on *policies*: population-based interventions aiming to optimize outcomes through guiding behaviors and decisions. Policies are developed for use by anyone from individuals and families to large groups and major organizations. While often considered a nebulous system of complex processes used by governments, policies are often very simple guidelines and can relate to very basic, everyday activities. This chapter introduces core concepts of policy, how it is distinct from – yet overlaps with – laws and regulations, the historical development of policy, and the making of policies as an area of scientific interest. This chapter sets the tone for the book, framing key terms and topics critical to maximizing the value of every section through the contributions of psychological and behavioral sciences to policy.

Learning objectives

- Gain an understanding of what policy is and what it is not
- Be able to describe what policies do
- Get a firm grasp on why policies matter
- Appreciate the history behind how policies came to be a major area of scientific research
- Explore the link between policies and psychological sciences

Introduction

Every waking moment of every day, people are faced with decisions. Once we make those choices, we then live them out through our behaviors. Many of us will have a set time we decide to wake up each morning, something that we base on our personal experience of getting ready for school or for work as well as how much sleep we need. That decision will influence almost everything throughout the day, as well as when to

DOI: 10.4324/9781003181873-1

set the time for waking up the following day once we have made the decision to go to sleep that evening.

Decisions we have to make vary between the most mundane choices about whether to wash our hands after we use the restroom and the most complex, multilayered processes involved with piloting a commercial airliner. With every decision we face, we confront contingencies related to its success, accuracy, efficiency, and influence on other people or aspects of our lives (Beach & Mitchell, 1978; Simon, 1957b).

Confident in our decisions?

But can we, as individuals, groups, or even entire populations, be confident making those decisions day in and day out? The average person may consume three full meals in a day, but is every meal equally planned and sufficiently healthy? On what basis do we choose the food we eat, when we eat, or how much we eat? When we take a moment to consider how directly our food consumption impacts almost everything about our health, it is exasperating to realize how little time we actually put into making such choices. The rational response to this is that it would be entirely unrealistic to put substantial amounts of time into making those decisions given we do it three times in a day, 21 times in a week, and possibly 11,000 times in a decade. Evolution has shown that humans are typically very good at making such choices as a species long term (Kenrick et al., 2009), as well as at adapting when supplies are short or commodities change (Payne, Bettman, & Johnson, 1988). However, there is reason to explore just how efficient and reliable we are in the ways we approach and decide on just about every behavior we make (Tversky & Kahneman, 1985).

When we are confronted with a choice, we are essentially tasked with comparing outcomes on the basis of the information we have, such as the probability of the best chance to "win" or the risk of "losing" (Kahneman & Tversky, 1984). Unfortunately, as will be discussed in Chapter 4, psychologists and statisticians have found that our understanding of probabilities and risks are limited in any context, even when simple numbers are provided to reduce complexity (Payzan-LeNestour & Bossaerts, 2011).

In 2008, 25 percent of American and 28 percent of German participants in a comparative national survey gave an incorrect answer when responding to the question, *Which of the following numbers represents the biggest risk of getting a disease? 1 in 100, 1 in 1,000, or 1 in 10?* (Galesic & Garcia-Retamero, 2010). How can such a large portion of the population get such a simple question – with such clear importance – wrong? If we are able to determine the difference between 10, 100, and 1,000, why should we be less successful in distinguishing 1/10, 1/100, and 1/1,000? If one-quarter of the population cannot discern something as basic as 0.1 (1/10 – the correct answer) being a much greater risk than 0.01 (1/100) or 0.001 (1/1,000), what threat does that pose to us as individuals and communities where we are faced with far more complex choices on a regular basis?

Much of this has been understood within **bounded rationality**, a concept developed by the economist Herbert Simon in his 1957 book *Models of Man*. Bounded rationality suggests that, while we may desire to give ourselves the best chance at a successful outcome, in the face of uncertainty and risk, we tend to make choices on the basis of our gut feeling or intuition (Gigerenzer & Selten, 2002). In the earlier example, it is presumed that many of those who chose incorrectly simply saw the larger numbers of 1,000 or 100 and quickly assessed them as being greater than 10. Rather than recognizing that they were denominators, participants' immediate response was that they presented larger values.

Beyond reliance on **confidence** or our **gut feeling** – the initial belief, reaction, or preference when confronted with information where an opinion, choice, or disposition is required, which may result in **implicit bias** (Jolls & Sunstein, 2006) – decision-making can be heavily biased by a number of other factors that may appear **irrational** (Spiegelhalter, Pearson, & Short, 2011). When we decide to buy a cup of coffee on our way to work every weekday, we are making a decision based on our previous experience of both having coffee (positive) and not having coffee (disastrous – for some), even if it causes us to be late for work or we realize the total cost in a year for buying coffee every day. When we skip our usual cigarette break at work because a new colleague mentioned how unhealthy smoking is, our choice is being influenced by the opinion of others. In the long run, we might decide to quit smoking altogether due to social norms and cultural views instead of the negative impact of smoking on physical health.

Our everyday decisions are also affected by our current emotional state. We might opt out of buying a new computer because a pushy salesperson evokes a negative emotional response such as anger or frustration. We might, however, purchase an identical product at another store after a more positive interaction with a different salesperson. Another factor that can influence decisions is level of perceived control. Students who perceive they have little control over the outcome (exam grade) of their decisions (study vs. watch TV) are less likely to try (choose studying over watching TV) than students who believe they have more control (Ajzen, 2002a). Thus, decision-making is susceptible to various extraneous influences that may seem illogical given they do not change the options being chosen from.

Intuitive choices, such as opting to eat breakfast before leaving the house, work well for us most of the time (Kenrick et al., 2009). However, they are not always optimal when we need to make more deliberate, calculated decisions (Kahneman, 2003b), such as when deciding between different medical treatments or making a choice among alternative financial loans. During these times, we are more likely to make use of risk estimates in the form of probabilities to aid our decision-making (Payzan-LeNestour & Bossaerts, 2011). For example, a cancer patient choosing between different treatment options might ask their doctor for the probability of each treatment's recovery prognosis and make their final decision on the basis of a deliberate evaluation of which treatment has the best chance of helping them recover.

Unfortunately, as mentioned earlier, probabilities pose a notorious challenge in terms of successfully conveying them to the general population and even to experts (Spiegelhalter et al., 2011). For example, in one classic experiment, medical doctors were asked to interpret the outcomes of mammography tests carried out to check for breast cancer among patients (Eddy, 1982). A large majority of the participating doctors confused the test's sensitivity (the proportion of positive test results among women with breast cancer) with the test's positive predictive value (the proportion of women with the breast cancer among those who received a positive test result). Thus, even people having rigorous training and expertise in a particular domain are subject to such decision-making fallacies. This difficulty with understanding probabilities – which is evident in experts and laypeople alike – affects our ability to make rational decisions (Hoffrage, Lindsey, Hertwig, & Gigerenzer, 2000).

So how confident can – and should – we really be in our ability to make good, rational choices? Going back quite a few years, multiple studies suggest that the confidence people have in their decisions exceeds their ability in terms of knowledge and judgment (e.g. Gigerenzer, Hoffrage, & Kleinbolting, 1991; Fast, Sivanathan, Mayer, & Galinsky, 2012; Alpert & Raiffa, 1982; Soll & Klayman, 2004; Pallier et al., 2002). This overconfidence tendency applies to both experts and laypeople (Einhorn & Hogarth, 1978). Students, for example, tend to overestimate their own performance on academic exams (Clayson, 2005), and most car drivers believe they are above average compared to other drivers (Svenson, 1981). People, in general, overestimate their time needed to complete tasks (Buehler, Griffin, & Ross, 1994), and the more difficult the task, the more likely people are to be overconfident (Lichtenstein, Fischhoff, & Phillips, 1982). More specifically, difficult tasks lead people to overestimate their actual performance on the task, while also incorrectly thinking they performed worse on it compared to others. Easy tasks, on the other hand, result in people underestimating their actual performance on the task, while incorrectly thinking they performed better on it compared to others (Moore & Healy, 2008). In sum, overconfidence appears to be a very common tendency in populations. Thus, one potential option to improve outcomes for populations is via guiding decisions and behaviors – whether tedious and seemingly inconsequential or complex and impactful – through policy.

What is policy?

So how can we confront our tendency to be misguided in our decisions? We often rely on a set of guidelines when faced with a decision (Jamieson & Giraldez, 2017). This is particularly true if that choice is significant or something we repeat regularly, such as deciding on a time to set our alarm clock every morning. These guidelines may not force one particular choice over another, but they provide a *process* to ensure the optimum choice is made, typically by including mechanisms that highlight better choices and safeguard against mistakes or higher risk options. When these are used across a group to the extent that everyone in that particular situation is influenced in some way, even if they do not abide, we consider these **policies**: population-based interventions that aim to guide behavior to the optimum outcome in the most efficient way over the life span of the choice (Ruggeri, 2017a).

Through guiding decisions, policies seek to either **optimize** (gaining the most through using up the least of finite resources, such as going to the market and buying the most food for the least money) or **maximize** (achieving the greatest result based on available resources, typically irrespective of expense, such as a traditional chess match, where the ultimate indicator is taking the opponent's king not how many pieces you have remaining when it happens) outcomes.[1] That is, policies aim to achieve the best practices or consistently repeated behavior, as often as possible. Hence, policies are sets of behaviors, decisions, and standards used by a group when dealing with significant or common challenges. Consistent approaches are therefore necessary to ensure the most ideal outcome, whether quantifiable, ideological, or simply for reliability.

At their most tangible level, policies are structured attempts to approach critical choices and practices that will have significant implications across a population (Schneider & Ingram, 1990). In these scenarios, they may be informed by a variety of sources while being carried out by a plurality of stakeholders, all by design. At their most basic, policies may be unwritten codes of practice that result in consistent actions or series of steps when a group or individual faces a common choice or obstacle (Schneider & Ingram, 1990). This may be as fundamental as deciding to wake up one hour before work every morning to get ready for the day ahead. We might think of a policy as a **lever** (see Box 1.1) that can be pulled to alter individual-, group-, or population-level behavior (Schneider & Ingram, 1990). Different policies are targeted toward different **populations** of interest, which may be individuals, groups, organizations, or the general public (Ruggeri, 2017a). Populations can, however, be established by design or by default (Howlett, Mukherjee, & Woo, 2015), as there are an infinite number of such potential tactics held by a complex overlap of individuals and groups (Ruggeri, 2017a).

BOX 1.1 POLICY LEVERS

Levers can be seen as the actions (interventions, policies) that identify specific areas for improvement, accounting for significant risks and contextual factors, leading to a population-level change if implemented as a (1) policy. The figure below represents the levers as (4) behavioral interventions that have (3) considered environments and exposures following the (2) identification of strengths and weaknesses in an educational intervention between age groups.

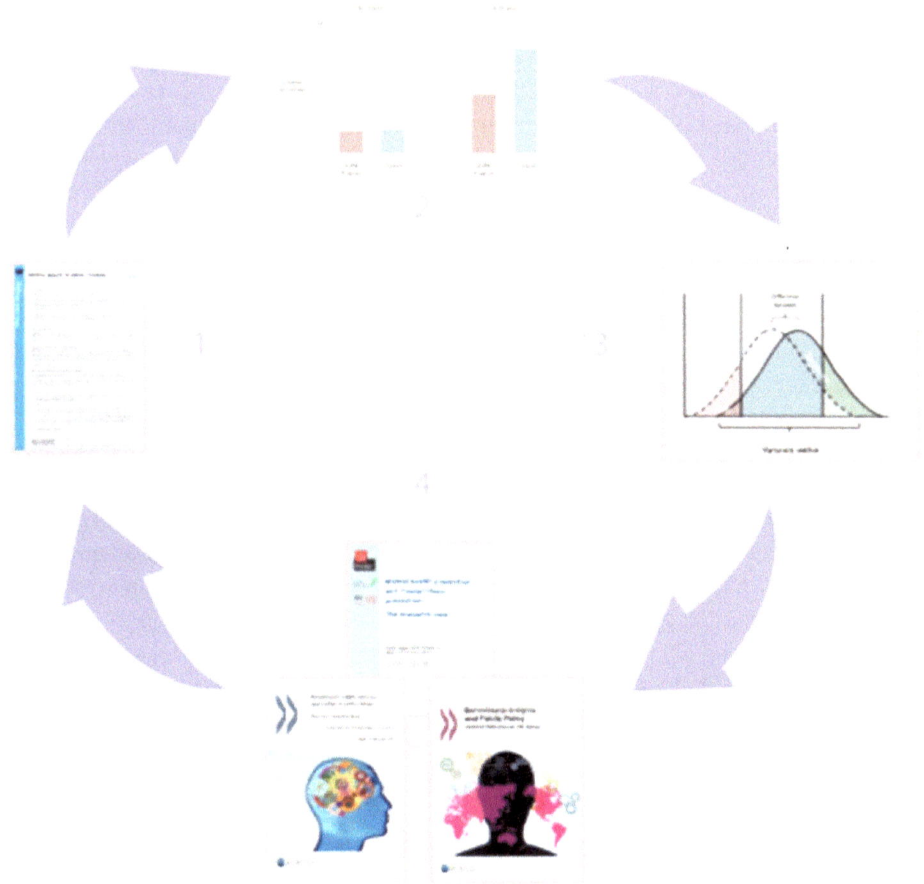

Policies: when push came to nudge

One common challenge in discussing policies is that there is a *general* understanding of what they seem to be, but no formal consensus on the *specifics* of what a policy is or is not (Oliver, Lorenc, & Innvær, 2014b). If we consider a policy as described earlier – a population-level intervention that focuses on guiding behaviors and choices – then we can see the overlap with **laws** and **regulations,** which are terms often used interchangeably with policy. However, while policies often heavily overlap with regulations and laws, they are not the same (Ruggeri, 2017a). For example, while an effort to reduce smoking without banning it is a policy, government legislation establishing bans and punishments for violating them are unmistakably laws. However, these are interrelated because a policy can lead to regulations or it can be the tangible response to meeting regulatory guidelines (Schneider & Ingram, 1990). In other words, laws may require organizations to have set policies for defined smoking areas, but the policies merely direct behaviors and are not laws themselves (Schneider & Ingram, 1990). Such a distinction may seem tedious to the casual observer, but as this book will demonstrate, it is fundamental to appreciating and developing effective behavioral insights, particularly in lieu of drastic and excessive regulatory conditions.

In spite of the overlap between policies and regulations, it is important to see the difference for both scientific study and application. Table 1.1 presents several domains where policies and regulations are used, distinguishing each intervention. In each case, the regulation disallows a certain behavior, which would be punished if violated, whereas the policies are an active attempt to discourage a behavior but the option remains.

> Policies often make use of so-called **nudges**, which involve adjusting any aspect of the choice architecture that alters people's behavior in a predictable way without forbidding options or significantly changing their economic incentives. To count as a mere nudge the intervention must be easy and cheap to avoid. Nudges are not mandates. Putting fruit at the eye level counts as a nudge. Banning junk food does not.
>
> (Thaler & Sunstein, 2008, p. 6)

Therefore, four key characteristics emerge from this definition: (1) a small choice architecture type of intervention that (2) has the ability to encourage optimal decisions while (3) preserving choice (4) without altering significantly the financial incentive structure.

Having a distinction between them means that policies can be seen as complementary tools to traditional laws and regulations. Whereas policies may employ nudges to steer behaviors, traditional regulations use command and control, such as punishments involving taxes or fees (sometimes referred to as "sticks") in combination with financial rewards and incentives such as cash back or subsidies (sometimes referred to as "carrots"), to regulate civic life. Not only can nudges be used to support an existing instrument, but in some cases they might also act as an alternative to enforcement.

Policies can be found anywhere (Whitty, 2015), including in families, in sporting teams, and at office poker nights, and they are ultimately the *do* of public, social, governmental, and organizational leadership. They are not the rules or laws (the *do not*) for which individuals may be punished for violating, but instead they are the strategies and approaches we take to achieve desired outcomes on the population level (Ruggeri, 2017a). In this way, policies can stem from wider strategies such that, while the rules and punishments may be very clearly presented, how to go about following them may not be as plainly prescribed. This means those with the most effective strategies for following the rules will likely have the most

TABLE 1.1 Policies and regulations*

Domain	*Regulation*	*Policy*
Smoking	Banning cigarettes and other forms of tobacco in restaurants.	Increasing taxes on cigarettes.
Transportation	Banning vehicles from nonresidents from driving on roads during certain hours.	Introducing a congestion charge that nonresidents pay to enter the city during working hours.
Energy	Limiting the amount of household energy use each month before power is cut.	Offering cash back for households that use less than the average monthly consumption.
Food	Making it illegal to have unhealthy snack food in school vending machines.	Placing health details on the front of vending machines so consumers can make choices.

**Note:* This is the perspective of the organization responsible for implementing the interventions. There are many instances where violating a policy may result in a penalty, but that is the perspective of the individual.

optimal outcomes in return (Werner-Seidler, Perry, & Christensen, 2016). This is equally the case for established laws and regulations as for unwritten rules or general principles. For example, governments may have specific rules for business practice that companies should establish strategies to avoid misconduct and corresponding penalties in the same way that they should have strategies in place to follow economic rules, such as how to meet demand in a growing market.

While social norms, standards, and binding agreements all have direct links to policy, they are distinct tools (Schneider & Ingram, 1990). However, in the face of a major social dilemma, it is likely that policies will inspire and utilize these behavioral insights in practice (Howlett et al., 2015).

What do policies *do*?

Policies are ultimately about guiding choices and behaviors to get the best outcome in the most efficient way, as often as possible (Ruggeri, 2017). However, in every case, we can redefine what we mean by each of these components: *best outcome*, *most efficient way*, and *as often as possible*. For this textbook, we will largely lean toward the optimization side of this discussion as opposed to the maximization side. While there are certainly many possible instances where a certain outcome may be non-negotiable, much of public policy must function with finite resources while recognizing cost-effectiveness – if the impacts do not outweigh the costs, it is unlikely the intervention will be continued (Allcott & Mullainathan, 2010). This means that seeking the best possible results while sacrificing the least in the way of resources will be a common theme in the development of any policy (Sunstein, 2015).

Policies seek to achieve consistency and effectiveness of choice and behavior. *Public* policy takes this to the level of supporting populations to make better choices in spite of those limitations mentioned earlier (Allcott & Mullainathan, 2010). This is particularly the case for ambiguous, repetitive situations or sustained challenges where having an established process produces benefits over those resulting from ad hoc decisions. An established policy process does not necessarily, or inherently, guarantee a standard decision or outcome (Schneider & Ingram, 1990). Rather, a consistent – even perpetual – pattern or algorithm is considered as steps are taken when faced with choice. The lack of policies can lead to erratic and unwise choices that ensure neither a likely positive outcome nor the potential for learning to be applied in future recurrences of an issue, challenge, or opportunity. In short, policies are an attempt to use probabilities in practice by consistently balancing potential gains and losses with their related risks.

You may understandably wonder why it matters to have such specific definitions and nuanced understandings of policies. Simply put: as will be explored throughout this book, a clear and agreed definition will go a long way toward ensuring impact and efficiency, particularly when faced with a complex challenge affecting a large population. A general view of policy as a nebulous combination of processes, organizations, and rules may be fine in some cases, but this is a textbook so we are allowed to be picky.

Policies will also aim for a particular outcome, whether it be the assurance of quality, protection against known risks, or the improvement of an important domain faced in the population (OECD, 2017a). To increase the likelihood of such an outcome, any policy must be specific, well communicated, and well designed (Howlett & Mukherjee, 2017). For example, policies have been successfully used to reduce spillage in public toilets (Thaler & Sunstein, 2008), effectively reducing unnecessary organizational costs. For this to happen, issues related to costs had to first be identified as problematic and compared to other concerns and then linked to possible interventions. The interventions needed to specifically target a behavior that had a direct or indirect impact on resources (Schneider & Ingram, 1990). Following this, a change in the behavior had to be observed, which was then matched to costs and compared to a baseline. To be confident that findings were a result of the intervention, similar spaces not involved with the intervention were monitored at the same time with the same observation methods, demonstrating different results from the trial location (see Chapter 3).

Beyond the improvement of public spaces, policies have the power to induce real social change through shaping and redefining social norms (Henrich et al., 2001; Schneider & Ingram, 1990). Hence, if the norm visibly changes, we may see a change in behavior. At Princeton University, through simply providing reusable water bottles to incoming undergraduate students, a social norm was fostered making it desirable to act sustainably by avoiding bottled water (Santos & van der Linden, 2016). Students receiving the free bottle were much more likely to support the statement, "Princeton should not sell bottled water," than those who did not receive the bottle. In many cases, policies are used to ensure that philosophical and ideological standards exist in practice (Ruggeri, 2017a), such as equal hiring policies disallowing consideration of race, gender, or age as a way to balance the distribution of employees across groups as well as to avoid discrimination. The outcome desired is a diverse workplace with the best candidates representing many groups. As such, policies reflect the values of those abiding by them and shape our everyday conduct (Schneider & Ingram, 1990).

Why do we need policies?

While people are generally good decision-makers (remember that at least 75 percent did get the *correct* answer about risk), we are still prone to making bad choices when relying on confidence in our abilities and knowledge (Moore & Healy, 2008). This remains true even for professionals with considerable expertise, including policymakers (Choi & Pritchard, 2003).

The Canadian government uses evidence on these topics to argue that these threats to good decisions could be better served by having systematic, algorithmic approaches, particularly for the most critical or repeated behaviors that have a significant impact on populations (Jamieson & Giraldez, 2017). Noting these, policies are a powerful tool to introduce those in a way that considers evidence on balance with meaningful outcomes, minimizing the influence of our biases in making choices. Additionally, they can be a tremendous tool in getting individuals to carry out actions that they may not otherwise do but that benefit themselves and, if so, their communities (Schneider & Ingram, 1990).

Policies hinge on the idea that we can create standardized, systematic approaches to various aspects of life at the large-group and population levels to encourage a perceived best behavior (Ruggeri, 2017a). Hence, policies *should* help people make good decisions, and those decisions *should* lead to better outcomes. There are certainly arguments to be made about safeguards against unethical policy guidance, where unnecessary harms may be created or where an individual group receives a disproportionate gain to the detriment of the group targeted by the intervention. However, this volume will focus largely on those that have been deemed to be sufficiently prosocial, to the extent that individuals and populations receive proportional gains through the methods and desired outcomes.

We also need policies to ensure the survival of entities that are shared or consumed by members of a group; these entities are often the defining features of a society. Consider how we aim to utilize our resources, particularly public goods in the context of social dilemmas. A **public good** is defined by two main characteristics: it is non-excludable and non-rivalrous (Kotchen, 2005). A public good is something that is available to every member of a group (non-excludable) and can be freely consumed by one individual regardless of the consumption of other individuals (non-rivalrous). That is to say that one person's use of a public good does not reduce the available amount to other people. Examples of public goods include parks, public radio, fresh air, street lighting, public health, and official statistical records.

Individual use of public goods can sometimes result in **social dilemmas**, which are decisions where individuals have to weigh personal interests against the wider collective group interest (Ledyard, 1995). Social dilemmas are common and can be found, for example, among waitstaff in certain restaurants. Each waiter can choose how much of their individual earned gratuity they want to either keep for themselves or put into a collective box that is shared among all the staff at the end of the day. The waitstaff as a whole will be best off if everyone contributes their entire tip money in the shared box. Each individual waiter, however, earns more by contributing nothing, or very little, to the box, while still receiving money from others' contributions, thereby "free riding" off the group (Ledyard, 1995). Hence, the self-interest of each individual waiter is at odds with the waitstaff's interest as a collective group. However, in social dilemmas, it cannot be assumed that everyone in a population will agree with what are deemed to be critical issues, appropriate methods, or desirable outcomes (Parks, Joireman, & Van Lange, 2013). It is for such situations that clearly defined policies and their intended outcomes can offer significant gains beyond simply the reward of the behavior but also through group cohesion.

Social dilemmas can also involve **common pool resources**, which is a type of good that benefits groups of people, but its benefits can be reduced by individual pursuits of self-interest (Ostrom, Gardner, & Walker, 1994). Thus, unlike public goods, common pool resources are rivalrous among consumers, in that one individual's use can reduce the available amount of the resource for another individual (Ostrom, 1990). Examples of common pool resources include forests, water basins, wildlife, agriculture, and parking lots. Excessive consumption of a common pool resource can result in the **tragedy of the commons**, which is where group consumption exhausts the supply of the good (Parks et al., 2013). While the strategy of grabbing the maximum amount available is the optimal strategy on an individual level, it is not ideal behavior on a collective group level.

One role of policy could be to encourage more sustainable usage of such resources. Policies designed to address common resource problems vary based on the nature of the resource (Adams, Brockington, Dyson, & Vira, 2002). Numerous social, economic, and environmental **drivers of change** in policies are used to address these challenges. Such drivers of change may be to transform the governmental management of the resource (transfer the resource from the public to the private sector), to commoditize the resource, or to change the ecological productivity of the resource (modifying the stocks of fish or forests) (Adams et al., 2002). Drivers of change used by governmental management of common pool resources can be divided into four fundamental processes (Adams, Brockington, Dyson, & Vira, 2001):

1 Excluding use of the resource
2 Regulating use of the resource
3 Monitoring legal and illegal use of the resource
4 Enforcing punishment of wrong usage of the resource

The likelihood that policymakers will have access to, use, and understand this knowledge of change to the same extent when designing interventions aimed at common pool resources is low, given the number of other factors they must consider (Adams et al., 2002). Furthermore, how these interventions will be received when implemented on a population level is also likely to differ. It is again for these reasons that clear frameworks and definitions for policies are critical.

What do policies consider important?

There is research in the social sciences spanning decades that provides insights into the likely responses of the public to any policy; this information was compiled in a comprehensive paper led by Craig Parks (Parks et al., 2013). This paper utilizes three distinct classifications for how to understand those responses: **prosocials** (those who support policies in the interest of society generally), **proselves** (those likely to reject prosocial concepts if there is no benefit to them or if they incur costs), and **competitors** (those who will support policies as long as they result in comparatively better outcomes for themselves). As demonstrated in Figure 1.1, there is a substantial amount that could be discussed about these classifications. For the purposes of this book, we merely note that anyone working toward policies should keep in mind public reactions and not assume uniform responses or support (see Chapter 2 for further information on scoring public acceptability).

As is reflected in the framework for Figure 1.1, there are a substantial number of elements to consider that are seemingly unrelated to a specific choice or behavior. These range from the number of siblings an individual has to their personal incentives for cooperating with or opposing a policy. While it may become possible in the age of Big Data to test this framework in practice, what is already clear is that considering these elements on a population level may offer tremendous insight for anticipating outcomes beyond the most direct effects considered when developing policy interventions. In other words, this approach may not perfectly predict a specific choice of a specific individual, but across a large group it should provide a reasonably accurate indication of what responses to expect from the public. This is ultimately a telling illustration of how policies are a direct use of probabilities in practice.

FIGURE 1.1 The Parks Framework for predicting public responses to policies in the context of social dilemmas

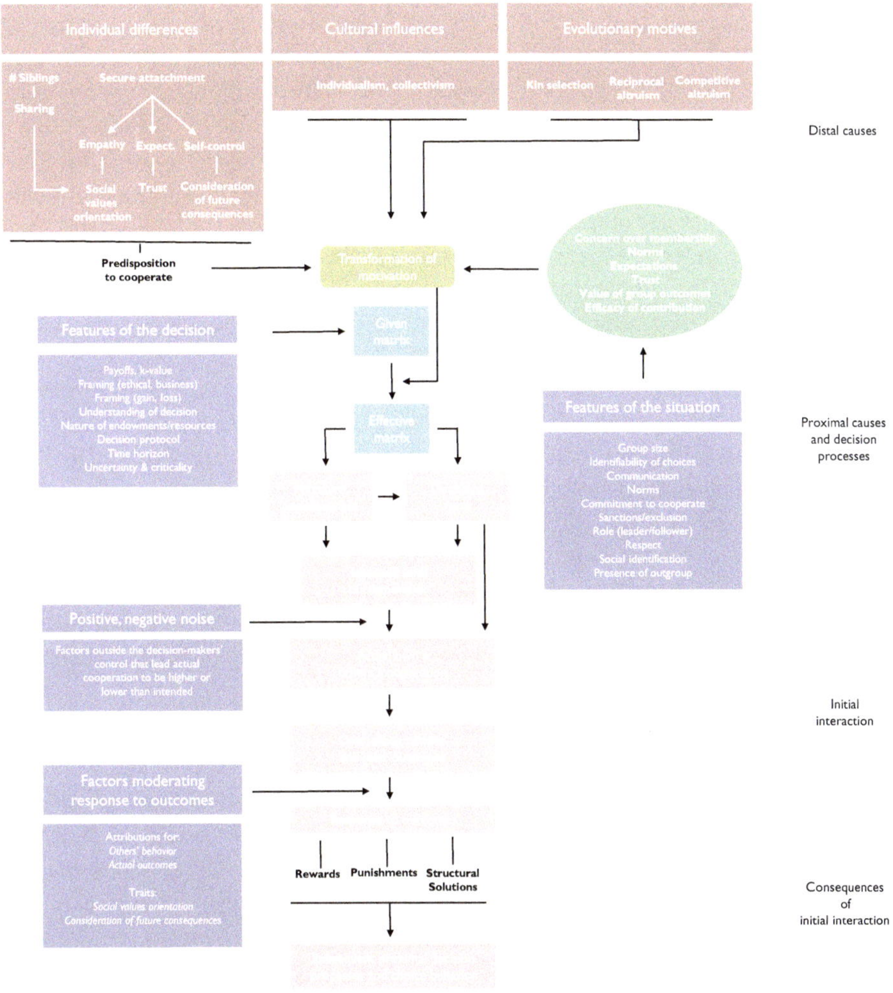

Source: Integrative model of decision-making in social dilemmas from Parks et al. (2013)

How are policies made?

As has been said previously, policies now stem from a variety of sources, and Chapter 2 will cover in more detail how they are developed in modern times. When considering public policy or other forms of interventions developed specifically by institutions responsible for population-level impacts and behaviors, we can typically expect somewhat more structure than when a family makes a policy. In other words, there tends to be an identifiable process for how these policies are developed rather than simply someone relying on their gut as with bounded rationality.

One common means of developing policies is through committees of experts or stakeholders (Fischer, Wentholt, Rowe, & Frewer, 2014). Approaches include unstructured deliberations in smaller groups of experts without any preestablished schedule or expected outcome of the meeting on the policy process. It can also involve highly structured meetings in larger groups, where experts engage in systematic discussions about various policy issues with a preset agenda that includes the aims of the meeting (Fischer et al., 2014). For example, 21 Spanish stakeholders reached a consensus regarding the best policy tools to address obesity issues through multistep structured interviews. In four steps – options, criteria, scoring, and weighing – each expert evaluated a set of policy tools, such as including more knowledge about physical health in school curricula or improving local sports facilities, which resulted in a prioritized list of recommendations for public policy addressing obesity (Gonzalez-Zapata, Ortiz-Moncada, & Alvarez-Dardet, 2007).

However, with a variety of expert opinions, there are challenges to consider when evaluating the relevance of expert suggestions (Fischer et al., 2014). Power dynamics can negatively influence most talkative group member, while others stay silent (Rowe, 1998). Group opinion may also be polarized toward controversial viewpoints, or the group may spend an insufficient amount of time reaching a consensus (Klenk & Hickey, 2011). One very common and prevailing approach developed by the RAND Corporation (Dalkey, 1967) is the Delphi method, which aims to resolve these issues of group interaction by ensuring that the "wisdom of the crowd" (Galton, 1907) is accessed through iterative, anonymous, group deliberation. The steps typically comprising a policy process using the Delphi technique are as follows (Turoff, 2002):

1 Formulating the problem(s)
2 Identifying relevant policy tools
3 Disclosing initial views on the problem(s)
4 Discussing causes of disagreement
5 Evaluating underlying causes
6 Reevaluating options

In the first round, expert opinions are provided anonymously through a computer. This anonymity is a central feature of the Delphi technique, limiting the influence of status on the group consensus (Thangaratinam & Redman, 2005). Results are summarized and returned to the experts, who are then able to revise their initial estimates. If the responses of individual experts are markedly deviant from the median response, they are asked to give some justification for their estimate (Dalkey, 1967). In this way, consensus is encouraged but outsider opinions are not neglected. Developed in the 1950s to forecast new technological innovations (Dalkey, 1967), the Delphi method now has a broad range of applications. It has been used to great effect in disciplines such as marketing, healthcare, medicine, and education (Thangaratinam & Redman, 2005). Many policy advisory organizations have since developed their own approaches, some of which are covered in Chapter 10, while Chapter 12 is dedicated specifically to the exact methods used by such an organization.

A brief history of policymaking

Even if they are becoming increasingly common for discussion in contemporary scientific literature, policies are not a recent phenomenon. The term has been used in writing for at least five centuries, and the concept has existed at least since Moses returned from Mount Sinai with the Ten Commandments, two of which could be considered policies (the others are unmistakably laws). As a form of leadership, the use of policies expanded significantly during Roman times across various domains, including economic, military, agricultural, and civil matters. Over time, such approaches have become more prevalent and structured, becoming a subject of scientific study and a mainstay in public discourse.

Such structured uses of policies employ **policy design**, which involves the way governments purposively seek to connect policy tools to the desired outcomes of the interventions (Howlett & Mukherjee, 2017). **Policy tools** (or **instruments**) are the strategies and interventions implemented in the expectation that they will achieve desired outcomes (Howlett et al., 2015). Examples of policy tools include taxation, sanctions, contracts, grants, and education (Schneider & Ingram, 1990). As improved understanding of these tools can help advance policymaking, their study has a central role in policy design. Despite being under-researched, this approach to policy has been undergoing continuous development since the 1950s (Howlett et al., 2015). During the early days of policy design (as an academic question), research focused on identifying types of policy tools and instruments. Since the 1960s, Theodore Lowi (Lowi, 1966, 1972, 1985) has attempted to categorize all such government policy tools into one of four groups according to their degree of coercion toward the desired population target and their likelihood of application (see Figure 1.2 for an overview; Howlett & Mukherjee, 2017):

Distributive policies: weakly enforced and targeting individuals (e.g. tax write-offs)
Regulatory policies: strongly enforced and targeting individuals (e.g. licensing)
Constituent policies: weakly enforced and targeting the public (e.g. mental health services)
Redistributive policies: strongly enforced and targeting the public (e.g. welfare programs)

Lowi's typological work was particularly influential among Canadian policy wonks[2] like Richard Simeon, whose work marked the beginning of formal Canadian policy studies in 1976 (Howlett & Mukherjee, 2017). Beyond merely classifying policy tools, scholars and policymakers realized the need to improve the understanding of their tools, which quickly became the predominant interest in the early stages of policy design. Accordingly, Doern and Wilson (1974) proposed a continuum model of tool choice on the basis of Lowi's initial typological approach. This model involved the differing levels of **legitimate coercion** that could be used by governments (Howlett & Mukherjee, 2017). Government involvement ranged from minimum action in private and self-regulated contexts to complete public ownership via mixed or crown corporations. They connected the degree of involvement to considerations such as policymakers' desire to be reelected and policy effectiveness. Doern and Wilson's continuum model continues to influence studies on policy design to this day (Howlett & Mukherjee, 2017).

Beyond categorizing policy tools, policy design studies became increasingly focused on the process of selecting specific tools for different interventions (Howlett & Mukherjee, 2017). This attention shift was evident in the work of Lester Salamon (1981) who investigated the changing forms of governmental activity in the United States through the use of different tools. Building further on this work, Linder and Peters (1989) proposed a

FIGURE 1.2 Classification of policy tools

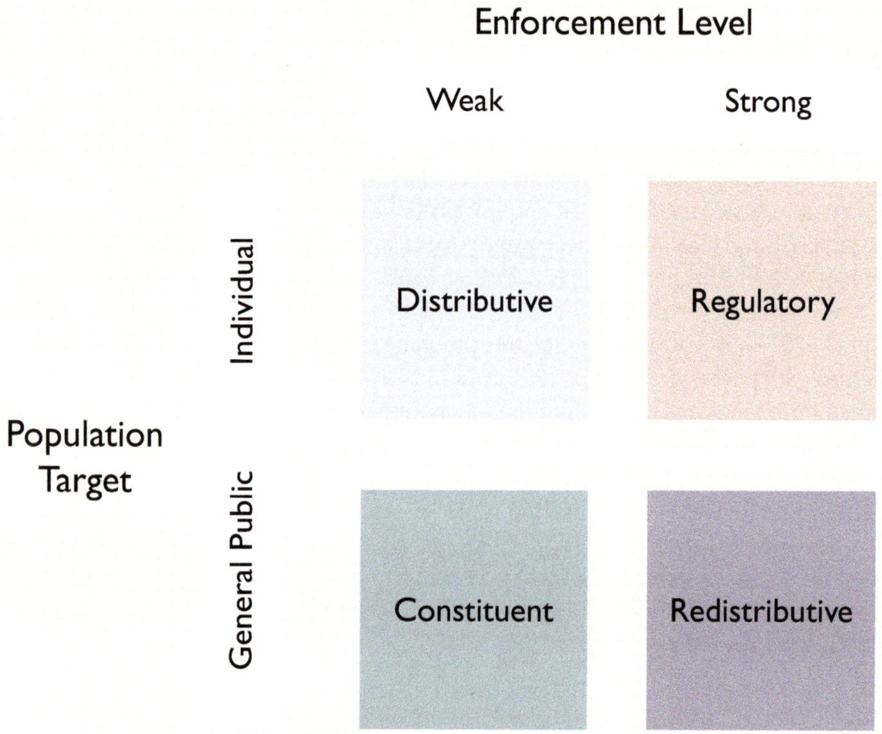

synthetic strategy (one that could be falsified by experience) for tool choice. This approach was focused on increasing the probability of governmental implementation by evaluating the political risk of each tool choice, making certain tools more viable depending on the specific obstacles confronting policymakers. This refocus was the first time a distinction was made between the design process and the policy tool, allowing for a more systematic comparison of the costs and benefits of each policy tool (Howlett & Mukherjee, 2017). Despite these advances, there was little regard for processes or evidence-based approaches, and policymakers did not seemingly follow any formal method of selecting the appropriate policy tool.

From interventions to toolkits

Today, policy studies seek to design effective levers that are most suitable for the environment in which the policies are to be implemented. Thus, while early policy design research focused on identifying tools, modern evidence-based design studies have shifted attention to identifying larger collections of policies, forming "portfolios" or **toolkits** (Howlett et al., 2015; Schneider & Ingram, 1990), which are compilations of tools used to aid in the policy process. Rather than an analysis of one choice made at one point during the policy process, policy portfolios include several tools directed at issues over a longer time period. Policy studies that adopted this portfolio concept witnessed a resurgence of interest in the aftermath of the global financial crisis of 2007–2008 (Howlett & Mukherjee, 2017). Realizing the need to elaborate on previously simplistic policy designs, researchers are now focused on gaining a greater understanding of the conceptual and methodological aspects of policy, which broadly make up the core of current evidence-based policy research.

Studies on contemporary policy design began in earnest in the 1990s (Schneider & Ingram, 1990) and have grown exponentially since (Howlett & Mukherjee, 2017). Recently, there has been a renewed interest in policy design studies, as more and more scholars are working toward finding the optimal constructs and discourse for developing policies (Howlett et al., 2015). Policy research itself has broadened its scope to incorporate who should create policies, the differences between design and nondesign, and evaluation by goodness of fit. Perhaps most importantly, there is growing consensus that more behavioral evidence should be considered in the evolution of policy design, consequently supporting the relevance of evidence-based policy research models in future studies.

Economic incentives and penalties as the classic policy levers

To return to the beginning of policy history with Lowi's influential classification of policies (Lowi, 1966, 1972, 1985), redistributive policies prevail in terms of application to this day. Taxation is a prime example of this – it remains the most common policy tool (Loewenstein & Chater, 2017) not because of its effectiveness, but more because it is familiar (Howlett et al., 2015). Taxation policies have been used by governments all over the world for centuries, and they have historically been used as an easy way to increase governmental and public revenues (Chaloupka, 1999; Feldstein, 2008). The revenue from taxed tobacco products, for example, at one time amounted to between 3 and 5 percent of total revenue estimations in several Western countries (Chaloupka, 1999). Taxes can also be a highly efficient tool in altering consumer behaviors due to higher prices or resulting in decreased consumption of saturated fat (Vallgårda, Holm, & Jensen, 2015). Accordingly, taxation is still frequently used as an economic incentive to influence population-based behavior.

However, it is important to go beyond public revenue estimates and behavioral change on the population level, as tax policies can have differential impacts on various subpopulations (Chaloupka, 1999). For example, despite strong empirical support for the effectiveness of taxing cigarettes in reducing smoking habits (Chaloupka, 1999), longitudinal behavioral data suggest that taxes may not be as efficient at reducing teenage smoking; higher prices on cigarettes seem to yield different responses in youths than in adults (DeCicca, Kenkel, & Mathios, 2002), and effects can often be very small in spite of very large tax increases (Callison & Kaestner, 2014). Furthermore, taxes as an economic incentive can also lead to negative changes in behavior, such as decreased labor effort and reduced saving (Feldstein, 2008). Hence, complex behavior patterns as revealed by behavioral insights ought to be taken into consideration when exploring policy tools, as will be the focus throughout this volume.

Future trends in psychology and policy

As this chapter has illustrated, there is great potential for the application of psychological principles to policymaking. Going forward, this book will present how governments, academic institutions, and nonprofit organizations around the globe have started and continue to implement so-called **nudge units** to support policymaking efforts through low-cost, yet effective interventions. In line with this, many organizations, particularly in the private sector, have begun creating new positions around behavioral insights, such as chief behavioral officers, choice architecture officers, behavioral economists, and behavioral science officers. Many of these positions focus on matters of internal, institutional policies aimed at improving efficiency, bolstering compliance, reducing cost, or promoting healthier lifestyles among employees.

The application of new tools such as predictive analytics, artificial intelligence, and machine learning to behavioral insights will continue to grow, with countless innovations resulting from this interchange between technology and behavioral sciences. With more innovation in applying behavioral sciences to policy and organizational challenges, new areas are emerging for potential application to behavioral sciences, especially in public policy for matters such as central banking, prevention of violent extremism, or international trade disputes. These will grow as universities continue to expand offerings in behavioral sciences, from added courses on behavioral economics to entire degrees. To be fully versed in this field, students will need to understand basic scientific theory and method in relevant fields such as psychology, economics, sociology, political science, and epidemiology. They will also require direct experience in applications when interventions run at scale, both on the implementation and on the evaluation. Many of these graduates will consider new work options that their predecessors have not considered before, both in government and in nongovernmental organizations. The impact may very well result in entirely new ways of designing and implementing public policy or doing business.

Psychological and behavioral sciences in policy: the road ahead

While the link to behavior and decision-making may make psychological science an obvious choice as a major contributor to evidence-based policies, we must not overstate its role and note that it forms only part of any wider policy agenda (Loewenstein & Chater, 2017). As this book will demonstrate extensively, psychological science's influence on major policies is now visible in almost every domain. While much of the work to be demonstrated will focus on local trials, many of the most pressing global challenges are behavioral in principle, hence the need for such volume. At the same time, there are many flawed approaches and interventions, which must be either corrected or avoided if behavioral sciences are to be relied on as effective in policy applications (Sunstein, 2017a).

The purpose of this chapter has not been to provide a comprehensive summary of policy or the science of policymaking. Instead, it has been used to frame the relevance of the 12 chapters that follow and has focused on providing necessary core information about what policies are and what they are not. The following pages aim to present policies not only as tools for solving problems but as catalysts for innovation and creating new opportunities. For this to be effective, what policies *do* and why they matter have been covered in detail.

This history is important not only to avoid repeating past mistakes but also to appreciate why it is meaningful in the first place. This book focuses on how high-quality work on this topic can both lead to and benefit from those interventions classified as behavioral insights, though obviously many others exist. It also aims to provide a diverse range of topics, regions, and outcomes, which has sometimes been ignored in similar work (Anderson & Stamoulis, 2007).

As an overview of the content that follows, Chapters 2 and 3 provide a detailed look at the history and science of behavior and decision-making by overviewing the critical people, theories, methodological approaches, terms, and tools that have brought the field to where it is today, both in study and in applications to policy. Chapters 4–8 then cover critical policy domains identified by major international organizations as areas where behavioral insights are already making an impact. Chapter 9 is a hybrid of both theoretical approaches to improving the way insights are delivered and examples of how insights are used in the delivery itself. Chapter 10 provides a detailed introduction on the principles of evidence-based policy. Chapter 11 dives into the evaluation of policies. Chapter 12 then provides an overview of the process used by an active behavioral insight unit. We conclude with a chapter defining the impact from policies and why behavioral insights are effective on the population level.

Our goal is for this volume to be a useful resource for teaching, catalyzing ideas, and generally promoting effective approaches to policies that will offer the greatest outcomes for the largest number. In future volumes, we aim to expand each section, add new policy domains, distinguish elements within current domains further, and provide more practical approaches toward the development, evaluation, and sustainability of effective policies.

Notes

1 Note that the key difference is that maximizing outcomes assumes there is an ultimate goal that is being sought, such as winning a championship or getting a dream job. Optimizing outcomes can have the same goal as a maximized outcome, but with the differences that optimization may not use such a binary concept and costs may create more harm after a certain point. The desire to win a gold medal at the Olympics may cost the athlete a substantial amount of personal time with friends and family, but this sacrifice does not change the value of the victory, which is the maximum. Alternatively, a dream job may require an employee to move far from friends and family, such that the sacrifice diminishes the value of the job and it is no longer an optimal outcome as the cost was too great.

2 We do not propose a specific definition for what a "wonk" is. We just feel readers of this book should be familiar with the term as they will likely be referred to in this way should they ever make the mistake of identifying themselves as policy advisors, experts, or – due to a catastrophic event – researchers.

2 A brief history of behavioral and decision sciences

Kai Ruggeri, Jana B. Berkessel, Philipe M. Bujold, Maja Friedemann, Hannes Jarke, Kamilla Knutsen Steinnes, Mary MacLennan, Sahana K. Quail, Felice L. Tavera, Sanne Verra, Faisal Naru, Filippo Cavassini, and Elizabeth Hardy

Chapter summary

Behavioral economics has a lot to contribute to effective policies and other applications. As evidence in this area accumulates, the field will increasingly provide direct insights for applications that maximize policy outcomes, particularly to those with a direct relationship to human choices and behaviors. To realize this potential, it is necessary to understand the psychological theory and the mechanisms currently used to study behavior, as well as the historic development of the field. While much was traditionally understood through the lens of classical economics, recent trends have expanded to include findings from psychology, neuroscience, and sociology, to name a few, leading to the areas of scientific study commonly referred to as behavioral science and behavioral economics. Findings from these domains are typically known as behavioral insights. They are often characterized by the use of behavioral constructs to explain patterns in the behavior of groups or single individuals. Many influential individuals from these domains have propelled our knowledge of the field, exploring the idiosyncratic ways in which behavior and decision-making affect our daily lives. This chapter provides a brief history of how this field came to be so academically influential while outlining the work of leading figures and concepts necessary to understand, study, and implement these behavioral insights.

Learning objectives

- Summarize common approaches to research in behavior and decision-making
- Understand major recent scientific advances leading to the field of behavioral insights
- Understand core terms and methods for studying behavioral insights
- Become familiar with leading experts that have had a major influence on the field

Behavioral science

Every day, people have to make countless decisions. Most of us have good intentions – we typically want to live long, plentiful, and fulfilling lives. However, we often struggle to translate

DOI: 10.4324/9781003181873-2

these intentions into behavior that truly maximizes our interests. As later chapters will show, people often base their decisions on factors that have no direct impact on the outcomes of the choices they make. Our current emotional state, for example, was once considered irrational and theoretically irrelevant, but it has now been tied reliably to our decision process. But what does it mean to be rational, or in this case *irrational*, and how is understanding rationality useful for policies? We'll come back to emotions in a moment.

Ultimately, we understand **rationality** as making choices and behaviors that are in our best interest, particularly when other options may be less beneficial or even harmful. Unfortunately, as we will see, human decisions can be highly unpredictable and susceptible to external influence, meaning we do not always behave in a "rational" way (Simon, 1955). For example, the choice between a fruit bowl and chocolate cake might turn out differently when feeling stressed out, when among friends, or when the fruit bowl is on the top shelf and the cake is within reach. This may even occur for someone who would otherwise value a healthy lifestyle similarly across various situations (Thaler & Sunstein, 2008).

Behavioral science aims to draw justifiable, objective conclusions about these seemingly incongruent behaviors and to understand the variability of these behaviors within and between individuals, groups, and populations. The term behavioral science itself gained popularity in the 1950s and was regularly used as a synonym for social sciences. While social sciences focus on studying the processes of a social system, behavioral science emphasizes the experimental study of behaviors common in a population, such as paying taxes or choosing when to see a doctor. Research in behavioral science is therefore empirical and data driven, focusing on decision processes and their consequences for individuals, groups, and social systems. The salient conclusions derived from behavioral science are typically referred to as **behavioral insights** and will be the focus of the following chapters.

Behavioral science consists of several disciplines that deal with the subject of human actions. This includes psychology, economics, sociology, law, social and cultural anthropology, marketing, political sciences, finance, ecology, epidemiology, and neuroscience – and potentially others. Each of these respective fields leverages different approaches to address the study of behavior, but regardless of discipline, most behavioral science research is conducted through experiments that systematically manipulate one or more variables (so-called *independent variables*) and measure the resulting changes in behavioral outcomes (so-called *dependent variables*). Through this approach, researchers aim to attribute observed changes in behavior to the variables that have been manipulated.

To illustrate, in a classic social psychological experiment, Nisbett and Wilson (1977) showed two different (staged) videotapes of psychology lecturers being interviewed to college students. In one video, the lecturer presented himself as very likable (emotionally warm), and in the other he was very distant, with much less emotional warmth. When asked to rate the lecturer on various dimensions, students rated the lecturer who was portrayed deliberately as less likable lower on all scales, even unrelated ones – despite explicitly claiming their dislike of him had not affected their ratings. In this case, emotional warmth is the independent variable of interest, and the judgments are the behavioral outcome (dependent variable) observed to assess any changes. Differences in judgments between groups can shed light on effective ways to foster beneficial decision-making in a classroom setting, even if it cannot be guaranteed to work for every student in every context. Generating insights in this way is therefore desirable, although not always feasible in the policy context. In these circumstances, science may be applied as a lens to help inform decisions. The behavioral effects of the policy can then be evaluated using program evaluation methods (see Chapter 11). Box 2.1 introduces you to some fundamentals of "classical" economic behavior.

BOX 2.1 A PRIMER ON THE FUNDAMENTALS OF CLASSICAL ECONOMIC BEHAVIOR

If you have read anything on behavioral economics, you will almost certainly have seen the terms "classical economics" or "traditional economic theory." In many cases, these terms appear alongside "violations," particularly when a behavior is observed that seemingly contradicts them – or at least deviates from expectation. While many people use these expressions often, it is important to understand exactly what is meant by them and not simply assume what is meant.

First, economic outputs are understood by market behaviors (see Figure 2.1), which are measured by supply (how much of a product is available for trade) and demand (how much of a product consumers are willing to purchase). These decisions are influenced by regulation (the rules of trading). It is assumed that the primary drivers of supply and demand are prices (P) and quantities (Q), so as prices increase, people will buy less, though as prices decrease, suppliers will produce less (and vice versa in both cases). The hope is that an equilibrium (PE, QE) is reached where consumers and producers are satisfied with prices and quantities, which is what regulation is meant to support and protect. Other drivers of demand exist and will be covered at various points in this book, including preferences, comparable goods, and complementary products (e.g. oil for a car). The same is true

FIGURE 2.1 Understanding economic theory through supply and demand: price (P), quantity (Q), equilibrium price (PE), equilibrium quantity (QE)

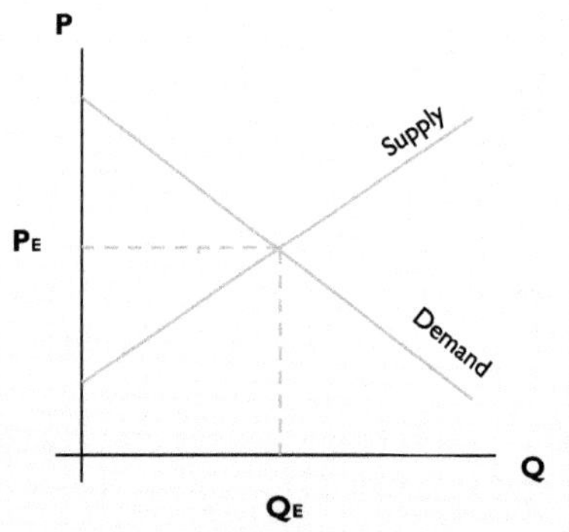

for supply, which can be driven by threats to the production of products, their cost to produce, and the number of other firms producing them.

Markets and economies can be defined by whoever is interested, so when you hear someone say, for example, "the German transportation market," this could involve automobiles produced in Germany, the cost of all related products for transportation entering or leaving Germany, or any number of other parameters. Ultimately, we understand how an economy is doing by measuring the accumulation of all markets. When we compare that accumulation to the same data for a prior period, it is known as **growth** and is typically calculated using **gross domestic product (GDP)**.

Finally, one of the pillars of classical economic theory is that human behavior in markets is rational – that we always seek to maximize those outcomes that are in our own, best interest. As this book will show, this assumption has been applied inadequately over time, and rather than being used as a static fact, rationality should be used as both a reference point and a context-specific matter. Other factors such as expected utility theory and fungibility are standard within classical economic theory, and those will be discussed in detail in this and other chapters.

Traditional approaches to the study of decision-making

Behavior is formed by many conscious and subconscious decisions. As a result, behavioral science is closely linked to the study of decision-making. **Decision-making** is the cognitive process that leads an individual to choose an opinion or action from a set of several possible options. The dominant theory of decision-making in economics is the **rational choice theory**, which proposes that individuals always seek to exchange their limited resources (e.g., money and time) for the alternative with the highest possible gain (Simon, 1955). If an individual is asked to choose between two alternatives – vanilla or pistachio ice cream, for instance – their choice should be the alternative that leads to the highest gain (in this case, the greatest personal enjoyment). If the customer prefers one scoop of pistachio ice cream over one scoop of vanilla ice cream, we could then say that the customer assigns more personal value to, or gets more enjoyment from, pistachio ice cream than vanilla ice cream.

According to rational choice theory, individuals act in a way that maximizes these personal gains, making the best decision for them by comparing all available options and choosing the one with the highest subjective value. The theory also implies that individuals have stable preferences over time, that they know exactly how much each option is worth to them, and that irrelevant situational factors are ignored by the decision-maker (e.g., the sudden availability of chocolate as a third flavor alternative, when the individual would never pick chocolate anyway). These assumptions, in particular, have led to much criticism from behavioral economists. In the real world, individuals often have to make decisions within a limited time frame, which makes it impossible to analyze every available choice in detail. Rational choice theory also leaves no space for contextual factors (such as **biases** or expectations), despite the substantial role of context in the decision-making process.

The idea that our decisions may be based on multiple factors is not new and, in fact, goes back to at least the eighteenth century when the famous Bernoulli family exchanged a series of letters on decision-making (Cowling, 1955). In those letters, they debated the role of context in how we understand the *value* and *probability* of a choice's outcome. This discourse paved the way for von Neumann and Morgenstern's **expected utility theory** (EUT): a formalization of the choices a rational individual ought to make and a key component of the modern rational choice framework (von Neumann & Morgenstern, 2007). The theory assumes that there is a precise functional mapping between our subjective preferences and the choices we make: in every decision-making situation, rational individuals assign subjective utilities (a metric of preference) to objective outcomes – and then act in a way that maximizes the utility they receive.

Importantly, the expected utility of an alternative is not the same as its expected value. Within the Bernoulli letters, in 1728, Gabriel Cramer wrote to Daniel Bernoulli, "the mathematicians estimate money in proportion to its quantity, and men of good sense in proportion to the usage that they may make of it." To put Cramer's words differently: alternatives with similar expected values do not always have the same expected utility. For example, consider the decision to go college for a degree or to start working. A degree might lead to a better salary (e.g., gain of $20,000 per year), but it also comes with risks (e.g., failing exams, dropping out). Say the probability of graduating is 75%; the expected value of attending college is 0.75 · $20,000 = $15,000. However, this gain has a different value for someone who already earns $200,000 per year compared to someone who only earns $20,000 per year. While the first person will likely decide against college, the expected utility is higher for the second person, leading to the alternate decision.

In the majority of economic scenarios, utility is an economic concept equivalent to human satisfaction (Thaler, 2015) and often depends on more than simple, general preferences (e.g., preferring apples to oranges). In fact, a key characteristic of utility is that it depends on the availability and the quantity of the commodity being considered. Each additional unit of a good or service provides **marginal utility**: increments of satisfaction that vary with the ease of access or the current consumption level of a good. If each additional unit of a commodity provides progressively more utility, we say that marginal utility is increasing; if utility increments instead decrease with additional units, we say that marginal utility is decreasing.

Most goods and services offer diminishing marginal utility. In other words, the more we have of something, the less we value each additional unit of it, even if the need to use it remains. This puzzle is described via Adam Smith's (introduced in detail later this chapter) paradox of water and diamonds: people will pay a substantially greater amount for a diamond (a good we have less of) than they will for water (a good we generally have more of), yet water is far more vital to our existence. This ultimately means that almost no product has a fixed inherent value and that the utility of all goods is contextual.

Another factor that comes into play when evaluating decisions is that, in the real world, some outcomes are probabilistic and predictable in nature, while others are not. The economist Frank H. Knight explored the dichotomy between predictable and unpredictable outcomes in his 1921 book *Risk, Uncertainty and Profit*, defining outcomes that occur with known probabilities as *risky* and outcomes whose probabilities are unknown as *uncertain*. In attempting to study behavior, we therefore treat risk as predictable while uncertainty is not; various economic theories attempt to address each of these types of situations. Indeed, individuals often make decisions where outcomes are truly uncertain, such as trying a new restaurant that just opened or deciding to move to a new city they have never visited for a job, not knowing if they will be happy in the location or the company.

EUT is one such theory that attempts to describe decision-making under risk specifically, meaning probabilities are possible to know. According to EUT, the satisfaction we expect from a choice is, in fact, dependent on both the utility of receiving the outcome and its probability of occurrence; the utility we expect, in turn, drives choice. In other words, **expected utility** is a product of utility and probability. So if you would win \$10 if you guess correctly on a coin flip (50:50), then the expected utility would be 5: (\$10 × 0.5) + (\$0 × 0.5). For choice options with multiple probabilistic outcomes, the expected utility is given by the sum of each outcome's expected utility.

Utility is not always a linear relationship (see Figure 2.2). Goods that offer diminishing marginal utility, for example, are best represented by concave utility functions (downward curving), while increasing marginal returns lead to convex utility functions (upward curving). But what do these mean in practice? Consider if you had a craving for chocolate. If you go to the store to buy some chocolate, you might buy one or even a few pieces. However, you probably will not buy a full year supply because really you just want to satisfy the craving. This would be concave – after you get the target amount, there is decreasing gain from having more. Alternatively, imagine getting dressed in the morning but finding only one shoe. That shoe does not offer great utility without its pair. As you find the second, the utility increases – convex – to its full potential (unfortunately, it will still not be able to help you find your keys). However, curvature reflects much more than the rate of change in utility, so let's try to be a little more precise and technical.

In EUT, utility function curvature allows us to predict how a "rational" individual would react when faced with risky choice options. For example, if we were to present you with the choice of a coin flip where you could win \$1,000 (\$0 otherwise) or a certain payout of \$500, your decision would vary depending on whether (1) the utility of money is linear for you; (2) your marginal utility of money is diminishing because you have an immediate

FIGURE 2.2 Linear, concave, and convex utility functions

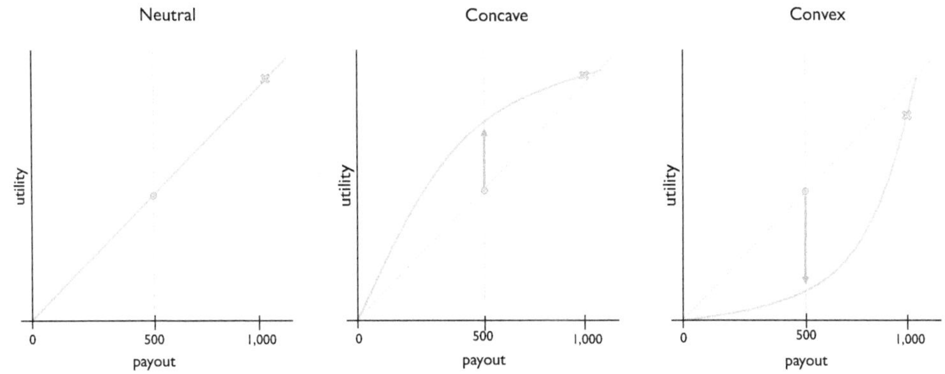

need for $500; or (3) you have increasing marginal utility for money because you have an immediate need for $1,000.

In the first case (linear utility), if the expected utility you get from $1,000 is 1,000, then the coin-flip option is worth $(1{,}000 \times 0.5) + (0 \times 0.5) = 500$ to you. Because utility, in this case, is linear, the certain payoff of $500 would also be worth 500 and you would therefore be indifferent between the options. This means that, if tested repeatedly over time or over a group, we should expect roughly a 50:50 pattern of choice, according to EUT.

In the second case (diminishing marginal utility), if the expected utility you get from $1,000 is again 1,000, the certain payout of $500 would now be worth more than 500 due to the concavity of the function. Because the coin flip is still worth 500 $[(1000 \times 0.5) + (0 \times 0.5) = 500]$ to you, you would prefer the safe option over the risky option. In other words, the guarantee of $500 has greater utility than the possibility of $1,000, which is the economic way of saying one in the hand is worth two in the bush.

In the third case (increasing marginal utility), we find the reverse: the certain payout of $500 would be worth less than 500. In such instances, we therefore expect you would pick the risky option. For whatever reason, lower amounts appear to have less significance than their objective values, resulting in a preference for risk over certainty. In each case, the difference in utility between the options depends on the curvature of the utility mapping.

Theory as a reference point

In some cases, you may find these insights to be rather obvious. However, such theories provide useful frameworks for studying, modeling, and predicting human behavior *with precision*. One of the key features in all social and behavioral sciences is that some of the most critical insights do not necessarily discover an unknown, but instead provide a more concrete understanding of how behaviors may appear across a population. As a framework, EUT has allowed economists to infer preferences and choices in a multitude of different situations, making it one of the most widely used theoretical models in economics. Without such references and their assumptions, it would be very difficult to carry out a study or debate insights, thus mitigating progress toward application. We should, however, also be mindful of EUT's restrictions, particularly when its assumptions do not hold true to behavior. We refer to such situations as *deviations from expected behaviors*, and a better understanding of these deviations almost always leads to better predictions.

In the case of EUT, we have to assume that for utility to reliably predict preferences, people need to decide rationally (von Neumann & Morgenstern, 2007). EUT establishes four axioms of rationality: basic assumptions that need to be satisfied for an individual to be a rational decision-maker. If all axioms are met, the individual is considered rational and their choices can be represented by a utility function. These axioms are as follows:

1 Completeness: well-defined preferences that lead to clear decisions
2 Transitivity: decisions remain consistent when presented repeatedly
3 Continuity: if one option is preferred over another, other options similar to the preferred option should also be preferred
4 Independence: preference for one option over another is independent of the existence of a third option

The first two axioms, completeness and transitivity, establish that decision-makers should be able to order their preferences. The continuity axiom, then, is necessary to establish the continuous scale (the utility function) upon which alternatives and their combinations can be compared. Finally, the independence axiom is necessary to define individual preferences as stable: that they keep to their order regardless of the way alternatives are presented, the scaling up or down of all alternatives simultaneously, or the addition of a decoy alternative (we will cover this later in the chapter). In other words, the independence axiom allows EUT to predict a rational individual's choices in different situations, once we know the general shape of their utility function (using the first three axioms). Together, these axioms allow us to predict the behavior of a rational individual in the way rational choice theory defines rationality.

Behaviors that systematically violate the assumption of independence have been widely documented. One popular but non-scientific example looked at subscriptions to the news magazine *The Economist* under two conditions (Ariely, 2008). The first condition offered an online subscription for $59 and a print subscription for $125 that included the online version for free. In this condition, a majority of respondents preferred the cheaper, online-only subscription. In the second condition, a third, decoy alternative was added: getting only the print subscription for $125. This is objectively worse: at the same price, consumers would receive less than the second option. In the new condition, the majority of people chose the combined print-online subscription over the other two options. This violates the independence assumption because a third option has inverted the relationship between the initial two options.

To account for these findings, psychologists and economists have developed models that attempt to explain when and how people deviate from the expectations of normative theories like EUT. Today, there are two broad classes of economic models. The first involves rational choice frameworks that aim to describe how people should behave to get the most out of a given choice. The second includes the behavioral models that try to capture how people actually behave in various choice situations. These approaches should *not* be considered as discrete but as complementary. Traditional rational models provide a prediction by which we can judge actual choices, and conversely, the behavioral models that capture systematic deviations from traditional models can lead to new ways of thinking about rationality. Many of the useful insights throughout this book come from these early observations. Deviations from these traditional models should be considered as areas for further study, and an understanding of the impact different scientific fields – and leading scholars from each – have had on behavioral research is a great place to start.

Behavioral economics

The explanation for the many violations of rational choice theory came in the form of **behavioral economics**, an interdisciplinary branch of economics seeking to include psychological insights in the study of economic decision-making. Behavioral economists stress that decision-makers are psychosocial **actors** who do not always behave optimally, as opposed to the ultrarational actors modeled in neoclassical economics. The focus of behavioral economics is therefore more experimental by nature, with conclusions that have tended to revolve around financial choices, incentives, and trade-offs where risk is involved. However, while many people believe that behavioral economics originated in the 1970s, its origins are very much entrenched in economic theory, going back to the pioneers of economic thought (ur Rehman, 2016; Camerer & Loewenstein, 2004).

As a field, behavioral economics is not without controversy, as many of the following chapters will demonstrate. Among its criticisms, for example, is that much of the early work was done with minimal sample sizes, and the results are therefore unreliable. Even leaders in the subject have expressed concern that some conclusions in the field, including from their own work, may be based on samples too small to provide reliable scientific evidence, which is central to concerns about replication in social science. Another focus of critics is that behavioral economics lacks a unified framework, perhaps best stated by Choi and Pritchard (2003):

> Instead of a theory, behavioral economics relies on a hodgepodge of evidence showing the ineffectiveness of human decision-making in various circumstances (often in a controlled, laboratory setting). Without such a theory, assessing possible methods for ameliorating such biases is a murky task at best.

More detail on this is contained in Chapter 3, but here, let's focus on how contemporary behavioral economics came to be.

Social psychology

The attempt to account for social context in the behaviors that we display is an essential aspect of behavioral decision-making. Much of the work in economic theory in the twentieth century happened concurrently with advances in social psychology, which is the study of the behavior of individuals in social settings. Because of this, social psychology has played a major part in the development of contemporary behavioral science. In particular, the concept of **social norms** has helped highlight the importance of contextual factors in influencing human behavior. The role of norms in human behavior was made prominent by Robert Cialdini. Social norms influence decisions and actions in many socially relevant settings. One notable example is littering. In an experiment by Cialdini, people returning to their car found a flyer under their windshield wiper. Some participants found themselves in an environment in which many identical flyers were already lying on the ground, making it seem like the norm was to simply throw them away. Indeed, when people found themselves in a littered environment, they were eight times more likely to drop the flyer themselves than when they were in a clean environment (Cialdini, Reno, & Kallgren, 1990). This scenario is an example of what Cialdini termed a *descriptive norm* – what people see others doing. More examples of this are included in subsequent chapters.

Key people and ideas

The following section is a brief list of some of the scholars that had the great influence in psychology and behavioral economics becoming so prevalent in policy. This list is not exhaustive, but instead includes individuals that were agreed on from researchers from different disciplines as being the most critical. See the suggested further reading at the end of chapters to come for more highly influential work – the following is only a brief overview of individuals and ideas that set the course for the field.

Adam Smith

In 1776, a Scottish academic by the name of Adam Smith published a book that would come to be seen as the magna carta of economics, titled *The Wealth of Nations* (or more accurately, *An Inquiry into the Nature and Causes of the Wealth of Nations*). This book enshrined the idea of the self-interested decision-maker, as well as the optimality of an open, freely competing market. Given how prevalent his frameworks and insights remain to this day, he could be likened to the Shakespeare of economics – he may not have invented the field, but his work is in many ways the standard against which all economic theorists are judged. What many tend to overlook, however, is the emphasis Smith placed on the role of uncertainty in the decision-making process, which goes against the idea that people make decisions in a normative, stable manner. Indeed, Smith included emotions, morals, and uncertainty as variables that could influence economic decisions.

John Maynard Keynes

Smith's work was further developed by John M. Keynes in his seminal work on the general theory of employment (1937). Keynes dedicated attention to the quality and quantity of information that people use to make their decisions, while also noting the challenge of predicting markets due to the collective irrational and unpredictable behaviors that people exhibit, especially in times of recession. While Keynes's work is widely referenced within the canon of traditional economic theory, his views on market interactions shifted the economic tradition away from purely rational models. **Keynesian economics** emphasizes that governments should invest in generating jobs: if people work – and are paid for this work – they can subsequently spend this money, which in turn stimulates markets to grow. Even decades later, this idea is still pursued heavily by modern economic thinking.

John Nash

John Nash, an American mathematician, made major contributions in the field of game theory. **Game theory** is the study of strategic decision-making, involving the mathematical analysis of situations with multiple participants, in which each individual's decisions affect the outcomes for themselves and others, typically in terms of cooperation (making choices that have mutual benefits) and defection (making choices where benefits are self-interested). Notably, during his time as a graduate student at Princeton University, Nash developed the concept that was later named the *Nash equilibrium*. This describes the situation in a non-cooperative game whereby neither player finds it advantageous to change strategy – for example, when knowing what the other players are doing, no unilateral change in strategy would yield better results (Nash, 1950). This influential concept led him to win the 1994 Nobel Prize in Economics.

The Nash equilibrium has been influential not only theoretically but also practically in its application to the understanding of real-world outcomes: for instance, the prevention of scenarios whereby competitors repeatedly undercut each other until neither makes a profit. An example of this can be seen in the case of the employment of medical students. As employers wanted to make offers of employment to candidates before any other employer, this pushed competitors to try to recruit even earlier. This continued until both employers and candidates were forced to make decisions further in advance than is advantageous (Holt & Roth, 2004). The introduction of solutions such as *clearinghouses*, which enable candidates to submit a list of preferred employers in order to produce a result in which employers and candidates are matched to produce a stable solution (Roth & Peranson, 1999), is based upon the concept of the Nash equilibrium.

Maurice Allais

The French economist Maurice Allais famously highlighted the failings of EUT. In a series of choice experiments, he showed that decision-makers reliably violated EUT choice predictions (Allais, 1953). The most famous of these experiments, and the phenomenon that would later be known as the *Allais paradox*, created behavior suggesting that probabilities were not processed objectively by decision-makers.

Consider the following gambles and choose which one you would prefer to play:

Gamble A:	100% chance of receiving 100
Gamble B:	10% chance of receiving 500
	89% chance of receiving 100
	1% chance of receiving nothing

Now choose between the following two gambles:

Gamble C:	11% chance of receiving 100
	89% chance of receiving nothing
Gamble D:	10% chance of receiving 500
	90% chance of receiving nothing

Most people prefer gamble A over B and gamble D over C, although the expected values are 100 (A), 139 (B), 11 (C), and 50 (D). In the first case (A vs. B), the lower risk of gamble A is preferred over the higher value of gamble B, while in the second case (C vs. D), the higher expected value of gamble D is preferred over the lower risk of gamble C. This finding illustrated that decision-makers behave incoherently and distort probabilities, ultimately paving the way for later work in behavioral economics.

Until Allais, there had been a general agreement that rational choice theory served as an accurate depiction of decision-making. That is, it described an expected norm for how people should behave in order to get the most out of a given situation. As many would come to show, however, its main strength (the assumption of rationality) would also prove to be the limiting factor in describing how people actually behave (Mongin, 2019). Since then, a large body of evidence has shown that people often depart from rational assumptions, demonstrating a variety of systematic errors in their reasoning (e.g., Allais, 1953; Ellsberg, 1961; Kahneman & Tversky, 1979).

In response to the limitations of neoclassical economics, several efforts emerged to provide models that could account for limited cognitive capacity, mental shortcuts, and restricted knowledge. As will be demonstrated shortly, this work introduced three key, influential streams of thought that have laid the foundation of the behavioral perspective in the study of decision-making: (a) Simon's concept of **bounded rationality** (Simon, 1957a, 1978); (b) Kahneman and Tversky's work on **heuristics** and **biases**, leading to their **Prospect Theory** (Kahneman, 2003b; Kahneman & Tversky, 1979; Tversky & Kahneman, 1992); and (c) Gigerenzer's concepts of fast, frugal heuristics and **ecological rationality** (Gigerenzer & Goldstein, 1996).

Herbert Simon

Herbert Simon is often considered the ultimate pioneer of behavioral approaches to decision-making (Sent, 2004). He was the first to suggest that humans lack the computational capacity to behave as assumptions of rational choice theory would predict (Simon, 1957b). This **bounded rationality** suggests that people often simply do not consider certain choices, as their mental capacity is too limited to compare them and make the optimal decision (Thaler, 2015). Instead, individuals follow their intuitive reasoning or **hedonic** desires (Kahneman, 2003a). Simon (1978) adapted the term **heuristics** to denote these intuitive techniques (cognitive algorithms) that enable quick and efficient decision-making.

Simon proposed that this bounded rationality leads individuals to satisfice rather than to maximize. To **satisfice** means that instead of maximizing (choosing the best outcome between choices), people set an aspiration (a target goal) that they want to achieve and select the first available option that reaches this target goal (Simon, 1978).

To illustrate the difference between the rational and the bounded rationality approaches, think about a woman shopping for a birthday cake for her mother. According to the rational approach (based on the maximization assumption), she should compare the costs and benefits of every cake available in the shop and then choose the one with the highest marginal return. According to the bounded rationality approach (based on the assumption that people satisfice), she should set target goals (e.g., price range, filling, the cake topping) and buy the first cake that meets these criteria, even if a better cake may exist. Over the last 60 years, the study of heuristics in such contexts has expanded to numerous branches within the behavioral sciences (see Gigerenzer & Gaissmaier, 2011; Kahneman, 2003b; Shah & Oppenheimer, 2008).

Daniel Kahneman and Amos Tversky

When Daniel Kahnemann and Amos Tversky published a series of experiments challenging EUT directly, it marked another milestone for behavioral economics and the study of decision-making in general. Their research program was the most prominent work on deviations from rationality in human decision-making (Shafir & Leboeuf, 2002) and formed the core of contemporary behavioral economics. Kahneman and Tversky's work also addressed heuristics as imperfect tools of the human mind that are responsible for undesirable systematic errors in decision-making (Tversky & Kahneman, 1974).

In 1973, Tversky and Kahneman published a study in which participants were asked to listen to two recorded lists. One list contained the names of famous celebrities and the other contained less-famous names. After listening to both lists, the participants were asked to indicate which of the two lists contained more names. A vast majority (about 80%) incorrectly chose the list containing the celebrity names, although it contained fewer names than the second list (19 vs. 20 names). Tversky and Kahneman suggested that the participants recalled more names of famous celebrities because the names were readily available in their memory, which led to the false impression that the famous celebrities list contained a higher number of names (the **availability bias**). Their 1974 paper "Judgements Under Uncertainty: Heuristics and Biases" also addressed what they called the **representation bias,** where people judge similar outcomes as more likely, and the **anchoring** effect, where people rely too heavily on initial pieces of information compared to subsequent information.

Most famous, however, is Kahneman and Tversky's formulation of **Prospect Theory** (1979), a model of decision-making under risk intended to serve as a more descriptive model of human choices than EUT (also see Chapter 4). Participants in a series of experiments were presented scenarios in which they could choose between two options with varying values and probabilities, such as a 25% chance of $100 or a 75% chance of $25. By analyzing responses across a range of values and risks – some higher, some lower, some gains, some losses – they concluded that many EUT violations exist. These violations were then addressed by Prospect Theory with three central tenets: subjective distortion of objective probabilities, reference dependence, and **loss aversion.**

First, Kahnemann and Tversky found that people do not weight subjective outcomes by their objective probability, but instead subjectively distort the latter. In fact, Kahneman and Tversky demonstrated that people reliably overweighted low-probability outcomes and underweighted high-probability outcomes

Second, Prospect Theory explored the role of reference points in decision-making. **Framing** involves a change in the description or presentation with no objective change in the choice options or values of outcomes. Consider this example: if you receive $5 out of the blue, you would most likely perceive it as a gain. Conversely, if you were first told you would receive $10 but instead only received $5, you would perceive it as a loss. Objectively, these two outcomes are the same: you have received an unexpected $5. However, the way the information was framed relative to an initial reference influenced how the outcome was perceived, irrespective of its objective value.

Third, according to Prospect Theory, losses are weighted more heavily than gains of the same magnitude. In combination with previous points, this explains why people tend to be **risk averse** for gains and risk seeking for losses when the probability of the outcome is high, and they are risk seeking for gains and risk averse for losses when the probability of the outcome is low (Tversky & Kahneman, 1992). Figure 2.3 provides an overview of how this loss aversion was demonstrated.

Prospect Theory is widely seen as the turning point for psychological research moving into the mainstream of economic science, and for it, Kahneman was awarded the 2002 Nobel Prize in Economics (sadly, Tversky had already passed away in 1996). Their research remains, to this day, some of the highest impact, most widely cited work across the behavioral, social, and

FIGURE 2.3 Prospect Theory

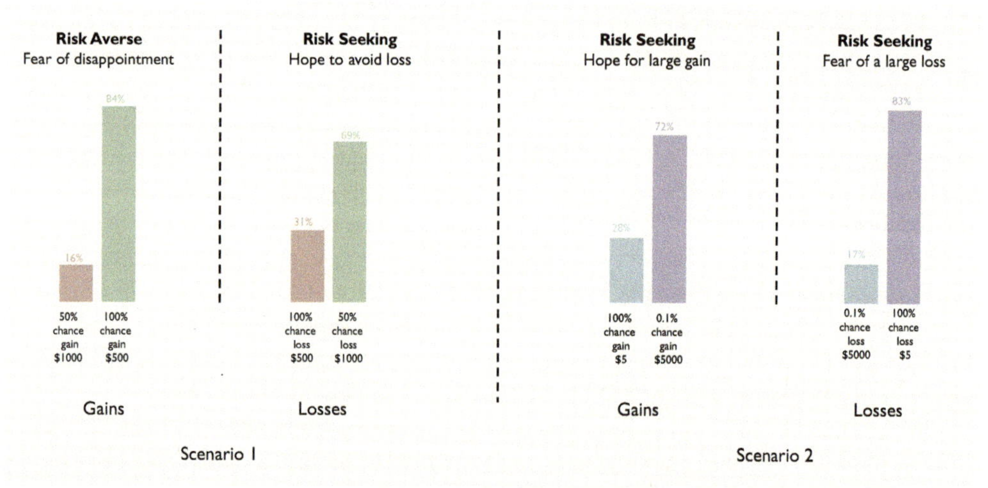

This figure presents four different outcomes as tested by Kahneman and Tversky (1979) in establishing Prospect Theory. The values above each bar represent the percent of participants that chose the particular option. The options are listed below each bar and present a series of uncertain outcomes versus certain ones. As the pattern indicates, individuals are much more likely to seek risk if it will help avoid a large loss or make a large gain.

economic sciences – and beyond (see Box 3.2) – and a great deal has been written about how their own relationship influenced their outcomes (see *The Undoing Project*, Lewis, 2016). (And not for nothing, many of the authors of this book were directly responsible for showing their initial findings replicated almost universally 40 years later, across many countries [Ruggeri et al., 2020a].)

Gerd Gigerenzer

The work of evolutionary psychologist Gerd Gigerenzer and his colleagues provides an alternative view on heuristics from Kahneman's work. Gigerenzer (2008) suggested that individuals do not need to follow neoclassical economic principles to make optimal decisions. Given the nature of human functioning, heuristics are more "rational" than the maximization approach, as heuristics represent the best possible use of humans' limited information-processing abilities. Under the framework they call **ecological rationality**, Gigerenzer and his colleagues emphasize that heuristics need to be used in an appropriate environment to provide optimal decisions (Gigerenzer & Brighton, 2009). His team described heuristics as fast and frugal adaptive mechanisms that enhance human functioning (Gigerenzer & Goldstein, 1996), contrary to Tversky and Kahneman (1973) who viewed heuristics as imperfect substitutes for rational reasoning.

Gigerenzer and his colleagues developed and compared computational models that simulated rational and heuristic reasoning. They demonstrated that a heuristic called "take the best" can – in some environments – outperform a rational model in both speed and accuracy (Gigerenzer & Goldstein, 1996). The key point made by Gigerenzer and Brighton (2009) is that rational models have a problem of data overfitting: they describe and fit existing data very well, but their predictive power for new data is poor. Heuristics, on the other hand, though they might fit data less reliably, offer falsifiable and often accurate predictions when it comes to out-of-sample data

To specify the environments where heuristics are optimal and suboptimal, Gigerenzer and his colleagues developed several theories. They note that the complexity and structure of a decision-making environment has a substantial influence over the efficacy of heuristics (see, for example, Gigerenzer & Brighton, 2009; Gigerenzer & Kurzenhauser, 2005; Todd & Gigerenzer, 2007). In line with research on ecological rationality, Gigerenzer also introduced the term **adaptive toolbox**. According to this concept, heuristics can be disassembled into building blocks and restructured to create a more suitable tool for a given environment (Gigerenzer, 2008). As a result, the human mind has only a limited number of strategies and reasoning techniques that can then be combined to address a range of situations.

Brigitte Madrian

In terms of individual studies with the greatest direct impact on real-world practice, perhaps the most significant is a 2001 paper by Brigitte Madrian and Dennis Shea. In their study on automatic enrollment in retirement savings plans for US employers, Madrian and Shea found that participation in employer-sponsored savings plans significantly increased when employees were faced with automatic enrollment with an **opt out** instead of an **opt-in** version (see Chapter 4 for a more detailed discussion). This *default behavior*, as they put it, referred to the general tendency of sticking to a default option instead of actively switching to a different choice alternative.

Since then, default approaches have become the standard means of influencing decision-making and have played an important role in behaviorally informed policies. **Default** behavior has been studied in decision-making insurance (Johnson, Hassin, Baker, Bajger, & Treuer, 2013) and environmental behavior (Sunstein & Reisch, 2014), as well as in healthcare decisions such as organ donation (Johnson & Goldstein, 2003), prevention, and vaccination (Brewer, Chapman, Rothman, Leask, & Kempe, 2017). Madrian has been, and remains, a true leader when it comes to advocating for integration of the behavioral sciences in policymaking (see Madrian, 2014).

Richard Thaler and Cass Sunstein

It is impossible to conclude a section on key figures in behavioral economics without mentioning Richard Thaler and Cass Sunstein. Their 2008 book *Nudge: Improving decisions about health, wealth, and happiness* presented a recent history of behavioral research, overviewing some of the peculiar decisions we make that do not seem to fit rational expectations. They also explored simple, low-cost interventions – **nudges** – that appear to steer large numbers of individuals away from those irrational decisions without actually requiring any major changes (Thaler & Sunstein, 2008).

Without a doubt, *Nudge* brought behavioral economics into the mainstream more so than any other article, study, or policy report. It also inspired a new generation of behavioral researchers to reposition their work so that they could apply theory to real-world problems. The following chapter describes Thaler's and Sunstein's writings in much further detail, along with key principles of their research.

While *Nudge* has led the rebirth of the behavioral side of economics, Thaler, Sunstein, and others will note that this multidisciplinary field is a lot more than just nudges. They would also note that many behavioral interventions are useful and can create an impact, but they are not a panacea – they will not cure disease nor will they prevent every case of poor decision-making. Yet, with a greater understanding of those behaviors and the interventions that may assist people in avoiding poor choices, we are likely to produce more informed policies that address real issues and real barriers, leading to better outcomes for more people.

Perhaps most critically, though, Thaler and Sunstein's work brought behavioral approaches to the attention of policymakers and governments around the world (Gino, 2017). As will be discussed in later chapters, this started with immediate applications to financial domains, such as taxes and regulating credit cards. However, as those chapters will demonstrate, it became evident almost immediately that behavioral insights are relevant for any policy domain, from energy to education and from healthcare to human rights. It is a remarkable achievement given that barely a decade has passed since the book came out, yet it has in some ways had as widespread an effect as many of the long-standing economic frameworks presented here.

BOX 2.2 NEUROECONOMICS

While the work of psychologists, sociologists, and economists often takes the forefront in the behavioral sciences, there has also been growing interest in understanding the biological building blocks that lead to our behavior. This is particularly the case for neuroscience, which is largely interested in the underpinning mechanisms between the brain and behavior.

In the early 1990s, once behavioral economics had been thoroughly established as a discipline, the field saw a deluge of new mathematical models that emerged to explain the ever-increasing number of rational choice violations. **Cumulative prospect theory** was developed to address the failures of Prospect Theory (Tversky & Kahneman, 1992), new heuristics described old ones, and a collection of new theories and algorithms began to amass, each describing specific choice biases in utmost detail. Simultaneously, in the 1980s, the field of neuroscience went through somewhat of a revolution. Until then, neuroscientists had been confined to the study of brain lesions in animals or patients with neurological injuries; that all changed when novel imaging techniques were developed that finally allowed researchers to explore the link between brain activity and behavior.

With the advent of modern brain imaging (where brain activity is measured using functional magnetic resonance imaging, or fMRI), many neuroscientists also began using the models of behavioral economics to correlate brain activity with quantifiable choices. Concurrently, behavioral economists had started tooling with the idea that rational decision-making models would run into biological constraints. It did not take long for like-minded psychologists, neuroscientists, and economists to collaborate, leading to neuroscientists using economics as a tool to understand the brain and economists using neuroscience to refine their models.

In the years since, neuroeconomics has sought to identify biological bases for framing and loss aversion (De Martino, Kumaran, Seymour, & Dolan, 2006) and probability distortions (Tobler, Christopoulos, O'Doherty, Dolan, & Schultz, 2008), and has shown that many animals share the behavioral biases described by behavioral economists (Heilbronner, 2017; Pearson, Watson, & Platt, 2014). The two main contributions of neuroeconomics to behavioral science, however, are perhaps the recognition that the biological limitations of our brain likely underpin context-specific preferences, as well as the inclusion of neural noise in choice models. The coding principles that govern our senses are likely to also govern our decision-making (see Figure 2.4) and might account for many of the cognitive biases identified by behavioral economics (Glimcher & Fehr, 2008). Likewise, neuroscientists have long known that the neural code is not as precise as rational choice models would suggest, and random noise in the firing patterns of our neurons would likely explain some of our more "irrational" choices.

Kahneman (2003) himself touches on these biological realities while describing his two-system model of human cognition that explains decision-making biases and errors: he describes the first system (system 1) as "fast, automatic, effortless, associative, implicit (not available to introspection), and often emotionally charged" (Ibid., p. 698), and the second system (system 2) as the one that utilizes deliberate, conscious control, requires effort, and is slower. He has also recently incorporated the concept of noise to his theories, as a source of error in human decision-making – a concept all too familiar to neuroeconomists. However, **noise** (Kahneman, Sibony, & Sunstein, 2021) – as captured by Kahneman's theory – does not reflect neural noise specifically but rather generalizes to all randomly occurring inaccuracies influenced by unstable situational factors. Thus, noise is difficult to explain using only cognitive or social shortcomings and is often *simply random*. Yet, Kahneman argues that it can be reduced by introducing reasoned rule to specific decisions, a form of simple calculation or algorithm that reduces the effect of noise through a tested process. Importantly, whereas noise can be corrected for without having to know the outcome, the removal of errors stemming from biases requires fixed algorithms and systematic analyses. If we want to understand the factors influencing decision-making, we need to account for both noise and heuristics, and to understand the mechanisms by which they occur.

While much more complex, the short history of neuroeconomics told here serves mostly to illustrate the current state of research in behavioral science. The birth of neuroeconomics led behavioral scientists to question past and current approaches to the study of decision-making and to begin formalizing the role of biological constraints in guiding our choices.

FIGURE 2.4 Neural adaptation and the reference effect

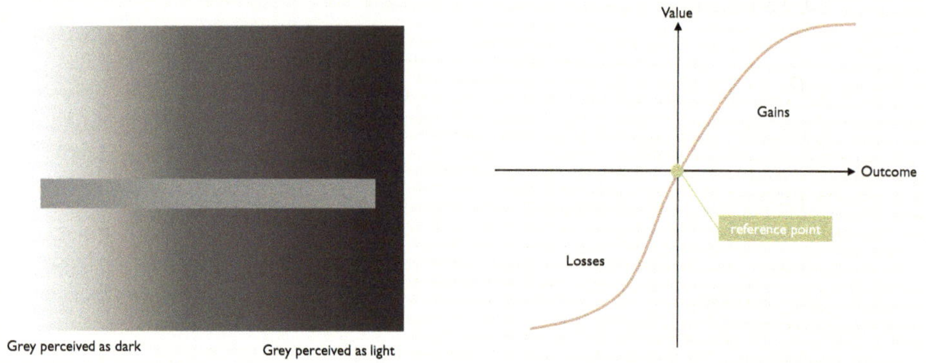

The perceived color of the bar depends on the reference provided by the background color. Similarly, the utility of an outcome in Prospect Theory depends on the reference point the decision-maker has at the moment of choice. This could be current wealth, anticipated wealth, or expectations formed out of past decision outcomes. Our reference point often shifts upward in reaction to gains and downward in reaction to losses.

Conclusion

While the fundamental economic theories and frameworks mentioned in this chapter continue to hold great significance in more traditional economic domains (financial decision-making, management, marketing), the behavioral sciences have also begun to play a major role in public policy and practice.

As we illustrated in this chapter, the last few decades have seen significant improvements in the way we understand and predict human decision-making, often counter to what had previously been assumed. Over time, the accumulation of new evidence, particularly from the psychological sciences, has led the broader behavioral sciences to play an ever-increasing role in understanding and shaping real-world behavior. The following chapters of this book will now present those cases.

Essay questions

1 When someone says "economic theory assumes people are rational," what do they mean? Are they correct?

2 Imagine you start a job at a big policy think tank consisting of classically trained economists. They know you have been learning about behavioral economics and ask you what exactly makes the field "behavioral" and if its theories contradict knowledge they have. How would you respond?

3 You meet your friend – who studies psychology – for coffee during a study break. She is preparing for her exam in economical psychology and tells you, "I don't even know why people still study economics. Behavioral scientists have shown that they are wrong anyway." Is she correct?

4 Three former students owe $10,000 after graduating and are offered a choice of payment plans for their student loans. They can choose from the following: (1) a 0% interest plan if they pay off the loan within 12 months; (2) a $100/month payment plan if they pay it off over 10 years; or (3) $25/month for the rest of their life. All three graduates are 25 years old. Student 1 has already found a high-paying job. Student 2 has found a job, but it only pays a little above the cost of living. Student 3 has decided to continue studying and will begin graduate school in three months. Use expected utility theory to describe what choice you expect each student to make, including any limitations.

3 An introduction to behavioral economics

Kai Ruggeri, Hannes Jarke, Maja Friedemann, Faisal Naru, and Francesca Papa

Chapter summary

Behavioral sciences have challenged the traditional view of a human as a wholly rational actor, the *homo economicus* in classical economic theory. Embracing these new findings, the field of behavioral economics formed to enrich traditional economic assumptions with evidence and theories from psychological research. These behavioral insights have been incorporated into public policy by governments all over the world. One tool in particular – nudging – has become a prominent, large-scale behavioral intervention. This chapter explores how the different aspects of behavioral economics, nudging and beyond, can come together to inform and enhance public policy.

Learning objectives

- Introduce critical terms and concepts from psychology and behavioral economics applied to public policy
- Explore contemporary tools from psychology and behavioral economics that have been successfully implemented into public policy

Behavioral insights and public policies

Over the last few decades, behavioral science has greatly advanced our knowledge of how humans think and how context shapes their thinking. By complementing traditional economic theory with ideas from cognitive and social sciences, behavioral research has gathered vast evidence of the ways in which humans deviate from rational decision-making and deepened our understanding of the psychological, social, and cultural variables influencing behavior. After almost a century of separation between the disciplines of economics and psychology, behavioral science has brought new interdisciplinary insights into economic and political discourse and launched a new policy agenda aimed at designing policies that are in line with how citizens actually behave.

National governments increasingly recognize the value of greater scrutiny of decision-making. Currently, over 200 government units, initiatives, and partnerships around the world work to apply behavioral principles to public policy (OECD, 2019a). As was covered in Chapter 2, much of this popularity came about after Daniel Kahneman was awarded

DOI: 10.4324/9781003181873-3

the Nobel Prize for Economics in 2002. That momentum rapidly accelerated after the success of Thaler and Sunstein's 2008 book *Nudge*, which is undoubtedly one of the most popular books on economics, policy, and behavior, and one of the motives for Thaler's Nobel Prize in Economics in 2017.

Despite the important roles that Thaler and Sunstein played in popularizing behavioral research, it is crucial to highlight that behavioral science and **nudges** (small changes in the choice architecture that encourage optimal decisions) are distinct concepts. Behavioral science is a scientific discipline encompassing a wide range of tools, and nudges are one of the ways in which we can apply its findings to policymaking (Lunn, 2014). The concept of nudging itself sits in a wider framework known as **libertarian paternalism** (Thaler & Sunstein, 2003), which is the idea that preferred behaviors should not necessarily be brought about through regulation, but rather be encouraged without banning other choices. In other words, people should be presented with the appropriate environment that encourages the most beneficial choice possible, but still be free to make the decision they prefer – even if that decision is not optimal for them.

Policymakers can make use of the psychosocial factors that affect individual decisions to promote those behaviors that are most valued by society and that might otherwise be neglected by single individuals. These could be conserving energy, increasing safety on the roads, or even saving for retirement (we will cover specific examples in the following chapters). Drawing on rigorous research from behavioral science, governments can improve the welfare of citizens in a variety of domains without compromising their autonomy, by tuning policies with the actual behavior of citizens and pretesting policy solutions before scaling them up.

In *Nudge*, Thaler and Sunstein (2008) present an anthology of examples demonstrating the peculiarities of human choice, centering on how what may appear to be minutiae in terms of aspects of a decision may ultimately have high **impact** and, therefore, be of substantial relevance to policy. Other popular books on this topic have followed. Titles such as *Scarcity* (Mullainathan & Shafir, 2013) and *Misbehaving* (Thaler, 2015) have further pushed behavioral insights into the zeitgeist of policy design and public discourse. While these have been successful in regard to reach and influence, the increase in the number of such volumes over recent years indicates that we are still very much in the early days – you may say the Wild West, even – of behavioral insights as a policy tool.

Traditional economic theory has long assumed that the approaches used by economists reflect the way people solve problems in reality (Thaler & Benartzi, 2004). This journey again goes all the way back to 1776 and Adam Smith's *Wealth of Nations* (see Chapter 2), and it is difficult to trace to what extent economic scholars fully incorporated behavioral factors into their work, largely because it was either not popular to discuss or simply not accessible to large groups. So these pages, much like many brief histories of behavioral economics, are more of a chronology for getting started, rather than a comprehensive narrative.

A brief history of behavioral concepts in economic thought

One of the central tenets of behavioral science is that decision-making is not only dependent on individual factors. A decision made alone may vastly differ from a decision made in the company of a friend, the family, or a group of colleagues; a decision made at home, work, or on vacation; or a decision considering how people in the neighborhood would judge you for it. **Social norms** – such as values or customs shared by a group or society – have been identified as a frame of reference for many decisions made by humans as early as the 1930s (Sherif, 1936). Moreover, individuals in different positions in a social group may have a different relative impact on shaping the behaviors and norms in their social network. In particular, a message will have a different impact depending on who conveys it (**messenger effect**), and it will be particularly impactful if communicated by an opinion leader (Katz & Lazarsfeld, 1957). As you will see in the following chapters of this book, these norms and social factors can be leveraged by policymakers in various areas, such as tax behavior, food choices, and more.

Another core aspect of behavioral economics is its criticism of the rationally acting human being – ***homo economicus***. As was briefly covered in Chapter 2, Herbert Simon – an American economist who later won the Nobel Prize in Economics – hypothesized in 1957 that people in fact behave only as rationally as they can within the boundaries of the information they have at their disposal. Their thinking is also influenced by factors outside their control or active perception. People make decisions within their **bounded rationality**, which may be limited by personal cognitive skills or simply time pressure to make a decision. For instance, if it is raining outside but you have a date in ten minutes, you are likely to buy the most easily available umbrella you can find, ignoring the economic implications of it possibly being overpriced or of poor quality.

Simon's notion of bounded rationality is therefore in sharp contrast with the long-standing theory of rational expectations by John F. Muth, who argued that our predictions do not systematically involve forecasting errors and are accurate on average. However, from an historical perspective, it is interesting to note that Simon's and Muth's conflicting theories originated from the same intellectual milieu. As Simon himself noted, "it is not without irony that bounded rationality and rational expectations . . . though entirely antithetical to each other, were engendered in and flourished in the same small business school at almost the same time" (Simon, 1991). But the core concepts from 1957 remained eminently in the economic canon.

Around 20 years later, Kahneman and Tversky (1979) produced another major shift by extending or countering **expected utility theory** (see Chapter 2) by adding the varying perception of gains and losses as a factor within **Prospect Theory**. They found that while people do calculate the expected utility of their choices, they act differently when presented with the chance of a loss than when presented with the same chance of a gain. Individuals evaluate possible gains and losses on the basis of their specific context (their reference point) rather than on absolute values. As a result, the pain of losing a certain amount of money tends to be greater than the joy of winning the same amount, as reflected in an asymmetrical and V-shaped value function (see Figure 3.1). The significance of reference points is also relevant for another key behavioral principle – the **anchoring effect** – whereby when making decisions or estimates, individuals tend to disproportionately rely on an initial piece of information (the anchor) and fail to accurately update their beliefs in light of new information (Tversky & Kahneman, 1986).

Similarly, Tversky and Kahneman (1981, 1986) found that preferences shift, to various extents, depending on the way in which a situation is presented – a process referred to as **framing**. For instance, *homo economicus* should not make a different decision when presented with the information that there is an 80% possibility that an investment in stock of

FIGURE 3.1 Hypothetical value function in Prospect Theory

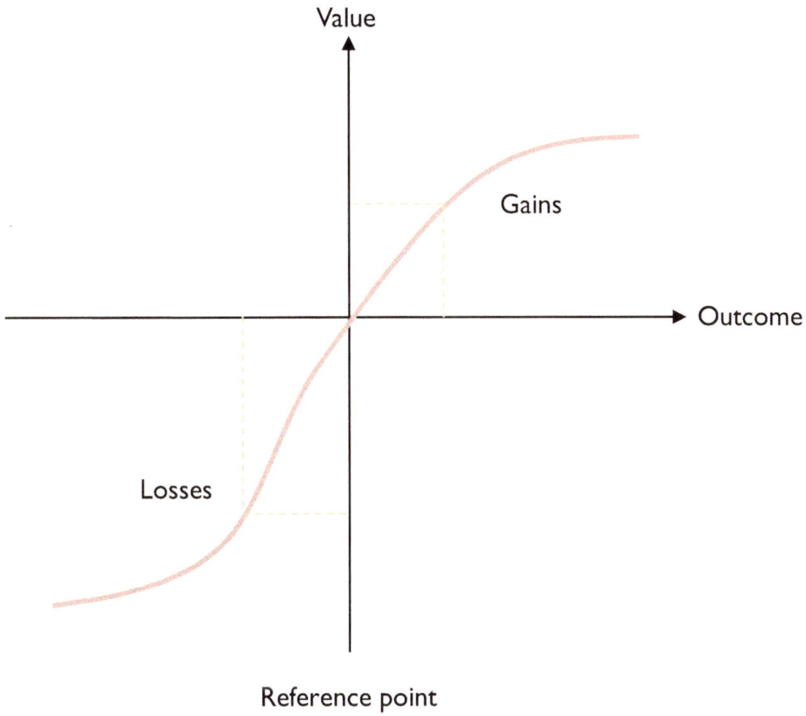

Source: Tversky and Kahneman (1986)

company Z will be profitable than when told that an investment in stock of company Z has a 20% possibility of generating a loss. However, there are many examples where people do: while framing may be reliant on, or associated with, a number of factors influencing its effectiveness, a meta-analysis suggests overall effects from small to moderate size in influencing decisions under risk (Kühberger, 1998).

But the field is not only about hypotheticals – it also specifically explores real behaviors, such as how our spending habits change depending on if we use cash or credit cards. For example, Thaler (1985) was the first to describe a process he labeled **mental accounting**. People tend to keep track of their financial activities in their head. However, they do not always use their full budget (like their current account, checking account, or even their savings account) as a point of reference; rather, they compare the price tag of something they desire to whatever amount they *think* they have available, such as the bills in their pocket or the paycheck that they just received.

Comparison of choices is more complicated than often treated in classical economics: imagine you are starting university and you want to open a new savings account. One offers an interest rate of 0.5% a year and another offers 2%. For both, you would have to sign a contract that binds you until the end of your studies. The first account with the lower interest rate gives you a $25 voucher for the student bar. Having a night out with friends right away can seem much more desirable than slightly more money stretched over several years. This process of valuing an immediate but smaller gain over a larger gain in the future is called **temporal** or **hyperbolic discounting** (Laibson, 1997). It describes our undervaluation of future benefits or how we put present, instant gratification in a different category altogether.

While standard economics conceptualized decision-makers as *rational actors*, and early work in behavioral economics considered them *quasi-rational actors* (influenced by the cognitive biases we just discussed), what has been referred to as the "second strand of behavioral economics" later advanced the notion of decision-makers as *enculturated actors, deeply impacted by sociocultural factors* (Hoff & Stiglitz, 2016; Demeritt & Hoff, 2018). This strand argues that judgments and behaviors are guided by entrenched social influences and, notably, by *cultural mental models or schemas* (DiMaggio, 1997). Our culture and social experiences shape both who we are and how we think, and they translate into sustained beliefs, narratives, worldviews, and social outcomes – as exemplified by national stereotypes or gendered divisions of labor, which are hard to eradicate.

During the 1990s, further investigation into the influence of group norms found that people may act in a way that confirms out-group or mainstream perceptions or stereotypes of a social group they belong to (or feel they belong to). This **stereotype threat** describes people as "being at risk of confirming, as self-characteristic, a negative stereotype about one's group" (Steele & Aronson, 1995, p. 797) and can even lower academic and cognitive performance, though those effects have been brought into question (Flore & Wicherts, 2015). Similarly, it was later found that belonging to a group that is associated with positive stereotypes can improve performance and is referred to as a **stereotype boost** (Shih, Pittinsky, & Ho, 2011).

Another concept from behavioral economics that has been particularly influential since the beginning of this century is the use of **default options** or settings. When people are faced with a choice between two or more options, making one of them predetermined unless the person deliberately chooses the other has a significant impact on a population level. For example, countries in which being an organ donor is the default – an **opt-out** approach – have much higher rates of organ donation than countries that do not (Johnson & Goldstein, 2003; see also Chapter 5 of this book). These findings have had a massive impact, including on European Union law such as the General Data Protection Regulation, which now dictates that (most) personal data collection without active consent (consent cannot be the default) is illegal and, since 2018, punishable by high financial penalties.

While one might get the impression that all of these phenomena make people less effective decision-makers than *homo economicus*, they can sometimes be useful in specific situations. As such, behavioral science does not universally endorse the idea that humans are fundamentally irrational creatures. In fact, since 2001, Gerd Gigerenzer has argued that many of the phenomena and biases mentioned are actually entirely plausible and advantageous, if activated within the domain for which they are designed. In an uncertain world where we are all "risk illiterates" (Gigerenzer, 2015), heuristics and biases are adaptive forms of reasoning that can constitute efficient mental shortcuts and intuitive judgments. Gigerenzer calls this framework the **adaptive toolbox.** A selection of emblematic examples of key heuristics and biases is presented in Table 3.1.

By building on a variety of the insights from behavioral economics, ranging from the effects of social norms to those of default options, one technique, in particular, is being applied by policies nowadays to help people make better decisions: **nudging**.

TABLE 3.1 Selected principles of behavioral economics

	Judgment	
Availability	*Representativeness*	*Unrealistic optimism*
Judging the likelihood of a future event based on the easiness of imagining/ recalling it	Judging the likelihood of an event based on its resemblance to an already familiar event	Overestimating chances of personal success and assuming immunity from risk compared to other similar people
	Decision-making	
Affect	*Salience effect*	*Discounting future rewards*
Evaluating an option based on the emotional response it evokes	When facing several options, the most explicity, simple, and direct option tends to be selected	Immediate rewards tend to be preferred to larger future rewards
Fairness	*Framing effects*	*Loss aversion*
Rejecting a positive outcome when it violates one's perception of fairness	The method of presenting choices determines the most likely chosen option	Tendency to avoid uncertain options with potential losses in favor of options with worse average outcomes but no risks of loss
	Choice architecture	
Accounting for human error	*Default options*	*Feedback*
Employing additional safeguards to prevent mistakes and avoid negative consequences	The pre-selected option that will be chosen by most people	Giving (direct) feedback after a decision has been made improves performance the following time
Incentives	*Structuring complex choices*	*Understanding consequences*
Rewards or costs intended to encourage or discourage specific behaviours	When choices grow in complexity, structure improves decision-making	Making poor short-term decisions simply by not grasping the likely outcomes

Nudges

As originally conceived by Thaler and Sunstein, a nudge is:

> Any aspect of the choice architecture that alters people's behavior in a predictable way without forbidding any options or significantly changing their economic incentives. To count as a mere nudge, the intervention must be easy and cheap to avoid. Nudges are not mandates. Putting fruit at eye level counts as a nudge. Banning junk food does not.
>
> (Thaler & Sunstein, 2008, p. 6)

With nudges and libertarian paternalism, Thaler and Sunstein (2008) also established the concept of **choice architecture**: the careful design of the environments within which people make choices. The word *careful* is key: behavioral researchers operate under the assumption that *any* (even a seemingly irrelevant) factor in the environment has the potential to influence choices (Thaler, Sunstein, & Balz, 2013). Choice architects seek to make use of the knowledge about factors that impact decisions. They use this to design environments that nudge individuals toward optimal decisions (Thaler & Sunstein, 2008). Similar to architects of train stations, for example, who adjust stairs or elevator positions in a way that optimizes moving from point A to point B, choice architects strategically alter factors in the environment to encourage people to make optimal decisions.

Presenting choice alternatives in a specific order (**order effects**), such as putting healthy meals on the front page of a menu, is one such example of a nudge. To grasp the importance of arranging choices strategically, consider the choice options in the two arrangements of Figure 3.2. Which cup would you choose? As can be guessed intuitively, some people who pick the small coffee in the first setting would actually choose the medium size in the second setting, because we all have a tendency to choose the middle option rather than extremes regardless of its actual value, which is known as the **extremeness aversion** (or sometimes as the **compromise effect**) (OECD, 2019b).

On the left, there is an illustration of differently sized coffee mugs, the smaller labelled with €2.50, the larger with €3.50. The caption reads "A. Which do you prefer?" On the right, captioned "B. Which do you prefer now?," the illustration shows three coffee mugs different in size. From smallest to largest, they are labelled €2.50, €3.50, and €4.50.

Another very popular intervention example is the fly in the urinal: while it might seem ridiculous, researchers found an 80% reduction in unsanitary splashing simply by adding a small sticker in the shape of a fly in the well of a urinal (Thaler & Sunstein, 2008). A small intervention, but one with very large downstream effects (less cleaning, avoiding the spread of threats to hygiene by those walking through).

Nudges are a subset of behavioral interventions that, when effective, can provide a relatively cost-efficient way to increase the frequency of positive behaviors (e.g. healthy eating, retirement saving, recycling, or charity donations) (Benartzi et al., 2017). By 2014, more than 50 governments were already implementing some form of choice architecture into their policies (Whitehead, Jones, Howell, Lilley, & Pykett, 2014), and their number continues to increase (Sunstein, Reisch, & Rauber, 2017).

A comprehensive study by Benartzi et al. (2017) showed that nudge-based interventions do particularly well in their impact-to-cost ratio; however, nudging should not be universally considered as "cheap." Many behaviorally informed policies are particularly cost-effective, as they build on slight changes in policy design or implementation, such as

FIGURE 3.2 Arranging choices – which do you prefer?

Source: OECD (2019b)

providing reminders to increase the uptake of a program, selecting the right timing to roll out a policy intervention, or effectively framing and ordering a set of options (World Bank Group, 2015). However, the development of new interventions can be resource-intensive, as substantial groundwork needs to be conducted before identifying which policy strategies to test (OECD, 2019b). Nonetheless, one of the strengths of behavioral public policy is precisely its experimental approach, which limits the risk of committing resources to the full implementation of a given policy solution that may have to be revisited at a later stage.

Behavioral public policy today

Behavioral insights, the lessons learned from behavioral, psychological, cognitive, and social science research, have gained increased popularity as tools to inform public policy around the world (OECD, 2014b, 2017a). This has led to the emergence of **behavioral public policy** (see Oliver, 2013) as a field of inquiry and has fostered a culture of experimentation to better understand how to adjust policies to citizens' actual behavior.

As the interest for behavioral policymaking grew more widespread, it became important to demonstrate that behavioral insights could effectively contribute to tackling complex policy problems. For this reason, in the early 2000s, a number of "nudge units" were formed within governments to demonstrate the positive return on investment of this new methodology. In order to set up the new units, governments worked in partnership with research institutions and policy laboratories to benefit from expertise and research outside government (OECD, 2017a). Famously, the first such unit – the Behavioral Insights Team (BIT) – was set up by the UK Cabinet Office in 2010 and started with a mandate to demonstrate a tenfold return on investment in two years.

Since then, hundreds of behavioral policy initiatives have been launched by public institutions around the world, encompassing both developed and developing countries (OECD, 2017a, 2019a). Despite international differences in the application of behavioral insights, the common thread among all behavioral initiatives is a nuanced understanding of human behavior, combined with a commitment to formulating evidence-based policies and utilizing rigorous research methods. The evidence-based approach is indeed key to the behavioral methodology, which is fundamentally grounded on actual, rather than hypothesized, behavior.

The motivation for behavioral public policy to be informed by rigorous experimentation processes has become all the more compelling in light of the recent "replicability crisis" in psychology and other social sciences (Schooler, 2014; Munafò, Smith, & Davey, 2018). As a number of scientific findings, including seminal theories in judgment and decision-making, are called into question by subsequent investigations, it is increasingly important for behavioral insights to be based on a culture of empirically testing policy solutions before scaling them up.

While methodological debates still exist, policymakers around the world continue to successfully apply behavioral insights to a range of policy areas, from energy and sustainability to financial decision-making, public health, and, more recently, poverty and development economics (World Bank, 2015). By the time of the global pandemic of 2020, behavioral researchers were at the front lines of urgent policy decisions to combat the spread of the disease around the world (Van Bavel et al., 2020). Anthologies of scores of examples across a dozen or more policy sectors are now compiled in OECD reports (2017), the first edition of this book (Ruggeri, 2019), and various online tools. We will explore many of these in the following chapters.

Ethics in applying behavioral policy

As behavioral and evidence-based methodologies are increasingly incorporated in policy-making, a number of key challenges persist, including ethical concerns, reliability, and questions regarding long-term effectiveness. In particular, behavioral approaches raise specific ethical concerns that are different from those of traditional public policy. This is primarily because behavioral approaches typically involve collecting primary data of individual- or group-level behaviors and leveraging biases to design policies. Moreover, libertarian paternalism builds on the assumption that the public institutions concerned can determine which policy outcomes are "better" and should be promoted – an assumption that is not uncontroversial (Lunn, 2014). Given the far-reaching consequences of public policy, it is therefore imperative to integrate ethical considerations whenever applying behavioral insights by adopting appropriate measures from the start to the end of the policy cycle (OECD, 2019b). In the conclusion chapter of this book, we present the **Golden Rule of Behavioral Policy**, which explicitly addresses these concerns.

While behavioral policy raises specific ethical considerations, the attempt to influence citizen behavior is nothing new for governments, as the primary purpose of all public policy is precisely to shape or regulate our behaviors in society. According to Schneider and Ingram (1990), "public policy almost always attempts to get people to do things they would otherwise not have done, or it enables them to do things they might not have done otherwise" (p. 5).

As was covered in Chapter 1, traditionally, governments have achieved this primarily through tools such as laws, regulations, or taxes compelling us to act responsibly. High taxes on harmful substances such as tobacco or beverages with large amounts of sugar are one example. Other traditional, but less coercive measures include the provision of information, for example, in the form of public health campaigns. These traditional instruments provide very powerful incentives for behavior, but they often come at a very high cost for governments and are sometimes ineffective at producing meaningful policy outcomes. For example, consumers might fail to internalize the long-term health cost of smoking despite heavy taxation, and public information may only have limited effects while also only reaching a small number of people.

In the last few decades, behavioral research has elucidated new opportunities to complement the traditional policy toolkit. Indeed, research has shown that in many cases, the adoption of a behavioral approach can determine the success of a policy intervention that otherwise would not have been as effective. For example, Devoto, et al. (2012) have shown, with reference to a program carried out in Morocco in 2007, that participation can greatly increase if we simply assist low-income populations to complete the application paperwork. In the specific case of this intervention, the rate of applicants asking for credit to finance a better water supply went from 10% to 69% of the targeted households when they personally received information and support to enroll in the program. Similarly, behavioral insights have been used to understand why housing vouchers alone fail to promote mobility of low-income households – these housing interventions, coupled with intensive counseling, targeted communication, programmatic support, and innovative policy features, can effectively help families and communities make better choices (Hall, Galvez, & Sederbaum, 2014). Similarly, members of low-income communities often have very poor attendance rates at free health-care clinics, yet simple adjustments such as assigning them to a regular care provider or not scheduling the appointment too far in advance has a meaningful impact on their ability to attend (Ruggeri et al., 2020a).

Law and behavioral policy

Many behaviors, particularly less-desirable ones, are already prohibited or otherwise regulated by law. But even in the areas of explicit government action, behavioral insights are still of great importance. The framing of laws and the provision of information are traditional policy tools that can benefit from inclusion of a behavioral dimension (Loewenstein & Chater, 2017). However, legislation cannot dictate all aspects of life and may not be flexible enough to achieve some shared societal goals. Governments employ public policies to promote goals that are valued but often neglected by society, such as pro-environmental behavior, healthy eating, and saving for retirement.

Governments have several tools at hand to motivate individuals to act more responsibly – the use of behavioral insights is one such tool that serves as an innovative alternative to traditional interventions like taxation, subsidies, and regulation (Loewenstein & Chater, 2017). For example, the imposition of high taxes on cigarettes would be classified as a classic traditional economics intervention.

Within these environments shaped by law and policy, individuals make decisions that have a direct impact on their health, wealth, and happiness. They often end up choosing an alternative that is more attractive at that specific time but less beneficial in the long run, such as choosing an unhealthy lunch option or buying a bigger TV rather than saving money for retirement. Choices such as these, though relatively harmless as one-time occurrences, might accumulate over time and result in decreased well-being and economic loss for society and the individual. As policymakers increasingly include citizens' well-being among their key priorities and among the key metrics to evaluate their own success (Adler & Seligman, 2016; Diener, 2009), the design of policies that account for psychological and behavioral components moves even higher on the policy agenda of the future (see Chapter 13).

What's next for behavioral public policy?

Following the initial phase of discovery and curiosity, new frontiers are now being explored by behavioral public policy. These include opportunities to explore new themes – such as embedding behavioral insights in macroeconomic models or in the organizational decision-making of public institutions – as well as opportunities related to new methodologies and other disciplines.

In particular, promising new methods are emerging in social science that empower researchers to study the collective-level dynamics of behavior. The mathematical analysis of social networks, for instance, allows researchers to map the structure of social connections among people in an organization and to generate predictions for how messages and norms will spread through that organization (Hannan, Pólos, & Carroll, 2007; Centola, 2018). These methods have the potential to identify more optimal ways of structuring communication networks to enhance the flow of ideas and behaviors through an organization. A growing body of literature shows that the structure of communication networks can be optimized to enhance collective intelligence within social groups, with the capacity to reduce individual-level **cognitive bias** and support more accurate judgments (Page, 2007; Pentland, 2012). For instance, this could have particular implications for climate change and environmental policies, as research has shown that bipartisan communication networks could be used to activate "social learning" that eliminates political bias in the interpretation of climate data

(Guilbeault, Becker, & Centola, 2018). These methodologies can thus be applied to strengthen our capacity not only to identify individual-level cognitive biases but also to develop effective policy interventions to reduce cognitive bias and improve group decision-making.

Furthermore, the contribution of network science to behavioral insights could also operate through enhancing behaviorally informed social norm interventions. Here, the most relevant lesson from network science is that the spread of information and influence through networks depends on one's position in the network and the structure of the network itself. By taking these features of the network into consideration, the degree to which social norms can be leveraged may be further enhanced. This has been alluded to in a few behavioral studies already, most notably in the 2015 World Bank Development Report, which discusses leveraging "highly connected students" and "highly salient clique leaders" in an anti-bullying campaign (World Bank, 2015). By targeting these individuals, a team of US researchers was effectively able to reach and influence a wider array of students than if they targeted connected students or students at random (Paluck & Shepherd, 2012).

More broadly, a much-debated next step for behavioral policy is its relationship with the neighboring discipline of data science. On the one hand, research has argued that behavioral principles constitute the very intellectual ground granting legitimacy to **Big Data** (Cardon, 2015). If individuals are prone to errors in judgment, are systematically overoptimistic, and do not reason probabilistically (Ayres, 2007), we then have a strong argument legitimizing algorithms to collect data on what individuals actually want and do online, rather than just relying on what they claim to want and do.

On the other hand, the use of data science to study and change individual behavior has delicate ethical underpinnings. With recent technological advances and the rise of interest and applications for Big Data, policymakers have new opportunities to utilize, on an unprecedented level, vast amounts of data. Though policies affect entire populations, they typically only represent the preferences of majorities and are rarely able to capture the nuanced interplay between policy-relevant subgroups (Ruggeri, et al., 2017). Through the expansion of Big Data, the identification of these subgroups has become easier, and they can now be targeted more specifically to gain the most from policies. Big Data not only provide information on more groups but also increase the amount and complexity of information for each individual. The data that policymakers can use are now more consistent, more flexible, more granular, and more natural (Sagiroglu & Sinanc, 2013), allowing for (potentially) better informed decisions.

However, apart from the increased targeting, the larger amount of information, and better assessment methods, Big Data also represent some risks for policymaking. Big Data cannot always be regarded as representing the entire population when the data are gained from specific websites or databases. Some of them may be biased, reflecting segmentation, stereotypes, and discrimination in society or not representing the population accurately – for example, underrepresenting minorities. This is known as the "*garbage in, garbage out*" (GIGO) problem, referring to the data used to train an algorithm. In policymaking, such biases are potentially dangerous and can systematically disadvantage populations. Additionally, the fast response rate to real-life actions through access to timely, real-life data can trigger premature overreactions to statistical anomalies or short-lived phenomena (Bell & Morse, 2013). It is the scope for future research to draw a conceptual distinction between the ethicality of this type of nudges in the corporate world and nudges in public policy – and it is the responsibility of future policymakers to ensure the ethicality of any behavioral insight interventions leveraging data science.

Overall, while data science is increasingly informing policymaking around the world, the field of behavioral policy has been late and cautious to incorporate it. However, promising applications of data science to behavioral insights policies exist. For instance, Young (2014) has shown that social media data can be a source of valuable information on the public's behavior, such as their probability of engaging in risky actions or contracting a disease, through the vast access to behaviors, choices, and influential sources of information.

What most distinguishes the behavioral approach as a framework for policy research is its uniquely interdisciplinary nature, which allows it to remain highly adaptive in both the tools it applies and the problems it can solve, as well as in the degree to which it is incorporated in different policy initiatives (Box 4.1). There has already been substantial progress in addressing some of the key open problems in policy design and organizational decision-making leveraging behavioral approaches. By adopting a collective-level perspective and new technological tools, the future of behavioral policy promises to make even greater advances in the capacity to design and implement social policies that enhance communities, from the productivity and well-being of individuals to the quality of their innovations and decision-making.

BOX 3.1 THE EUROPEAN TAXONOMY FOR BEHAVIORAL INITIATIVES

The European Commission (EC) uses a taxonomy to classify whether an initiative is behaviorally tested, behaviorally informed, or behaviorally aligned (Lourenço, Ciriolo, Almeida, & Troussard, 2016). The different categories describe the degree to which behavioral considerations were used in shaping an initiative. The taxonomy is helpful to identify policies that are both explicitly and implicitly informed by behavioral insights.

Behaviorally tested initiatives

Initiatives that are explicitly tested using behavioral insights or scaled out after an initial experiment. For example, the EC report provides self-commitment strategies for gamblers to fight their overconfidence using the results of previous related studies.

Behaviorally informed initiatives

Initiatives designed according to already existing behavioral practices. For example, national lawmakers do not test the effects of plain tobacco packaging beforehand, but they assume that the behavioral insights on framing and social norms will succeed on the basis of previous evidence.

Behaviorally aligned initiatives

Initiatives that can be aligned to behavioral evidence, but do not rely explicitly on any behavioral insights. Many European countries record motoring offenses as penalty points on drivers' licenses, which is assumed to have a preventive function on the basis of the principle of loss aversion.

Case selection for this volume

Through a more applied and holistic approach, psychology includes topics that are particularly relevant for evidence-based policy. Consequently, this textbook will have a predominant focus on the behavioral insights derived from psychological research. As this is a narrative resource meant for learning about current insights on the behavioral and decision-making sciences, examples have not been compiled as a systematic review. Instead, all chapters follow a more general set of guidelines on what was included, what elements were extracted for discussion, and what insights were of interest. For every chapter, those guidelines included three standing principles:

1 Any interventions, whether original studies or policy initiatives, had to have a fundamental element of behavioral concepts, such as nudges, framing, social norms, or public messaging. Simple interventions that had no underlying theoretical consideration related to behavioral science were left out. This supported a focus on teaching and understanding, rather than universal or comprehensive collections.
2 Any studies or policies had to be attempted on a meaningful scale. This varies by the nature of the topic and the decade the study was performed, so there is no set sample size or power, nor specific potential for impact. Instead, this volume contains studies that address an issue of genuine interest on a scale relevant to that issue. Some borderline cases have been included as side box examples, but niche or purely anecdotal insights have largely been excluded, as anecdotes are not archetypes. Where relevant, we have attempted to present relevant cautions and caveats.
3 A clear outcome of interest had to be stated or implicit, with little room for interpretation. Even in trials where it was not assessed or findings were not significant, all examples had to include a clear, intended impact, mainly for the purposes of assessing fidelity and efficacy.

The material in the following chapters is for educational and training purposes and should be considered as such, not as a systematic depiction of any kind (e.g. highest impact, ranges of impacts, ranges of domains or topics).

Conclusion

Behavioral insights have rightfully received considerable attention from the public policy community, particularly since the turn of the century. Without the behavioral dimension, many policies were arguably less effective and utilized an unrealistic understanding of our needs and cognitive functions. As such, behavioral and decision sciences have offered substantial contributions toward the impact of policies, by using a number of the tools that will be covered in this book. While it is not always obvious in each example, one or many of these core insights have been applied. Most examples show some sort of positive success, but to be representative, some show minimal or underwhelming results, whereas others may show no effect or even negative impacts. Each of these cases is an opportunity to build more knowledge of this burgeoning area of study and application.

Essay questions

1 Discuss the limitations of applying behavioral economics to public policy and lawmaking.

2 Using the concepts discussed within this chapter, design an intervention to promote a more active lifestyle in the working environment.

3 Is *libertarian paternalism* a paradox? Discuss.

4 Discuss the ethical implications of governmental interventions implementing nudges.

Additional insights and further reading

Benartzi, S., Beshears, J., Milkman, K. L., Sunstein, C. R., Thaler, R. H., Shankar, M., . . . & Galing, S. (2017). Should governments invest more in nudging? *Psychological Science, 28*(8), 1041–1055.

Hausman, D. M., & Welch, B. (2010). Debate: To nudge or not to nudge. *Journal of Political Philosophy, 18*(1), 123–136.

Hertwig, R., & Grüne-Yanoff, T. (2017). Nudging and boosting: Steering or empowering good decisions. *Perspectives on Psychological Science, 12*(6), 973–986.

Madrian, B. C. (2014). Applying insights from behavioral economics to policy design. *Annual Review of Economics, 6*(1), 663–688.

Michie, S., Van Stralen, M. M., & West, R. (2011). The behaviour change wheel: A new method for characterising and designing behaviour change interventions. *Implementation Science, 6*(1), 42.

O'Neil, C. (2016). *Weapons of math destruction: How big data increases inequality and threatens democracy*. New York, NY: Broadway Books.

Thaler, R. H., & Sunstein, C. R. (2009). *Nudge: Improving decisions about health, wealth, and happiness*. New York: Penguin Books.

Troussard, X., & Van Bavel, R. (2018). How can behavioural insights be used to improve EU policy? *Intereconomics, 53*(1), 8–12.

4 Economic, financial, and consumer behavior

Kai Ruggeri, Maja Friedemann, Jakub M. Krawiec, Hannes Jarke, Sahana K. Quail, Alessandro F. Paul, Tomas Folke, and Enrico Rubaltelli

Acknowledgments: Joe J. Gladstone

Chapter summary

To understand human decision-making, policymakers have traditionally turned to classical economic theory. However, human behavior often deviates from the expectation of rationality put forward by these classical approaches. One area where these deviations are clearly observable is in economic and consumer choices. Mapping out these examples of consumer irrationality has helped establish the field of behavioral economics over recent decades, catalyzed through early work by Daniel Kahneman and Amos Tversky on risk in the 1970s. The study of factors that influence consumer decisions has led to a better understanding of questions such as why people avoid paying taxes, often save too little for their future, or spend money in ways that fail to improve their well-being. These insights have provided new opportunities for developing efficient, evidence-based policies aimed at tackling problems from improving consumer protection to encouraging tax compliance and waste reduction.

Learning objectives

- Gain an understanding of factors influencing financial decision-making and everyday consumer choices
- Become aware of the importance of behavioral economics in policymaking worldwide
- Become acquainted with examples of successful policy interventions that have been informed by behavioral research, as well as examples of unsuccessful interventions

Introduction

Every day we are faced with monetary decisions we need to make. How much should I tip the waiter? Should I buy a coffee? Can I use a coupon to get a discount? We generally do not spend a lot of time making these decisions. Yet, when you really think about it, they are not quite so simple.

Consider the coffee example. You need to assess how much the pleasure you will get out of drinking the coffee is worth to you, how much the effort of going to the coffee shop

DOI: 10.4324/9781003181873-4

costs you, what else you could be spending your money on, and so on. We usually rely on rules of thumb – **heuristics** – to make these decisions, and sometimes these rules of thumb can lead to decisions that are not optimal. However, knowledge about those predictable errors can help us to realize what to watch out for when making financial decisions. Did you know, for instance, that we tend to spend more money when using credit cards instead of cash (Morewedge, Holtzman, & Epley, 2007)? Or that we tend to select suboptimal health insurance plans when we are faced with too many different options (Benartzi, 2015)? In this chapter, we will examine these phenomena and many other aspects of financial decision-making.

Attempts to explain economic decision-making in science and policy have traditionally been dominated by classical economic theory, which assumes that people's main concern is maximizing benefits while minimizing costs for themselves. Classical economic models usually assume humans to be fully rational actors who have stable preferences and make optimal financial decisions across their lifespan. However, such models often fail to explain consumer behavior in the real world. After all, people tend to save too little and spend too much, and their preferences often fluctuate considerably over time and context. As mentioned in the preceding chapters, an expanding body of research within psychology and the behavioral sciences has catalogued a number of cognitive biases that impede individuals from making optimal decisions with their money. This work helps to explain why we find consistent violations of rationality, with a majority of consumers being shown to be highly influenced by the social, psychological, and environmental contexts in which financial decisions are made.

Behavioral economics and financial decision-making have long and rich histories as areas of study. As early as the eighteenth century, writers and scholars were interested in the psychological underpinnings of economic life. In the 1950s, Herbert Simon, a professor at Carnegie Mellon University in Pittsburgh, introduced the influential concept of bounded rationality. In this concept, he argued that human decisions are not always optimal because there are limitations to human information processing (see Chapter 3 for a more detailed discussion). The understanding that consumer decisions are suboptimal because of limitations in cognitive processing has helped academics explain why behaviors that reinforce financial hardship – including excessive borrowing, excessive consumption, and inadequate savings – are so widespread. For example, consumers often pay off the smallest rather than the most expensive forms of debt first (Besharat, Varki, & Craig, 2015), and many individuals fail to accurately forecast and budget for future spending (Sussman & Alter, 2012).

An understanding of the psychological motivations driving financial behaviors not only offers a description of why people often make suboptimal financial choices but it also provides a source of new insights into ways for improving these decisions (Camerer et al., 2003). As behavioral economics has matured and demonstrated increasingly robust and reliable effects both in- and outside the lab, policymakers have begun to take notice. For example, recent large-scale policies informed by insights from behavioral economics include the Credit Card Accountability Responsibility and Disclosure (CARD) Act of 2009 in the United States and the ban on pre-checked boxes for online purchases in the European Union.

Following high-profile success stories of policy interventions informed by behavioral science research, recent years have seen various governments establishing their own national agencies tasked with incorporating these insights into policymaking (e.g. the Behavioural Insights Team in the United Kingdom and the Social and Behavioral Sciences Team in the United States). These developments reflect the emerging influence of behavioral science on economic study and public policy.

Financial literacy

Do people fully understand the financial choices with which they are faced? A large body of research indicates that they may not and that this gap in comprehension may lead to poorer outcomes for consumers. This understanding – or lack thereof – is typically defined as **financial literacy**: "a combination of awareness, knowledge, skill, attitude and behavior necessary to make sound financial decisions and ultimately achieve individual financial well-being" (OECD, 2016c, p. 47).

Following the 2008 financial crisis, financial literacy interventions received unprecedented interest from policymakers worldwide (OECD, 2009). Interventions aimed at improving financial knowledge and skills were introduced globally (e.g. Atkinson & Messy, 2013; OECD, 2016b, 2017b) with the aim of improving individual financial well-being. A large-scale survey comprising 54,650 adults from 29 different countries showed not only the relatively low levels of financial literacy on average (13.2 out of 21 possible points) but also the considerable variance within countries (OECD, 2016c).

Differences in financial skills and knowledge within a population need to be considered when planning interventions. This is because interventions that are specifically tailored to more homogeneous subgroups within a population tend to produce stronger effects on average than do universal interventions (Miller, Reichelstein, Salas, & Zia, 2015). For example, an advertising campaign that educates recipients about available investment methods may be highly valuable for those who have yet to start investing, but it may be a poor use of resources for those who are already investing their assets.

While policymakers have largely embraced financial education (OECD, 2016b), there is ongoing debate among researchers about its effectiveness (Fernandes, Lynch Jr, & Netemeyer, 2014; Miller et al., 2015). Financial literacy itself has been found to correlate positively with prudent financial decisions and the use of formal savings products (Xu & Zia, 2012), but the effectiveness of financial literacy interventions remains controversial. Two meta-analyses diverged in their conclusions. Fernandes et al. (2014) describe the effects of education interventions to be minimal, with interventions explaining just 0.1 percent of the variance in downstream financial behaviors such as savings rates. In contrast, Miller and colleagues (2015) suggest that financial education may have a positive effect in some domains, such as savings behavior or financial skills, but not in others. While further work may help develop greater consensus on this matter, it is important to note that, ultimately, the effectiveness of educational interventions is likely to be determined by which outcomes and which groups are targeted. What is more, work by Statman, Fisher, and Anginer (2008) illustrates that the errors that investors make are tied to the use of their affective reactions. It is hard to change such reactions with traditional financial literacy programs.

Though there are still uncertainties about exactly how our brains function when making financial decisions, and thus about how to use education to improve financial literacy, work by Kahneman and Tversky (1979) has made a significant contribution to understanding how and why people, in certain contexts, behave in a way that would be considered financially illiterate or at least not fully rational.

Prospect Theory

If you were picking a college degree with the aim to one day win a Nobel Prize, psychology might not be an obvious choice. There is, after all, no Nobel Prize offered in psychology.

This makes the achievement of Daniel Kahneman all the more impressive. In 2002, together with economist Vernon L. Smith, Kahneman was awarded the Swedish National Bank's Prize in Economic Sciences in Memory of Alfred Nobel (commonly referred to as the Nobel Prize in Economics) for his work with Amos Tversky on decision-making that ultimately led to **Prospect Theory** (Kahneman & Tversky, 1979; see also Chapter 2 of this book). This theory represents a milestone in behavioral economics as it depicts how people *actually make* decisions (descriptive approach) and how this differs from the assumptions traditionally made by economists based on the **expected utility** paradigm, which is concerned with how decisions *should* be made (prescriptive approach). To understand what makes Prospect Theory so influential and why it is so relevant when designing behaviorally informed policies, we will take a look at a rather gloomy hypothetical example from a paper by Tversky and Kahneman (1981). Participants were faced with two scenarios (Ibid., p. 453):

> Problem 1: Imagine that the US is preparing for the outbreak of an unusual Asian disease, which is expected to kill 600 people. Two alternative programs to combat the disease have been proposed. Assume that the exact scientific estimate of the consequences of the programs are as follows: If Program A is adopted, 200 people will be saved. If Program B is adopted, there is 1/3 probability that 600 people will be saved, and 2/3 probability that no people will be saved. Which of the two programs would you favor?

Before Prospect Theory, the most common framework for approaching decision-making under uncertainty was expected utility theory. A decision made according to an expected utility calculation would ask the decision-maker, "In each possible option, which one has the greatest net utility?" According to this model, people would be indifferent to the options: a 100 percent chance of saving 200 people is equal to a 1/3 chance of saving 600 people (because one-third of 600 equals 200).

In a strictly mathematical sense, the outcomes should be perceived as equal. However, 72 percent of the participants favored program A, whereas only 28 percent chose program B. It appeared that people did not want to take the risk of everyone dying but would rather ensure that at least some number of them survived for certain. This is a demonstration that people tend to be risk averse, meaning that they behave as if uncertainty is costly. But are people risk averse in all situations? What would happen if the probabilities were different? Let's have a look at the second part of the same study, where Tversky and Kahneman presented another group of students with a slightly different version of this dilemma:

> Problem 2: If Program C is adopted 400 people will die. If Program D is adopted there is 1/3 probability that nobody will die, and 2/3 probability that 600 people will die. Which of the two programs would you favor?

We saw before how people tend to be more risk averse; however, that is not the case in this example of a negatively framed problem. The choice here is between a sure loss or a risk of a loss. Here, individuals tend to become risk seeking, showing a preference for the risky choice. This time, 78 percent of participants chose the riskier program D, whereas 22 percent of the participants chose the more certain program C. What is the difference between this situation and the first? Again, in terms of utility, the programs are identical (two-thirds of 600 equals 400), but people clearly make different decisions in each scenario. In decision-making under uncertainty, people tend to underweight those outcomes that are probable and uncertain, while often overweighting certain or secure options.

Expected utility theory assumes people are aware of the outcomes associated with each choice, as well as their respective probabilities. This means they can make decisions that produce the best outcome on average (the highest expected utility). However, this model ignores how people might value options differently based on their point of reference. Prospect Theory extends the expected utility model by adding personal weights to various components of the choice.

The context of the decision influences how people value risk. In the original example about the rare disease, the wording of the scenario **framed** the options differently, and these frames influenced how participants responded to the uncertainty. Specifically, people tend to prefer certain gains to risky gains but tend to prefer uncertain losses to sure losses. In the first situation, Tversky and Kahneman gave both a guaranteed option that some lives would be saved and an option where all lives could be lost. In the second situation, the reference frame was lives lost rather than lives saved. While the net outcomes of the different options were the same, the patterns of choice were inverted between the two scenarios. Since the original publications by Kahneman and Tversky (1979) and Tversky and Kahneman (1981), research has shown that the same people respond to uncertainty differently based on how the options are framed (De Martino et al., 2006), as presented in Box 4.1.

BOX 4.1 REDUCING COMPLEXITY BY REFRAMING FINANCIAL RISK

Gentile, Linciano, Lucarelli, and Soccorso (2015) investigated how the framing of risk-return representations can affect investors' perceived complexity, usefulness, and understanding of content. Investors were presented with information about the risk, return, and costs of four products: one outstanding structure bond, one newly issued structure bond, and two stocks varying in risk levels. These four products were presented in different formats.

1 The first approach presented market information in a synthesized form – aggregating market, liquidity, and credit risks
2 The second approach presented information in an unbundled format – not aggregating information
3 The third approach was based on what-if scenarios, discussing risks as a function of relevant indicators
4 The fourth approach used probabilistic modeling of expected returns

Investors had to rate the presentation formats on complexity and usefulness and indicate how risky they perceived the presented products to be. Information presented via the synthesized form was most easily understood, followed by the unbundled and probabilistic forms, and least easily understood via the what-if format. The less complex representations were perceived to be more useful. Moreover, complexity of information format affected investors' accuracy of judging the products' risk. Investors' assessments were more likely to be correct for the less complex formats. When the respondents were asked how much money they would invest in the products, perceived complexity seemed to be a main driver behind the willingness to invest in presented products. This indicates that even investors scoring higher than average on financial literacy are affected by the way financial information is disclosed and that highly financially literate individuals are not immune to behavioral biases. Therefore, financial education initiatives need to consider removing bias from programs as well, in order to effectively protect investors.

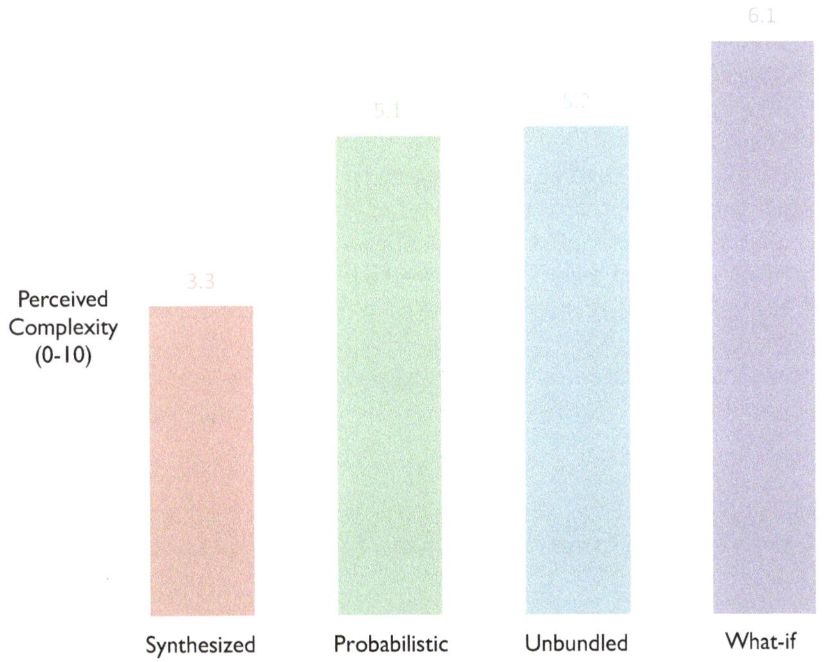

Choices today impact tomorrow: the biggest nudge so far

During your student years, you are probably not thinking a whole lot about retirement or how much money you will have when you are 70. Your immediate concerns are more likely to be your grades, your peers, and what you will do next in your life. The more immediate (proximal) the results of our actions seem, the more value we place on them. Unfortunately, this means, at the same time, that outcomes that seem further in the future (distal) are given less importance and may lead to us missing out on optimal choices today simply because they do not seem to matter until tomorrow . . . or ten years from now (Green, Myerson, & Macaux, 2005). While thoughts of retirement may not excite you now, this precise idea is the basis for one of the most influential and highest impact interventions in behavioral economics.

In the United States, one of the most common retirement savings plans is known as a 401(k). It involves individuals and their employers making regular deposits into an account under what is known as a **defined-contribution scheme**. These accounts are backed by the government, making them a lower risk option for investing in retirement, and are often considered as part of a general benefits package to entice potential employees. Critically, participating (investing) in a 401(k) is entirely voluntary.

In the late 1990s, about 50 percent of Americans working in the private sector did not have any retirement savings (EBRI, 2005). Individuals working in the public sector were slightly better, with almost 77 percent enrolled in a plan (EBRI, 2005). This difference between the private and public sectors caught the attention of Madrian and Shea (see Chapter 2), who decided to study pension enrollment in the case of a large, publicly traded Fortune 500 company. One of their main interests was to test the application of a **default** option (Madrian & Shea, 2001). Defaults refer to a pre-planned route of action that will take place unless the decision-maker actively chooses otherwise (Thaler & Sunstein, 2008). In other words, the default option is what you get unless you specifically ask for something else.

In the study, newly hired employees were defaulted into the 401(k) program, with a preset regular contribution equal to 3 percent of their salary. Workers had to actively opt out of the program if they wanted to, and doing so was not burdened with any additional costs or punishments. The default option worked: participation in the pension program increased, rising from 37 percent prior to the trial to 86 percent of newly hired workers (see Figure 4.1).

However, some cautions have to be applied. Employees hired under automatic enrollment retained the default contribution rate of 3 percent, whereas employees hired

FIGURE 4.1 Participation rate in a savings plan after the introduction of automatic enrollment

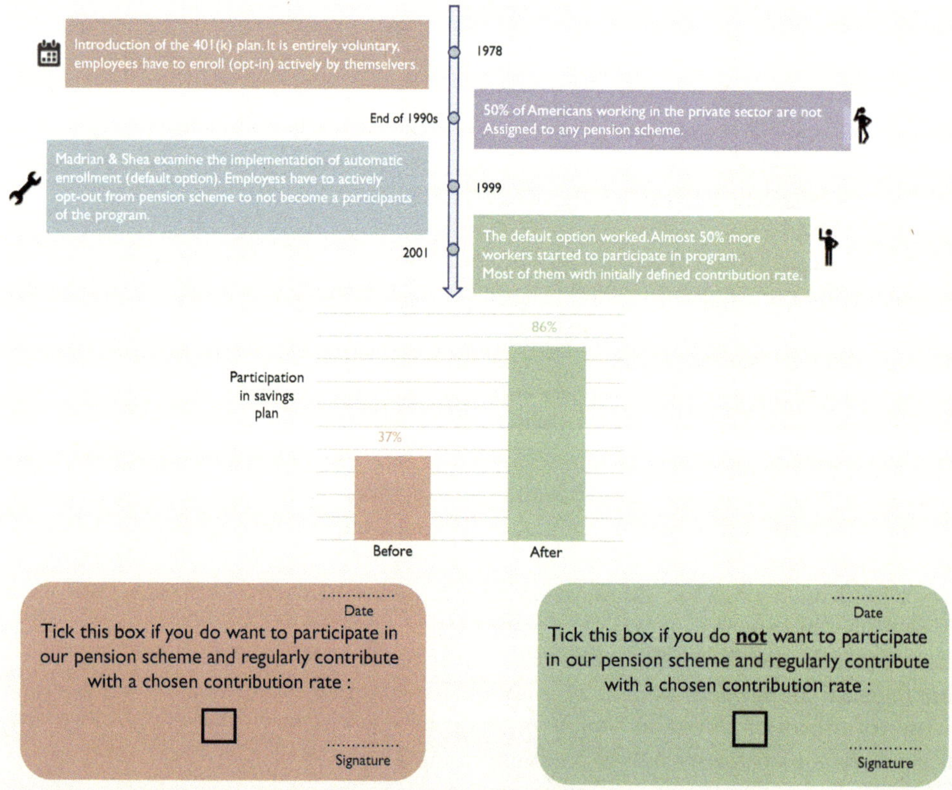

before automatic enrollment usually chose a contribution rate equal to 6 percent. So while more people enrolled, they enrolled at a lower rate, indicating that the default option needs to be implemented carefully. For many employees, 3 percent may not be enough to retire on, but this may not be evident to an employee seeing it as the suggested plan.

Researchers try to explain these results as an outcome resulting from multiple factors (Madrian & Shea, 2001; Choi, 2015). One of them is employee **inertia**: before the enrollment changes, employees were not enrolling in a retirement program because they were not used to it and thus were more likely to exhibit no action as it may have been seen as safer not to defer income. In turn, this could have led to procrastination in thinking about saving for retirement and delaying committed savings behavior. Researchers do not stop here with this possible cause-effect link. Inertia and procrastination could lead to or indicate a more complex cognitive bias called **status quo bias**. For employees, making a decision on their saving behavior could have been a situation involving a lot of costs, such as learning about new financial solutions or long-term planning. The high complexity of this decision, involving a considerable amount of uncertainty about myriad new factors, made employees even more eager to stick to the well-known present situation (Samuelson & Zeckhauser, 1988).

Madrian and Shea (2001) believed that lack of financial knowledge and substantial complexity in the task are two factors that raise the anticipated costs of gathering knowledge and choosing the most optimal savings plan. By introducing automatic enrollment, individuals did not have to struggle with those factors. Additionally, from the employee perspective, automatic enrollment in a savings plan by an employer might be seen as a piece of advice from a more knowledgeable entity. Consider that employees with the shortest tenure were the most likely to participate in automatic enrollment. With less time in their position, it is likely that those employees lack detailed financial knowledge and experience from previous jobs, which in turn may encourage them to rely on the employer's initial suggestions (Madrian & Shea, 2001).

The default study quickly became a catalyst for researchers to test tools that might similarly increase participation in pension plans. One of the most successful interventions is the Save More Tomorrow™ program, developed by Thaler and Benartzi (2004). This intervention is based on the concept of delaying perceived saving costs, and it helped to raise the rate of individuals enrolled in pension plans. The program enables employees to make the decision about starting to save money for retirement purposes long before the system actually begins to charge them. Thanks to this delayed commitment, participants do not perceive the immediate costs of their decisions. Additionally, program contributions are related to employees' salaries to avoid violation of their current living standards. Researchers found that after the intervention's roll out, 78 percent of employees previously unwilling to participate in standard pension plans had chosen Save More Tomorrow™ (see Chapter 8 for a more detailed discussion).

These principles have been tested in other financial contexts as well, such as charitable donations. In the Give More Tomorrow program, Breman (2011) showed that average increases in donations were higher when existing monthly donors were asked to make a *future* increase (in one or two months) in their contribution, as opposed to being asked to increase it immediately. Many of the nudges covered here can be applied to digital environments, to help people make better choices in consequential domains such as healthcare, see Box 4.2.

BOX 4.2 DIGITAL NUDGING

Are there any implications of behavioral insights for the digital world? In *The Smarter Screen*, written by Save More Tomorrow™ co-founder Shlomo Benartzi, numerous examples of interventions are presented that can help to create more user friendly and easy-to-understand digital applications. One of them is healthcare.gov, a website that helps Americans choose the optimal health insurance program for their needs. Initially, the website launch was considered a fiasco with an overwhelming amount of information not digestible for an individual. For instance, in one of the states, users were confronted with 169 different healthcare plans coming from eight different insurers. To make it worse, each plan had its own unique features such as different drug benefits or different doctor networks.

After a series of online experiments, Benartzi proposed a two-step intervention to facilitate better individual decision-making. First, the number of options was decreased to only 16 offers. Each was labelled as either low, medium, or high medical use. Second, users encountered a tournament of options. Benartzi uses this term to describe the process of presenting users with a group of options per round, where users have to choose the best one matching their preferences.

The 16 remaining offers left after the first step of the intervention were randomly assigned to one of four rounds where people were asked to choose the one they preferred. During each round, four offers were presented. In the final fifth round, users had to decide by choosing one offer from the four previously selected ones. The results have shown that users were able to choose more appropriate offers according to their needs. On average, individuals saved more than US$300 per year (Benartzi & Lehrer, 2015). After the application of the two-step intervention, it was easier for users to compare available insurance offers from different perspectives and to find which were the most relevant for them. By splitting the decision architecture into a longer process, including assigning offers to a variety of categories and presenting them as smaller groups, the result was that information was easier to process by participants and thus it was easier for them to make appropriate decisions.

Encouraging tax compliance

In the United Kingdom, billions of pounds are lost in tax revenue each year, simply because many citizens are late in making their payments (OECD, 2017f). In 2012, the Behavioural Insights Team ran a large-scale, **randomized controlled trial** (RCT) manipulating real reminder letters by the tax authorities to nudge taxpayers by using **social norms** (Hallsworth, List, Metcalfe, & Vlaev, 2014). The RCT included five different versions of the letter:

Version 1: emphasized the *basic norm* of paying taxes on time; letting individuals know that tax compliance is not as low as they might think
Version 2: emphasized a *country norm;* increasing the salience of the message
Version 3: emphasized that the recipient was committing a *norm violation* by not paying as opposed to the majority of people; the *minority norm*, increasing the salience even further
Version 4: emphasized the *gains* that society makes from taxes
Version 5: emphasized the *societal losses* suffered from missed tax revenue

Around 100,000 self-assessment tax debtors were sent different versions of the letter, and the rate of response was compared to that of the standard letter (see Figure 4.2).

FIGURE 4.2 Tax letters in the United Kingdom

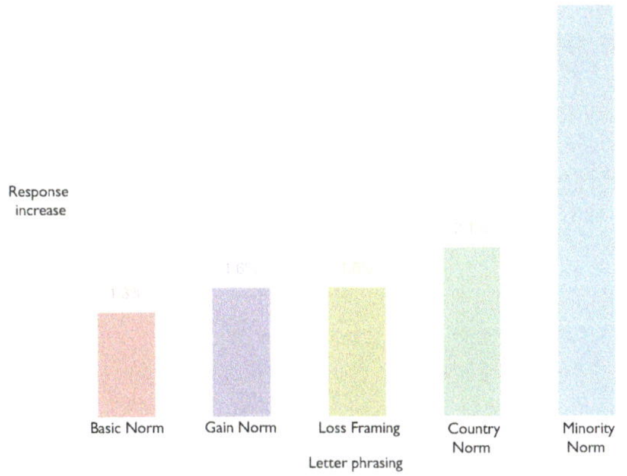

Overall, the tax authorities collected a surplus of around GB£9 million (about US$14.4 million at the time) over a 23-day period. The trial was considered so successful that the reminder letters were soon implemented into a nationwide policy, meaning that social norms were now standard practice in tax letters in the United Kingdom. On aggregate, the savings due to these letters really add up. It is estimated that the intervention led to GB£210 million (about US$326 million at that time) more in tax revenue in the 2012–2013 financial year (Behavioural Insights Team, 2014).

A further example of a successful intervention persuaded people to register their unlicensed vehicles in the United Kingdom. The Driver and Vehicle Licensing Agency (DVLA) aimed to increase compliance by experimenting with more harshly stated reminders (e.g. pay your taxes or lose the vehicle) and **personalized** letters. Letters were personalized to include either the brand of the unregistered vehicle (for which tax still needed to be paid) or a picture of the vehicle. The personalization alone was not very effective (2 percent increase); however, when the picture of the vehicle was added, the personalization produced stronger results (9 percent increase; Behavioural Insights Team, 2014).

Another way in which tax compliance was encouraged was through the use of **salient** information. When an enforcement order – which is issued to people who fail to respond to penalty notices and penalty reminders – included changes that made it more salient (i.e. a stamp stating "Pay Now"), the payment rate increased by 3.1 percent. This intervention rolled out throughout New South Wales and translated to an increase of AUD$1.02 million in payments (Behavioural Insights Team, 2014).

Simplifying information

In addition to social norms, alternative approaches to improve tax payments include **simplifying** the information. The Canadian tax authority simplified the way people could pay their taxes by adding a link to a website that sent taxpayers directly to the tax form. This replaced direction to an overview website that required additional searching for the form. The response rate increased from 19 percent to 23 percent (Behavioural Insights Team, 2014), which is modest, yet equates to a large number when applied nationally. However, while people are often more likely to engage in tasks made simpler by design, it does not always work out that way. For example, a similar method was introduced to encourage individuals to consider better health insurance options in Colorado (Ericson, Kingsdale, Layton, & Sacarny, 2017). While there was a modest increase in the number of individuals that did respond to the email when simplified information was presented, there was no indication that behavior changed on the basis of receiving more simplified information.

Mental accounting and the CARD Act

Is $5 in your wallet worth the same as $5 in a piggy bank? While classical economists would say yes, behavioral economists have shown otherwise. The theory of **mental accounting** describes how consumers organize their finances by mentally ascribing money for different purposes. It is defined as "the set of cognitive operations used by individuals and households to organize, evaluate, and keep track of financial activities" (Thaler, 1999, p. 183). In other words, people treat money differently depending on factors such as its origin and intended use, and they do not think about money in terms of formal accounting. For example, someone might spend the same amount of money in a completely different way if it was received as a gift than if they received it as part of their wages from work.

To put it more formally, in contrast to basic economic principles, research on mental accounting suggests that people do not treat money as fungible (interchangeable); instead, they segregate their money on the basis of its function, which in turn influences their financial decisions. A mental accounting experience frequently encountered in everyday life is when people gain money unexpectedly – for example, by finding money on the street or receiving an unexpected tax return. These types of earnings are labeled **windfall gains**. In many cases, people spend unexpected gains on pleasurable things they might not normally buy, such as visiting a high-end restaurant or treating themselves to a massage.

BOX 4.3 MENTAL ACCOUNTING

In an experiment by Kahnemann and Tversky (1984), participants were asked to imagine that on their way to a show, they lost either the theater ticket worth $10 or a $10 bill. Next, the researchers wanted to know if they would go home or buy a new ticket for the theater. The discrepancy between the responses is remarkable but can be explained by the principle of mental accounts. The people who had lost the ticket felt like buying a second one would increase the cost of seeing the show to a price that had become unacceptably high. The participants who had lost a $10 bill instead seemingly did not post this to the mental account of the show and thus were more likely to attend the theater anyway.

Be careful not to misinterpret this: while the vast majority chose to pay for the ticket in the first scenario, and a thin majority chose to go home in the second scenario, note that there were exceptions in both instances. It should not be concluded that *everyone* will *always* choose as the majority does, as is unfortunately how behavioral insights are sometimes described. See Chapter 13 for a more detailed discussion on this and why it is both a blessing and a curse in behavioral insights for policy.

A tick box displaying participants' response to the question "would you still pay $10 for a ticket" when either having discovered that they had lost a $10 bill, or after having lost the ticket. 88% of participants said they would still pay $10 for a ticket after losing the $10 bill, as opposed to 54% after losing the ticket.

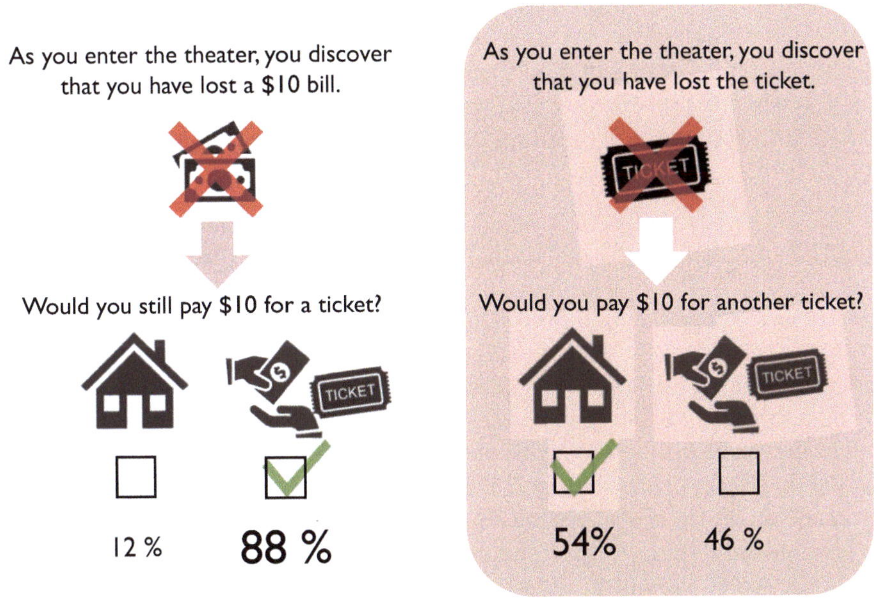

Mental accounting can also be observed in how people spend less money in supermarkets when paying in cash (typically a fixed amount they hold in a wallet) than when paying by credit card, which has a more flexible limit (Morewedge et al., 2007). While both of these ultimately come from the same source – our bank account – it has long been evident that our spending behaviors vary substantially between the two. Recognizing this, policymakers have sought to apply this insight for the benefit of consumers.

The Credit Card Accountability Responsibility and Disclosure (CARD) Act of 2009 reformed credit card regulations in the United States in such a way as to limit financial institutions from taking advantage of consumer biases (Consumer Financial Protection Bureau, 2013). Two regulations within the CARD Act in particular were informed by behavioral insights like mental accounting:

1 Creditors were forced to decline transactions that exceeded credit limits in order, rather than simply charging a fee for each overdraft. This regulation is designed to protect consumers who generally discount future costs in the presence of immediate needs or gratification.
2 The second regulation introduced a nudge mandating that lenders include additional information on the credit card bill. Specifically, the bill is required to show the time it would take for debtors to pay off their debt via minimal monthly repayments, concurrently with the cost of repaying their debt over 36 months. The method aimed to steer consumer attention away from the default of repaying the debt via minimal monthly installments – which is associated with higher costs of borrowing money – toward paying the debt more swiftly, which has greater long-term value in most scenarios.

Agarwal, Chomsisengphet, Mahoney, and Stroebel (2014) estimated that the CARD Act has saved consumers around US$11.9 billion per year, mainly by reducing the fees that are charged when customers go over their credit limits. This example illustrates how nudges making *hidden fees* more salient can substantially benefit customers by reducing borrowing costs. It also demonstrates the potential value of mixing a mandate (the first feature) with a libertarian approach (the nudge feature) in the context of behaviorally informed policy.

Reminders help make savings information salient

Savings accounts are a common product offered by retail banks. However, although these accounts exist, many people seem to struggle with saving money. One reason for this is the **present bias**, which assumes that we place greater value on matters in the moment than similar matters in the future. One manifestation of this is that people tend to prioritize the immediate gratification of spending over the gratification of having money saved (O'Donoghue & Rabin, 1999), which is a future benefit. When we consider whether to treat ourselves to a spontaneous dinner in an amazing new restaurant, it is easy to forget about that plan we had to increase our retirement fund and instead just enjoy the here and now.

In a successful attempt to reduce overdraft charges in the United Kingdom, a sample of 500,000 customers at a large British bank received alerts that provided them with their bank account balance and impending overdraft charges (Financial Conduct Authority, 2015). A reduction in overdraft charges of 6 percent (approximately GB£0.23 in average monthly charges) was found for customers who signed up for the text alerts, and those using the mobile app showed a reduction of 8 percent (GB£0.33). Interestingly, when consumers both received text alerts and used the mobile app the effect was amplified, reducing overdraft charges by 24 percent (GB£0.93). The combination of providing customers with timely and important information and empowering them through technology to act upon it seems to be a promising approach to improve consumer financial outcomes. It is worth noting that the effects varied considerably between age groups, suggesting that younger (those more familiar with technology) and older (those least familiar with technology) individuals may have more to gain from these reminders.

Another case reports that three banks in Bolivia, Peru, and the Philippines tested ways to help customers increase their savings (Karlan, McConnell, Mullainathan, & Zinman, 2016). In order to increase the salience of saving options and benefits, they sent out randomized reminders to customers who had recently committed to a savings account, using letters in Peru and text messages in the Philippines and Bolivia. Overall, there was a small but robust effect of reminders: the likelihood of meeting their savings goals increased by 3 percent for those who received messages compared to the control group, who did not receive reminders.

Commitment contracts to encourage saving

Another attempt to improve savings rates is the use of **commitment contracts** – formalized, self-imposed plans an individual places on themself, in this instance to limit their own access to their savings accounts. A rural bank in the Philippines conducted an RCT aimed at encouraging people to reach their savings goals through a commitment contract (Ashraf, Karlan, &

FIGURE 4.3 Application of commitment contracts in savings programs

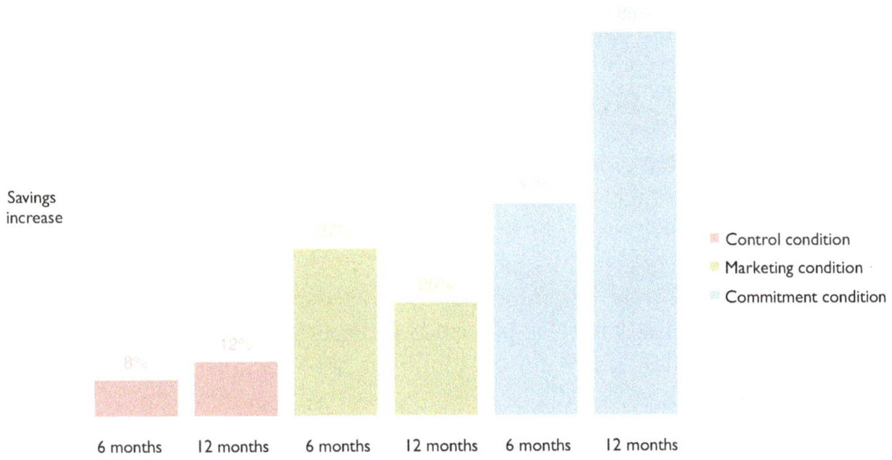

Yin, 2006). In the control condition, participants simply had a standard savings account. In the treatment condition, consumers had a standard savings account but were visited by a bank representative who encouraged them to save money. There were then two commitment conditions offered as options by another bank representative, who also encouraged them to save: they were to open a savings account that restricted withdrawal until a specific month (date-based goal) or until a certain savings goal was reached (amount-based goal). Customers in the control condition, who kept their standard account, increased their savings by 8 percent after six months and by 12 percent after 12 months. Those in the treatment condition showed a 37 percent increase in savings in the first six months, but these increases in savings dropped to 25 percent after 12 months (reported in Behavioural Insights Team, 2014, p. 36). Customers with a commitment account, however, showed an average increase in savings of 47 percent after six months and even 82 percent after 12 months (Ashraf et al., 2006, p. 658), though no split between commitment conditions was reported (see Figure 4.3).

Cognitive biases in the car market

One of the most commonly studied markets in industrialized countries is automobile sales, with particular attention paid to variations in prices between locations and models. Given the high rate of private car ownership in the United States, it might be assumed that most individuals have a reasonably strong understanding of the relationship between car prices and their features. Lacetera, Pope, and Sydnor (2012) tested this notion by looking at used-car sales prices based on the number of miles driven. At first glance, this pattern (see Figure 4.4) is not particularly surprising: the more miles driven, the lower the average price of the car. However, on further examination, you may notice that there seems to be a drop in price at intervals of approximately 10,000 miles. What is causing these sudden drops? Surely there is no substantive difference between a car – controlling for other features or issues – with 19,900 miles and a car with 20,001 miles. One way to explain this is as a result of **anchoring**, a heuristic where people weight most heavily the first piece of information they receive and put less weight on the information that follows. In this case, that means the first digit in the miles driven appears to influence the perceived value of the car and people's willingness to pay, as there are multiple instances where cars with an almost 10,000-mile difference had more similar prices than cars with only a few miles' difference, simply due to having the same first digit.

These differences have direct implications for policymakers. On one hand, such behaviors influence consumer welfare, so it may benefit individuals to be informed of their own biases. If we are aware that we may pay too much for a car simply because the first digit gives an impression of greater value, this might encourage us to be more critical with such choices. Alternatively, the loss in revenue for a used car solely on the basis of the first digit in its mileage could certainly be perceived as harmful for an economy, particularly one as vital as automobiles, which employs millions of workers within the United States alone. The latter perspective could perhaps be considered from the lens of classical economic theory, which is a direct application for why it has become so critical for behavioral economics to be integrated into many forms of policy. The presence of both perspectives offers better balance between impacts for wider economic outcomes and the well-being of individuals.

Another feature customers assess when evaluating the desirability of a car is fuel efficiency. In the US, this is commonly assessed through miles per gallon (MPG).

FIGURE 4.4 Heuristics and price drops

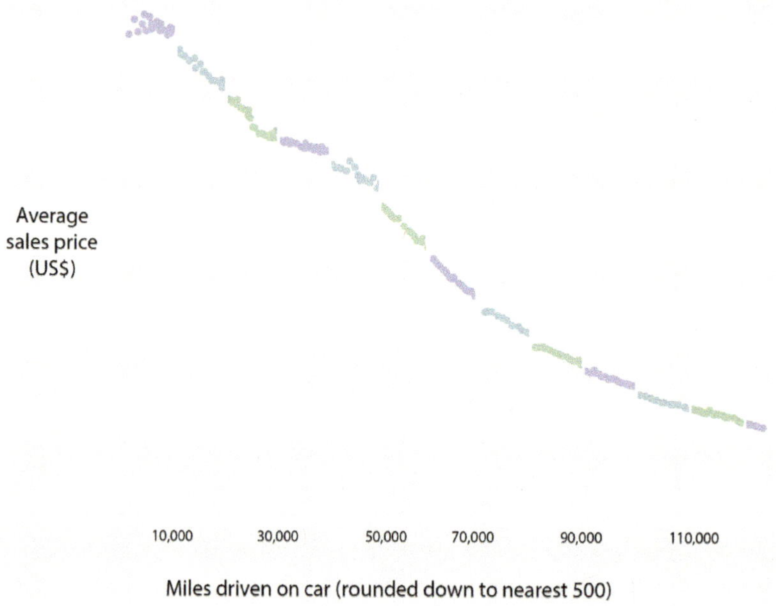

However, Larrick and Soll (2008) showed this is frequently misunderstood. A common misperception is that the relationship between MPG and gas used per 10,000 miles is linear; however, it is in fact curvilinear. The authors detailed that this means that over the course of 10,000 miles, more fuel is saved by replacing a 12 MPG vehicle with a 14 MPG vehicle than that saved by replacing a 28 MPG vehicle with a 40 MPG vehicle. Within their study, they found that when fuel efficiency was expressed as MPG, participants frequently undervalued small improvements on inefficient vehicles and overestimated improvements when the MPG was already high. However, when expressed as gallons per 100 miles (GPM), the majority of participants correctly chose the more fuel-efficient option. These results show a clear influence of information format that the authors hope implicates public policy to aid customer understanding of fuel consumption in order to make informed decisions.

Nudges with unintended consequences

There are many cases where theoretically sound nudges delivered with the best intentions still fail to produce the desired effects. Sunstein (2017a) describes various examples and discusses possible explanations for such failed nudges. Potential reasons include the difficulty of overriding strongly held preferences. For example, for people engaged in the unhealthy habit of smoking, the use of pictures illustrating the adverse effect of the activity on health might be ineffective in getting them to refrain from a behavior anchored by addiction. In another example, the Dutch Government introduced a reform to prevent websites from automatically tracking user data. Many companies responded to this "Don't Track Me" default by making access to their website contingent on the user giving permission to be tracked. As individuals had potentially strong reasons to make use of the website, giving permission to utilize data was a formality. It also may have ultimately strengthened the position of the website as it now had full consent.

Consider how social norms were used to improve tax compliance (Hallsworth et al., 2014). To implement this approach, the researchers had to present averages across the community to noncompliant individuals. While the vast majority in this descriptive norm did follow the desired behavior, it also highlighted that there were at least some others that did not comply, not just the letter recipient. In other words, those who were not following the rules were essentially told that others break the rules too. This may be interpreted as reason to continue the behavior or, worse, to encourage those who had previously been compliant to stop paying taxes (Cialdini, 2003). Such negative norms can lead to issues where the normative behavior differs from the desired or optimal behavior. In such cases, use of an **injunctive norm** outlining the desired behavior, rather than a **descriptive norm,** can be more beneficial (see Chapter 6 for further discussion).

When financial incentives are counterproductive

Financial incentives – and disincentives – may seem like an easy approach to change behavior, but in fact, they have many drawbacks (Gneezy, Meier, & Rey-Biel, 2011). We are used to giving and receiving material incentives when doing something for other people. Policymakers are also interested in changing individual behavior through financial means. For example, incentive schemes can be employed to encourage blood donations, vaccinations, or attendance at health screenings. However, researchers have found that in some cases, instead of fostering desired behavior, financial interventions can in fact be counterproductive (see Box 4.3).

In one famous study at a childcare center in Israel, parents had been routinely showing up late to pick up children at the end of the day. In an attempt to make more parents show up on time, a small penalty charge was introduced. However, after the fee was implemented, late pickups actually *increased* and stayed significantly higher over time (Gneezy & Rustichini, 2000). Along with many possible points, one of the general conclusions is that this charge was not a deterrence, at least not at the price point chosen, and may have instead made parents feel entitled to be late by creating a fee for a service. As they were already late to pick up their children, paying the fee may have allowed for greater utility in continuing other activities such as work or running errands, thus encouraging the exact behavior that had been targeted for reduction.

Another example of financial backfires is the case of a small Swiss town whose residents were asked about their views of a nuclear waste facility being built nearby (Frey & Oberholzer-Gee, 1997). While nuclear waste facilities are necessary for a country that relies on nuclear power, few people want such a facility in their backyard. When no financial incentive was presented, around half of the residents approved (50.8 percent). When asked again, but with an individual financial incentive highlighted for opening the facility (amounts varied between US$2,175 and US$6,525), approval rates were much lower (24.6 percent). This indicates that compliance with prosocial behavior requests may stem in part from a sense of social duty, which could be reduced when prosocial problems are framed in terms of monetary compensation. In other words, when presented with a choice that appears to be between socially supportive and not, we are more likely to be prosocial. When financial incentives are introduced, we may interpret that as an indication that the option may not be desirable ("Why would they pay me if it were a good thing?"). We further explore how financial incentives might undermine prosocial behavior in Box 4.4.

One approach studied nutritional outcomes after subsidizing food costs in two Chinese provinces. Jensen and Miller (2011) found that people did not use the money saved by the subsidy to purchase more highly nutritional, low-cost staple foods such as rice and wheat. Instead, individuals tended to use it to buy higher cost, lower nutritional foods, mainly meats. They concluded there was no evidence of a nutritional benefit produced by the program and found that nutritional intake even declined in one province.

BOX 4.4 WHY ECONOMIC INCENTIVES CAN UNDERMINE PROSOCIAL BEHAVIOR

When policymakers try to incentivize people financially, there are certain aspects they must be aware of in order to avoid unintended consequences. According to Bowles (2008), there are four ways in which economic incentives can undermine prosocial behavior:

1 The provision of incentives might frame a decision as being about self-interest

rather than ethical or social behavior. For example, in an experiment conducted by Liberman, Samuels, and Ross (2004), participants behaved more selfishly when the game was labeled as "Wall Street Game" compared to "Community Game." The presence of financial incentives might lead to an overjustification of the prosocial behavior, thus crowding out the original intrinsic motivation.

2. Financial incentives, though effective in the short term, can be counterproductive in the long run by altering individuals' endogenous preferences. This was illustrated in an experiment by Falkinger, Fehr, Gächter, and Winter-Ember (2000), where participants who did not receive any incentives contributed more to a public good than participants who had gotten used to an incentive scheme before, which had then been terminated. However, it has to be noted that, in some cases, short-term incentives can foster long-term intended behavior. For example, incentivizing a healthy lifestyle in the short run can help individuals experience the positive effects it has on them and thus lead to good habits that continue even after the extrinsic motivator is terminated.
3. Incentives convey information that may undermine the recipient's motivation. Prosocial behavior often involves trust, whereas incentives can indicate distrust. Distrust signals pessimistic expectations indicating that poor performance is the norm, thus making it acceptable. Consequently, low incentives, incomplete contracts, or the absence of fines can in some cases yield better results than high levels of control or high incentives would (Ellingsen & Johannesson, 2005).
4. Finally, financial incentives can backfire by undermining the recipient's feelings of autonomy and self-determination. For instance, it has been shown that providing young school children with material rewards can undermine their intrinsic motivation and can thus negatively affect high-quality learning (Deci, Koestner, & Ryan, 2001).

These examples illustrate that policymakers need to be cautious when employing financial incentives and that the potential long-term consequences of terminating a policy have to be considered before implementing it. The use of economic incentives without considering other factors involved in influencing people's actions when trying to promote a certain behavior might not be as effective as you would think.

Behavioral insights can help us predict when financial incentives will have positive effects and when they will lead to unintended consequences instead. By knowing about the various cognitive biases that were presented in this chapter, we can adjust for our own irrationality, anticipate others' behavior, and create environments in which individuals are more likely to be in positions to make choices beneficial for their own financial well-being.

Improving life satisfaction by buying tailored products

Can money buy happiness? This question has long engaged researchers, policymakers, and the entire public. Thankfully, behavioral science has shed some light on this, which may likely only stir the debate further. The conclusion? Maybe, but not necessarily so straightforward.

First, consider that Kahneman and Deaton (2010) found that more money does not necessarily buy more happiness, but less money is associated with emotional pain. Under this pretext, themoney-happiness link would not be linear. Instead, a basic level of money would alleviate some pain while also indicating a ceiling of when money may no longer yield a positive effect. In an American sample, this upper limit was estimated at US$75,000.

However, studies have questioned this conclusion, arguing that if money does not buy happiness, perhaps it is because people are not spending it the right way (Dunn, Gilbert, & Wilson, 2011). These studies suggest that money can indeed elevate well-being if we obtain experiences instead of material goods (Carter & Gilovich, 2010; Howell & Hill, 2009; Van Boven & Gilovich, 2003), if we use it for others rather than for ourselves (Dunn, Aknin, & Norton, 2014), and if we spend it on many small items instead of a few large ones (Nelson & Meyvis, 2008). Additionally, it may simply indicate that at lower income levels, the negatives that can harm well-being are more likely, but their removal can only bring us to a modest level of well-being.

While there are numerous studies highlighting that there might be general rules on how to spend money to improve well-being, these relationships are not likely to be the same for everyone. For example, spending more on others does not increase happiness for those who care little about others (Hill & Howell, 2014).

These results show how important it is to understand the way spending affects the happiness of individuals, as opposed to the happiness of entire groups. Matz, Gladstone, and Stillwell (2016) provide such an approach based on individuals' behavior. In a correlational field study, they analyzed over 76,000 bank transaction records. Additionally, the 635 bank transaction record owners were sent a questionnaire where they rated their personality traits (measured in terms of their Big Five personality traits) as well as their life satisfaction. Additionally, a separate set of participants had rated which personality traits best fit 59 spending categories (such as books, entertainment, jewelry; "If this 'spending category' was a person, how would it best be described?"). After the data from the bank transaction records and the two questionnaires were combined, the results showed that individuals who spend more on products matching their personality report higher levels of life satisfaction (Matz et al., 2016, study 1).

As the science underlying spending and happiness continues to grow, and given these results, it may be possible in the future for companies to try to improve customer well-being by providing tailored suggestions based on the personality traits of the consumer. Similarly, policymakers might use these findings to design policies in a more tailored way, as personalization of consumer messaging also comes with many risks and opportunities for manipulation.

Conclusion

The application of behavioral economics to better understand and influence economic and consumer decision-making is a rapidly growing field of study, as is evidenced by interest in the topic from governments around the world. Lessons from behavioral economics and consumer psychology potentially have broad applications relating to areas as diverse as public health, consumer protection, environmental impact, and national and personal finances, as described in this chapter. From simple interventions such as a small charge for plastic shopping bags to complex endeavors like educating the public about financial issues, these insights have the capacity to provide powerful individual and societal benefits. While the science of behavioral economics is now a well-established discipline of study, the application of behavioral economics to policy has only just begun, and there is still tremendous potential for growth. It is important to avoid known pitfalls, such as the ways financial incentives can backfire, or how knock-on effects may offset initial gains. However, if done effectively, this can have considerable benefits not just for economic impact and growth but also for the well-being of entire populations.

Essay questions

1 Think of a significant policy challenge that has not been addressed through behavioral economics. Describe how the insights described in this chapter could be applied to this policy area.

2 Are financial incentives always the best solution to influence behavior? Describe some of the problems that arise when financial incentives are used.

3 Find an existing policy based on classical economics and suggest how a behavioral approach could improve the effectiveness of the policy if implemented.

4 Imagine you are in charge of financial regulation for the country you live in. What do you consider the most important area of regulation that would benefit from insights from behavioral economics? Explain the problem, how you would approach it to help solve the issue, and what behavioral concept or theory your approach is building from.

5 Will reducing the complexity of information provided to investors improve their investment decisions? See the paper by Gentile et al. (2015) and justify your conclusion. Remember that a decision not to invest can be good (if it would have created losses) or bad (if it would have created gains).

Additional insights and further reading

Approaches used to increase people's saving behavior

Choi, J. J. (2015). Contributions to defined contribution saving plans. *Annual Review of Financial Economics, 7*, 161–178.

Behavioral biases might work differently in developing countries

Anderson, C. L., & Stamoulis, K. (2007). *Applying behavioural economics to international development policy*. UNU-WIDER Research Paper No. 2006/24.

Alternative descriptions of a problem can lead to different decision preferences

Tversky, A., & Kahneman, D. (1986). Rational choice and the framing of decisions. *The Journal of Business, 59*(4), 251–278. https://doi.org/10.1086/296365

How to improve the climate between taxpayers and authorities to foster compliance

Gangl, K., Hofmann, E., & Kirchler, E. (2015). Tax authorities' interaction with taxpayers: A conception of compliance in social dilemmas by power and trust. *New Ideas in Psychology, 37*, 13–23. https://doi.org/10.1016/j.newideapsych.2014.12.001

The influence of multinational economic policies

Hodson, D., & Maher, I. (2001). The open method as a new mode of governance: The case of soft economic policy co-ordination. *Journal of Common Market Studies, 39*(4), 719–746. https://doi.org/10.1111/1468-5965.00328

Committing to a scheme in advance can increase savings

Benartzi, S., & Lewin, R. (2012). *Save more tomorrow: Practical behavioral finance solutions to improve 401K plans*. New York: Portfolio/Penguin.

Interventions to enhance financial literacy in Brazil and Spain

Bruhn, M., Legovini, A., Zia, B., Leão, L. de S., & Marchetti, R. (2014). *The impact of high school financial education: Large-scale experimental evidence from brazil*. Washington, DC: World Bank Group. Retrieved from http://bit.ly/2xo6T4f

Hospido, L., Villanueva, E., & Zamarro, G. (2015). Finance for all: The impact of financial literacy training in compulsory secondary education in Spain. *SSRN Electronic Journal*. IZA discussion paper no. 8902. https://doi.org/10.2139/ssrn.2559642

Small cash transfers can be effective as educational support programs

Benhassine, N., Devoto, F., Duflo, E., Dupas, P., & Pouliquen, V. (2015). Turning a shove into a nudge? A "labeled cash transfer" for education. *American Economic Journal: Economic Policy*, *7*(3), 86–125. Retrieved from www.nber.org/ papers/w19227

Personalization of financial aid information has an impact

Busso, M., Dinkelman, T., Martínez, A. C., & Romero, D. (2017). The effects of financial aid and returns information in selective and less selective schools: Experimental evidence from Chile. *Labour Economics*, *45*, 79–91. https://doi.org/10.1016/j.labeco.2016.11.001

Monetary incentives might lead to positive schooling outcomes

Kilburn, K., Handa, S., Angeles, G., Mvula, P., & Tsoka, M. (2017). Short-term impacts of an unconditional cash transfer program on child schooling: Experimental evidence from Malawi. *Economics of Education Review*, *59*, 63–80. https://doi.org/10.1016/j.econedurev.2017.06.002

This chapter was adapted from the following:

Ruggeri, K., Folke, T., Jarke, H., Paul, A. F., & Gladstone, J. J. (2019). Economic, financial, and consumer. In K. Ruggeri (Ed.), *Behavioral insights for public policy: Concepts and cases* (pp. 80–93). New York and London: Routledge.

5 Health behavior and decision-making in healthcare

Hannes Jarke, Kai Ruggeri, Johanna Graeber, Markus R. Tünte, Olatz Ojinaga-Alfageme, Sanne Verra, Dafina Petrova, Amel Benzerga, Zorana Zupan, and Matteo M. Galizzi

Acknowledgments: Mari Louise Berge, Andrijana Radukić, David Rosenthal, Nastja Tomat, and Keying Wang

Chapter summary

Where people live, what they eat, how careful they are about taking their medications, and even what they do in their spare time are very much related to the quality of their lives and their health-related outcomes. While our genetic makeup accounts for a significant portion of our health outcomes, we know that health is also heavily influenced by what are known as social determinants: education, wealth, neighborhood safety, housing, and health literacy, among many others. Throughout the day, we face many decisions that have a direct or indirect impact on our health and quality of life. Many of these choices can be influenced toward healthier options by behavioral interventions. This chapter presents behavioral insights and interventions that have a high potential to impact the health of community members, reduce disparities, and improve their overall quality of life. These insights and interventions range from increased medical adherence to improved nutritional choices using nudges, regulations, provision of information, or rewards for positive behaviors.

Learning objectives

- Describe the relationship between health policy and health outcomes
- Apply key features of behavioral insights to interventions that focus on health outcomes
- Distinguish intervention approaches targeting treatment, prevention, and promotion, and consider their implications
- Understand the impact of interventions such as incentivizing healthy behaviors or using environmental restructuring

DOI: 10.4324/9781003181873-5

Introduction

High blood pressure, tobacco use, high levels of blood glucose, physical inactivity, and obesity have been repeatedly identified as the leading causes of mortality worldwide (WHO, 2009). In addition to the immense harmful impacts on population health, these conditions also create a significant economic burden. The annual net cost of illnesses associated with obesity for healthcare in the United Kingdom alone is estimated to be GB£2.47 billion (approximately US$3.2 billion), equaling about 2 percent of the health budget and 0.3 percent of the country's GDP (Tovey, 2017). However – in many cases – these conditions can be prevented or reduced not only by medical interventions but by changes in behavior. Interventions that successfully promote healthy behaviors on a wider level can range from very simple to complex and can be effective across the general population or only for specific groups (see also Box 5.4 later in the chapter). Before we discuss such interventions, let us first take a look at the factors that influence population health.

The key determinants of health in general and specifically the onset, development, and progression of diseases can be found on multiple levels:

1 Structural, socio-economic, and environmental factors
2 Our health-related behaviors, lifestyles, and everyday decisions

As such, the development of interventions – and a framework for them – that can influence behavior toward better health outcomes may be critical for improving population health and reducing the economic burden of disease.

Public Health England (PHE) is an executive agency of the UK Department of Health and Social Care that works to improve public health and reduce health differences. It aims to do this through promoting healthier lifestyles and providing evidence-based support and advice to governmental bodies and industry. According to PHE, "while individual behaviour change is extremely important, a comprehensive and coherent framework to address these problems needs to draw more broadly on behavioral and social sciences to identify and solve structural and social issues" (PHE, 2018, p. 5). PHE proposes a collaborative and comprehensive strategy and framework to apply behavioral sciences to improve population health and well-being, which is the first strategy of this kind in the world. The goal of the framework is to help public health professionals to leverage insights and methodologies from behavioral and social sciences for their work. As such, this chapter is structured following the PHE framework to introduce concepts and cases where behavioral sciences are applicable to health (see Box 5.1).

BOX 5.1 A COMPREHENSIVE PUBLIC HEALTH POLICY FRAMEWORK FOR BEHAVIORAL INTERVENTIONS

PHE's high-level strategy and framework distinguish between several categories of public health policies, which include behavioral interventions in (1) legislation; (2) regulation; (3) fiscal measures; (4) guidelines; (5) environmental and social planning; (6) communication and marketing; and (7) service provision.

In particular, Galizzi (2014, 2017) presents five classifications of behavioral interventions in health policy: **preference-based** policies; **information-based** policies; **financial incentives**; **regulation** policies – which include legislations, bans, taxes, and subsidies; and **nudges**.

Preference-based policies are based on the idea of providing the public, patients, and healthcare professionals broad sets of choices from which they can pick their favorite option: the broader these sets of choices are, the larger the set of possible profiles of preferences that can be satisfied. A typical example is a website comparing private insurance plans, as described by Thaler and Sunstein (2008).

Information-based policies are policy interventions providing information to the public, patients, and healthcare professionals to enable them to make healthier decisions. Some typical examples are the "Smoking kills" messages on packets of cigarettes or the nutritional labels on food items.

Financial incentives are policies providing monetary incentives conditional to a specific change in behavior. Some examples are paying GB£100 to smokers when they quit or giving obese patients lottery vouchers when they lose weight.

Regulation policies – including legislation, regulations, bans, taxes, and subsidies – are a cluster of policy interventions that directly interfere with markets and market prices in order to overcome market failures, particularly "externalities." Taxes and subsidies, for example, act as hedges between the producers and the consumers, and market prices are increased or decreased by their introduction for all consumers. Some examples are the taxes on cigarettes and spirits or the current discussions on introducing "fat taxes" or "soda taxes," that is, taxes on sweetened fizzy drinks in the US, Mexico, UK, France, and Italy.

Finally, *nudges* are essentially policy interventions that leverage changes in choice architecture and the decision environment to promote better choices without changing, limiting, or forcing a preferred behavior (see Chapters 2 and 3).

Application of behavioral insights to health policy

In 2006, the European Union made a significant stride in rethinking all forms of public policy under the banner "**Health in All Policies**" (HiAP). The premise is that all policies have some direct or indirect impact on the health of the population concerned (Koivusalo, 2010). HiAP is defined as "an approach to public policies across sectors that systematically takes into account the health and health systems implications of decisions, seeks synergies, and avoids harmful health impacts, in order to improve population health and health equity" (WHO, 2014a, p. 2). However, to fully realize the aims and potential of HiAP, targets have to be clearly identified and suitable policy levers need to be developed in order to achieve them. Policies shape the conditions in which people live, and the development of all policies will impact individual and community health. For example, policies that influence how we care for our environment, the type of transportation systems we use, and our access to education will all have implications for the health of all those living in our community.

Some of the most widely impactful global health issues, such as cancer, obesity, and diabetes, are not purely the result of our genetic makeup or environmental factors. Many of these may be prevented by changing certain behaviors, in particular smoking, alcohol consumption, and lack of physical activity (WHO, 2009). Some infectious diseases, such as HIV, are also possible to prevent through changing behavior, such as using condoms. However, large amounts of government and healthcare budgets are often allocated to treatment of disease, rather than public health and disease prevention. For example, in 2017, only 2.5 percent of US healthcare spending was used for public health (Rama, 2019). As a consequence, public health budgets are often comparatively small, highlighting the need for designing low-cost interventions to encourage and move people toward healthier behavior (Nurse et al., 2014).

Promotion, prevention, and treatment

Rose (1985) draws a distinction between providing treatment to high-risk individuals as opposed to a population-based strategy that seeks to create the conditions for improved population health. This idea has been extremely influential and has been cited in over 4,000 publications, including official guidelines of professional communities (e.g. Perk et al., 2012). Consider the case of smoking: if cigarettes are cheap and easily available and nobody speaks out against people smoking in public spaces like restaurants, a fundamental change in smoking behavior appears unlikely. While some have argued that this view poses a simplistic binary reduction (e.g. Malik, 2006), the idea in itself provides a starting point for thinking about all levels of interest in addressing health problems. Without a coherent and comprehensive policy approach aimed at restructuring the environment to eliminate or reduce exposure to unhealthy stimuli, the effect of targeted individual interventions within a hindering environment will be limited.

Building from Rose, policies to improve the overall health status of a population can make use of three different levers: targeting the treatment of known issues (**treatment**); preventing issues from occurring (**prevention**); and improving the overall status of a population (**promotion**) (Ruggeri et al., 2017). For example, to tackle the issue of obesity, rewards can be used to encourage healthy eating and physical activity (promotion); children at risk of diabetes can be targeted directly in schools (prevention); and lotteries can be used to encourage overweight people to reach their weight-loss goals (treatment). It is not always easy to distinguish these approaches completely: sometimes they will overlap. For example, a healthy eating habit program for obese children hopefully affects their general health behavior (promotion), could prevent further complications such as diabetes (prevention), but may be mainly used for them to lose weight as a measure to reverse their condition (treatment). To distinguish between the three, it is therefore advisable to consider the overall objective of the intervention, whether it is mainly to promote, prevent, or treat. By using this framework, this chapter provides an overview of interventions exemplifying each of the three approaches.

Promotion

The WHO defines **health promotion** as "the process of enabling people to increase control over their health and its determinants, and thereby improve their health" (WHO, 2005, p. 1). Health promotion goes beyond targeting individual behaviors and includes changing behavior on a larger scale through social and environmental interventions. We can extend this definition to include any initiative aimed at any individual, regardless of their current health status, that focuses on achieving improved health outcomes. Behavioral insights can support health promotion in various areas. For example, nudging people can improve eating habits and physical activity, encourage participation in regular tests and screenings, and can even improve the conditions of others by encouraging registration as a blood or organ donor.

Nudges

Changes in the environment to promote well-being

Our physical environment directly shapes our daily behavior and in turn has considerable impact on our health. In **environmental engineering**, certain properties of an environment are modified with the aim of making desired actions more salient, more accessible, or more attractive. This might include more efficient signage to improve traffic flow on busy roads, safer bicycle paths in urban areas, and clean outdoor spaces for physical activity and social gatherings. Those attractive and pleasurable public spaces are known to promote engagement in physical and social activities and can benefit population well-being (Anderson, Ruggeri, Steemers, & Huppert, 2017; Anderson, 2015).

The importance of public spaces being engaging also caught the attention of the Global Happiness Policy Report of 2018 (Diener, 2018). The report highlights, among other research, an observational study by Anderson and colleagues (2017) that was carried out in the Northern Quarter of Manchester, United Kingdom. The aim was to examine whether improving outdoor space in a residential community would elicit any increase in three activities that are closely related to well-being and also easily observed. These are (1) connecting with other people (e.g. talking and listening), (2) engaging in physical activity, and (3) taking notice or being aware of the external environment (Aked & Thompson, 2011). Interventions to increase well-being were selected by the community residents themselves through participation in workshops (Anderson & Baldwin, 2017).

These interventions included the introduction of public art exhibitions, high-speed Wi-Fi, shade-tolerant planting, a lawn, vegetation management, recycled seating, painting, and cleaning. After the community-led change in the neighborhood space, observed and self-reported behaviors associated with well-being increased. Physical activity, for example, increased by 23 percent over a period of one year.

Promotion of healthy eating through salience and rewards

A balanced diet and nutrition can help prevent a number of chronic diseases such as coronary heart disease, cancer, and type 2 diabetes (World Health Organization, 2003a). However, when unhealthy fast food choices are so much more easily accessible and affordable (Jones, Conklin, Suhrcke, & Monsivais, 2014), how can we encourage healthier food choices in everyday life?

In Denmark, authorities decided to promote healthier diets by implementing an intervention aiming to increase fruit and vegetable sales – and subsequent consumption – in supermarkets (OECD, 2017g). The trial included 12 intervention stores and 12 control stores. In the intervention stores, pre-cut vegetables were placed next to minced meat (hamburger) coolers to encourage people to add vegetables to their meal. This is an example of a **coat-tailing** intervention: pairing a preferable (in this case, healthier) option with a popular option (related or otherwise), with the aim of making it visible in a convenient way and thereby increasing the likelihood of the preferable option being chosen (or a bundle intervention; see Milkman, Minson, & Volpp, 2014). Sales per customer of pre-cut vegetables in the intervention stores increased by 61.3 percent compared to the control stores, while minced meat sales also increased by 32 percent.

Use of reciprocity to increase organ donor registrations

More than 110,000 people are currently on the national transplant waiting list in the United States (Health Resources and Services Administration, 2018). While 34,770 organs are donated annually, 20 people die *daily* because they did not receive an organ transplant in time. At the same time, 95 percent of Americans support organ donation, but only 54 percent are registered donors. The application of behavioral insights to organ donation policies is a heavily debated topic that raises major ethical questions and the possibility of grave negative outcomes.

As discussed in a blog by Richard Thaler (2011), in cases where it is extremely complicated or difficult for a person to opt out of an option, utilization of opt out (i.e. being signed up to an option until you actively object to it) effectively becomes a mandate. For example, consider two fictitious, extreme scenarios: country A's population is highly educated and digitally literate on average, with citizens that can easily access and change legal documents on a secure system online. They are already informed once they start school that they are organ donors by default and may change this by simply removing a check mark from a box, which they can comfortably and securely do from their couch. Country B on the other hand has a population with low socio-economic status and low literacy. Most citizens are not aware of the law and the fact that they are organ donors. For those who are aware, to switch their status requires a lot of bureaucracy and paperwork, effectively preventing most of them from actively choosing the non-default option. While a high number of organ donors is certainly desirable from a public health perspective, policies that threaten or undermine individual free will are violating some of the key ethical and practical principles of nudges and many other behaviorally informed interventions.

How could behavioral insights be used in an ethical way to increase organ donations then? Use of **reciprocity** by reframing questions and propositions to inform individuals how they may benefit from a certain behavior has been shown to be a promising cost-effective – and non-restrictive – tool. In the United Kingdom, a randomized controlled trial examined whether the use of different messages would encourage people to join the organ donor register. After citizens completed an online form to renew their car tax or apply for a driver's license, one of eight different messages to join the organ donor register was presented to them, each using different behavioral strategies. Based on the principle of reciprocity, one of the messages displayed was "If you needed an organ transplant would you have one? If so please help others" (BIT, 2013, p. 7). This was the most influential message out of the eight and has since been put into practice and, based on results from the trial, may increase organ donations by up up to 69,000 annually.

Incentives

Use of rewards to promote physical activity

On average, 54 percent of people living in OECD countries are considered overweight, and 19 percent are considered obese (OECD, 2017h). In Canada, six in ten adults and nearly one in three children are overweight.

Financial incentives are often considered to promote physical activity. Charness and Gneezy (2009), for instance, randomly assigned university students to three groups to investigate this sort of incentives. A control group was given handouts explaining the health benefits of regular physical exercise. A second group was given the handouts and additionally received $25 if they attended the gym at least once in the following week (low incentive). Finally, there was a high-incentive group, where participants were given the handouts and received an additional $100 if they attended the gym at least eight times in the following month. Participants were observed up to seven weeks after the incentives were removed. Despite the absence of financial incentives at that point, gym attendance was significantly higher for the high-incentive group than for the other two.

The Public Health Agency of Canada (PHAC) designed an **incentive**-based pilot project to encourage greater physical activity (OECD, 2017g). It was intentionally designed as a loyalty program, rewarding those who reached physical activity milestones at designated fitness facilities with loyalty points (i.e. Air Miles). The project was implemented in 15 locations across Canada with a total of 98,000 participants registered over approximately three years. Incentivized visits to fitness facilities were compared to 11 control sites that did not offer the incentive. Members who were enrolled in the project visited fitness facilities 17 percent more often than members who were not enrolled in the project. The effect was strongest in the first few months of the intervention, while the long-term effects of the pilot project are still being evaluated. Although this project was seemingly successful in Canada – where these kinds of loyalty programs are widely used and popular – the situation may be different elsewhere in the world.

Faulkner, Dale, and Lau (2019) investigated the effect of loyalty points on the frequency of YMCA Health and Fitness Centre visits in Canada. They collected data at 13 YMCA locations amounting to a sample of 459,146 YMCA members. Visiting rates were observed during a pre-program period, an incentive period, and a post-incentive period over four years. The average rate of center visits during the incentive period was indeed higher among those YMCA members who collected Air Miles. However, Air Miles rewards collectors not only had higher visiting rates during and after the incentive period but also already had higher rates before. After they adjusted for visiting rates in the pre-incentive period, the authors found no evidence for an association between the Air Miles rewards and visiting rates.

Although it seems like rewarding physical activity has potential, it is not always successful. To motivate new gym members to reach their exercise goals, Carrera, Royer, Stehr, and Sydnor (2018) tried an incentive-based approach. New members were offered a reward for visiting the gym at least nine times during the first six weeks of their membership. Goals were intentionally set low to specifically support people who exercise the least. The 690 participants were allocated to four conditions: two groups received monetary incentives (US$30 or US$60), one group could earn a pre-selected item worth approximately US$30, and a control group received US$30 regardless of the outcome. Overall, visits to the gym plummeted over the course of two months. While taken together, participants in incentivized groups were more likely to reach the threshold than those who were simply given US$30, the increase in average number of visits was still small, especially for people who did not work out much in the first place. During follow-up measurements within the next six weeks, no differences between the groups were found.

One possible explanation for the failure of the US$60 incentive group could be the **discouragement** effect. People can become discouraged as a result of not meeting a previously set goal, which can, in our example, result in even fewer gym visits than they would have made without the incentive being present. Webb, Chang, and Benn (2013) summarize further evidence in support of the existence of this phenomenon – avoidance after failure – which they accordingly label "the ostrich problem." Similarly, Kangovi and Asch (2018) argue that while meeting certain thresholds in, for example, reducing weight or blood pressure can serve as an effective motivational boost, not meeting these thresholds can elicit a feeling of failure. Depending on the personality of a person, these experiences may then be followed by an actively avoidant behavior toward individual health-related data. Nevertheless, encouraging people to reach their own exercise goals is still worthwhile: large-scale evidence suggests that **monitoring goal processes** is an effective self-regulation strategy that is likely to invoke positive changes in behavior (Harkin et al., 2016). However, success may be dependent on the size of the incentive and individual personality.

Findings from a large-scale multicountry study ($N = 422{,}643$) indicate that **loss-framed incentives** can be more effective at promoting physical activity than standard rewards (Hafner, Pollard, & Van Stolk, 2018). Customers of a large insurer in the United States, United Kingdom, and South Africa were offered an Apple Watch for only a small activation fee ($29 in the US). However, participants' activity levels were tracked monthly over the next two years using the Apple Watch, and the insurer required customers to pay money if they did not meet certain activity levels. Participants did not have to pay anything once they reached a certain threshold, but had to pay up to $12.50 if they were inactive. For reference, the highest amount charged each month would result in an amount equal to the retail price of the device, including the activation fee. Compared to another group, which received purely gain-framed incentives (such as coupons, cinema tickets, etc.) for being physically active on similar levels, participants in the loss-frame condition were more active – meaning they reached the threshold for at least light exercise (as defined by the study) more often. The increase in activity was strongest in South Africa (44.2% increase in activity, equaling an increase of 6.1 more active days with physical activity), followed by the United States (30.6% / 4.7 days), and then the United Kingdom (27.7% / 3.6 days). Among the three intensity levels of exercise (light, standard, or advanced) the largest relative increase was observed in advanced exercise, and the largest relative increase in physical activity was observed in a subpopulation of obese individuals with low pre-intervention activity (109% in South Africa, 160% in the UK, and 200% in the United States). The increased activity levels were still present 24 months after the repayment period had concluded.

Motivating people to donate blood using health checks

The global need for safe blood is increasing every day (WHO, 2006). As the number of accidents, injuries, and treatments involving blood transfusions, such as for cancer, are increasing, the demand for blood is rising. Therefore, the acquisition of new donors and motivation of existing ones are challenges many nonprofit organizations face. In the past, financial incentives have been used for this purpose, but they can have potential side effects, such as demotivating donors who are already intrinsically motivated to donate (Lacetera, Macis, & Slonim, 2012).

Leipnitz, de Vries, Clement, and Mazar (2018) suggest using complementary health checks as a nonfinancial incentive. These health checks are relatively cost-effective for blood donation services, barely require extra effort for donors, and might appeal to regular donors – who have been found to display increased health consciousness (Atsma, Veldhuizen, De Vegt, Doggen, & De Kort, 2011) – in particular. Two field experiments in Germany examined the effect of a comprehensive blood test, framed as a health check, on blood donation behavior. Participants were donors groomed for their third donation within 52 weeks. The experimental group received coupons for this health check with their invitation to donate, while those in the control group did not receive any incentives. Participants whose invitation included the incentive were 33 percent more likely to donate again than those who received the standard invitation. Repeating the procedure, the authors found a 13 percent increase in people who donated again. Interestingly, the effect was also found in participants who were already eligible to receive the same health checks free of charge through their family doctor (General Practitioner or GP). The positive effect was retained for donors receiving the coupon a second time. For the German Red Cross, this strategy has proved so successful that they have started to adopt it in different blood donation services across the country.

BOX 5.2 HEALTH LITERACY

In a world of ever-increasing complexity in medicine and health, understanding and being informed about health-related topics become increasingly important. The term **health literacy** has been used to describe this competence. A prominent, integrated approach defines the ability to (1) access information relevant to health, (2) understand information relevant to health, (3) appraise, judge or evaluate information relevant to health, and (4) apply or use information relevant to health across the domains of healthcare, disease prevention, and health promotion as the crucial elements of health literacy (Sørensen et al., 2012, p. 10). Behavioral insights allow for new approaches to informing people about the consequences of behaviors related to health – such as nutrition, vaccination, or physical activity – in order for them to make educated decisions. Critically, by targeting better health literacy, interventions do not need to wait until someone is unwell but can form a wider strategy to reduce risk and improve the health of a population.

Prevention

Prevention aims to reduce the burden of disease and associated risk factors by reducing the number of people becoming ill or by detecting disease at an early stage (WHO, 2017a). Prevention strategies focus on groups that are at risk of developing ill health or sickness. The aim of prevention is then to avoid manifestation of a disease or development of poor health outcomes by manipulating social determinants. We also extend this definition to include any initiative aimed at strengthening the barrier between risk and illness. This includes interventions that may not explicitly seek to improve health but aim to decrease the risk of becoming unwell. It might not directly improve current health situations, but those who follow the guidance will reduce their risk of experiencing the associated illnesses or ill-being (see also health literacy, Box 5.2). Prevention efforts that have effectively utilized behavioral insights include HIV screening, overdose prevention, reducing medical complications in hospitals, and increasing vaccination rates.

Information-based interventions

Notifying medical professionals of opioid-related deaths

Overdose-related deaths have become a major problem in the United States with the increased availability certain of drugs (Ballantyne & Fleisher, 2010). In particular, opioid-related deaths have increased exponentially in recent years, with most deaths occurring in patients for whom the risks of prescribing outweigh the benefits (Leung, Macdonald, Stanbrook, Dhalla, & Juurlink, 2017; Seth, Scholl, Rudd, & Bacon, 2018).

In a randomized controlled trial in the US, an intervention was trialed for 861 clinicians who had prescribed opioids to patients who suffered a fatal overdose (Doctor et al., 2018). Half of the prescribers received a personal letter informing them of the death of their patient and giving them information on safety guidelines for prescriptions, while the other half did not receive any notification. Rates of milligram morphine equivalents (MME) prescribed were compared before and after the intervention. Professionals who received a personal letter prescribed 9.7 percent less in MMEs in the three months following the intervention, while no change was observed in the control group.

Nudges

Reduction in over-prescription of pharmaceuticals with social norm letters targeting prescribers

The issue of over-prescription is not limited to opioids, and it causes harm in vulnerable populations while also being a financial burden to healthcare providers (Department of Health and Human Services, 2013). To tackle this issue, the use of messages containing social norms directly targeted at prescribers (such as doctors) to reduce unsolicited prescribing rates as an inexpensive intervention method has been subject to investigations (Sacarny, Yokum, Finkelstein, & Agrawal, 2016; Sacarny et al., 2018a).

A first attempt in 2016 targeted a specific class of drugs in a randomized controlled trial (Sacarny et al., 2016). In the United States, drugs are categorized in relation to their potential for abuse and dependency, with Schedule II being the category of drugs that are the highest risk but that are still legal. The top 0.3 percent of prescribers – physicians and other practitioners – who were responsible for 10 percent of all Schedule II drug prescriptions were identified. Half of them received a letter containing a **social norm** message stating that their prescription behavior was highly dissimilar to that of their peers. These letters showed how much more they had prescribed compared to other doctors (e.g. "You prescribed 362% MORE Schedule II controlled substances than your peers"), including bar charts illustrating the high discrepancy. The other half served as a control group and did not receive a letter. In the 90 days following the letters, no difference in prescription rates was observed between the groups, indicating that the intervention had no effect. However, the researchers were able to identify several areas that might have contributed to the lack of impact. First, letters might simply not have reached many recipients in time (for example, 131 of 760 letters were returned initially). Further, 21 percent of the prescribers had already been under investigation for fraud or abuse in the past, making it plausible that the letters simply had been ignored.

A second randomized controlled trial targeting the antipsychotic drug quetiapine – which is commonly used in treating schizophrenia and bipolar disorder – offered the opportunity to apply insights from the first intervention (Sacarny et al., 2018a). Out of the 2.8 million annual quetiapine prescriptions in the United States, 75 percent lack sufficient clinical evidence, which makes the drug an appealing target for the development of interventions that could reduce off-label prescriptions. This led to changes in the protocol from the original study: the top 5 percent of prescribers in primary care were identified. Half of them received a series of three letters stating that their prescription rates of quetiapine were under review as they were much higher than those of their peers. The other half received an unrelated control letter.

Quetiapine prescriptions over a nine-month period were then compared. This time, results showed that prescription rates in the target group decreased by 11.1 percent, and the number of new patients being prescribed quetiapine decreased by 27.1 percent, highlighting a change in prescription behavior. Taken together, these two studies emphasize how the path to a working intervention is often paved with failure and how small changes made in the design of an experiment or an intervention can have a major influence on results (see Figure 5.1 comparing both studies).

FIGURE 5.1 Comparison of two interventions targeting the over-prescription of drugs

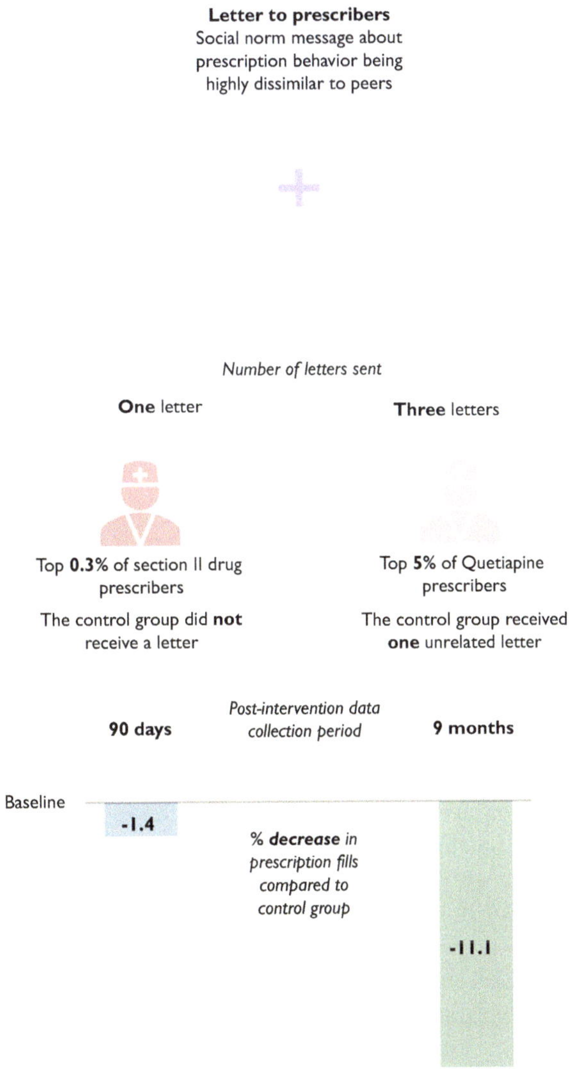

Reduction of over-prescription of antibiotics through justification prompts and peer comparison

Unnecessary use of antibiotics increases treatment costs unnecessarily and exposes patients to possible adverse effects of the drug. Unique to antibiotic prescription, however, is that it is the main driver of the spread of antibiotic resistance (Centers for Disease Control and Prevention, 2013). The majority of antibiotics prescribed in the US are used to treat respiratory tract infections. However, in many cases, such as bronchitis, they are not suitable as treatment (Smith, Fahey, Smucny, & Becker, 2014).

Meeker et al. (2016) employed a cluster-randomized trial to test whether behavioral interventions targeted at physicians might be effective in reducing over-prescription for respiratory tract infection treatment. Three interventions were tested and compared to a control group. One group of physicians received a suggestion for nonantibiotic treatment alternatives through a pop-up on their computer screen every time they were about to prescribe an antibiotic. Another group of physicians was asked for accountable justification for their prescription (in writing). Doctors sorted into the third group were subject to **peer comparison**: they received emails that compared their prescription rates to those of clinicians with the lowest inappropriate prescription rates. A comparison of prescription rates at the start of intervention to those 18 months later showed no measurable effect when alternatives were suggested. However, clinicians held accountable via written confirmation reduced their prescription rates by 7 percent, and those who were subject to peer comparison reduced their prescription rates by 5.2 percent. As with the letters in our previous example, the component of a **social norm** appears to be key in the change in prescription behavior.

Use of social norms to reduce alcohol consumption in college students

Though alcohol consumption is especially common during college, students overestimate the amount of alcohol consumed by their peers, creating a **self-other discrepancy** (Borsari & Carey, 2003). This perceived difference in our own behavior and that of our peers can create emotional discomfort, and students may try to resolve this discomfort by behaving similarly to their peers. To target this discrepancy, a multisite RCT employing **social norms** was implemented across 18 different educational institutions in the US (DeJong et al., 2006).

The institutions were divided into control and intervention groups. In the intervention group, a social norm–based, multimedia campaign ran from 2000 to 2003. Building upon previously obtained survey results, the core social norm messages of the campaign targeted students' average number of drinks during a week and at a party (e.g. "67% of XYZ University students have 4 or fewer drinks when they party," p. 869). At first glance, the messages did not show an effect, as changes in drinking behavior in the intervention group varied between a 1.1 percent decrease and a 10.6 percent increase, depending on the measure. In the control group, increases in drinking behavior from 17.5 percent to 24.7 percent were observed over the three-year period, indicating that although the use of social norms did not reduce drinking behavior, a protective effect had occurred. Specifically, rates of drinking behavior went up strongly in the control group, while smaller changes were observed in the intervention group.

However, a second study utilizing an almost identical social norm approach failed to find a similar effect (DeJong et al., 2009). A three-year social norm campaign targeted students attending 14 different institutions in the US. In contrast to the first study, results revealed no relevant change in drinking behavior in either group. Baseline drinking levels were different in the first and second studies: while students in the first study drank, on average, 4.6 alcoholic beverages per week, 6.2 drinks were recorded in the second study. Hence, campaigns utilizing social norms may be less effective at institutions with an already relatively high level of student drinking.

Use of checklists to reduce complications in hospitals

When performing common actions on a daily basis, we often switch to "autopilot," a more automatic form of behavior and decision-making that is less conscious and does not require engaged thinking (Kahneman, 2011; Robertson, Darling, Leifer, & Footer, 2017). This may be more or less beneficial in different contexts. For example, the switch to autopilot mode is common during routine and repetitive tasks to save cognitive resources. However, in healthcare settings, a switch to autopilot mode during routine tasks such as surgery may increase medical errors.

One way to overcome the limitations of our cognitive abilities is to make the steps of a task more **salient** by arranging them into a **checklist**. Checklists arrange salient, necessary steps into a guideline, often presented in a mandatory, chronological (or other procedural) order. There have been several attempts to study this approach, often with positive results. A total of 17 operating room teams from three different medical institutions in Boston (US) participated in 106 simulated, surgical-room crisis scenarios, such as cardiac arrest, anaphylaxis, or hemorrhage. Each team was randomly assigned to manage the scenarios with a checklist or manage by memory alone. The results showed that only 6 percent of steps were missed when a checklist was available, compared to 23 percent missed when the scenario was managed only by memory. Nearly all participating healthcare practitioners (97 percent) stated that they would prefer to use such a checklist during operations in crises (Arriaga et al., 2013).

Similar results were found in 103 intensive care units in Michigan, where another checklist was introduced to ensure adherence to infection-control practices in order to reduce catheter-related bloodstream infections (Pronovost et al., 2006). After the checklist was implemented, infection rates were reduced by up to 66 percent in comparison to baseline rates. This effect was sustained throughout the 18-month study period (Figure 5.2).

On a large scale, the WHO Surgical Checklist has been used to improve team communication and consistency of care to reduce complications and deaths related to surgery in eight hospitals in Canada, India, Jordan, New Zealand, Philippines, Tanzania, England, and the US (Haynes et al., 2009). The results of the intervention showed declines in death rates from 1.5 percent before introduction of the checklist to 0.8 percent after its introduction. Further, inpatient complications significantly declined from 11 percent pre-intervention to 7 percent post-intervention. A similar reduction was found by an investigation in a hospital in the Netherlands, where overall mortality decreased after introduction of the checklist compared to before (odds ratio 0.85; van Klei et al., 2012).

Increasing vaccination rates

While the WHO estimates that vaccinations prevent approximately 2.5 million deaths each year, vaccine-preventable diseases still remain a major cause of morbidity (suffering from a disease) and premature mortality in the world (WHO, 2013). Why are some people reluctant

FIGURE 5.2 Catheter-related bloodstream infection rates

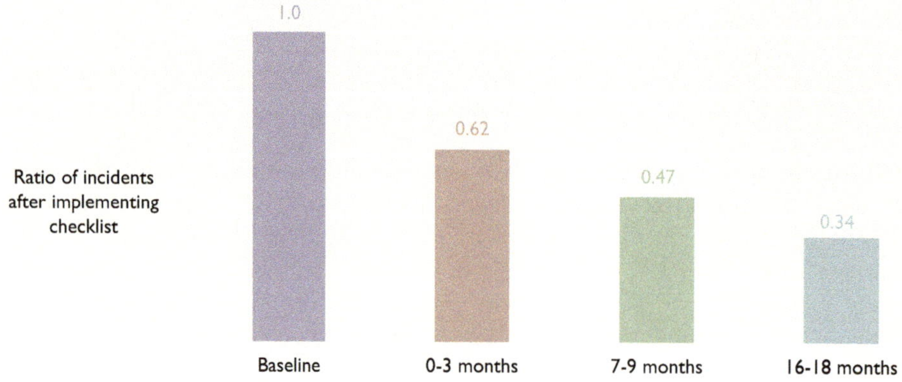

to make use of vaccinations? Betsch, Böhm, and Chapman (2015) suggest that it might be due to (1) not caring about immunization (complacency); (2) inconvenience in terms of physical availability, affordability, or geographic accessibility; (3) lack of confidence in the vaccine itself or the healthcare system; or (4) estimates that the pros do not outweigh the cons (utility calculation). Fortunately, several strategies targeting different aspects of the decision-making process show promising findings for increasing vaccination rates.

The use of **default** options may be one way to increase vaccination rates. Chapman et al. (2010) tested this assumption by randomly assigning employees and staff from a university into an **opt-in** or **opt-out** vaccination condition. In the opt-out condition, participants received an email stating that they had been scheduled for a flu shot appointment, with the date, time, and location provided and with the option to change or cancel the appointment. This way, the default option was to have the vaccination appointment: people had to actively change or cancel the appointment if they preferred not to have it. In the opt-in condition, participants received an email explaining that free seasonal flu shots were available with the option to schedule an appointment.

The results showed that only 8 percent of opt-out participants *canceled* appointments, whereas only 21 percent of opt-in participants *made* appointments. Overall, more participants in the opt-out group (45 percent) were vaccinated than in the opt-in group (33 percent) (see Figure 5.3). This highlights not only that default can be a powerful option but also that specification of appointments is worth considering in extending its impact.

Another way in which vaccination compliance may be increased is by using **active choices**, where the decision-maker is required to make a choice without a default option (Carroll, Choi, Laibson, Madrian, & Metrick, 2009). Keller, Harlam, Loewenstein, and Volpp (2011) tested a procedure called **enhanced active choice**, which highlights the preferable option through its advantages. They conducted a series of studies to test and compare the effect of different choice options on flu shot compliance and prescription refills. For example,

FIGURE 5.3 Use of defaults to increase vaccination rates

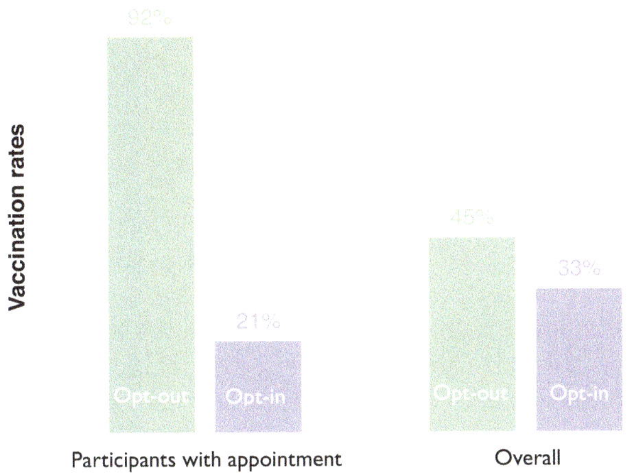

Source: Based on Chapman et al. (2010)

in one experimental study, 110 participants were allocated to one of four choice-structure conditions:

1 Default opt-in ("Place a check in the box if you want a reminder to get a flu shot")
2 Opt-out ("Place a check in the box if you DO NOT want a reminder to get a flu shot")
3 Active choice ("I don't want a reminder to get a flu shot/I want a reminder to get a flu shot")
4 Enhanced active choice ("I want a reminder to get a flu shot/I want to remind myself to get a flu shot")

Results from the four conditions show that enhanced active choice was the most effective strategy, with 93 percent of participants requesting a reminder. Active choice respondents were more likely (72 percent) to request a flu shot reminder than those in the opt-out condition (52 percent) or those in the opt-in condition (45 percent). It should be noted that actual vaccination behavior was not observed, but the desire to get the flu shot was recorded.

The use of **implementation intentions** could increase vaccination compliance by prompting people to have specific plans about when and how to carry out an action. Milkman, Beshears, Choi, Laibson, and Madrian (2011) tested this approach by randomly sending three different types of emails about workplace vaccination clinics to all 3,272 employees of a large firm. The employees received information about dates and times of clinics at their work location. Additionally, for two groups these emails contained a **prompt** for the employees to write down either the date or the date *and* time they planned to get the vaccine. The third group only received details about the vaccination and served as a control. Vaccination rates were higher for those with more specific implementation intentions. While no statistically significant differences in vaccination rate between the control and the date only group were observed (33.1 and 35.6 percent, respectively), those who were prompted to write the date and time had a 4.2 percent higher vaccination rate.

These findings highlight how a range of behavioral techniques offer the potential to increase vaccination rates. Although, as with many nudges, the long-term impact of such interventions is oftentimes unclear. For example, could these approaches be used each year and remain effective?

Incentives

Small cash incentives and HIV screening

As of 2018, there were over 36 million people in the world living with HIV, and nearly one million people died in 2017 from AIDS-related illnesses (UNAIDS, 2018). To prevent the spread of HIV, it is important that people are aware of their infection as early as possible. However, getting people to learn their HIV status is difficult due to social and psychological barriers, such as the fear of social stigma or worrying. The potential of **financial incentives** to increase individuals' knowledge of their HIV status and to impact behavior change was examined in a study conducted in rural Malawi (Thornton, 2008). More than 2,800 individuals were screened for HIV in a free door-to-door test, and they received randomly assigned vouchers worth up to US$3 that could be redeemed after they collected their test results. The findings suggested a significant difference based on monetary value. Among those without any cash incentive, 34 percent of participants collected their test results. Across all participants who received a cash incentive in any amount, 80 percent collected their results.

Two months after test results became available, individuals were interviewed about their sexual behavior following the testing and their attitudes toward condom use. To measure attitudes toward protective measures, at the end of the interview 30 cents were given as appreciation for participation with the option of using it to buy condoms for a reduced price. HIV-positive individuals who were aware of their status were more than twice as likely to purchase condoms as HIV-positive individuals who did not learn about their results. However, for HIV-negative individuals, knowledge of HIV status had no effect in terms of condom purchase.

Although this result suggests that learning their own HIV status had little impact on purchase of protective measures by HIV-negative individuals, it has to be taken with caution as a number of alternative explanations seem plausible. For example, participants might have had a sufficient number of condoms at home and did not need to purchase any at the time of the visit, or they might have been in a committed relationship in which HIV prevention is of low relevance. Also, regarding the unexpected 30-cent gain, psychological constructs such as the **windfall gain** (see also Chapter 4) have to be taken into account: people have been more inclined to spend this money on atypical purchases, as they did not expect to have it available for spending. In sum, this study highlights the potential cash incentives can have in increasing personal knowledge of HIV status in rural areas, while also outlining the problems that can arise when attempting to measure sustained changes over time.

Regulation

Rethinking barriers as a useful tool for reducing overdoses

Throughout many countries, a variety of medications are readily available in stores. While certainly convenient to get rid of an unwanted headache or other minor ailments, this availability comes with risks that should not be underestimated. Acetaminophen-related (paracetamol) adverse events remain a public health burden, accounting for an estimated 38,000 hospitalizations annually in the United States alone (Major et al., 2016). Acetaminophen overdose has long been linked to liver damage (Yoon, Babar, Choudhary, Kutner, & Pyrsopoulos, 2016) and, even though numbers are declining, is a common method for self-harm and suicide attempts (Hawton et al., 2003).

In the United Kingdom, **legislation** reduced the permitted acetaminophen pack sizes in regular stores (not pharmacies) from 25 tablets per pack to 16 tablets per pack (The Medicines Amendment Regulations, 1997). This legislation limited the amount of acetaminophen that could be bought in a single purchase, acting as a preventive measure for any suicidal impulses. Following its implementation, a 43 percent reduction in suicide rates and a 61 percent reduction in registrations for liver transplants resulting from acetaminophen poisoning were reported between 1998 and 2009 (Hawton et al., 2013).

Such examples again show that the combination of behavioral techniques and legal restrictions can elicit behavior change. Although this strategy did not directly target the root of the problem (i.e. addiction or the desire to commit suicide), it prevented behaviors related to one of the most common and accessible methods used to commit suicide.

Banning multibuy promotions to reduce alcohol consumption

Measuring the effectiveness of a policy is not always a straightforward endeavor. Consider the following measure taken against high alcohol consumption and abuse. In 2015, a total of 41,161 adults (age 16 and above) in Scotland were admitted to a hospital because of a condition that could be attributed to alcohol consumption. At least 3,705 died as a result of alcohol abuse – which makes up 6.5 percent of all deaths in Scotland that year (Tod et al., 2018). Alcohol consumption and abuse are connected to a variety of direct and indirect health outcomes, including liver damage, higher risk for polyps, higher risk for multiple types of cancer, and – depending on the amount of intake – higher risk of hypertension or even sudden cardiac death (Mostofsky, Mukamal, Giovannucci, Stampfer, & Rimm, 2016). Furthermore, an analysis of data from more than 28 million individuals across 195 countries concluded that there is no safe level of alcohol consumption (GBD 2016 Alcohol Collaborators, 2018).

To tackle the health risks associated with alcohol consumption (especially abuse), the Scottish Parliament introduced legislation in 2010 that banned multibuy promotions (increasing volume of purchasing, decreasing price per unit) of alcoholic beverages in retail stores. Multibuy promotions may easily elicit the impression of a quick gain, or even a windfall gain. A person who is about to buy, for example, four bottles of beer may now be able to buy – and thus consume – six bottles for the same price. Following the ban on multibuys, an investigation of 22,356 households between January 2010 and June 2012 revealed that the number of products purchased per trip decreased by 8.1 percent (Nakamura et al., 2014). However, the frequency of shopping trips involving cider and beer increased by 9.2 percent, and overall alcohol purchases did not decrease. No effects were found in relevant specific populations (such as individuals with low socio-economic status or heavy drinkers) either. This highlights the need to evaluate such interventions in context, monitor groups that are affected more strongly, and investigate further explanations for results. For instance, when policymakers in Philadelphia tried to reduce consumption of sweetened drinks through taxation, they found that while the higher price did work as expected, people living close to the state border started buying more and more beverages in neighboring states (Roberto et al., 2019).

Robinson and colleagues (2014) used another timeframe (January 2009 to September 2012) to evaluate the Scottish multibuy promotion ban. They compared alcohol sales in Scotland to those in England and Wales (combined as one group), which had not introduced such a ban, and found that total alcohol sales went down by 1.7 percent during that period. Notably, this reduction was due to a decline in specific beverages: wine (4 percent reduction) and pre-mixed beverages (8.5 percent reduction). No other forms of alcohol showed a decline in sales. If these kinds of policies are to succeed, investigation into the groups buying these beverages and their specific spending behavior seems crucial.

Reduction in standard serving sizes to reduce alcohol consumption

Does your family own old wine glasses that seem smaller than your own? In England, the capacity of an average wine glass has increased from 66 ml in 1700 to 449 ml in 2017, with the steepest increase having occurred during the past 20 years (Zupan, Evans, Couturier, & Marteau, 2017). Just as glass sizes have increased, so has alcohol consumption, raising the question of whether the increase in glass size might be contributing to the increased consumption. If so, would serving or selling alcoholic beverages in smaller portions reduce consumption?

A study in the United Kingdom tested this strategy by **reducing serving sizes** (Kersbergen et al., 2018). In a first experiment, 114 students at the University of Liverpool were invited to take part in a study. Initially, they were told that the study was examining the impact of social drinking on opinions. Over the course of the experiment, participants then had several opportunities to purchase alcoholic beverages. One-half of the participants received drinks containing 2.07 standard UK unit serving sizes of alcohol (e.g. 460 ml of beer or 165 ml of wine), while the other half of the participants received their drinks in a container with 25 percent less capacity (345 ml of beer or 125 ml of wine). Researchers then compared the number of alcoholic beverages consumed, while controlling for a range of variables. Participants in the reduced serving size group drank between 20.7 and 22.3 percent less alcohol. In addition, participants in both groups reported perceiving the provided serving size and the amount of alcohol they consumed as normal.

Having established an effect of reduced serving size on alcohol consumption, in a second step, the researchers aimed at validating their results in a real-world setting. At four quiz nights hosted at different pubs in Liverpool, 166 participants were recruited (each attending only once). For two quiz nights, UK standard sizes of beer and wine were served (568 ml of beer or 175 ml of wine), while for the other two quiz nights reduced serving sizes were used (379 ml of beer or 125 ml of wine). On average, 28.1 percent less alcohol was sold during the reduced serving size condition, and participants drank 32.4 to 39.6 percent less alcohol. By using a mathematical model built upon the results of the two experiments, the researchers estimate that a reduction of 25 percent in standard serving sizes could reduce deaths related to alcohol by between 5.6 and 13.2 percent per year.

Treatment

We refer to **treatment** as any intervention that focuses on moving an individual or group from a negative health status or behavior (e.g. illness, obesity, addiction) to no longer meeting the criteria for classification in that category. While most of these treatments are medical interventions – such as undergoing surgery – many have a behavioral component that is core to the success of that treatment (e.g. adhering to a nutritional plan before and afterward or taking medication on time). In other cases, the intervention itself can be behavioral, as is the case with physical activity to combat obesity.

Nudges

Reduction in complexity and use of reminder cues

Failure to adhere to medication intake instructions and plans has been identified as one of the biggest problems in healthcare globally (WHO, 2003b). Medical adherence rates of patients with chronic illness in developed countries average around 50 percent (WHO, 2003b), leading to an increase in hospital admissions, medication waste, overall health impairment (WHO, 2003b), and avoidable healthcare costs of approximately US$100 billion to US$300 billion per year in the United States (McGuire & Iuga, 2014). Medication-taking behavior, and therefore adherence, is a complex concept involving patient-, physician-, and health system–related factors (Brown & Bussell, 2011). Improvements in patient medication adherence could even have greater effects on health than improving specific medical therapies themselves (WHO, 2003b).

To be able to adhere to a medication schedule, patients should be educated about their particular disease and how their medication works. However, clinicians simply explaining to patients that consistently taking their medication is in their best interest does not guarantee that they will actually do so. They may simply forget to take their medication, especially in situations when they are required to follow complex medication regimens for extended periods of time (Haynes, McDonald, & Garg, 2002). Medication adherence could therefore potentially be enhanced by making the instructions more salient in everyday life, such as by reducing the complexity of the medication intake process and by using reminder cues.

The Federal Study of Adherence to Medications in the Elderly (FAME) employed this approach by providing a pharmacy care program that included individualized patient education and drug **reminder** packaging in the US (Lee, Grace, & Taylor, 2006). The drug reminder cue consisted of customized blister packs, with 31 numbered blisters for each day of the month and a sticker with the intake instructions. Each blister contained all the medications the patient had to take that day, removing the need for several different pill bottles. After a 14-month follow-up period, medication adherence had increased from 61.2 percent at baseline to 95.5 percent after the intervention and was maintained in the long term. Reminders can also be very useful within smartphone apps, as explored in more detail in Box 5.3.

Use of technology to increase tuberculosis treatment adherence

Tuberculosis (TB) is dangerous and infectious. At the beginning of the nineteenth century, the disease was so widespread in Sweden that every fourth death could be attributed to it (Wallstedt & Maeurer, 2015). Despite an available vaccination now, TB remains the ninth leading cause of death worldwide and is especially dangerous to vulnerable populations such as infants or HIV-positive individuals (WHO, 2017c). To ensure that medication is taken as needed, Moldova currently follows WHO guidelines, which require patients to travel to the doctor and take the medication in front of their physician (OECD, 2017g). This is known as directly **observed treatment** (DOT). However, DOT does not work for all patients: the travel is costly, time-consuming, and tiring. Many patients tend to discontinue treatment once they leave the hospital, a behavior that in turn is connected to increased rates of multiple drug-resistant TB strands within the country.

To reduce such costs, the United Nations Development Programme (UNDP), in partnership with a local NGO and the Behavioural Insights Team (BIT) in the United Kingdom, tested the use of a virtual adaptation of DOT – the virtually observed treatment (VOT). In VOT, patients take the pill in front of a camera and send a video message via an app, instead of having to be physically present at the hospital. Patients also receive personalized feedback and reminders if they do not send the video. In a RCT with 178 patients, the BIT found a significant advantage in adherence for VOT over DOT. In the directly observed condition, physicians were able to confirm average treatment adherence on 44 percent of the days indicated for the medication, while adherence in VOT was observed on 84 percent of days (BIT, 2018). A first synthesis of evidence available so far concludes that VOT is generally connected to high adherence rates and is widely accepted among patients (Garfein & Doshi, 2019).

Incentives

Use of financial incentives to support smoking cessation

In 2000, tobacco use was the leading preventable cause of death in the United States (Mokdad, Marks, Stroup, & Gerberding, 2004). The use of financial incentives to induce smoking cessation has been explored in clinical settings. An early randomized controlled trial by Higgins at al. (2004), for instance, provided pregnant women with vouchers that were either contingent or not contingent on quitting smoking. The vouchers were also delivered for 12 weeks postpartum. Cigarette smoking levels were observed during pregnancy, 12 weeks postpartum, and 12 weeks after the vouchers were removed. As expected, contingent vouchers were more effective in inducing smoking cessation, and effects were sustained up to 12 weeks after the end of the vouchers. A similar study by Volpp et al. (2006) considered 179 smokers who were participating in a five-session nicotine patch program over 8 weeks. They randomly gave some participants $20 for each session in which they participated, plus $100 if they actually quit smoking at the end of the program. In the short run, 75 days after the end of the program, cessation rates were significantly higher in the incentive group. Six months after the end of the program, however, smoking rates were not significantly different across the treatment and the control groups.

While there have been many attempts to reduce smoking, and programs for smoking cessation show some success, participation in such programs is typically low (Zhu, Melcer,

Sun, Rosbrook, & Pierce, 2000). In an effort to reduce dropout rates, Volpp et al. (2009) used financial incentives in a smoking cessation program for employees of a large firm.

In the incentive group, participants received US$100 for participation, US$250 for not smoking until six months later, and US$400 for not smoking an additional six months. Abstinence was measured through a cotinine test, which uses a biomarker to check for nicotine consumption. Participants in the control group only received information about the program. Overall, the rate of enrollment in the cessation program was low, though it was higher in the incentivized group (15.4 percent vs. 5.4 percent). Of those that participated, the completion rate was also higher for those who received money (10.8 percent vs. 2.8 percent). Across all participants in the study who received incentives, 20.9 percent stopped smoking, even though not all of them had participated in the cessation program. In the control group, 11.8 percent stopped smoking. After six months, 14.7 percent in the incentive group and 5 percent in the control group were still abstinent. One year after the intervention, 9.4 percent (incentive) and 3.6 percent (control group) passed the test (see also Figure 5.4).

In sum, participants showed higher abstinence rates after the introduction of financial incentives. While there is no information from the time period after the incentives ended, evidence suggests that most relapses occur in the first eight days after cessation (Hughes, Keely, & Naud, 2004). While using financial incentives to motivate people in their progress of quitting smoking appears to be a useful tool, it still remains to be seen which amounts are most cost-effective and how beneficial these interventions can be in the very long run.

FIGURE 5.4 Use of financial incentives to support smoking cessation

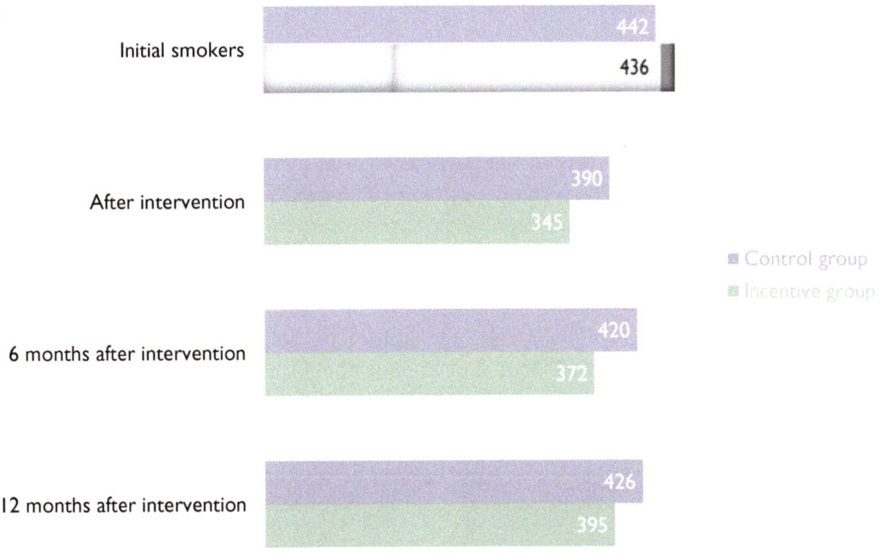

Source: Volpp et al. (2009)

Use of lotteries to reduce obesity

A report by the Global Health Observatory found that 15.4 percent of males and 39.6 percent of females in South Africa were obese (WHO, 2017d). Obesity was particularly high among office workers with few opportunities to engage in physical activity. The Walk4Health program was created with the aim of increasing physical activity and other healthy behaviors among

BOX 5.3 THERE'S AN APP FOR THAT?

In today's world, smartphones and mobile applications (apps) are commonly used. Therefore, they offer the opportunity to reach a wide range of individuals and populations and can also act as powerful health promotion tools. They hold great potential for use in prevention efforts, by targeting at-risk individuals, as well as in treatment, or as reminder systems in a variety of situations.

Take smoking as an example. There are already a substantial number of apps and other mobile phone based interventions made specifically for the purposes of smoking cessation (Abroms et al., 2011). Studies of these interventions indicate both short-term and long-term effects (Ybarra et al., 2016). For example, Free et al. (2011) found in a large-scale study with 5,800 participants, that after six months, the success rate of people trying to quit smoking was more than double for those using a text-message based intervention (10.7 percent) compared to those who tried to quit without support (4.9 percent).

It is clearly worth further exploration of how mobile technologies may facilitate meaningful interventions utilizing behavioral insights. Future mHealth interventions will have to consider (possible backfire-) effects of such apps on sub-populations and how to ensure that all groups can benefit equally.

employees of the Western Cape government through the use of competition, saliency, and role models (OECD, 2017g). During a six-week pilot study, 50 participants were given pedometers that tracked their daily steps. In addition, teams of four employees competed to take the most steps. Results were publicly displayed to track progress and ranking. Among those who participated, 70 percent lost weight and lowered their body mass index (BMI) (OECD, 2017g).

Volpp et al. (2008) trialed two financial interventions in the US to encourage weight loss in a group of 57 overweight individuals between the ages of 30 and 70 years with BMIs from 30 to 40. The goal for participants was to lose 16 lbs. (7.3 kg) of weight over 16 weeks. Participants had to keep track of daily weight loss and return to a clinic at the end of every month to be weighed. In the two money-based interventions, daily and monthly weight-loss goals were computed. In a lottery condition, participants had a one-in-five chance of receiving a US$10 reward and a 1 in 100 chance of receiving a US$100 reward upon achieving the daily goal. Participants also had to reach a monthly goal for the money to be paid. In a deposit-contract condition, participants were given the opportunity to contribute between US$0.01 and US$3 for each day they achieved their set goal. When a monthly goal was accomplished, this amount was matched 1 to 1 by the researchers, and an additional payment of US$3 was added as an incentive.

Both financial interventions positively impacted weight loss: participants in the lottery condition reported losing, on average, 13.1 lbs. (5.9 kg), with 52.6 percent reaching or exceeding the initial goal of 16.0 lbs. (7.3 kg). Participants in the deposit-contract condition reported losing 14.0 lbs. (6.4 kg) on average, with 47.4 percent reaching or surpassing the initial goal of 16 lbs. (7.3 kg). At the same time, participants in the control group only lost 4.4 lbs. (2 kg) on average, with 10.5 percent reaching or surpassing the 16.0 lbs (7.3 kg) target. To see whether the change in behavior was permanent, participants were weighed again seven months after the the start of the intervention. On average, participants in the lottery group weighed 9.2 lbs. (4.2 kg) less, those in the deposit group 6.2 lbs. (2.8 kg) less, and participants in the control group 4.4 lbs. (2 kg) less. After seven months, participants in the treatment groups had lost weight but not those in the control group, indicating the effectiveness of using of lotteries to reduce obesity.

BOX 5.4 INTEGRATION OF BEHAVIORAL INSIGHTS WITHIN HEALTHCARE SYSTEMS AND SERVICES

The need for a systematic approach to the implementation of behavioral insights within healthcare settings to ensure better clinical delivery and improved health outcomes is highlighted in a report by Robertson et al. (2017). The proposed model involves the integration of behavioral design teams into healthcare settings, an approach that has already been successfully implemented within governments to improve citizen outcomes. These teams are made up of trained behavioral science experts that have the ability to design, implement, and test behavioral interventions. The presence of behavioral design teams within hospitals and other care settings could help drive the systematic integration of behavioral concepts into every stage of healthcare delivery and could thus improve health outcomes. Figure 5.5 illustrates opportunities across the care spectrum for applying behavioral insights to improve healthcare delivery, some of which have been addressed in this chapter.

FIGURE 5.5 A conceptualization of opportunities for behavioral insights in health and healthcare

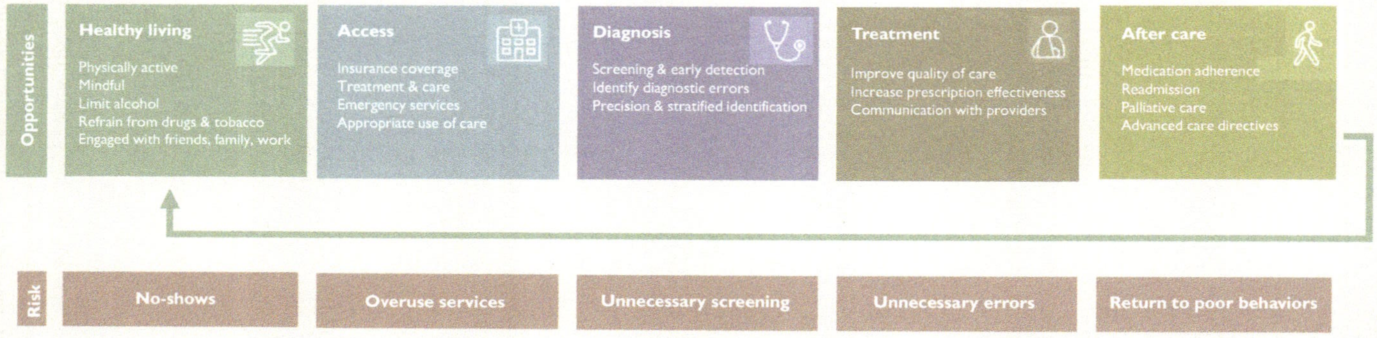

Source: Inspired by an original image produced for the report by Robertson et al. (2017)

FIGURE 5.6 Three pillars of healthcare

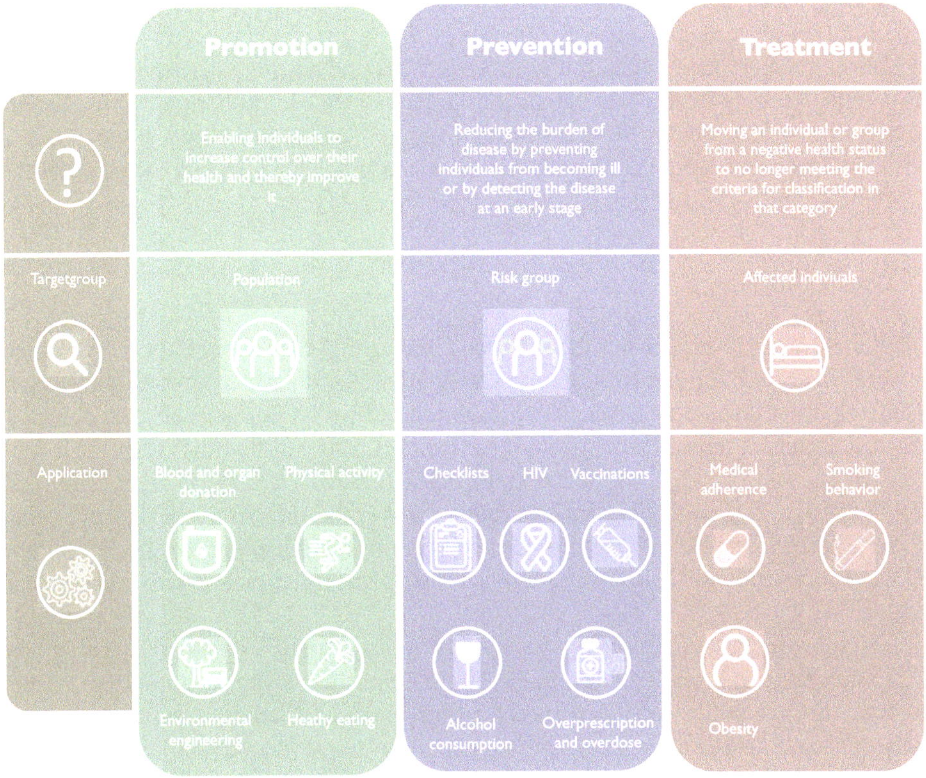

Cautions and concerns for applying behavioral insights to health policy

Two main challenges remain in developing effective behavioral interventions in health, which are currently also the two main gaps in the evidence. First, there is little systematic evidence on the **carryover** longer-term effects of nudges and other behavioral interventions in health, that is, whether and how long their effects persist over time on the same targeted health behavior. This is a key limitation for real-world health policy and practice applications where health outcomes are typically assessed over years or even decades.

Second, there is little systematic evidence on whether and how behavioral interventions targeting one health behavior also affect other, non-targeted behaviors, that is, the "*behavioral spillover*" effects of health nudges and other interventions (Truelove, Carrico, Weber, Raimi, & Vandenbergh, 2014; Dolan & Galizzi, 2015; Nash et al., 2017; Galizzi & Whitmarsh, 2019).

Take, for example, smoking cessation: when someone quits smoking with the help of an intervention, is it permanent? How long will it last on average? Will cigarettes be replaced by another form of tobacco, e-cigarettes, or another addiction? For which kind of individuals will it actually work? Are recovered smokers more likely to take up a more active lifestyle again once lung functions increase?

Many of the issues related to the overall impact and sustainability of intervention effects arise because having a single intervention is often not enough. Especially in the case of population-based interventions, we need to be wary of having *a single* intervention (see Chapter 10) instead of truly implementing an entire and coherent **policy platform** within a longitudinal framework. An intervention may show an effect when used once, but if it can be established within an organization or extended to a population, those effects are far more likely to offer genuine value. This means that policymakers would benefit from developing strategies that look beyond achieving narrowly defined targets in a single attempt and consider how to **monitor** overall changes in behaviors, ramifications, and impacts over time.

Conclusion

While there are a substantial number of broad and complex challenges in health globally, behavioral insights have demonstrated promising results when it comes to the treatment and prevention of disease, as well as the promotion of health. This goes beyond clinical and health-specific approaches. The scope of these insights is so vast that they should be applied in a coordinated and synergic way, making use of the Health in All Policies vision. The exploration of the heterogeneity of the intervention effects could inform the design of personalized and tailored interventions, benefiting specific groups within a population. This not only pertains to socio-economic and health characteristics but could extend as far as personality or values.

Insights from behavioral economics and psychology can be applied to designing behavioral interventions spanning the entire set of health policies, from information provision to regulation, through nudges and incentives (see Figure 5.6). Behavioral insights will – likely – not directly cure diseases, but they can contribute to preventing new infections, contribute to better health choices associated with better health outcomes, and may very well save lives and improve population health. By keeping this focus in mind, governments and other organizations can better secure and improve the health of the populations they serve by making use of behavioral insights.

Essay questions

1. How can policies from non-health domains (such as education, economics, finance) affect health, and what are the implications of recalibrating outcomes to focus on health no matter what the policy is? Justify your responses with examples.

2. What are the strengths and weaknesses of treatment, prevention, and promotion interventions? Give examples to back up your response.

3. According to the WHO, in 2014 there were 1.9 billion overweight and 600 million obese adults in the world. Imagine that you are a policymaker and you are designing an intervention to treat and prevent obesity in your community. Describe your approach to treating and preventing obesity using behavioral insights. What impact is your approach likely to achieve?

4 Now imagine that you are minister of health in a low-income country with limited monetary and human resources. Explain how you would approach the same task as in question 3 and reflect on how the impact of both approaches could differ.

5 Consider the study of Thornton (2008) who used financial incentives to increase individuals' knowledge of their HIV status and the way long-term effects were measured. Can you think of possible downsides to this approach and biases that might be in play? Design your own follow-up measurement and explain the behavioral science underpinning it.

6 Your country's government could reduce vaccination hesitancy by employing behavioral techniques (such as nudging or social norms) or by introducing a law that makes vaccination mandatory. Explain the general differences between these two approaches, elaborate on ethical implications, and then take into account country-specific factors. What are possible adverse effects of either option?

Additional insights and further reading

Redesign of hospital forms to reduce prescription errors

Behavioural Insights Team. (2014). *EAST: Four simple ways to apply behavioural insights*. London: Behavioural Insights Team.

Use of voluntary commitment products to help people quit smoking

Giné, X., Karlan, D., & Zinman, J. (2010). Put your money where your butt is: A commitment contract for smoking cessation. *American Economic Journal: Applied Economics*, *2*(4), 213–235. https://doi.org/10.1257/app.2.4.213

Use of lottery incentives to increase medication adherence

Volpp, K. G., Loewenstein, G., Troxel, A. B., Doshi, J., Price, M., Laskin, M., & Kimmel, S. E. (2008). A test of financial incentives to improve warfarin adherence. *BMC Health Services Research*, *8*(1), 272. https://doi.org/10.1186/1472-6963-8-272

Lottery incentives did not help increase medication adherence

Kimmel, S. E., Troxel, A. B., Loewenstein, G., Brensinger, C. M., Jaskowiak, J., Doshi, J. A., . . . & Volpp, K. (2012). Randomized trial of lottery-based incentives to improve warfarin adherence. *American Heart Journal*, *164*(2), 268–274. https://doi.org/10.1016/j.ahj.2012.05.005

Use of normative messages to encourage the use of stairs

Slaunwhite, J. M., Smith, S. M., Fleming, M. T., & Fabrigar, L. R. (2009). Using normative messages to increase healthy behaviours. *International Journal of Workplace Health Management*, *2*(3), 231–244. https://doi.org/10.1108/17538350910993421

Use of nonfinancial incentives to increase immunization among Indian children

Banerjee, A. V., Duflo, E., Glennerster, R., & Kothari, D. (2010). Improving immunisation coverage in rural India: Clustered randomised controlled evaluation of immunisation campaigns with and without incentives. *British Medical Journal, 340*. https://doi.org/10.1136/bmj.c2220

Use of text messages to encourage people to quit smoking

Free, C., Knight, R., Robertson, S., Whittaker, R., Edwards, P., Zhou, W., . . . & Roberts, I. (2011). Smoking cessation support delivered via mobile phone text messaging (txt2stop): A single-blind, randomised trial. *The Lancet, 378*(9785), 49–55. https://doi.org/10.1016/S0140-6736(11)60701-0

This chapter has been adapted from Ruggeri, K., Radukić, A., Ojinaga-Alfageme, O., Benzerga, A., Zupan, Z., Verra, S., . . . & Rosenthal, D. (2019). Health and healthcare. In K. Ruggeri (Ed.), *Behavioral insights for public policy: Concepts and cases* (pp. 94–113). New York and London: Routledge.

6 Energy and environmental behavior

Sara Morales Izquierdo, Manou Willems, Johanna Emilia Immonen, Amel Benzerga, Ondřej Kácha, Kai Ruggeri, and Sander van der Linden

Chapter summary

The most pressing environmental concerns of the twenty-first century include climate change, sustainable energy production, and access to clean air and water. In order to promote sustainable behavior, effective energy and environmental policies are needed beyond polarized debates around regulation. Although public willingness to utilize sustainable and pro-environmental options is increasing, actual behavior trends have not followed suit, with few exceptions. Largely through the use of social norms, a variety of behavioral insights present clear opportunities to achieve desired outcomes, with evidence ranging from better engaging local communities to improved public campaigns. Other approaches, such as setting default choices in favor of green energy, appear to result in "optimal" policy outcomes. In this chapter, we explore several techniques and their potential for impact.

Learning objectives

- Understand why evidence-based policy is a relevant tool in addressing environmental and energy issues
- Become familiar with current approaches to evidence-based policy in the energy and environment sectors
- Establish links between human behavior and environmental issues, particularly energy consumption
- Understand how evidence-based policies succeed to different extents in addressing the value-action gap
- Understand how behavioral insights can be used to address imperfect decision-making and to encourage pro-environmental behavior
- Understand the value that can be gained from evidence-based behavioral environmental policies compared to traditional policies

DOI: 10.4324/9781003181873-6

Introduction

Recognizing the significant threats to sustainability, the World Bank launched the Energy and Environment program in 2014 (World Bank, 2017). The purpose of this program was to bring together industrial leaders, elected officials, scientific experts, and non-governmental organizations. These groups were to outline a path toward addressing the major challenges related to accessing, using, and optimizing energy sources, while protecting the environment. As a development organization, the World Bank sees inequalities in access to electricity as a major barrier to meeting the United Nations Sustainable Development Goals, particularly for the poorest regions. At the same time, it recognizes the opportunity that providing clean, renewable energy options to those groups can act as a way to protect the environment without sacrificing economic growth. Developing countries not only lack proper and widespread access to electricity but they also suffer disproportionately from the consequences of climate change due to their limited access to financial and institutional resources (OECD, 2008b).

Energy consumption and human impact on the environment are clearly not only matters for developing regions. A considerable amount of research has been carried out to understand how human behavior in OECD countries impacts the environment. The economy in the Western world remains highly dependent on non-renewable fossil fuels, further contributing to human-induced climate change. It has been shown that excessive energy consumption by households and the energy requirements of the economy are significant challenges worldwide, because a global nexus between energy consumption and economic growth has been formed (Marques & Fuinhas, 2016; Apergis & Payne, 2009, 2010).

Direct negative consequences for the environment include loss of water supplies and glaciers (Chevallier, Pouyaud, Suarez, & Condom, 2011), threats to human health (Patz, Frumkin, Holloway, Vimont, & Haines, 2014), deforestation (Ahmed, Shahbaz, Qasim, & Long, 2015), production of electronic goods waste (Robinson, 2009), and pollution of natural habitats. This happens at the same time as extensive losses in biodiversity (Liu, Daily, Ehrlich, & Luck, 2003) comparable to that caused by major catastrophic extinctions in pre-human world history (Ceballos, 2015). Besides these direct consequences, there are other alarming processes occurring (see Box 6.1). For example, energy consumption not only contributes to climate change but is also expected to rise by 40 percent by 2030 if no major policy changes are introduced (International Energy Agency, 2009).

Another area that is also directly linked to many environmental issues is the agriculture domain. Livestock, with its high production of greenhouse emissions, is a major contributing factor to climate change (United States Environmental Protection Agency, 2012). The impact of meat production activities on the environment is rarely discussed in environmental policies despite the call for urgent action. However, consumer-oriented policy approaches seem to be more realistic than imposing taxes on landowners or interventions directly targeting the activities (Dagevos & Voordouw, 2013).

A great example of a consumer-oriented policy is the promotion of purchasing **green products**. Green products are defined as products that, when consumed, do the least possible harm to the environment. Consumer demand under a free market generally is not a sufficient path toward the extensive adoption of green products (Battisti, 2008). Regulation and fiscal incentives are also needed to ensure the accelerated usage of green products. Consequently, human behavior can be directly linked to such challenges, making decision-making and other behaviors natural levers for impact (Sovacool, 2014; Weber, 2013).

However, if the consequences of behavior are not considered, the impact of those regulations and incentives may be ineffective or even counterproductive (Giest & Mukherjee, 2018). More specifically, improvements in energy efficiencies may increase the demand for other services or devices, which results in an increase in energy consumption. This phenomenon is also known as the **rebound effect** by which a significant gain in energy efficiency is expected, while instead a reduction has been found as a consequence of changes in human behaviors (Greening, Greene, & Difiglio, 2000). To illustrate: even though someone saves money on energy bills because of their solar panels, this money might be spent on an extra holiday flight.

BOX 6.1 ENVIRONMENTAL CHALLENGES

With the current climate trend continuing, and assuming the economy will be directly affected by climate change, the World Bank Group estimates that an additional 3 to 122 million people (depending on future policy decisions) will be living in poverty by 2030 due to climate change (Rozenberg & Hallegatte, 2015), reversing decades of decline in poverty rates. It is also estimated that by 2030, 47 percent of the global population (3.9 billion people) could be living in areas under severe water stress, and 67 percent (5.4 billion people) could still lack access to public sewage systems (OECD, 2008b; see Figure 6.1). The combination of these two factors contributes significantly to diarrhea, which is already one of the leading causes of child mortality (WHO, 2016).

FIGURE 6.1 World population living in areas under water stress: 2005 vs. 2030 projection

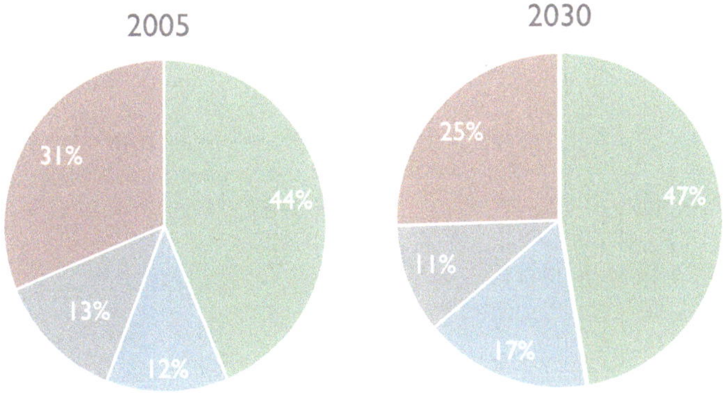

Behavioral scientists have been actively studying ways to change how we think about and behave toward the environment (Steg, Bolderdijk, Keizer, & Perlaviciute, 2014; van der Linden, 2015b). Such initiatives have had an impact on proactive steps to improve the environment (i.e. De Leeuw, Valois, Ajzen, & Schmidt, 2015), involving land reclamation, reforestation, and redesign of community spaces in urban areas (Wolch, Byrne, &

Newell, 2014). Furthermore, researchers have been focusing on the influence of environmental factors on human behavior, making it a tool on its own for influencing choices and outcomes (Schultz, Bator, Large, Bruni, & Tabanico, 2013). For example, in the United States, it was estimated that a national behavioral program related to energy may generate up to US$2.2 billion in economic benefit (Allcott & Mullainathan, 2010), which may be seen as a cost target for establishing large-scale interventions.

Whether behavioral insights can lead to increased sustainable environmental practices is a major area of ongoing study and debate (e.g. Cerutti, 2017; Weber, 2013, 2015), though the available evidence indicates a clear potential for impact (e.g. Sustainable Energy Authority of Ireland, 2018; Xanthos & Walker, 2017). Currently, energy policies often focus on energy efficiency, securing the supply, and balancing markets (see Box 6.2 for an example).

Next to economic incentives, market-based solutions, and regulatory processes, the knowledge gained from environmental psychology and behavioral insights is an important addition to shaping and evaluating environmental policies. In this regard, Big Data analysis posits a great opportunity for the design and analysis of environmental policies, as it allows us to monitor individual behaviors across time and to generate interventions targeting very specific subgroups (Giest & Mukherjee, 2018), or even personalized nudges based on personality and individual habits (Anagnostopoulou et al., 2018). However, although biases are part of human nature, several pitfalls emerge when studying the impact of behavioral insights on **pro-environmental behavior** (i.e. behavior that reduces the negative impact of individual actions on the environment).

BOX 6.2 THE EUROPEAN PARLIAMENT'S ENERGY UNION

The European Parliament's Energy Union introduced a strategy to combat climate change on a global level (Erbach, 2015). Building upon the 2030 Framework for Climate and Energy, this program encourages member states to prioritize energy-efficiency policies. This means that most policies are focused on major entities as opposed to individual ones. At the same time, it further aims to address energy security to strengthen the cooperation between the member states and the EU's role in global energy markets. By using such a holistic strategy, the EU-wide energy market aims to match the energy supply with demand, and these goals are targeted through new legislative means. Transport and buildings are identified as targets for energy-efficiency measures, and research on energy-neutral buildings and sustainable transport systems is sought.

The more you know

Climate change and the greenhouse effect are complex phenomena, and the public often holds misconceptions about them (van der Linden, 2017). For example, although climate change is considered to be real and dangerous, many individuals are not able to distinguish between concepts such as climate and weather. Moreover, some people even hold incorrect beliefs, such as global warming being caused by the "entrance" of heat through the hole in the ozone layer (Bostrom, Morgan, Fischhoff, & Read, 1994). Also, not everyone cares about the environment or values pro-environmental behavior, and some may even deny the existence of climate change and other major environmental threats (Hoffman, 2011;

Whitmarsh, 2011). Whitmarsh (2011) concluded that around 10 percent of a representative sample of residents of the United Kingdom did not believe in climate change, and about 30 percent agreed that the media exaggerated its impact.

When climate change was first recognized as a major global challenge, efforts were centered on providing the public with information about the benefits of pro-environmental behavior in order to influence their choices (e.g. Luyben, 1982; Staats, Wit, & Midden, 1996). In order to achieve this, governments and civil services expected that informing the public about environmental issues would lead to better awareness. This would hopefully lead populations to take up opportunities to act in a more pro-environmental way.

For example, in the mid-1990s, the Dutch Ministry of the Environment designed a mass media public information campaign to increase public awareness of the nature and causes of greenhouse gas emissions. National television, newspapers, and billboards conveyed the message to the public for approximately two and a half months. The impact of the campaign was evaluated by surveying more than 700 people before and after the campaign to assess changes in knowledge, problem awareness, and reported pro-environmental behavior, among others (Staats et al., 1996). Results showed a slight increase in knowledge about the greenhouse effect after the campaign, especially among the group that reported having noticed the campaign in all three media sources through which it was conveyed. Disappointingly, knowledge and awareness did not appear to have a strong relationship with self-reported pro-environmental behavior.

This phenomenon is referred to as the **knowledge-action gap** (see Figure 6.2; Barth, Fischer, Michelsen, Nemnich, & Rode, 2012) and is likely heavily moderated by egoistic, altruistic, and biospheric value orientations (van der Linden, 2017). A meta-analysis of the effect of knowledge about climate change showed that the effect size was rather low (Hornsey, Harris, Bain, & Fielding, 2016). Similarly, another meta-analysis showed that interventions aimed at changing first-level beliefs about the environment did not predict energy consumption behavior (Jachimowicz, Hauser, O'Brien, Sherman, & Galinsky, 2018).

As we will explore in the upcoming section, awareness of the need for pro-environmental behavior does not always predict its implementation (Hornsey et al., 2016). Beyond that, the implication is that simply having more information is not a guarantee of public concern or improved behavior across a population (van der Linden, 2017).

FIGURE 6.2 Knowledge- and value-action gaps

Thinking green

How much water do you think is required to produce 1 kg of meat? 100 liters? 1,000 liters? 2,000? It may surprise you that it is between 5,000 and 20,000 liters! Although many of us may have heard from various sources that the consumption of meat impacts the climate (Fox & Fimeche, 2013), this has not led many of us to switch to a vegetarian lifestyle.

Surprisingly, many people generally *want* to act green (Frederiks, Stenner, & Hobman, 2015; Hornsey et al., 2016; van der Linden, 2018), yet for many reasons they struggle to convert those beliefs into practice. For example, a national survey in Canada of over 1,500 participants showed that 72 percent of the participants reported a gap between their pro-environmental intentions and their actual actions, caused by individual, household, and societal constraints (Kennedy, Beckley, McFarlane, & Nadeau, 2009). This has generally been called the **value-action gap** (see Figure 6.2; Blake, 1999), which happens when individuals hold a certain belief (in this case, the desire to act pro-environmentally) but fail to carry it out in practice. The value-action gap is in fact a major challenge for energy and environmental policies.

One potential explanation for low engagement in specific behaviors may be our tendency to minimize the value of future events and outcomes, while weighting immediate needs higher (Weisbach & Sunstein, 2008). This is referred to as **temporal discounting**: a small immediate reward can seem more attractive than a larger one in the future (Frederick, Loewenstein, & O'Donoghue, 2002).

Green alternatives, such as solar energy and electric vehicles, sometimes require investments in the short term, and their advantages can only be seen in the distant future (Teng, Wu, & Chou, 2014). van der Linden (2015a) summarizes that climate change is seen as distant, both in time and in space, which reduces engagement in pro-environmental behavior. Besides, it is difficult to be concerned about something that you cannot directly or emotionally experience.

Annual Pew Research Center surveys of how Americans rank top national public policy priorities have systematically shown that concerns about the environment lag behind other issues, such as the economy, healthcare, and terrorism (e.g. Pew Research Center, 2014, 2018). This could partly be explained by people's tendency to predict that the consequences of climate change are going to be stronger in distant locations than in places close to their own communities and (Gifford et al., 2009), hence, less likely to affect them than others.

Given the immediate challenges posed by climate change, such as extreme weather and rising sea levels, behavioral insights aimed at engaging the public with this issue are becoming increasingly urgent. Other than that, not all nations can afford to buy land on higher ground in response to rising sea levels, like the Republic of Kiribati did when it bought land on the Fijian islands to prepare for future migration (Caramel, 2014).

To find out more about the public approval of **green nudges**, some opinion polls have been conducted. Green nudges can be seen as indirect techniques to promote pro-environmental behavior. While some variability among attitudes across different Western nations exists, in many cases the majority approve of the usage of green nudges (Hagman, Andersson, Västfjäll, & Tinghög, 2015; Jung & Mellers, 2016; Reisch & Sunstein, 2016). Whether green nudges lead to more pro-environmental behavior is a highly discussed topic (Weber,

2013), though several studies indicate positive results. These studies have proposed several strategies to promote individual pro-environmental behavior, and in the upcoming sections, we will discuss some of them in more detail.

A nudge toward more pro-environmental behavior

Even if wider national policies are accepted by communities, small actions and daily pro-environmental behavior can also have a huge impact on the climate. For that reason, it is important to design policies that promote the choices that are best for the environment. So, given the difficulty of trying to encourage pro-environmental behavior through the promotion of knowledge about climate change and pro-environmental values, what else can we do?

In the following paragraphs, we will present several nudging tools that have previously been used in the domain of pro-environmental behavior, with both high and low success rates. We start by describing the success of the globally used plastic bag charge policy. Then, we will describe several techniques focusing on the use of **social norms** and **social status competition** to influence behavior. Next, we review techniques focusing on influencing **intrinsic** and **extrinsic motivation** for such behaviors. Finally, we will give an overview of techniques that can aid consumers who already value pro-environmental behavior to actually act in such ways.

Five pence none the richer?

In 2010, 275 million metric tons of mismanaged plastic waste were generated by people living in 192 coastal countries, with the potential to enter the ocean (Jambeck et al., 2015). While convenient for many purposes, plastic bags contribute to a high proportion of worldwide pollution. Several policies to reduce the use of plastic bags have been introduced successfully in previous decades (see Figure 6.3 for a world map of plastic bag laws) using different strategies, such as charging customers for them, banning their sale, or putting a tax on plastic bags for stores that sell them. The latter strategy had a higher impact than would be predicted by traditional economics, as described in Chapter 4, for such a small tax.

For example, in the Republic of Ireland, a €0.15 tax passed on to consumers led to a 94 percent decrease in plastic bag use compared to before the introduction of the plastic bag levy (Convery, McDonnell, & Ferreira, 2007). Similarly, in 2015, the UK government introduced a mandatory GB£0.05 charge for plastic bags in England. Prior to this, the seven main retailers in England (i.e. Asda, Marks and Spencer, Sainsbury's, Tesco, The Co-Operative Group, Waitrose, and WM Morrison) reportedly issued 7.6 billion single-use carrier bags in the 2014 calendar year (Department for Environment, Food & Rural Affairs, 2016). In the first six months after the introduction of the five-pence charge, this number dropped to 0.6 billion, the equivalent of only 8 percent as many as the previous year!

How can such a small charge have such a powerful effect? **Prospect Theory** offers a possible explanation: as the reference point was that each bag was provided for free before

FIGURE 6.3 World map of single-use plastic bag legislation

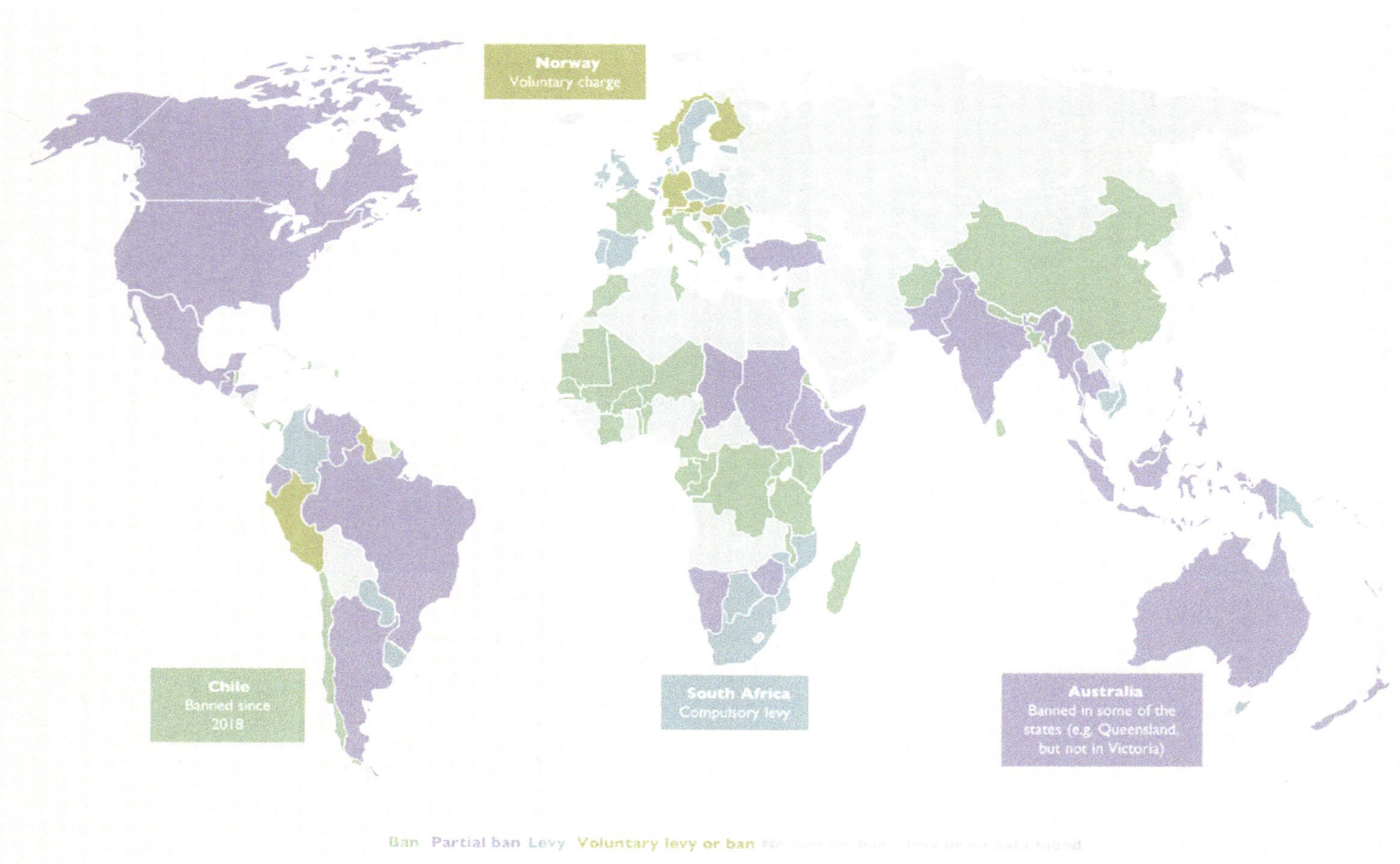

An example for each of the policy-types (ban, partial ban, levy, voluntary agreement on ban or levy, and no ban or no data found) is shown in the figure. Note that not all of the colored countries enforced legislations successfully or countrywide. This figure is inspired by an original image produced by Wikipedia contributors ("Phase-out lightweight plastic bags," n.d.).

the introduction of the fee, the financial loss experienced from the charge was made more salient (see Chapters 2 and 3 for more about Prospect Theory). Therefore, to avoid losing any money, consumers do their very best to not pay the charge, which has resulted in an overall reduction in plastic bag usage.

Since then, plastic bag usage has slightly increased, but it is still much lower than compared to the period before the charge. To be more specific, an estimated 1.3 billion single-use plastic carrier bags were used between April 2016 and April 2017 (Department for Environment, Food & Rural Affairs, 2017) and 1.0 billion between April 2017 and April 2018 (Department for Environment, Food & Rural Affairs, 2018). To put this into context, if we compare 2014 to the 2016–2017 period, each resident in England consumed, on average, 140 bags per person in 2014. This dropped to 25 bags per person per year in 2016–2017.

More tangibly, a decreasing trend in plastic bags on the sea floor of the Greater North Sea has been demonstrated between 1992 and 2017 (Maes et al., 2018). This suggests that such (comparatively) easy policies can make a huge contribution to combat marine litter worldwide. Nevertheless, there is still much ground to be gained as, in some countries such as Nepal, legislation efforts have poorly been enforced (Bharadwaj, 2016).

Follow the crowd

Social norms are rules and standards of behavior that are considered acceptable in a given group within a given context (Cialdini & Trost, 1998). To promote pro-environmental behavior, energy and environmental policies have tried to influence such social norms. For example, at some point in your life, you may have heard the phrase: "Reduce, Reuse, and Recycle," referred to as the "3R initiative." The 3R initiative was launched during a ministerial conference in Tokyo in April 2005 and aimed to promote effective use of resources and materials globally (Ministry of the Environment Government of Japan, 2005). This was one of the most common initiatives to induce pro-environmental behavior, namely, by cutting out unnecessary usage, getting more out of something before replacing it with a new item, and making sure old products were disposed of in the most environmentally friendly way. In 2018, another yearly worldwide initiative to enhance global awareness of the need to protect the environment was introduced by the United Nations' World Environment Day (see Box 6.3).

BOX 6.3 WORLD ENVIRONMENT DAY: BEAT PLASTIC POLLUTION

"Beat Plastic Pollution – if you can't reuse it, refuse it!"

To combat plastic pollution, this call to action was introduced as the theme for the World Environment Day in India, 2018 (United Nations, 2018). Ever since 1974, the United Nations has been raising global awareness of the significant difficulties we have to combat in order to protect the environment by designating June 5 as World Environment Day. Every year, more than 100 countries participate in the celebration of this day by focusing attention and awareness on environmental concerns. Interestingly, in 2018, a global game was initiated that encouraged people to upload a photo or a video on social media. They were asked to show a reusable green alternative for a single-use plastic item, while challenging friends to do the same. Thereby, a social norm was introduced on a global level to promote pro-environmental behavior.

Apart from the global initiatives previously described, other **green options** have been introduced. These options include products, services, and behaviors that preferably lead to either reduced consumption of nonrenewable resources or increased uptake of replacement products that have a less harmful impact on the environment. Presentation of the green option as socially desirable may then increase people's willingness to actually engage in such actions (Thaler & Sunstein, 2008). Studies focusing on the effect of social norms on pro-environmental behavior approached this by utilizing social comparisons and social status competitions, which will be discussed next.

Social norms and comparisons

Did you ever get a really high grade on a test, but then suddenly your good mood was tempered by seeing a classmate get an even higher grade? Or the other way around, when you perked up after observing the worst player on your sports team and thinking, "Well, at least I am faster than that!"

These upward and downward social comparisons occur from an early age, and human beings are highly sensitive to them. Social comparisons have widely been used as a tool to activate certain behavior. In the environmental domain specifically, it involves comparing how the environmental behavior of one group relates to the average behaviors of others, thereby revealing a **social norm**.

When utilizing social norms in environmental policies, a policymakers need to watch out for a potential pitfall that is referred to as the **boomerang effect** (Schultz, Nolan, Cialdini, Goldstein, & Griskevicius, 2007). The boomerang effect got its name from its two-level function: one intervention can promote a positive effect for one group, while prompting an undesired effect for another. In relation to pro-environmental behavior, this means that for some groups a certain **nudge** will be followed by a decrease in, for example, energy consumption, whereas another group might display an undesired increase in energy consumption (see the upper section of Figure 6.4 for an example). The argument used to explain this is that individuals utilize social norms as a way to center their own behaviors compared to others, which pulls everyone to the mean, regardless of whether the norm is positive or negative by comparison (Frederiks et al., 2015).

Several methods have been introduced to avoid the boomerang effect. In the most compelling and widely cited example, Schultz et al. (2007) tried to counter a boomerang effect from reliance on social norms in the context of energy conservation, so that the net gain would remain positive. They introduced a common distinction between **descriptive norms** (what others are doing) and **injunctive norms** (what others think we *ought* to be doing). The authors noticed that when people received descriptive normative information (e.g. that they were acting greener than their peers), they often increased their energy consumption to conform to the social norm (see the upper section of Figure 6.4).

To counter this undesired boomerang effect, an injunctive message was provided to households by the use of smiley faces for those who showed a higher level of pro-environmental behavior than their peers. Results showed that such an injunctive norm was mostly effective in keeping consumption low, while concurrently resulting in lower consumption of those above the average (see the lower section of Figure 6.4). That is to say this study is a perfect example of an illustration of the fragility of behavioral interventions: subtle nudges cannot only be rendered ineffective by other psychosocial factors (Thaler & Sunstein, 2008) but they may also backfire in parts of the population who were originally doing well.

FIGURE 6.4 The boomerang effect and how to counter it

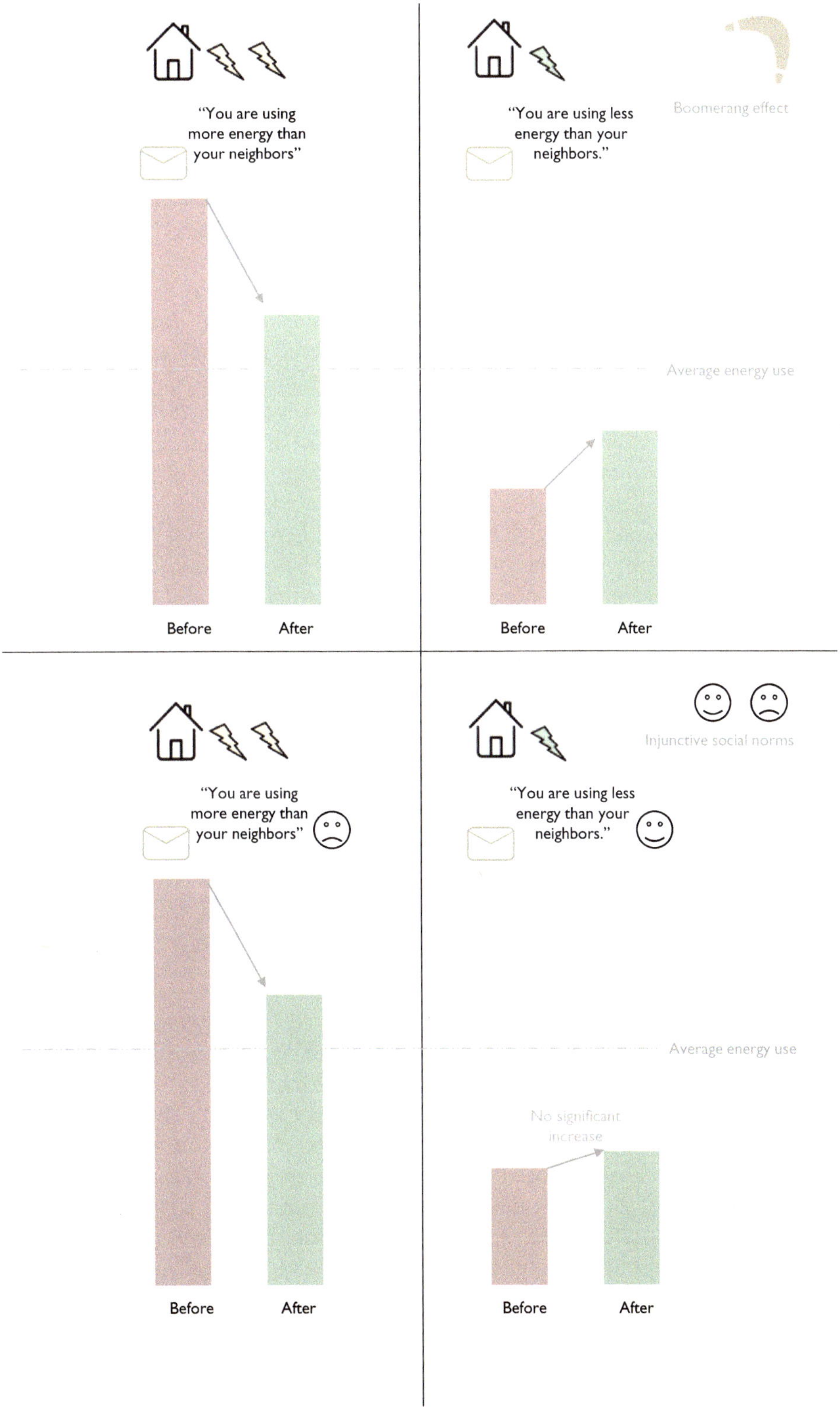

Another example of a study that explored the effect of social norms is a study by Brandon, List, Metcalfe, Price, and Rundhammer (2018). They combined descriptive and injunctive norms in an attempt to reduce the energy consumption in over 40,000 households. The descriptive technique consisted of a bimonthly Home Energy Report (HER), which stated the use of energy in comparison to average neighbors and efficient neighbors. The injunctive technique consisted of the Peak Energy Report (PER), which informed customers of an expected peak in energy consumption. The PER further stated their rank position in energy efficiency during previous peaks compared to their neighborhood's, prompting them to reduce their energy consumption. After the peak, customers received feedback on their rank position of efficiency during the peak and encouraged them to perform better during the next peak.

Customers received either the HER, the PER, both, or nothing (control group). Results showed that customers receiving the HER consumed 2.1 percent less energy than customers in the control group, whereas the ones receiving the PER reduced their energy consumption by 3.8 percent. Interestingly, the energy reduction of customers receiving both the HER and the PER was 6.8 percent, which was a significantly larger reduction than the HER and the PER techniques alone. Therefore, this study shows how the use of descriptive and injunctive norms combined do not crowd out effects, but possibly even yield better results than each of the techniques alone.

Further experimental studies have examined whether the use of social comparisons is a viable strategy to promote other pro-environmental behaviors such as decreased water usage, with many studies showing positive results. For example, a study by Ferraro, Miranda, and Price (2011) used social norms as a strategy to promote water conservation by using a natural field policy experiment. In 2007, residents of Atlanta, Georgia, were sent three different types of information on their monthly water bill:

1 Information only: included tips on how to save water at home;
2 Promoting pro-environmental behavior: in addition to the information only message, it included a personalized message with a norm-based appeal (e.g. "We all have to do our part to protect Cobb County's precious water resources");
3 Social comparison: in addition to the information only and norm-based appeals, it included a comparison of the total household water consumption over the past few months compared to the county's average (e.g. "You consumed more water than 73 percent of your neighbors").

In the short-term, results showed positive effects for the last two groups (promoting pro-environmental behavior and social comparison) and no effect was found in the information only group. More strikingly, this study showed that only the social comparison condition revealed a long-term effect, which was even present two years after the message was sent (see Figure 6.5). That is, effects dissipated when social comparison was not used.

Social comparison has also been used to encourage greener transport choices. A study by Anagnostopoulou et al. (2018) developed a pilot version of an app that analyzed and ranked tailored transport alternatives for a given route on the basis of parameters such as distance, available transport options, individual habits, and personality. The app aimed to increase the choice of greener transport alternatives, such as walking, cycling, or using public

FIGURE 6.5 Social comparison messages to save water

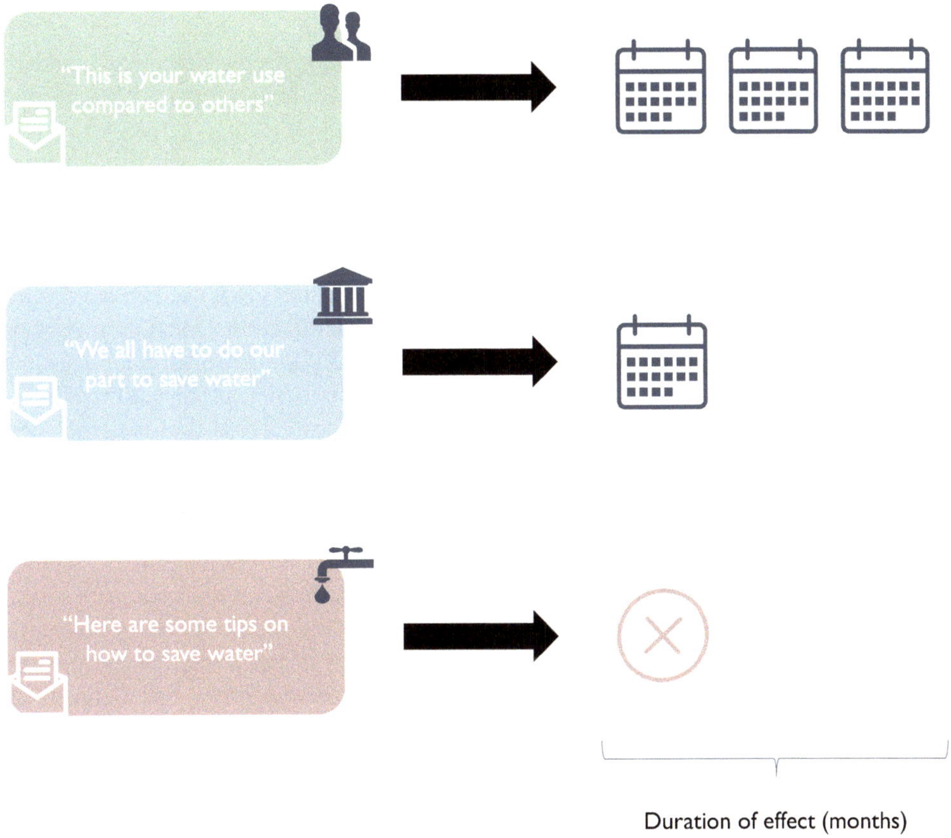

transportation. This app used several different nudges, including social comparison. More concretely, it informed participants about the share of people that had chosen that route (social norms) and about how their CO_2 consumption compared to others. Although the actual behavioral impact of the nudges was not evaluated, participants reported that social **comparison messages** had increased the likelihood of them choosing a greener transport alternative.

Similar evidence for an effect of comparison messages has been shown in other environmental domains as well, such as electricity consumption (Allcott & Rogers, 2014), food waste recycling (Linder, Lindahl, & Borgström, 2018), bottled water usage (van der Linden, 2015b), and hotel towel reuse (see Nisa, Varum, & Botelho, 2017 for a meta-analysis).

Behavioral insights from such studies suggest that the use of social comparison to some sort of reference group is more effective in promoting long-term changes, while the provision of information alone is unlikely to be sufficient. Note that, in longitudinal studies, the effect of social comparison shows a decaying trend over time. It is therefore probable that, after a while, the occurrence of the desired behavior gradually comes to an end. This suggests that future policy research should identify with more precision not only how, when, and why people tend to stop displaying the targeted behavior but also how we can put a halt to this negative trend.

Furthermore, even if the use of social norms has been shown to be effective in prompting the increase in pro-environmental behavior, the extent of their effect remains variable. Thus, which specific factors make this technique more or less successful? Findings from a meta-analysis by Jachimowicz, Hauser et al. (2018) may shed some light upon this question. Their research included studies from 30 states in the United States that used an intervention based on social norms with comparison messages (they compared the consumption of participants to that of their neighbors and added a smiley face if their consumption was lower than the mean consumption). They found that second-order beliefs predicted the effectiveness of the intervention. More specifically, participants who believed that their neighbors thought that reducing energy consumption was a positive behavior were the ones for whom the social norm intervention showed a stronger effect.

In addition to the meta-analysis, the researchers further explored the effect of second-order beliefs. They conducted an experiment in which all of the participants were presented with a descriptive norm about the energy consumption of their country. In addition, half of the participants were presented with a higher second-order belief stating that most of the residents of their country held a positive view of reducing energy consumption, whereas the other half were presented with a low second-order belief stating that awareness about energy consumption in their country was low. The participants in the first group stated a higher willingness to reduce their energy consumption (Jachimowicz, Hauser et al., 2018).

Social status competition

Another way to tailor pro-environmental behavior is by using **social status competition**. Social status can be described as the relative ranking of individuals within a specific society on the basis of, for example, personality traits, merits, or actions. A concept referred to as **competitive altruism** proposes that social status can be used as a tool to motivate human beings to behave in a more altruistic manner (Hardy & van Vugt, 2006). Competitive altruism can potentially be extended to pro-environmental behavior too, because such behavior often implies a degree of self-sacrifice for the common good (e.g. spending more money to buy a less polluting car that will have lower CO_2 emissions).

Some studies have focused on social status as a tool to promote pro-environmental behavior. For example, in an experimental study, Griskevicius, Van den Bergh, and Tybur (2010) investigated whether inducing status competition can enhance pro-environmental behavior by comparing green, nonluxurious product choices to similarly priced nongreen, luxurious product choices. In the experimental condition, participants read a story about a person graduating from school, finding a job with high-status features, and ending up in a higher position than same-sex peers. Participants were required to imagine the story as if it were theirs, with the purpose of eliciting the *desire for social status and prestige* (i.e. status competition). Participants in the control condition read a story of similar length, without any status competition activation.

As expected, when status competition was activated, participants were more likely to choose green products than the control group (Figure 6.6, Study I). Interestingly, a follow-up experiment showed that in the experimental condition, green choices were made more often when prices of green products were higher than those of the nongreen products (Figure 6.6, Study II). In contrast, if green products were cheaper than the nongreen counterparts, the difference between the desire to buy green products and nongreen products was not significant (Figure 6.6, Study III). A similar phenomenon can be observed in the success of the Toyota Prius (see Box 6.4).

FIGURE 6.6 Social status activation and purchase of green products

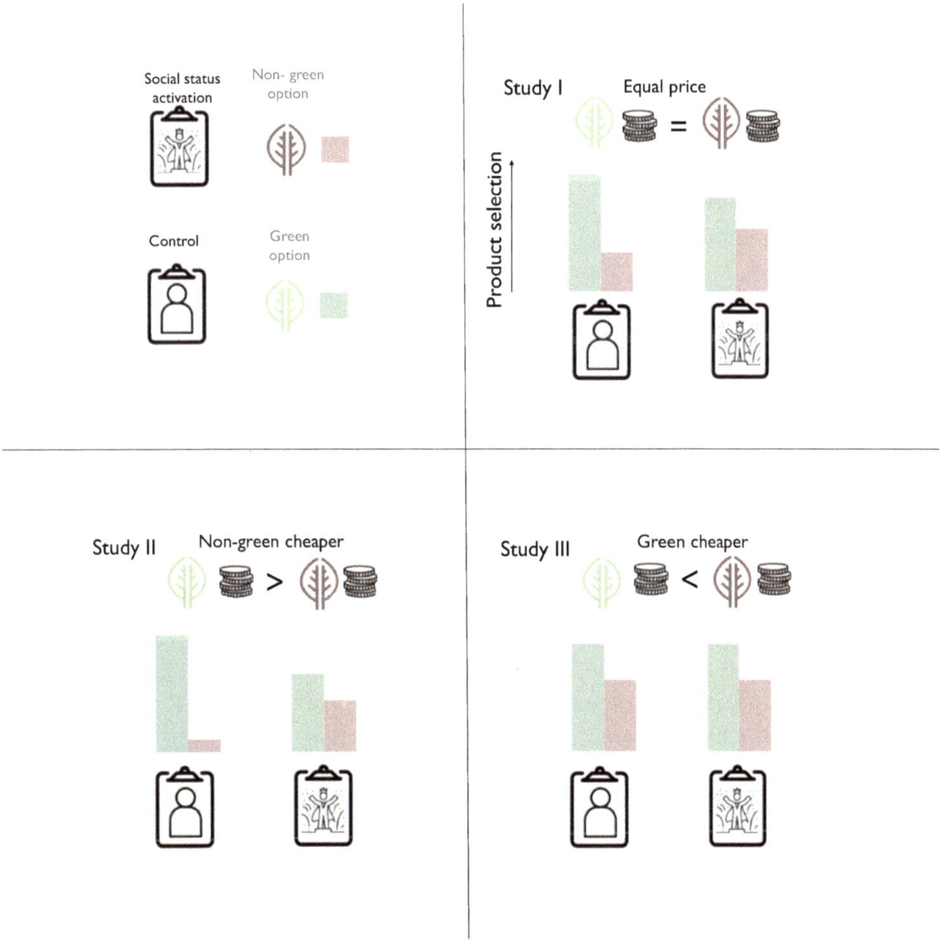

BOX 6.4 TOYOTA PRIUS: A STATUS SYMBOL?

Have you ever seen someone carrying the "I'm not a plastic bag" bag or heard about proud plans to install solar panels on the roof? Intentionally or not, it seems that people are becoming increasingly willing to pay higher prices for green goods to signal their environmental concern to others. This concept has been dubbed **conspicuous conservation** (Sexton & Sexton, 2014). There is no better example to illustrate this phenomenon than through car ownership decisions, one of the most visible consumer decisions that people make.

It has been shown that people are willing to pay higher prices for ecologically friendly hybrid cars, such as the Toyota Prius, compared to cheaper cars from the same brand. To stress this, a survey by the *New York Times* showed that the main reason buyers purchased the car was that it "Makes a statement about me" (Maynard, 2007). Contrastingly, environmental reasons (i.e. lower emissions) were listed as the fifth most frequent reason for buying the car. Therefore, policymakers should be careful with their attempts to reduce green product costs to promote pro-environmental behavior. Especially for cases in which products are expensive, cost reduction may not have the desired effect on wealthy consumers if they wish to signal their wealth to others through the selection of green products.

The Western Cape Government in South Africa has also examined the influence of status competition on pro-environmental behavior (OECD, 2017i). A program called "Too Wise to Waste" was used as an information campaign to promote pro-environmental behavior over a two-year period. The aim of the campaign was to reduce energy consumption in government office buildings, as these buildings were noted to utilize 1.5 times more energy than the industry standard. Four different levers were used in emails that were sent to 991 employees, including the following:

1 Information about energy use, including tips for translating knowledge into action;
2 Reminders to switch off devices at the end of the day;
3 Social competition by comparing energy consumption across different floors;
4 Assignment of responsibility to one person for "wise" energy behavior through sharing duties, while enhancing social competition between colleagues.

During the first four months, the average baseline energy consumption per person for all of the different floors was calculated. Then, the various floors were randomly assigned into a control group or one of the two experimental groups. The control group did not receive any emails during any phase of the intervention. During the first three months of the intervention, the experimental groups received similar emails containing information (1) and reminders (2). Over the next six months, one experimental group received monthly emails including social competition statements (3), while the other experimental group received emails including responsibility statements on top of the social competition statements (4).

After the first three months, the experimental groups showed a 2 percent reduction in energy use, but this result was not statistically significant. Only the groups receiving emails including both social competition and responsibility statements showed a significant 14 percent reduction in energy use, whereas the social competition only condition did not lead to a significant reduction in energy use. As will be discussed later, it appears that information disclosure alone does not automatically offer a significant contribution to pro-environmental behavior, while social status activation seems to be a much more powerful tool.

What drives us

Why do you turn down the heating when you are gone for the day? Why do you sometimes shower fewer minutes than you ideally would want to? Is it just because you think everyone acts in such ways, or are there other reasons behind it?

To engage in any behavior, we not only follow or compete with the herd, we also need to be motivated to do so. For example, our intention to turn down the heating might be driven by a range of motivations: we might do it to save money because of a financial incentive, to comply with our neighbors as a motivation to adhere to the social norm, or because reducing the risk from climate change is inherently important to us (Ackerman, 1997; Kollmuss & Agyeman, 2002; Schultz et al., 2007).

Under **self-determination theory** (see Box 6.5), it is common to understand motivation by two key drivers of human behavior: extrinsic motivation and intrinsic motivation (Deci & Ryan, 1975, 1985; Ryan & Deci, 2000). Motivation is extrinsic if one pursues an action to receive an external reward such as money or acknowledgment from others. Contrastingly, when we turn down the heat because protecting the environment is embedded within our personal values, our motives are intrinsically based. Previous research has shown that intrinsically motivated action is primarily associated with interest, persistence, behavioral quality, and well-being (Ryan & Deci, 2000; Kácha & Ruggeri, 2018; van der Linden, 2015b, 2018), therefore making it an interesting tool to use in behavioral studies about pro-environmental behavior.

BOX 6.5 AUTONOMY AND PRO-ENVIRONMENTAL BEHAVIOR

Under self-determination theory (Ryan & Deci, 2000), autonomy is a huge part of human well-being. In fact, it is one of the three pillars that researchers have concluded are innate to our psychological needs. Vugts, van den Hoven, de Vet, and Verweij (2018) found that, in the context of the debate about nudges, autonomy refers to any of the following aspects:

- The possibility of making a choice among a set of available options (freedom of choice)
- The capacity to choose and decide by reflecting about how possible options match our ultimate goal (agency)
- The possibility of holding our own values and acting coherently (self-constitution)

Do you think that giving people choices where they are able to choose pro-environmental options (such as energy and paper use in this chapter) will influence their well-being? Do you think the effect will be stronger if there is a clear value-action gap? It seems like a simple win given that all the ingredients are there: a desire to act in a certain way without being able to, providing a mechanism to do so, and letting that mechanism be a purely independent (autonomous) choice. However, this has not been fully reflected in studies on the topic. What might explain the lack of conclusive evidence in support of this? How does it relate to each of the three definitions of autonomy?

Leveraging intrinsic and extrinsic motivation toward pro-environmental behavior

Messages can be framed so that they leverage intrinsic motivation to engage in pro-environmental behavior. Several studies have examined the influence of intrinsic motivation on pro-environmental behavior, showing positive results. Therefore, it may also function as a promising policy lever for improving food-purchasing behavior as the next case example will illustrate.

In 2015, on behalf of the European Commission, the Consumers, Health, Agriculture and Food Executive Agency (CHAFEA) conducted a lab experiment at the Milan Universal Exposition (Elsen, van Giesen, & Leenheer, 2015). In their experiment, CHAFEA aimed to increase the acceptance of "imperfect foods" that do not reach the high visual standards for supermarket foods (i.e. "perfect" foods), thereby promoting the purchase of imperfect food. Five hundred visitors to the exposition were presented with either a message about avoiding food waste ("Embrace imperfection: Join the fight against food waste!"), an **authenticity message** stressing that imperfect food is natural and therefore just as desirable as perfect food ("Naturally imperfect: Apples/carrots the way they actually look!"), or no message at all. The anti–food waste message was intended to target extrinsic motivation, whereas the authenticity message targeted the intrinsic motivation of people to evaluate food from a more naturalistic perspective. Results showed that visitors receiving the anti–food waste or the authenticity message reported preferring to buy the imperfect food more often (42 percent and 43 percent, respectively) than the visitors who received no message (26 percent; see Study I in Figure 6.7). These findings suggest that both messages succeeded in helping participants identify the benefits of buying imperfect foods.

To assess the extent of the effect, the prices of perfect and imperfect foods were varied; the researchers expected that lower prices for imperfect food would undermine intrinsic motivation. As described earlier, when the prices for perfect and imperfect foods were similar, individuals receiving an anti–food waste message or an authenticity message had higher intentions to buy imperfect foods as than the control group. More interestingly, when the price reduction for imperfect foods was large (i.e. 30 percent less), the anti–food waste and authenticity messages were followed by greater intentions to purchase imperfect foods (51 percent and 50 percent, respectively) as compared to no message (39 percent; see Study II in Figure 6.7). Although it appeared that prices had some influence on consumer behavior, a considerable variability in findings across a number of scenarios was found. Therefore, results from this study have to be carefully interpreted. Furthermore, note that, in most of the conditions, consumers were still more likely to choose perfect foods over imperfect foods.

Another study on the influence of targeting motivation to promote pro-environmental behavior was conducted by Schwartz, Bruine de Bruin, Fischhoff, and Lave (2015). In this study, over 1,000 participants were presented with hypothetical energy-savings programs that emphasized intrinsic incentives (reducing one's environmental footprint), extrinsic incentives (saving money on one's energy bill), or both. As was found in other studies as well (Asensio & Delmas, 2015; Bolderdijk, Steg, Geller, Lehman, & Postmes, 2012), the results showed that a greater number of participants of those who were presented with intrinsic incentives were willing to enroll in the energy-savings program (24.2 percent) compared to participants who were presented with extrinsic incentives (12.2 percent). Additionally, they found that only 16.7 percent of the participants who received messages containing both intrinsic and extrinsic incentives were willing to enroll in an energy saving program, a significantly lower share than that of participants who received messages containing intrinsic incentives alone (see Figure 6.8).

This study has provided further evidence that extrinsic incentives undermine intrinsic interests (Deci, Koestner, & Ryan, 1999; Frey & Oberholzer-Gee, 1997). A range of behavioral

FIGURE 6.7 Influence of different messages on intention to buy imperfect foods

In the first study, the price of imperfect food was equal to the price of perfect food, while in the second study, the price of imperfect food was 30 percent lower than the price of perfect food.

FIGURE 6.8 Reasons for willingness to enroll in an energy-savings program

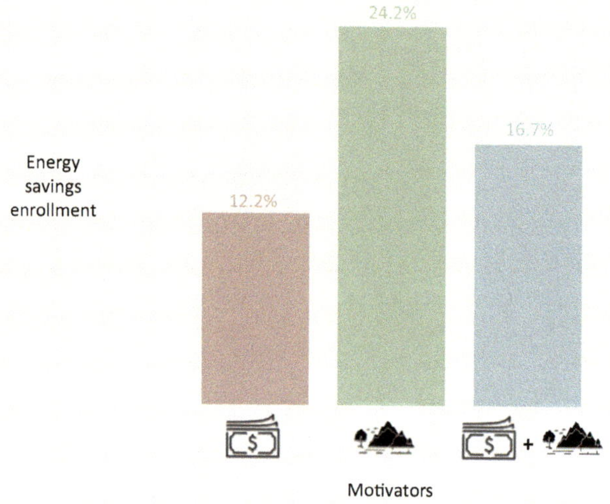

studies have pointed out the double-edged nature of extrinsic motives. For example, Frey and Oberholzer-Gee (1997) conducted interviews in which citizens from Switzerland were asked whether they agreed with the placement of one of two nuclear waste repositories close to their village. Strikingly, the approval rate of 50.8 percent dropped to 24.6 percent when the citizens surveyed were offered monetary compensation for the placement of the waste repository in their proximity. The authors offered an explanation that the presence of extrinsic incentives crowded out altruistic tendencies (see Chapter 4 for a more detailed discussion of this study and financial incentives in general).

Nonetheless, a study by Kácha and Ruggeri (2018) did not support the crowd-out effect of extrinsic motives. In their study, over 100 participants from the Czech Republic were given four weekly tasks to encourage them to act as *socially responsible individuals*. Furthermore, they were randomly assigned to three conditions:

1 Autonomy-supportive communication: designed to target intrinsic motivation;
2 Descriptive social norms: designed to target extrinsic social motivation through a comparison message;
3 Control group: no specific target.

Interestingly, the pro-environmental behavior of participants in all three groups increased during the study period, with no differences in increase between groups. In other words, participants receiving messages that targeted intrinsic and extrinsic motivation did not display a higher number of pro-environmental behaviors than the control group. In addition, it was shown that the use of social norms did not undermine intrinsic incentives. These study examples do not necessarily suggest that extrinsic incentives cannot be effective in promoting pro-environmental behavior. Merely, they should be aligned with behavioral tools, as the motivational basis for engaging in a certain behavior can vary.

Chater and Lowenstein (2016) argue that **sense-making** and the pursuit of things fitting the image of the "good life" are underestimated drives for decision-making in human beings. Sense-making refers to the desire to understand our experiences and the world around us. If pro-environmental values are embedded in individuals' sense-making, they may be more likely to engage in pro-environmental behavior and to seek more information about it.

An example of a policy that was built upon the possibility of changing behavior through extrinsic motivation was a project called the "Green Deal" that was launched by the Department of Energy and Climate Change in the United Kingdom in 2013 (National Audit Office, 2016). Its purpose was to improve household energy efficiency, while removing the high upfront costs associated with investment in energy-efficient renovations. Households could, for example, take out a Green Deal loan to improve their loft (attic) insulation or replace their old windows with double-glazed (double-paned) ones. The loan was then repaid from the savings that resulted from the improved energy efficiency. To further incentivize people to adopt the Green Deal, immediate monetary rewards were included: part of the Green Deal was entitlement to a one-month council tax holiday and vouchers for products and services.

Fundamentally, the Green Deal was a creative financial mechanism with the purpose of increasing pro-environmental behavior. Together with another scheme called "the Energy Company Obligation," it improved the energy efficiency of 14,000 households, with an expected savings of 0.4 million tons of carbon dioxide over the project's lifetime (Department of Energy & Climate Change, 2012). Although evaluation of the success of the Green Deal was not easy as clear expectations were not defined before the program was implemented, it turned out not to be cost-effective (National Audit Office, 2016). An independent empirical evaluation by Pettifor, Wilson, and Chryssochoidis (2015) showed that the low uptake of the Green Deal was partially explained by consumer uncertainty about its possible long-term financial benefits. Unfortunately, the Green Deal has therefore been a costly example of a case in which a nudge has not been effective in the real world.

So far, we have seen how the addition of external incentives can undermine our drive to act green just because it is the "right thing to do." But how do these external rewards interact with other nudges? Earlier we showed that social norms are of great importance in promoting pro-environmental behavior; next we will describe another example of how extrinsic incentives can undermine the effect of messages including a social comparison (i.e. comparison messages).

In a field experiment by Pellerano, Price, Puller, and Sánchez (2017), households in Quito, Ecuador, whose energy consumption was between 100 and 125 kWh/month (considered low use) were randomly assigned to one of two experimental groups or a control group. On their monthly energy bill, one experimental group received a comparison message showing their individual household consumption compared to the neighborhood's consumption, whereas the other experimental group received an additional financial incentive message ("If you reduce your monthly energy bill nearly XX,XX percent, you will save approximately US$XX per year").

As expected, households receiving the comparison message reduced their energy consumption by 1 percent, which was significantly different from the control group. Further, it was found that the extrinsic incentive crowded out the effect of the comparison message. Therefore, it seems that exposure to information about some financial benefits may have an effect that reduces the initial impact on pro-environmental behavior. However, this does not necessarily mean that financial tools can never be used as a lever to impact pro-environmental behavior, as shown by the successful introduction of small charges for the use of plastic shopping bags earlier in this chapter.

Pitfalls

A potential difficulty to consider is that emphasizing intrinsic motives often appears to drive easier, low-cost behavioral changes rather than difficult, high-cost behavioral changes. For example, van der Linden (2018) showed that the satisfaction ("warm-glow") that participants anticipated they would obtain from pro-environmental behavior predicted their actual behavior in the following four weeks when the costs were low (e.g. buy locally grown and produced foods), but the effect was reduced for high-cost behavior (e.g. purchase home energy from a green source). In addition, intrinsic motives tend to be most effective when the personal values of the target population align with the actions promoted or when the actions are framed in line with personal values.

In practice this often means that individuals need to sufficiently value pro-environmental behavior prior to the intervention in order for it to succeed. A few instruments exist that increase intrinsic interest in sustainable practices but have yet to find their way into actual policies. On the other hand, the cost-benefit trade-off is potentially high, as the benefit of intrinsic engagement lies in its self-sustaining nature and its independence of external rewards, making it particularly suited to deliver lasting policy outcomes (van der Linden, 2015a, 2018).

Focusing on the positive to improve energy consumption

Think of the last time you were told to do something environmentally friendly: you were probably more likely to be asked to consume less instead of saving money. However, van der Linden (2015b) argue that climate change should be framed around the gains from immediate actions instead. As was covered in more detail in Chapter 3, people tend to be, but are not always, **loss averse** (Tversky & Kahneman, 1991).

Losses related to pro-environmental behavior can prevent people from engaging in this type of behavior, even if there are benefits to be gained. Besides, people are also more willing to take a chance to avoid a loss than to secure a gain. Therefore, one way to increase their acceptance and willingness to engage in beneficial behavior is by selecting the proper **framing**. This suggests that in order to increase pro-environmental behavior through environmental policies, the immediate negative aspects of it should be diminished and gains should be highlighted.

Several studies have focused on the effect of framing on pro-environmental behavior. For example, a study by Hurlstone, Lewandowsky, Newell, and Sewell (2014) examined the effect of framing messages on emission policy preferences. A group of Australian citizens was informed about the influence of a reduction in CO_2 emissions on predicted income per capita in two different ways. In the "loss-frame scenario," the participants were told how much a 25 percent reduction in national CO_2 emissions would lower the predicted income level by 2020, compared to the income level that would have been predicted without the emission reductions. In the second scenario, a "gain-frame scenario" was used: individuals were told how much the income level would rise from the current level despite the reduction.

Results showed that by framing emission reductions as gains rather than losses (as in the gain-frame scenario), individuals were more likely to report willingness to reduce CO_2 emissions. This supports the notion that framing may go a long way toward increasing support for the broader environmental policies described in the introduction to this chapter (see Figure 6.9).

FIGURE 6.9 Effect of framing on willingness to accept carbon emission cuts

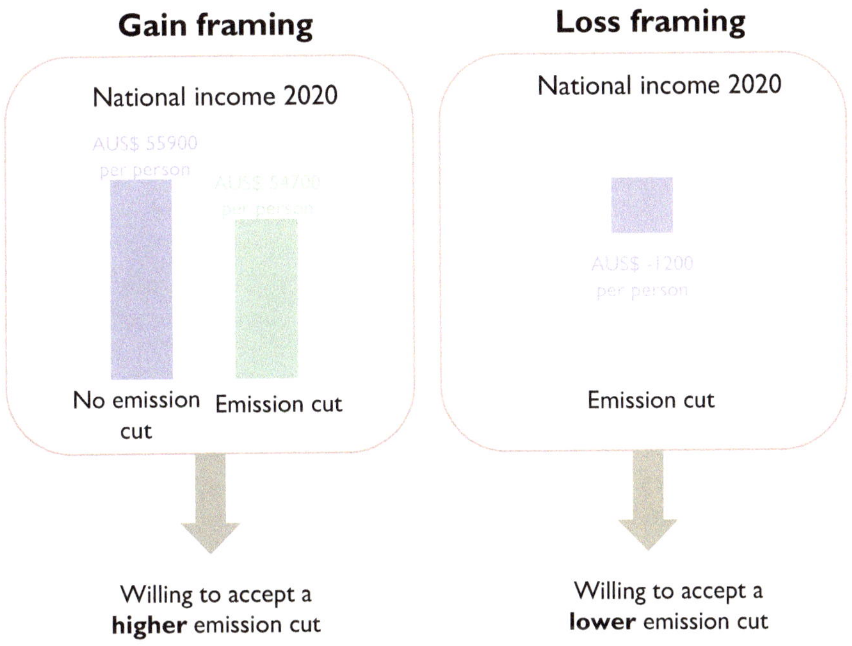

Participants were willing to accept higher emission cuts when the information regarding its impact over predicted national income was presented in gain framing in comparison to loss framing. Note that the black line represents the reference value.

Green consumers

So far, we have reviewed some strategies to motivate and promote pro-environmental behavior. But what about those consumers who generally *want* to act pro-environmentally, but are not doing so? How can we help them? And does behavioral economics actually have a say in it?

One way to do so is by **labeling** green products, so that they are easily recognized as such. Another option is setting the green option as a **default**, making it less effortful to act in a pro-environmental way. Next, we will review these two techniques, how they have been used so far, and what potential pitfalls we need to bear in mind when using them.

Use of salient labels to increase pro-environmental consumer choices

The use of **ecolabeling** is one of the techniques that is used to nudge consumers that already hold pro-environmental values into choosing environmentally sustainable options. An eco-label provides consumers with information about the relative environmental friendliness of the product. By providing information about the environmentally friendly properties of the product in a salient manner, labeling is a simple way to possibly influence pro-environmental behavior. For example, a Danish study showed that putting an ecolabel on everyday products makes grocery shopping convenient and effortless for people who are already interested in these products (Thøgersen, Jørgensen, & Sandager, 2012). When one is designing a label, however, it is important to consider how to make the distinctions between the different categories salient enough.

A good example of this is the labeling system used to define the energy class of "electrodomestics". In 1995, the European Union introduced a mandatory energy labeling scheme for electrical appliances. This labeling scheme classified the appliances on a seven-point, colored scale that marked the most energy-efficient appliances on the market with an "A", whereas the least energy-efficient ones were marked with a "G." In less than 10 years, around 90 percent of refrigerators, washing machines, and dishwashers sold in stores had reached class A (Olander & Thøgersen, 2014; European Commission, 2010).

Due to industry resistance against revising the criteria, three new classes were introduced for class A, namely, A+, A++, and A+++. Furthermore, the color-coding scheme was kept the same and the lowest three values (E, F, and G) were dropped. Unfortunately, this simple change has seemingly led to undesirable outcomes. In a study by Heinzle and Wüstenhagen (2012), 187 German consumers answered questions about what product choice they preferred. The researchers presented the consumers with different television models in a quasi-realistic shopping scenario. The consumers were assigned to two different groups, which differed in how the energy labels were presented for the different television models. The group presented with the old energy label list of A to D were more likely to choose the highest category (i.e. A) than the group that was presented with the new list of A+++ to A (see Figure 6.10).

FIGURE 6.10 The effect of labeling types

Pitfalls

Why did this simple change in letters influence decision-making in such a way? Consider two cognitive biases: **anchoring** and **satisficing**. Anchoring occurs when the first piece of information is used as a reference to evaluate the remaining pieces of information (Tversky & Kahneman, 1974). When selecting an option, it is common to take the first or more salient piece of information as a reference point (i.e. an anchor) and limit the weight given to additional information.

Anchoring may explain how seeing the letter A in the first place influences the perception of the remaining information (Olander & Thøgersen, 2014). In that sense, all categories that are labeled with A are similar, no matter how many pluses have been added. This may create the assumption that the difference between A and A+ is smaller than the difference between C and D, although the difference is the same. Another cognitive bias to consider is satisficing, which relates to people accepting their minimum requirement rather than choosing the best option (Simon, 1957a). In combination, these two biases most likely explain why people change their decisions when presented with different labeling lists.

The idea behind the energy label is to help consumers make a well-informed decision (Heinzle & Wüstenhagen, 2012). However, the extension of the list to include A's with different plus signs only confuses customers, as the information is perceived differently from what was actually intended. This is a great example of how some behavioral techniques that aim to nudge pro-environmental behavior produce undesired effects if heuristics and biases are not carefully considered. Therefore, when labels are used as a decision aid for customers, the they need to be easily understood and it is best to avoid unfamiliar rating systems.

Nevertheless, anchoring and satisficing biases can be used in an effective way to promote pro-environmental behavior. A study by Kim and Hyun (2020) used a survey asking 333 participants how much of an environmental aviation tax they would be willing to pay when using an aircraft. Inclusion of an anchor of €25 was followed by a significant increase in the amount of money participants were willing to pay for around 65 percent of the sample.

Making green the default option

Another technique to combat the value-action gap and encourage a certain desired behavior, such as acting more pro-environmentally, is by generating easier and more convenient opportunities to act in such ways. By the settlement of **default options**, the **status quo bias** is tapped into (Samuelson & Zeckhauser, 1988), which is the reluctance to move away from an established point of reference. People tend not to change their behavior unless the motivation is strong enough (Samuelson & Zeckhauser, 1988).

Inspiring such motivation is one of the challenges faced when promoting pro-environmental behavior. Therefore, a shift in the status quo is a hopeful possibility for environmental policymaking (Weber, 2015). In addition, setting of a default can also be interpreted as a way of setting a social norm in which the default option is perceived as the socially desirable option (Everett, Caviola, Kahane, Savulescu, & Faber, 2015; McKenzie et al., 2006). This adds to the explanation of the effectiveness of this technique: people select the default option because actively changing their choice requires enough motivation to do so and to conform to the social norm.

A new and pro-environmental point of reference may be used through a process called the **default effect.** The default effect is the idea that a desired behavior can be promoted by making it the predetermined first choice, without mandating it or impeding other choices. A default choice is one that is passively made unless someone chooses differently. In cases where a default choice is already pre-selected, an individual might not even actively make a choice but just merely accepts the default option by not making a choice at all.

In 2015, the paper and pulp production industry accounted for 5 percent of the total production-related waste disposal in the United States (United States Environmental Protection Agency, 2017). Campaigns encouraging reduced paper consumption are widespread, and by utilizing knowledge of human cognitive biases, policymakers can develop interventions to promote pro-environmental behavior by making default choices environmentally friendly.

An example study conducted by the US Department of Agriculture's Economic Research Service (ERS), in collaboration with the Social and Behavioral Sciences Team, aimed to encourage the conservation of resources by testing the ability of a green default printing option (i.e. double sided) to reduce the amount of paper used in ERS offices (Social and Behavioral Sciences Team, 2015). They tried to prompt printer users who had initiated a single-sided print job with a dialog box encouraging them to change their default printer settings to double-sided. The treatment condition was randomized throughout the ERS, where people, depending on which printer they habitually used, would either be exposed to the prompt or not.

As shown in Figure 6.11, users who were prompted by the dialog box used double-sided printing 5.8 percent more often than those who were not. While this difference may appear marginal, it was significant spread across a large organization, which is why it is not negligible, especially when applied to larger print jobs. As a result, the ERS adopted double-sided printing as their default setting on all of their printers, thereby increasing the likelihood that users will print on both sides of a piece of paper. Such outcomes have implications both for the environment and for cost savings in an organization, as they can lead to a reduction in the amount of paper used.

Setting defaults to green alternatives may also be effective for improving energy efficiency. The OECD ran a randomized controlled trial in one of its offices during the winter months to see if changing the default thermostat setting elicited any change in the temperature choices of the employees (Brown, Johnstone, Hascic, Vong, & Barascud, 2012). It was shown that after the thermostat default setting was decreased, the mean office temperature decreased compared to that of the control group. The most effective strategy was to decrease the default thermostat setting progressively by 1 °C each week rather than changing the default temperature setting more rapidly (2 °C per week), which made the employees more likely to adjust the thermometer setting by increasing the temperature.

As with other behavioral tools, the effectiveness of the defaults in promoting pro-environmental behaviors depends heavily on the context. According to **dual process theory**, defaults work best in environments where individuals are driven by their **fast, automatic processing system** as opposed to their **slow, conscious processing system** (see Kahneman, 2003b). In the printing study, the change in the default option was effective as people tend to select the "print" button as soon as the dialog box appears, rather than spending additional time thinking about possible printing options such as single- vs. double-sided printing. In the office temperature study, the default effect proved to be most effective in reducing energy usage when the change of temperature was small and less likely to interfere with employees' conscious processing. This example shows how the change in the default option, as with any other behavioral intervention, needs to take into account and anticipate possible consequences in order to avoid opposite outcomes.

FIGURE 6.11 Encouraging change with defaults to green options

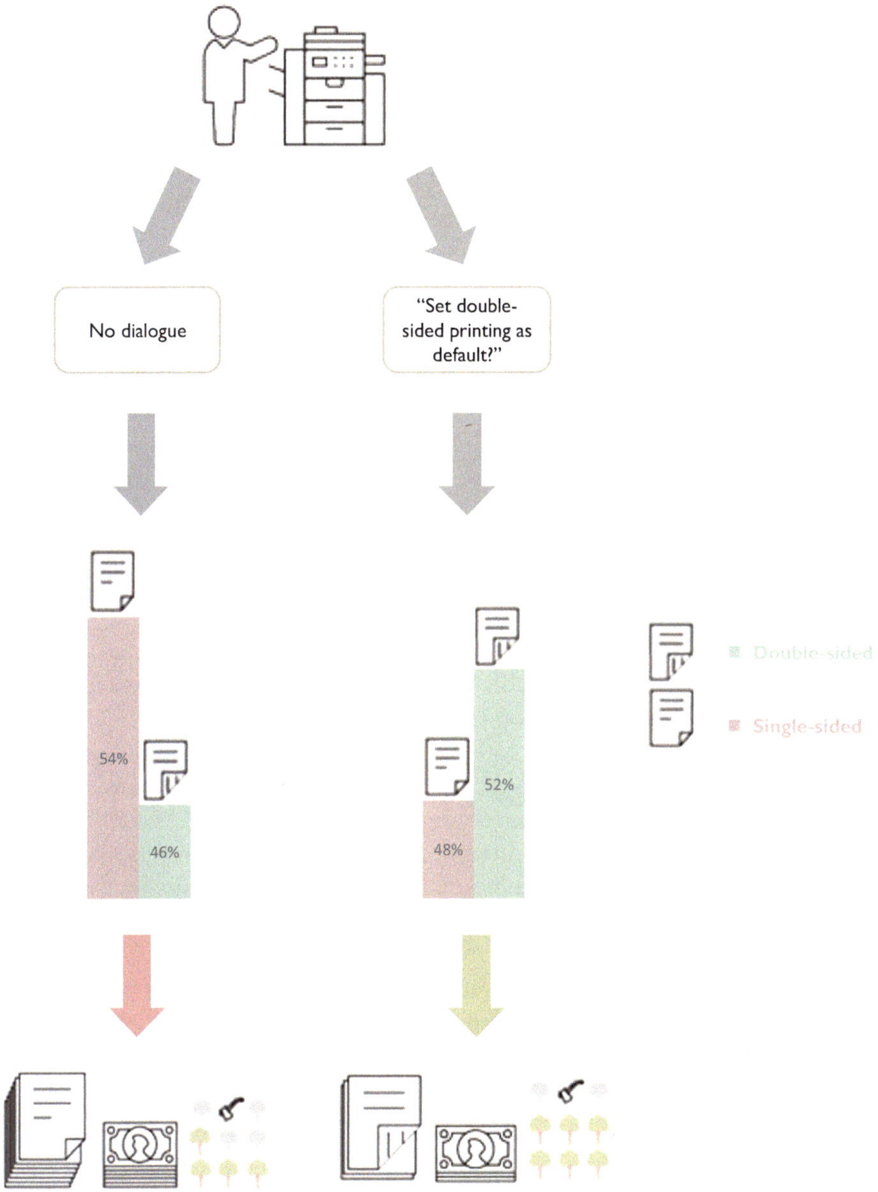

Changes in default options have also been tested in the context of long-term decisions, such as the purchase of green options when choosing an energy contract. Ebeling and Lotz (2015) carried out a randomized control trial in which they designed two different versions of a web page for the purchase of an electricity contract. In the **opt-in**

version, prospective customers needed to actively select the green option in their energy contract, which guaranteed that their energy would come from renewable sources and was slightly more expensive. In the **opt-out** version, the green option was already selected. Therefore, customers had to deselect it if they did not want to purchase the green option.

From over 40,000 prospective customers visiting the page, 0.62 percent purchased the green option in the opt-in condition, compared to 5.58 percent in the opt-out condition. This difference was shown to be significant. When the effect of the default option was explored not relative to the prospective customers who visited the web page but relative to those who actually purchased a contract, 7.2 percent purchased the green option in the opt-in condition, compared to 69.1 percent in the opt-out condition. More interestingly, when the relationship between the percentage of customers purchasing the green option in a region and the percentage of votes for green parties in that region was explored, the researchers found that both correlated with the opt-in condition, but not with the opt-out condition.

The authors wondered whether this effect was due to participants not being aware of the option that they were purchasing. In order to explore this possibility, they conducted a lab-based study with a representative sample of 290 Americans in which they asked the participants to imagine that they were purchasing an energy contract. They found parallel results regarding the effect of the default option, and they also found that 100 percent of the participants that selected the green option in the opt-in condition and 84.13 percent of the participants having selected the green option in the opt-out condition correctly recalled having done so. This result was interpreted as showing that most of the decisions regarding the purchase of the green and more expensive option were conscious.

Overall, we can see that changing the default option may be a useful technique to nudge pro-environmental behaviors both in daily decisions with a short-term impact and also in long-term decisions with a clearer economic impact.

Aside from making the green alternative the default option, other techniques changing the choice architecture have been shown to be effective in influencing environmental behavior. As described before, livestock and meat production are two of the biggest contributors to greenhouse emissions and water consumption (United States Environmental Protection Agency, 2012). In this context, some studies have explored effective nudges for the reduction of meat consumption. For example, a field experiment by Vandenbroele, Slabbinck, Van Kerckhove, and Vermeir (2019) analyzed how the location and visibility of vegetarian meat alternatives impacted their purchase in several supermarkets. They found that sales of vegetarian "meat" increased when its visibility was increased and when it was paired with real meat products. According to the authors, pairing vegetarian alternatives with meat products accentuated the similarities between the products, making the vegetarian alternatives seem more familiar and, thus, increasing the likelihood that consumers would purchase them.

Conclusion

Why does it matter that we implement behavioral policies in the environmental domain? It has been argued that ineffective energy and environmental policies can be seen as unethical, as they take time and effort away from more effective policies designed to address urgent environmental issues such as climate change (Schubert, 2017). This means that there is a tremendous opportunity to utilize insights that directly demonstrate how pro-environmental behaviors may be increased. However, ethical concerns around nudges – green or otherwise – arise because of their **libertarian paternalism** (see Chapter 3 for more details). For example, changing a default can be seen as distrustful of individual judgment and as a way to manipulate decisions in a direction that is convenient for policymakers (Schubert, 2017). However, it can be counterargued that there are always many (competing) influences exerted on the unconscious and conscious decisions people make.

Policies are not laws and can therefore, in many cases, only address voluntary behavior. This means that many are implemented without setting legal restrictions on choices. As mentioned at the beginning of this chapter, it has been questioned whether consumer demand under a free market is sufficient for the extensive adoption of green products (Battisti, 2008). Energy and environmental policies based on sound behavioral science are useful, but even if they are scalable and successful, it is still questionable whether they have the power to forge a more sustainable energy system, reduce the unwanted effects of climate change, and result in a cleaner environment globally. In this chapter, we have presented a range of options that have so far had some positive effects, together with some others that have not. Expansion of this toolkit and building on relevant theories, both within this book and beyond, may offer greater potential toward sustained benefits for the environment through changing human behavior and decision-making.

Essay questions

1. Why are behavioral insights important in energy and environmental policies?
2. What might help bridge the knowledge- and value-action gaps?
3. What are the limitations of evidence-based policies in the energy and environmental domains? Think of environmental issues where you could not use behavioral insights.
4. Next to Prospect Theory, what other behavioral economic concepts might explain the success of the plastic bag levy around the world?
5. Discuss the pros and cons of using defaults, social norms, labeling, intrinsic motivation, and providing information.
6. How can nudges facilitate autonomy? How can they threaten it? Answer these questions by using the three definitions of autonomy described in Box 6.5.
7. Which of the behavioral insights presented is most effective in promoting pro-environmental behavior and why?
8. In their study, Kácha and Ruggeri (2018) used social norms and autonomy-supporting messages to encourage pro-environmental behavior, but the participants receiving them did not display more behaviors of this kind than the control group (see a description of the study in the section Leveraging intrinsic and extrinsic motivation toward pro-environmental behavior). These techniques have been shown to work in other studies. Why do you think they did not work similarly this time?

Additional insights and further reading

Behavioral interventions and energy efficiency

Allcott, H., & Mullainathan, S. (2010). Behavior and energy policy. *Science, 327*(5970), 1204–1205.

Disclosure and green energy choice

Litvine, D., & Wüstenhagen, R. (2011). Helping “light green” consumers walk the talk: Results of a behavioural intervention survey in the Swiss electricity market. *Ecological Economy, 70*, 462–474.

Social values driving pro-environmental purchasing decisions

Norazah, M. S. (2016). Consumer environmental concern and green product purchase in Malaysia: Structural effects of consumptions. *Journal of Cleaner Production, 132*, 204–214. https://doi.org/10.1016/j.jclepro.2015.09.087

Combined intervention strategies for reducing energy consumption

Dolan, P., & Metcalfe, R. (2011). *Better neighbors and basic knowledge: A field experiment on the role of non-pecuniary incentives on energy consumption*. Oxford: University of Oxford.

Strategies for behavioral influence

Dolan, P., Hallsworth, M., Halpern, D., King, D., Metcalfe, R., & Vlaev, I. (2012). Influencing behaviour: The Mindspace way. *Journal of Economic Psychology, 33*, 264–277.

Methods of influencing choice architecture

Johnson, E. J., Shu, S. B., Dellaert, B. G., Fox, C., Goldstein, D. G., Häubl, G., . . . & Weber, E. U. (2012). Beyond nudges: Tools of a choice architecture. *Marketing Letters, 23*(2), 487–504.

Ecolabels as environmental nudges

Sammer, K., & Wüstenhagen, R. (2006). The influence of eco-labelling on consumer behavior – results of a discrete choice analysis for washing machines. *Business Strategy and Environment, 15*, 185–199.

Defaults for light bulbs

Dinner, I., Johnson, E. J., Goldstein, D. G., & Liu, K. (2011). Partitioning default effects: Why people choose not to choose. *Journal of Experimental Psychology: Applied, 17*, 332–341.

Simplifying efforts to reduce energy consumption

Scholl, G., Rubik, F., Kalimo, H., Biedenkopf, K., & Söebech, Ó. (2010). Policies to promote sustainable consumption: Innovative approaches in Europe. *Natural Resources Forum, 34*, 39–50.

Reducing thermal energy demands

Hafner, R. J., Elmes, D., & Read, D. (2019). Promoting behavioural change to reduce thermal energy demand in households: A review. *Renewable and Sustainable Energy Reviews, 102*, 205–214.

Defaults and smart defaults for policy

Smith, N. C., Goldstein, D. G., & Johnson, E. J. (2013). Choice without awareness: Ethical and policy implications of defaults. *Journal of Public Policy & Marketing, 32*(2), 159–172.

Determinants and outcomes of belief in climate change

Hornsey, M. J., Harris, E. A., Bain, P. G., & Fielding, K. S. (2016). Meta-analyses of the determinants and outcomes of belief in climate change. *Nature Climate Change*, 6(6), 622–627. https://doi.org/10.1038/NCLIMATE2943

This chapter has been adapted from Ruggeri, K., Immonen, J., Benzerga, A., Kácha, O., Kunz, M., & van der Linden, S. (2019). Energy and environment. In K. Ruggeri (Ed.), *Behavioral insights for public policy: Concepts and cases* (pp. 114–130). New York and London: Routledge.

7 Education and behavior[1]

Carly D. Robinson, Thomas Lind Andersen, Clair Davison, Emir Demić, Hamish Evans, Mafalda Fontinha Mascarenhas, Shannon P. Gibson, Renata Hlavová, Wing Yi Lam, Silvana Mareva, Aleksandra Yosifova, and Kai Ruggeri

Chapter summary

Education is a critical resource for sustaining economic development and social cohesion, as well as individual and population health. Policies aimed at improving education could have a positive impact far beyond classrooms, particularly given that improved educational outcomes are associated with greater well-being. In this chapter, we present a number of behavioral insights that address current challenges in teaching and learning. We explore interventions that could alleviate the corrosive effects of inequality and ensure smoother transitions across different educational stages. We focus on various approaches for improving educational practice, such as providing incentives and fostering motivation, which have been selected specifically to highlight findings that have implications for education policy.

Learning objectives

- Recognize the behavioral barriers that hinder learners' ability to achieve educational goals
- Understand the role of simple behavioral interventions in education and their potential for impact through targeting short-term choices or long-term beliefs
- Identify specific behavioral insights that apply to education, such as engaging students on a personal level, targeting social norms, and simplifying the way information is presented
- Describe and evaluate the relative strengths and weaknesses of behavioral interventions in education regarding implementation, cost-effectiveness, and generalizability

Introduction

Education, considered by UNESCO (2014) as a prerequisite for sustainable development and maintaining peace throughout the world, is a promising lever to facilitate changes in global values, habits, and consumption. Early and consistent investment in education provides a wide range of positive outcomes, including promotion of mental and physical health;

DOI: 10.4324/9781003181873-7

reduction in crime, improved socio-economic success; fostering of workforce productivity; and higher economic return (Campbell et al., 2014; Lochner, 2011). By cultivating a host of positive outcomes for individuals and society, education has the potential to reduce social grievances and conflict (Østby & Urdal, 2011; Thyne, 2006).

Currently, issues in education policy, such as curriculum, equity, and procurement, are typically tackled through national or state-level regulations and laws (see Box 7.1). These policies often employ a top-down approach, which is mostly divorced from the experiences of relevant stakeholders, namely, students, teachers, administrators, and family members (Anderson & Togneri, 2005). These top-down educational policies often fail to account for the **behavioral barriers** that impede student success or barriers that hinder people's ability to achieve their educational goals.

For example, despite the high estimated financial and nonfinancial returns from higher education, the annual enrollment rate for postsecondary institutions has been gradually declining since 2010 in the United States (National Center for Education Statistics, 2017; McFarland et al., 2019). One behavioral barrier students and parents face relates to the trade-off between immediate costs, such as tuition fees or investment of effort, and future benefits, such as higher future income. In such trade-offs, the decision-making of students and their parents might be affected by present bias and temporal or hyperbolic discounting.

BOX 7.1 GOOD TO KNOW FOR EDUCATION POLICY – GROWTH VS. PROFICIENCY

In industrialized nations, current educational policies tend to utilize test-based accountability that adopts both national and international measurement benchmarks for monitoring educational objectives (Anagnostopoulos, Lingard, & Sellar, 2016; van der Sluis, Reezigt, & Borghans, 2017).

Supporters of test-based accountability argue that standardized tests within literacy, numeracy, and science, such as the Program for International Student Assessment, provide data to measure and evaluate schools, teachers, and students' academic performance (Anagnostopoulos et al., 2016). A pitfall of these measures is that they are often used for accountability and sanctioning within the policies (van der Sluis et al., 2017) rather than for evaluating the policies themselves (OECD, 2015b). Furthermore, the overreliance on such measures can unduly simplify the complex process of teaching and learning while also failing to account for the behavioral barriers that may affect educational outcomes (Anagnostopoulos et al., 2016).

When considering test-based accountability, one must also take into account the growth vs. proficiency debate (Ho, 2008). Should tests be used to evaluate whether students have reached a certain "proficiency" threshold, or should they be used to evaluate student improvement or "growth" over time? By assessing students as either proficient or not, standards rely on arbitrary cutoffs that can distort perceptions of gains made by students (Ho, 2008).

Moreover, proficiency does not take into account a student's starting point, therefore potentially becoming more discriminatory and leading schools to invest more resources on students closer to the proficiency threshold rather than on students who have much better or much worse performance (Booher-Jennings, 2005). According to a survey conducted among American Education Finance Association members, 68 percent of participants found growth or value-added metrics that take into account student characteristics to be a better tool to evaluate school quality (Stiefel, Schwartz, & Rotenberg, 2011).

An understanding of how beliefs and biases affect educational decision-making is the first step toward overcoming behavioral barriers. Behavioral insights can then be leveraged to support engagement or follow-through with the desired behavior. In the context of increasing postsecondary enrollment, immediate incentives can be used to offset current costs and thereby encourage students to remain on track with their long-term educational goals. Those designing educational policies and interventions must grasp the relevant barriers to promote better attainment of educational outcomes.

In this chapter, we review behavioral barriers commonly encountered in educational contexts and present evidence suggesting that behavioral insights may be useful in overcoming them. For instance, a behavioral intervention might address students' limited attentional resources by **simplifying** the university application process and providing **reminders** about important deadlines in order to improve enrollment rates in higher education (Bettinger, Long, Oreopoulos, & Sanbonmatsu, 2012; Hoxby & Turner, 2013; Castleman & Page, 2015). Another behavioral intervention might aim to reframe children's patterns of thinking about their abilities, which would improve their motivation to succeed (e.g. shifting students from a fixed mindset to a growth mindset; Paunesku et al., 2015). Through examples, we illustrate how behavioral insights can impact educational outcomes by targeting cognitive, social, motivational, and self-regulatory obstacles.

We have organized the chapter according to three types of interventions: *social interventions* aimed at mobilizing social support for students; *motivational interventions* that boost students' motivation; and *self-regulatory interventions* that help students take control over their actions to achieve educational goals (Figure 7.1). The chapter will guide you

FIGURE 7.1 Overview of the chapter

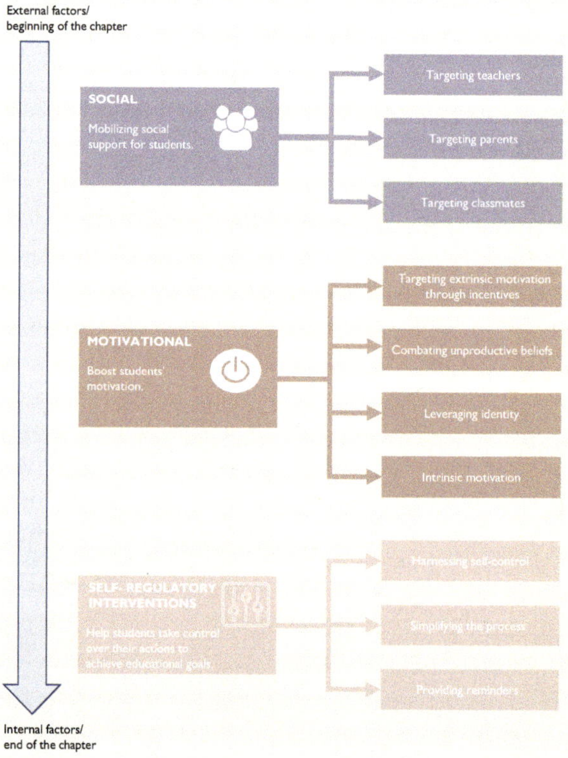

through various interventions that might impact a wide variety of educational outcomes, including enrollment, attendance, persistence, and academic achievement. We will start with interventions targeting more external factors, such as students' social networks and extrinsic motivation, and proceed to explore more internal factors, like intrinsic motivation, behavior-relevant beliefs, and self-management.

Social interventions

We will begin by discussing interventions that promote social support for students. Educational success is often attributed to individual student abilities, but the process requires the involvement of many interdependent stakeholders, including teachers, classmates, administrators, and families. Behavioral interventions that target students' social networks can mobilize support for students to improve educational outcomes. In the following sections, we highlight interventions that target students' families, peers, and teachers.

Targeting parents to improve student outcomes

Baby steps go a long way

Starting school represents an important step in children's lives. While the age of entering school varies across countries, the initiation of primary education appears to bring substantial changes to the lives of children and their families (Fabian & Dunlop, 2007). Many children find the sudden introduction of new relationships, environments, or contexts for learning to be overly stressful (Fabian & Dunlop, 2007). Pianta, Kraft-Sayre, Rimm-Kaufman, Gercke, and Higgins (2001) emphasized the importance of building relationships in easing the transition into school. A successful transition to school requires collaboration between the child, their family, teachers, peers, preschools, and the wider community. Parents, in particular, play a key role in preparing children for this transition through promoting school readiness and early academic success (Taylor, Clayton, & Rowley, 2004). However, the degree of parental involvement can vary substantially. Parents often lack information about effective parenting practices, which can be a barrier to smooth educational transitions. Almost all parents want to support their children's education, but seemingly unattainable long-term parenting goals may become overwhelming (York, Loeb, & Doss, 2018).

One way to support parents in preparing their children for school involves **segmentation**, the process of breaking down complex, long-term tasks into smaller steps. Interventions that communicate realistic actions and specific plans may make it easier for parents to keep track of their goals and to stay motivated.

For example, READY4K! is an eight-month, text messaging program that employed segmentation to promote at-home literacy activities in support of children's long-term development (York et al., 2018). In the first year, the program involved 519 4-year-olds and their families in the United States and targeted the early literacy development of these preschool children. In the second year of the program, 512 families received support for literacy, math, and socio-emotional development. Every week during the school year, parents received three messages aimed at increasing children's academic development through positive parenting practices. The three messages consisted of the following: (1) a fact informing and highlighting the importance of a specific academic skill; (2) a tip suggesting easily accessible and specific family activities; and (3) an encouraging and reinforcing text relating to parental involvement and a follow-up tip. The tips focused on short, simple, highly specific activities that built upon preexisting family routines. The program was structured as a spiral curriculum, starting simple and advancing over time, with topics being reintroduced throughout the year for reinforcement.

The program had a positive effect on both parents and their children, with parents in the intervention group reporting higher parental involvement at home. These parents were more likely to engage their children in shared activities, such as storytelling, looking at pictures in books, and reciting nursery rhymes than parents who did not receive the intervention. Correspondingly, children whose parents received READY4K! texts experienced gains in their literacy performance and had greater awareness of letter sounds. Additionally, the program was found to be more effective in the second year when it focused on literacy, math, and socio-emotional development. The results suggest that providing parents with actionable strategies and continuous encouragement may be an effective, feasible, and inexpensive approach to fostering parental involvement and school readiness. The study also highlights the potential of using text messaging as a vehicle for breaking down complex tasks into small and easy steps, which could help address behavioral barriers in parenting practices more generally. However, the scalability and generalizability of the approach for other areas of childhood development remain to be explored, particularly for domains such as language, motor, or social skills.

Closing the attainment gap: encouraging growth mindset in parents

Carol Dweck's (2006) highly influential work on mindsets (people's beliefs about their abilities) has emerged as one of the most popular theories of motivation in the past decade (see Box 7.2). The theory posits that people who have a **fixed mindset** tend to believe that intelligence and skill level are innate and unchangeable, regardless of effort. People who hold fixed mindset beliefs are less likely to exert effort on tasks once they encounter obstacles and setbacks (Blackwell, Trzesniewski, & Dweck, 2007). In contrast, people who have a **growth mindset** consider abilities to be a product of work and effort, rather than innate talent (Dweck, 2006). Those with a growth mindset tend to regard failure as an indication that one should increase the amount of time and effort spent on a given activity (see Figure 7.2). Mindset theory has many implications for improving educational success. In this section, we highlight how parents' mindsets can serve as another behavioral barrier that can impede effective parental engagement.

BOX 7.2 GROWTH MINDSET

The growth mindset approach may be successful because it reinforces a positive academic identity, which may improve educational outcomes by decreasing the likelihood of small failures leading students and parents to believe that academic success is unachievable (Yeager & Walton, 2011). As Dweck's approach has been widely cited and debated throughout the literature, particularly in education policy and behavioral insights, we strongly recommend you explore these theories further, as we only present a basic overview here.

FIGURE 7.2 Fixed and growth mindsets as proposed by Carol Dweck (2006)

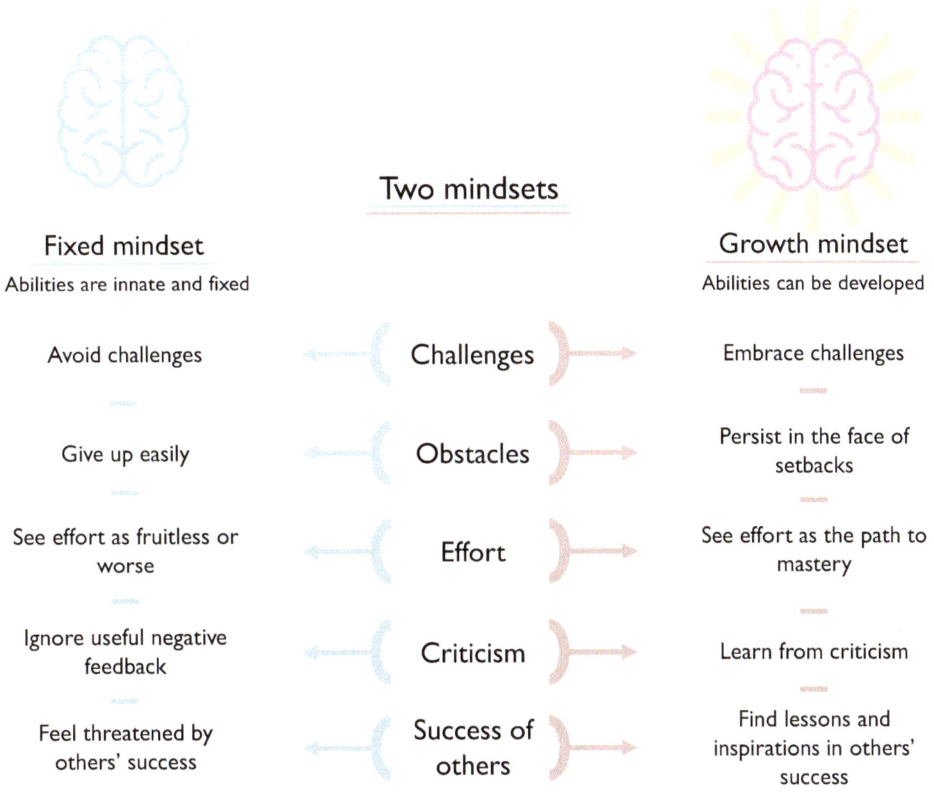

Source: Dweck (2006)

Research suggests that parents' beliefs about education may affect student success. Parents who think that the factors contributing to success are fixed may be less likely to encourage their children to improve their educational outcomes, which may put their children at risk of underperforming due to a lack of encouragement and motivation. For instance, a study found that given the same level of previous performance and parental education, 9-year-old children whose mothers hoped they would enroll in university scored, on average, 2.5 percentile points higher at age 11 compared to children of mothers with no such aspirations (Gregg & Washbrook, 2011). Thus, the fixed beliefs of many lower socio-economic status (SES) families that higher education is simply not for them and that improvement in their child's educational outcomes is unattainable may constitute a behavioral barrier for children's educational outcomes.

Thankfully, intervention studies show that people's mindsets can be shifted. In a large-scale study in Denmark, Andersen and Nielsen (2016) implemented a growth mindset intervention to improve reading outcomes in second graders. The intervention emphasized the malleability of children's reading ability by providing parents with information on how their child's reading skills could be improved, regardless of the child's current abilities. This study was a **randomized controlled trial** (RCT) in which 1,587 second-grade children from 72 classrooms in 28 schools were randomly assigned to either a treatment or a control group.

Researchers provided parents and children with books to read together, while providing parents with additional information on parent-child interactions they could engage in to improve their child's reading abilities.

The effects of the program were greatest for children whose parents initially believed that their child's reading ability was fixed. The growth mindset intervention was combined with the distribution of books, meaning that it is difficult to isolate the unique contribution of the growth mindset approach as compared to additional materials. Nonetheless, the pattern of results is a promising suggestion that relatively simple and inexpensive interventions may successfully shift parents' perceptions of their children's education, therefore resulting in improved educational outcomes for students who are traditionally at risk.

However, the effectiveness of growth mindset theory was challenged by a recent RCT involving 5,018 pupils in England who received a growth mindset–based intervention delivered by their teachers (Foliano et al., 2019). Teachers received one day of training on mindset theory and its implementation. On the basis of that training, they delivered sessions to students for eight weeks. Results indicated that the intervention had no effect on academic attainment, self-efficacy, test anxiety, or self-regulation. Furthermore, there was only a small and nonsignificant impact on intrinsic value or perceived meaningfulness of the academic tasks. In addition, in a subsequent exploratory analysis, children who demonstrated a fixed mindset before the intervention showed no effect of the intervention. The only aspect positively affected by the intervention was teachers' perception of pupil perseverance and attitudes.

The authors suggested that the lack of impact could be due to widespread familiarity with growth mindset theory among teachers, which was not controlled for in the control group. When we think about growth mindset interventions, it is important to consider that the effectiveness of these interventions might be dependent on the children's age or the involvement of their social network, namely, their parents.

Targeting parental misbeliefs to boost student attendance and grades

During the 2015–2016 school year, more than 7 million students were absent from school for 15 days or more in the United State (U.S. Department of Education, 2019). Students who are absent from school are more likely to have lower grades and withdraw from education before completing high school (Nauer, White, & Yerneni, 2008). An increase in student attendance rates has the potential to increase instructional time, improve instructional quality, and bolster academic performance. In turn, these outcomes may contribute toward reducing dropout rates and narrowing the achievement gap (Balfanz & Byrnes, 2013; Nauer et al., 2008).

Working with parents to help get their children to school has shown to be a promising way to reduce student absenteeism. Specifically, sending letters to parents about their children's attendance results in reduced student absenteeism. One randomized experiment of 28,000 households sent personalized mail to parents of children in kindergarten and the 12th grade (Rogers & Feller, 2018). Each letter informed parents of the number of days that their child was absent from school and compared this to the absence rates of others in their class. Students whose parents received the personalized mail showed a 10 percent reduction in chronic absenteeism (missing more than 10 percent of all school days) in comparison to students in the control group, whose parents received no personalized mail. A conceptual replication of this experiment with parents of over 10,000 elementary school students also found that sending parents personalized mail about their child's attendance resulted in a 15 percent reduction in the number of students who were chronically absent over the course of the school year (Robinson, Lee, Dearing, & Rogers, 2018a).

Both of these interventions targeted parents' inaccurate beliefs about the number of school days that their child had missed and included motivating messages emphasizing the importance of daily attendance. These insights can be useful for school administrators who want to communicate effectively with families to address common misconceptions about attendance.

When it comes to improving attendance, mail-based communications may actually be more effective than other means of communication, such as text messages, because letters become social artifacts that capture and maintain parents' attention with accurate information about their child's attendance. Text messages, on the other hand, tend to be read upon receipt and are more likely to be forgotten. A study conducted with 11 high schools and nearly 4,000 students in New York City found that sending text messages to parents with updates about their children's attendance had no impact on student attendance (Balu, Porter, & Gunton, 2016).

Text message interventions may be more effective when they are used to bolster students' social support (see Box 7.3 on how student's performance was impacted when feedback was provided through information and communications technology) by providing members of their social network with personalized information about upcoming exams and course content (Groot, Sanders, Rogers, & Bloomenthal, 2017). For example, Bergman and Chan (2019) sent parents weekly text messages providing timely information about their children's missed assignments, grades, or class-specific absences. Experimentally tested in 22 schools in the United States, this simple intervention was linked to a 28 percent reduction in course failure and a 12 percent increase in class attendance when compared to students whose parents did not receive text-message reminders.

BOX 7.3 TEACHER-PARENT FEEDBACK AS A TOOL FOR IMPROVING STUDENT PERFORMANCE

Feedback is broadly understood as the process of being provided with information regarding aspects of one's performance, behavior, understanding, choices, or general demeanor (inspired by Hattie & Timperley, 2007). Often, in an educational context, feedback is given directly by a teacher to a student regarding their work.

However, giving parents feedback on their child's academic performance appears to also be valuable because it provides parents with an opportunity to engage in their child's education. Parental involvement has a positive relationship with children's educational attainment and success in school (Damgaard & Nielsen, 2017; Kraft & Rogers, 2015). Despite the existence of encouraging evidence, schools rarely share information with parents to a level where they are fully engaged (Kraft & Rogers, 2015).

So how do we usefully tap into this resource? Information and communication technologies (ICTs) are any form of equipment or machinery used for the explicit purpose of linking people and information. They can provide easy-to-use methods to share feedback with both students and parents. Several studies have shown that providing parents with feedback through ICTs (e.g. over the phone or through text messaging) can mobilize parental involvement, as well as student engagement and success. Systems like learning management systems (LMS; software used by teachers to track student progress and provide information, assignments, and course materials to students) make it even easier to deliver feedback to parents.

For example, Kraft and Rogers (2015) tested the effect of high school teachers providing parents with weekly feedback on their child's performance in a credit recovery program. In the positive feedback condition, teachers reported what the student had done well in their work. In the improvement feedback condition, teachers advised parents on what their child could improve on. In the control condition, no feedback was given to parents. The provision of feedback gave parents the opportunity to discuss this with their child.

Overall, they found that this type of teacher-parent communication increased the probability of students passing their courses by 6.5 percent and decreased student absenteeism by 2.5 percent. The difference between the positive feedback condition and the improvement feedback condition was not statistically significant. However, parents who received improvement feedback were 1.6 times more likely to talk to their children about what could be done better in comparison to parents in the control condition, whereas no such difference was evident in the positive feedback condition.

Targeting parents to promote student interest

Expectancy value theory is widely applied in the field of education as a model for understanding students' achievement motivation. According to the theory, a person's performance, persistence, and choices are predominantly determined by their expectation of success and the subjective value they place on the task (task value; Eccles & Wigfield, 2002). Task value consists of four subcomponents, including attainment value, intrinsic value, utility value, and cost (Eccles, Adler, Futterman, Goff, & Kaczala, 1983). We will focus on **utility value** in this section, which refers to the usefulness and relevance that a person attributes to a task (Eccles & Wigfield, 2002; Wigfield & Cambria, 2010).

Individuals tend to gravitate toward and persist in tasks that they believe will be useful and relevant to their future goals (Wigfield & Cambria, 2010). For instance, 14- to 18-year-old students perceive science, technology, engineering, and math (STEM) subjects to be increasingly desired by employers in the twenty-first century workforce (National Foundation for Educational Research, 2011). Yet, students report having insufficient information about STEM career paths, which may reduce the likelihood that they will pursue STEM careers.

Maltese and Tai (2011) found that students who perceive science as valuable and want a science-based career are more likely to take upper-level STEM courses in college. Therefore, increasing the perceived value of STEM courses for students may result in higher enrollment in these courses. Parents may be particularly effective at helping students realize the utility value of taking STEM courses. For example, an intervention providing parents of 10th- and 11th-grade students with handouts and links to a website promoting the value, usefulness, and everyday relevance of STEM courses positively influenced students' STEM course choices (Harackiewicz, Rozek, Hulleman, & Hyde, 2012). These students opted for at least one additional semester of mathematics and science classes during their final two years of high school compared to students whose parents received no STEM materials. By providing parents with the relevant information on the utility of STEM courses, they can become powerful partners in the effort to drive students toward STEM classes and careers.

Targeting classmates to improve student outcomes

While school attendance is closely linked to academic achievement and is critical to educational success, children who face obstacles at home are more likely to be absent, which can negatively affect their performance and increase the likelihood of them dropping out of school completely (Musser, 2011). Certain African countries, such as Malawi (Jukes, Jere, & Pridmore, 2014) and South Africa (van der Berg, 2008), have succeeded in enrolling high numbers of children in their elementary schools, but there are also high **dropout** rates. Case studies in Malawi showed that dropping out was more common among children with additional household responsibilities, such as caring for siblings or chronically ill parents (Moleni, 2008; Pridmore & Jere, 2011).

One behavioral intervention designed to address the problem involves **partnering**, which taps into social norms and provides peer support by assigning certain at-risk children a "buddy." Buddies are fellow students responsible for helping at-risk children with daily school tasks and providing them with general support. The aim is that these partnerships will improve the behaviors, choices, or sustained commitment of at-risk children through social support and modeling. The SOFIE (Strengthening Open and Flexible Learning for Increased Education Access) project in Malawi implemented a partnering intervention to decrease school dropout rates for at-risk children (Jukes et al., 2014). Out of 40 participating schools, 20 schools were randomly assigned to receive the intervention, which consisted of identifying 15 students who were at risk of dropping out. These 15 students received supplementary educational materials, community support, and a school buddy whose role was to support their learning and follow up with them if they missed a day of school. These children were 55 percent less likely to drop out than similar at-risk children who did not receive any support (see Figure 7.3). In the 20 intervention schools, there was also a 35 percent reduction in dropouts overall, suggesting that the intervention may have had a spillover effect that indirectly benefited children – particularly older children – in the intervention schools who did not receive any program materials.

Targeting teachers to improve student outcomes

Improving teacher-student relationships

According to the National Center for Education Statistics in the United States, the proportion of White teachers in public elementary and secondary schools was 80 percent in 2015–2016, while the percentage of White students was 49 percent (de Brey et al., 2019). These racial mismatches between teachers and students can be problematic and can result

FIGURE 7.3 The impact of partnering on reducing dropout rates

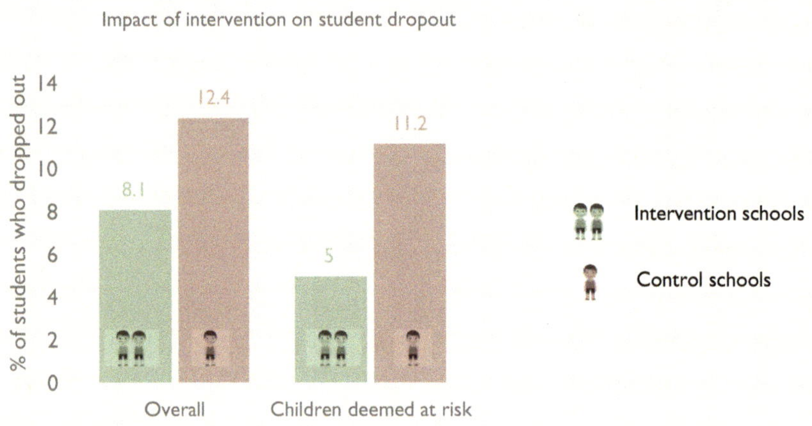

Source: Jukes et al. (2014)

in worse outcomes for Black students (Gershenson, Hart, Hyman, Lindsay, & Papageorge, 2018). However, strengthening teacher-student relationships offers a promising solution.

In educational settings, positive teacher-student relationships have been closely linked to student achievement and motivation (Roorda, Koomen, Spilt, & Oort, 2011; Wentzel, Russell, & Baker, 2016). One of the ways to improve teacher-student relationships is by targeting their perceived **similarity**. Similarity refers to the closeness to others, namely, their attitudes, values, interests, and personality (Tesser & Campbell, 1980). Therefore, increased perceptions of similarity could be a foundation for developing positive interpersonal relationships.

A study conducted in the United States administered a short "get-to-know-you" survey to 315 ninth graders and 25 ninth-grade teachers (Gehlbach et al., 2016). Gehlbach and colleagues provided teachers and students with feedback on what they had in common. Both students and teachers reported an increase in perceived similarity to each other at the end of the semester. However, only teachers perceived more positive relationships with students. Exploratory analyses suggested that highlighting commonalities differentially impacted the quality of the teacher-student relationship depending on the race of the student. Specifically, learning about similarities and common interests was associated with improvements in the relationships between teachers and their African-American and Latino students, as well as improvements in student academic performance. This resulted in a 60 percent reduction in the achievement gap between White students and traditionally disadvantaged minority students. These results indicate that targeting perceptions of similarities may promote teacher-student relationships and foster downstream benefits on student grades.

Framing student gains and losses for teachers

Teachers also demonstrate **loss aversion**. An experiment by Fryer, Levitt, List, and Sadoff (2012) awarded bonuses to teachers on the basis of their students' improvement in test scores throughout the year. In one condition, the bonus was distributed to teachers at the beginning of the year. If a teacher's students did not meet the criteria for receiving the bonus, the teacher had to return it (a loss frame). In the other condition, teachers received the bonus at the end of the year if their students met the bonus criteria (a gain frame, more aligned with traditional incentive structures). Students whose teachers would have had to give the bonus back saw their test scores increase by 6.8 percentile points compared to controls. This effect was meaningfully higher than the effect observed for students whose teachers would receive the bonus at the end of the year. These findings suggest that **reframing** teacher bonuses as losses may positively influence student grades, though there may be practical and ethical concerns about applying such methods in practice.

Motivational interventions

Many issues that impede student success can be attributed to the unproductive beliefs students hold about their own ability or identity (Steele & Aronson, 1995), a lack of motivation (O'Rourke, Haimovitz, Ballweber, Dweck, & Popović, 2014), or not having relevant information to act upon (Hulleman & Harackiewicz, 2009). Behavioral interventions attempt to increase student motivation by addressing these issues in order to have a positive impact on educational outcomes. These interventions provide **incentives** that are based on external factors such as financial rewards or public recognition, which may target students' **extrinsic motivation**, or incentives based on internal factors such as feelings of accomplishment or application of values, which tap into students' **intrinsic motivation**.

Targeting extrinsic motivation to boost performance

Improving performance by providing financial incentives

There is a vast literature on monetary incentives in education, which is beyond the scope of this chapter. We will, however, examine the extent to which these incentives may act as an extrinsic motivator for students. In general, studies that assessed the effect of financial incentives offered for academic performance suggest that large financial incentives foster better performance than small incentives.

One study, conducted in the Netherlands, examined an intervention that offered financial incentives to university students if they completed their first-year requirements by the start of the second academic year (Leuven, Oosterbeek, & van der Klaauw, 2010). Students were randomly assigned to earn either a small reward, a large reward, or no reward. Results showed that high-ability students in the large-reward group had higher pass rates, whereas low-ability students in the same group completed fewer requirements. Therefore, the offer of a financial incentive resulted in better outcomes for high-ability students, but worse outcomes for low-ability students.

Another study, conducted in the United States, also found that the offer of large monetary rewards to university students significantly improved overall grade point average (GPA; Angrist, Lang, & Oreopoulos, 2009). The Student Fellowship Program, which offered students the opportunity to earn monetary awards for grades, and the Student Support Program, which provided study groups and peer-advising services, were combined to make the Student Fellowship and Student Support Program (SFSP). The monetary rewards were awarded on the basis of student ability. That is, students were categorized according to how they previously performed in the GPA quartile and then rewarded an amount ranging from $1,000 to $5,000, depending on the improvement in their GPA. First-year students in SFSP had a 0.17 higher GPA than students who were offered no incentives (see Figure 7.4).

In contrast, another study by the same lab found that the offer of large monetary rewards did not significantly affect overall GPA (Angrist, Oreopoulos, & Williams, 2014). The Canadian Opportunity Knocks (OK) program offered large monetary rewards to 400 first- and second-year college students for earning course grades above 70 percent. Students were awarded $100 for every class grade they received above 70 percent and then an additional $20 for every additional grade point thereafter. The program also provided email-based peer mentoring services by pretrained third- and fourth-year students. While grades improved above 70 percent in second-year courses, the effects were small and there was no significant GPA difference between students assigned to the OK program and students who were not in the program (see Figure 7.4).

The SFSP and OK program both offered university students financial incentives for their grades, but they employed different criteria for awarding them to students. The SFSP adjusted reward requirements according to student ability, so that the grade requirements for earning a reward were different for each student, whereas the OK program offered uniform rewards for grades above 70 percent, regardless of students' baseline academic performance

FIGURE 7.4 The impact of monetary incentives on grade point average (GPA)

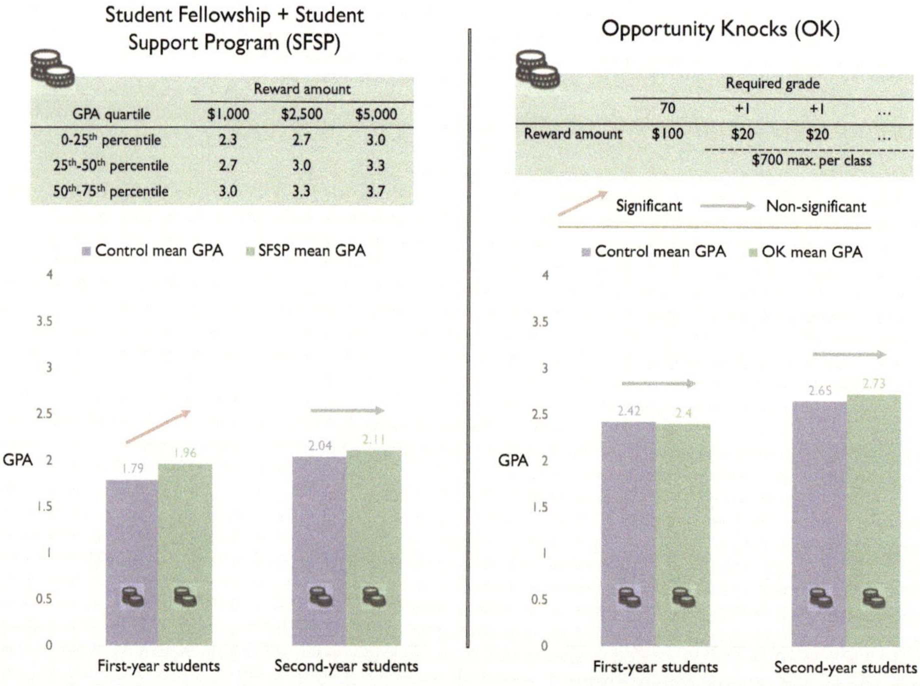

Angrist et al. (2009) found improvements in GPA* (left, SFPS), whereas Angrist et al. (2014) saw no impact on overall GPA (right; OK). Both incentives offered rewards around the annual tuition fee.

*The maximum achievable GPA is 4.0.

(see Figure 7.4). This might potentially explain why monetary incentives improved GPA in the 2009 study by Angrist et al., but had no impact in their 2014 study.

Another study found that financially rewarding exam performance improved the exam scores of girls at a primary school in Kenya (Kremer, Miguel, & Thornton, 2009). Conducted in two neighboring districts in Kenya (Busia, a larger, more populous city, and Teso, a smaller city), findings showed that exam scores improved by 0.27 standard deviations in Busia and by 0.09 standard deviations in Teso. The latter result, which was not statistically significant, may have been due to fewer schools choosing to participate in that city. Nonetheless, the success of the program may have been due to the substantial value of the prize offered; girls with test scores in the top 15% of their grade received a scholarship, which included two grants to cover school fees and supplies, and public recognition at an awards assembly. The study also increased teacher attendance, which may explain the positive spillover effects reported for boys, who were not eligible for the scholarship.

In addition to the amount, the timing of rewards also appears to influence the effectiveness of monetary incentives. In a study conducted in the United States, Levitt et al. (2016) offered students financial incentives for performing well on a low-stakes test. Students were not expected to prepare for the test, and their performance did not have any bearing on their academic standing. Additionally, students were only notified about the reward immediately prior to the test, so any changes in student performance would be due to students exerting more effort on the test (as opposed to studying more in advance). When students were told that the reward would be given immediately after the test, they demonstrated improved test scores. Conversely, when students were told that they would receive the reward after a one-month delay, performance was not affected by the monetary incentive. These findings suggest that providing students with rewards immediately after the target behavior may be more effective than the popular practice of recognizing students at the end of the term or school year.

Improving performance by providing social incentives

Nonmonetary incentives represent another potential tool for fostering motivation and improving learners' self-control. There is an extensive literature suggesting that people may adjust their behavior when provided with information about **social norms,** as discussed in Chapter 3. Similarly, informing students about how they perform in comparison to their peers could shift their perception about what is desirable and acceptable behavior. Such social comparisons could motivate students to perform better through introducing the social incentive of obtaining a higher rank within the reference group. Rank-based or relative grading taps into social norms by providing students with information on how they rank compared to other students in their class.

Jalava, Joensen, and Pellas (2015) conducted a RCT with 1,045 sixth graders in Sweden and found that children were more driven to succeed when they were informed that a test would be marked using rank-based grading, with only the top three students in the class being rewarded. Use of rank-based grading resulted in better test scores when compared to objective grading (giving absolute grades based on a fixed A–F scale).

In another study, Azmat and Iriberri (2010) compared the effect of receiving only absolute grades to receiving absolute and relative grades together. Over the course of the academic year, high school students received their own GPA, as well as the class average GPA, giving them a clear idea of where they stood in the classroom. This resulted in a 5 percent increase in the grades of both high- and low-scoring students when compared to the previous and following years, when only absolute grades were provided.

Increasing perseverance by rewarding effort

O'Rourke et al. (2014) modified the language of a widely used online educational game that helps elementary schoolchildren to learn fractions. The RCT they conducted, involving 15,000 children, adapted an old "fraction points" reward system to a new "brain points" system, whereby players were rewarded for effort as opposed to outcome (e.g. rewarding players based on level completion). In addition to effort, the brain points system rewarded children for the strategies they used and the progress they made. Children who were rewarded for their effort spent more time engaging with the game than children who were rewarded for completing levels. Children playing the brain points version completed an average of 6.7 levels compared to only 5.5 levels completed by the children playing the old fraction points version. The most marked increase occurred among children who were initially low performing. In a second study with 25,000 children, O'Rourke, Peach, Dweck, and Popovic (2016) further assessed the efficacy of five different variations of the brain points system. A control version, identical to the 2014 study, included the brain points system and a growth mindset narrative that presented players with animations teaching them about growth mindset throughout the game. The four other variations either (1) excluded growth mindset animations; (2) removed brain point rewards; (3) awarded brain points at random intervals; or (4) excluded a visualization of the player's progress. Results showed that children played the game for longer and completed more levels in variations of the game from which growth mindset animations were excluded. Overall, these results provide an insightful strategy to increase perseverance and educational outcomes, such as material retention, by rewarding a child's effort.

However, symbolic awards do not necessarily increase recipients' intrinsic motivation – they are still external motivators. In a randomized experiment with over 15,000 students from sixth through 12th grade, Robinson, Gallus, Lee, and Rogers (2019) found that offering students symbolic awards for having perfect attendance in the upcoming month (a prospective award for their future behavior) did not impact student attendance, on average. At the same time, another group of students received an award for having had a perfect month of attendance in the past (a retrospective award for their past behavior). Compared to students in the control condition, who received no information about the awards, students who received a retrospective award for their past attendance missed 8 percent more school and were 2 percent less likely to attain perfect attendance in the following month. To explore the reasons behind the unexpected negative consequences of the awards, the researchers conducted a follow-up study online with 311 participants between the ages of 18 and 29. Results suggested that the awards were sending unintended signals to students about the social norms for attendance (i.e. that they were attending school more than their classmates) and their school's expectations for their attendance (i.e. that they were attending school more than the school expected them to attend). Both symbolic and material incentives should be carefully monitored as they may override intrinsic motivation, which we will discuss at the end of this section.

Enhancing motivation by combating unproductive beliefs

Nudging away gender stereotype threats

Psychological factors also contribute to the development of a negative academic identity that hinders performance, particularly negative stereotypes about the general abilities of individuals on the basis of gender and race. Unfortunately, such stereotypes are commonplace in educational contexts and may lead to what Steele and Aronson (1995) defined as the **stereotype threat** (the tendency to perform worse when one is reminded of a negative stereotype concerning the abilities of their own group). This phenomenon represents a potential contributing force for the gender gap in mathematics and other STEM subjects.

For example, there is a common misperception that women are not as gifted as men in the field of mathematics (Kiefer & Sekaquaptewa, 2007). This view is likely worsened by a troubling pattern: there are far fewer female mathematicians than male, with women being less likely to apply to major in STEM subjects (Hill, Corbett, & St Rose, 2010). The National Science Foundation (2009b) reported that, in their first year of university, 29 percent of male students planned to major in a STEM field in 2006 compared with only 15 percent of female students in the United States. Although more recent statistics suggest that this has improved, with 49 percent of males and 37.5 percent of females planning to major in a STEM field in 2014 (National Science Foundation, 2016), there is still a prevalent gender disparity, particularly within specific subjects such as engineering and mathematics.

Gneezy, Niederle, and Rustichini (2003) examined the mechanisms behind this tendency and present evidence that females often shy away from competitive settings and are particularly likely to avoid environments where males most often dominate, such as STEM fields. Further evidence has shown that, when women take math tests, the stereotype threat can introduce toxic anxiety, which negatively impacts their test performance (Spencer, Steele, & Quinn, 1999). However, Spencer et al. (1999) offered a powerful example of how the removal of stereotype threat primes can improve educational performance: a reduction in the saliency of the gender stereotype can reduce gender differences in performance. Saliency can be manipulated by removing any immediate prompts or primes about belonging to a stereotyped group from the testing environment. Thirty female and 24 male participants were informed that inconsistent results had been found regarding gender differences in math ability and that they had been selected for the study due to their strong background in mathematics. Participants were informed that the first test had been found to produce gender differences, while the second test had not. The order of these descriptions was counterbalanced across participants. Women who learned that gender was associated with performance underperformed relative to men, but those who were told that there were no gender differences performed equally to men (see Figure 7.5). Although this study had a small sample size, it provides evidence that a reduction in the saliency of the stereotype threat may improve performance, particularly among women.

In another study, Danaher and Crandall (2008) reanalyzed the data from Stricker and Ward's (2004) experiment comparing alternative methods to reduce stereotype threat. Using a less conservative statistical approach ($p < .05$ and $\eta \geq .05$), they compared the effects of the standard administrative practice of placing demographic and gender questions at the top of the exam sheet to an alternative of placing them at the end of the exam. On the Advanced Placement Calculus exam, females passed the test at about a 6 percent higher rate when the questions were placed at the end of the exam, whereas males had a 4 percent lower passing rate. The difference in passing rate between males and females decreased from 16 percent to 5 percent. Given the large number of students taking the test annually, this would translate to almost 3,000 additional young women starting college each year with calculus credits in the United States. Danaher and Crandall's work (2008) suggests that making gender less salient in educational contexts can enhance women's mathematics performance. Simply the removal of potentially negative primes before tests can alleviate the hindering effects that stereotypes have on educational outcomes and may work toward narrowing the gender gap in STEM fields.

FIGURE 7.5 Gender stereotypes and test scores

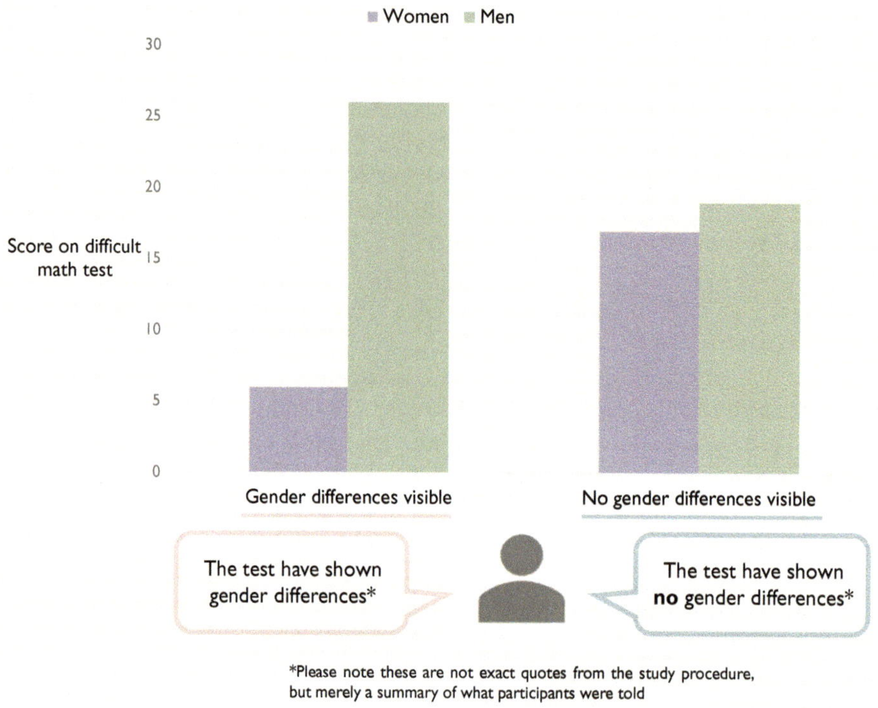

The mean scores for each condition were only reported in a figure in the study (Spencer et al., 1999). Therefore, this figure relied upon an approximation method to be reproduced.

Nudging away racial stereotype threats

The stereotype threat phenomenon can also apply to a person's race and ethnicity. Steele and Aronson (1995) found that when race was emphasized, Black college students significantly underperformed on standardized tests compared to White students.

Aronson, Fried, and Good (2002) experimentally tested one way to combat unproductive beliefs among students. They had African-American and White university students engage in a long-distance student mentoring program and asked them to write letters to young, struggling, middle school children. The students were assigned to one of three conditions: in the first condition, they were asked to inform their middle schooler that intelligence is malleable and can be increased with hard work and determination. In the second condition, they were asked to inform the middle schooler that there are different types of intelligence, with individuals having varying strengths and weaknesses in different domains, and in the control condition no letter was written. Among African-American students, those who wrote letters about the malleability of intelligence viewed intelligence as more malleable than participants in the other two conditions. They also had a higher GPA at the end of the next semester than students in the other two conditions. White students in the same condition also briefly modified their beliefs, but there was no longitudinal impact on their GPAs.

Another study, conducted in the United States, involved 243 school children taking part in a self-affirmation exercise emphasizing self-integrity and sense of self-worth (Cohen, Garcia, Apfel, & Master, 2006). Children completed either a 15-minute, in-class assignment focusing on their own values and why they are important to them or a similar assignment that focused on values that they indicated were not particularly important to them. The study found significant improvements in grades for African-American children focusing on their own values compared to those focusing on trivial values. The exercise had no impact on European-American children's grades.

In addition, a follow-up study including the original 243 children and a new cohort of 385 children found that the effect of the self-affirmation exercise was even greater for low-performing African-American children two years later. The initial effect on African-American children who were high performing dissipated, but the exercise still reduced the achievement gap in GPA between Black and White children (Cohen, Garcia, Purdie-Vaughns, Apfel, & Brzustoski, 2009). The authors suggest that an emphasis on the positive aspects of one's identity may help minority students alleviate the stress arising from negative stereotypes.

Notably, Dee (2015) failed to replicate this effect in a study comprising 2,500 US students. The self-affirmation exercise appeared to be effective only for minority students within classrooms with strong peer achievement. However, in these high-performance (and potentially more competitive) classrooms, the self-affirmation intervention was associated with negative effects for female students. These results emphasize the need for further examination of the interplay between educational context and student characteristics in order to understand the various mechanisms that self-affirmation interventions may trigger.

Behavioral insights and socio-psychological interventions aiming to lessen the effects of negative stereotypes have shown mixed effects. Nonetheless, stereotype threat is a widely studied and debated topic in the field of social psychology, and it should be explored beyond the basic overview presented here.

Encouraging university applications

While enrollment in postsecondary education (i.e. universities) has increased steadily worldwide (UNESCO Institute for Statistics, 2018), there are still a substantial number of young people who choose not to attend despite being qualified to do so (Walker & Zhu, 2013). A large **attainment gap** (the difference in attainment between groups that are otherwise equal in ability) remains when it comes to postsecondary education enrollment. Students from low-income backgrounds apply to university less often or they apply to less selective universities than students from high-income families, even when they have the same ability (Hoxby & Turner, 2013). Students from high-income families are 2.4 times more likely to enter universities than students from low-income families in the United Kingdom (UCAS, 2016).

One possible explanation could be that students from disadvantaged backgrounds are less likely to aspire to attend university (Anders, 2012; Sanders, Chande, & Selley, 2017). Once ability is accounted for, most of the difference in university entry between students from advantaged and disadvantaged backgrounds is linked to application decisions, with those from disadvantaged backgrounds submitting fewer applications (Anders, 2012).

Personalized messaging is a potential solution to encourage students to apply to university. For example, informing prospective applicants about the university experiences of older students from similar backgrounds could bolster students' motivation to apply. Sanders et al. (2017) tested this approach using a cluster RCT with over 11,000 high school students in the

United Kingdom, where potential applicants learned about university students who shared a similar background and could serve as a role model. Students were randomly assigned to one of four conditions. Students received either (1) a letter addressed to their school from a male student in November, (2) a letter sent to their home from a female student in April, (3) both letters, or (4) no letters at all. Researchers found that receipt of both letters increased a student's chance of applying to a Russell Group university (an elite group of public research universities within the United Kingdom) from 19.9 percent to 23.2 percent and their chance of accepting an offer from a Russell Group university from 8.5 percent to 11.4 percent (Sanders et al., 2017). However, these findings should be interpreted with caution as no statistically significant effects on the overall likelihood of applying were found.

Targeting intrinsic motivation when improving performance

Improving performance by increasing utility value

Fostering students' interest and making education relevant to their lives may be a way to increase their intrinsic motivation and improve learning outcomes. The following examples suggest that targeting the utility value of education could be a useful way to improve engagement and academic performance.

A randomized field experiment conducted among 262 ninth graders tested the effect of an intervention designed to foster interest in and reflection on the relevance of science material to one's life (Hulleman & Harackiewicz, 2009). Students were asked to write either about the value of the course content to their own lives (the treatment group) or a summary of the information covered in their ninth-grade science course (the control group). Students who had lower expectations for their own science performance and who were assigned to make connections between class content and their lives showed an increased interest in science, and in turn, their course grades improved by nearly two-thirds of a letter grade (Hulleman & Harackiewicz, 2009). The intervention had no effect on students who already had higher expectations of succeeding in science.

In another study of 237 undergraduates from an introductory psychology class, Hulleman, Godes, Hendricks, and Harackiewicz (2010) examined the effects of a utility value intervention on students' course grades and interest in the subject. In the middle of a 15-week semester, students in the experimental group wrote two essays depicting the relevance of the course material to their lives, while the control group wrote essays making connections between the course and psychology research. Students' interest in the course and intention to major in psychology was measured at three time points: on the second day, second week, and 13th week of the semester. The study found that the intervention sustained student interest in psychology, especially for individuals with lower grades on the first two exams. At the end of the semester, students with increased perception of utility value were found to have higher final course grades, and those with higher levels of utility value expressed more interest in psychology (Hulleman et al., 2010).

Self-regulatory interventions

The prevalence of self-control failures has resulted in an array of strategies that help people delay gratification and control their impulses in the service of achieving their long-term goals. Self-regulatory behavioral interventions can be particularly helpful in education, as they aim to help students overcome common failures of self-control that result in lack of follow-through on educational goals and intentions (see Box 7.4 on how text message reminders may aid students in their commitment to enroll in university).

In educational contexts, where the return on effort invested in learning is likely to occur far in the future, failures of self-control represent a prominent behavioral barrier. Children and adolescents are particularly sensitive to this as their brains and self-regulatory functions are still developing (Bettinger & Slonim, 2007; Green, Fry, & Myerson, 1994). In this section, we review various behavioral approaches to tackling barriers related to failures of self-control in order to improve educational performance.

Harnessing self-control through prior commitment

One strategy for addressing behavioral barriers related to self-control is to introduce pre-commitment or a commitment device. You may remember **commitment devices** from Chapters 4 and 5, which described their function to deliberately limit future choices by allowing people to voluntarily impose costly restrictions or penalties on themselves for failing to accomplish their goals (Bryan, Karlan, & Nelson, 2010; Rogers, Milkman, & Volpp, 2014). For example, students who want to ensure that they study for an exam may ask a friend to change their Netflix password until they finish the exam.

Commitment devices might be an effective way to address temptations. Duckworth, White, Matteucci, Shearer, and Gross (2016) tested an intervention aimed at improving self-control in 285 high school and university students in two consecutive studies. Participants were asked about a goal they wanted to achieve. In the **situation modification** condition (aimed at changing circumstances to foster self-control), researchers asked students to remove any temptations that might distract them. In the response modulation condition, students received the instruction to exert willpower over temptations. Finally, students in the control condition only had to set a study goal.

Students who were told to proactively remove temptations that might distract them reported increased study quality and were more likely to achieve their goals. Students who were just told to exert willpower over temptations showed no improvement over the control group. For university students, a reduction in temptation partially mediated goal performance in the situation modification intervention, but not in the response modulation intervention (Duckworth et al., 2016). These findings suggest that directly advising students to change their study environment may allow them to be more likely to achieve their study goals.

Another study examined the effects of commitment by comparing student performance across three deadline conditions, where missing the deadline was equally costly for all groups (Ariely & Wertenbroch, 2002). Participants proofread assignments and received monetary rewards based on the number of errors detected. Students were assigned to three conditions: one group had full flexibility to hand in assignments at any time before the final deadline (maximum-flexibility group), another group was assigned interval deadlines (evenly spaced assignment schedule group), and a final group was allowed to set their own deadlines (self-imposed deadline group).

Students in the self-imposed deadline group performed better than students in the maximum-flexibility group. Those following an evenly spaced assignment schedule performed best of all. The results suggest that providing students the ability to pre-commit may improve their performance, but that students themselves may not always be able to set their own optimal commitments.

BOX 7.4 USE OF TECHNOLOGY TO IMPROVE BEHAVIORAL INTERVENTIONS

Technology can be used to enhance or adapt existing behavioral interventions in education. For instance, an intervention that delivered text messages with personalized reminders significantly reduced the number of college-accepted students who failed to matriculate in the fall (also known as the "summer melt"; Castleman & Page, 2015). Building on the rationale underlying this intervention, another study aimed to increase the number of matriculating students by utilizing an artificial intelligence (AI) platform to deliver personalized reminders to students (Page & Gehlbach, 2017). Results showed a 3.3 percentage point increase in enrollments for students who had already committed to attend the university (Page & Gehlbach, 2017). Incorporation of the AI platform – which could recognize familiar student questions and provide relevant responses – into ICTs may further scale the availability of effective behavioral interventions.

Increasing awareness of financial aid availability

Many students from disadvantaged backgrounds in the United States fail to apply to university because they are discouraged by the substantial cost of higher education and are unaware of potential financial aid or lack the means to obtain it (Commission on the Future of Higher Education, 2006). Personalized, timely, and informational interventions may again be a very effective way to address this problem.

In an attempt to increase awareness, the White House Social and Behavioral Sciences Team (SBST) developed an initiative that sent personalized text messages over the summer months reminding low-income, college-accepted high school graduates to complete the necessary tasks to successfully matriculate, including forms for financial aid, before they were due (SBST, 2015). Low-income students in the treatment group were 5.7 percentage points more likely to enroll in college than low-income students in the control group who received no texts (see Figure 7.6). In the broader sample, there was a 3.1 percentage point increase in enrollment.

A test of the same approach with college students to help with their loan repayments had similar results. Over 77,000 students who had missed their first repayment received an email reminding them of their first installment. An additional 22,000 students did not receive the email. After one week, 3.5 percent of students paid their first installment following the email reminder, whereas only 2.7 percent paid without a reminder. Three months later, this modest but meaningful difference still persisted.

As with many behavioral insights, it appears that the provision of useful information targeted at the appropriate population may offer relatively substantial impacts at a low cost. Another intervention targeted low-income individuals who were receiving tax preparation assistance and helped them complete the Free Application for Federal Student Aid (FAFSA) for themselves or their children. In a randomized field experiment, Bettinger et al. (2012) provided low-income students and their families with information about financial aid for college tuition in one of three different forms: a generic brochure; personalized eligibility information; and personalized eligibility information along with direct help with applications. Compared to the first two groups, those in the personalized information and direct

FIGURE 7.6 College enrollment rates among low-income students

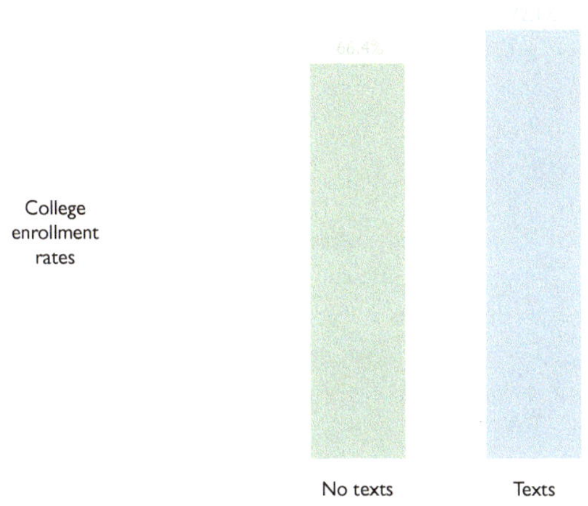

Percentage of lower-income high school seniors matriculating in the following summer with 95 percent confidence intervals.

Source: SBST (2015)

support condition were more likely to apply, receive financial aid, and ultimately attend college. Specifically, college enrollment rates increased from 28 to 36 percent for that group. This intervention was effective because it accelerated the financial aid process, made it more convenient, and provided relevant (yet often hard to access) information.

Technology in education

The examples we have presented so far in this chapter show that social, motivational, and self-regulatory behavioral interventions may help students achieve positive educational outcomes, such as obtaining higher levels of education (e.g. Jukes et al., 2014; Page & Gehlbach, 2017), performing better academically (e. g. Aronson et al., 2002; Cohen et al., 2009), and attending school more often (e.g. Robinson et al., 2018a; Rogers & Feller, 2018). However, limited resources may hinder some students' access to these interventions. One possible solution is to utilize technology to scale interventions. Through the use of technology, we can reach more people, in less time, and in various locations.

As ICTs develop at a rapid pace, there tends to be growing pressure to apply their benefits to modernize schools. However, employment of ICTs can be challenging, particularly in countries where innovations have only started to be introduced in educational settings (McGarr, 2009). Efforts to accelerate the use of technology in schools could be a beneficial way to address several important issues that impact educational success (McGarr, 2009; UNESCO, 2014).

For instance, in many lower- and middle-income countries there tends to be an imbalance between supply and demand of advanced teaching qualifications (UNESCO, 2006), leading to a greater need for more high-quality teachers. ICTs may help teachers obtain better qualifications and facilitate their professional development (Mourshed, Farrell, & Barton, 2013; UNESCO, 2017). ICTs may also enable the professional development of recent graduates, equipping them with the skills required for a competitive job market. Technology can be useful for educational systems in all countries, but the unequal distribution of ICTs and access to digital devices between countries will affect current options and introduces the need for structural development (UNESCO, 2014).

Utilization of technology for educational improvements

Learning management systems (LMS) and other similar tools for active teaching are becoming increasingly popular. These tools may include online curricula, assignments, feedback, and general communication (de Castro e Lima Baesse, Grisolia, & de Oliveira, 2016; Macfadyen & Dawson, 2010). LMS have been used effectively to increase student attendance and reduce course failures by increasing and simplifying communication between teachers and parents (Bergman & Chan, 2019) and facilitating parents' participation in their children's education (Kraft & Rogers, 2015).

But can we explain the effectiveness of LMS by the way in which these systems are implemented? Educational leaders can leverage the power of **defaults** (a predetermined choice that is applied unless an individual deliberately selects another option). For instance, Bergman, Lasky-Fink, and Rogers (2019) developed a field experiment with the parents of 6,976 students to test different ways of implementing a text messaging service informing parents about their child's school performance. Parents were allocated to one of four conditions: a control condition, in which they were not informed of the existence of this service; a standard condition where they were told how to enroll in the text message service; a simplified condition where they could enroll by replying to the text message; or an automatic enrollment condition where parents were automatically enrolled in the service but could choose to opt out (only 5 percent of the parents did so). Students whose parents were in the automatic enrollment condition failed classes less often, had a GPA 0.07 points higher than students in the control group, and failed 0.23 fewer courses, on average (Bergman et al., 2019; see Figure 7.7). There was no significant effect of the other conditions. This suggests that automatic enrollment (with the option to opt out) might be a better approach when implementing new technologies.

ICTs can also allow individuals more freedom to pursue their own educational goals, which may promote individual autonomy and convenience of access with less reliance on active educators or specific settings (de Castro e Lima Baesse et al., 2016). In this category, **massive open online courses (MOOCs)** are made available to a large number of people in multiple geographic locations, often without formal registration, prerequisites for attendance, or assessment. They are increasingly common when it comes to higher education and skill-specific courses, though most of them exist as self-engaging and voluntary. Several studies have shown that the completion rates for MOOCs can be very low, normally estimated to be just under 10 percent (Yeomans & Reich, 2017).

In these cases, learning analytics can be utilized to prompt students about their own planning, goals within the course, and missed assignments, while promoting self-regulation in general (Littlejohn, Hood, Milligan, & Mustain, 2016; Yeomans & Reich, 2017). These provide methods of maintaining students' engagement with their learning, keeping them on the intended trajectory, and giving an overview of their progress. With increased autonomy and the vast number of online distractors, this may be useful for optimizing the benefit of using

FIGURE 7.7 How to implement a text message–based intervention

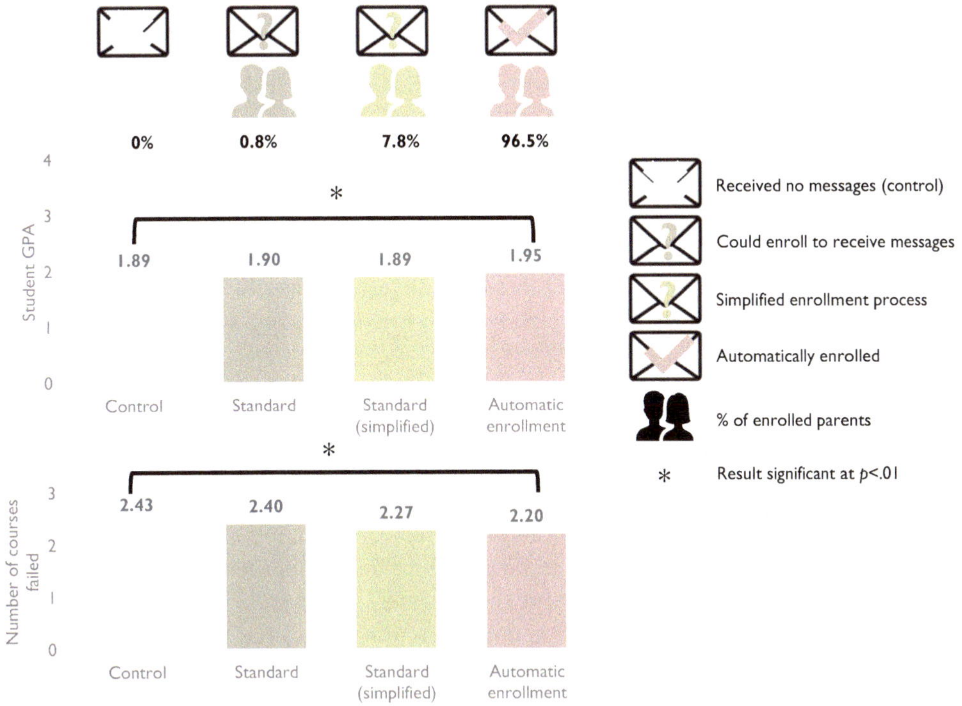

Source: Bergman et al. (2019)

ICTs in education (Littlejohn et al., 2016; Yeomans & Reich, 2017). This kind of pedagogical monitoring can utilize alerts through text messaging, email, and phone calls. They can be both reminders and inquiries about the student's goals, expectations, and participation, with the purpose of helping students follow through on their educational goals (de Castro e Lima Baesse et al., 2016; Saqr, Fors, & Tedre, 2017; Yeomans & Reich, 2017).

de Castro e Lima Baesse et al. (2016) used a continual monitoring system in a **virtual learning environment (VLE)** for public health students. The platform utilized messaging through apps, SMS, and email if the module was not regularly opened. Results showed that the dropout rate for the class in which the system was employed was much lower (30.6 percent) than that for the class that did not employ it (43.2 percent).

Still, it is important to keep in mind that these technologies may also fail to achieve the desired impact. For instance, research on **student facing dashboards** (digital platforms that inform and give feedback to students about their performance relative to others) has found mixed results in terms of their effectiveness (Teasley, 2017). In one case study on student interactions with a digital platform during a first-year engineering course, Khan and Pardo (2016) found no significant effect of frequency of dashboard usage on midterm scores.

Similarly, in another study, researchers gave students a summer bridge program (a program aimed at reducing retention and promoting academic success in at-risk populations in postsecondary education) access to an online dashboard with information about their engagement, performance, and relative standing among their peers (Lonn, Aguilar,

& Teasley, 2015. Researchers found that throughout the program there was a significant decrease in students' **mastery goal orientation** (a tendency to focus on competence and task mastery, also referred to as growth mindset; Lonn et al., 2015). This decrease was associated with how often students reported viewing the platform with data about their performance and how they compared to others (Lonn et al., 2015).

A general and important note on the use of technology: ICTs should be seen as a means of enhancing and supporting traditional education – not replacing it (de Jong, Linn, & Zacharia, 2013; Smetana & Bell, 2012). Teachers' and students' attitudes toward ICTs in education may not always be positive (Adukaite, van Zyl, Er, & Cantoni, 2017; Agudo-Peregrina, Hernández-García, & Pascual-Miguel, 2014; Artino, 2010; El-Masri & Tarhini, 2017; Lochner, Conrad, & Graham, 2015), thus making ICTs a potential behavioral barrier themselves. This means a **blended learning** approach, where both face to face and **e-learning** (a teaching and study method utilizing web-based platforms for various classes) are used, may be necessary to meet the needs of all participants.

Conclusion

In this chapter, we reviewed several common barriers in education and provided examples of how we can use behavioral insights to tackle them. Behavioral insights may offer simple and inexpensive solutions for helping students, parents, and teachers overcome barriers at every step of the educational process. It is important to acknowledge that many of the challenges in education are systemic and reflect structural inequalities or prejudices that cannot be addressed effectively by low-cost behavioral interventions. Behavioral insights are not a silver bullet, but an opportunity to augment more comprehensive educational reforms and improve student success.

In light of the evidence presented here, policy initiatives may be more effective if they leverage low-cost, scalable interventions that can overcome specific, relevant barriers. Although the evidence is promising in terms of producing positive changes, it is important to remain cautious of the current limitations of behavioral approaches.

For instance, when applying behavioral interventions to students, educators need to consider whether certain interventions are developmentally appropriate for the targeted population. While certain behavioral interventions may work for adults, they may not be appropriate for children and adolescents – especially if they are not in a position to act meaningfully. For example, text message reminders to complete an assignment may be an effective strategy for adults but not for elementary school students (Chande et al., 2017), and commitment devices may improve high school and university students' performance, but not that of middle schoolers (Robinson, Lee, Dearing, & Rogers, 2018b).

In addition, the cost-effectiveness and scalability of these behavioral interventions are factors that we need to take into consideration when interpreting the magnitude of effect sizes (Kraft, 2019). Low-cost and highly scalable interventions with modest effect sizes may be worth the investment. Finally, practitioners and policymakers need to be informed when interpreting the results of the increasing number of behavioral interventions in education, as some of these interventions may only work for a subset of people and/or in specific settings (Hanselman, Rozek, Grigg, & Borman, 2016). The increasing number of studies with pre-registered hypotheses testing the effectiveness of behavioral insights (Gehlbach & Robinson, 2018) could be a useful tool for consumers aiming to make an impact at a larger scale.

Ultimately, behavioral insights may offer a powerful addition to ensuring high-quality and lifelong education. While many behavioral interventions target relatively small changes, when successful these may lead to a range of significant and positive outcomes. As we have discussed, these outcomes may include reducing social inequalities, promoting economic growth, and increasing earnings (UNESCO, 2011), but they may also come in the form of improved health and well-being as well as improved social mobility (Campbell et al., 2014; Lochner, 2011). With such a powerful role in the lives of individuals, communities, and populations, there is certainly more room to explore the potential impact of applying behavioral insights to educational contexts.

Essay questions

1 Discuss the relative strengths and weaknesses of using behavioral interventions in education to reduce the current SES inequalities in educational outcomes.

2 Can you think of a general or specific issue in education that could not be resolved by behavioral insights?

3 Alternatively, think about a problem in education that *could* be solved through a behavioral insight but is currently neglected. How would you design a study addressing this problem?

4 There are several different actors in education, including students, educators, parents, and administrators. Explain how you would approach these actors, in similar and different ways, using a specific behavioral insight.

5 What are the challenges of implementing behavioral insights related to technology in educational practice?

Note

1 This chapter has been adapted from Ruggeri, K., Hlavová, R., Lind Andersen, T., Evans, H., Mareva, S., & Robinson, C. D. (2019). Education. In K. Ruggeri (Ed.), *Behavioral insights for public policy: Concepts and cases* (pp. 131–155). New York and London: Routledge.

Additional insights and further reading

Summary of behavioral interventions in postsecondary education

Ideas42. (2016). *Nudging for success: Using behavioral science to improve the postsecondary student journey*. Retrieved from http://bit.ly/2dy9C3S

The effectiveness of different nudges in education

Damgaard, M. T., & Nielsen, H. S. (2018). Nudging in education. *Economics of Education Review*, *64*, 313–342. https://doi.org/10.1016/j.econedurev.2018.03.008

Growth mindset predicts educational outcomes

Claro, S., Paunesku, D., & Dweck, C. S. (2016). Growth mindset tempers the effects of poverty on academic achievement. *Proceedings of the National Academy of Sciences, 113*, 8664–8668. https://doi.org/10.1073/pnas.1608207113

Habits and beliefs guiding self-regulated learning vary with mindset

Yan, V. X., Thai, K., & Bjork, R. A. (2014). Habits and beliefs that guide self-regulated learning: Do they vary with mindset? *Journal of Applied Research in Memory and Cognition, 3*(Cognition and Education), 140–152. https://doi.org/10.1016/j.jarmac.2014.04.003

Key factors explaining e-learning satisfaction among high school teachers

Cheok, M. L., & Wong, S. L. (2015). Predictors of e-learning satisfaction in teaching and learning for school teachers: A literature review. *International Journal of Instruction, 8*(1), 75–90.

Success in integrating technology remains restricted by several obstacles

Derbel, F. (2017). Technology-capable teachers transitioning to technology-challenged schools. *The Electronic Journal of E-Learning, 15*(3), 269–280. Retrieved from www.ejel.org

Attitudes, subjective norms, and self-efficacy as predictors of teachers' intention to use digital learning materials

Kreijns, K., Van Acker, F., Vermeulen, M., & Van Buuren, H. (2013). What stimulates teachers to integrate ICT in their pedagogical practices? The use of digital learning materials in education. *Computers in Human Behavior, 29*(1), 217–225. https://doi.org/10.1016/j.chb.2012.08.008

Students' perceptions of systems influence their intention to use e-learning systems

Moreno, V., Cavazotte, F., & Alves, I. (2017). Explaining university students' effective use of e-learning platforms. *British Journal of Educational Technology, 48*, 995–1009. https://doi.org/10.1111/bjet.12469

Improving academic performance in children using metacognitive self-regulatory strategies

Duckworth, A. L., Kirby, T. A., Gollwitzer, A., & Oettingen, G. (2013). From fantasy to action: Mental contrasting with implementation intentions (MCII) improves academic performance in children. *Social Psychological and Personality Science, 4*, 745–753. https://doi.org/10.1177/1948550613476307

Handy Tools

Free version of the get-to-know-you survey for teachers to use
https://backtoschool.panoramaed.com/

8 Work and workplace decision-making

Ralitsa Karakasheva, Jascha Achterberg,
Jana B. Berkessel, Alessia Cottone, Julia Dhar,
Jon M. Jachimowicz, Yuna S. M. Lee, Ashley Whillans,
and Kai Ruggeri

Acknowledgments: Ludvig Bjørndal

Chapter summary

Work is a major part of many of our lives. While individual experiences with work will differ – from how long we work to what jobs we have and to what extent we enjoy them – everyone is affected by employment, whether they have a job or not. Over the decades, research in the behavioral sciences has focused specifically on the workplace, dating back to some of the most influential studies in psychology. Given the wealth of accumulated research, a tremendous opportunity now exists to link theory and results to successful interventions. This chapter introduces several approaches to workplace interventions and looks at how certain tools such as commitment devices, nudges, personalized incentives, framing, and even the physical environment itself may lead to better outcomes for employees and organizations. We present these interventions as opportunities for change, from the earliest steps in finding a new job through the later stages of career progression. We consider not only job performance but also the health and well-being of employees, employers, and the communities they serve.

Learning objectives

- Identify major topics in workplaces for the behavioral sciences
- Understand how behavioral insights can ensure a fairer and more effective recruitment process
- Understand how behavioral interventions may boost performance at work
- Understand how healthier behavior can be encouraged and how incidents can be prevented
- Learn how behavioral insights can be applied to promote retirement savings

Introduction

The roots of experimental psychology are closely intertwined with the earliest psychological research in the workplace, a field then referred to as applied psychology. This work largely started in Wilhelm Wundt's laboratory in Leipzig, Germany, and William James's experimental rooms at Harvard University in the nineteenth century (Landy, 1997). Some of the most

DOI: 10.4324/9781003181873-8

insightful and enduring findings from that era continue to influence our thinking today. Among them is the **Hawthorne effect** (also known as the "observer effect"), which suggests that individuals may change their behavior simply as a result of being observed (Muchinsky, 2005; Roethlisberger & Dickson, 1939). It has its origin in a series of experiments conducted at the Hawthorne Works in Cicero, Illinois, which investigated whether the working environment influenced worker productivity. Since then, the relevance of the workplace and its complexity have demanded careful experimentation and behavioral insights.

It is especially important to understand workplace behavior given that we spend a substantial portion of our lives at work. The average working German aged between 18 and 64 years spends more than three times as much time working as engaging in hobbies or sports (Statistisches Bundesamt, 2017). In 2015, the Association of Accounting Technicians found that the average British person spends 47 years of their life working, which is considerably more than half of an average lifetime (AAT, 2015). Much of what we do at work is challenging and has direct consequences for us as employees, our families, our colleagues, our communities, and our organizations. Similarly, the spectrum of activities at work ranges from different social behaviors (like collaborating, competing, or communicating), to deciding whom to recruit, promote, or fire, to the influence of how we feel at work, to the decision to quit a company and go work somewhere else.

In this intricate patchwork, behavioral insights have much to offer toward developing the means and ends of evidence-based workplace interventions to foster productivity and support employees. In some cases, this may require complex exploration of nuanced aspects of each workplace and individual, whereas in others it may be as direct as finding ways to give employees greater autonomy (Ne Gagné & Deci, 2005). In particular, if we look at the general structure of the workplace as the basic point of action for workplace interventions, transformation of the mere physical environment alone may have an impact on behavior (Leaman & Bordass, 1999; Spreitzer, Garrett, & Bacevice, 2015; Burt, 2004). Interventions with regard to workflow and the procedures of work also offer possibilities for improvements. Examples of these could include goal formulation (Locke, Shaw, Saari, & Latham, 1981; Locke & Latham, 2002) or task-switching behavior (Lu, Akinola, & Mason, 2017; Becker, Alzahabi, & Hopwood, 2013).

Where health and stress management supports employees and thus can help organizations to reach their goals (Hourani, Williams, & Kress, 2006; Chandola, Brunner, & Marmot, 2006), good recruitment processes may help to avoid the occurrence of problems by providing a good employee-employer fit in the first place (Schneider, 1987; Chatman, 1991). Additionally, task structures, perceptions of acknowledgment, and incentives can influence the perceived meaning in work and thus the motivation and productivity of employees (Ariely, Kamenica, & Prlec, 2008; Bareket-Bojmel, Hochman, & Ariely, 2017).

Given how critical working, seeking work, and the workplace itself are in the life of an employee, this chapter presents behavioral insights that can play an important role in solving everyday challenges. From the first steps of selection and recruitment to the final stage of one's working career, we will follow employees over their entire career path. To begin with, improvements in recruitment and selection through knowledge gained from behavioral studies could increase job satisfaction through a better employer-employee fit, benefiting both employers and employees. In addition, significant steps could be made toward a fairer recruitment process and creating and sustaining a more diverse workforce. Once employees are already working, interventions can be implemented to increase productivity through monetary and nonmonetary incentives. Regarding employee health, employers may not only promote healthy behavior and prevent incidents but also apply behavioral insights to help

FIGURE 8.1 Working life timeline

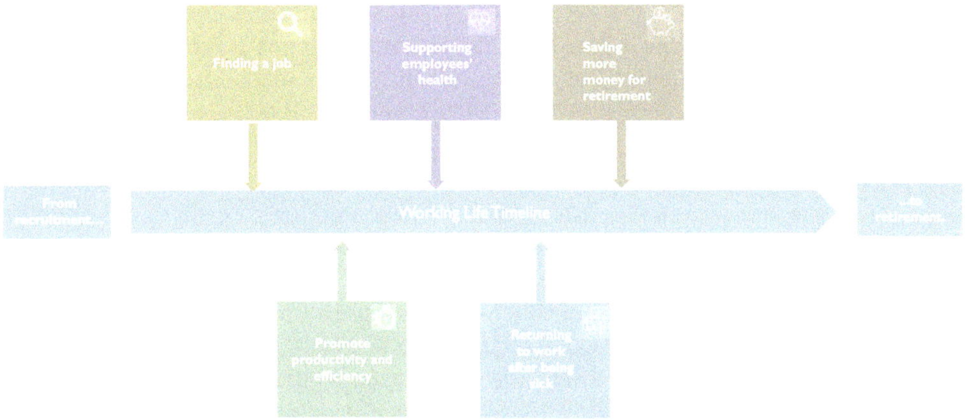

Timeline overview over the chapter (from recruitment to retirement)

those who already suffer from a long-term condition return to work faster after recovery. Last but not least, behavioral insights can be successfully applied to stimulate the accumulation of savings by employees to make sure that they have the financial means to retire after their careers.

Behavioral insights for successful job-seeking and recruitment

Job-seeking can be a long and arduous process. Oftentimes individuals may be under pressure to secure a job if they are unemployed. Behavioral insights can thus be applied to improve the job-seeking journey. However, policymakers should not only want to increase job-seekers' engagement with the process but also seek ways to ensure that the recruitment journey is fair. Undoubtedly, fair recruitment of candidates can benefit all parties involved. For instance, Herring (2009) found a 3 to 9 percent increase in an organization's revenue for every 1 percent increase in the gender and ethnic diversity of its workforce.

Taking this lead, the Behavioral Insights Team in the UK designed a platform (called "Be Applied") to help organizations find the best candidates on the basis of their talents by reducing the influence of different biases that could be at play. For example, specific features could be used such as anonymizing applications, randomizing the order of applications, and using work sample–based assessments. However, despite new advancements in the field of recruitment, challenges remain. In the following examples, we illuminate how behavioral science can be applied to increase job-seekers' engagement with the search process and increase fairness during recruitment.

Increasing job-matching service use through nudging

The Government of Canada developed a national service to connect job-seekers with employers, known as Job Match (OECD, 2017j). This service matches specific job-seeker profile criteria (skills, education, experience, and location) with job postings requiring similar criteria on Job Bank. One of the challenges for the service was the struggle to increase its total number of accounts created (OECD, 2017j). About 750,000 people visited its pages per week, but only some of them followed the link that was provided to Job Match and created a profile. Over a five-month period in 2015, the Government of Canada attempted to increase the number of clicks on the link to their webpage and therefore increase the number of accounts created by implementing different nudges on the job posting pages. Each nudge was presented on a rotating weekly basis and was reintroduced at least three times during the period. Nudges came in the form of either social norms or framing. Other nudges tested were a **sense of commitment** and a **call to action** combined with **salience.**

Nudges generated between 67 and 122 percent more clicks than a control posting, depending on the nudge. Additionally, those who clicked on a nudge on a Job Bank job posting page had a higher probability of creating an account once they went to the Job Match website. These results are compared to those who saw only the control posting, which did not contain any nudges but otherwise had the same appearance. The analysis demonstrated that the nudging intervention had a persistent effect on Job Bank users. Given the wide sample of 750,000 participants, sustained effects from such an intervention have clear implications for improving labor market effectiveness.

Even though the first approach was effective at increasing the creation of accounts, many users did not go on to complete and activate their profiles. Out of the registered users, approximately 50 percent had only partially completed profiles. Over a two-month period in 2015, Job Match administrators attempted to increase the rate of completion by introducing emails that either used **social norms** or **framing**. For example, the email containing the social norm nudge said, "Thousands of Canadians have already completed their Job Match profiles and are being matched to new job opportunities." Other versions of the email used a sense of commitment or a call to action/salience. For instance, to increase commitment some participants read "You are only one step away from being matched with an employer looking for your skills and experience" and were then presented with positive options such as "I want to find a new job" or "I already have a Job Seeker Account" (Audet, Gascon, Rahbar, & Soliman, 2017). A RCT was carried out with 3,784 users with incomplete accounts, each of whom received one of five different emails (four experimental groups, one control; 757 users per condition on average). Intervention groups were 77 percent more likely to respond to the email by following the link than those in the control group. On average, 43 profiles were completed for each of the intervention groups, compared to only 21 in the control (an increase of 106 percent). The overall differences between the intervention groups were not statistically significant, so all nudges had rather similar effects. This experiment suggests that behavioral insights may offer multiple simple and cost-effective ways to increase the use of government programs.

Improving the consultancy process to boost job-seeker commitment

One innovative intervention includes a behavioral approach that the Ministry of Manpower (MoM) in Singapore has effectively developed. The service offers career centers to motivate and support unemployed citizens to find work (OECD, 2017j). While analyzing its consultancy process, the ministry observed poor commitment, passive behavior, and a lack of motivation and self-esteem in individuals who used its career center services. A revised process was needed to better support these job-seekers. The consultancy process was redesigned by implementing behavioral insights, and the intervention was then evaluated by randomly allocating career consultants to a treatment (new consultancy process) or a control group (old consultancy process). The new consultancy process included four changes: a **commitment device**, **chunking**, an **incentive**, and **social norms** or **priming**.

The commitment device is a means to avoid procrastination while supporting self-control by making a commitment visible and the promise credible. In this case, job-seekers signed the top page of a job booklet they received in the first meeting with their consultant. By performing this small action, job-seekers committed themselves to the task of finding employment.

The second element in the intervention by the MoM was chunking, a strategy that consists of breaking down the bulky job search process into smaller, more manageable pieces with the aim of raising the individual's perceived ability. The incentive was designed to motivate job-seekers by rewarding individuals who either successfully attended five sessions with their consultant or found a job by giving them a SG$100 voucher. Finally, messaging and visual cues in the form of pictures on the wall of the consultant's room were used to convey social norms and prime the job-seekers (subtle motivational messages).

The integrated redesign resulted in a significant increase of the rate of placements. While the control group had a success rate of 32 percent, superior results were observed for the treatment group with a 49 percent employment rate (see Figure 8.2). While no conclusions were offered regarding which of the four interventions had the greatest impact, this case study suggests that both the career center and the job-seeker can potentially benefit from a general redesign of the consultancy process on the basis of behavioral insights. The government of Singapore reported a rise in the ownership and morale of job-seekers with rather minor changes to their program.

FIGURE 8.2 Improving the consultancy process

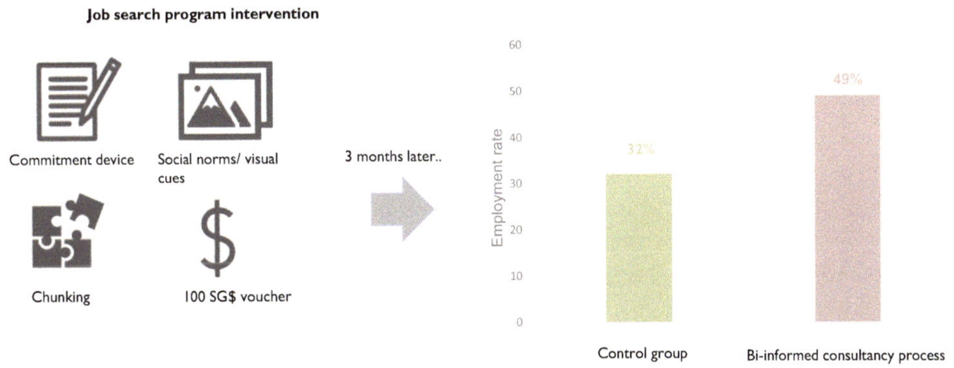

A depiction of a study from the Ministry of Manpower in Singapore OECD, 2017j).

Increasing fairness in the recruitment process

One primary objective of occupational psychologists is to ensure a fair recruitment process, which translates into having a more diverse and effective workforce. Numerous studies have investigated the impact of unconscious bias on the fairness of the recruitment process. Laboratory experiments have demonstrated that cues in the applicants' résumés (also known as *curriculum vitae* or CV) can have a strong impact on the rating of the suitability of the applicant. For example, in an experiment in the Netherlands, Derous, Ryan, and Nguyen (2011) manipulated the applicant names to be either or Arab or Dutch and asked the participants to rate suitability of each for a pre-selected job. Suitability ratings for job applicants with the minority name were significantly lower than those of the nonminority applicants.

Because the information enclosed in an CV often signals personal characteristics that may lead to discrimination, one proposed intervention to tackle this problem has been to anonymize job applications. Åslund and Skans (2012) analyzed the data from a government pilot project initiated by the city council of Gothenburg, Sweden. Two districts volunteered to implement the anonymous job application screening procedure. A third district, where the screening process remained unchanged, was selected on a nonrandom basis as a comparison group. In the new anonymous procedure, applicants had to complete a specifically designed form that did not reveal any information regarding ethnicity or gender. Applicants were also asked to submit their CV separately from the form. Recruitment managers had to invite applicants to an interview on the basis of the information given in the anonymous form. Once filtered, recruitment managers could see the CVs of the applicants who were invited for an interview.

Under the standard application process, females and non-Westerners had significantly lower probabilities of being invited for an interview than under the anonymous job application condition. However, when it came to actual job offers, only female applicants showed a significant increase in the probability of receiving an offer. The difference between the comparison and anonymous job application conditions was nonsignificant for non-Western applicants. When evaluating the effectiveness of the intervention, the authors noted that although the intervention could improve the CV screening procedure, in the anonymous job application condition there were fewer applicants on average. One interpretation is that this may stem from the added effort of adjusting one's application to the strict criteria. Additionally, the researchers did not have any guidance or input regarding the job interview procedures. Thus, this intervention could further benefit from applying behavioral insights to the interview stage as well.

It is important to address unconscious bias and stereotyping in the selection process. However, recruitment is a two-sided process; thus, interventions should also take into account the effect that stereotypes have on applicants when it comes to their motivation to apply for a particular job. Previous studies have shown that stereotype threats negatively affect the performance of minority groups, as they may increase anxiety (Linos, Reinhard, & Ruda, 2017).

A RCT in the United Kingdom conducted by Linos et al. (2017) attempted to use mechanisms from **self-affirmation theory** to increase the diversity of police officer applicants through the use of an online situational judgment test. Applicants that passed the first stage of selection received the test link attached to an email, which was designed to reduce the anxiety of underrepresented groups. The test contained several manipulations: there was an absence of any anxiety-provoking material (for instance, technical specifications were presented at the end of the test rather than at the beginning); positive sentences were included (such as "Good luck!" and "Congratulations"). In addition, the participants in the experimental condition were asked to think about what it meant for them and their community to be a police officer, so that their social identity and sense of belonging were activated. As a result, non-white participants in the treatment group were 21 percent more likely to pass the test than non-white applicants in the control group.

On the other hand, no significant change was observed for white participants exposed to the treatment condition, indicating that the intervention specifically targeted the minority group and significantly lowered the racial gap. Although this study had significant results, it is important to highlight that it analyzed the cumulative effect of different framing mechanisms. Future studies should isolate single manipulations to disentangle their influence. Additionally, it is not yet known whether increased diversity is maintained during successive application stages, such as interviews and assessment centers.

Behavioral Insights for productivity and efficiency

Targets and incentives

The desire to increase productivity and efficiency is a fundamental goal for companies in order to be competitive and stay in the market. A common technique used by employers to increase productivity and efficiency is to reward employees for their effort or for reaching

FIGURE 8.3 Overview of incentives as behavioral tools

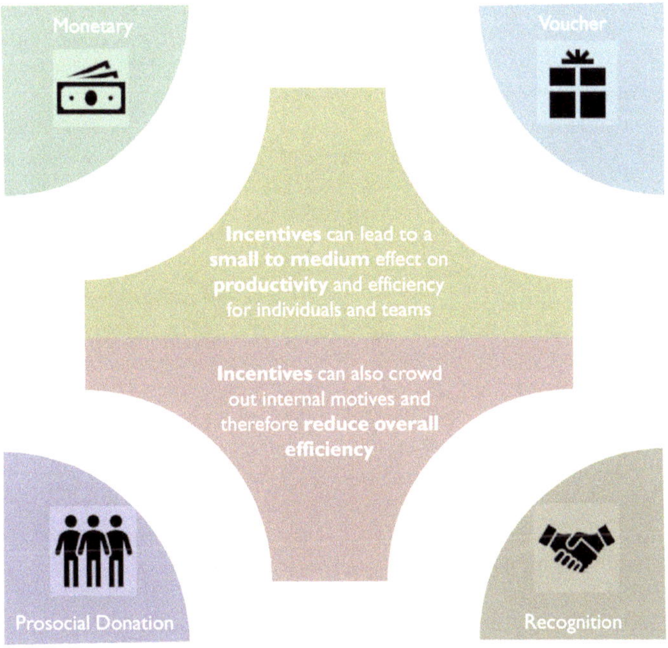

a predefined goal. Traditionally, employers have relied on monetary rewards to boost productivity; however, as the behavioral insights field develops, we are seeing that individual differences such as personal motives come into play and may impact individuals' reaction to a monetary reward (Frey & Goette, 1999). For this reason, researchers have begun to investigate whether alternative tools such as nonmonetary rewards and professional recognition can be used to boost productivity.

Brief review of financial incentives in the workplace

Financial incentives play a large role in the workplace as rewarding workers financially often tends to have a positive effect on performance. In a meta-analysis of 146 studies with a total sample of over 30,000 participants, Garbers and Konradt (2013) observed that financial incentives on average have a positive influence on performance. The authors found a small-to-medium effect size for individuals and teams across a wide variety of studies. However, they also noted the effect of certain moderators, such that financial incentives seemed to have a larger positive impact on teams and for more complicated tasks. Such nuances should be considered whenever incentives are implemented as a behavioral tool (see Box 8.1).

BOX 8.1 SPECIAL FACTORS TO CONSIDER WHEN IMPLEMENTING INCENTIVES

Incentives can be a powerful tool; however, situational factors and individual differences may also come into play when it comes to predicting the behavioral reaction to an incentive. Those factors should be carefully considered when designing the reward system in a company. The following examples illustrate areas in which such complex interactions are observed.

Interaction with personal motives: Studies have highlighted that different types of motives (internal and external) are not additive-separable but interfere with each other (see Chapter 6 for further discussion). This conflict of motives can be found in psychological literature (Deci et al., 1999) and is known as **motivation crowding theory** in economics. For instance, one study found that paying volunteers a small amount of money was associated with a 16% decrease in volunteer time compared to not paying them at all (Frey & Goette, 1999).

Rewards in teams: The choice of the right incentives becomes more complicated when designing them for teams. Garbers and Konradt (2013) use a meta-analysis to conclude that equitably distributed rewards tend to result in a more positive effect than equally distributed rewards within teams. Additionally, the labor economics literature highlights that relative rewards within a team seem to increase effort and efficiency but may also harm voluntary cooperation (Irlenbusch & Ruchala, 2008; Carpenter, Bowles, Gintis, & Hwang, 2009).

"Free nudges" might do the job just as well: Application of financial incentives to induce desired behaviors comes with the additional costs of paying the incentives. This may ultimately make them less cost-effective, given that another intervention may have the same effect without providing the incentive. For example, a study by the National Bureau of Economic Research (NBER) conducted in the UK highlights that just giving out information or setting goals by default can have a similar effect on employee behavior as when incentives are present (Gosnell, List, & Metcalfe, 2016).

While financial incentives certainly offer behavioral insights, they are typically treated as their own tool and not considered, for example, as nudges (see Selinger & Whyte, 2012). This is because implementation of a financial incentive fundamentally changes the trade-off of a decision. The principle of libertarian paternalism (see Chapter 3) posits that external factors will influence decisions even though they are not relevant to the possible options. For example, one might decide to eat healthier just because of how food is arranged in the cafeteria, even though the options per se stay the same. While the rearrangement of food would clearly classify as a nudge, the implementation of an incentive (e.g. lowering the cost of healthier foods) essentially changes the relative values and thus the trade-off between the options.

Regardless of their classification, a consistent trend can be observed across studies of financial incentives: they already play an important role in the workplace and they tend to have a positive effect. Therefore, it is worthwhile for students new to the field to have a look at the interventions.

Prosocial incentives and target setting for efficient behavior

The ability to meet targets and manage resources efficiently are crucial for organizations, especially when resources are costly and damage the environment. One such type of resource is fuel. The consumption of jet fuel is not only a major cost factor for airlines but also a burden on the environment. In a field experiment, Virgin Atlantic Airways partnered with the NBER to check whether behavioral insights could be used to make pilots save fuel (Gosnell et al., 2016). A total number of 335 pilots were split into three experimental groups and one control group. A baseline measurement of fuel-related behavior at three time points (before takeoff, during the flight, and post-landing) was collected as well. Pilots in the first group received only feedback about their fuel efficiency at the three different time points. The second group received feedback and a personalized goal for saving fuel. Pilots in the third group received the feedback and the personalized goal for reduced fuel consumption, and they were offered an additional prosocial incentive for reaching the goal (for every goal reached the company would donate £10 to a charity of the captain's choice); the fourth group was a control group. Although this group did not receive any feedback, pilots in this group were aware that their behavior was being monitored.

The results showed that pilots in the feedback condition did not reduce their fuel consumption before takeoff or during the flight, compared to the control group. However, pilots in this experimental condition managed fuel consumption significantly more efficiently once they had landed. In contrast, pilots who received feedback and a personalized goal had significantly lower fuel consumption at all three points of measurement compared to the control group. However, there was no significant difference between the feedback and personalized goal group and those in the condition in which a prosocial incentive was introduced as well. One interpretation of these results is that addition of the prosocial incentive to the target setting did not significantly contribute to increasing fuel efficiency. In other words, the data suggests that the prosocial incentive was not effective in motivating pilots to save fuel. These results could be used for future implementations as they highlight that use of appropriate targets might be sufficient to reach the desired outcomes and that specific rewards are not necessarily needed.

At the end of the experiment the authors also provided rough estimates of the fuel that was saved over the course of the trial. According to the calculations, groups were able to save roughly between 266,000 and 704,000 kg of fuel altogether, which corresponds to savings of between $209,000 and $553,000 for the airline. Another interesting observation made by the authors was the presence of a possible Hawthorne effect, as the control group pilots started to save fuel as soon as they were informed that there would be a study taking place.

Short-term incentives: monetary vs. nonmonetary

What about other kinds of incentives and rewards for increasing employee productivity? Until now we have only considered incentives that are linked to a certain amount of money, whether given to the worker directly (financial incentive) or to a charity of the worker's choice (prosocial incentive). To determine whether nonmonetary incentives also work as short-term incentives, Bareket-Bojmel et al. (2017) conducted a field experiment at a manufacturing plant for high-tech semiconductors in Israel. They compared the effect of different incentives on the productivity of 156 employees, divided into four experimental groups. A baseline measurement captured the productivity of employees three weeks before the trial. The researchers tested four types of bonuses: $25 in cash, a voucher for a family meal (worth roughly $25), and a letter from the senior manager. Participants in the fourth condition were offered a choice between the voucher and the cash incentive.

Researchers found that, on the day in which employees were given the chance to earn a bonus, higher productivity was observed in the conditions where cash incentive, meal voucher and recognition letter were provided. There was no significant difference between those three conditions. Additionally, there was no change in productivity when the incentives were removed from the letter and choice groups, while productivity decreased in the conditions where a cash incentive and meal voucher were used. These findings suggest that managers may have to consider a wide variety of tools to reward employees, depending on whether they want to achieve a short-term or a sustained impact. Additionally, different types of rewards may be have to be used to produce different outcomes (e.g. increasing productivity vs. reducing staff turnover).

Professional recognition as an incentive

While incentives have primarily been discussed in terms of their effect on productivity and efficiency, research highlights that incentives can influence a wide range of variables that should be considered when implementing incentives. These spillover effects can take the negative shape of harming cooperation (see Box 8.1), but they can also bring additional positive effects. Casini, Hubert, and Kaelen (2016) presented a case for professional recognition being a protective factor against burnout (relating to the verbal incentive in the previous case study). Professional recognition is defined by researchers as acknowledgment of skills and qualities coming from colleagues, superiors, or other parties within the organization. To investigate whether professional recognition might be a protective factor against burnout, the researchers administered an online questionnaire to 326 workers, which consisted of the Professional Recognition Scale and the Oldenburg Burnout Inventory (OLBI). Casini et al. (2016) found a strong negative relationship between recognition and burnout. Additionally, correlational studies suggested that professional recognition predicts low turnover intent among nursing staff (Abualrub & Al-Zaru, 2008). Even though this study is correlational and results should be interpreted with caution, these results are consistent with those of Bareket-Bojmel et al. (2017) and suggest that nonmonetary rewards in the form of receiving recognition for one's effort are well-received by employees.

Behavioral insights for maintaining employee health and well-being

As working adults tend to spend more time at work than anywhere else, the workplace environment may potentially have a large impact on employee mental and physical health (ENWHP, 1997), which may in turn impact employee performance. For instance, one major factor that creates risks for employee well-being are low levels of physical activity. Low levels of physical activity contribute to the development of cardiovascular diseases, obesity, and type 2 diabetes (Booth, Roberts, & Laye, 2012). Though the WHO advises that adults aged 18 to 64 years should commit to 30 minutes of moderate physical activity at least five days a week (WHO, 2010), office-based employees lead an increasingly sedentary lifestyle. One study found that employees of a UK-based university spend up to 71 percent of their work time in a sedentary position (Clemes, O'Connell, & Edwardson, 2014). Therefore, considerable effort has been put into exploring how behavioral insights can be used to prevent unhealthy behavior in the workplace.

Workplace safety is another major area of concern to employers, governments, and insurers. Figures show that during 2016 and 2017, over 600,000 cases of self-reported, non-fatal, workplace injuries were registered in the United Kingdom alone. It is estimated that for 2015–2016, workplace injuries have cost the British economy 5.3 billion pounds (HSE, 2017). Previously, behavioral insights were mainly used to prevent accidents. However, recent evidence suggests that behavioral insights can be used to facilitate and speed up the process of returning to work after a long-term sick leave. The following section will discuss how behavioral insights can be used in the field of employee well-being.

Effective workload management

Heavy workload has been reported as a predictor of burnout and poor employee mental health (de Beer, Pienaar, & Rothmann, 2015). All employers have a duty to ensure that their work environment is not causing adverse psychological or physical effects on their employees. However, extra care should be taken when employees are dealing with vulnerable individuals, such as patients, as errors in judgment may occur.

In 2016, the British National Health Service faced a serious problem: wait times for seeing a specialist sometimes exceeded a year, and it was largely due to mismanagement. One major factor contributing to this mismanagement was the way available options were presented to general practitioners (GPs) when referring patients on. When a GP searched online for a specialist, nearly 100 options would be automatically generated, resulting in a presentation format that was extremely difficult to navigate for optimal management. To address this, Hallsworth and Burd (2018) attempted a behavioral RCT. In the experimental group, slight changes were introduced into the e-referral system that GPs used in one hospital that volunteered to participate. The changes aimed to present the available options in a comparative fashion based on waiting times and location. The first change included displaying three local clinics at the top of the screen highlighted in green. This indicated that wait times for these options were short. The remaining options were listed below in a separate box. The options that had an exceptionally long wait time were marked with the label "Limited capacity" in red. If a doctor still opted for one of the options in red, a pop-up message appeared on the screen warning of the long wait time. The results suggested that there was a significant reduction in the selection of clinics with a long wait time when the options were labelled as Limited capacity. Referrals to those options dropped from 11.6 percent in the control group to 7.1 percent in the experimental group. However, highlighting of options with short wait times in green did not lead to a significant increase in their selection.

In a follow-up study, the same authors reapplied these principles to both GPs and their patients. Patients were nudged via an online app in which referrals were made directly. This time, the authors observed that referrals to the clinics with long wait times were 20 percent lower for the experimental group than for the control group. Additionally, referrals to the options with short wait times increased by 14 percent when they were positioned at the top of the screen and highlighted in green. The authors also estimated that if the intervention was applied on a national level, up to 40,000 referrals per month could be redirected to healthcare providers who have the capacity to treat patients faster.

Increasing physical activity at work

For myriad reasons, on-site gyms are not a realistic option for most organizations. As an alternative, Thomas and Williams (2006) investigated whether providing employees with **pedometers** and daily **reminders** about achieving a goal of 10,000 steps per day would increase employee physical activity levels. In the first week of the intervention, the daily step counts of over 1,000 employees were recorded via pedometers as a baseline measure. From the second week onward, employees had a daily goal of reaching 10,000 steps and received regular reminder emails. The results revealed that during the fourth week of the intervention, employees were 10 percent more active compared to baseline (Figure 8.4). Additionally, there was a

FIGURE 8.4 Making employees more physically active

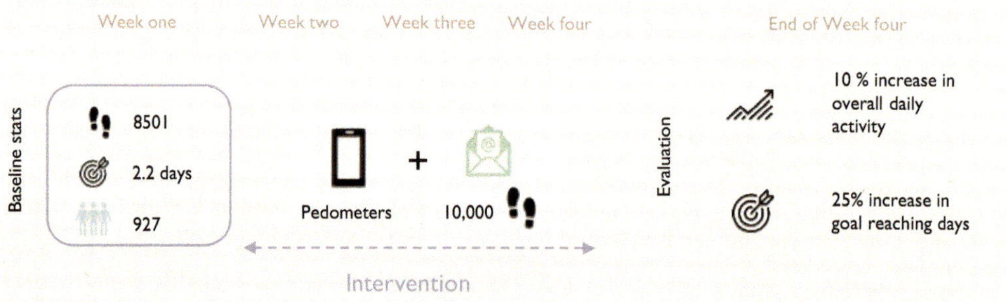

Source: Thomas and Williams (2006)

25 percent increase in the number of days in which employees achieved their goal compared to the baseline measurement. Notably, those who had the lowest physical activity levels were the ones who showed the largest increase. These results are important as they override one of the major limitations of physical activity interventions: that they work only for those who are already active. The follow-up study also revealed that after three months, 63 percent of employees had retained or further increased their physical activity levels, suggesting that the intervention may have been effective in producing sustained increases in activity.

Another study by Venema, Kroese, and De Ridder (2017) investigated how a change in the **default** option may encourage to increase the use of a sit-stand desk in the standing position. Sit-stand desks are workstations that can be easily converted into standing desks, thus providing employees an opportunity to spend less time in a sedentary, seated position (we note such desks have shown limited benefits in research so far; Pronk, Katz, Lowry, & Payfer, 2012). One of the main reasons is the effort required for converting the desk to the standing position (Wilks, Mortimer, & Nylén, 2006). The intervention implemented by Venema et al. (2017) consisted of changing the default position of all sit-stand desks by converting them to the standing position. The results (Figure 8.5) revealed that, during the

FIGURE 8.5 Reducing sedentary time among employees

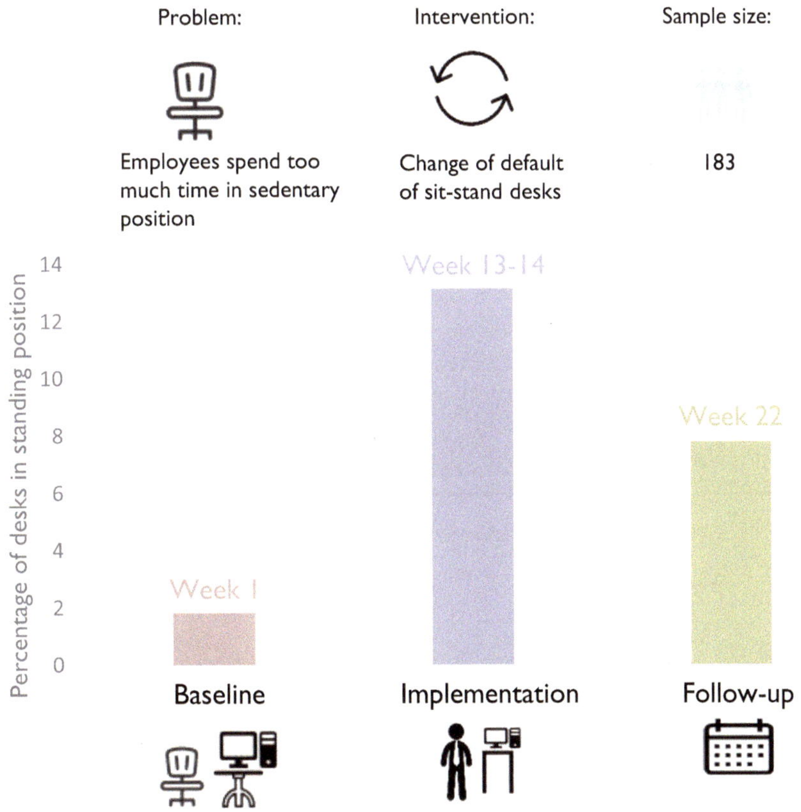

Source: Venema et al. (2017)

baseline measurement, fewer than 2 percent of employees were standing, compared to over 13 percent during implementation. The follow-up study revealed that two months after the nudge was removed, retention was 7.8 percent, which was still significantly higher than the baseline measurement.

Improving safety in the workplace

When the health of employees is at stake, it is imperative that companies invest in accident prevention interventions. Behavioral insights can offer an easy and cost-effective way of increasing adherence to safety practices. Ferguson, Bibby, Leaviss, and Weyman (2003) explored how the **framing** of messages in leaflets may increase adherence to safety guidelines. The sample consisted of two groups: 263 workers who engaged in manual handling and 188 employees who worked in a noisy environment. Participants in each group were given either a positively or a negatively framed leaflet relevant to the employee's occupation. Intent to follow safety guidelines was measured through self-report before and after the leaflets were distributed. For employees who worked in a noisy environment, intent to follow safety guidelines was influenced differently depending on how often they adhered to safety practices. Those who used ear protectors the majority of time were more influenced by a positively framed message. Employees who used ear protectors less than half of the time were more influenced by a negatively framed message. In the manual handling group, intent to follow safety guidelines was influenced by the positively framed message, especially when employees had already suffered from back problems. Negatively framed messages did not influence employee intent.

Overall, this study demonstrated that, although employees can be encouraged to follow safety guidelines, the framing should be specific to the target group. In addition, the effectiveness of framing for different purposes should be tested before being implemented, though this is true of all interventions. One particular limitation to note is that the study measured employee intent rather than actual behavior. Thus, the results should be interpreted with caution.

BOX 8.2 DECREASES IN PRODUCTIVITY LOSS DUE TO DEPRESSION THROUGH ACCESSIBLE THERAPY

Absenteeism is the habitual pattern of absence from work and is often seen as an indicator of psychological, medical, or social obstacles (Johns, 2007). Additionally, absence frequency is predicted by low levels of job satisfaction (Ybema, Smulders, & Bongers, 2010). The European Labour Force Survey data suggest that 11.4 million working days were lost in Britain in 2008–2009 due to work-related stress, depression, or anxiety. This is the equivalent to 27.3 days lost per affected worker. The average annual cost of lost productivity in England attributable to an employee with depression was estimated as GB£7,230, and for anxiety it was GB£6,850 (McCrone, Dhanasiri, Patel, Knapp, & Lawton-Smith, 2008). Given the costs associated with poor mental health, it is important that employers invest in the prevention of mental health problems.

McDaid, King, and Parsonage (2011) proposed a workplace-based intervention that could save a company of 500 employees up to £19,700 in year one and £63,478 in year two. Their proposed procedure was as follows: after a screening via questionnaire, those identified as being at risk of depression or anxiety disorders would be offered a course of cognitive behavioral therapy (CBT) delivered in six sessions over 12 weeks. Savings were calculated as the difference between intervention costs plus social healthcare and productivity losses due to absenteeism (being absent from work) and presenteeism (significantly impaired work performance due to working while suffering from a physical or mental illness, being distracted, or not being motivated). The authors estimated that a successful intervention could lead to a reduction in presenteeism to the equivalent of an extra 2.6 hours of work per week. Additionally, if depression, anxiety disorders, and work-related stress are averted, 27.3 days of absenteeism per worker per annum would theoretically be avoided. However, it is unclear whether this approach has been tested empirically, which invites further study before wide application should be considered.

Use of behavioral insights to make returning to work easier

Recovery from a long-term illness or injury can be challenging, especially when there is an additional burden of having to return to work. In Australia, for example, the return to work after an injury is frequently a protracted experience for all involved, as it requires substantial paperwork from doctors, insurers, employers, and employees. Redesign of this process could therefore support workers during difficult times.

The Behavioral Insights Unit, Allianz (an insurance company), and the Department of Education ran a ten-month program in 2013–2014 applying behavioral insights for a faster return to work in Australia. They used several interventions (NSW Premier & Cabinet Behavioral Insights Unit, NSW Government Education, & Allianz, 2016) that were based on the EAST (Service et al., 2014) and Mindspace (Dolan et al., 2012) frameworks. These were used to redesign both the process and the documents that go along with the process of getting back to work.

Interventions were built on the following:

1. **Simplification**: communicating by highlighting key messages and responsibilities of all parties concerned and reducing total volume of documents
2. **Personalization**: increasing employee ownership by giving documents personal names and headers, for example, Jon's Recovery at Work Plan
3. General positive **priming**: renaming the Injury Management Plan as the Work and Health Plan and positive framing for recovery (supporting motivation by highlighting the positive aspects)
4. Fostering **commitment**: asking workers to make active, specific, realistic, and personal commitment statements for the near future
5. **Timeliness**: improving the timing at which employees send their recovery at work plan to encourage engagement with recovery at an earlier stage
6. **Case conferences**: implementing meetings between the department, the insurer, and the treating doctor to improve communication between the three parties

This approach was applied to 1,700 cases of injured employees, who returned to work faster than the control group. The treatment group's return-to-work rate within the first 90 days was reported to be about 5 percent faster (Figure 8.6). The support of employees throughout their

FIGURE 8.6 Behavioral insights for easing return to work

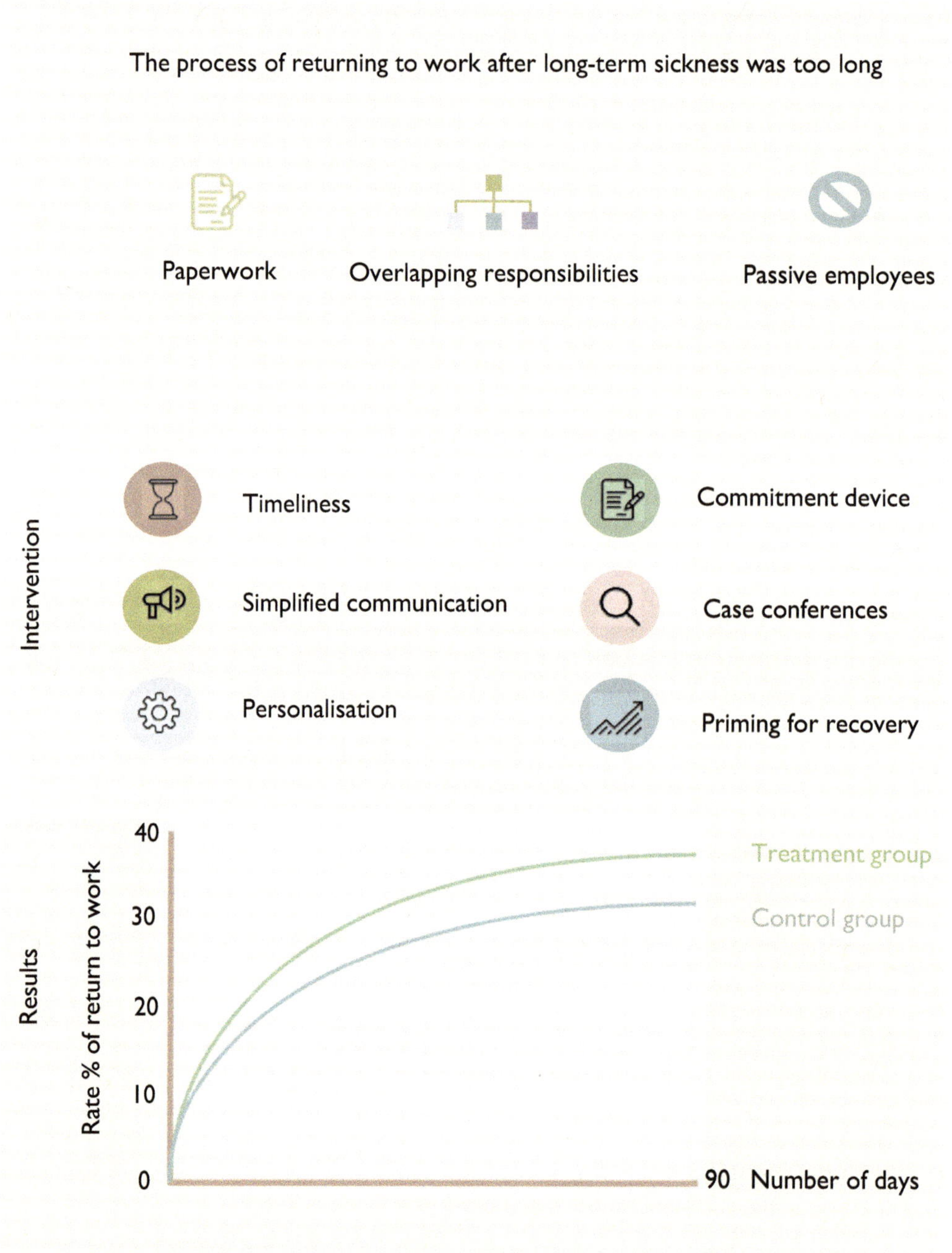

Source: NSW Government Education & Allianz (2016)

recovery is equally as important as investing in incident prevention. Notably, this approach can be tailored to situations in which there is no insurer involved. Furthermore, employees who have no insurance may benefit the most from such an intervention, as long-term sick leave may pose a serious threat to their financial stability.

The substantial amount of paperwork, however, is not the only factor slowing down the process of employees returning to work after suffering from illness. Countries providing full wage replacement usually reduce or eliminate the incentives that employees receive while ill so that they will return to work as soon as recovery is over. As sick pay is costly for employers, insurance companies, and governments, behavioral insights can be applied to stimulate those who are ready to return to work, while preserving the full wage replacement for those who need it.

In 2007, the Norwegian government introduced a *compulsory dialogue* meeting to promote the resumption of work for employees with long-term conditions. Three weeks before the meetings, employees received a notification letter. During the meeting, the employer, the employee, and their physician discussed a plan for returning to work (part-time or full-time) and any adjustments to the working environment that needed to be implemented. Markussen, Røed, and Schreiner (2017) analyzed data from January 2009 to December 2010 and compared this period to the one prior to the introduction of the compulsory dialogue meeting. The authors reported that faster resumption of work was achieved through both notification and attendance effects following the implementation of the intervention. For each compulsory meeting, sick leave days taken for long-term conditions were approximately 7 work days less. The authors estimated that an employee returning to work 7 days earlier saves the welfare system around US$1,885.

Behavioral insights for retirement age

Retirement can seem a long way off when facing the daily stress of work; thus, we often treat it as a stage of our lives that we do not focus on until late. The approach to retirement age is a significant period of change in any working life, yet all the working years up to that time are just as important. As retirement is a period in which our incomes will decrease and our barriers to work will increase, financial plans for after we finish working are critical to our well-being long before we reach that stage.

Use of nudges for retirement planning through behavioral interventions

In order to increase the number of people who plan retirement savings, the Behavioral Insight Unit in Canada, together with the Ontario Investor Office, tested five different messages aimed at encouraging participants to use Canada's online Retirement Income Calculator, a tool that helps people to estimate and plan retirement savings. The messages were included in a newsletter that was emailed to 76,565 employees from the public service in Ontario (Wilcoxen & Tregebov, 2018). This field experiment compared five different messages to see which one was the most effective in increasing the number of people clicking on the link that led to the landing page of the retirement calculator (Figure 8.7). The first message used no behavioral insights and reflected the traditional approach

FIGURE 8.7 Behavioral insights to increase savings for retirement

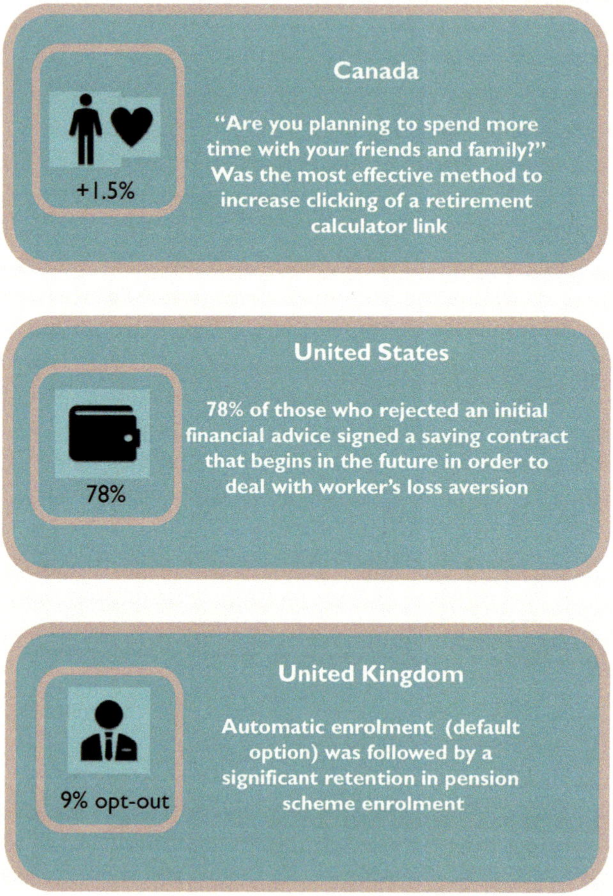

Source: Wilcoxen and Tregebov (2018), Department of Work and Pension (2013), and Thaler and Benartzi (2004)

that the government uses to inform people about the available service. The second message emphasized the short-term benefits of having a retirement plan, such as experiencing higher levels of financial security. The third message highlighted the value of having a retirement plan in terms of social engagement: spending more time with friends and family. The fourth message nudged individuals to think about the personal benefits of having more savings during retirement such as being able to devote more time to hobbies. The fifth message emphasized the simplicity of using the retirement calculator. Of the four messages that used behavioral insights, the one that stressed the social value of having a retirement plan was the only one that had a statistically significant effect. In this condition, 7.7 percent of the participants clicked on the link that leads to the calculator compared to the message with no behavior insights, for which engagement with the link was 6.35 percent. However, when the researchers examined which message was associated with more people proceeding to the actual calculator page (sustained engagement), the one that focused on simplicity was the most effective at 2.16 percent compared to the message with no behavioral insights at 1.57 percent. These results suggest that, in the future, different framings might be used at different points in the customer's journey to maximize the number of people that make use of the online calculator. For example, an emphasis on social value might be effective in attracting people to the online calculator landing page. Once participants have opened the website, another nudge stressing the simplicity of the calculator could be used to get people to engage with the calculator.

Use of defaults to increase retirement savings

In line with Madrian and Shea's default study highlighted in Chapters 2 and 3, the Department for Work and Pensions in the United Kingdom (2013) conducted a field experiment with large organizations. The pension scheme of 1.9 million employees working for 42 companies was changed to an automatic enrollment (default option) plan. The goal was to encourage more employees to maintain a pension plan. Total participation in the pension scheme before the intervention was 61 percent. Of the remaining employees, 24 percent (460,000) were eligible for an occupational pension. Those employees were automatically enrolled. After one month the average opt-out rate was 9 percent.

While the report emphasized that these findings were limited to the environment of large employers, similar conclusions were made in a paper by Beshears, Choi, Laibson, and Madrian (2006) from the NBER. Although their review of the empirical evidence resulted in a similar observation, they also point out that default options can be used to promote contributions at all the stages of the savings life cycle (savings plan participation, contributions, asset allocation, rollovers, and decumulation).

But what are the underlying mechanisms of automatic enrollment, and why do some people adhere to the default option while others decide to opt out? Prabhakar (2017) conducted a qualitative focus group study with 44 participants to investigate the matter and identified **status quo bias** and simplicity, among the main reasons, not to opt out of the automatic pension scheme in the United Kingdom. This may be a double-edged sword, as it implies individuals may also not opt in circumstances where they should, particularly (according to those 44 individuals) if critical information is unclear or unavailable. On the other end, some people may only choose to drop out because of issues of affordability (in particular women and young people) and the presence of better alternatives.

Although the use of defaults has generally become an important tool in interventions focusing on modifying **choice architecture**, there have also been null findings as well as backfires (Reiter, McRee, Pepper, & Brewer, 2012). For that reason, Jachimowicz, Duncan, Weber, and Johnson (2018) conducted a meta-analysis of 58 studies to determine the average influence of default strategies in various domains. While their findings indicate substantial, positive effects of defaults on choice, they also highlight certain factors that need to be considered for effective implementation. Such influences may include the intensity and distribution of the initial preference. The authors also noted that participants' perception of the trustworthiness of the choice architect influences their compliance with the pre-selected option. Additionally, the effort that is required for switching from the pre-selected option has an effect on the effectiveness of the default.

Overcoming temporal discounting to increase retirement savings

One phenomenon that offers some explanation as to why employees may not save for the future is **hyperbolic discounting** (Benartzi & Lewin, 2012; Service et al., 2014): giving more value to having money now than to having money at a future, distant retirement age. Thus, individuals often procrastinate when it comes to saving because the perceived value of high immediate costs is higher than the remote gains (Ainslie, 1975). To overcome this bias, Thaler and Benartzi (2004) developed a behavioral intervention they called Save More Tomorrow™. This is a retirement savings plan that avoids the high immediate costs by making individuals sign a savings contract that begins in the future (e.g. the beginning of next year), as opposed to right away.

In a field experiment conducted in a mid-sized manufacturing company, they observed that 90 percent of the employees saw a financial advisor for planning their retirement, but only 28 percent accepted the advice and started to save money. By presenting their scheme to all of the employees who rejected the initial advice, 78 percent of that group signed up to the new scheme. Though this may have also been due to having a follow-up session, the plan may still be a valuable option to offer alongside more traditional retirement saving schemes. This may be particularly the case for individuals who have substantial near-term expenses, such as graduate hires with student loan repayments.

Another concern is that many individuals do not take the opportunity to save for retirement even when a well-structured plan is already offered by their employer. So how can we best design messages and information to support better saving behavior before it is too late? Croy, Gerrans, and Speelman (2010) studied which factors most effectively promote saving behaviors. To do so, they analyzed data from 2,300 respondents to a randomly distributed questionnaire. The framework for questions utilized the **theory of planned behavior** (TPB; Ajzen, 2002b), which states that attitudes toward behavior, subjective norms, and perceived behavioral control shape behavioral intentions and, therefore, behaviors.

Croy et al. found that the predictors explain up to 75 percent of participants' intentions to increase their contributions. A more detailed analysis highlighted that **injunctive social norms** (making evident the approved and disapproved behaviors) were the strongest predictor of the outcome variable, whereas **descriptive social norms** (most common behavior) were not a significant predictor.

While the importance of long-term financial planning applies to individuals and employers, there are some general limitations of these studies. Apart from some insights being limited to theoretical behavior, the mixed effects of different trials indicate that approaches again must be tailored to the immediate context. As such, this is further support for organizations, particularly large ones, to have behavioral scientists on staff to look at institutionally specific approaches to financial planning. Such personalization is likely to go a long way toward addressing the risks presented by temporal discounting of financial well-being, particularly in retirement.

Conclusion

Behavioral insights can be used in many areas of working life, spanning from recruitment to retirement. While some insights may be easily implemented, like adding nudges to emails, others are associated with a higher cost, such as rethinking office furniture. Ultimately, the aim of all insights is to produce better workplaces and work experiences, leading to more competitive organizations, healthier employees, and stronger economies. If implemented effectively, these interventions may offer an impact beyond the office and deliver positive secondary effects to employees and their communities. However, there is still a great deal of evidence yet to be established with regard to the effectiveness and sustainability of many workplace behavioral interventions. As such information becomes available, there will be greater opportunities to determine if, when, and how these tools may be better implemented into policies by managers and organizations.

Essay questions

1 Which theories or constructs of behavioral insights are most vital for managers to understand? What specific issues might these be applied to in the workplace?

2 Imagine you are working for a large company. Think of three creative examples of policies you could apply to increase job satisfaction. What are the possible difficulties you might encounter?

3 How would you characterize the potential trade-off of applying behavioral approaches in workplaces that benefit employees vs. those that benefit the company?

4 How would you design an intervention to encourage young people to increase their retirement savings while they are still paying off student loans? What financial and ethical influences should you consider?

5 Are all nudges ethical? Think of examples when the use of nudges could be considered unethical.

Additional insights and further reading

Empowering leadership fosters creative performance

Audenaert, M., & Decramer, A. (2016). When empowering leadership fosters creative performance: The role of problem solving demands and creative personality. *Journal of Management and Organization*, *24*(1), 4–18. https://doi.org/10.1017/jmo.2016.20

Intrinsic and prosocial motivation can increase performance

Grant, A. M. (2008). Does intrinsic motivation fuel the prosocial fire? Motivational synergy in predicting persistence, performance, and productivity. *Journal of Applied Psychology*, *93*(1), 48–58. https://doi.org/10.1037/0021-9010.93.1.48

Working from home increases productivity

Bloom, N., Liang, J., Roberts, J., & Ying, Z. J. (2014). Does working from home work? Evidence from a Chinese experiment. *The Quarterly Journal of Economics*, *130*(1), 165–218.

Timing your mindfulness meditation right at work

Hafenbrack, A. C. (2017). Mindfulness meditation as an on-the-spot workplace intervention. *Journal of Business Research*, *75*, 118–129.

Listing obstacles and solutions for return to work

Van Oostrom, S. H., van Mechelen, W., Terluin, B., de Vet, H. C., & Anema, J. R. (2009). A participatory workplace intervention for employees with distress and lost time: A feasibility evaluation within a randomized controlled trial. *Journal of Occupational Rehabilitation*, *19*(2), 212–222. https://doi.org/10.1007/s10926-009-9170-7

Participatory intervention improves mental health and job performance

Tsutsumi, A., Nagami, M., Yoshikawa, T., Kogi, K., & Kawakami, N. (2009). Participatory intervention for workplace improvements on mental health and job performance among blue-collar workers: A cluster randomized controlled trial. *Journal of Occupational and Environmental Medicine*, *51*(5), 554–563.

Creating personal job titles reduces emotional stress

Grant, A. M., Berg, J. M., & Cable, D. M. (2014). Job titles as identity badges: How self-reflective titles can reduce emotional exhaustion. *Academy of Management Journal*, *57*(4), 1201–1225. https://doi.org/10.5465/amj.2012.0338

Mindless work may improve creativity

Elsbach, K. D., & Hargadon, A. B. (2006). Enhancing creativity through "mindless" work: A framework of workday design. *Organization Science*, *17*(4), 470–483. https://doi.org/10.1287/orsc.1060.0193

Results Only Work Environment (ROWE)

Ressler, C., & Thompson, J. (2010). *Why work sucks and how to fix it: The results-only revolution*. New York: Penguin Publishing Group.

Introducing behavioral alternatives to combat bullying

Strandmark, M., & Rahm, G. (2014). Development, implementation and evaluation of a process to prevent and combat workplace bullying. *Scandinavian Journal of Public Health*, *42*(15, Suppl), 66–73. https://doi.org/10.1177/1403494814549494

How flexible working can improve gender equality in the workplace

The Behavioural Insights Team. (2017). *How flexible working can improve gender equality in the workplace*. London: Behavioural Insights Team, Cabinet Office. Retrieved from www.behaviouralinsights.co.uk/news/how-flexible-working-can-improve-gender-equality-in-the-workplace

Teaching behavioral strategies to fight gender bias habits

Carnes, M., Devine, P. G., Baier Manwell, L., Byars-Winston, A., Fine, E., Ford, C. E., . . . & Sheridan, J. (2015). Effect of an intervention to break the gender bias habit for faculty at one institution: A cluster randomized controlled trial. *Academic Medicine*, *90*(2), 221–230.

A meta-analysis of workplace stressors and their health outcomes

Goh, J., Pfeffer, J., & Zenios, S. A. (2015). Workplace stressors and health outcomes: Health policy for the workplace. *Behavioral Science & Policy*, *1*(1), 43–52.

Companies structure jobs to encourage innovation

Bock, L. (2015). *Work rules! Insights from inside Google that will transform how you live and lead*. London: John Murray.

"More than public service: A field experiment on job advertisements and diversity in the police"

Linos, E. (2017). More than public service: A field experiment on job advertisements and diversity in the police. *Journal of Public Administration Research and Theory, 28*(1), 67–85. doi: 10.1093/jopart/mux032

This chapter has been adapted from Ruggeri, K., Berkessel, J. B., Achterberg, J., Prinz, G. M., Luna-Navarro, A., Jachimowicz, J. M., & Whillans, A. V. (2019). Work and workplace. In K. Ruggeri (Ed.), *Behavioral insights for public policy: Concepts and cases* (pp. 156–173). New York and London: Routledge.

9 Communications and behavioral economics

Marlene Hecht, Nejc Plohl, Bojana Većkalov, Julia P. Stuhlreyer, Kai Ruggeri, and Sander van der Linden

Chapter summary

No matter how important and valuable a message is, it will not yield the desired outcome if it does not reach its audience. This lesson is taught in many areas of our everyday life, such as in education or relationships. For communicating policies, there is no difference. To ensure that a message is understandable for the public, appropriate communication strategies must be adopted. Therefore, it is important for policymakers to know how different elements of a message can be used to deliver its content effectively. In this chapter, we focus on providing an overview of case studies that tested different elements of communication, largely related to message content. We suggest that the use of principles such as personalization, temporal distance, framing, participation, operational transparency, simplicity, and salience may result in better policy outcomes through increased public engagement. We highlight both the opportunities and potential pitfalls of implementing those strategies at scale. To show the practical value of these guidelines, we discuss different attempts at translating scientific findings into policy and engaging the public in new policies.

Learning objectives

- Understand different forms of communication between policymakers and the public
- Learn about principles that can facilitate successful communication
- Understand potential concerns of using behavioral insights for communication, specifically linked to personalization and the use of Web 2.0
- Derive knowledge from examples of effective communication and understand factors that may have contributed to their success

Introduction

Communication is an essential element of interventions. Every message sent out to the public includes distinct features (such as message content, design, and the medium used for delivering it), and all of these features can have an impact on the perception and action of the receiver, even when not intended.

DOI: 10.4324/9781003181873-9

Think about the tax compliance messages in Chapter 4. What if these were sent out via email or social media instead of including them in a letter? Would this have made a difference in engaging the public? Similarly, remember the study that tested if health behavior, more specifically the enrollment in automatic refills for chronic medication, differs between individuals having received the option of enhanced active choice (i.e. in which the preferable option is highlighted by stressing the disadvantages related to choosing the nonpreferred alternative) compared to those who received an opt-in option (Keller et al., 2011; for a complete review, see Chapter 5). In this study, the effect of enhanced active choice was tested by providing the information either via telephone (Study 3) or via a website (Study 4). While this was not the focus of the authors' research, response rates between these two channels differed, even though the same intervention messages were tested (see Figure 9.1). Thus, it is hard to design and evaluate an intervention without considering its communicative features, such as the medium (see also Box 9.1) or the message itself. What if we additionally change the design of a message or its content? This is all part of communication and is not negligible in the policy context.

This chapter differs from the preceding ones in that its aim is to highlight principles that might lead to elevated public engagement using a methodological approach, instead of illustrating how behavioral insights can be used in one specific domain. As such, it is focused on effective communication strategies and is meant as a pragmatic guideline and toolbox for using behavioral insights appropriately and effectively.

It is important to note that the principles presented are by no means an exhaustive list of all useful communication strategies. They instead represent a selection of principles that have been shown to be highly effective in the literature and are simple and practical enough to be used by policymakers without much training. While we acknowledge that the use of different media can lead to different behavioral outcomes, we will mainly focus on features of the message itself. However, some of the principles we mention (e.g. personalization, salience) can be applied to the selection of an appropriate medium as well.

FIGURE 9.1 Delivery of default messages over different channels

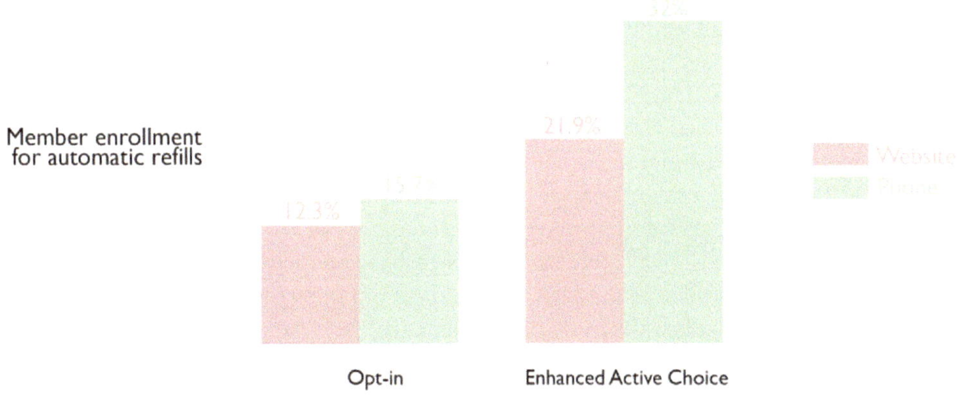

BOX 9.1 CHALLENGES OF USING WEB 2.0 SERVICES FOR POLICY IMPLEMENTATION

Despite the many opportunities offered by Web 2.0 services, there are numerous hurdles that need to be overcome in order to tap their full potential. First, the highly participatory nature of such services, which is usually understood as an advantage, can also have adverse effects. For example, viewer comments on health-related YouTube clips were shown to have an influence on other audience members' evaluations of these clips. Specifically, the comments either supported the content from the video or opposed it, which can alter the effectiveness of an intervention if individuals identify with the commenters (Walther, DeAndrea, Kim, & Anthony, 2010). In other words, negative user-generated comments can outweigh the potential positive effects of carefully designed interventions.

Second, there is general concern regarding the credibility of information sources and the accuracy of information on different platforms, which infamously peaked in the discussion of "fake news" during the 2016 US election (Allcott & Gentzkow, 2017). Because any user can generate content, it is difficult to monitor its quality and protect users from inaccurate information. As such, it is often left to users to decide what they should (and should not) believe. For example, one study suggests that user-generated social media content in health contexts is often inconsistent with existing scientific evidence (Steinberg et al., 2010). Hence, rather than supporting the distribution of scientific findings, if false, user-generated content may hinder it. Correcting this will require policymakers and scientists to not only communicate findings effectively but also address existing beliefs that may have been influenced by flawed information – a step that can be even more bothersome because false beliefs, the potential results of initial misinformation, seem to be very difficult to change (e.g. Nyhan & Reifler, 2010).

Effective communication of policies – a bridge from policies to the public

The translation of scientific discoveries into policies is a difficult task (for an overview of this process, see Box 9.9). Not only does the use of evidence-based policies differ between countries, but sometimes it can be different even within a country, such as in the United States.

To examine how many states in the United States make use of evidence-based policy actions, the Pew-MacArthur Foundation reviewed various federal documents, including publicly available ones as well as internal sources. They examined six actions of evidence-based policymaking, such as how much funding is allocated to evidence-based programs, in four public areas (for a more detailed description of their report, see Chapter 10). The results showed that most states had already taken at least a modest level of evidence-based policymaking actions, with Washington, Utah, Minnesota, Connecticut, and Oregon leading (see Figure 9.2). In contrast, evidence-based policymaking played only a minor role in seven states (Pew Charitable Trusts and MacArthur Foundation, 2017).

Despite the fact that not all states use evidence-based policies yet, the case studies presented in this book demonstrate the high effectiveness of policies based on research insights and with this the potential for effectively communicating ideas and information to the public.

In the following sections, we will emphasize a number of key principles that have previously been identified as valuable for engaging the public. Most of these principles show that very subtle differences in the way we communicate can have a strong impact on how recipients, in this case

FIGURE 9.2 Use of evidence-based policies in the United States

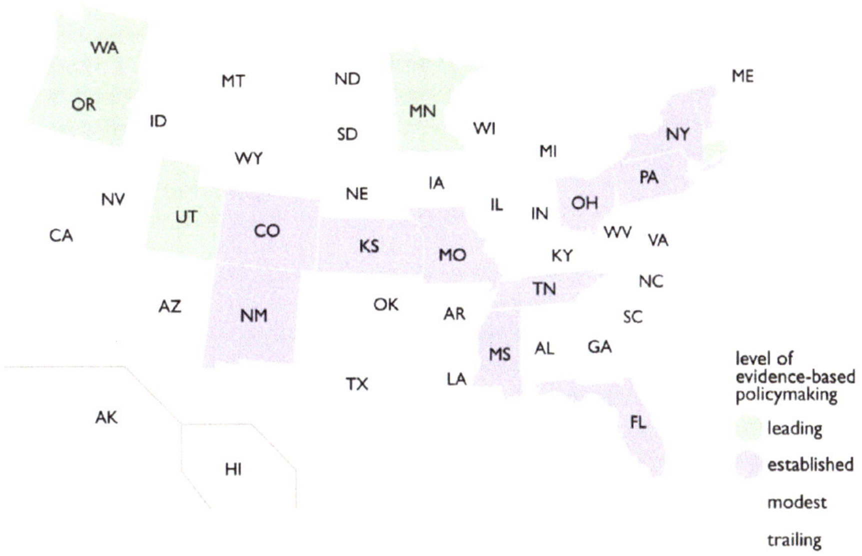

Source: Pew Charitable Trusts and MacArthur Foundation (2017)

the public, respond to a message. On the basis of this, we suggest some guidelines that can promote better policy outcomes, and we illustrate examples of the principles being used in practice.

Personalization

Tailoring messages to increase the use of mammography

One in eight women in the United States will develop breast cancer during her life (DeSantis, Ma, Bryan, & Jemal, 2014). One of the most important factors determining the outcome of the disease is early detection (Berry et al., 2005). Mammograms are recommended either every year or every two years after the age of 40 (American Cancer Society, n.d.). However, approximately one-third of women in this age range have not attended a proper checkup within the last two years (National Center for Health Statistics, 2017). To tackle this problem, Lauver, Settersten, Kane, and Henriques (2003) tested whether personalized messages (for further information on **personalization**, see Box 9.2) could be used to increase the utilization of mammography and clinical breast examination for high-risk women.

The effect of tailored messages was investigated through a randomized controlled trial with three conditions – (1) no message, (2) a message containing professional recommendations for breast screening (e.g. clarification of mammography procedures), and (3) a message containing professional recommendations as well as a tailored message (related to individual beliefs about and barriers to breast screening). After participants consented to take part in the study, the messages in conditions 2 and 3 were provided by nurses over the telephone. As opposed to participants in group 2, all participants in group 3 were additionally asked about their personal reasons for why they had not attended a clinical breast examination in the past. After this, tailored messages were adapted to tackle these self-reported barriers. After the telephone contact, all participants in both groups 2 and 3 were further sent pamphlets containing the messages via mail.

Women in both message conditions were more likely to report that they had undergone mammography and a clinical breast examination in the short term (3–6 months after the intervention) than those in the control group. In the long term (16–22 months after the intervention), however, mammography utilization was greater for the tailored-message group (56.6 percent) than for the recommendations-only group (47.0 percent; Lauver et al., 2003). The findings of the study are further supported by a meta-analytic review conducted in 2007. Based on 28 studies, the meta-analysis concludes that women exposed to tailored interventions are significantly more likely to get a mammogram. However, it must be noted that, despite making a significant change, the tailored interventions displayed only a small effect size (Sohl & Moyer, 2007). This means that, when we look at all studies combined, there is only a small increase in the number of women who got mammograms when they received a personalized message compared to those who did not receive such a message. However, because of how important early detection is for determining the outcome of cancer, every opportunity to equip individuals to identify the option that may benefit them most is important.

Promotion of parent-child interaction through personalized text messages

Would you be more motivated to study if you received weekly text messages focused on your individual skills and how you can improve them? Do you think this could improve your grades? Doss, Fahle, Loeb, and York (2017) tested an intervention similar to the one just mentioned: they wanted to find out if an existing text message–based education program for kindergarten students would have different effects if it included personalized messages.

The intervention, implemented in the San Francisco Unified School District, started in October 2014. The 388 participating families (540 children) were divided into three groups: (1) a tailored-message group, (2) a text-only group, and (3) a control group. Families in both groups 1 and 2 received three texts per week for eight months, which informed them about the skills that the student should attain and the tasks that the student should complete for each week. However, the tailored-message group's texts provided additional information on the children's learning progress (based on prior assessments) and suggested one out of four learning activities (tailored to individual academic information). The control group (3), in contrast, received one text every two weeks which included only general district information.

The results showed that children whose parents received tailored messages were 1.47 times more likely to move up a reading level in comparison to the control group. Additionally, parents in the tailored-message group more often reported that they were engaged in literacy activities (e.g. by reviewing their children's direction of reading) compared to parents in group 3. This might partly explain children's higher literacy levels. Additionally, parents in group 1 had less parent-teacher contact than parents in group 2 (according to teachers' self-reports). The authors suggest that this finding might be due to parents being less incentivized to talk to teachers about their children's progress at school, given that they had already received information on this through the tailored messages.

As the intervention was based on an existing program and only required small changes in text messages, the use of tailored messages in education programs might be a cost-effective option to increase academic gains and to promote interactions between parents and their children (Doss et al., 2017).

Personalizing processes to increase university applications and matriculation

What was it like for you to apply to university? If you remember a very complex application procedure and a lack of centralized information about prospective universities, you might not be alone. Prospective students may be overwhelmed by all the available information and the number of deadlines in the application process (Page & Scott-Clayton, 2016). To simplify application procedures, personalized messaging may be useful. Several behavioral interventions attempted to personalize and simplify the information about available universities, such as by reminding students of critical deadlines and providing them with support.

Such an approach was used as part of the expanding college opportunities (ECO) project. In the ECO-C intervention conducted in the United States, high-achieving students from low-income backgrounds were provided with semi-customized information about the application process and costs of college (Hoxby & Turner, 2013). The intervention was intended to take advantage of the economies of scale that arise when a central organization efficiently uses large databases to inform the intervention that each person encounters. The students who received personalized information submitted 19 percent more applications and were accepted to 12 percent more colleges than those in the control group. They also enrolled in colleges with higher graduation rates and more generous resources in comparison to the control group. In such ways, simplification and personalization may have the potential to narrow the educational attainment gap (Hoxby & Turner, 2013). However, it must be noted that students in the control group did not receive any informational materials at all. Thus, we cannot attribute the change solely to the personalization principle. Nevertheless, it seems that providing students with information might generally be helpful for motivating prospective students to apply.

After a successful application, students have to matriculate in order to be able to start their studies. To do this, they need to keep a critical deadline. A phenomenon called *summer melt* refers to college-accepted students failing to matriculate into universities in the year after high school (Castleman & Page, 2015). Simplification of information about colleges and helping students to access professional assistance can improve students' postsecondary outcomes. In a study by Castleman and Page (2015), two interventions were tested to mitigate summer melt. In one intervention, young people aspiring to study at a university received automated and personalized text messages reminding them about pre-matriculation tasks and enabling them to request counselor support. In the second intervention, peer mentors were tasked with supporting students who intended to enroll. Students who received text messages were around 3 percent more likely to apply for 2-year university programs, while students who received mentor support were around 4.5 percent more likely to apply for 4-year university programs. Positive effects of both interventions were more pronounced for students who did not have clear college plans or who had few previous opportunities for college counselling and support. While the numbers seem to indicate different effectivity, further analyses comparing the two interventions revealed that their effects on enrollment were not significantly different from one another (Castleman & Page, 2015). These results suggest that, generally, the provision of information at the moment when action needs to be taken may be critical for the success of such interventions – regardless of whether support is provided by mentors or via text messaging.

BOX 9.2 PRINCIPLE #1: PERSONALIZATION

Personalization refers to customizing messages to fit recipients' characteristics or preferences (White, Zahay, Thorbjørnsen, & Shavitt, 2008). The resulting messages may be more effective in eliciting favorable responses than standard messages that address the broad population rather uniformly (e.g. Hirsh, Kang, & Bodenhausen, 2012). The ability to implement personalized communication at scale has been facilitated by technologies used for digital marketing communication, which allow companies to learn much more about individual consumers than ever before by tracking their behavior (e.g. Ansari & Mela, 2003). The level of personalization can vary from simply changing the name of the recipient to tailoring messages according to recipients' demographics, purchase histories (White et al., 2008), and even psychological profiles (Matz, Kosinski, Nave, & Stillwell, 2017b). For instance, Hirsh et al. (2012) prepared five different advertisements for a single product (a mobile phone), each designed to target one of the five major dimensions of personality (McCrae & John, 1992). The text on these advertisements was manipulated to highlight the motivational tendencies associated with different personality characteristics (for instance, "With XPhone, you'll always be where the excitement is", for high extraversion). Additionally, participants' Big Five personality traits were measured. Results showed that participants rated advertisements that matched their personality traits more positively than the other advertisements, showing the potential value of personality-based communication strategies (Hirsh et al., 2012). These findings, which are mostly coming from the field of marketing, have already been translated into the field of policymaking as well.

While personalization has previously been shown to be an effective principle that can increase public engagement, concerns about its (mis)use (especially on social media) have been raised.

Online firms collect enormous amounts of personal data from their users and allow advertisers to use this data to target and personalize ads (Tucker, 2014). Facebook, for example, says that it does not share users' information with advertisers without their consent. This statement is true per se, but in reality, users have to agree to its privacy terms in order to use Facebook, and there is no opt-in or opt-out option (Fuchs, 2011).

Research suggests that online data can reveal a lot more about consumers' habits and preferences than first meets the eye. For example, Kosinski, Stillwell, and Graepel (2013) showed that Facebook likes can be used to accurately predict a range of attributes, such as sexual orientation, ethnicity, religious and political views, personality, and intelligence. For example, by automatically analyzing Facebook likes, one can correctly discriminate between homosexual and heterosexual men in 88 percent of cases.

On one hand, prediction of users' individual attributes and preferences may be used to improve products and services by personalizing advertisements and potentially increasing consumers' satisfaction (e.g. Matz et al., 2016). On the other hand, it is not hard to imagine negative implications of these actions; the same principles could easily be applied to profile and manipulate large numbers of people without their consent and without them noticing (Matz et al., 2017b). Hence, while personalization of advertising and communication may benefit individuals and society at large, privacy concerns will have to be addressed more thoroughly by governments and policymakers. At the moment, there are no simple guidelines or regulations on where to draw the line between maximizing the potential of social media and violating privacy.

Temporal distance

Encouraging financial compliance through temporal distance

Mutual societies are organizations owned by their members, and their purpose is usually to bring profit either to the community or to the owners (Financial Conduct Authority, 2016). Each year, mutual societies in the United Kingdom are supposed to send their annual returns and financial accounts to the Financial Conduct Authority (FCA). However, not all societies submit their returns on time, and some of them do not submit returns at all. Late submissions not only result in losses of time and resources for the FCA, but they can also have consequences for the societies themselves, such as losing their registration or receiving a fine. How can we prevent financial noncompliance? By using the cases presented in previous chapters, try to come up with your own solution before reading how the FCA proceeded.

The FCA decided to redesign their communication materials in a way that would increase compliance. Overall, the FCA sent letters to 7,984 mutual societies. Each society was randomly allocated to one out of three treatment groups or to a control group. The first group received a letter including salient information about penalties, while the second group received a letter that included a warning. To examine whether the time interval between receipt of the letter and the deadline would have an impact, the third treatment group was sent letters on different dates. In the following 10 months after the intervention, the FCA measured whether societies submitted their annual returns and whether societies had changed toward losing their status (in other words, whether the societies were closing).

Surprisingly, neither the salient message nor the warning showed a significant increase in the return rate. However, societies that received the letters shortly before the deadline submitted their annual returns on time more often than the societies that received the letters earlier (see Figure 9.3). Specifically, societies that were sent a letter in July (and had, on average, a shorter deadline with a median of approximately 3 weeks) were 2.4 percent more likely to respond than those that were sent a letter earlier (with a median of approximately 2 months' time until the deadline) (Smart, 2016).

FIGURE 9.3 Use of temporal distance to increase financial compliance

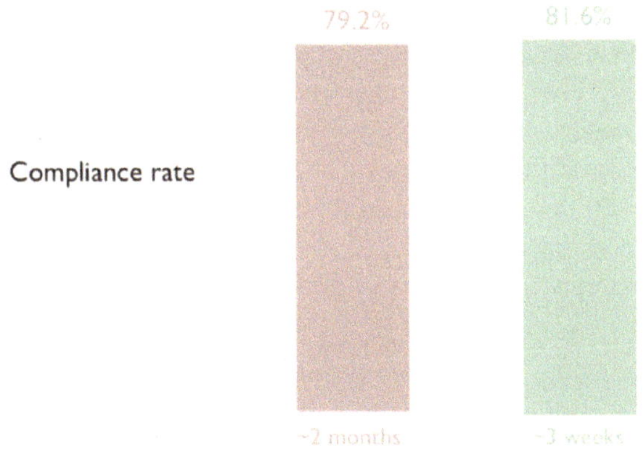

Overall, these results highlight that the timing of an intervention might be just as important as all the other principles used to deliver policies to the public. The phenomenon influencing the results of the intervention may be referred to as **temporal distance** (see Box 9.3).

BOX 9.3 PRINCIPLE #2: TEMPORAL DISTANCE

Temporal distance (temporal discounting) refers to the perceived proximity of an event in time. The observed distance in time between the announcement of a specific event and its actual occurrence influences the way individuals think about the event itself (Trope & Liberman, 2003). As temporal distance increases, mental representations become less concrete and increasingly abstract (van der Linden, Maibach, & Leiserowitz, 2015). Concurrently, if an event is mentioned shortly before it takes place, individuals have more concrete thoughts about the event itself and plan their actions differently than for events that will take place further in the future (Trope & Liberman, 2003). Therefore, immediate concerns take precedence over planning for the future (Vugt, Griskevicius, & Schultz, 2014).

Framing

Motivation of businesses to register for an online tax service by using framing and social norms

One central element of behavioral economics is **loss aversion**: the notion that we place more value on not losing something than on obtaining an equivalent gain (for a more detailed review of Prospect Theory, see Chapters 2 and 3).

How can we use Prospect Theory to design communication materials? The Behavioral Insights Team collaborated with the city of Denver, Colorado, and used loss aversion **framing** in redesigning letters. The aim of these letters was to motivate businesses to register for an online tax payment service. The existing letters focused on environmental conservation and thus motivated businesses to "Go Green!". The treatment letters, in contrast, either focused on the disadvantages of not using the online service (i.e. included a loss frame) or stated that most of the receivers' peers had an online account already (i.e. stressed a social norm). Overall, 32,866 letters were sent out to businesses.

Compared to businesses that received the control letter (1.7 percent), more businesses registered online after having received the loss frame letter (3.0 percent) or the letter stressing social norms (3.4 percent). Did these businesses also use these online services, or did they merely register for the service? Results showed that businesses that received the loss frame letter (1.7 percent) or the social norm letter (2.0 percent) also filed their taxes online more often than the control (1.2 percent). Therefore, message framing (as well as use of social norms) in letters can be a cost-effective way to lead to a more successful policy implementation (Behavioral Insights Team, 2016).

Increases in online vehicle license renewals by using framing and salience

Vehicle owners in Ontario, Canada, are required to renew their vehicle license annually. There are two ways this can be done: at a service counter or through an online platform. The government of Ontario collaborated with the Behavioural Economics in Action research hub

(BEAR) at the Rotman School of Management (University of Toronto) to encourage more vehicle owners to renew their license online. More specifically, their aim was to increase the use of online services by modifying notice reminders and applying behavioral science principles, particularly framing and salience.

An RCT was designed with a randomly selected sample of 626,212 vehicle owners who were due to be sent renewal notices at the time of the trial. Changes in the notice reminder were implemented for randomly assigned subsamples of participants. The aspect of salience was tested by presenting the information about the online option on a blue background, while the framing principle was applied by either highlighting the advantages of using the online system or highlighting the disadvantages of not using the online system. This led to three experimental conditions that were tested against the standard notice: (1) salience, (2) salience and loss framing, and (3) salience and gain framing. The intervention started in December 2013 and lasted for 8 weeks.

Participants in each of the three treatment conditions used online renewals more often than those who received the standard letter. Whereas 10.3 percent of the control group renewed their license plate online, this number was higher in groups 1 (11.6 percent) and 2 (13.3 percent), and it was highest in group 3 (14.7 percent). Thus, individuals in the salience and gain framing group (3) were most likely to use the online renewal service (see Figure 9.4).

The eight-week trial alone resulted in participants avoiding CA$28,000 in transaction fees, convincing the government to apply salience and gain framing interventions to all renewal notices sent to vehicle owners in Ontario. Since then, the pace of year-over-year increase in online service uptake has accelerated by 1 percent (Castelo et al., 2015).

Note that, in this study, messages with gain framing exhibited a greater effect (in combination with salience) than those with loss framing. Yet, in the study discussed previously (Behavioral Insights Team, 2016), letters including loss framing yielded the strongest effect. This highlights that the effectiveness of frames can differ, depending on the specific intervention that is tested. Thus, there does not seem to be a one-size-fits-all strategy for choosing which frame to use. For further information on framing, see Box 9.4. The principle of salience is further explained at the end of this chapter (Box 9.8).

FIGURE 9.4 Use of framing and salience to increase online license renewals

BOX 9.4 PRINCIPLE #3: FRAMING

An important part of communicating with the public, regardless of the communication channel, is **framing**: the presentation of logically equivalent information in different ways, which influences perception of the message itself (Druckman, 2001). For example, if we state that a certain political candidate has a 49 percent disapproval rating, this may lead to the perception that the candidate is disliked and unlikely to win an election. However, if we highlight a 51 percent approval rating, it creates a different impression, although the two statements could be considered logically equivalent (assuming no third option). Framing has been studied extensively by some of the most eminent researchers in behavioral science (e.g. Kahneman & Tversky, 1979; to read a more detailed description of Prospect Theory, return to Chapters 2 and 3). Of particular importance to this chapter is that framing effects can help to make policy communication more effective. For example, research has identified gain frames as facilitators of pro-environmental attitudes (Hurlstone et al., 2014) and illness prevention behaviors, such as smoking cessation (Gallagher & Updegraff, 2012).

Participation

Increases in commitment to job-seeking through participation

Extended unemployment is harmful to physical and mental well-being (Black, 2008). Improvement of the return to work rate has therefore been one of the main goals of Jobcentres in the United Kingdom (Behavioural Insights Team, 2012). To help individuals find employment faster, the Behavioural Insights Team tested the effect of a redesigned job-seeking process that motivated active **participation** by encouraging job-seekers to set themselves clear goals.

In a first pilot study, job-seekers received either a commitment-focused intervention (where they were asked to inform their job advisor about their commitment to job-seeking activities for the upcoming fortnight) or the standard treatment (which simply required job-seekers to document what they had done retrospectively). The commitment-focused intervention further included resilience training and strength identification for individuals who were still searching for a job after eight weeks, as well as making sure that the job-seekers discussed options for returning to work with Jobcentre staff earlier than the usual practice. The results showed that job-seekers in the treatment group were 15–20 percent more likely to be off benefits 13 weeks after they signed on to receive benefits than those who received the standard treatment.

After this successful pilot study, the use of commitment interventions was tested for 10 months in 12 Jobcentres across Essex, with 110,838 job-seekers participating. Similar to the pilot study, the results of this larger trial showed a greater proportion of people flowing off benefits for the commitment-focused intervention (58.5 percent) in comparison to the standard treatment (56.8 percent). Even though this difference was significant, it is important to note that the effects of this larger scale trial were smaller than those of the pilot.

Overall, the results led to the additional training of 25,000 job advisors, and the commitment tools are now used in all Jobcentres in the United Kingdom, as well as in Singapore and Australia (Behavioural Insights Team, 2012, 2014, 2015). For further information on the participation principle, see Box 9.5.

BOX 9.5 PRINCIPLE #4: PARTICIPATION

The **participation** principle refers to providing people the opportunity to take part in different forms of decision-making. Thanks to the continuous development of Web 2.0 services, participation has been made much easier and cheaper to implement than ever before (Lilleker & Jackson, 2010). While traditional communication channels (e.g. letters) made it time-consuming and expensive to communicate with customers, social media allows companies to engage with customers interactively and in real time (Sashi, 2012) and can thus serve as a new tool for customer engagement (Rishika, Kumar, Janakiraman, & Bezawada, 2013). However, participation is not limited to the company-consumer interaction; it can just as easily be applied to the interaction between government and the public.

Operational transparency

Increases in trust in government services through operational transparency

Imagine you had an app to report work that your city needs to perform, such as a pothole on the street that needs to be fixed. Would you use it? What if you received a photo of the completed work once the issue had been resolved? Would this change your answer?

In Boston, Massachusetts, such an application exists: by using the app "Citizens Connect", residents can send requests on the work that needs to be performed in the form of photographs. In order to explore how modern technology and policies can strengthen the partnership between residents and the city government of Boston, the Boston Mayor's Office of New Urban Mechanics tested whether an updated version of this app could impact citizens' behavior. The office's self-declared strategy is to facilitate civic involvement by increasing the residents' trust in the government. One way to achieve this is to increase **operational transparency** (i.e. by increasing the visibility of otherwise "invisible" government work, see Box 9.6).

Resident submissions captured by the application (e.g. "a sidewalk that has not been shoveled") previously received a "closed" badge when the issue was resolved. In September 2014, however, the city launched the new version of the app, which could also distribute images of the work performed. To test the effectiveness of increased operational transparency, two conditions were created – an operationally transparent condition and a control condition. When an issue was resolved, residents in both conditions received a notification of the completed work, but those in the operational transparency treatment additionally received an image of the work that had been completed.

Overall, 21,786 residents reported more than 370,000 monthly observations (withholding high submitters who sent in more than 20 requests in a given month) during the 13 or 14 months after the implementation (only 12 of the residents received the transparency treatment for 14 months).

Residents who were exposed to increased operational transparency submitted 59.8 percent more service requests to the city government in the months following the treatment than in the preceding months. Furthermore, these requests were made in 37.7 percent more service categories. Additionally, while these increases were especially strong in the month immediately following residents' initial exposure to operational transparency, the effects persisted in 11 of the 13 (or, respectively, 14) months that followed (Buell, Porter, & Norton, 2017). While this persistence shows that the updated application was also effective on a long-term basis, it is not entirely clear why the effect vanished after some time.

BOX 9.6 PRINCIPLE #5: OPERATIONAL TRANSPARENCY

Operational transparency in policy contexts refers to revealing the otherwise hidden work that the government performs by making it more visible to the public (Buell et al., 2017). It has previously been shown to be an important factor influencing attitudes toward the government, including trust (Buell et al., 2017, Studies 1 and 2). Next to participation (see the previous principle), transparency in a more general sense is one of the main communication strategies that can lead to higher trust in government (Kim & Kim, 2007). This is of particular importance in the policy context, as trust in the government improves the level of public policy acceptance and reduces administrative costs, while encouraging compliance with regulations and contributions to public good (e.g. Levi, 1998; Parks, 1994).

Simplicity

Increases in letter response rates by using simplicity and salience

How many letters do you receive per week? Which ones do you open right away, and which ones do you set aside to read later? Have you ever wondered about what makes you open, read, and act on some letters earlier than others?

The FCA, the body of financial regulation in the United Kingdom, tested exactly this in an RCT. It wanted to find out which elements of a letter get people to take action, and it was particularly interested in the effects of seven design features, mostly deriving from **simplicity** and **salience** principles. The FCA collaborated with a firm to apply these features to an original letter sent out to the firm's customers addressing inadequacies in past sales processes. The letter asked those customers who felt misled to call the firm's hotline. The outcome measure thus was the number of customers who called the helpline in order to get a refund. While a plain envelope and the original letter served as a control, the treatment mail included one of the six following alterations:

1. a message to "act quickly" on the envelope
2. a logo on the letterhead
3. replacement of existing bullet points with more salient bullet points
4. a simplified message that included only 60 percent of the original text
5. a sentence explaining (and stressing the quickness of) the claims process
6. the CEO's signature at the bottom of the letter

Overall, 195,140 letters were sent out. The treatments were assigned and combined in a balanced and randomized procedure. The FCA additionally tested the effect of a reminder letter, which we will not focus on in this section as the intervention was tested on another sample and thus effect sizes cannot be compared directly.

FIGURE 9.5 Response rates to letters with differently phrased messages

Note that response rates in the logo condition (2) did not differ from the control letter and are therefore not displayed in the graphic.

Whereas the control letter received a response rate of 1.5 percent, response rates were higher for those who received a letter with bullet points (+3.9 percent) compared to the control, as well as for the simplified message group and the claims process message group (both +1.4 percent). The logo letter and the envelope with the message to "act quickly" did not change or only negligibly changed response rates compared to the control, and individuals who had received a letter with the CEO's signature were slightly less likely to respond (−0.3 percent).

Overall, it seems that adding small changes to a letter that follow the simplicity (see Box 9.7) and salience (see Box 9.8) principles can make a difference in the way people respond (see Figure 9.5) (Adams & Hunt, 2013).

However, note that parts of these findings stand in contrast to those of Smart (2016), who found that people responded to letters about their interest-only mortgages less often when information was summarized in bullet points (−1.8 percent compared to the control). Yet, Smart's (2016) results also suggest that groups who received a simplified letter without a risk warning or a letter written in a friendlier, more informal way replied more often. Thus, simplicity might still have an effect on response rates. The efficacy of interventions might depend on message content. Smart (2016) concludes that, in her study, the letter content might have been too complicated, making the call to action less visible when it is simplified in bullet points. Another factor that influences efficacy might be the desired outcome: while Smart (2016) investigated how to increase customer payments, the study by Adams and Hunt (2013) encouraged consumers to request a refund.

Enhancement of central bank communications by using simplicity

Did you ever voluntarily read your bank's policy summaries? Probably not. Despite the central role that the banking system and monetary policies have in our lives, not everyone spends time reading bank documents. One of the reasons for this might be their incomprehensibility. For example, Fullwood (2016) found that in order to understand an average recent report from the Bank of England, one must have the literacy level of a university graduate. Given this finding, it is no surprise that the Bank of England was looking for a way to improve the communication of economic information and reports. In cooperation with the Behavioural Insights Team, they prepared an online experiment consisting of four conditions: one control condition and three treatment groups. A total of 2,275 participants were recruited for the experiment, yielding approximately 500 participants per condition.

For the control condition, the original Monetary Policy Summary from the February 2018 Inflation Report was used. In the first treatment group (visual summary), participants received a visual summary of the original report. According to the Flesch-Kincaid readability metric (which is calculated with regard to the number of words, sentences, and syllables), this summary was written in a simpler way and required the literacy level of an average 13- to 14-year-old. Despite its improved comprehensibility, the visual summary was longer than the original report. The second treatment group (reduced text summary) therefore received a shorter textual version of the visual summary. In the last treatment group (relatable summary), the key messages from the Inflation Report were made more relatable to the public by increasing the use of first- and second-person pronouns and reducing third-person abstractions, using everyday language instead of technical jargon (e.g. "rising prices" instead of "inflation"), and adding personalized visuals (such as an option to display the unemployment rate in the reader's region).

To evaluate the level of their comprehension, participants were asked five multiple-choice questions on the summary content after they had read the reports. Overall, groups in all treatment conditions showed higher levels of comprehensibility than the control group. More specifically, compared to the control group, the visual summary group showed a 0.5 point higher average comprehension score, whereas it was 0.6 point higher for the reduced text summary group and 0.8 point higher for the relatable summary group (see Figure 9.6). To understand how the comprehension scores relate to the five questions asked, take the example of the 0.8 point increase for the relatable summary group: this translates to answering an average of 2.85 out of

FIGURE 9.6 Comprehension scores of groups receiving different policy reports

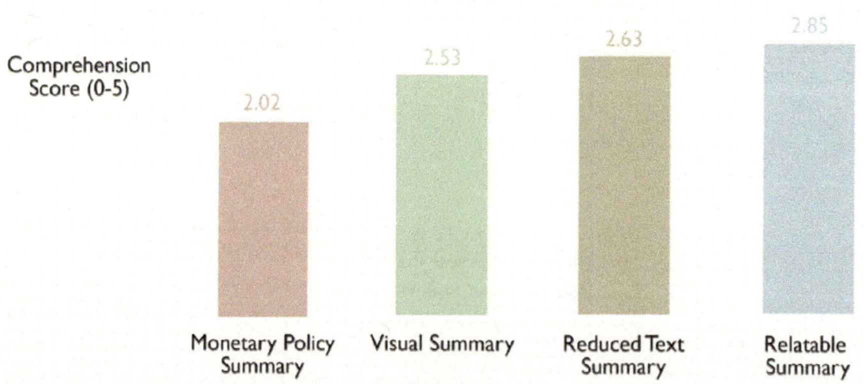

5 questions correctly, compared to an average of 2.02 in the baseline Monetary Policy Summary condition.

The increasing level of comprehension in all treatment conditions was also reflected in self-report ratings: participants in the treatment conditions more often reported that they were able to understand the content and material they had read.

The experiment also aimed to investigate how the different treatment conditions influence the participants' perception of the bank. In all conditions, the average perception score was about three points (out of five). The largest difference was noticeable in the relatable summary group: their reported perception of the bank was, on average, 0.28 points better than those who had read the baseline Monetary Policy Summary. Another variable examined was the participants' trust in the information they had read. However, in comparison to the control group, no treatment condition showed a difference in participants' trust levels at the .05 level of statistical significance. Thus, the different ways of presenting information did not seem to affect participants' trust in the organization (Bholat, Broughton, Parker, Ter Meer, & Walczak, 2018).

BOX 9.7 PRINCIPLE #6: SIMPLICITY

Generally speaking, the more complicated a message is, the less likely it will be understood and result in the desired outcome (Zarcadoolas, 2010). We refer to the idea that messages often need to be simple to be effective as the **simplicity** principle. The main barriers in message delivery often stem from experts using themselves as model audience members (De Bruin & Bostrom, 2013). Hence, policymakers may tend to present the information in ways that they personally find most fitting, while the actual needs of the target audience remain unaddressed. This cognitive bias, often referred to as the "curse of knowledge" (Birch & Bloom, 2007), can impede successful communication between policymakers and the public. While simplicity can facilitate the translation of knowledge, we cannot ignore its potential pitfalls. Simplification of a text without considering its actual content (e.g. by exclusively focusing on sentence length) can, counterintuitively, make the text harder to understand because readers must draw inferences themselves (Zarcadoolas, 2010). Additionally, simplification of a message by reducing the amount of text can sometimes lead to the omission of caveats, limitations, and other indicators of uncertainty (e.g. words like "may"). The inclusion of such indicators, however, is important for ensuring that the information conveyed is not exaggerated, and some studies have shown that indicators of uncertainty (especially when coming from the authors of a scientific study) improve the perceived credibility of the source (Jensen, 2008).

Salience

Improvements in climate change communication by using salience

Delivery of messages to the general public might be a tricky task. For example, even though climate change and its consequences are widely discussed topics, research suggests that less than half of Americans believe that "most climate scientists think global warming is happening" (Leiserowitz, Maibach, Roser-Renouf, Feinberg, & Howe, 2013). Note that, in contrast, in the same study almost two-thirds of Americans indicated that they themselves believe that global warming is real. Therefore, it seems that the discrepancy lies mainly within how Americans perceive scientific opinions.

So what is the most effective way to communicate consensus about global warming research? Van der Linden, Leiserowitz, Feinberg, and Maibach (2014) tried to answer this question by providing information about the scientific consensus on human-caused climate change in 11 different conditions – 10 treatment and one control condition. As the total number of participants was 1,104, each of these conditions contained about 100 participants. The general message was the same for all participants in the treatment groups: "97% of climate scientists have concluded that human-caused climate change is happening." What differed between conditions was the way in which the consensus was communicated. For two groups, the message was presented simply in the form of plain text or a pie chart. Other conditions included metaphors in varying forms. In contrast, no information was provided for the control group.

The results suggested that participants who received any treatment, and therefore any form of communication, displayed higher estimates of the scientific consensus than the control group. However, these levels differed between treatment conditions. More specifically, the pie chart and plain text groups showed the greatest change in comparison to the control group. The post-test to pre-test increase in the estimation of scientific consensus was 14.4 percent for the pie chart condition and 17.88 percent for the descriptive text condition. For metaphors, the average increase was 11.9 percent.

The weaker effects in the metaphor conditions were reported as a surprising result, considering how popular the use of metaphor is for scientists in the climate change discourse. The authors concluded that metaphors might be more effective in explaining complex information, whereas plain text might be more suitable to depict a straightforward concept such as scientific consensus.

Use of a "Pay now" stamp and letter rephrasing to increase the payment of fines

There are not many people who would say that they like paying penalties. Many people do not pay them on time, and some of them do not even answer the notices. To change this, New South Wales' Department of Premier & Cabinet, the Office of State Revenue, and the Behavioral Insights Team collaborated to design an intervention that aimed to test whether small changes in reminder notices could promote better policy outcomes. Their study used "Enforcement Orders," or letters for those who responded to neither a Penalty Notice nor a Penalty Reminder Notice to pay their fines. A total number of 48,445 letters were sent out. The control group received the standard form of Enforcement Orders, while the letters for the trial group were changed to make the messages more salient. Alongside those changes, a red "Pay Now" stamp was included on the first page of each letter.

Individuals in the trial group had a 3.1 percent higher payment rate than those in the control group (see the Figure 9.7). Even though this difference might seem small, the changes translated to AUS$1.02 million increase in payments for the New South Wales Government (Behavioural Insights Team, 2014).

FIGURE 9.7 Use of a "Pay now" stamp and letter rephrasing to increase the payment of fines

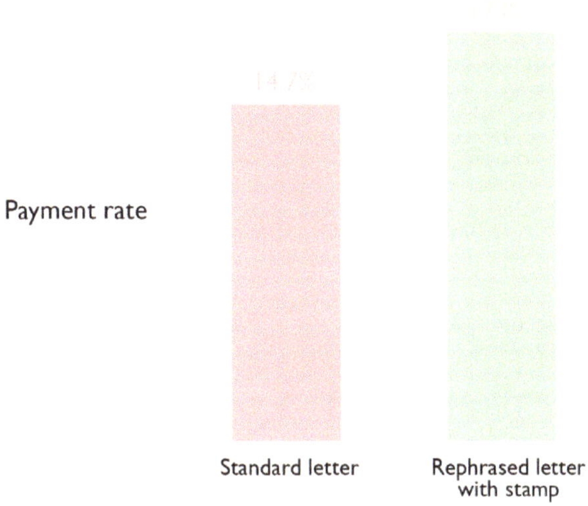

BOX 9.8 PRINCIPLE #7: SALIENCE

The principle of **salience** refers to an object that captures attention and is easily memorable (Min Kim & Kachersky, 2006). The principle of salience may be applied to written communication by highlighting text, adding headlines or pictures, and, more broadly, by visualization.

Additionally, advances in the field of communication research suggest that there is an alternative way to enhance the salience of a message through utilizing narrative communication. This form of communication involves a temporal sequence of events influenced by the actions of specific characters (Dahlstrom & Ho, 2012). Put differently, narrative communication often refers to a form of giving and receiving information through stories (Kreuter et al., 2007).

BOX 9.9 A BRIDGE FROM SCIENTISTS TO POLICYMAKERS: EFFECTIVE SCIENCE DISSEMINATION

To develop an evidence-based policy, the insight gained from scientific research first has to be communicated by scientists to policymakers, before it can be further communicated by policymakers to the public. In a first step, the insight gained from scientific research is communicated by scientists to policymakers in order to develop an evidence-based policy. In a second step, the resulting policy is then implemented and communicated to the public. These steps are necessary for effective **scientific dissemination** (step 1), as well as the successful implementation of policies (step 2) (see Figure 9.8).

Of course, in reality, the communication between scientists, policymakers, and the public is not as unidirectional as it first appears. While this is not the focus of the present chapter, the public also communicates with policymakers and policymakers also communicate with scientists. For example, the public can push an issue so that policymakers commission researchers to study it. The principles mentioned throughout this chapter may be used for scientists to communicate with policymakers as well with the public. As important as this step is, it is also a difficult one. Research has identified both major barriers to current science dissemination and solutions to overcome them. One example of applying the principles presented in this chapter to science dissemination is Insights for Impact (Policy Research Group, 2016), a report of the Policy Research Group at the University of Cambridge. As can be seen in Figure 9.9, the Policy Research Group summarizes and illustrates findings in the behavioral sciences by using salience and simplicity principles, with the goal of communicating their potential implications to policymakers.

FIGURE 9.8 A conceptualization of communication from scientists to the public in the policy context

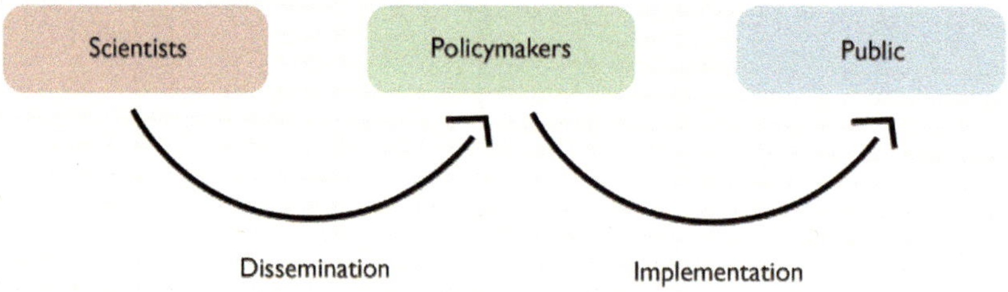

FIGURE 9.9 An example of a salient and simple science communication

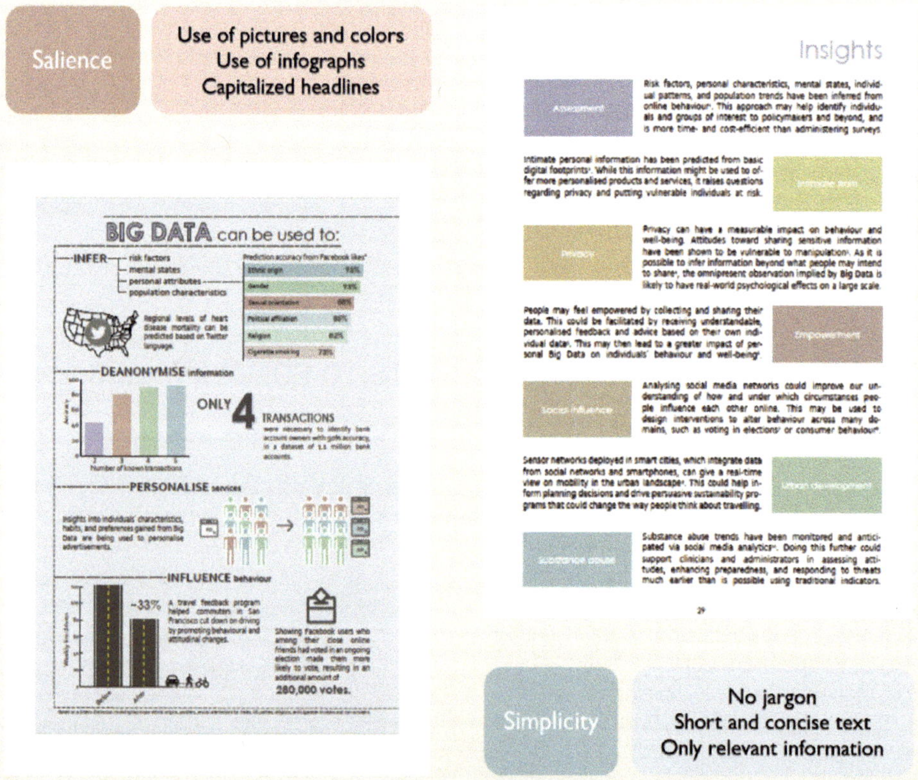

Conclusion

Communication is an important but challenging mechanism to connect governments and the public. While the exchange between these stakeholders can lead to many positive consequences, external barriers as well as potential mishaps by people involved are a constant. Various communication principles are permanently at work and can be utilized as instruments for optimizing this interaction. In any case, they must be considered when applying behavioral insights to public policy.

Effective communication also carries risks, beginning with how information such as personal data is handled, given the potential for its misuse. Additionally, these principles and tools may result in unwanted outcomes. Therefore, it is important to acknowledge that the quality of content should always be the priority, while effective communication strategies are a valuable asset that can help us share this content with others.

Essay questions

1 How could you get more people to attend the office Christmas party? Describe three principles that could be utilized and demonstrate how they could be applied in this context.

2 Which principles of communication are particularly suitable for engaging the public via Web 2.0 channels? Why?

3 Imagine a Facebook campaign about the importance of vaccination. How could the participatory nature of Facebook facilitate the implementation of this message, and how could it lead to adverse effects?

4 In this chapter, we described two important steps – science dissemination and policy implementation. Describe two examples, one for each of these steps, that illustrate how these steps can be performed effectively.

5 The response rate to an email offering a new benefit program for employees was pretty low. Just about 5 percent of employees registered for the program before the deadline. Try to use the communication principles described in this chapter to bring up possible explanations as to why the campaign was not successful.

Additional insights and further reading

Salience and framing did not reduce the number of errors in registration forms

OECD. (2017). Behavioural insights case studies: Public service delivery (Incomplete Company Registration Forms). In *Behavioral insights and public policy: Lessons from around the world*. Paris: OECD Publishing. https://doi.org/10.1787/9789264270480-en

Simplified contracts lead to increased involvement in the conditions of service delivery

OECD. (2017). Behavioural insights case studies: Telecommunications (Simplification of Telephone and Internet Contracts). In *Behavioral insights and public policy: Lessons from around the world*. Paris: OECD Publishing. https://doi.org/10.1787/9789264270480-en

Price transparency increases consumer welfare

Duke, C., Huck, S., & Wallace, B. (2010). *Experimental economics research: Final report*. London: Ofcom. Retrieved from www.ofcom.org.uk/__data/assets/pdf_file/0023/31865/experiments.pdf

Additional principles of persuasion

Cialdini, R. B. (2001). *Influence – Science and practice*. Boston, MA: Allyn & Bacon.

The type of academic information provided to parents impacts their choices and preferences

Hastings, J. S., Van Weelden, R., & Weinstein, J. (2007). *Preferences, information, and parental choice behavior in public school choice (No. w12995)*. National Bureau of Economic Research. Retrieved from www.nber.org/papers/w12995

This chapter was adapted from Plohl, N., Ruggeri, K., Stuhlreyer, J. P., & Matz, S. C. (2019). Communication and public engagement. In K. Ruggeri (Ed.), *Behavioral insights for public policy: Concepts and cases* (pp. 174–199). New York and London: Routledge.

10 Evidence-based policy

Kai Ruggeri, Olatz Ojinaga-Alfageme, Amel Benzerga, Jana B. Berkessel, Maja Friedemann, Renata Hlavová, Marvin Kunz, Nejc Plohl, Felicia Sundström, and Tomas Folke

Acknowledgments: Brian Head and Michael Howlett

Chapter summary

There are many types of policies that originate from many sources. In this chapter, we review these and how they have been developed over time. We illustrate how many policies initially targeted at-risk or problematic groups and how more recent approaches have shifted toward thinking about entire populations. All such approaches include strengths and weaknesses, which often relate to the lack of a clear evidence base prior to implementation. Scientific evidence is increasingly regarded as a helpful addition to many theories of behavioral interventions, hence the increased use of evidence-based policy frameworks. As theory has to be balanced with pragmatics to be useful in policy, a practical pathway model for the development of evidence for policy evaluation is introduced.

Learning objectives

- Understand the various types of policies
- Understand the Rose Hypothesis and the implications of high-risk vs. population approaches
- Define evidence in the context of policy
- Learn the value of systematic approaches to policy and the integration of evidence throughout
- Appreciate the strengths and limitations of evidence-based policy

Policy shapes and sizes

In the first chapter, we covered what policies are, what they aim to do, how they often come to exist, and a brief history of how they get made. However, the word "policy" itself can relate to many topics, aspects of life, and sources, meaning there are many forms of policies. While policies may ultimately seek to deliver a positive outcome across the relevant groups, there is no one specific way policies are decided, developed, implemented, or evaluated.

DOI: 10.4324/9781003181873-10

In terms of the study of policy, the twentieth century was a period of substantial interest, and as a result, classifications, typologies, taxonomies, and methodological frameworks for studying policy began to emerge (Howlett & Mukherjee, 2017). As described in the first chapter, Lowi's (1966) approach stood for a long time as the prevailing classification of types of policies. More recent classifications have placed greater emphasis on other characteristics of policy design. This has included the type of political risk a policy choice can have (Lamborn, 1998), the strengths and weaknesses of different policy tools (Linder & Peters, 1989), the combination of different policy tools into bundles (Gunningham & Sinclair, 1999), and the reworking and adaptation of existing policies to new contexts (Howlett & Rayner, 2013). However, perhaps the most broad-ranging approach to the study and development of policy in recent literature is **evidence-based policy (EBP)**.

Since the 1990s, the idea of having evidence formally integrated into policies has been promoted by a number of academics, institutions, government leaders, and international organizations (Cartwright & Hardie, 2012). The appeal of this is that it presents a systematic form of validation for decision-making in leadership: those responsible can refer to "the evidence" at the front end ("this is why it is a good decision") and for any outcomes ("this decision was made on the best information available at the time"). Thus, the use of evidence in policymaking should improve civic trust in the people making the decisions and increase the perceived legitimacy of policies (Head, 2015). To an extent, evidence appears to rise above partiality, politics, bias, and naiveté, ostensibly reassuring an audience that policies are not about the opinions or preferences of those in charge, but rather are informed responses to specific issues and the best options available to resolve them for the greatest benefit. Yet, agreement on how each of these exists and is defined in reality – "evidence," "best," "benefit" – is far more complex in practice.

What is evidence?

To understand EBP, its implications, strengths, weaknesses, and applications, there are many aspects that require clear definitions. Beyond what was discussed in Chapter 1 about policies themselves, it is most critical to have a clear understanding of what *evidence* is. In this book, the term **evidence** refers to scientifically supported conclusions that are primarily identified through peer-reviewed sources. However, understanding of the term differs among contexts and use, so there are many other possible definitions for it. For our purposes, we will focus on the context of applications of evidence derived from scientific study to policy.

The term evidence-based policy (Bowen & Zwi, 2005; Lin & Gibson, 2003) is a paradigm that incorporates research evidence into the process of **decision-making**, namely, the process of identifying the best option to tackle the defined problem. It provides a framework for making **policy** decisions on the basis of **evidence** to help address and resolve problems so that more effective policies can be implemented. Nevertheless, in the policy literature, the term evidence-based policy is often defined simply as a review of empirical research findings (Marston & Watts, 2003). Evidence-based policy evolved from **evidence-based practice** and **evidence-based medicine**, where clinicians try to achieve better outcomes by basing their interventions on evidence (Grimshaw, Eccles, Lavis, Hill, & Squires, 2012). Evidence-based medicine represents an integration of clinical expertise, high-impact research findings, and the interests of patients and caregivers in clinical services (Marston & Watts, 2003). It is the conscientious, explicit, and judicious use of the current best evidence in making decisions about the care of individual patients.

Altogether, the aim of EBP is to promote interventions that are supported by the best evidence available at the time but, of course, later evidence may contradict the existing theories, leading to better interventions as evidence accumulates. As we will show, however, this is perhaps an oversimplified view of EBP, and many challenges to this notion do exist (Cartwright & Hardie, 2012; Cartwright & Stegenga, 2011; Cartwright, Goldfinch, & Howick, 2010; Cartwright, 2009).

In order to apply EBP, it is essential to have a good understanding of what constitutes evidence. However, definition of the word evidence might be a challenging task because many textbooks dealing with evidence in terms of EBP discuss the term but do not provide a single, explicit definition (i.e. Parkhurst, 2017; Pawson, 2006). This lack of a definition does not imply a disinterest by the authors, but rather the complexity of the construct. In fact, there seems to be no clear and absolute meaning of evidence; it varies depending on its context and use (Thistlethwaite et al., 2012). Even though several authors repudiate the possibility of having an evidence base from which policymakers can draw to achieve agreement (Bennett & Jessani, 2011), there are still a few different authors who have attempted to give a definition for evidence within EBP. For Jones and Higgs (2000), evidence equals knowledge arising from a variety of sources that can be considered as credible. Guyatt, Rennie, Meade, and Cook (2002) contemplate potential evidence as any empirical observation about relationships between events. Evidence encompasses all of the systematically obtained information or facts (Rycroft-Malone et al., 2004).

"Evidence" in the context of EBP is generated by applied research, namely, research that attempts to apply lessons from more abstract research to the real world (Head, 2008). To be able to aid in the design of effective policy, scientific evidence needs to be based on wide, rigorous, and systematic research. In order to properly support policy design, scientific evidence might also need to be combined with other forms of knowledge. According to Head (2008), three important types of evidence relevant for policy arise from (1) political knowledge, (2) rigorous scientific and technical analysis, and (3) practical and professional field experience. Though all of these information sources can be useful, scientifically generated evidence should still remain the foundation for evidence-based policymaking. Other sources, such as political knowledge and practical and professional field experience, should be considered afterward as means to specify how the scientific evidence can best be implemented in the current context.

If we consider the three types of evidence relevant for policymaking in more depth, political knowledge includes contextual judging of activities, determining priorities, communicating key messages, and making compromises (Head, 2008). Conversely, scientific knowledge is based on research and provides a more systematic analysis of current and past observations and possible generative models that could account for these observations. Because of the combination of methodological approaches and perspectives used, cross-disciplinary knowledge might be particularly valuable in informing policy design. However, the practical wisdom of professionals and organizational knowledge connected to program management and implementation offer good sources of evidence as well (Head, 2008).

Yet, not all collected evidence is commonly used in policymaking. As Nutley, Davies, and Walter (2002) indicate, a more limited range of evidence is typically used. In practice, policymakers' concepts of what constitutes good evidence markedly differ from those of researchers (Davidson, 2017). Nonetheless, there are key characteristics that determine the quality and usefulness of evidence used in policymaking (Parkhurst, 2017; Shaxson, 2005; Spencer, Ritchie, Lewis, & Dillon, 2003):

1 Relevance: the impact that the evidence can create and its generalization. Generalization refers to sampling and the context of the study, namely, whether the study is widely applicable or context-specific and how the findings might change in different contexts.
2 Quality, accuracy, and objectivity: statistical problems of evidence generated. If we take into consideration whether the methods were used properly and whether the findings were not determined by the investigators or policymakers, we are able to reduce bias in the evidence base and strengthen our interpretations.
3 Credibility: the internal reliability of the evidence, relying on a clear argument and using appropriate methods and presentation of the conclusions. It is important to distinguish the sources of evidence (expert or lay knowledge) and identify whether the analysis methods were appropriate for the available data.
4 Practicalities: how accessible the evidence is for policymakers along with its feasibility and affordability.

The forms of scientific evidence most commonly used in policymaking are (1) randomized controlled trials, (2) systematic reviews, and (3) meta-analyses (Parkhurst, 2017). A **randomized controlled trial** is a type of scientific experiment in which individuals, groups, or regions are assigned randomly to either an intervention group or a control group not receiving any intervention (for an overview, see Chapter 11). **Systematic review** is an extensive review of the literature that rigorously summarizes the work about a certain topic, analyzing multiple research studies. **Meta-analysis** is a statistical analysis based on combining multiple data sources or studies testing the same intervention, and it typically forms the pinnacle analysis of a systematic review (Parkhurst, 2017). Although systematic reviews seem to be the most common source of evidence in policymaking, their utility is still under discussion, as is the value of their associated meta-analyses (Stegenga, 2011). This is typically because a broad evaluation of impact, such as from a cancer drug, may show no major differences when compared to similar interventions, even though subgroups within an analysis do show an effect (Ruggeri, Maguire, & Cook, 2016).

In sum, there is no single, universal definition for either evidence or EBP (Cartwright & Stegenga, 2011). This is not necessarily a problem, and it can be seen as both an opportunity for meaningful debate and a chance to find consensus through converging insights from differing perspectives, as with any such construct (Stewart-Brown, Middleton, & Ashton, 2015). While no single definition is mandatory, for the purposes of understanding in this book, we suggest that the term refers exclusively to scientifically supported conclusions that have been primarily identified from peer-reviewed sources.

Strengths and weaknesses of evidence-based policy

The growing use of EBPs in governments is a response to an increasing demand for more effective policy interventions and represents a shift away from traditional approaches that may have been informed predominantly by a small number of stakeholders or ideologies (OECD, 2017a). Using the scientific method as a basis, EBPs draw from previous knowledge and test new hypotheses before they are broadly applied, therefore reducing the risks and costs associated with potentially unsuccessful interventions. Another advantage is that

EBPs may offer cheap and effective solutions to change behavior that otherwise might not have been considered. One example comes from the airport in Copenhagen, Denmark. This intervention was developed from observations of smoker behavior outside the airport, and it demonstrated that by simply indicating the location of a specified smoking area, people were much less likely to light their cigarettes in nonsmoking zones than when only the non-smoking areas were indicated (OECD, 2017a). This simple conversion of observed data into intervention embodies many of the features to covered in earlier pages of this book.

Although there is still a lack of robust evidence demonstrating that the use of evidence in policy implementation leads to reliably better outcomes, it is accepted that the collaboration between academia, government, and laypeople will increase the likelihood that it will have an impact (Armstrong, Doyle, Lamb, & Waters, 2006). For now, we will consider the strengths and weaknesses of EBPs in terms of the credibility of evidence and by addressing the political aspects of policymaking.

The credibility of evidence

Public opinion has a major influence on policy (Burstein, 2003), which means that scientific evidence alone may not, for example, convince someone that flying is safe or that certain foods should not be served in schools. Such evidence, therefore, should not be overvalued as the only credible source of knowledge in policymaking (Oliver et al. 2014b). This focus on experimental evidence can sometimes underestimate the complexity of issues that are addressed by policies (Smith & Joyce, 2012), which may, for example, also involve context-dependent cultural or political influences. In fact, empirical research may sometimes have its own specific value-laden assumptions, that could strongly influence the operationalization or measurement of important concepts (Tetlock, 1994).

An overly simplistic approach to evidence-based policy might also imply a unidirectional relationship between those producing scientific evidence and those taking up the knowledge and "translating" it to policy. While being experts on their own research, scientists can often miss other important aspects of the policymaking process (Oliver, Innvar, Lorenc, Woodman, & Thomas, 2014a). The shift away from a unidirectional idea of knowledge transmission to an idea based on collaboration and mutual learning may create a sense of shared accountability toward the target outcome of a given policy (Wehrens, Bekker, & Bal, 2011). A policy should therefore be informed by a breadth of evidence collected through a collaborative process between the government, policymakers, researchers, and laypeople (Kogan & Henkel, 1983; Oliver et al., 2014a; Resnik & Elliot, 2016). This is becoming increasingly possible with tools produced by groups such as the Behavioural Insights Team in the United Kingdom, which has developed the EAST Tool (Behavioural Insights Team, 2014) that stands for Easy, Attractive, Social, and Timely – features it has determined are critical to make a behavior policy effective. This pragmatic framework seeks to assist in making more efficient and effective policies with the use of behavioral insights.

The politics of evidence-based policy

Policymaking almost never involves purely technical decisions based solely on empirical evidence and would rarely base decisions on value calculations alone. Policymaking is in fact political and involves constant trade-offs between multiple stakeholders with competing interests. The effective development and application of EBPs rely on a compromise between the values, capacity, and resources of a particular government and the evidence made available by researchers. It has consistently been found that two of the main factors influencing the use of evidence in policy are the quality of the relationship between researchers and policymakers and the accessibility of research evidence (Oliver et al., 2014b). Yet, the idea of using more evidence in policymaking is not always sufficient.

Our own values and beliefs are major influences on how we view evidence, and the same is true for policymakers. For example, a government that believes in the dangers of climate change is more likely to develop policies aimed at encouraging people to switch to a more sustainable energy provider than a government that does not believe there is a danger. Such contextual variability can therefore limit the generalizability and replicability of EBPs. A particular EBP might not necessarily produce the same outcomes across countries or even across communities within the same country. It is clear that, in the context of EBPs, there should be consideration of the variety of social values and concerns that exist, as well as how these can influence different evidence bases relevant to each concern (Parkhurst, 2017).

One of the challenges in evidence-based policymaking is the utilization of sound research in controversial or value-laden policy areas. Evidence might be regarded in a biased rather than an objective and balanced way, such that partisans only consider available evidence that supports their own point of view (Head, 2015). Take the legalization of cannabis, for example. This debate is mainly discussed in terms of health risks versus benefits. On the one hand, cannabis has been considered a gateway drug to other more addictive and damaging drugs. On the other hand, it has been considered beneficial for a number of medical conditions. Yet, although the arguments for the risks versus the benefits of cannabis can, in fact, be empirically studied and directly compared, they do not necessarily come in with equal weight. Our individual belief system influences what we accept as evidence, or how we balance between two competing pieces of evidence. The types of policies developed surrounding the use of cannabis therefore depend on the chosen evidence base of the particular community or government, influenced by their specific belief systems. This means the comparison between risks and benefits is not likely to be the only feature in the policy debate or in establishing related legislation.

In sum, the question of what exactly constitutes good evidence and what good evidence use is within a policy process can be interpreted differently depending on the context (Parkhurst, 2017). With better collaboration and an increase in understanding between the academic community, laypeople, and governing bodies, the challenging questions of how and in what contexts different types of evidence should be used to develop effective policies could begin to be answered.

A subtle caution about "evidence" and "evidence-based policy"

Greenhalgh and Russell (2006) argue that to improve the policymaking process, we first need to acknowledge that it is both a socially and a politically charged process – a "social drama" (Turner, 1980; Greenhalgh & Russell, 2006), per se. They suggest that improvements in the amount, clarity, and communication of evidence will not make policymaking more efficient. In fact, it is the policymakers themselves that can ultimately improve the process by developing a better awareness of their own biases and values and how these can influence their arguments for what constitutes evidence and what is considered an acceptable action. It is through the open reflection on and acknowledgment of all motives behind the respective arguments of policy stakeholders that "evidence gaps" might be more systematically identified and the frustrations involved in policymaking might be reduced. In other words, to improve the policy process, there has to be commitment from those involved on all sides to acknowledge biases, limitations, opportunities, and risks, rather than simply trying to find evidence to justify a decision. This applies to policymakers as well as to the population at large.

What else gets into policies?

There has been a rapid increase of investment in evidence-based policies as well as in thinking about entire populations. When we explore the literature associated with these approaches, two clear dimensions emerge: one is the level to which a policy is driven by evidence or ideology, and the other involves how much a policy is seeking to correct a problem or to proactively maximize outcomes (see Box 10.1). However, to create discrete classifications would diminish the appreciation for how these are, in fact, balances rather than binary. Instead, it can be useful for identifying multiple elements of a single policy, for instance, to see each quadrant and axis as part of a checklist to ensure that multiple perspectives are considered prior to implementation. To illustrate this, Figure 10.1 presents two axes for mapping out policies. Note that these sections are meant to help with learning the processes and features of policies, but they are not absolutes that apply in all cases.

Evidence–ideology continuum

The first axis in the model presents the continuum from ideological to evidence-driven approaches. While this distinction is supported in literature (e.g. Waarden, 1992), it is often subject to misinterpretation. Many may believe that the use of evidence automatically leads to a better outcome, yet in reality, not all evidence is equally valuable; in addition, sources and uses of evidence also have to be considered (Oliver et al., 2014a). To understand all ideological policies as inherently bad is wrong as well; in many cases, ideological policies align with rational solutions and lead to positive outcomes (Grossman, 2013). For example, imagine if a family only chose to eat at restaurants that received five-star ratings in online reviews. If their close friends happened to open a restaurant and invited them to the opening, would the evidence base (lack of a five-star rating) keep them from going to support their friends (ideological)? Probably not. As such, instead of labeling one side of the scale as universally good and the other one as bad, it is important to be aware of the advantages and disadvantages of both.

Perhaps the biggest advantage of ideological policies is their convenience. Policies often align by default with the core beliefs of policymakers and broadly with those of their constituents (Grossman, 2013). Evidence-based policies, on the other hand, can challenge core beliefs by taking an empirical approach to design and evaluation. In such cases where evidence-based policies challenge core beliefs, these may prove to be more difficult to implement than ideological policies. Additionally, many of those readily available beliefs create a great deal of benefits, so they are not universally incorrect (Gigerenzer, Todd, & The ABC Research Group, 1999).

A common disadvantage of ideological policies, though, is that being effective in a specific context at the time of implementation does not guarantee effectiveness in changing circumstances or adaptation when new evidence becomes available (Grossman, 2013). Consider if policies were not updated in the light of new evidence – we might still use hot whiskey as a sleeping drug for infants (e.g. Harding, 1920). This treatment seemed reasonable at the beginning of the twentieth century because it did put babies to sleep, but it would be indefensible now because of the accumulated evidence on the negative effects of alcohol on the neonatal brain.

While it is important to understand advantages and disadvantages of extreme points of the spectrum, few policies can be classified as purely evidence-driven or purely ideological. Instead, most policies lie between these extremes, indicating at least some amount of each except in extreme cases, though it is difficult to present a policy that lacks *any* ideology, given that a preference for the use of evidence in making a decision is itself an ideology. In this way, it becomes quite evident that having both scientific evidence and ideologies (whether social, political, cultural, or other forms) explicitly considered in the development of policy may be the most responsible and reliable approach anyway. Additionally, while this is one helpful approach to classification, it is not the only continuum on which policies are understood. Where extreme applications of ideology come into play, it may be more useful to consider the rhetoric used by those in leadership positions – this is an important topic but not one we are able to cover in this volume.

BOX 10.1 DESCRIPTION OF POLICY SCALES

Treatment – Treatment policies aim to counter a known problem or concern, often in urgent situations where the status quo or no response may lead to worsening outcomes. In many cases, such policies do not emphasize the long-term implications, but instead focus on fixing an existing issue.

Proactive – Proactive policies have the goal of creating opportunities and better outcomes for a situation in which a problem is not yet present. These kinds of policies therefore have a better opportunity to focus on long-term goals compared to the more acute treatment policies.

Evidence-based – Classification of a policy as evidence based means that there is, to some extent, a use of existing scientific knowledge and information in the creation and choice of an intervention. Such policies use insights to demonstrate that a better outcome (e.g. reduced risk or increased chance of success) is more likely if one option is used over the others.

Ideological – An ideological policy is one that focuses on implementing a particular belief rather than maximizing an outcome (e.g. closing a store on Sundays in observance of a religious custom). In these instances, action in line with the belief is the important outcome, rather than any measurable benefits that accompany it.

Proactivity–treatment continuum

Another general philosophical lens through which policies can be scaled involves the extent to which they are targeted to address a known issue or to advance the standing of a population (Torjman, 2005). Essentially, every policy can be understood in this way, though it is rarely clear that one policy is purely one or the other. For example, exercise can help an overweight individual lose weight (treatment), reduce the risk of certain illnesses associated with sedentary behavior (prevention), and improve overall function (promotion). To illustrate this, we present the second axis as a continuum from proactive to treatment. What makes this particularly

FIGURE 10.1 A conceptualization of four features of policy: evidence, ideology, proactivity, treatment

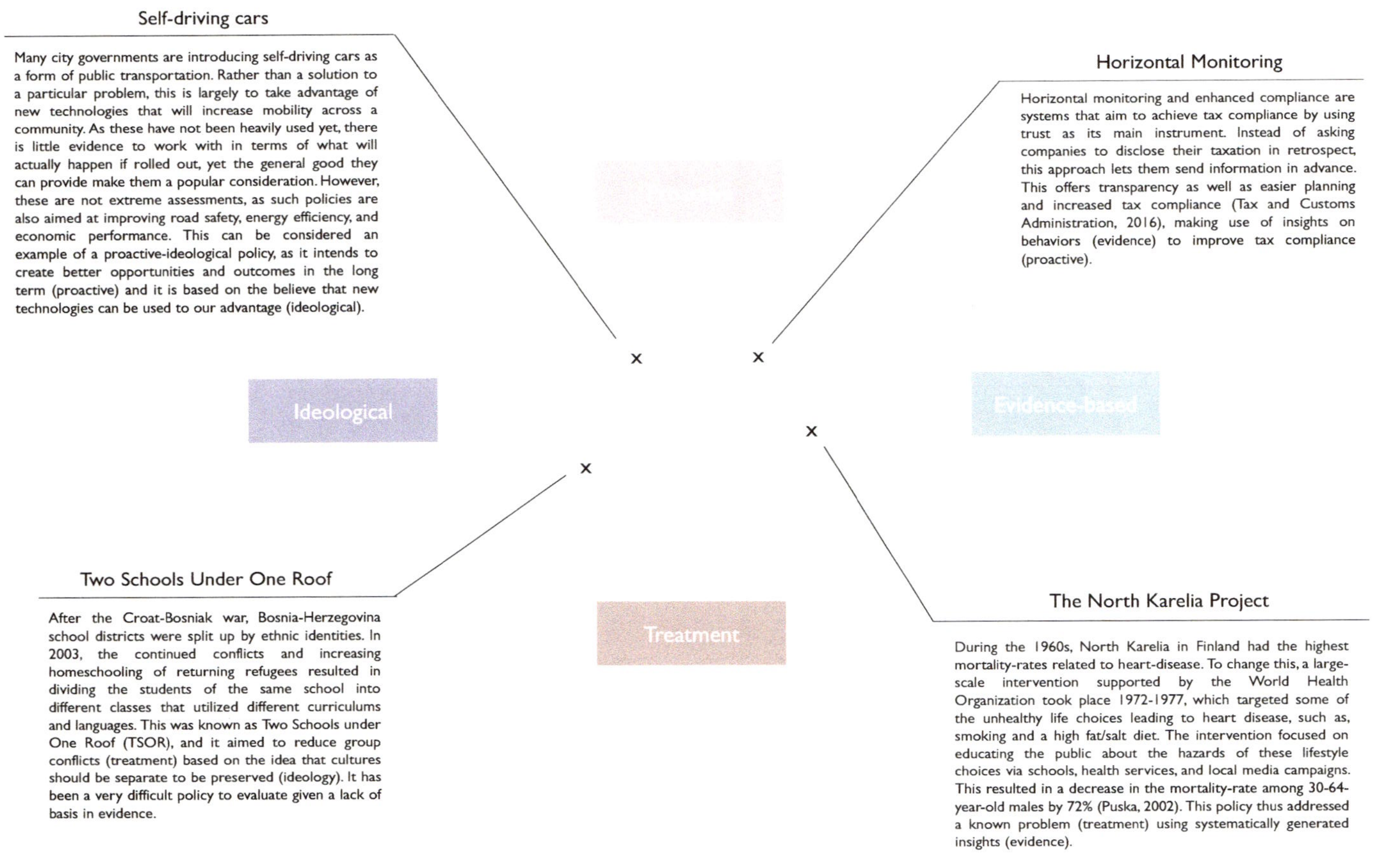

This figure presents a conceptual understanding of different policy types. It is not an absolute nor a robust depiction, but can be useful in understanding the use of evidence and other features of policy across a number of challenges or for multiple policies addressing the same issue.

relevant to the first axis is the broad theory of *purpose*, which is the relationship that links the two. While other features of policy that will be discussed later include costs, effectiveness, implementation, and so on, these elements speak to the application of policy not the concept of it. Combining these two into a single diagram demonstrates collectively what purpose a policy is aiming to carry out, which is critical for understanding likely impacts and implications later.

Perhaps the biggest difference between such policies is the sense of urgency of the problem. Although the consequences of proactive policies are often distant and uncertain, studies from different fields show that proactive policies may sometimes be more cost-effective than treatment policies (e.g. Drechsler, Eppink, & Wätzold, 2011). For example, ecological policies for species conservation are often implemented only when populations are at critically low numbers. Once policies are finally decided, solution of the problem often requires additional conservation measures and a high level of support, resulting in higher costs than would have been required if conservation efforts had started earlier (Drechsler et al., 2011). The implications of these distinctions are quite significant, as will be discussed later, because policies are often seen as responses to problems, which can limit outcomes to focus only on short-term objectives. In the absence of having any proactive policies that seek to break negative cycles, long-term objectives and gains may be forsaken and near-term issues might be repeated.

Ultimately, treatment policies focus on fixing a known problem, whereas proactive ones promote a given potential in the absence of a specific threat. However, this is again not a binary classification, and unlike the evidence–ideology continuum, it is much easier to present a conceptual explanation for landing in the middle: **prevention**, which refers to interventions that seek to avoid a problem prior to it materializing through actions that reduce exposure to known risks. This does not mean that all policies in the middle focus on preventing negatives, but that placement on the axis itself can represent a policy type as well as a combination of types.

Plotting across both axes

When combined to form a spectrum, the two axes create a useful conceptualization of policy approaches. The purpose of this tool is not to rate one approach, cover all possible features, or even compare approaches to the same challenge. Instead, the aim is to be able to map out a number of policy approaches for an organization or for a single issue. In this way, it can assist with understanding the ongoing interventions and can anticipate impacts as well as likely gaps. Furthermore, it can help with seeing policies as intervals, not single points on a quadrant or in a binary group. For example, the North Karelia health policy is widely seen as the archetype for population health promotion. However, the initiative itself was in response to identified public health issues related to behavior. The initiatives used covered a large spread of the proactive–treatment axis, which may have also contributed to their effectiveness over a long period of time. This particular conceptualization of policy approaches is not new, yet it has gained momentum in recent years due to a highly discussed concept known as the **Rose Hypothesis**.

From treating individuals to boosting populations

In 1985, the British epidemiologist Geoffrey Rose published an article titled "Sick individuals and sick populations," which was republished verbatim in the same journal in 2001 and has been cited nearly 4,000 times in scientific literature as of 2017. Given the notoriety this piece received at the time and how it has been sustained since, it is inaccurate to call this article prescient.

Yet, with the rapid boost in EBPs described in this chapter, the philosophy he has presented has perhaps never been a more relevant framework within the discourse on population-level interventions. This is largely because Rose's argument operates on a fundamental availability and understanding of evidence that can be interpreted for decision-making and applications, typically in the form of population-level data that identify variability, risks, and exposures.

While the work has been widely cited, it is not without controversy, particularly regarding applications of the population approach. A number of examples of this misuse were highlighted by Sally Davies (2014) and William Davies (2015) – no relation – showing that a large amount of the work claiming to utilize the Rose Hypothesis falls short on method and impact. However, many of those issues are in fact the fault of those citing the model as opposed to the model itself, largely due to researchers overlooking the principles Rose presents for effective population-level effects.

In the original paper (which was formed from a wider book), Rose presents two general approaches to health policy: the high-risk strategy and the population strategy. In the high-risk strategy, Rose outlines the classical approach to the treatment of sick individuals in a population, which involves identifying those groups of people who are either already unwell or most likely to become unwell. In the population strategy, interventions seek to shift the means of the entire population and not focus solely on those who are worst off, though that proportion should also decrease if the curve increases uniformly. In the latter case, Rose argued, the high-risk approach means that even effective treatments will not lead to improvements in average health across a population. This creates an argument for thinking beyond treatment for ways to improve public health, which then form the basis for considering population approaches.

In the population approach, Rose essentially presents four "rules" for a policy to be effective at shifting the curve (see Figure 10.2). The first is that there must be appreciation that the

FIGURE 10.2 Nuanced visualization of the Rose Hypothesis

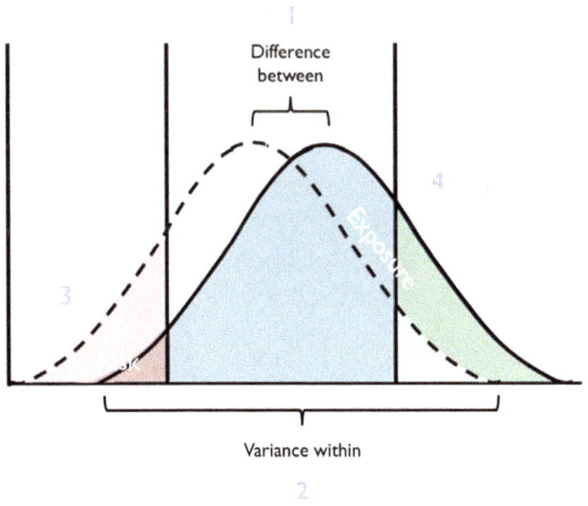

The Rose Model has four major components. First, the difference in means (1) between two populations will always be less than the variation (2) within one population. Next, risks (3) within populations must be identified and contrasted with risks in other groups. Following this, differences in exposures (4) to both positive and negative environmental aspects must be identified between populations, as everyone within a population would be affected equally and therefore no differences would be visible. With these identified and factored into an intervention, policies may now be effective at shifting the mean and not simply treating those at the bottom.

variation seen within one population (meaning the distance from top to bottom) will always be greater than simply comparing the means of two groups. In other words, while differences in incomes between genders may show that males earn more than females, the difference between the highest and lowest earning females is substantially greater and indicators will have much better power in identifying those. Second, Rose states that risk factors have to be understood within populations, whether they are genetic or other innate features or patterns observed within a group but not found in others. Additionally, and perhaps most critically, Rose says that exposures within and between groups have to be considered as those will have substantially greater impacts than individual behaviors in terms of population outcomes. For example, two very active people may have generally good health. However, if one person lives in a rural area with minimal air pollution and the other lives in Beijing, we can expect that, more often than not, the active individual in Beijing will have worse health than the one in a rural area. Likewise, we would expect that the rural population – regardless of activity level – would have better health than people living in Beijing (again, removing activity level). Thus, an attempt to simply improve activity levels in Beijing may not drastically improve the health of the population, whereas addressing the quality of the air would. It is important to state that positive exposures can also create positive differences, such as greater exposure to education at an early age resulting in better population outcomes than a group with lower exposure. The final "rule" in this approach is that, for any intervention to be effective at shifting the curve, the three prior rules must be addressed (variation, risk, and exposure) alongside any specific intervention. Rose uses the example of drinking water in Scotland: while behavioral policies might have shown anecdotal improvements, the risk factors associated with disease and the poor quality of the drinking water – to which the entire population was equally exposed – were the greatest influences that needed to be addressed prior to any specific behaviors. Likewise, Rose points to the North Karelia interventions in Finland (Puska, 2002), where genetic factors, behaviors, and education were all useful in a long-term effort to improve health in what had been a region of high disease, poor health choices, and low physical activity.

To attempt to determine which risk factors could explain why some individuals in a given population are more susceptible to an illness than others automatically assumes a heterogeneity of risk factors within a population. However, disease risk differs not only between individuals but also between different populations (Rose, 2001). If individually focused policy research ignores the heterogeneity between populations, then it aims to find the causes of cases yet fails to look for the causes of incidence (why the base rate of a problem may differ between populations). To illustrate, it is generally understood that water hardness is inversely related to cardiovascular disease rates (Burton, 2008). In the mountainous regions of Scotland all drinking water is soft, so water hardness cannot explain any individual variations in cardiovascular disease for that population. However, if the population is compared to other parts of the UK, the lack of hard water might explain lower incidence rates in the Scottish Highlands relative to other UK populations.

The two approaches to policy should not be seen as discrete, but as complementary and as useful in different contexts. While they have fundamental differences in terms of ideology (i.e. one presumes that focusing on those with the greatest risk will bring a maximum benefit, whereas the other presumes that only by addressing the entire population regardless of individual risk will impact be maximized), this is not to say that one is better than the other, but that they each offer unique strengths. They therefore achieve different goals, meaning a combination of both approaches might lead to the best outcomes (Doyle, Furey, & Flowers, 2006).

The strengths and weaknesses of population-level interventions largely mirror those of targeted interventions (see Figure 10.3). A primary strength is the explicit aim to decrease

FIGURE 10.3 Strengths and weaknesses of Rose's two policy approaches

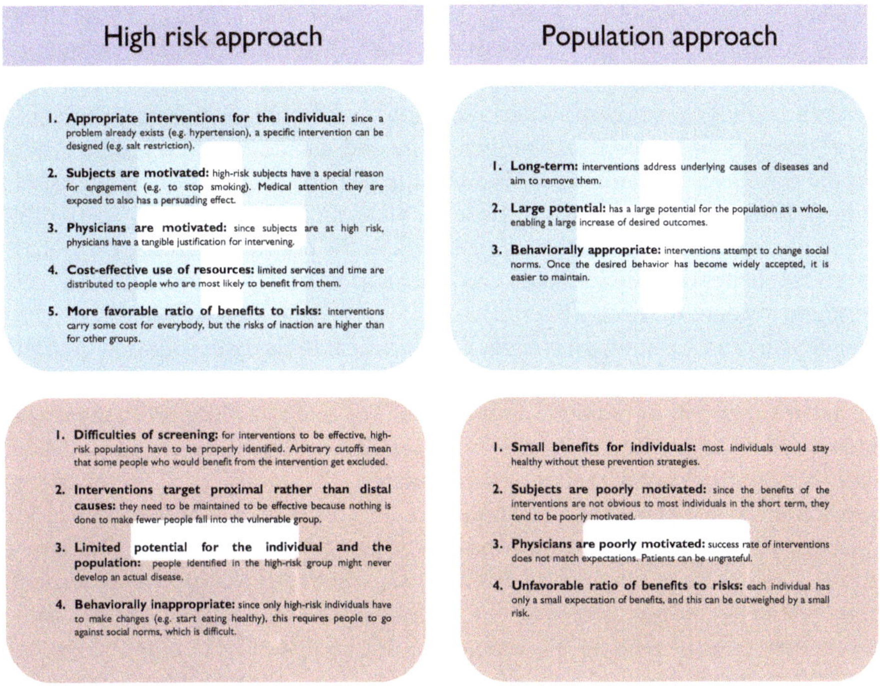

the risk of the full population by attacking the core causes of the underlying problem (Hawe & Potvin, 2009). If we return to the cardiovascular example, a population-level intervention might urge fast food restaurants to downsize their portions and thus hopefully reduce the fat intake of the population. This has the benefit of addressing one of the core causes of cardiovascular disease and may perhaps bring incidence rates down by preventing people who were at a low-to-moderate risk from ever joining the high-risk or sick groups. The inverse is that the population as a whole might be less motivated to change their diets than those people who know their life may depend on it. Similarly, the cost-benefit ratio is lower because resources will be spent on modifying the behavior of people who may never develop heart disease.

More than 20 years after Rose's initial paper contrasting individual-focused interventions with population-level interventions, his framework is still relevant and frequently discussed. In a follow-up paper, Doyle et al. (2006) demonstrated that focusing exclusively on one approach over the other may be problematic and could lead to an increased gap between different parts of a population. For instance, while general life expectancy for babies born in the UK is rising, the gap between mean life expectancy and that for babies in the lowest socio-economic quintile is also widening (Flowers, Bailey, Streather, & Wilkinson, 2004). In this case, the distribution has shifted, but left behind individuals at high-risk, expanding inequalities. If policymakers only focus on population strategies, they may exacerbate those inequalities, meaning high-risk strategies are necessary. As such, many would argue that policy should make use of both approaches to address the majority and minorities.

Libertarian paternalism

It is important to note that population-level interventions through policy will almost always require some involvement of the state. This may come in the form of policies themselves, or in terms of regulating various initiatives that reach the public on a near-ubiquitous level, such as advertising and transportation. In the context of population approaches to policy, this presents a rather controversial aspect regarding the extent to which governments should determine (directly or indirectly) what behaviors and choices are best and to what extent they should be explicitly mandated or just encouraged. This topic is often discussed under the frame of **libertarian paternalism** (Thaler & Sunstein, 2003), which is when individuals are steered in a certain direction through changes in the choice architecture toward what is deemed to be a better decision or behavior (paternalism) without forcing it, thus preserving their ultimate freedom of choice (libertarian).

While it may be less controversial for a government to regulate pollution to protect citizens from poor air quality, deterring people from making poor individual choices may appear to infringe on a cornerstone of liberal democracies. For example, there are many reasons that individuals will be tempted to consume food high in fat, which is generally considered an unhealthy option that is not in their long-term interest (O'Connor, 2015). In situations where these choices are so pervasive that they become commonplace on a problematic level across a population, **structural interventions** may be necessary to address them (Loewenstein & Chater, 2017). Much like changing the drinking water in Scotland, this may require a broad-level intervention to reduce or remove the population's exposure to this unhealthy choice. While this may offer benefits to all, unlike the drinking water example (where only one option was available in the first place and there is no clear argument for having unhealthy water), this scenario has direct implications for choices and thus is not necessarily accepted by all. Such approaches have often been referred to as "the nanny state" (Macleod, 1965), whereby government approaches are seen as telling people what to do rather than allowing them self-determination over their lifestyle. In any case, such approaches are clearly in need of reliable, robust evidence for making the best decisions, hence the expansion of EBP, at least in name.

Practical vs. theoretical models

As is explained in Chapter 1, there are many different frameworks for developing policies. Since at least the 1950s, there have been clear arguments and proposed frameworks for the inclusion of scientific insights into policymaking (Lindblom, 1959), yet not all frameworks explicitly consider evidence in their cycle (Fox, 2005; Schneider & Ingram, 1990). Both the arguments for including evidence and the methods for doing so have evolved considerably since these early proposals.

In the classic, evidence-driven policy cycle, there was no established approach for how evidence was integrated into the decision-making process. For many decades, this represented a considerable number of the evidence-based approaches, particularly in terms of economic policy. While the shift to more systematic uses of evidence has increased in recent decades, the most notable expansion of this thinking occurred in the aftermath of the global market crash of 2008. Through the growing recognition of both the flaws in relying on unproven theory and the increased availability of relevant scientific insights, the demand for evidence in policies – from development through evaluation – continues to expand.

A pragmatic model for developing and studying evidence-based policies

The role of scientific research in policy has been debated in academic literature for at least the last 60 years. One of the challenges that has long been highlighted is that scientific theory is often broad, whereas policy applications require precision and nuance (Lindblom, 1959). There have also been disagreements about where evidence fits into the policy cycle, how evidence should influence decisions, and even who the main actors should be (Howlett, McConnell, & Perl, 2017). Previous studies on the policymaking process have typically focused on elements rather than the process as a whole (Oliver et al., 2014a), and many policy cycle frameworks have been simplified to be useful for teaching and study, but are not realistic enough for robust understanding or application (Howlett et al., 2017).

BOX 10.2 BARDACH'S EIGHT-STEP APPROACH TO POLICY ANALYSIS

1 Defining the problem
2 Assembling evidence
3 Constructing alternatives
4 Selecting criteria
5 Projecting outcomes
6 Confronting trade-offs
7 Deciding
8 Telling the story

One prevailing framework for the development and evaluation of policies as solutions to problems comes from Eugene Bardach. His eight-step approach (see Box 10.2) has influenced a number of major policy organizations, as well as academic policy institutes, and has expanded to a nine-step approach that was revised in 2015 (Bardach & Patashnik, 2015). What has perhaps made it so resilient in terms of relevance in the science and application of policy are its clear and distinct components, which may be applied to all areas of policy. According to the most recent version from 2015, the authors suggest that the model could also benefit from the addition of a ninth step for repeating steps one through eight as necessary.

While Bardach's and other general policy frameworks are useful for a variety of purposes, such as teaching and research, the steps are predominantly based on theory, which limits their utility for the development and application of actual policies. This is because the practical realities of policy are rarely so chronological or concisely restrained to one step or another (Howlett et al., 2017), nor are many policy outcomes revealed at all (Cheung, Mirzaei, & Leeder, 2010). To address these limitations, we present an updated pragmatic model that offers more robust coverage of policy development for application (Ruggeri, 2016).

The model in Figure 10.4 offers a theoretically driven but pragmatically focused framework for study and application. It pieces together a substantial number of frameworks already in use or widely cited in the relevant literature, particularly in the context of major, complex, multisectoral policies. In this way, it can mobilize classical and contemporary policymaking approaches (Howlett & Mukherjee, 2017; Howlett et al., 2017; Resnik & Elliot, 2016; Bardach & Patashnik, 2015; Howlett et al., 2015; Oliver et al., 2014a; Parks et al., 2013;

FIGURE 10.4 A pragmatic model for the development and evaluation of policies

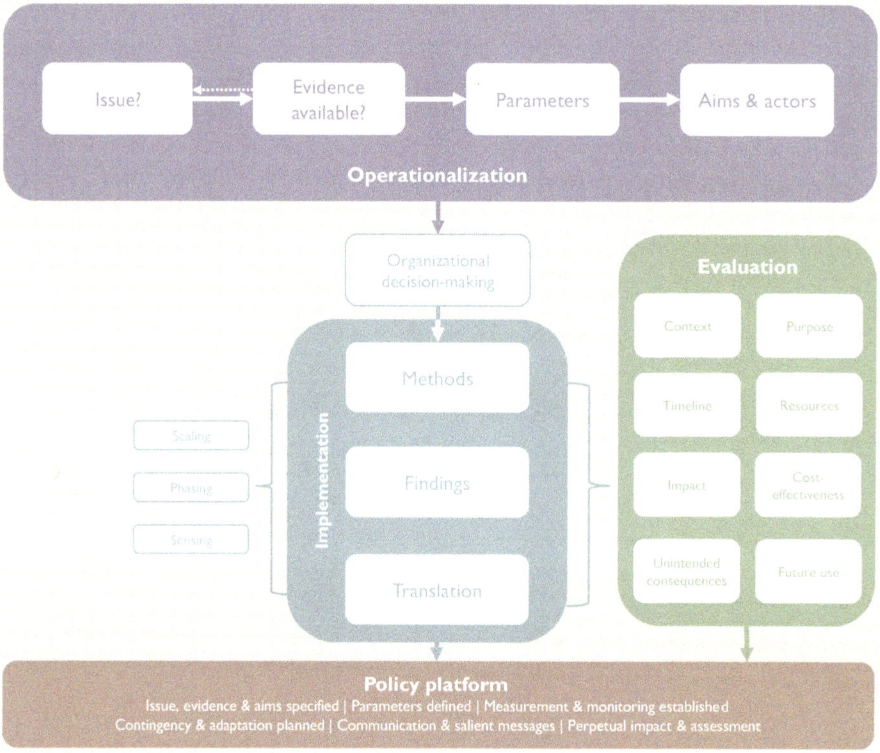

Allcott & Mullainathan, 2010; Insel, 2009; Choi & Pritchard, 2003; Schneider & Ingram, 1990; Lindblom, 1959) while retaining properties that are useful for scientific study. It is important to note that no single pipeline model can robustly cover all policy domains and initiatives (Oliver et al., 2014a), but a uniform structure that fits a wide variety of interventions makes comparisons of impact easier and may reduce bias in the evaluation process (Pollitt & Shaorshadze, 2011).

Operationalization

As with any empirical study, particularly those involving interventions, there must be an established approach that defines the key terms. This is referred to as **operationalization,** which means to define terms and constructs specifically and precisely for a given context, often a research project or policy initiative.

For example, imagine how challenging it has been to deal with the effects of climate change – because what is it, actually? Without properly defining what is meant by the term "climate change," it could merely be interpreted as changes in temperature. If the concept is limited to this understanding, the complexity of its meaning related to a variety of factors may be overlooked, such as the increasing amount of carbon dioxide in the atmosphere and the role of fossil fuels, in addition to changes in climate patterns. Such an example highlights how difficult it can be to create a policy that will successfully make an impact if what the policy is trying to address is not precisely established beforehand.

Another example is to consider the term "single parent": what exactly is a single parent? If separated into its individual parts, "single" would be defined as being of one unit or as a person who does not have a romantic partner, and on the other hand "parent" would be defined as a person who has a child. In the context of each other, however, single parent may take on a different meaning altogether, signifying a person who is raising a child without a partner. Then again, if both biological parents raise their child together but are not in a formal relationship with each other, should they be considered single parents? Also, if one parent passes away and the surviving parent remarries, should the surviving parent then be considered a single parent? In a similar way, if the key terms of a policy are not defined and agreed upon early and within the particular context in which they are intended to be used, their ambiguity might lead to disagreements and debates throughout multiple levels of the process, limiting the potential of any initiative.

There are four key subcomponents that contribute to the operationalization in the context of policy: (1) the issue, (2) the evidence, (3) the parameters, and (4) the aims and actors. The issue needs to be identified and its definition agreed upon in order to determine the intended outcomes of the intervention. The evidence available about the given issue must then be reviewed, and it can either reinforce or cause one to adjust the key terms of the issue accordingly. Parameters outlining the specific variables under observation are necessary to determine the success or failure of an intervention. Finally, the aims and actors are to be identified, engaging the right people linked to the right indicators or outcomes in order to ensure the intervention has the desired impact.

Issue

For a policy to have a chance of making a significant impact, the particular issue being addressed in an intervention needs to be clearly defined and agreed upon by those primarily responsible for its development, implementation, and evaluation (Resnik & Elliot, 2016). It is important to note that "issues" are not always bad things. In many cases, they may be very positive (e.g. how should a company decide how much to give employees for annual bonuses) or neutral, where some decision has to be made but no specific problem exists (e.g. deciding the ideal location for a stop sign on a road near a school).

Take flu shots, for example (see Chapter 5). If we observe low rates of vaccination in a specific group, is the low vaccination rate the issue itself? Is it a matter of public trust in the vaccination, where people believe there is either a risk involved or no actual value in being immunized? While there may be general agreement that the rates of vaccination are low, if we are not in agreement over what the core issue is, imagine how difficult it will be later when we establish possible interventions! In an example intervention, the low rates among employees were addressed by establishing a scheduled vaccination appointment by default; unless they opted out, employees had a shot scheduled. This successfully resulted in increased rates of flu shots among employees (Chapman, Li, Colby, & Yoon, 2010).

While this may seem like an obvious step, it cannot be overstated just how critical it is to have clarity on the issue. Without that, the establishment of our desired aims and outcomes will lack clear reference and the steps to build evidence will have no clear foundation.

The more systematic and efficient way is to be as clear as possible, as early as possible, about what the core issue is.

Evidence

Once an issue is defined, it is important to gather relevant evidence that explains critical information. As discussed, evidence here refers to scientifically supported conclusions identified through mainly peer-reviewed sources, though it may also come in other forms. Only once the issue has been established can relevant evidence be gathered to further inform parts of the intervention, though it can also be the case that, as evidence is considered, how the issue is understood may change.

When looking for relevant evidence, there is an obvious risk that we will be biased and merely confirm our preconceived notions of an issue. This is why it is important to have a structured approach for gathering evidence from a variety of sources and types of evidence (Figure 10.5), which may offer a more varied and reduced-bias perspective of a given issue.

One of the ways in which evidence is methodically gathered and reviewed for policy use is through **systematic reviews**: extensive, structured compilations of empirical evidence that rigorously collate the research on a certain topic, ideally toward convergence. Although the use of systematic reviews is quite common in policy decision-making, not all meta-data or meta-analyses lead to the best and most accurate policy decisions (Ruggeri et al., 2016). In fact, systematic reviews can multiply the amount of error compared to a single study. Reliance on a number of studies for evidence, as with systematic reviews, might therefore not necessarily yield a more reliable conclusion than evidence from a single study (Oliver et al., 2014a). This is not to say that systematic reviews are not a useful tool, but they should not be seen as an absolute source in all cases, and relevant contextualization is also critical.

Parameters

The success or failure of an intervention is identified by making comparisons between the same measurable characteristics of a population before and after the implementation of a policy. In order to make these comparisons, the measurable characteristics, or parameters, need to be identified. **Parameters** are the measurable characteristics of a study, policy, or population. In an empirical context, they are the specific variables under observation or the headline points of impact that are necessary to determine the success or failure of an intervention. If these are not specified early on in the policymaking process, it will be impossible later to be able to evaluate the effectiveness of a policy in influencing a given outcome. How can we know something is successful if we have not established what it is supposed to achieve?

For example, when we consider a policy aimed at reducing climate change, what parts of climate change would the policy be addressing? Reducing the use of fossil fuels? Increasing use of renewable energy? Attempting to slow down desertification? How can the policy truly be considered successful at reducing climate change if the parameters under observation are not identified beforehand?

This does not mean that other variables that might have influenced or have been influenced by the intervention should be ignored. In fact, other variables might highlight the side effects, trade-offs, or unintended consequences of an intervention. For example, while an

FIGURE 10.5 Forms of evidence used in policies

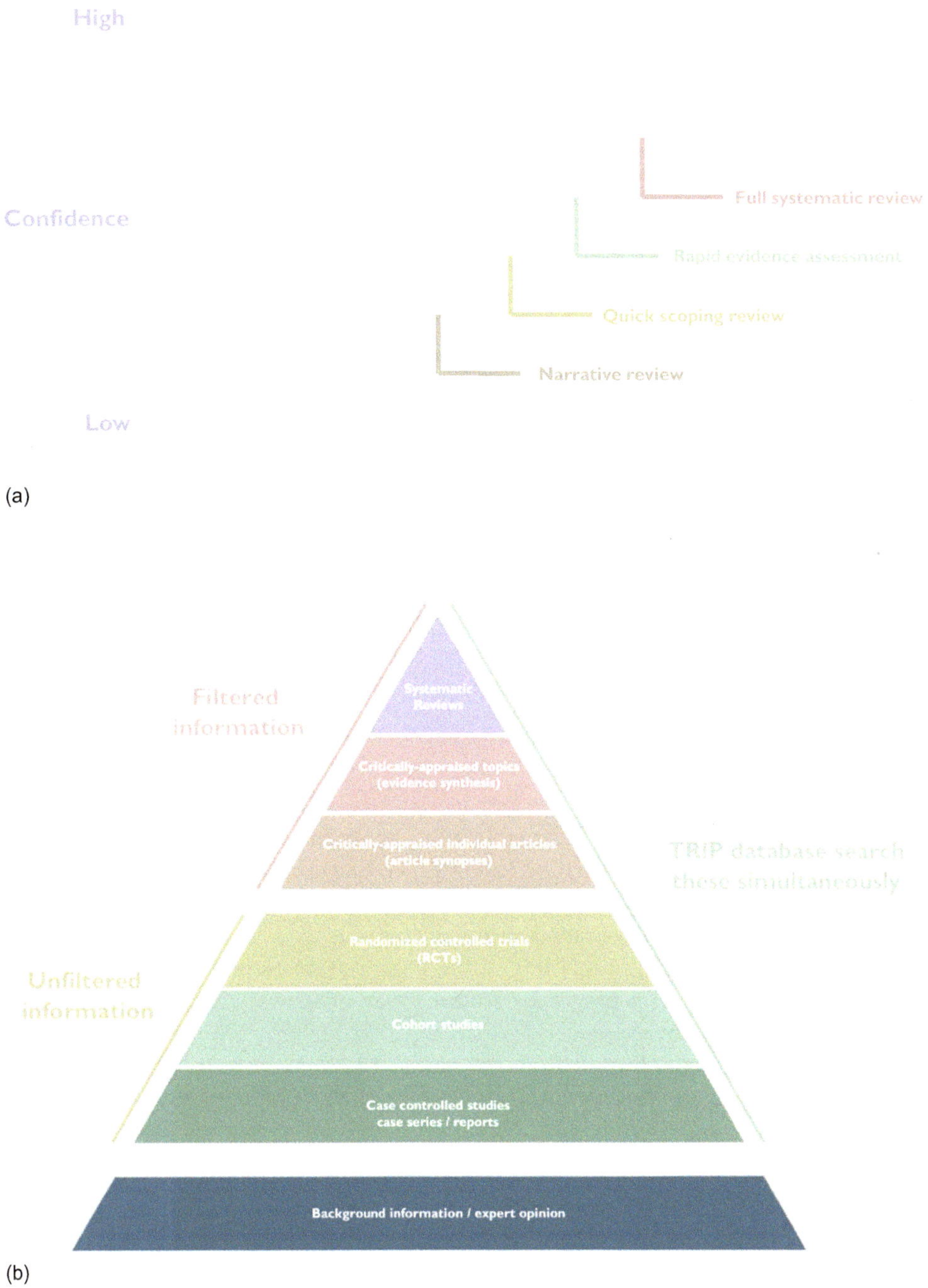

environmental policy might be effective for its intended purpose of reducing carbon emissions by changing a flight trajectory, it might also come at a cost to public health by increasing noise pollution and its associated health consequences.

Aims and actors

Aims refer to the defined goals to be achieved as part of an action, behavior, or decision. They are the kind of impact the policy is seeking to achieve for a successful result. **Actors** are the participants carrying out a defined role as part of an action, decision, or process. They signify the population that is involved and that will be affected by the policy. Once the parameters are identified, the stakeholders and what they consider successful or impactful can be determined. Otherwise, how can the people involved in a policy be determined without having already identified the variables that will be impacted?

The aims and actors are in the same step of the policy model because of how they are inherently linked. What is considered successful is dependent on who the actors are and how they consider a policy to be effective in fulfilling their interests. In a similar way, the actors involved in a policy might change depending on the aim of the policy. It is clear that the success of a policy cannot be expected if the right people are not engaged and linked to the right indicators or outcomes. The aim of the policy and those who are involved are therefore dependent on each other and will vary and adapt to each other as well. By clarifying who is involved and what their interests are in the outcomes of a given policy, a sense of transparency is created between the public and the decision-makers, which is an essential part of the policymaking process (see Chapter 12).

Identify decision-making processes within responsible organizations

As EBP has blossomed as an area of academic study, so too has recognition that much of the effective policy work must be understood in context. While this could relate to geographical, political, economic, or other social ambient indicators, it is also vital that **organizational behavior** is understood as policies are developed (Beshears & Gino, 2015). This specifically relates to the decision-making functions of the organization responsible for implementing a policy, as ignoring such pragmatic features may otherwise render a systematically developed policy futile. For example, while an organization may wholeheartedly endorse a robust approach to policy formulation, the remit of leadership may require anticipated costs and impacts to fit within a certain frame before considering any particular option. In such instances, operationalization may offer a useful exercise in framing the approach, but recommendations may end up ignored or dismissed if those aspects are not presented with the proposed levers.

Methods

After the operationalization phase, the method of the intervention needs to be determined. A **method** is the process by which empirical insights are generated. It is typically an exact series of steps or instructions that are followed when carrying out a scientific study that would allow someone to directly replicate it. An intervention is any action taken with the aim of making a change from an already established process and/or outcome. Interventions occur in the context of a study where a variable is acted upon to lead to an intended change in outcome (see levers in Chapter 1). Method design is a crucial step in the policymaking process and needs to be carefully considered for an intervention to be successful (Insel, 2009).

In the policy context, methods involve particular levers or areas of improvement being identified and exploited in order to influence a population-level change in outcomes when implemented as a policy. As previously mentioned, taxation is perhaps *the* classic (Howlett et al., 2015) lever, though not necessarily the most efficient or effective one (see Chapters 3 and 4). Other classic methods include standard setting, subsidies, sanctions, public takeover, grants, arbitration, direct legislation, persuasion, education, and licensing. Such methods have long been recognized as being limited in their creativity and scope (Howlett et al., 2015; Choi & Pritchard, 2003; Schneider & Ingram, 1990; Lasswell, 1955), although this does not necessarily mean that they are all ineffective (Oliver et al., 2014a).

The addition of behavioral insights to the methodological toolkit allows one to go beyond the classic taxation model of influencing behavior by penalizing unwanted behaviors, and instead encourages the use of behavioral patterns to either support wanted behaviors or prevent unwanted behaviors. Later chapters outline specific examples of how behavioral insights have been applied to policy, addressing issues in a variety of fields such as finance (Chapter 4), health (Chapter 5), the environment (Chapter 6), education (Chapter 7), and the workplace (Chapter 8).

Many policies have attempted to address an issue by developing a solution without having clearly identified the problem being addressed beforehand. In other words, many policies skip over the operationalization phase and go directly to developing a method to come up with a solution to the issue. This is a fundamentally flawed approach; an understanding of the context is necessary before jumping to solutions and making uninformed assumptions about improvements.

Findings

After the method has been implemented, the data are analyzed to see whether the intervention has been proven effective according to the parameters identified in the operationalization phase. Ideally, any analytical plans to generate findings would be planned during operationalization, but this may not always be practical. This step may better be seen by dividing it into two parts: one where the ideal plan is established, and another where adjustments are made to account for what data are ultimately available.

Translation

One of the most important steps for the use of evidence in policy is **translating** findings for conclusion and, potentially, further application. Due to the varied backgrounds of policymakers, it is essential that the findings of an intervention evaluation are presented in a way that cannot be misinterpreted and is easily accessible to the general public. Although such information has traditionally been communicated through extensive and exhaustive reports, other styles of communication can be used too. For instance, the *Insights for Impact* publication (Ruggeri, 2016) provides a brief report on behavioral insights that is widely accessible.

Implementation

Implementation is the process of enacting a given intervention and its necessary features. Implementation is not a binary process (implemented or not) but falls along a continuum in relation to a number of factors, such as how long the policy is implemented, what resources are devoted to it, and whether it is modified by practical considerations. Policymakers have developed several conceptual tools to better capture this complex system, including scaling, phasing, and sensing processes.

Scaling refers to moving from smaller projects or controlled trials to wider implementation, potentially to full populations. The resources (i.e. human, monetary, physical) needed for the implementation of the intervention should be stated and considered when determining whether a policy is scalable (El Chammay, 2017). **Phasing** occurs when an intervention is broken down into different parts and implemented in different stages. For example, the phasing of a policy would occur if it is first implemented with adults, next it would be applied to include adolescents, and it would continue expanding until the policy is implemented for the whole population. This incremental process allows for changes to be made from one stage to the next based on the information gathered from the previous phasing stages (Oliver et al., 2014a). Finally, for long-running or expensive interventions, it is often useful to make an informal evaluation of the policy as it is being implemented. This informal evaluation is known as **sensing**.

Evaluation

Evaluation refers to the empirical assessment of decisions, costs, processes, and outcomes related to the development and implementation of a policy. Policy evaluation involves the assessment of five key aspects: efficacy, effectiveness, efficiency, fidelity, and sustainability (see Chapter 11 for more details).

As with findings, the evaluation step occurs at a later stage, yet ideally should be planned throughout the policymaking process. Policy evaluation also does not end once a policy has been implemented; it later acts as a monitoring mechanism within a policy platform, guiding policymakers to make informed decisions about future scaling, further adoption, and the wider translation of the policy. Policy evaluation and its value in EBPs will be further discussed in Chapter 11.

BOX 10.3 EVIDENCE-BASED POLICY IN 50 AMERICAN STATES

In 2017, a consortium between The Pew Charitable Trusts and the MacArthur Foundation released a report on how individual states in the US engage in evidence-based policy, if at all. The consortium defined evidence-based policymaking as *the systematic use of findings from program evaluations and outcome analyses ("evidence") to guide government policy and funding decisions (p1)*. While this definition focuses more on information generated by and from policies specifically (as opposed to other forms of evidence, such as clinical trials or product testing), they demonstrate how this approach is being used in most of the 50 states and the District of Columbia. From this, they were able to:

1 Identify six distinct methods to integrate research into policy decision-making

A. Define levels of evidence

B. Inventory existing programs

C. Compare program costs and benefits

D. Report outcomes in the budget

E. Target funds to evidence-based programs

F. Require action through state law

2 Evaluate and quantify these six action areas between four policy domains

3 Produce a categorical scoring of each state based on these activities

Using this approach, they found:

40 states have definitions for levels of evidence, 23 of which have advanced actions in at least one policy area

All 50 states have an inventory of existing policy initiatives making use of evidence

34 states require evidence through law, though only 11 have advanced actions on this

The report considered domains: behavioral health, child welfare, criminal justice, and juvenile justice.

Specifically for behavioral health policy, they found:

29 states define levels of evidence, though only **13** are advanced

17 maintain an inventory of behavioral health interventions, though only **6** are advanced

40 states target funds toward evidence-based programs, but only **2** are advanced in this practice

Only **three** states – all advanced – directly compare costs and benefits between programs

Collectively across the four domains, each state was categorized as leading, established, modest, or trailing (Map 1). In sum, what the Pew-MacAarthur report shows is that there is concurrent growth in use of evidence in policymaking and opportunity for better standards to be implemented, particularly in the context of behavioral health policies. However, there was no clear indication that states had to be overall leading to be attempting evidence-based behavioral policies.

Policy platforms

One of the key limitations of just about every policy is the lack of follow-up (Oliver et al., 2014a) and many policies are never assessed for impact. Given their substantial levels of potential impact, as well as implications for resources, we suggest that policies should be seen as platforms rather than simple interventions. Unlike a static policy report, a policy platform can be thought of more like a website, with not only the key information about the intervention but also interactive features and updates. In the context of policy, a **policy platform** is a space that accommodates real-time information on policies and their impact, as opposed to one-off interventions. It considers policies as a long-term process, where the long-term impact is continually monitored and the issues addressed are regularly revisited to be adapted and adjusted as required, just as websites also undergo regular updates of content and/or software to function properly. One of the key elements of a policy platform is that it includes ad hoc monitoring of behaviors and outcomes as interventions are implemented and beyond. For an understanding of why this is especially critical in an age of greater appreciation for evidence use in the policymaking process, see Box 10.3.

Summary of model

It should be noted that the features that have been outlined act merely as a checklist for what should be addressed in the policymaking process, and they might not always be done in that precise order, such as with Bardach's eight-step approach. In fact, there will always be overlaps of processes and actions, simply because policies are rarely highly contained interventions that always have a controlled implementation as designed in a theoretical framework (Howlett et al., 2017). This framework utilizes many of the features of prevailing policy cycles, but it expands to include additional features from well-known policy institutes active on both the academic and implementation sides, one of which is presented in full in Chapter 12. Other approaches are described in various sections in other chapters.

As a final note, use of this process does not necessarily guarantee successful policy outcomes. Human behavior is notoriously complex and therefore difficult to accurately predict. Even when a behavioral intervention has been shown to be successful, the causal mechanism of the intervention is almost never clearly established. The intervention might fail to translate to a different place or time because of contextual differences (Parks, 2014). What evidence-based policy does promise is a more objective understanding of whether an intervention is working and why, so that policies may iteratively improve over time.

Conclusion

So, ultimately, what is the value of evidence in the context of policy? It is seemingly uncontroversial that *some* form of evidence should be part of many major decisions, but clearly this is not always the case, such as when multiple pieces of information appear to contradict one another or are viewed as unequal on the basis of source, age, or complexity. Policies are often created in complex environments involving the interaction of people, organizations, and the environment. Reliable and understandable evidence that all parties involved can broadly agree on, even if not on its utilization, is what can help to better encapsulate the complexities of responses. Ultimately, this is where the genuine value of evidence exists. Where information is controversial on the basis of source, ambiguity of interpretation, or ambivalence, insights may not even be considered as evidence by all parties and may only offer an obstacle in the decision-making process.

While the traditional focus of policymaking has been to address and, more recently, prevent problems, we are moving into a new era, where policies seek to realize opportunities. In this age, access to both personal and population-level data has reached unprecedented levels, which allows for more systematic, evidence-driven approaches, particularly for policies that will impact large groups.

This book has largely covered how to understand the outcomes of those policies and how new behavioral interventions might improve them. However, no matter how appealing or novel a new approach may sound, the only way to determine its success and optimize its implementation is to have a systematic plan in place before it commences. Such a plan will also enhance the capacity to translate the intervention for more widespread use, even when there are many features to consider beyond scientific evidence – or when no such evidence is available. The theoretical underpinnings for these points are clear and long established, making it a perfect time to seek those innovative approaches while maintaining a firm, evidence-driven base, at least to the point that this maximizes effectiveness for the greatest number.

Essay questions

1. Why is it difficult to produce a theoretical model to robustly describe the features of policymaking?
2. What are the implications of the two different approaches to policy described by Rose (high-risk vs. whole population)?
3. What are the strengths and weaknesses (theoretical and established) of "evidence-based policy"?
4. Design a policy to improve mental health for children in a deprived region of your country using the evidence-based process described in this chapter.

11 Policy evaluation and behavioral economics

Kai Ruggeri, Julia P. Stuhlreyer, Johanna Emilia Immonen, Silvana Mareva, Maja Friedemann, Alessandro F. Paul, Matthew Lee, and Rachel C. Shelton

Acknowledgments: Annalisa Robbiani, Frederick W. Thielen, Amiran Gelashvili, Filippo Cavassini, and Faisal Naru

Chapter summary

Empirical policy evaluation is necessary to answer the question: what is a good policy? To answer this question, this chapter will review the management of policy evaluation and cover key performance indicators for evaluation, such as efficiency and fidelity. On the basis of these indicators, common frameworks for policy evaluation are explained. Some of the challenges in conducting policy evaluation, though, are the complex and variable aspects of all policies, as well as their context-specific antecedents and outcomes. This makes comparison between policies very challenging, if not impossible; hence, we close with an example of strategies for standardizing the evaluation of policies across domains and approaches. Ultimately, the purpose of this chapter is to identify not only what comprises a strong policy but also *how* to produce effective policies that maximize the number of people reached and impacted.

Learning objectives

- Understand the important aspects and necessary steps of policy evaluation
- Distinguish key policy performance indicators: efficacy, effectiveness, efficiency, fidelity, adaptation, and sustainability
- Recognize the main elements of common approaches to evaluate policy
- Be able to develop a general policy evaluation framework
- Utilize a standardized scoring system for evaluating different types of policies

Introduction

In the second chapter of this book, we covered processes of policy development and implementation, particularly as they relate to evidence. In these processes, the ultimate aim is to generate the best possible outcomes for the lowest costs in resources. Clear structures to

DOI: 10.4324/9781003181873-11

implement, manage, and track policies are paramount for establishing accountability among stakeholders and facilitating later analysis (see, for example, Ministry of Foreign Affairs, 2009; Australian Development Agency, 2009). However, no matter how much we invest in systematic structures or uses of evidence to inform the policy content, we cannot know if a policy is effective unless we perform an appropriate evaluation.

There are many possible ways to evaluate a policy. Besides being based on scientifically rigorous evidence, Lindblom (1959), for instance, classically suggested that a "good" policy is one that achieves agreement about a particular desired outcome across key decision-makers. While this may suffice on some superficial levels, a more robust and comprehensive assessment of the benefits and shortcomings of policies can be obtained through rigorous **evaluation**, which entails generating information on expected and actual impacts of specific policies, as well as the processes involved in their development, implementation, sustainability, and use of resources (OECD, 2015a). Evaluation is also to be distinguished from **monitoring**, which refers to the continuous assessment of implementation against an agreed-upon schedule (OECD, 2015a).

To explain policy evaluation, the chapter is structured as follows – first, we discuss policy implementation and how evaluation is embedded within it. On this basis, we provide a coarse **framework** (an overarching guideline with principles for a construct that can help direct the approach taken without specifying or itemizing all content) detailing what should be established in an evaluation process and how it could be managed. Subsequently, common approaches to policy evaluation are presented in a simplified framework with special emphasis on key indicators, such as efficacy, fidelity, adaption, and sustainability. Further, the chapter reviews how data could be collected and interpreted to assess whether a given policy is a "good" policy beyond Lindblom's classic description. Finally, we present a systematic scoring system that allows the comparison of different policies across topics and contexts and their present and potential uses.

Beginning with the journey in mind

The degree to which the insights generated by evaluations are useful strongly depends on the quality and type of data and evidence gathered: claims about a policy's effects on an attribute of interest would only be appropriate if relevant supportive data were obtained. Ideally, to enhance generalizability and external validity, the data should be obtained across different types of contexts and populations. It is good practice to determine and define the criteria for interpreting whether a policy has met its goal or reached the desired outcome a priori. Additionally, in order to promote transparency and maintain accountability, these criteria can be determined in collaboration with policymakers and other key stakeholders and then be shared publicly (e.g. using an **open data framework**) (Zuiderwijk & Janssen, 2014). Retrospectively applied effectiveness criteria are often chosen arbitrarily and are easily disputable. The observation that a decision had a beneficial outcome does not readily mean that the decision was good or that the outcome was planned. Therefore, plans for impact or outcome assessment should have already been considered and determined as the selection of the most suitable policy for a given issue is made. To facilitate policy design and planning, two common approaches are used: ***ex ante*** (before the policy implementation) and ***ex post*** impact (after the policy implementation) (OECD, 2014a).

Ex ante *evaluation*

Ex ante assessment focuses on the planning and design of the policy itself and poses the question, "Will this policy have an impact and, if so, in what way?" To do this, *ex ante* also has to consider "What is the problem that needs to be resolved?" as well as "What are the likely intended and unintended outcomes of this policy?" The *ex ante* assessment is useful to establish the need for a policy prior to the actual implementation. An *ex ante* assessment provides the advantage of choosing among different policy options on the basis of expected impacts – the flexibility in changing implementation strategies, through planned and well-documented adaptation, comes from the implementation design and real-world practice. The implementation design includes the means through which the policy objectives are realized as well as the objectives themselves. An example of an approach to *ex ante* impact assessment is presented in Box 11.1.

BOX 11.1 EUROPEAN COMMISSION GUIDELINES FOR POLICY PLANNING

There is no "gold standard" for how policies ought to be planned and designed, and the process may differ considerably across organizations, contexts, and levels of policymaking (e.g. local, state, national). Nevertheless, it may be valuable for the various stakeholders working in different segments of the policy cycle to have a schematic understanding of how such a process may be applied in practice. As an example, the guidelines for *ex ante* policy planning applied by the European Commission (2016) are presented next.

1 Bring together an inter-service group consisting of people who work in fields related to the subject that will be evaluated
2 Inter-service group prepares the impact assessment
3 Announce to stakeholders and policymakers that they can provide feedback about the potential challenges and the impact of the implemented policy
4 Commence a 12-week, open public consultation to make sure that the stakeholders and policymakers have the chance to voice their opinions
5 Collection of data, input from stakeholders, and further evidence
6 Write the impact assessment report
7 Send report to the Regulatory Scrutiny Board for review; the review includes a closer look at what can be improved and formulates advice for future policies
8 If the report is accepted by the board, submit further policy initiatives to inter-service consultation

Policy implementation

After considering these many factors, the move toward systematically realizing policies can begin. It is important to establish the implementation plan early to avoid potential biases as well as structural barriers (financial, organizational, transactional) that can lead to bottlenecks and other challenges later in the process. The policy implementation plan translates an idea into policy – it details how a policy is put into action, defines the monitoring process, and ensures that all planned aspects are performed (Centers for Disease Control and Prevention, 2015). Implementation plans comprise a set of selected implementation strategies intended to achieve desired outcomes (e.g. enhancing the speed and quality at which a policy is adopted, implemented, and sustained). For example, implementation strategies include steps such as accessing new funding, starting a dissemination organization, or conducting educational meetings (Powell et al., 2015). Further, the implementation plan should contain clear guidelines defining at which point a policy is considered fully implemented. In practice, policies often need to be rolled out incrementally over time and space; thus, it is useful to distinguish between initial, medium, and longer term policy implementation when designing a policy evaluation. For example, some policies are immediately ready for enforcement and monitoring, whereas more complex policies (e.g. the Paris Agreement on climate change) require several years to achieve full implementation. Similarly, some areas within a jurisdiction are immediately ready to implement a new policy, whereas other areas require additional capacity building first. The knowledge about how an intervention was executed provides the basis for assessing its effectiveness and impact. The information about what policy aspects were implemented and the extent to which they were achieved allows us to evaluate how the policy components that were originally planned relate to the observed effects. Furthermore, an understanding of these factors allows policy evaluators to recognize when and to what extent a policy is not being implemented as planned (e.g. with low fidelity) which can lead to the termination of potentially effective policies and the continuation of ineffectively implemented policies (Brownson et al., 2015). Knowledge of how to adapt policies that are being mis-implemented to get them back on track and even when to de-implement (e.g. replace, terminate, or defund) ineffective and potentially harmful policies are key actions that all policy evaluators must consider.

Ex post *evaluation*

To assess whether a policy has been implemented appropriately and effectively, robust assessment is critical (Howlett et al., 2015). This is known as *ex post* policy evaluation, which is a systematic assessment of progress made toward meeting objectives, implementation processes, and the integration of relevant evidence and methods (World Health Organization, 2007). An *ex post* assessment explores whether a policy's impact goal was reached and, thus, determines the effectiveness of an intervention and the need for any alternative action (for example, revising or adapting existing policies and adjusting the implementation plan). Without evaluation, it is impossible to determine effectiveness and whether further adoption and wider policy dissemination are appropriate. The World Health Organization (WHO) divides policy evaluation into two forms. First, the evaluation focuses on the content of the policy – its vision, objectives, and target areas. Second, the evaluation of the plan refers to assessing the proposed implementation strategies, targets, and their indicators. Furthermore, because there are numerous possible ways to approach an evaluation, every evaluation team can choose the procedure that is most suitable to a given policy and its implementation (Trochim, 2009). It is important to note that evaluation is not a static process, but it can be iterative and flexibly adjusted according to the context (Menon, Karl, & Wignaraja, 2009).

Process

According to the WHO (2007), it is critical to evaluate the full scope of the development process of a policy. This includes considerations of whether the development followed the best practice guidelines, whether the key stakeholders were involved in the process, and the extent to which the plan was checked against the available resources and the best available evidence. Further, a strong policy plan would take local conditions and needs into account when detailing key areas of action and steps necessary for successful implementation by specific stakeholders (Menon et al., 2009). The evaluation assesses whether these actions are taken, and in instances where this is not the case, it analyzes the reasons behind the failure to adhere to the plan. Evaluation, therefore, may inform all aspects of a given policy and may provide insights into iterations of related initiatives, regardless of whether the planned outcomes are met or not. For this reason, the United Nations Development Programme (Menon et al., 2009) considers policy planning, monitoring, and evaluation to be interrelated processes, which provides an important link between past, present, and future initiatives and development results. Equally important is the need to evaluate the quality of the regulatory and policy tools that are being used to develop the policy (OECD, 2014b).

Monitoring

Have you ever made a New Year's resolution? If you are like many people, you probably committed to changing something, but shortly after January 1 the effort going into those changes started tapering away, and achieving the goals you set out became increasingly unlikely. But how early were you aware that things were not going as planned, and what could you have changed had you known? This is not so different from monitoring policies, which is often a critical feature of interventions during and after implementation.

Monitoring is a key element in evaluations because there are numerous factors, such as changes in the environment or staff, that make policy implementation challenging (WHO, 2007). This is important given that the contexts and settings in which policy implementation is taking place are complex and dynamic. Monitoring is defined as the ongoing process of assessing the progress of the policy implementation strategies toward the set goal (Menon et al., 2009; WHO, 2007). In this regard, it is necessary to determine whether the pre-specified actions were performed, if the progress proceeded as planned, and whether any difficulties or unanticipated challenges arose (Menon et al., 2009; WHO, 2007). On this basis, the planned and performed implementation strategies can be adjusted to ensure that the desired goals and policy objectives are successfully met (Menon et al., 2009). The resulting findings may be used to communicate and engage with the key stakeholders about the status and the advances made toward the objectives (Menon et al., 2009).

There is no fixed timeline for when monitoring should begin or how long it should last. However, Waterman and Wood (1993) outline the four key stages of monitoring, each being an iteration of the previous one:

Stage 1 – Collect the facts: examine qualitative information to understand if a policy-related issue exists
Stage 2 – Identify relevant stimuli: produce a database of information for regular evaluation
Stage 3 – Statistical analysis: evaluate changes over time to understand impacts
Stage 4 – Re-examine initial information: use all insights once policy is fully implemented to go back to policymakers to understand and consider further actions

In some cases, these approaches may be outdated in modern policy contexts, yet the general nature of the timeline remains relevant.

The main contribution of monitoring is that it identifies adjustments needed within implementation of the policy, particularly when the data indicate problems and the need for redirecting course. When this occurs, "patches" can address the identified issues and help to avoid repeating mistakes (Howlett et al., 2015). As policies usually comprise bundles of multiple policy tools, instead of abandoning existing policies and replacing them with new ones, policy designers can restructure policies by adding or subtracting elements or objectives to or from the existing policy mix. Of course, the specific context and likely results of the policy redesign need to be taken into account when introducing changes over time (Howlett & Rayner, 2013).

Monitoring itself should not replace a full evaluation, but the information that it produces may be a useful tool in terms of transparency (i.e. ad hoc reporting on progress to stakeholders) and overall effectiveness (by allowing one to identify and correct issues earlier in the process). While monitoring is different from evaluation, monitoring activities often produce the data needed to inform and drive key evaluation activities.

Evaluation management

Evaluations are often complex processes that surpass the workload capacity of individuals and instead require full teams. This includes the input and engagement of stakeholders and partners, as they may provide feedback and contribute to decision-making across every step of the evaluation (Menon et al., 2009). Roles and responsibilities should be attributed on the basis of competencies and, when necessary, external expertise (e.g. from statisticians, analysts) should be contracted. Additionally, an evaluation team should oversee the whole evaluation process and should compile the information acquired by the different members of the evaluation group. The evaluation team is also responsible for maintaining communication with, and disseminating key findings to, policymakers, key stakeholders, and community partners.

The European Commission (EC; European Commission, 2016) states that to evaluate policies effectively, the evaluation team should fulfill the following features: political support, resources, expertise, coverage, integration, and structure. To plan and perform the evaluation process, the evaluation group and defined stakeholders should designate an evaluation manager, who intermediates among the involved parties and takes on the daily responsibilities of the evaluation (Menon et al., 2009). According to the United Nations Development Program (UNDP) (Menon et al., 2009), the evaluation manager should lead the evaluation process, debrief the evaluators, coordinate the different parties involved, provide the relevant data to the key stakeholders, manage the contract agreements, and review the evaluation plan and reports. Following the evaluation, a management response, consisting of a statement about recommendations and further procedures, should be written and monitored until all planned actions are taken or canceled (Fertman & Allensworth, 2016; Rogers, 2014).

There are many different approaches to performing an evaluation. The choice of which approach to use is based on the questions one is trying to address, the feasibility and resources available, the criteria that will be used to judge program performance, and the performance standards that must be reached for the program to be considered successful (Community Tool Box, n.d.). Although there is no single "just" approach to evaluations, similar considerations apply to most planned and applied evaluations (see Figure 11.1).

The following steps outline practical elements within an adapted evaluation framework of the WHO (WHO, 2007) and the UNDP (Menon et al., 2009). Evaluations are complex

FIGURE 11.1 A pragmatic framework for evaluation and monitoring

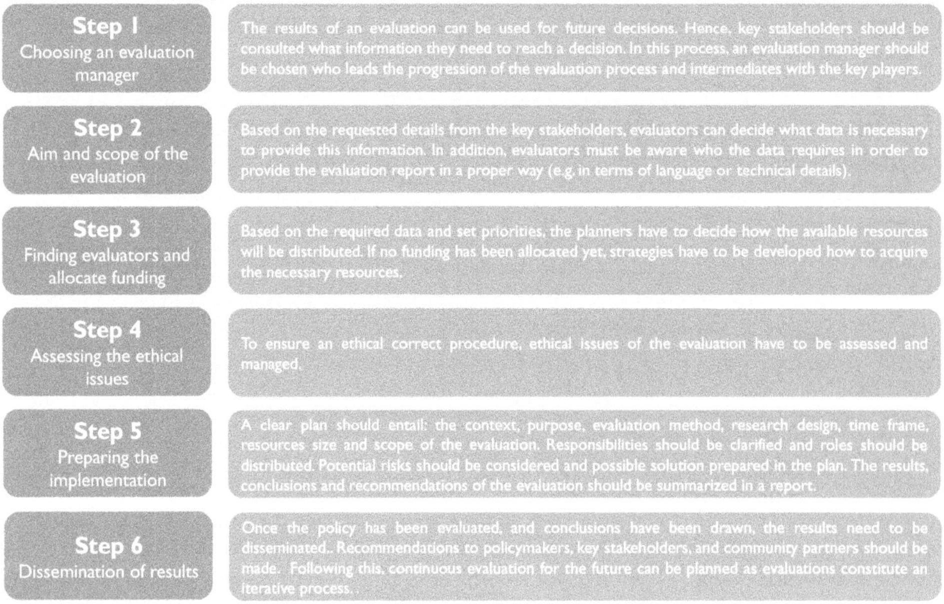

processes that require numerous considerations beyond the ones mentioned in the oversimplified version outlined here. Nonetheless, the framework provides a useful basis for evaluation planning.

Features of evaluation

The literature on policy evaluation converges on several features (see Table 11.1) considered to be **key performance indicators (KPIs)** in any policy evaluation. The features are applied and explained in an example concerning a municipality that aims to reduce the use of personal cars to reduce traffic congestion by distributing free public transport tickets.

When one evaluates the sustainability of a policy in the long term, it is necessary to establish that the effectiveness is not a mere **superficial effect** in which the expected results are initially shown but do not last (Loewenstein & Chater, 2017; Sunstein, 2017a). Consider an example from the New York City (NYC) Human Resources Administration Department of Social Services (HRA-DSS), which is the largest US social services agency combating poverty and income inequality. For decades, HRA-DSS workforce development programs tried to help NYC residents to move out of poverty and off welfare. This target was pursued by placing individuals into jobs as quickly as possible, without much consideration of the sustainability of this impact or unintended consequences. This approach inadvertently resulted in individuals not being trained in line with long-term employability goals. This placed them in lower wage positions with little access to higher wage sectors. The resulting

TABLE 11.1 Features of evaluation

Feature	*Definition*	*Application*
Efficacy	Efficacy refers to the ability of a program to achieve the overall planned purpose (Gertler, Martinez, Premand, Rawlings, & Vermeersch, 2016).	Efficacy would measure whether the overall goal to reduce the use of personal cars is met.
Effectiveness	Effectiveness examines how the observed effect relates to the desired outcome by comparing the observed outcome to a baseline measure. Thus, effectiveness indicates the extent to which the intervention made a difference toward that goal (O'Donnell, 2008; Gertler et al., 2016).	Effectiveness measures the extent to which the distribution of free public transport tickets truly led to a decrease in the use of personal cars.
Efficiency	Efficiency describes the relationship between the used resources (e.g. funds, expertise; Menon et al., 2009) and the achieved success. This could require the estimation of optimization and maximization points, which reflect the use of the smallest amount of resources to gain the greatest possible level of desired output.	Assessment of efficiency focuses on the extent to which outcomes were maximized with the fewest unwanted effects in the shortest time and smallest resource use. Most efficiency measures are likely to overlap with cost-effectiveness, though would offer more scalar understanding rather than static calculations.
Fidelity	Fidelity denotes whether an intervention was implemented the way it was planned (Bradshaw & Klein, 2007; O'Donnell, 2008). A high-fidelity program would have been implemented exactly as planned, whereas a low-fidelity program would have been carried out with considerable difference from how implementation was envisioned (Bradshaw & Klein, 2007).	Fidelity would indicate whether the public transport tickets were distributed as planned.
Adaption	While fidelity is an important feature of policy interventions, in some cases adapting the original intervention may be necessary. Policies may need to be adapted for new settings, for new populations, or for changes in contextual factors, such as environmental, political, sociocultural, or economic ones (Allen, Shelton, Emmons, & Linnan, 2018). Adaption may also be required in order to promote the sustainability of an intervention (Shelton, Cooper, & Stirman, 2018).	The intervention might need to be adapted if it turns out that distribution of free public transport tickets leads to overcrowded buses during peak hours. A possible adaption could be to also encourage the use of bikes in the city by offering free minutes for bike-sharing platforms.

Feature	*Definition*	*Application*
Sustainability	Sustainability indicates the estimated life of the observed effect and whether it is expected to continue after the implementation is completed. The assessment evaluates the ability of the population addressed to maintain and manage the obtained results in the future (Fertman & Allensworth, 2016; Pollitt, 2013). Additionally, sustainability may also involve the continued assessment of the ongoing delivery or implementation of the policy over time (Shelton et al., 2018).	Sustainability would be met if the effect of the intervention (reduced use of personal cars) is maintained in the long term.
Termination	Termination refers to the reality that not all policies should be, can be, or are meant to be sustained. Over time, policies are often adapted, defunded, replaced, or fully terminated. Termination may be required if the evaluation reveals that the unintended consequences negate the intended impacts of the policy or if the policy intervention is actually causing harm.	An appropriate evaluation would also consider what impacts termination may have, such as an unwanted increase in individual use of personal cars or the reduced use of public transport requiring changes to standard schedules.

lack of sustainability soon materialized in an observed low retention rate for the placements. One in four who took a position was back to receiving cash assistance within 12 months (Glen, 2017). On a superficial and short-term level, the program achieved success in connecting individuals to jobs. However, it suffered long-term shortcomings in failing to keep people employed or placing them in jobs that could not meet their financial needs. This example illustrates that in some cases a meaningful evaluation requires assessment of both the immediate and long-term effects of a policy. Policy evaluation should not stop when the policy implementation phase comes to an end. On the contrary, *ex post* assessment should be performed to assess the sustainability of the policy (ideally at least a year after policy implementation) by using the policy platform concept described in Chapter 10.

Use of policy models to form *ex post* evaluations

As described in full detail in Chapter 10, a pragmatic model for evidence-driven policies should include a robust framework for evaluation. While it is not exhaustive, that framework covers the primary features and some additional indicators that are common in the evaluation literature (see Table 11.2). It is recommended that the parameters of the target indicators be defined in as much detail as possible during the operationalization of the issue. Definition of the parameters is crucial for ensuring that the primary objectives of the policy are tangible.

TABLE 11.2 Primary indicators for evaluation analysis

Term	*Questions*
Context[1]	What is the context in which the policy was initiated? What are the key features (size, scope, nature, behavioral barriers) of the problem or opportunity involved? Did the context change during the policy implementation? What is the final status of the context?
Purpose	What is the purpose of the policy? Are fidelity and efficacy ensured?
Timeline	What are the key dates from identifying the issues through the evaluation? How long did the implementation process last? How much time was needed before the data and the insights were available?
Resources	What resources (e.g. financial costs, human costs, social capital) were required for the policy?
Impact	What are the specific benefits or harms for individuals, groups, or populations that the policy delivered (usually compared to a baseline or status quo method)? Were the benefits and impacts equitably distributed?[2]
Reach	What proportion of the population is reached by the intervention? How representative of the overall population are the individuals participating in the intervention? What is the absolute number of people affected by the intervention?
Cost-effectiveness	What is the financial value based on what was invested in relation to total gain?
Population gains	Does the entire population benefit even when they are not targeted, affected, nor participating?
Future uses	What should stay in place? How can others use it? Will the policy continue to make an impact? Should the policy be put back into the toolkit until it becomes necessary again?

Notes:

1 See also: Allen, P., Pilar, M., Walsh-Bailey, C., Hooley, C., Mazzucca, S., Lewis, C. C., . . . Brownson, R. C. (2020). Quantitative measures of health policy implementation determinants and outcomes: A systematic review. *Implementation Science, 15*(1), 1–17.

2 See also: Emmons, K. M., & Chambers, D. A. (2021). Policy implementation science – An unexplored strategy to address social determinants of health. *Ethnicity & Disease, 31*(1), 133–138.

Methods and data collection

In order to evaluate the effect of an intervention, relevant data should be collected and analyzed. The main objective guiding the choice of methodology would be to adequately address the evaluation questions, while performing a fair and unbiased assessment (UNEG, 2016). The specifics of the research design would often depend on the effect that one is trying to assess and the available resources (e.g. time, evaluators). Before time and resources are invested in a large-scale evaluation, pilot studies are highly recommended. Pilot studies are usually quick and small in scale. They allow researchers to obtain an idea about the expected outcome as well as to forecast any challenges that may arise in the evaluation process (Van Teijlingen & Hundley, 2001). Equally important is to be selective and targeted. Not everything can be evaluated, and the depth and scope of evaluations should be proportional to the size, scope, and impact of the policy (OECD, 2015a; OECD/Korea Development Institute, 2017). In addition, experiments can be an effective way of evaluating the effectiveness of policy implementation from a user perspective and can therefore be performed in a lab or a field environment.

There are numerous research designs to evaluate the success of a given intervention. Most frequently researchers conduct **experimental designs**, **nonexperimental designs**, and **economic evaluations** (see Table 11.3). The various approaches are not mutually exclusive and evaluators often triangulate different methods (e.g. quantitative and qualitative methods) to enhance reliability and ensure valid results (Menon et al., 2009).

TABLE 11.3 Research designs

Type of design	*Description and key features*	*Further reading*
Experimental design	• Manipulation of at least one predictor variable • Assess the effect of the manipulated variable(s) on (an)other variable(s) of interest • Aims to detect a cause-and-effect relationship	WHO (2007)
Randomized controlled trial (RCT)	• Considered as the gold standard methodology for evaluating an intervention • Comparison of at least two groups • Individuals are randomly assigned to an intervention or control group	WHO (2007) Behavioural Insights Team (2014) Jamieson and Giraldez (2017) Cartwright (2007)
Quasi-experimental design	• In some cases, more ethical, feasible, and cost-effective than RCTs • Compares (natural) groups without a randomized allocation	WHO (2007)
Natural experiment	• Studies policy reform as an experiment itself • Often classified together with quasi-experimental design	Blundell and Costa Dias (2002)
Nonexperimental design	• No variable manipulation • Examines naturally occurring relationships between variables (e.g. through surveys or focus groups) • Relies on observation, interpretation, or interactions • Only correlational statements are possible • Usually high in external validity	Glasziou (2004)
Economic evaluation	• Considers the cost-effectiveness and sustainability of policies • The type depends on the objective and the features of the intervention evaluated	Menon et al. (2009) Drummond, Sculpher, Claxton, Stoddart, and Torrance (2015)
Cost-minimization analysis	• Compares the costs of policies • Aims to identify the least expensive policy among two or more options that have identical benefits	Menon et al. (2009)
Cost-effectiveness analysis	• Compares the relative values of competing interventions • Costs are measured in monetary terms, and effectiveness is assessed independently	Menon et al. (2009)

(*Continued*)

TABLE 11.3 (Continued)

Type of design	*Description and key features*	*Further reading*
Cost-utility analysis	• A particular form of cost-effectiveness analysis, which is used when effectiveness or utility is hard to quantify in monetary or metric terms • Compares the consequences of policies on the basis of set criteria • It is used to compare interventions with different (nonmonetary) benefits	Dernovsek, Prevolnik-Rupel, and Tavcar (2007) WHO (2009)
Cost-benefit analysis	• Estimates the net monetary cost of achieving a particular outcome • Based on the principle that the monetary benefits of an intervention should exceed the costs of its implementation • Considers costs and benefits in monetary terms	Treasury (2013)

Common data collection methods

Along with selecting the research design, researchers make a choice about which specific data collection methods to use. The choice of which methods to use is driven by several factors: the objectives, the design of the research or the intervention, practical factors related to time and the available resources, and the type of analysis that would best capture the effect of interest. The data obtained can either be quantitative, qualitative, or mixed methods, which integrates both quantitative and qualitative methods (WHO, 2007; Palinkas & Rhoades Cooper, 2017). Quantitative data encompass information expressed in numbers (typically from surveys) and are analyzed with statistical techniques. In contrast, qualitative data are typically nonnumeric (involving text and words) and are analyzed through a separate set of techniques depending on the research question (Bryman & Burgess, 1994). In some cases, researchers may gather and triangulate both quantitative and qualitative data to test the effects of an intervention (Johnson & Onwuegbuzie, 2004). The required data may be readily available (e.g. existing texts or survey data) and may merely require collation and analysis. This is, for example, the case when using archival records or existing reports and documents of previous initiatives. More frequently, however, the data necessary to answer the research question need to be collected using primary data collection (Menon et al., 2009). Data collection initiatives typically reply on standardized instruments and questionnaires, interviews, and observations (Menon et al., 2009); ideally, the quantitative measures that are used have been psychometrically tested and validated. In recent years, Big Data approaches have become increasingly prominent (Jin, Wah, Cheng, & Wang, 2015).

Standardized instruments and questionnaires provide a common approach to obtaining information on a wide range of topics from a large number of diverse individuals. They are typically administered online and have the advantage of being relatively quick and inexpensive, which is particularly convenient when data are collected from large samples of respondents. Large samples are typically required to ensure that a given investigation has sufficient **statistical power** to detect the effect of interest. The statistical power refers to the probability that, if it is false, the null hypothesis, which predicts no significant statistical difference between the observed variables, will be rejected. Typically, the larger the effect is and the larger the sample size is, the greater power the study has to detect a significant and real impact (Cohen, 1992). Statistical power and sample size are important considerations because inadequately powered studies can lead to false rejection of the null hypothesis or failure to detect a real effect. Equivalently, cluster randomized trials, which may be used for policy-related studies, require large numbers of clusters or units to power the study.

BOX 11.2 PRIMARY AND SECONDARY DATA

Primary data are firsthand data gathered by the researchers themselves for the specific purpose of the study.

Secondary data are data previously collected and readily available, like archival records or existing reports and documents of previous initiatives.

While standardized tools and questionnaires allow for large samples of respondents, they often provide just a general snapshot of the issue and can be lacking in the depth of information provided. In order to obtain more detailed information about individual impressions and experiences, researchers often conduct individual interviews (Menon et al., 2009). Qualitative interviews can often be used to complement and provide richer context to responses to questionnaires and surveys; interviews are also useful to provide insight into issues or phenomena that are not well understood. **Focus groups** in particular can be a quick and useful way to explore both similar and divergent points of view across diverse stakeholders (Menon et al., 2009). Nonetheless, interviews often require trained facilitators, and data collection and data analysis can be time-consuming and resource intensive.

One relative weakness of interviews and questionnaires is their frequent reliance on self-report of one's past behavior or perceptions of the environment or social context, which is known to be prone to several biases. For example, self-reports are particularly vulnerable to **social desirability bias**, which refers to a tendency of respondents to answer questions in a way they think may appear more favorably to the interviewer (Phillips & Clancy, 1972). This response bias can distort the interpretation of mean tendencies and individual differences, as it can introduce an overestimation of positive and an underestimation of negative attitudes or behaviors. Further, retrospective assessments can be prone to **cognitive biases** of recall, where memory of individual behaviors can be shaped by current moment and mood (Schacter, 2012). People are often found to misremember and provide inaccurate judgments of their performed behavior (Behavioural Insights Team, 2014). Similarly, individuals can also be poor at predicting their behavior. For instance, respondents have been found to perform much less exercise than they predicted they would (Behavioural Insights Team, 2014).

On-site observations provide a potential means to overcome some of the biases associated with self-reports. In this approach, direct observation protocols are used to evaluate how a program operates, encompassing the ongoing processes and activities, as well as the results that are observed along the course of the initiative (Menon et al., 2009). While observations allow real-time tracking of the program's implementation and progress as they occur, including the extent to which a full program is being implemented with fidelity or the extent to which it is adapted, they can be very costly and time-consuming. In order to ensure comparability of results across sites, data collectors must be trained to use the protocols in the same manner, and clear guidelines should be set to facilitate consistent interpretation of protocols from different sites.

Alternative methods to overcome these biases and test the effectiveness and impact of policies can include experiments in a controlled environment (OECD, 2017a, 2017b). Because extraneous variables can be controlled in experimental studies, and experimental research designs may be replicated, this form of research should be considered when it is likely that results from qualitative research, such as focus groups or individual interviews, are skewed due to biases or other interfering factors.

Big Data

Another potential tool for overcoming issues related to self-report that has generated substantial excitement in recent years is the use of **Big Data**: collated sets of digital footprints acquired at large volume, velocity, and variety, often matched from multiple sources (Jin et al., 2015). One of the most significant changes that the digital era has brought to policymaking is the availability of constant, user-generated streams of digital information. Digital traces such as social media posts, Google searches, financial transactions, and bus card swipes are automatically collected by various devices and constitute large, often inexpensive data sets with ecologically valid information about individual choices and behaviors. The information they contain is exceptionally rich, encompassing geographical locations, social connections, financial choices, physical activity, audio, video, etc. (Kosinski, Wang, Lakkaraju, & Leskovec, 2016). These Big Data samples can offer time- and resource-efficient opportunities to explore natural human behavior (Kosinski et al., 2016).

Big Data provide a direct means to address concerns such as those expressed by Lindblom (1959) over the limited utility of insights based on retrospective and unrepresentative evidence. Big Data sources can help to overcome such concerns by allowing regular, flexible, and granular access to larger populations (Back et al., 2010). They bring many advantages, including the opportunity to capture even small effects (given the large samples sizes often available), as well as the opportunity to obtain behavioral insights free from the potential social desirability bias associated with self-reported surveys (Kosinski et al., 2016; Matz, Gladstone, & Stillwell, 2017a). Nowadays, online patterns of behavior such as Facebook likes can be used to reliably infer personal characteristics such as ethnicity, gender, sexual orientation, political affiliation, and personality traits (Glenn & Monteith, 2014; Bachrach, Kosinski, Graepel, Kohli, & Stillwell, 2012; Lambiotte & Kosinski, 2014). The analysis of these data sets can help governments and organizations identify individuals and groups of interest, as well as population trends and risk factors. For example, analysis of the volume of Google searches for illegal substances can provide insights about interest in these substances and their popularity (Deluca et al., 2012). Such insights allow governments to monitor and predict potential public threats and assess the effectiveness of interventions designed to tackle them. Additionally, access to Big Data when implementing policies affords researchers the possibility to quickly evaluate and flexibly revise interventions according to how they are received, ultimately allowing for improved regulation (Schintler & Kulkarni, 2014). Of course, this will only *occur if the information is used* to inform the design of new policies and regulations or to modify existing ones.

The use of Big Data analytics affords numerous advantages, but governments and organizations must also address various challenges, including issues of representation, accuracy, access, and privacy. Big Data are not always accurate and balanced representations of entire populations, and failure to appreciate this can leave policy-relevant groups ignored (Ruggeri et al., 2017; Bentley, O'Brien, & Brock, 2014; Taylor & Schroeder, 2015). Big Data are not always equally accessible to all parties and often either are generated outside public administrations or are not available to all departments within administrations. Further, there are various ethical concerns about organizations and governments collecting and using Big Data to target consumer behaviors without the explicit consent of the users. Without clear ethical standards about how Big Data approaches should be implemented, there is a risk that they may be used to manipulate or disproportionately benefit specific groups (Ruggeri et al., 2017), with lower income and disparity populations at greater risk for being less likely to receive benefits. To ensure that such approaches have society's best interest in mind is a challenging but necessary task that requires clear guidelines around individual control of shared data, confidentiality, and transparency about the ways in which these data are used and accessed

(Ruggeri et al., 2017). Ultimately, one of the most important roles of Big Data in policymaking may be to demonstrate empirically that interventions capitalizing on such data result in broad public benefit (Ruggeri et al., 2017). In this way, it may prove to be a powerful tool both for generating evidence and for establishing standards for scientific insights to be used in policy.

Standards for evidence

To inspect the evidence, the evaluation design should employ a research method and data collection strategy that are rigorous and well-suited to the specific evaluation questions. This is critical because the final decision from an evaluation will be to determine whether a policy has been a good one, in some form. It is therefore important to also have standards for the valuation of evidence available in advance.

To assess the extent to which evidence is available for a topic (e.g. from a scientific study or a policy), the Cambridge Policy Research Group produced the **Index for Evidence in Policy (INDEP)** (see Figure 11.2; Policy Research Group, 2016). INDEP

FIGURE 11.2 Index for Evidence in Policy (INDEP)

assigns the evidence of interest a rating ranging from 0 (theory proposed) to 10 (impact validated), reflecting the quality, amount, and consensus regarding existing scientific evidence. While evidence of any rating could be used to inform policies, the insights with lower ratings should be treated with caution and may require additional scientific grounding. Further, INDEP also considers the evidence around the generalizability of the given insight (e.g. the settings, contexts, populations, and conditions in which the policy may be effective). As reflected in the INDEP, the evidence for the policies should not be produced only in controlled or niche environments, but ideally experiments in real-life, less-controlled, and lower resource settings should occur after an intervention is established in a controlled trial.

Scoring policies

In the United States, one of the tensest periods (for direct stakeholders, at least) is when the Congressional Budget Office (CBO) releases its estimates of financial and human impact after legislation has been presented by Congress. While the CBO is technically nonpartisan and offers only estimates, its projections often set the tone for public and political discourse about a given bill. While it is rare that public attention returns to these estimates in follow-up laws that are eventually passed, government and political structures often rely on these evaluations in both future development of prospective legislation and related debates. Most countries have similar structures in place for such legislation, but policy scoring is considerably less institutionalized, with few parallels to draw from across countries.

Much like with policy cycles, there are a substantial number of theoretical approaches to the evaluation of policy (Trochim, 2009). Most, if not all, of these frameworks present very useful information for classifying and organizing critical features, but they provide little practical direction (Howlett et al., 2017). Furthermore, many of these frameworks offer concepts for measurement without producing actual metrics or scales, nor detailing how to weigh various aspects on the basis of their overall impact on or value to outcomes. It is likely that many policymakers, researchers, and stakeholders from invested organizations will refer to these only to find general agreement about the importance of theory but will be disappointed with the lack of detail on specific application. While this is a genuine challenge, it is largely viewed as a matter of broad categorization intended for simplifying teaching and research (Howlett et al., 2017). This is not meant as a criticism of published models; it merely represents an important gap in the field, which is a clear opportunity for scientific contribution to policy.

How to understand policy evaluations

The work of Cheung and colleagues (2010) offers an exceptional glimpse into policy evaluation through a framework for scoring *policy reports*, which include the evaluations but go beyond simply the policies and tools themselves. Through eight general criteria (outlined next), they propose measures for assessing the information and approach in *health* policy reports. The criteria encompass the content, how robustly the information is provided, and which fundamental elements are included. These domains are useful not only for shedding light on what is important in reporting but also for *a priori* thinking about and planning for policy implementation.

1 Accessibility
2 Policy background (i.e. the source of the health policy)
3 Goals
4 Resources
5 Monitoring and evaluation
6 Political opportunities
7 Public opportunities
8 Obligations

There are many examples of how to generally weight and standardize indicators relevant to policies. The OECD has been a leader in producing systematic approaches to policy evaluation through combining and standardizing social and economic indicators (see Nardo et al., 2005). However, in most cases, policy indices are established discretely between domains, though they may have significant overlap with a variety of sectors. An example of this is the Small and Medium-Sized Enterprises (SME) Policy Index, which is built for the scoring of frameworks and capacities of governments to optimize growth through supporting local business development. It is an excellent tool for a general review of SME policies. Such instruments may be relevant for cross-country comparisons in certain policy areas, but they are not a tool for robust policy evaluation.

Similarly, one of the most powerful indicators of national economic stability is inequality (Piketty & Saez, 2014; Piketty, 2000). Within this area of work, the **Gini coefficient** (a measure where 0 equals perfectly equal incomes and 1 equals perfectly unequal incomes across a country) is commonly used as a score for assessing national economic inequality, which is useful for predicting a number of likely barriers to growth and stability (Gastwirth, 1972). The Gini coefficient is widely reported in academic, government, industry, and third-sector initiatives, which is likely due to its simplicity in scoring and use. Gini scores have catalyzed a substantial number of policies aimed at reducing inequality to spur growth, but the coefficient is entirely focused on incomes and is less useful for broad application.

Drawing from an entirely different source, one measure widely reported in the media is the World Press Freedom Index, assigned annually by the organization Reporters Without Borders. This multidimensional index is able to score and standardize a number of indicators (e.g. media independence from government, legislative protections, censorship, violence toward journalists) critical to members of the press. This score is useful for understanding the media freedom within a country. Further, for countries that value freedom of the press, it can indicate potential areas for improvement.

In spite of the value that many existing scoring approaches provide in specific contexts, at present there is no scientific, systemic approach to standardized scoring of policies that can be applied across different domains. At the same time, a substantial amount of research on policy – theoretical and applied – has converged on a set of common indicators deemed critical (Allcot & Mullainathan, 2010). This presents a tremendous opportunity to standardize the policy evaluation process to help policymakers to determine the effectiveness of interventions that have already been applied or are currently being considered.

While there is no standardized scoring tool available for all policies, it is possible to utilize the extant indicators on which policy researchers have converged. It is recommended that a common scale is used as often as possible, followed by appropriate waging similar to the approach used by the OECD. This also serves as a guide for the minimum information that should be included in high-quality policy reports, similar to the framework provided by Cheung and colleagues (2010). Ideally, such an approach would maximize the accessibility of the policy evaluation to policymakers, experts, and stakeholders, as well as to the general public.

In the example presented in Box 11.3, 20 indicators are assessed: most are scored from 0 to 5, the evidence assessment scoring ranges between 0 and 10, and some items range from negative to positive. A separate scale for evidence assessment is introduced as a means of correcting for policies where most projections are not based on empirical evidence. The purpose behind this is to provide a scale ranging from 0 to 100 that is easily understood and requires no advanced knowledge of statistics or policy evaluation. In Box 11.3, each indicator in the scoring is itemized, with a suggested framing for each score. Indicators cover populations involved, clarity of important indicators, cost and resources, critical social factors, infrastructure, and scientific quality. These indicators closely correspond to the principles employed by major international organizations involved in behavioral policy (OECD/Korea Development Institute, 2017). This approach allows for a policy to be scored *ex ante* to assess its overall impact as well as likely strengths and areas of concern across specified dimensions. For example, in the generic version in Box 11.3, items 9 to 12 could be rephrased about realistic potential as opposed to empirical outcomes. This would assist with identifying potential weaknesses of or gaps in a given policy that can then be addressed through modifications or the introduction of additional policy tools.

BOX 11.3 A GENERIC POLICY SCORING SYSTEM

Populations involved

1 Which of the following population strategies will be directly or indirectly influenced by this policy? (0 – Not at all; 1 – Indirectly; 2 – Directly; 3 – Exclusively)

• Severely impaired or disadvantaged	0	1	2	3
• Impaired or disadvantaged	0	1	2	3
• Prevent	0	1	2	3
• Sustain	0	1	2	3
• Promote	0	1	2	3

2 At what level are effects expected? (0 – Not at all; 1 – Indirectly; 2 – Directly; 3 – Exclusively)

• Rare or isolated	0	1	2	3
• Small group or tribal	0	1	2	3
• Community	0	1	2	3
• Large region or national	0	1	2	3
• International	0	1	2	3

3 High-risk or population-level approach? (0 – Not at all; 1 – Indirectly; 2 – Directly; 3 – Exclusively)

• High risk	0	1	2	3
• Population	0	1	2	3

Indicator clarity

4 Are the indicators targeted by the intervention clear? (0 – Not at all; 2 – Entirely clear)
5 Does/did the evaluation refer to the intended outcome and was there a clear reference comparison (e.g. baseline, control) for determining effect? (0 – Not at all; 2 – Entirely clear)
6 Is information about the policy accessible to the public? (0 – Not at all; 5 – Entirely transparent)

Impact and resources

7 How cost-effective is the intervention?

• Costs	Lower (2)	Same (1)	Higher (–l2)
• Effectiveness	Lower (–3)	Same (–1)	Higher (3)

8 How long will it take to go from implementation to impact? (0 – Unknown; 1 – Lag after implementation; 2 – During implementation; 3 – Lag after launch; 4 – With launch)
9 How long will the impact last or how soon will outcomes regress to mean? (0 – Additional interventions will be required immediately; 5 – Once implemented, effects should be sustained for the foreseeable future)
10 To what extent was the policy implemented as intended? (0 – Not at all; 3 – Precisely as designed)
11 To what extent did the policy achieve its intended, primary aims? (0 – Not at all; 5 – Completely)
12 To what extent was there a return on the investment? (–5 – Loss; 0 – No return; 5 – Measurable return greater than amount invested)
13 Are/were there significant risks associated with this policy? (–5 – Risks for the whole population; –4 – Risks for the most vulnerable; –3 – Significant risks to a large group; –2 – Moderate risks to a large group; –1 – Moderate risks within reason; 0 – No known risks)
14 Are there any significant trade-offs? (–5 – Significantly more harms than benefits; 5 – Only benefits, no harms)

Social considerations

15 To what extent is/was this supported by the public? (–5 – Extremely unpopular; 0 – No support or dissent; 5 – Extremely popular)
16 To what extent is the policy politicized? (5 – Completely apolitical; 0 – Explicitly biased for or against a political group)

Infrastructure

17 To what extent are there legal or regulatory structures to support this approach? (0 – No regulatory backing; 5 – Well defined with oversight)
18 Is it possible to replicate the policy in other locations? (0 – No; 5 – Directly and without modification)

Scientific quality

19 Evidence assessment: using the 0–10 scale from the PAI, rate the level of evidence in support of this intervention.

Well-being

20 What is the impact on well-being? (–1 to 1 for every dimension measured)

It is important to utilize any such tool with some caution, as it is merely for the purpose of standardizing and informing policy discussions and for comparing policy options, but should not be perceived as the absolute word on policy decisions. Additionally, as earlier chapters have presented, there are strong reasons for expanding the number of critical outcomes measured. Along with well-being, these could encompass the reduction of inequalities or the increase of economic stability and physical security.

What is a good policy?

The ultimate test to deem a policy *good* reflects its success at improving desired outcomes with little or no harm. Notably, there are different paths of varying levels of efficiency and sustainability through which a policy can arrive at this effect. In the spirit of the famous quote, "If you treasure it, measure it" by Lord Gus O'Donnell (Copps, 2011), we can estimate the valuation of a policy by considering its performance across various dimensions such as context, purpose, impact, side effects, costs, resources, timeline and implementation, population gains, and future uses. Following this multidimensional approach, a good policy considers the relationship between the outcome and the necessary resources to increase the overall gain, while an even better policy has high external validity and can be translated into other domains and used in the future (Figure 11.3). Crucially, future applications may carry novel challenges, and these should be carefully evaluated before future uses are pursued and implemented (Bloom, Genakos, Martin, & Sadun, 2010). Sufficient evaluation of a policy and the consideration of its features are recommended to assess the evidence, which facilitates the statement of whether a policy is *good*. In this way, it is more likely that we can understand whether a policy has produced the most positive outcome for the greatest number of relevant individuals, groups, and populations.

FIGURE 11.3 Valuation of a policy

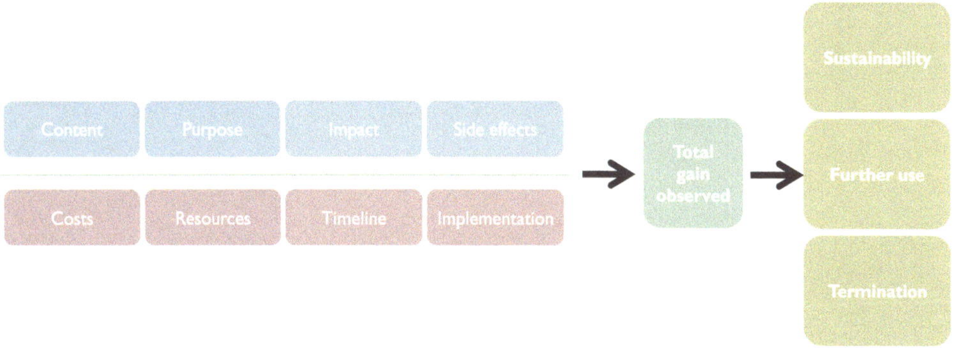

Essay questions

1 If you were only given 5 minutes to present the implementation plan for a major policy, which elements would you focus on and why? Give a policy example to illustrate.

2 Think of a possible example for a policy and explain the features of evaluation based on this example. (Hint: Use the examples from Chapters 4–8.)

3 Imagine that you are part of an evaluation group and you want to support individuals to stop smoking. Name a possible policy and decide which research method you would use to assess the success of the implementation. Explain.

4 A previously implemented policy was terminated. You are asked to rate the policy. How would you approach this and on which points would you base your rating? Explain.

5 What is the benefit of failed policies or having a very bad approach to a major challenge? How can evaluation help?

6 What are the implications of not planning an evaluation early in the process of developing a policy?

7 Describe five mistakes that could be made in designing a policy evaluation.

8 How might policy evaluations differ for various domains, such as health policy, energy policy, and school policy?

9 If a policy evaluation was interested in assessing whether the policy and its impacts were equitably distributed, how might you go about determining this?

12 Behavioral insights – a Government of Canada perspective

Elizabeth Hardy, Haris Khan, and Meera Paleja

Summary

At all levels of government in Canada, there has been a growing movement toward evidence-based decision-making. This movement has roots as far back as the 1970s. The availability of data has enabled the growth of policy research areas that support evidence-based decision-making by providing impartial research that informs the policy development and implementation process. Behavioral insights and experimentation are tools for generating and incorporating more evidence in the implementation of policies and programs. The Government of Canada made a commitment to devote a fixed percentage of program funds to experimenting with new approaches and measuring impact to instill a culture of measurement, evaluation, and innovation in program design and delivery. This chapter details the development of behavioral insights use in Canada, provides an overview of key institutions, and showcases examples of putting behavioral insights into practice.

Learning Objectives

- Learn about the use of behavioral insights (BI) in the public sector in Canada
- Understand the challenges of implementing behavioral insights into governments and strategies to help overcome these challenges
- Understand the relative costs and benefits of different operational models for behavioral insights units in governments
- Learn about the practical application of BI using case study examples of recent work conducted by the governments of Ontario and Canada

Introduction

Located between the Arctic, Atlantic, and Pacific Oceans and the United States of America, Canada is home to approximately 35 million people spread over the second largest country in the world by land area. Indigenous peoples inhabited the land now known as Canada for thousands of years before the arrival of French and English settlers beginning

DOI: 10.4324/9781003181873-12

in the sixteenth century. A modern and independent Canada was established in 1867. Canadians enjoy some of the highest living standards in the world, ranking at number ten in the United Nation's 2016 Human Development Index (UNDP, 2016). Multiculturalism and diversity are defining features of Canadian society; the country is home to people of more than 200 reported ethnic origins, more than one-fifth of Canadians were born elsewhere (Statistics Canada, 2011), and cultural protections (including official bilingualism) are enshrined in the constitution.

Canada operates in a federal system in which the Government of Canada and the governments of each province or territory in the country have distinct jurisdictional roles and at times jointly administer policies and programs. Each jurisdiction is generally independent of each other in terms of legislative authority, with the Constitution of Canada dividing jurisdiction between the federal and provincial or territorial governments. The Government of Canada primarily administers policy areas that are of a national interest such as foreign relations, national defense, taxation, immigration, and indigenous relations. The provincial and territorial governments are primarily responsible for the delivery of education, healthcare, and property and civil rights.

Each of these governments is supported by a nonpartisan public service that provides advice and implements the mandate of the elected officials. In general, the public services comprise "line" departments and agencies, which are tasked with policies and programs in specific policy areas (e.g., Health Canada or the Financial Consumer Agency of Canada). In addition to departments, central agencies help coordinate and support departments in order to help the public service as a whole implement the government's agenda.

At all levels of government in Canada, there has been a growing movement toward evidence-based decision-making. In the Government of Canada, this movement has roots as far back as the 1970s with the advent of program evaluation as a component of decision-making; it continued into the 1980s and 1990s and was then incorporated into the results-based management approach in the early 2000s. Evidence-based decision-making leverages the best available objective evidence from research to generate policy and programmatic advice to decision-makers in order to deliver the desired outcomes as effectively as possible. The availability of data has enabled the growth of policy research areas that support evidence-based decision-making by providing impartial research that informs the policy development and implementation process (Townsend & Kunimoto, 2009).

Behavioral insights and experimentation are tools for generating and incorporating more evidence in the implementation of policies and programs. In 2016, the Government of Canada made a commitment to devote a fixed percentage of program funds to experimenting with new approaches and measuring their impact to instill a culture of measurement, evaluation, and innovation in program design and delivery. The following year, the most senior public servants in Canada endorsed the Federal, Provincial, and Territorial Declaration on Public Sector Innovation, in which they committed to "experimenting and measuring results by identifying what works and what doesn't" among a set of other actions that support the mainstreaming of behavioral insights and experimentation into governments across Canada.

Teams at all levels of government – municipal and local, provincial, and federal – are being launched across the country. Table 12.1 provides a snapshot of the top five largest teams in Canada.

TABLE 12.1 Government Behavioral Insights Teams in Canada

Team name and institution	*Year established*	*Objective*	*Key project completed to date*
Behavioural Insights Unit, Treasury Board Secretariat, Government of Ontario	2013	Ontario's Behavioural Insights Unit (BIU) collaborates with the Government of Ontario and broader public sector partners to create more efficient processes, improve outcomes, and deliver better services to Ontarians. Applying the knowledge and methodologies of behavioral science, the BIU designs and tests low-to-no-cost solutions and generates evidence on what works – and what does not work – before scaling up.	Modifying Bin Labels to Increase Accurate Recycling Behavior: The team tested different variations of public space waste and recycling bin labels. While all new labels increased accurate recycling rates, the highest performing label increased correct organics recycling by 82%, led to 55% more coffee cups being disposed appropriately, and increased accurate recycling of mixed containers by 32% relative to the control labels.
Behavioural Insights Research and Design, Employment and Social Development Canada, Government of Canada	2014	The Innovation Lab at Employment and Social Development Canada (ESDC), Government of Canada, works with multidisciplinary teams within the department and with stakeholders to integrate experimentation and end-user experience in the development of services, programs, and policies.	Employment Assistance: JobBank.ca offers a wide variety of services to its users, including the Job Match service. This tool allows employers and job-seekers to be matched on the basis of their respective needs and profiles. Six trials have been conducted to test whether behavioral insights experimentation could be leveraged to increase the take-up of the Job Match service. See Chapter 9 for more details.
Accelerated Business Solutions Lab, Canada Revenue Agency (CRA), Government of Canada	2015	The Accelerated Business Solutions Lab (ABSL) was created as a dedicated space to improve business outcomes through testing new approaches, engaging in intelligent risk-taking, and catalyzing innovation throughout the Canada Revenue Agency (CRA).	Encouraging Online Tax Filing with Environmental Messaging: The CRA conducted a randomized controlled trial to encourage paper filers to switch to online filing through the use of environmental text, images, and pledges (i.e., the promise to plant a tree on behalf of a filer if they filed online).

Team name and institution	*Year established*	*Objective*	*Key project completed to date*
Impact and Innovation Unit (IIU), Privy Council Office, Government of Canada	2015	The IIU explores how new policy and program tools can address public policy challenges. They work with departments to design and implement solutions, measure results from program experimentation, and document best practices.	Increasing Recruitment of Women into the Canadian Armed Forces: Building off an extensive research study, a social media trial applying behavioral insights to social media marketing was completed in 2017. The ads were displayed over 2.5 million times, and differences in unique click-through rates are supporting evidence-based recommendations for future campaigns.
Behavioural Insights Group, Public Service Agency, Government of British Columbia	2016	The British Columbia Behavioural Insights Group (BC BIG) is a central research and evaluation unit in the Government of British Columbia dedicated to using insights and methods from behavioral science and service design to solve behavior-based policy challenges.	Provincial Sales Tax (PST) Compliance Project: Sending a set of email reminders to businesses closer to their PST payment due date (i.e., 5 days and 1 day prior) reduced delinquency in payments by 50% and saved 2,500+ hours in compliance-related time during a six-month period.

Building the practice

As governments around the world begin to discover the benefits of leveraging behavioral science to help improve outcomes, an increasing number of organizations are setting up in-house behavioral insights (BI) teams. Whether in the form of a dedicated team or simply embedding behavioral scientists into specific policy or service areas, building the practice of BI in government can be challenging.

The start-up

The pressure to build a portfolio of work in an effort to demonstrate the value of the BI approach is extremely high during the first year or two of a team's existence. Typically, BI units are set up with temporary funding and must prove their value to senior decision-makers in order to be made permanent. Projects need to be selected carefully in order to provide evidence that the application of behavioral insights is resulting in the desired effects – increasing performance, achieving efficiencies, or improving service delivery to citizens.

Oftentimes, there can be resistance toward a new, innovative approach to policy work. To take an experimental approach to policy and service delivery, where assumptions are continuously tested, is a strong departure from the way policy design is traditionally done. Wherever possible, a rigorous approach to measurement, such as the application of randomized controlled trials, should be incorporated into the trial design in order to effectively measure impact. Until the recent growing movement toward evidence-based policy, an experimental approach was not commonplace, nor one that most public servants were familiar with.

While the trend continues toward the increased use of evidence in policy and program design, there are significant and persistent barriers to change in government.

Silos

Government silos refer to the phenomenon in which groups of people within government become isolated from the greater public service. This isolation means that these groups' ideas and experiences are not disseminated through the rest of government, and conversely, ideas from other parts of government do not penetrate these groups. In these situations, knowledge and data sharing become more difficult across the agencies and departments of government. These limitations in sharing hinder the use and application of innovative tools like behavioral insights. Silos often focus solely on their assigned areas and experience lower levels of knowledge and information sharing.

Path dependence

In many areas, the Government of Canada and its provincial and territorial counterparts have been implementing policies and programs in a particular way for several decades. The accumulated history of over a century of policy development means that processes can often be rigid and resistant to change, even if the individuals who administer them are amenable to change. Often, policy directives are ossified in legislation that can require lengthy political action to amend. In addition, the Canadian public service continues to age. The average Canadian public servant was 45 years old in 2016, up from 40.4 in 1990 (Government of Canada, 2016), which means that hiring decisions made decades ago inform the skill set available in the public service today. In addition, drastic changes to a service and rigorous measurement of its results are often (and erroneously) seen as risky because they may challenge expectations about program performance and reflect poorly on a program's administration.

Legacy systems

In addition to institutional path dependence, often the technical systems that underpin program delivery pose barriers to doing things differently in government. Randomized controlled trials (RCTs) are the first-choice experimental design for testing the use of behavioral science in public policy, but randomization at the individual level can be challenging when using current systems. In Box 12.1, a case study of a trial conducted by the Canada Revenue Agency describes the technical challenge posed by legacy systems and how its Accelerated Business Solutions Lab addressed it.

BOX 12.1 WORKING INCOME TAX BENEFIT CASE STUDY

Overview

The Accelerated Business Solutions Lab at the Canada Revenue Agency (CRA) is tasked to improve business outcomes through a wide range of initiatives, including behavioral experiments, quantitative analyses, ethnographic studies, and reports on emerging issues in tax administration.

To help ensure that Canadians receive the tax benefits to which they are entitled, the Accelerated Business Solutions Lab conducted an experiment to test the impact of a behaviorally informed, informational insert on take-up of the Working Income Tax Benefit (WITB).

Opportunity

The WITB is a refundable tax credit intended to provide relief for working, low-income individuals and families. To claim the WITB, tax filers must complete a separate form that is completed at the same time as their Income Tax and Benefit return. While the estimated take-up rate for the WITB among eligible tax filers is relatively high (85%), it drops to 49% when considering only those who file by paper (instead of using tax software or going to a tax preparer). There are a number of factors that may contribute to this low take-up rate, including the absence of an automatic application process, the complexity of the application form, and lack of awareness of the benefit. As resolution of the first two factors would have required longer term legislative or administrative changes, the Accelerated Business Solutions Lab decided to focus on addressing the lack of awareness about the benefit.

Solution

An informational insert advertising the WITB was created for the 2017 tax filing season. The insert was placed in the middle of the paper tax forms book, so that it would easily be seen by those opening the book. The design of the insert was informed by insights gleaned from prior behavioral research and experiments. Notably, a field experiment (Bhargava & Manoli, 2015) on incomplete take-up of a similar benefit in the United States (the Earned Income Tax Credit) found that awareness, simplification, and heightened salience of benefits led to substantial additional claims. To this end, various features were included with the insert to make it more appealing to tax filers:

- A physically separate document that could be pulled from the forms
- An attention-grabbing headline ("Stop!")
- Short, simple, plain language
- Specific benefit amounts and income ranges
- An emphasis on short-term benefits ("get the WITB on your 2016 return")

While the Accelerated Business Solutions Lab generally advocates for randomized controlled trials when undertaking experiments, that approach was not feasible in this situation due to the way these paper forms are printed and distributed. Therefore, an alternative approach called difference-in-difference analysis was used (see Wing, Simon, & Bello-Gomez, 2018 for more information about DiD designs).
To test the effectiveness of the behavioral intervention, the insert was placed in all paper forms books in the province of New Brunswick (140,000), which served as a treatment group. Paper forms books in all other provinces and territories did not include this insert and served as a comparison group.

Results

The insert was very successful at increasing WITB claims among low-income paper filers in the province. Comparison of New Brunswick's performance to the rest of the country suggests that claims increased by as much as 35% in New Brunswick as a result of the intervention. If the insert had been included in tax forms books nationwide and had the same proportionate effect as in New Brunswick, it could have resulted in over 18,000 new claimants and an additional CA$12.5 million in WITB payments. Following the success of this experiment, the CRA scaled up to include a similar behaviorally informed insert in all paper tax forms books during the subsequent tax filing season.

Mainstreaming BI in government

Effective administration of a BI trial typically involves working through various phases. Although different BI teams use different methodologies (as broadly described in Chapter 10), in essence they follow a similar approach. One framework involves four different stages: understand, design, test, and scale/implement.

Understand

The purpose of this phase is to gain an understanding of the context of the broader policy challenge, to understand the implications of changes in behavior, to develop a concrete and measurable target behavior change, and to understand the barriers surrounding the target behavior.

FIGURE 12.1 The Understand-Design-Test-Scale/Implement model for BI in Canada

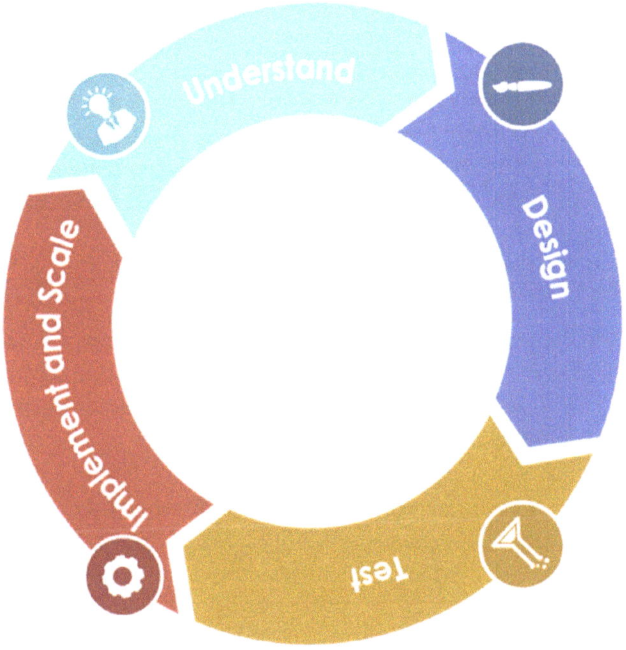

Source: Graphic created by Laurie Cat Bennett

Context and implication analysis

Here we wish to understand the following types of components of the program or policy challenge.

- Understand the degree of the problem: what quantitative or qualitative evidence do we have to understand how big the problem is?
- Make sure we are prioritizing positive social impact: are individuals and society benefiting and is individual choice always persevered?
- What behaviors act to make this problem better or worse?
- What evidence do we have that a change in behavior would have policy implications?
- What evidence do we have that a change in this behavior would result in benefits to government and to the citizen (e.g., improved efficiencies, cost savings, citizen welfare), and if it would, what would the degree of impact be?
- What evidence do we have that a given behavior is not occurring to the desired frequency?
- Is there an obvious traditional tool (e.g., regulation or fine) for behavior change that does not need to be tested for us to conclude with reasonable confidence that it would likely work better than a BI solution?

An example might be beneficial to illustrate how the preceding could be applied to solve a specific policy problem. Suppose we wish to run a trial to reduce flu transmission in a hospital. As a first stage, we conduct a context and implication analysis to understand both the problem (e.g., How substantial an issue is flu transmission in the hospital? What are the relevant behaviors that lead to flu transmission or prevention?) and implications (e.g., If we increase hand hygiene behavior by healthcare workers, what impact will that have in reducing overall transmission?). We learn some very valuable information that would allow us to understand the context of the problem and relevant behavior and also help us to understand whether targeting of a behavior would have a meaningful impact on flu transmission in hospitals. For instance, we may learn that rate of acquisition of the flu in the hospital is much higher than desired and that preventing flu transmission in the hospital by targeting healthcare worker behavior would likely lead to beneficial outcomes for patients. This information would be beneficial in helping us to understand how behaviors fit into the overall context of the problem and whether changes in these behaviors could make a sizable impact.

Behavioral metric development

Often the policy challenges faced by organizations are quite general and broad. The BI approach will act to decompose a broader challenge into its component behaviors, solving for a small piece of the bigger puzzle. The questions we should ask ourselves about the component behaviors include the following:

- What specific behaviors are involved and what specific behavior change is hoped for?
- Is the behavior quantitatively measurable? (e.g., completing a benefit form is a measurable behavior, whereas a user's attitude about the benefits program is *not* a measurable behavior)
- Do administrative data exist that capture the behavior in some form? If not, would it be possible to set up administrative data collection?

- If it is not possible to capture target behavior data directly, is there a proxy we can use to infer that a behavior is likely to have occurred? (e.g., we may not have data on whether someone actually went to get a flu shot, but we may be able to capture data on whether they made an appointment to get one)
- What touchpoints do we have to make contact with the population where changes in behavior are considered to be important?

In the example related to reducing flu transmission in a hospital, we can consider various specific behaviors related to this broad objective. These might include improving hand hygiene, encouraging workers to take sick days when they are not well, or increasing rates of flu vaccination by healthcare workers. Our behavioral metric development process would enable us to uncover some useful findings that would help us to focus on and solve for one specific target behavior in our intervention. For instance, our analysis may reveal that targeting the flu vaccination rate in healthcare workers may be the behavior with the highest impact. Therefore, increased rates of flu vaccination would make an ideal target behavioral goal to help achieve part of this broader policy objective.

Assessment of behavioral barriers

It is often helpful to create a behavioral map for the entire decision process from start to finish and identify "weakest links" where data or other evidence suggest there is a drop-off in the process. In our flu transmission example, healthcare workers receive an email from the hospital encouraging them to book an appointment for a flu shot. When we map the behavior, we find that individuals tend to ignore the email and do not phone the available telephone number to book an appointment. We believe that the hassle factor of booking an appointment might be an impediment to obtaining the vaccine. Using a BI approach, we may design an intervention to make this part of the process easier. To understand both the context and the behavioral barriers, we can use the following approaches:

- Literature review
- Jurisdictional scans
- Interviews with policyholders
- Interviews and focus groups with stakeholders
- Surveys
- Departmental reports
- Review of relevant internal and external data

Design

In the design phase, we will generate potential solutions and design a trial by using the appropriate research methodology. This phase will involve a careful balance of policy and good science to ensure that we have designed a trial that not only has scientific rigor but meets the policy objectives and can be feasibly carried out in practice.

Solution generation

Here, the BI practitioner should work closely with the policyholder. The practitioner may decide to generate solutions on the basis of BI principles and previous work and then consult with the partner. The main advantage of this approach is that the BI practitioner could come up with solutions based on their BI expertise and findings from the literature, without the constraint of feasibility limiting their scope at first pass. Once the partner is consulted, the ideas could be modified to account for policy considerations.

An alternative approach is for the practitioner and policyholder to co-create solutions. The main advantage of the co-creation approach is that the partner has expert knowledge of the policy, and they would be in the best position to assess whether the proposed intervention is feasible and has any potential for implementation. When we design solutions, we ultimately want to assess four different components of the solutions we develop:

- Is this solution *feasible*?
    - The best BI interventions are small changes to an existing program or process. A more substantial change that may involve plenty of time and additional cost may not be possible.
- What is the potential *impact* of using this intervention?
    - Assess whether this solution is likely to make a substantial change in the target behavior.
- Is this solution *testable*?
    - Determine whether each intervention can be applied to a subset (one test group) of our sample. If it requires a systemwide change that applies to all individuals in the sample, it likely would not be a testable solution because we cannot compare it with other solutions or a control.
- Is the solution ultimately *scalable*?
    - If it is determined that the solution is feasible for testing, we should also confirm that the solution, if successful, could ultimately be scaled up and implemented. Here it is crucial for the BI practitioner to work with the policyholder and, if possible, seek the advice of the decision-maker who would ultimately approve the implementation.

For example, after we conduct literature reviews and a co-creation session with a small number of healthcare workers in the hospital (who would not be included in our trial), we develop various solutions that fit our criteria. Through the co-creation session, we confirm that email is a good way to reach healthcare workers in a reasonably timely way so we can then develop solutions on the basis of the feasibility of this communication medium. As mentioned, our behavior map identified the hassle factor as being a major impediment to employees scheduling and receiving flu vaccinations. Because healthcare workers use Outlook to check their email, we can easily include a calendar invitation with a prespecified time to attend their appointment, which of course they can always change. Another feasible solution is that we could create a clickable link in the email we send so that healthcare workers can flexibly book an appointment online without having to phone.

Trial design

There are several important considerations when we run a trial using BI. It is crucial to consider factors such as randomization, sample size, and appropriate controls and policy considerations such as trial length and data privacy.

Potential for randomization

It is important to assess the extent to which complete randomization is possible. In an ideal experiment, complete randomization is the gold standard that brings us closest to inferring causality by accounting for confounding variables. Here, the BI practitioner must learn whether it would be possible to place different individuals or organizations into different experimental conditions and whether they would be able to track each experimental group's outcome behavior. In our flu example, we would want to know the current rate of flu vaccination specifically for each group. We would also want group-specific vaccination rate data for individuals in our calendar condition and control condition. An ability to form this link would allow us to draw conclusions about the effectiveness of each intervention in producing the desired behavior. If complete randomization is not possible, it is helpful to consider alternative, quasi-experimental approaches such as difference-in-difference or cluster analyses.

Sample size

Obtain an estimate of sample size. A sample size in the thousands is usually best, but trials can also be run with smaller samples (see Chapter 10). The advantages of a larger sample size are that (1) our sample is more generalizable to the broader population and (2) we are more likely to detect a true difference between experimental conditions by using inferential statistics. By obtaining an estimate of sample size, we will be able to run a power analysis so that we know how many conditions we can have in our trial without compromising statistical power. For our flu vaccination trial, if we find that our hospital has 3,500 healthcare workers whom we could include in our sample, this would likely be a good sample size for the proposed trial.

Use appropriate control(s)

In many cases, the control will be the status quo, such as an email or a letter that is normally sent by the program, for instance. Where there is no comparable touchpoint for our experimental conditions, we may choose to introduce a null control group (a group that receives no intervention). This would allow us to understand what would have happened had no intervention been used at all. In Box 12.2, you will learn about a trial where a null control group was introduced.

In a case where substantial changes are made to an existing touchpoint, we may wish to include an enhanced control alongside our experimental conditions and status quo control. In the case of a letter for example, an enhanced control would include non-BI changes to the letter, such as color, formatting, and font, so that we can directly isolate the effects of a visually appealing touchpoint from the effects of the BI interventions.

BOX 12.2 CANADA LEARNING BOND CASE STUDY

Overview

The Canada Learning Bond (CLB) is an educational savings incentive that helps low-income families save for their children's education. In 2016, only about one in three eligible children received the CLB. In response, the Impact and Innovation Unit of the Government of Canada, in collaboration with Employment and Social Development Canada, conducted a randomized controlled trial (RCT) to test the effectiveness of behavioral insights in correspondence sent to the primary caregivers of children eligible for the incentive.

Opportunity

The CLB is designed to encourage and reinforce the importance of saving for a child's postsecondary education. Eligible children from low-income families can receive up to CA$2,000 deposited into their Registered Education Savings Plan (RESP), which is a savings account designed to help people save for their children's education. In order to receive the CLB, the primary caregiver of an eligible child must open an RESP.

Solution

In February 2017, 37,751 primary caregivers of CLB-eligible children were sent letters describing the incentive and how to access it. In order to isolate the impact of sending a reminder, an additional 4,719 primary caregivers received a letter only at the end of the trial (the null control). The trial tested two different base letters, as well as three behavioral insight additions for a total of eight different treatments. The three additions were the following:

A **mock check** designed to make the benefits of the CLB appear more tangible in a physical form that was already familiar to recipients

A **checklist** of required steps to help potential recipients navigate the process of enrollment by providing instructions and a concrete call to action

Imagery of a group of students at a graduation with accompanying text designed to make the child's enrollment in postsecondary education feel closer in time for the primary caregiver reading the letter

FIGURE 12.2 CLB trial results

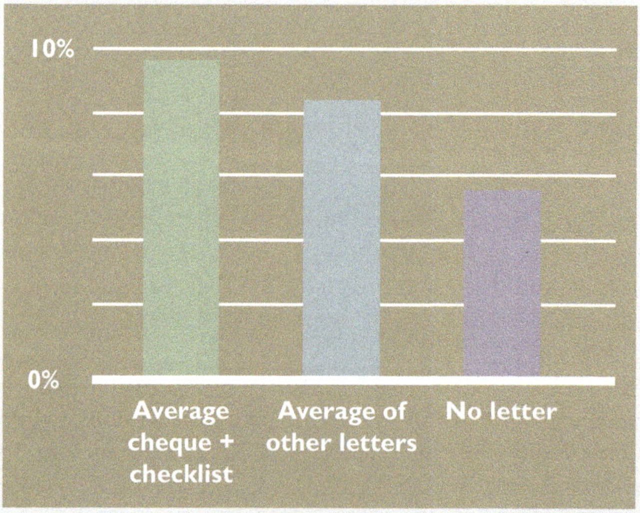

Results

The most effective letter additions were the mock check and the checklist, both of which resulted in increased take-up rates of 9.6%, compared to 8.5% for those receiving a letter without the additions and 5.2% for those not receiving a letter. There was no statistically significant difference in take-up rates between the two base letters.

These results suggest that making simple and cost-effective changes to communications, such as highlighting the value of social benefits by making them more tangible, and making the process of signing up easier to navigate are effective ways of increasing take-up rates for the CLB.

Length of a trial

Trials can vary considerably in length depending on the behavior we are attempting to capture. For instance, consider our flu transmission example. If the vaccination appointments can be booked over a period of five months, we may choose to collect data over a period of five months to ensure we have captured all available data related to our trial. If we decide to examine timely vaccinations, because getting the vaccination earlier in the season has a greater benefit anyway, we may choose to look at appointment booking data for the duration of the month after the behavioral intervention. The time period of the trial might also be affected by the policyholder's deadline to implement a certain program or make a change in a process. In this case, it is possible that fewer data would be collected in order to suit policy considerations.

Data privacy and anonymity

It is critical to account for the data privacy concerns of the policyholder. If this is a concern of the policyholder, we should request to receive anonymously coded or aggregated data with the identifying information removed. This should be sufficient for a statistical analysis where we are comparing behavior between groups and not between individuals.

Once we have accounted for the preceding concerns, we can set up our experimental trial. In the case of a full RCT, we want to ensure that we use random sampling, whereby each individual in the population has an equal chance of being selected for our sample. In many cases, this may not be practical, but this is the ideal to ensure that our sample is free of bias. It is also important to ensure random assignment, in which each individual in our sample is equally likely to be assigned to any experimental condition. This approach minimizes confounding variables where the relationship between an intervention and outcome behavior is actually due to a factor other than the intervention itself. For example, if a sample is not randomly assigned, we may have individuals in Vancouver assigned to receive letter A and individuals from Montreal assigned to receive letter B. In this case, the differences in outcome behavior between letter conditions can just as easily be attributed to the location of the individual as it can to the intervention itself.

Test

During this phase, we run the trial testing our solutions against one another and against a control. Generally speaking, this should be done in line with standard guidelines for RCTs in behavioral research, though with the added perspective of a real-world setting and the involvement of broader populations. An experiment conducted in a real-world setting means there are a number of potential influences over which we have substantially less control than in a contained laboratory experiment.

Similarly, the BI approach is different from a traditional evaluation. In a traditional evaluation, we implement one potential solution and evaluate the target behavior before and after the intervention. In cases where a trial is not feasible, this type of approach can be valuable. However, one major shortcoming is that the process does not allow us to conclude whether a change of behavior can be attributed to the intervention itself or whether some other co-occurring factor affected the outcome behavior over the same time period. In other words, a traditional evaluation does not allow us to draw conclusions related to *causality*.

In order to establish whether an outcome behavior can be directly attributed to our intervention, we would need to test multiple solutions in a RCT. The solutions should be based on the BI literature and would be measured (most often) against a status quo control condition. This approach allows us to conclude that our intervention *caused* the behavioral response of interest, rather than other factors that could have affected the outcome over the time period during which the evaluation took place.

In a BI intervention to increase the rate of flu vaccination of healthcare workers, we may test different ways to reduce the hassle factor surrounding booking flu vaccinations. As discussed earlier, for individuals in one condition, we may send out a calendar invitation with an appointment prebooked for the individual. In another condition, individuals will receive a clickable link to book an appointment online. We can test these two solutions against the control condition – the original email prompting employees to call in to book an appointment.

To ensure that a trial is conducted smoothly, it is crucial that the party executing the trial (usually the policy, program, or touchpoint holder) be provided explicit instructions by the BI practitioner. This would include the randomization scheme, final versions of all approved trial materials in the correct format, mailing lists or other contact information for individuals in the sample (if appropriate), and written data collection procedures. After all data are collected, they will typically be analyzed using inferential statistics and reported to the policyholder.

Scale/implement

During the scale/implement phase, the policyholder will decide what intervention to scale up. To scale up means to apply the intervention to the broadest possible population. Implementation means to apply the intervention to all activities moving forward, and the result of both is that the intervention becomes the "new normal" of doing business. While this phase marks the end of a particular trial, it is also usually a time for policyholders to begin to ask questions about what else could benefit from a behavioral insights approach and deepen the understanding of the barriers assessed during the understand phase.

Often the implemented or scaled solution is the intervention that performed best in changing behavior. However, in some cases the policyholder may decide to go with a solution that did not produce the greatest behavioral change. This might be a case where the cost-benefit analysis does not warrant using the more effective, but more expensive intervention. For example, in Box 12.3, you will learn about an organ donor registration trial where one of the best performing interventions – a simplified form with brochure – was *not* selected for implementation due to its elevated cost and impact on the environment.

BOX 12.3 ORGAN DONOR REGISTRATION CASE STUDY

Overview

In the province of Ontario, more than 1,500 people are currently waiting to receive life-saving organ transplants. Every three days, one of these individuals dies while waiting. An increase in organ donor registration rates is critical. We know the majority of people across the province are willing to register as an organ and tissue donor, yet only 25% of Ontarians are registered.

Opportunity

The province of Ontario has a prompted-choice system to register organ and tissue donors – this means that Ontarians are asked whether they consent to be a donor during health card, driver's license, and photo card transactions at government service centers across the province. Individuals can also proactively register online at BeADonor.ca. The registration rate remains significantly lower than other jurisdictions that use a prompted-choice system, despite the fact that research shows broad public support of the program and willingness among Ontarians to register.

In an effort to increase registration rates in the province, the Ontario Behavioural Insights Unit partnered with the University of Toronto's Behavioural Economics in Action at Rotman School of Management (BEAR), the Trillium Gift of Life Network, ServiceOntario, and the Ministry of Health and Long-Term Care to pilot the use of behavioral insights to increase organ donor registration.

Solution

To begin, a number of barriers were identified that could prevent individuals from registering as donors. These barriers included a complex registration form that was difficult and time-consuming to complete and customer service representatives who at times, due to the lengthy process and high volume of customer traffic, did not always prompt individuals to register.

After careful analysis of the donor registration process, the team designed a pilot project based on the established principles of behavioral insights. The goal of the project was to improve the in-person organ donor registration process and increase registration rates. Four types of interventions were tested.

Simplification: a simplified version of the current donor registration form
Timing: handing the form out sooner, at the reception desk rather than at the service counter
Nudge: one of three nudge statements were added to the top of the simplified form
Information: handing out the current Trillium Gift of Life Network brochure rather than not handing out anything

Results

The pilot project was a success. Registration rates increased up to 143% compared to current registration rates. Three of the conditions outperformed all others, each significantly increasing an individuals' likelihood of registering compared to the control condition. The best three conditions applied behavioral insights interventions, including simplification of the form, nudge statements, and addition of an information brochure to the simplified form. As a result of this trial, the simplified form, with the best performing nudge statement, is being implemented. Although the information brochure condition performed slightly better than the other conditions, the decision to not implement the form with the brochure was made due to increased implementation costs and environmental considerations of that particular intervention.

Once implemented, these successful changes could garner over 450,000 new registrations in Ontario annually, approximately 200,000 more than the status quo (Government of Ontario, 2016).

In some cases, the trial may glean additional opportunities for testing that could lead to even more improvements. Therefore, there may be iterations on a trial to identify what works the best at the lowest cost.

The relationship with the policyholder

A key part of running a behavioral insights trial is the relationship between the BI unit and its partners. In virtually all circumstances, the BI unit will be separate from the group that is actually delivering a given program or policy. Therefore, the relationship between the unit and the partner must be managed with two objectives in mind. The first is to ensure buy-in in order to actually run the trial in the short term. The long-term objective should be to share knowledge and experience such the partner becomes more capable of running experiments and applying behavioral science principles in their own right. These partners are often strategic policy or program delivery and administration units in departments or agencies.

Co-creation of interventions

One great way to create a positive relationship with implementation partners is to work together to create the interventions for a given BI trial. Not only does this method help generate buy-in among partners, it is also highly likely to create better interventions. While the BI unit brings expertise and knowledge about behavioral science and experimentation methodology, implementation partners have experience with the people whose behavior the trial is meant to change, as well as the systems that will actually deliver the intervention. Combination of these backgrounds should result in interventions that are informed by academic behavioral science as well as policy and program knowledge.

Data sharing and analysis

Data sharing and analysis are another opportunity to collaborate positively with implementation partners. In an ideal situation, implementation partners are able to share raw, individual-level data with the BI unit for analysis. Due to privacy and data sharing constraints, however, this is not always possible, and the BI unit may have to rely on implementation partners for some level of analysis. In either case, the data analysis phase is about using experimental data to answer questions and generate insights that are useful for both partners. While the results of the experiment itself are central, the data can often provide other insights that could be useful for the implementation partners moving forward. By asking partners if there are particular questions they would like to have answered by the data, this phase can be made a collaborative experience that creates value for all parties.

Presentation and case study

The presentation of results is the culmination of the trial, and one cycle of the process from understand to test/implement, and is usually given to the senior executives who championed the project but may not have been involved in the day-to-day of running it. This is an opportunity to highlight not only the work of the BI unit but also the work of any partners who helped implement the trial. It is also important to be clear and transparent about the process that the BI unit undertook when designing, running, and analyzing the trial in order to help demystify experimentation. If senior executives can be made more comfortable with the process and the advantages of experimentation, they will be more likely to request its use from their staff, which in turn helps mainstream the use of behavioral insights and experimentation in government.

Conclusions and considerations

This chapter has outlined a framework for testing solutions using BI. Although a framework like this could be useful for structuring a BI project, it is often necessary to be flexible and willing to deviate from this approach if necessary. There are often external factors, such as political implications, time sensitivity, and the scientific constraints of field research, that can prevent a perfect trial from being run. For instance, there may not be time or resources for a deeper examination of the literature during the understand phase. If this is the case, then solutions might have to be generated with limited background information. However, the testing itself will provide important insights and evidence, even if a proper background review was not possible.

Another common constraint could concern the feasibility or ethics of complete randomization. Often there are both scientific and policy considerations that could prevent a trial from being run as a perfect randomization. To return to our flu vaccination example, in a perfect randomization, we may want to assign each healthcare worker to a different experimental group. However, a scientific consideration is that two healthcare workers in the same department may receive different emails and then speak to each other about it, ultimately affecting their behavior (spillover). Therefore, we may decide on a different trial design, such as a cluster design where we randomize our conditions by department rather than by individual healthcare worker. In our flu shot example, an ethical constraint may be that placing healthcare workers into a control group with no intervention during flu season may result in higher flu acquisition rates for the workers and for their patients. Therefore, with a problem that has public health implications, we may want to consider inclusion of a control condition only if there is a status quo intervention already being utilized and not if the control means no attempt would be made to encourage flu shot behavior, for example. From a policy perspective, in many trials exposure of people to different experimental conditions may be deemed unfair or unethical, and this is another case where fully randomized trials may not be appropriate and cluster trials could be useful.

It is important to keep these realities in mind to make sure that BI is used to fit a given context, rather than attempting to shape a context to suit BI. The ultimate goal of using BI is to improve policies and programs and, as such, a flexible approach is often necessary to ensure valuable evidence is generated for the policyholder.

Centralized versus diffuse systems

Across organizations, two main approaches have been used to integrate BI expertise and methodologies into government.

The **centralized model** involves placing a dedicated BI team in a central location in an organization. This team then acts as cross-domain and cross-departmental BI experts and take on a consulting role with partner departments when BI-compatible projects arise.

The **diffuse model** involves embedding BI expertise within multiple departments across an organization. These team members would possess both BI expertise and some subject-matter knowledge for the particular domain, and they would lead projects when it meets the priorities and objectives of the department. With this approach, the BI team may be housed in a central location in a department, acting as consultants to meet the priorities and objectives of the department. Alternatively, the BI experts may be placed on a team with a specified policy goal. In the former case, the diffuse approach would likely also require collaboration with the policyholding team in order to ensure access to necessary approvals, problem-specific knowledge, relevant touchpoints, and data. In the latter, the BI practitioner(s) would be expected to have or build subject-matter expertise to develop optimal solutions for a precisely defined set of priorities.

Both the centralized and diffuse approaches have their respective advantages and disadvantages, which often mirror those of the other.

Centralized model

Advantages

Introduction of a novel evidence-generating approach to a department. The BI team is removed from the scope that a particular department has developed. The centralized BI team has the ability to take a step back and assess whether the behavior challenge presented is the most impactful way of tackling the overall policy objective.

Cross-domain insights to apply to new area. Findings from the behavioral sciences about human biases and heuristics are not necessarily confined to particular domains. Behavior-based insights may be brought in from other areas to solve challenges that have a common behavioral or cognitive thread. For instance, centralized BI practitioners might suggest the application of a self-control nudge that was successful in encouraging people to recycle in order to increase physical activity.

Greater focus on what works. Rather than designing interventions dictated by political pressures around a program area, a centralized team might design interventions focused on what is expected to produce the greatest overall benefit.

Ability to select from a broader range of projects. Not all projects are suited to behavioral insights. A centralized team allows for the generation of useful insights from a variety of areas, potentially illustrating the full cross-domain impact of the approach.

Disadvantages

Lack of area expertise. A lack of dedicated experts in the relevant department may result in the BI team missing key considerations when attempting to understand problems and develop solutions.

Lack of understanding of how to acquire relevant data and navigate departmental structures. A centralized unit may have a less sophisticated understanding of political considerations in a program area, which may lead to an intervention design that is not likely to be granted approval to be tested or implemented. A centralized unit is also likely to have less familiarity with the data landscape of a particular organization and less experience navigating complex departmental structures and processes. This may result in the centralized unit spending additional, unexpected time and resources navigating the inner workings of the department. A potential outcome of this lack of understanding may be that the solutions proposed by the centralized unit are less feasible in practice.

TABLE 12.2 Advantages and disadvantages of a centralized model

Advantage	*Disadvantage*	*Sample undesirable scenario*
Novel evidence-generating approach introduced to partner department	Lack of area expertise means BI practitioners may miss key contextual considerations when developing interventions.	A trial to increase use of a quit-smoking phone line is proposed by a centralized team to a health-related government department. It is learned that no funding is available for the development of a new, phone-based intervention, and as a result, the intervention is unable to move forward.
Cross-domain insights applied to new area	Proposed intervention may be less feasible in practice.	A centralized BI team proposes an intervention to increase jury duty attendance but learns that data about jury attendance are not compiled and that it would require additional expensive resources to capture the relevant data.
Greater focus on what could work based on previous evidence	May have difficulty obtaining buy-in from decision makers. Lack of familiarity with departmental processes may lead to difficulty in data acquisition and navigation of departmental structures.	A centralized BI team engages the relevant policy team to tackle the challenge of increasing diverse hiring in government. A relevant decision-maker is particularly prideful of the diversity training program they have been championing and sees the BI intervention as challenging their efforts. As a result, the decision-maker does not see the need for an additional intervention and does not approve access to necessary data.
BI practitioners have the ability to select potentially high-impact projects across policy areas.	BI may be used only on occasion in a given area and fail to be embedded in departmental processes.	Individuals in a department know that the application form for a social benefit is overly complicated, but without a designated BI team, they are unable to leverage expertise on how to improve and test an improvement.

May have difficulty obtaining buy-in. A centralized unit would need to partner with a team from the relevant program area within a department to fully execute a trial. It may prove to be difficult to find engaged partners as BI is likely not an embedded part of their process, and these projects are often additional tasks on top of their job descriptions. Further, a centralized unit may not have key contacts with decision-makers in partner organizations. These restricted networks mean it may be more difficult to obtain buy-in from the people that would be able to approve the project.

The centralized model means that BI may not be successfully embedded within the processes and procedures of a department or organization. One of the most fundamental disadvantages of a centralized model is that BI expertise is detached from the inner day-to-day workings of departments, meaning that it may be viewed by those in the organization as a transient, project-specific engagement and not a core policy tool leveraged for behavioral change.

The centralized model presents a useful framework for utilizing BI in government. There are some challenges to this approach, but many of these can be overcome with effective partnerships and communication.

One way to augment the previously mentioned challenges is to foster strong partnerships between the centralized BI unit and the partner department. The partner department should be actively involved to act as a bridge between organizations, communicating importance to senior management and obtaining necessary approvals, providing subject matter expertise, balancing political priorities with impactful insights, assessing the feasibility of proposed interventions, acting as a liaison between BI scientists and data holders, and ensuring the intervention is aligned with program objectives. At the outset of such a partnership, a collaborative project charter or statement of work could act as a commitment device and should identify key dates, milestones, deliverables, and respective responsibilities to ensure agreement between the partner organization and the centralized BI unit.

One important challenge mentioned is that having a centralized model means that it will be harder to entrench BI practices and procedures into different departments and areas. The BI approach may be viewed as something that requires a high level of expertise, and the requirement to make a connection with an extradepartmental team may act as a small hurdle for those interested in its application. This can be mitigated through hosting workshops and talks where the process for working with the centralized team is clearly outlined, cross-domain findings are clearly explained to show the benefits of the BI approach, and contact is maintained with previous project partners who have benefited from BI to stay abreast of their current work and find opportunities for future collaboration.

Diffuse model

Advantages

Ability to embed the BI approach. Perhaps the greatest advantage of the diffuse model is that the BI approach, including academic insights and rigorous experimentation, has the potential to be entrenched into internal processes within an organization.

BI practitioner would be knowledgeable in the subject matter and not a generalist. The BI team or practitioner would be able to acquire subject matter expertise for a particular program area, meaning that the hypotheses tested are informed by what has worked well in the past in that particular domain.

Navigation of departmental structures and processes may be simple when the BI team is embedded and has familiarity with internal processes. The familiarity gained with key decision-makers in a department over time may make it easier to tailor communication materials and gain necessary approvals. A working understanding of internal data collection processes and practices, as well as methods and key contacts for acquiring relevant data, would make it simpler to run trials in a timely manner.

Trials that are feasible and implementable based on the political landscape may be proposed and conducted. Embedded BI teams have an understanding of the department's workings and political priorities, which means that they are able to design trials that effectively accomplish the objectives of a particular policy or program.

Disadvantages

Projects suited to BI approaches may be limited in some departments. Some departments are more suitable for this approach than others. For instance, it may be difficult to utilize BI in a department where there are no easily available touchpoints with the target population, or where there are insufficient data and little ability or will to obtain relevant data.

Political pressures around certain program areas may lead to ill-fitting applications of BI. An embedded BI team may be required to take on projects that are meant to fulfill the department's priorities but are not the best fit for a BI approach.

TABLE 12.3 Advantages and disadvantages of a diffuse model

Advantages	*Disadvantages*	*Sample undesirable scenario*
Ability to embed BI approach in a department	Projects suited to BI approach in some departments may be limited.	In a department with few touchpoints or limited data capabilities, the BI approach may be difficult to use.
BI practitioner may be knowledgeable about a particular subject matter and not a generalist.	Embedded BI units may become highly specialized and miss key literature that could be used to apply behavioral interventions across domains to their area of expertise.	A social norm nudge to improve electricity conservation behavior has the potential to be applied to improving employee exercise frequency in a department, but this link might not be apparent if the embedded BI team is only examining literature specific to improving physical activity.
Navigation of departmental structures and processes may be simple when the BI team is embedded and has familiarity with internal processes.	Political pressures in certain program areas may lead to inappropriate applications, where BI is not the best fitting approach for a particular problem.	A priority for a department is to promote a cultural change around environmental issues. Because culture change is not a measurable behavior, it would not be possible to use a quantitative BI approach with testing. It is possible that a BI team would be expected to be a part of this type of initiative, even if the problem is not well suited to the BI approach.
Propose and conduct trials that are feasible and implementable based on the political landscape.	BI team may find it difficult to develop creative solutions while being aware of the constraints and capabilities of their department.	A BI team wants to design an intervention to improve the uptake of preventative cervical cancer screening among eligible individuals. Mailing letters would be an easy and inexpensive way to reach the targeted individuals. However, previous experience of the team showed that due to the way letters are printed in the department, randomization of mailing would not be possible. Therefore, the team may draw the conclusion that the letter option is not feasible and decide to go with a different communication route, without attempting to explore the possibility further or examining alternative approaches for quasi-randomization.

Embedded BI units may become highly specialized and miss key literature that could be used to apply behavioral interventions across domains to their area of expertise. The ability to apply findings from different domains may be limited as their scope of knowledge narrows to their area. Staying up to date with broader literature and methodological innovations that could have applications for their area will be useful in augmenting this possibility.

The diffuse model provides a promising approach to embedding BI in the processes and procedures of a given department. Key challenges may be mitigated in several ways.

As discussed, there may be a shortage of projects that are a clear fit for a BI approach in a given department because of the lack of touchpoints or data, leading to improper applications of BI. In cases such as these, partnerships with external organizations such as community organizations, schools, or other levels of government may be valuable in obtaining relevant touchpoints and data that would support a BI approach and benefit the department in achieving a piece of the broader policy objective.

To ensure breadth and that relevant interventions are applied in different contexts, maintenance of strong connections with other embedded BI teams would help ensure that teams are aware of the latest literature and methodologies across domains. One way to achieve this is by holding conferences and meetings for BI practitioners in government, which will keep teams up to date on the latest work in different areas.

For example, in response to a broad and growing interest in behavioral insights across the federal public service, the Impact and Innovation Unit in the Government of Canada launched a Behavioural Insights Community of Practice (BI CoP). This horizontal network of employees, practitioners, and researchers meets quarterly to share information, research methodologies, and experimental results. BI CoP membership is open to all public servants interested in BI and experimentation, at all levels. To complement the internal BI CoP, the IIU is bringing together provincial, territorial, and municipal governments working in the field of behavioral insights with the Behavioural Insights Network (BIN). This network facilitates stronger communication and collaboration on behavioral insights across the country at all levels of government, by providing a forum to share experiences and make linkages and potential project partnerships.

Conclusion

This chapter has outlined the current state of the application of behavioral insights to public policy in Canada, provided an understanding of the challenges to this work, provided some solutions to help overcome them, and discussed organizational models for behavioral insights units in government. Since 2014, Canada has seen a rise in the adoption of behavioral insights into government's policy and program design toolkit. The proliferation of BI capacity in federal, provincial and territorial, and municipal governments is matched by a growing ecosystem of academic, corporate, and nonprofit organizations that are applying BI and experimentation to every sector of society. Given the emergent nature of the field, there is much more to learn about how best to apply this approach to public policy challenges.

Over the coming years, the field is likely to grow in both the breadth and depth of its application to public policy. Application of BI to a broader set of problems will involve the need to increase the capacity of local governments to use BI and experimentation, as well as the application of BI to improve internal government functions to drive efficiency and impact. To apply BI more thoughtfully requires the use of behavioral science principles earlier in the policy process in order to design policies and programs in a way that is likely to improve behavior, while also applying BI to areas with proven problems. The evolution of the practice over the coming years will see BI being applied to more persistent problems by a more diverse set of organizations and individuals in order to drive greater impact for citizens.

Further readings

Large-scale randomized controlled trials

Barratt, H., Campbell, M., Moore, L., Zwarenstein, M., & Bower, P. (2016). Randomised controlled trials of complex interventions and large-scale transformation of services. *Health Services and Delivery Research, 16*(4), 19–36.

Real-world challenges to randomization

Heard, K., O'Toole, E., Naimpally, R., & Bressler, L. (2017). Real-world challenges to randomization and their solutions. *J-PAL*. Retrieved from www.povertyactionlab.org/sites/default/files/resources/2017.04.14-Real-World-Challenges-to-Randomization-and-Their-Solutions.pdf

Prevention of spillover effects in RCTs, example from criminology

Ariel, B., Sutherland, A., & Sherman, L. W. (2018). Preventing treatment spillover contamination in criminological field experiments: The case of body-worn police cameras. *Journal of Experimental Criminology, 15*, 569–59. https://doi.org/10.1007/s11292-018-9344-4

Difference-in-difference designs

Wing, C., Simon, K., & Bello-Gomez, A. (2018). Designing difference in difference studies: Best practice for public health policy research. *Annual Review of Public Health, 39*, 453–469.

13 Behavioral *impacts* for public policy

Kai Ruggeri

Instead of a theory, behavioral economics relies on a hodgepodge of evidence showing the ineffectiveness of human decision-making in various circumstances (often in a controlled, laboratory setting).

Choi and Pritchard (2003)

Chapter summary

It is nearly impossible to overstate the influence behavioral economics now has in academic science and applications to policy. Essentially all domains covered in public and political debates – from social services to social media – are now fair game for interventions derived from psychological science and their subsequent evaluations. While this trend may have started over a decade ago and certainly existed long before that, a number of prevailing concerns have overshadowed behavioral economics as a field of scientific study, which could be summarized simply as "But *why*?" In this concluding chapter, we critically review the concepts and cases discussed in the preceding chapters, highlighting strengths and general insights, as well as pointing out concerns regarding ethics, failures of behavioral policy, and the lack of a cohesive theoretical framework. This chapter seeks to explain why combining psychology and behavioral economics seems to be such an effective tool as opposed to merely being an interesting experimental technique. We use all of these topics to highlight the most critical insights across the field, as well as what it could mean for the future of policymaking, its impact on economic stability, and most importantly, its impact on improving the well-being of entire populations.

Learning objectives

- Define impact in research and policy
- Understand the value of behaviorally informed interventions on two levels: achieving immediate goals and wider impacts on population well-being
- Define well-being, its measurements, and its place as the ultimate policy outcome
- Critique the strengths and limitations of evidence-based policy and behavioral economics
- Consider the impact of social and economic inequalities on well-being

DOI: 10.4324/9781003181873-13

Where we are

There is an unmistakable, sprawling trend of applying insights from scientific research in the social and behavioral sciences to policies. As demonstrated in the previous chapters, every aspect of our lives – from what we eat to how much we save for retirement – is a potential area of interest for research and policy related to our behaviors. As the general trend toward behavioral approaches continues, this will likely only continue to expand the range of evidence-backed tools offered within behaviorally informed policy.

In spite of this recent trend, it is important to note that the conversion from insight to impact is not necessarily a tradition, particularly for social psychology. Whereas policy applications may be clear from a study on how tax letters could encourage better compliance in a group of delinquent nonpayers, they are less so from a study on implicit attitudes toward an out-group held by a group of students. Thankfully, increasing evidence is available on the potential cost-effectiveness of nudges in comparison to other policy options (Benartzi et al., 2017). For this final chapter, we will consider the bigger picture regarding behavioral insights for policy, including positives, negatives, opportunities for impact, priorities, and what to expect in the future in this field.

Limitations of behaviorally informed policies

With their dominance in the field, there is a tendency to assume that nudges are low-cost in comparison to other policy options (or no policy at all). While there is some evidence to support this view (Benartzi et al., 2017), such claims may understate the substantial investment required for indirect study from behavioral sciences, leading to the final applications. In other words, once implemented, behavioral interventions may be excellent value for cost, but establishing and validating underlying theory for the most effective ones typically require long-term investment to reach this point. As there is now clear momentum in utilizing behavioral approaches to policy, particularly from work in psychology and behavioral economics, it is critical that we consistently improve standards in the field, from terminology to toolkits and from theory to validated impact.

One way to begin to improve the pathway from insight to impact is through better attempts at **replication** in the social and behavioral sciences. A major issue that has expanded substantially in recent years has been that a number of well-known and widely cited studies from the psychological sciences failed to produce the same findings when tested again by other researchers (Camerer et al., 2016). In many cases, this was largely due to reliance on very small sample sizes or not paying attention to critical aspects of statistical analyses, such as confidence and error (Matjasko, Cawley, Baker-Goering, & Yokum, 2016).

While this has many implications for research generally, it is specifically relevant to behavioral policy in that it requires greater investment in basic science, by using a variety of methods to check that ideas are likely to work when implemented in the real world. This is especially important because there is a lot of variability in potential effects (positive and unwanted side effects) between groups and locations, and for even a simple method it may be the primary limitation of behaviorally informed policies.

To discuss this more tangibly, we will consider some very real and very recent examples that attempted to apply simple interventions with the use of financial incentives. Recall the famous Gneezy and Rustichini (2000) studies from Chapter 4: while the addition of a price tag to things might seem like a simple solution, the actual results can be problematic. Each of our examples considers policies along those lines by either adding a fee or taking one away.

In analyzing these results, we get a more sober view of behavioral interventions, but one that provides a critical perspective.

Hospital visits in the Czech Republic

Like most countries in Europe, the Czech Republic has a national healthcare service that provides universal care without cost at the point of entry. While this is sometimes referred to as "free healthcare," what it really means is that treatment is provided irrespective of one's ability to pay, as the system is funded through social health insurance that is mandatory for residents to pay into as a portion of their income, rather than through fees for service collected at the point of entry or discharge (with only a few exceptions).

However, also like many countries in Europe, the Czech healthcare system has faced two major issues in recent decades: a lack of sustainable funding and an increase in avoidable utilization. In other words, there are concerns that there is not enough money and too many unnecessary visits to maintain service and quality standards. While a number of solutions to this problem have been considered, one initiative stands out as particularly unpopular.

In 2008, the government decided to introduce small user fees of between 30 Czech crowns (around US$1.60) and 90 crowns (about US$4.80) for visiting a doctor, receiving prescribed medicine, spending a day in the hospital, or using services outside of standard working hours (see Kalousova, 2015, for full evaluation). The absolute maximum amount that anyone could be charged in a year was less than 1% of annual median income.

The idea behind the user fees is not to generate revenue or offset costs as a primary aim. Instead, much like charging a few cents for plastic bags in the grocery store (see Chapter 6), user fees are mostly meant to make people explicitly aware of their behavior, so that they are less likely to be wasteful in their use. When the cost of healthcare is considered in comparison to its critical role, such a small amount is seemingly inconsequential if it can help reduce costs to a system under pressure.

So everyone was happy about this, right? Obviously no, or it would not be in this section.

In fact, there was an almost immediate backlash in terms of negative public reaction to the user fees, formally known as the Public Budgets Stabilization Act of 2007. By March 2008, public reactions were so strong that the courts became involved, and the opposition party was able to get nationwide support to the extent that the ruling coalition was in disarray by October. By March 2009, the government had collapsed following its failure to win a vote of confidence. This coincided with a series of court battles and interim attempts to change the law, which was a feature of multiple election cycles in subsequent years.

Initial evaluations of user fees did show a significant decrease in healthcare utilization, but by the second year, the numbers had already returned to levels similar to those before 2008. However, those effects have hardly been relevant to the widespread disapproval of the policy across the country.

Plastic bag use

Sorry, now we have to ruin the plastic bag story too. While Chapter 6 painted a generally positive picture regarding a reduction in plastic bag use by introducing a small fee, subsequent work has highlighted convincingly that there are **substitution effects** that may undermine those policies. In California, where single-use plastic bags were banned outright, the effect on usage was immediate and extreme, as would be expected. Over the 12 months following the ban, there was a 40 million pound reduction in plastic bags (Taylor, 2019), which seems like a major impact. However, as pointed out by Taylor (2019), single-use plastic bags are not truly single use, which you probably already knew.

Why? Because like most people, somewhere around your home, you have a stash of plastic bags that you use for things like lining small garbage containers, picking up excrement from the family dog, separating shoes from clothes in a suitcase, and so on. In this way, many of those plastics were actually used more than was realized in a way that *avoided* the need for thicker plastics, mainly heavy-duty garbage bags. Taylor raises this as a critical concern: in that same period, there was a 12-million-pound increase in the use of heavy-duty plastics, which are in fact more problematic for the environment for a number of reasons, particularly manufacturing.

To be clear, this does not mean the policy failed. On the contrary, it very much achieved its primary purpose of reducing single-use bags. But this **leakage** (a policy reduces one behavior but results in its substitution with another, potentially more harmful behavior) cannot be ignored.

Disappointingly, similar points have been made generally about attempts to encourage household behaviors that reduce negative impacts on the climate. Such behaviors are increasingly scrutinized as climate change becomes taken more seriously around the world. While one meta-analysis gave a generally positive review on the impact of behavioral interventions in this domain, these were limited to a small number of behaviors (Nisa, Bélanger, Schumpe, & Faller, 2019). Worse, the overall findings concluded that behavioral interventions more broadly – even if viewed positively by the populations involved – had minimal effects on mitigating climate change and no evidence of sustained change.

Provision of free access to healthcare

Last, we will consider removing the cost to make something free. In Philadelphia, a team of researchers was trying to solve a long-standing issue in healthcare: too many people simply miss their appointments, called no-shows. In low-income communities, these rates can be especially high, even for clinics where care is provided free of charge. However, "free" is not really free: parents have to find childcare, patients with jobs have to take time off work, and everyone has to find a way to get to the clinic.

To address this, Chaiyachati et al. (2018) worked with a healthcare clinic that provides care to disadvantaged people across the city to provide free, app-based, ride-sharing services to get people from home to the clinic. This seemed like a good candidate for impact, as it was well known that many people from these communities struggle with access to transportation and public options are not always helpful. It was also a likely candidate because the cost of providing these rides was far less than the cost of patients missing appointments (or even arriving late). But you know where this is going.

Unfortunately, after a trial of the free rides, the team found no improvement in attendance rates in this population. In spite of having all the right ingredients and focusing on a population that might benefit the most, no-show rates remained about the same after the intervention was implemented.

Getting back on track

The point of these three examples is not to discourage behavioral interventions or to undermine everything we have discussed in the preceding chapters. Instead, they are here to raise some very important questions about behaviorally informed policy. First, how can we know when to expect one to work and one to not only fail but backfire so miserably? Second, even when things do not work, what can we learn from these "failed" interventions? To answer these questions, we can begin by asking ourselves, "what is the real purpose?"

The point: means and ends

So what makes a good policy? In Chapter 10, we outlined the extensive process of evaluation required to answer this very question. On one hand, a good policy is one that meets the goals it sets out to achieve. Ideally, this occurs in line with the specific process that is envisioned beforehand. But this typically limits the identification of good policies to treating mere symptoms (e.g. better eating habits, less risk-taking with savings accounts, not procrastinating before an exam), rather than making a lasting change. Although these are important outcomes, they are ultimately the means to an end. But what end should that be?

Scientists are often required to produce a statement of the anticipated **impact** of the study they are conducting. In most cases, this involves explaining a process by which meaningful findings, discovered during or after the study, could be translated into applications. Those applications should then offer tangible changes toward relevant challenges or needs, such as an increase in the number of people that have access to healthcare or a reduction in pollutants in the air for the area around a city.

Due to the *publish or perish* mindset within academia, impact has previously focused primarily on scientific dissemination. As argued by many, this alone creates a number of concerns (to put it generously), and scientific publication naturally should not be considered the only form of impact. Facilitation of a better dissemination process for many may expand opportunities for impact (Ruggeri, 2014; Insel, 2009), but that is a topic for another time. However, even with scientific evidence, policies will vary in how likely they are to create any form of meaningful gain (Howlett et al., 2015). Some argue that such an impact cannot happen at all without closing the gap between the development of evidence and its application in practice, whether for policy or otherwise (Insel, 2009). Still others argue that pushing scientists to focus on application can threaten advancement by discouraging discovery (Jogelkar, 2012), indicating resistance to the concept from the outset.

There is no consensus about a definition of impact. However, with the increasing prominence impact has gained in science and policy discourse, organizations such as the Economic and Social Research Council of the UK offer some of the most explicit descriptions, such as "a considerable contribution to society and the economy" (ESRC, 2017). With this definition, it becomes clear that research impact, even in a classical sense, goes beyond understanding and advancing the scientific method and theory. It implies that impact is not (or should not be) limited to academia, and at best it should focus on how outcomes *improve* society and the economy, with benefits for individuals, organizations, and nations.

Somehow, all of this leaves a rather dissatisfying depiction of value. To study behavioral insights in the context of public policy is to believe that a better understanding of our decisions and actions should eventually make life *better*, at least by enabling us to carry out the values we hold and the choices we desire to make. There may be a number of findings that influence legislation, for example, but is that automatically a good thing, justifying further work on a topic? Clearly not, but that is not much of a conclusion, either. No, much further than simply showing what *could be used*, the genuine impact from behavioral insights should be understood as *improving things that matter*. In this way, we can directly ask if policies are supporting us to carry out those choices we value and then follow up by asking if behaviorally informed approaches are doing a better job of that, whether alone or as a complementary tool.

Take, for example, Box 13.1. In a democratic society, can there be any more important activity than voting? *Any* intervention that seeks to change voting behaviors, even if apolitical, such as a neutral party seeking to increase voter registrations, will have consequences. In democratic systems, voting has a direct and substantial effect on norms, taxes, laws, schools, health systems, and almost any other domain (whether covered in this book or not). Furthermore, on the issues that are most contentious, where a small shift in voting patterns affects the entire outcome, interventions such as this have a direct and unmistakable impact on a society. But to what end? Is the purpose of policy simply to *get* people to vote, or is the purpose of voting to get the most accurate representation of a population into leadership positions? Or is there some inherent good that comes directly from civic participation, regardless of outcome? In short, interventions can be effective in their own right, but we have to ask ourselves, "*to what end?*" (Note: This approach was also – seemingly effectively – applied in various locations to encourage individuals to get a vaccine during the COVID-19 pandemic; no data on those attempts were available during the writing of this chapter.)

BOX 13.1 SIGNIFICANT IMPACT: USE OF LOTTERY PRIZES TO INCREASE ELECTORAL VOTES

In collaboration with the Behavioural Insights Team (BIT), John, MacDonald, and Sanders (2015) ran a RCT that investigated the use of a lottery prize as an incentive to encourage electoral participation in the United Kingdom. Compared to those reached by traditional door-to-door canvassing, those in the lottery group had 3.3 percent more registrations when the prize was £1,000 and 4.2 percent more when the prize went up to £5,000. These increases were significantly different from the control group, but not from each other.

While this is a clear victory for institutions who want to encourage voting participation, when we consider the demographic of people who would most likely be affected by this intervention, a controversial quality comes to light: lower income individuals are more likely to participate in lotteries (Haisley, Mostafa, & Loewenstein, 2008). From a political standpoint, this could be considered controversial, instigating an uncommonly high influx of low-income voters who might have the capacity to tip the balance for or against a given political agenda. The counterargument, naturally, is that the prize remains available to all, and thus no one is punished for existing behavior, even if the reward has varying relative value. Ultimately, by encouraging more participation from groups traditionally underrepresented in voting, governments are more likely to accurately reflect the views of the population and variability in needs therein.

Competing policy agendas

One specific challenge with the notion of impact is where discrete policy agendas come into conflict. For example, LaGuardia Airport in Flushing, New York, sits in a densely populated area. Anyone living near the airport will no doubt be familiar with the sights and sounds of aircraft, as it is one of the busiest transportation hubs in the United States. There are a number of policies and regulations to guide how planes can use the airport, such as the hours of the day flights are scheduled, noise thresholds for takeoffs and landings, and flight patterns for all planes entering or departing the airspace (Jiao et al., 2017).

In one policy area, fuel efficiency may be seen as the most critical topic and lead to policies that direct the most environmentally friendly routes in and out of the airport. Given the importance of air quality to both physical health and subjective well-being, there is no doubt an argument for energy-efficiency policies (Van Kamp, Leidelmeijer, Marsman, & de Hollander, 2003). At the same time, the noise thresholds to which flights must adhere around the airport also have a direct impact on the same outcomes (Ising & Kruppa, 2004). What happens when the fuel-efficient path generates the most noise? What determines the most important components when the primary outcomes of interest come into direct conflict? Such challenges are not isolated to aviation and can be expanded to a number of economic and social challenges. Thus, certain approaches may increase an effect, but where there are potential conflicts or unwanted side effects, a higher order consideration not only is a philosophical consideration but may also serve as a pragmatic guide for decision-making.

Furthermore, to have some way of identifying an end across all policies, there must be conceptual clarity in what is measured and how (Oliver et al., 2014a). Thus, current approaches to assessing behaviorally informed policies can focus on their ability to deliver immediate goals, but this may change as evidence becomes more robust. Over the long term, for those approaches to produce meaningful results when studied, impact evaluations of evidence must go beyond looking at the reduction of a particular problem or successfully informing more effective policies (OECD, 2014a). They need to identify what *matters most*.

GDP and beyond

In traditional policy reporting, well-being has often been defined in the context of national prosperity, most commonly indicated by the gross domestic product (GDP): the total value of all goods and services produced in an economy. Over the past century, GDP has been the undisputed gold standard for estimating how well the population of a country is doing (Adler & Seligman, 2016; Allin & Hand, 2017). This stems in large part from the economic view that an increase in GDP should indicate more people in gainful employment, which was long considered the fundamental building block for countries to sustain and flourish.

GDP uses economic measures to evaluate the prosperity of a country, suggesting that an increase in national prosperity should equate to an increase in population well-being. However, while countries with a higher GDP tend to have higher population well-being, it has been noted on many occasions that increases in GDP rarely coincide with increases in well-being (Easterlin, 2013). Thus, to equate well-being for a group or country to its economic growth is insufficient; other approaches must provide better measurement and insight (Ruggeri, Garcia-Garzon, Maguire, Matz, & Huppert, 2020b). However, there has been reluctance on the part of many to move past GDP as the best indicator, though recent reframing as GDP *and beyond* (complementing traditional economic measures with other major outcomes, such as health and social mobility) has seemingly settled a few nerves (Allin & Hand, 2017).

The last 40 years have seen an encouraging acceleration in approaches to the measurement of well-being, which reflects not only improved science in the field but also greater interest in relevant policies (Allin & Hand, 2017). While GDP is still the default outcome of interest when looking at national social indicators, the inclusion of more diverse and scientifically developed measurements for well-being has advanced globally (Huppert & Ruggeri, 2018). There has also been greater emphasis on a more dynamic (i.e. nonlinear) understanding of income and well-being, such as Daniel Kahneman and Angus Deaton's conclusion that wealth and happiness are only correlated up to a certain level; beyond that point (in their study, this amount was US$75,000), they found, income is not a clear predictor of emotional well-being (Kahneman & Deaton, 2010).

This expanded thinking about what qualifies as the most critical outcomes has been spurred largely by academics, national governments, and international organizations. Perhaps none have been more influential than the OECD, which even goes so far as to release an annual report on well-being titled *How's life?* Even more, and perhaps not coincidentally, the last word in the title of Thaler and Sunstein's famous book *Nudge* is "happiness."

Well-being as the priority in policy

The use of behavioral insights for policymaking has drawn a great deal from the field of positive psychology, which has championed the view that well-being is one of or the most important outcome in policy (Adler & Seligman, 2016). The philosophy from this discipline has been influential toward how recent interventions are conducted. This largely took the form of a shift from *resolving problems* to *improving circumstances*, which means a focus on the ideal outcome above all else. Work from this field has attracted the interest of the general public toward positive psychology, as well as highlighted potential implications for policy, which has set much of the terminology and direction of current political and social discourse (Allin & Hand, 2017).

Variability is a mainstay across how well-being is assessed, though some convergence in the field has led most current approaches to include one or more of three "traditions" of definition and measurement: **hedonic** (the feeling or perception of positive experiences about life), **eudaimonic** (positive functioning), and **evaluative** (broad assessment of circumstances, typically past and present) (Huppert & Ruggeri, 2019).

Definitions of well-being can largely be distinguished into two approaches: (1) definitions that attempt to quantify it in objective terms, such as an aggregation of factors (e.g. education, income, employment); or (2) definitions that view it as a subjective state that varies over time and changes in circumstance. The former approach is more common in traditional policy and economic evaluations, whereas the movement spearheaded by psychologists (positive or otherwise) has pushed the latter to be considered more often, given how it covers genuine experiences unique to an individual in a manner similar to diagnosing illness (Ruggeri et al., 2020; Huppert & So, 2013). Without this, it would be assumed that anyone who is, for example, low on a social indicator such as income or education must always have low well-being and vice versa, ostensibly precluding the existence of **positive deviants** (favorable exceptions within a group having traditionally negative outcomes), which include high-performing students from low-income households or flourishing individuals in deprived regions (Ruggeri & Folke, 2021).

The WHO defines well-being as a subset of health synonymous with mental health. It explains that mental health can be understood as "a state of well-being in which every individual realizes his or her own potential, can cope with the normal stresses of life, can work productively and fruitfully, and is able to make a contribution to her or his community" (WHO, 2001). Clear definitions of well-being are difficult (Dodge, Daly, Huyton, & Sanders,

2012) but vital for the recalibration of policies that explicitly aim to secure or improve well-being (Huppert & Ruggeri, 2019).

To set well-being as the ultimate outcome is meant not only for social appeal but as a pragmatic tool that allows standardization across policy domains (see Chapter 10). Such a clear objective as a universal indicator of effectiveness can center debates on policy challenges, provide a reference across domains, and assist policy researchers and evaluators in seeking patterns for many interventions and dimensions of well-being. Consider some of the following highest impact interventions in this textbook.

Economic: tax payments increased after social norms were used in letters.
Health: unwanted patient outcomes declined after checklists were introduced during surgeries.
Energy: water consumption reductions were sustained when social comparisons were used.
Education: minority children showed reduced stress when positive features were affirmed.
Employment: return to work was faster for those who received personalized messages.
Communication: payments happened sooner when reminders were sent closer to deadlines.

In each of these, entirely different – though socially valuable – outcomes are considered. But again, we should ask two questions: does it meet its first aim and, if so, to what end? Does an increase in tax payments offer something inherently valuable to a community? Does reduced water consumption protect my future well-being? While each offers clear value within their respective domains, a standardized approach to outcomes may offer transparency in both purpose and future policymaking toward improved population well-being. As demonstrated in Figure 13.1, across the combination of these approaches – and a vast number of others – we

FIGURE 13.1 Conceptualization of successful interventions toward improved population well-being

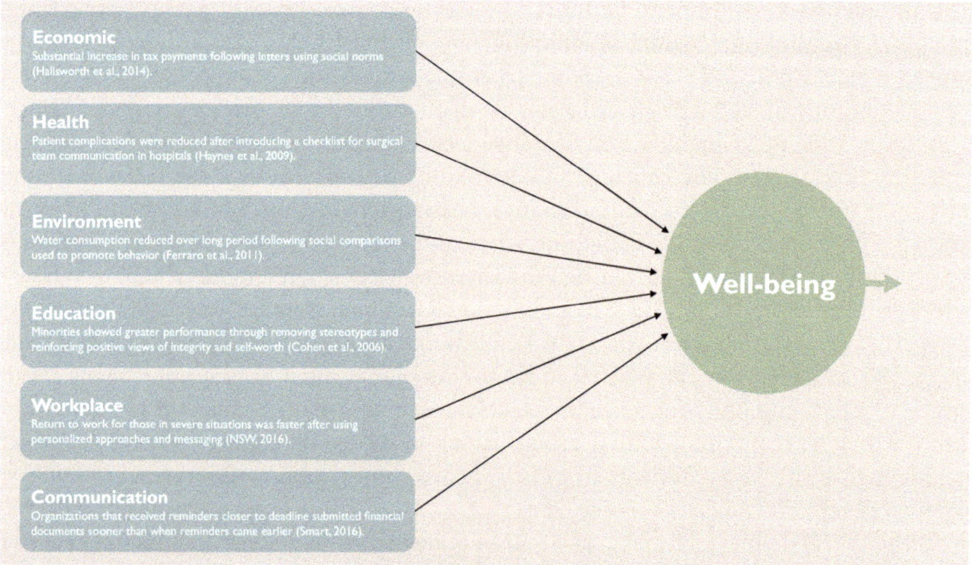

The concept depicts how five different policy domains might improve population well-being. Note the arrow to the right of well-being: one does not simply reach a point and then no further issues arise to any aspect of health, social standing, or physical security. Well-being is not something to be achieved, but that requires effort to maintain and improve.

may be better able to argue for both individual and cumulative effects of behavioral insights in policies with the most important of aims in sight.

Placement of well-being as the core outcome is a substantial challenge

Thankfully, as work on behavioral insights has expanded, it has become abundantly clear that there will be a great deal of evidence on a number of other vital domains. While this book has covered some of these, critical insights are being delivered in others, particularly those related to physical safety, financial *security* (as opposed to prosperity or GDP growth), maintenance of government integrity, and national security (Benartzi et al., 2017). If it has not been made explicit already, it may be worth noting that, along with well-being, these features, especially economic stability and physical safety, are also outcomes we argue should take priority and be used for comparison across policy interventions. Whether or not behavioral insights are yet delivering in each of these is a matter for debate, yet the evidence and knowledge generated alone offer substantial value, and this will hopefully continue to expand as it is critical for policy-related decisions (Sunstein, 2014).

It has been argued that only individuals who are already performing well will benefit from interventions that focus on well-being, whereas those with lower well-being do not gain anything from such policies. This raises concern about the best approaches to improving well-being without creating or furthering inequalities through policy. Likewise, it is important to avoid developing behavioral interventions that benefit only the most reachable populations, so that the most isolated are not left worse off, resulting in new or expanded inequalities.

Huppert (2009) raises that point by using the example of national investment in training Olympic athletes: doing so will improve the overall abilities of those who are exceptional but will have little value to the general population in terms of increasing the number of high performers. While investment in Olympic competition can certainly be valuable at a number of levels, particularly related to community cohesion and driving aspirations, unless that investment is used to mobilize activity levels generally, as a behavioral policy it will have negligible population impact.

While these are genuine concerns that require consideration, there is evidence to suggest that the promotion of well-being and the prevention of mental illness were more effective at delivering greater economic benefits than other interventions (Hawe & Potvin, 2009). Similarly, interventions aimed at reducing obesity in the population must go beyond just the reduction of weight in those already classified as obese to address the exposure to unhealthy foods and large portion sizes across the population. This will address both those who may already be obese and those who are at risk of becoming so (Loewenstein & Chater, 2017). Broadened out, these concerns also apply to matters of structural inequalities, institutionalized discrimination, and the absence of efforts to correct system flaws: simply trying to correct negative outcomes after they occur will not prevent them from continuing in others. Thus, overall shifts in the population mean are greater when interventions do not focus solely on fixing where problems exist, but on overall improvement of systems across the entire population, not only those worst-off. However, this may leave an unsatisfactory feeling for many, as it may fail to provide immediate relief to those suffering most.

Opportunities vs. problems

As has been mentioned throughout this volume, policies have often been thought of as solutions to problems, but this substantially limits their potential. To wait until an issue exists ensures that the issue will *always* be a threat, like not exercising or not eating healthy foods until you are objectively unhealthy.

To change this, policies should also be thought of as opportunities before a problem exists. For example, the world's population is aging rapidly; imagine what impacts there will be if we see that as an opportunity for healthier, longer lives, rather than only as a threat to the health system when today's young become tomorrow's old. It is imperative that we start thinking of how tools such as behavioral insights can improve lives prior to when problems arise and that through successful implementation of these we reduce the negatives in spite of the challenges faced.

Barriers to well-being

As appealing as it may sound, it is important to stress that there are considerable challenges and barriers to implementing and realizing well-being as the goal of policy. Researchers and policymakers alike face myriad difficulties in effectively delivering a successful policy in any domain, and this should be taken into account. Those difficulties are far from constant, and variability within populations is itself a barrier.

Inequalities

If we consider the heterogeneity within populations, one of the biggest barriers to improving well-being across a population is **inequality** (Cingano, 2014). While there may be many ways to understand inequality, most simply it is the distance between those doing the best and those doing the worst in a particular domain (e.g. income, wealth, health, well-being, education).

Because economic wealth is considered to be one of the most common indicators of social prosperity, inequality, too, has mostly been defined in economic terms. There is no denying that income inequality is a global issue. In fact, in spite of their tremendous wealth, the United States and the United Kingdom are home to some of the world's largest economically unequal populations (Stiglitz, 2012). While there is an increasing proportion of people earning high incomes, there is also a growing number of people earning below-average incomes. This produces a curve that is stretching wealth toward the rich, but skewing volume toward the middle and lower classes. The rising inequality in wealth and income has even been identified as the most important trend likely to determine global developments in the next 10 years (World Economic Forum, 2017).

Harvard philosopher T. M. Scanlon (2018) highlights four primary reasons to be concerned about economic inequality:

1. It gives undue power to a small number of people
2. It damages fairness in political institutions
3. It damages general economic fairness in our systems
4. It takes away the gains of economic growth from those who are partially responsible for it

In short, inequality is rising and it is a major problem, both by impeding growth and by threatening the well-being of populations (Cingano, 2014; Piketty, 2014); thus, it must be asked, do behaviorally informed policy approaches offer an effective mechanism to reduce them?

Greater income inequality is associated with a number of negative outcomes in mental (Oishi, Kesebir, & Diener, 2011) and physical health (Pickett & Wilkinson, 2015), increases in poor quality risk-taking (Payne, Brown-Iannuzzi, & Hannay, 2017), and in lowered economic stability (Ostry & Berg, 2011). However, it should not be treated in isolation in human development, economic, and political outcomes (Binelli, Loveless, & Whitefield, 2015). Policy that only targets income inequality will not necessarily lead to a reduction in other aspects of inequality (Payne, 2017), such as education or health. For example, in families with substantial financial wealth, education level (of parents or children) is not a significant indicator of outcomes for children. However, for lower income families, the educational attainment and quality of education of parents become a substantial predictor of how well children will do in life (Cingano, 2014). To an extent, this is illustrated by the example in Figure 13.2 based on the Economic Policy Institute finding that, even when test scores are similar, children from higher income homes graduate from college at a much higher rate than children from lower income homes. In fact, even children with high test scores from low-income families are less likely to graduate than children with low test scores from high-income families.

Concurrently, while overall health across Europe has generally improved in recent years, this outcome has not been experienced equally when divided between Eastern and Western Europe (Mackenbach, Karanikolos, & McKee, 2013). This means that inequalities have to be understood as something that cannot be addressed through economic policy alone (see Box 13.2), and in order to consider those worse off, there needs to be a wider reach of policy impacts (Allcott & Mullainathan, 2010).

FIGURE 13.2 College graduation rates based on income and test scores

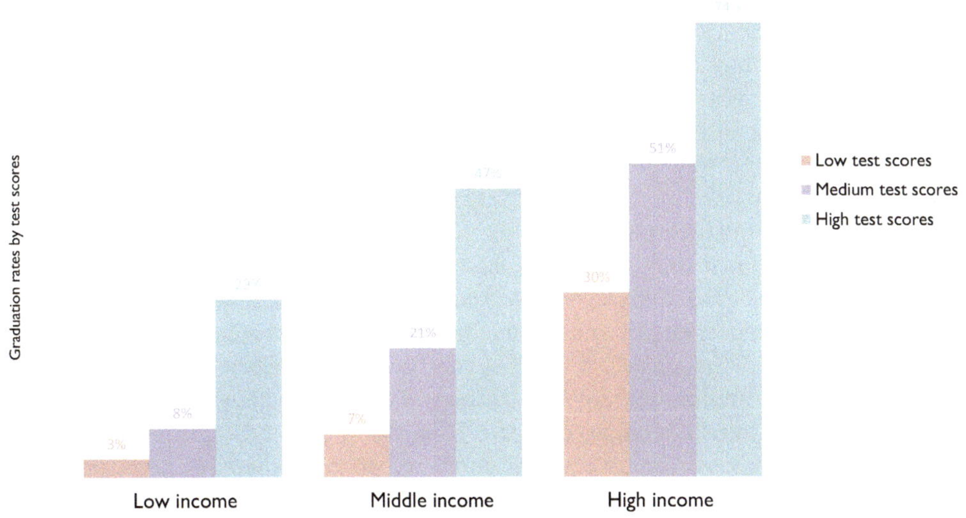

Source: Economic Policy Institute

BOX 13.2 BEHAVIORAL POLICY AND DEVELOPING ECONOMIES

Global development is an area of considerable inequality. There are some doubts about whether behavioral economics is a relevant tool at that level or just in highly industrialized countries where populations have generally high living standards. However, as this book has shown, successful examples of behavioral policies around the world demonstrate broad potential (Sunstein, 2014). For example, financial decision-making might be even more influenced by behavioral components in developing countries (Anderson & Stamoulis, 2007).

Developing economies are often characterized by multiple smaller, informal, poorly functioning markets. In such markets, behavioral components may have an even bigger impact (Falk et al., 2018) and are also associated with a shadow economy more than double (41 percent on average) the size of OECD countries (18 percent on average) (Schneider & Klinglmair, 2004). In transition countries, circumstances are similar, but citizens face changes in how resources are distributed – that is, from the smaller, personal markets toward one big market. This creates a tremendous opportunity for impact, if existing methods can be translated or new ones can be developed and successfully applied. As such, behavioral insights could be used to avoid increasing inequalities if applied appropriately in relevant contexts. Such an approach may prove either complementary or even more effective than traditional economic interventions (Anderson & Stamoulis, 2007).

Addressing inequalities in well-being

Inequality is multidimensional and taps into various aspects of human life, be it economic or social. With that in mind, well-being may be a more useful predictor to consider than GDP or any single measurement alone, encompassing a range of influencing factors. This is underscored by Diener and Seligman (2004): although national income has consistently increased over time, life satisfaction remains relatively stable. Ultimately, economic prosperity and the desirable outcomes associated with it are merely a means to the end goal of better population well-being.

Who, then, should be the main target of policy? One option is to target those in the worst circumstances. Layard (2016) believes that elevating the "most miserable" will have a greater effect on average well-being than moving those who already have a higher well-being even higher. This might initially seem like a relatively simple and effective approach. However, by considering only those at the bottom, we incorrectly assume that anyone doing well will always remain that way. Conversely, remember Huppert's (2009) argument that targeting only those at the top may improve the outcomes for those individuals, but it does nothing to increase the number of high performers.

Research on increasing well-being has commonly focused on increasing average well-being by targeting the majority, but it has not taken into account who exactly would benefit most from a given intervention and whether those who are most in need will, in fact, be positively affected by it. Although such difficulties consistently act as a barrier to effective insights, the presence and awareness of these inequalities and differences between people can also be considered an opportunity for targeted impact. Doing so may offer the greatest gains for those in the worst situations, but it must consider public reception to where resources are allocated as well as not creating stigmatization for those groups (Hansen, Bourgois, & Drucker, 2014).

It is important to know about and compare national averages of well-being to inform policy. It is even more important to be aware of the contextual variations and inequalities within a single country in order to appropriately target policy to a specific issue or demographic. For example, a high national average well-being does not necessarily mean that the country is prospering in all aspects of life or that all people are well off (Farver-Vestergaard & Ruggeri, 2017). Awareness of inequalities will ensure that policymakers do not miss those who are most vulnerable within a national population and will also inform them regarding the particular factors that contribute most to a country doing exceptionally well. Inequality can therefore be an opportunity for impact because it makes us aware of variations within a population. This enables policymakers to target unique problems that might affect a specific demographic, the details of which would be lost if only a generalized, average score of well-being is taken into account.

Overcoming barriers

Reduction in inequality is a fundamentally political process (Ruggeri & Folke, 2021), and those politics can sometimes even drive the inequalities deliberately (Lerman, Sadin, & Trachtman, 2017). Although there is rarely general agreement on how such inequalities should be rectified, inequality is – without doubt – widely acknowledged as an issue that needs to be addressed (Payne, 2017). While a definite approach on how to solve inequality does not exist yet, the most fundamental way to address inequality is by changing the policies, rules, and regulations that uphold or enforce the current wealth gap and other inequalities (Ruggeri & Folke, 2021). To properly address them, it is important to assist those in the worst circumstances to improve but not assume that those doing well will automatically remain that way, among other challenges (see Box 13.3). If policies are only focused on the general population, those most in need might not benefit, and other effects may be difficult to quantify due to the general diffusion of impact. Yet, if policies are only focused on the most vulnerable, they are more likely to elicit the policy antagonism identified by Parks and colleagues (2013) in the general population.

How can this be reconciled? According to Rose (2001), it is important that at least *some* policies not exclusively target the most vulnerable (high-risk) individuals but do target the entire population. This is a substantial challenge, as understanding the population is critical given that the variations within it may be extreme. Yet to focus *only* on high-risk individuals is not likely to generate benefits across the population. Therefore, an understanding of the challenges and incentives across the spectrum is necessary for a reasonable chance of impact (Bowles, 2008).

The point of behavioral insights for public policy

This provides us with an *ideal aim for policy*: to shift an entire population distribution *forward*, benefiting those who are most vulnerable, the general population, and those who are doing well. To do this requires an understanding of the population not just trying to involve everyone in what appears to be a useful intervention.

This is, however, not always a realistic goal. Populations are heterogeneous and unequal at baseline and in outcomes (Rözer & Kraaykamp, 2013), so it is close to impossible to develop a single policy that can equally benefit an entire population (Ruggeri & Folke, 2021). For real impact, behaviorally informed approaches must be nuanced and targeted appropriately, or they will fail to be as robust as populations require. To overcome this, policymakers must consider inequalities – from income and race to health and education – as much as possible in order to effectively influence and increase well-being, particularly through better understanding of their social determinants (Sadana & Harper, 2011). This may be where behavioral insights offer the greatest potential for impact.

BOX 13.3 RELEVANT AND RESPONSIBLE POLICY IMPACTS USING BEHAVIORAL INSIGHTS

1 Standardize frameworks and outcomes, but make them appropriate and adaptive

Organizations – particularly governments – should have clearly established approaches, definitions, measurements, and appropriately assessed outcomes for policies.

2 Include population variability when designing policy interventions

Whether scientific studies of behavioral insights or other methods are the core, inequalities must be addressed by having policies that appreciate within-population differences. This includes variabilities in impact, such as boomerang effects and unwanted side effects, and must avoid creating or expanding inequalities.

3 Highlight how gains for one group are a benefit for the entire population

To reduce the risk of antagonism in policies addressing social dilemmas, the impact for the entire population should be highlighted rather than focusing only on those directly targeted by interventions.

4 Communicate effectively

All aspects of policies should be presented in a way that can engage the widest possible audience (as described in detail in Chapter 9). Exclusion of people or groups from information will only exacerbate inequalities.

5 Anticipate resistance – appreciate the perspective of antagonists

Policies should never be presumed as a cure nor be expected to please all parties. This does not mean those who resist should be ignored, nor that a policy should be written off due to lack of unanimity.

6 Be transparent

Policies should be transparent from start (identification of the issue) to finish (evaluation) – not only when they work, but especially when they do not.

7 Do not run policies in isolation

All policies should find common denominators with other interventions, even if only in the evaluation of outcomes and impacts, but ideally in looking across agendas (e.g. how education impacts health or how one successful policy may harm another domain).

8 Celebrate gains, even small ones

Policies not only should be in the public discourse when issues arise but they also should be monitored and disseminated to reassure stakeholders of their value, even for moderate effects. Remember: better beats perfect.

9 Test for replication

Just because something worked once does not mean it will work always and everywhere. Make sure findings can be replicated – in a good way – especially before going from experiment to the real world.

Better beats perfect

Perhaps one of the greatest messages from the early days of research on behavioral insights is the power of personalized messaging (Matz et al., 2016). This has less to do with the effects found in such interventions and more to do with the unprecedented ability to identify those personal traits and then exploit them through various platforms, particularly social media. When done for positive reasons, these approaches demonstrated clear value to both the individuals (better links to products, services, behaviors, and outcomes of direct benefit) and the organizations, which presented efficient and optimal gains without obvious unwanted consequences (stressing *positive reasons* here). Yet, are these gains *meaningful for things that matter*, and are all behavioral approaches so easy to assess?

In 2017, a *New York Times* article challenged the value of behavioral economics in health, arguing that it will never be a *cure* for human illness (Carroll, 2017). This is an accurate point but not a helpful argument: behavioral interventions were never meant to be a *cure*. If a cure is the only meaningful outcome, then almost no policies can be considered useful. Instead, all policies should be complementary: the addition of marginal taxes alone will not create a significant reduction in tobacco use in the same way the addition of green labels to eco-friendly food products will stop global warming; prevention of disease from spreading can be applied along with treating disease once afflicted. Major impacts require a variety of interventions working together, behavioral policies and beyond.

For teaching purposes, this book has largely used nudges as examples for psychological interventions in public policy, but they are certainly not the only form of behavioral policy. They are easily the most widely discussed right now and typically offer a framework that is helpful for understanding, but other tools exist.

For example, another popular method is **boosting**, which focuses on better understanding of choices rather than simply encouraging an optimal one (Hertwig & Grüne-Yanoff, 2017). Consider a situation in which there are no optimal choices, such as how much money to save every month. Nudges would assume there is a set target amount, such as the classic rule that 20 percent of your income should go to savings – but is that true for everyone in all circumstances? Obviously not and, in fact, advising everyone to follow the same financial planning guidelines has been shown to result in harmful effects, particularly for disadvantaged populations (Sussman & O'Brien, 2016). Instead, boosting would provide rapid ways to estimate the optimal balance between spending and saving, such as is found in the quick calculators on many online banking platforms. If this supports a broad level of optimal saving for individuals, then it meets the highest level criterion for *good* behavioral policy: better outcomes than existing or absent policy. In sum, behavioral policy is not a cure, but good behavioral policy will improve outcomes.

In other words: *better* beats *perfect*.

Ethics of behavioral insights

One thing that has not been stated explicitly up to now but probably should be is that, unlike most policies, *laws* have typically been mandated through a democratic (or other governing) process. This means they have to follow guidelines and protocols before they are decided upon. Policies, on the other hand, are often used to deliver on those laws but are not necessarily forced to go through the same processes and can be implemented separately from any formal governance.

Consider attempts to reduce text messaging on mobile phones while driving. In many places, it is now a crime to send a message while driving (with varying guidelines between jurisdictions). Those laws did not come about overnight and, in many cases, are in continued legislative battles. For punishment to occur, these processes must be established formally and implemented widely.

However, to *encourage* people to stop texting while driving requires no such processes. Any individual could put a sign on their car to discourage the practice. Any telephone company could put locks on phones when movement is consistent with being in a car. Any app developer could create a tool that disables messages from appearing while the owner is driving.

While transparency in government has been a theme in several examples in this book, consider the principles of behavioral insights in application such as engineering situations in anticipation of behavior and choice (Sunstein, 2017b). Without knowing more, this reeks of underhanded manipulation, especially without having information about the context, intentions, or actors involved. Does this not cut directly back against one of the drivers of behavioral approaches to policy, which is improving the transparency of policymaking? (Sunstein, 2014).

While the counterargument to this is noting that other options are still available, it is understandably a not very convincing one, and it would be reasonable to ask what the real trade-off is (i.e. is it really *worth it*?), and if other forms of self-regulation are possible. Thus, surely it can at least be asked, would the behavior be the same if individuals targeted by behavioral interventions were made explicitly aware of the shaping and framing (i.e. the choice architecture) being applied? If the answer is clearly "no," then naturally there are two further questions to ask:

1 Does the impact (for individuals as well as populations) of a behavioral policy outweigh the consequences of doing nothing, or of choosing a less effective approach?
2 What are the ethical principles that guide the decision about whether or not to implement?

The Golden Rule of behavioral policy

More work on ethical standards is needed as policy approaches using behavioral insights expand and become more standardized. However, one standard that can be applied immediately is to answer this very simple question: is the outcome something individuals want (or would want) for themselves?[1] We refer to this as the **Golden Rule of behavioral policy,** and Box 13.4 summarizes a wider set of such points made by Jachimowicz, Matz, and Polonski (2017).

BOX 13.4 TRANSLATION OF THE BEHAVIORAL SCIENTIST'S ETHICAL CHECKLIST INTO POLICY APPLICATIONS

1 Are the interests of those involved aligned? In other words, are we certain that the outcomes we hope for are what the people they will affect want?
2 Is the process transparent to participants?
3 Does the design and analysis plan allow for evaluation of the effectiveness?
4 Are data collected and stored safely to ensure privacy and anonymity?
5 Can participants easily opt out?
6 Do the potential benefits outweigh the potential harms?

Source: Adapted from Jachimowicz et al. (2017)

What if they do not work?

Nudges fail (Sunstein, 2017a). Perhaps the most widely discussed, critiqued, and divisive political topic of the early twenty-first century – at least in the United States, but receiving worldwide attention due to the global implications of US healthcare and related markets – was the Patient Protection and Affordable Care Act (ACA) of 2010. If this does not ring a bell, perhaps you have heard of it by its more common name: Obamacare.

To be clear, the ACA is not at its core a nudge or a policy. In fact, it is very much a legal standard with clear rules and penalties for violating them. While some could argue that certain elements include aspects of behavioral insights (e.g. the mandate for insurance for which a penalty is levied against those who opt out), the ACA is unquestionably a law. However, as it presented such a dramatic change in social norms around accessing healthcare, a number of interventions have attempted to "improve" population behavior in the choice of appropriate insurance plans. One in particular was carried out in Colorado, which aimed to get more people to the website during the enrollment period and used various methods to improve plan selection (Marzilli Ericson, Kingsdale, Layton, & Sacarny, 2017). Unfortunately, while the approach did seem to be effective at getting more people to visit the site, there was essentially no difference in getting individuals to choose better plans between those in the nudge groups and the controls.

Similarly, a study on environmental behaviors in Czechia using nudges to induce intrinsic motivation found that the intervention appeared to be effective at boosting a number of positive features, including well-being, yet had no overall impact on the specific behaviors targeted (Kácha & Ruggeri, 2018). After committing over 1,000 words to arguing that well-being is the most important outcome, it would understandably come across as hypocritical to go back on that now.

When behavioral approaches do not achieve their primary purpose, it is easy to write them off, yet this would be a mistake. In the two cases presented, noticeably valuable insights were actually elicited. In the first, the insight could be summarized as *leading a horse to water but not making it drink*. This is not a trivial matter: it highlights that behavioral interventions may require nuanced or stepped applications where multiple phases are necessary to identify change – in this case, not only entering the marketplace but identifying the best option. In the second example, it was clear that very positive features were associated with intrinsic motivation, particularly well-being, even if the desired behavior change was not observed. In this scenario, the behavioral approach elicited critical insights between important features of well-being and relevant correlates but came up short as levers for change, which means an ethical principle is now evident for any further attempts at intervention: make use of the positive and do not risk those associations in doing so. It goes without saying, though, that there are also many possible ways to assess why the intervention was not successful, and by addressing those we may achieve a better outcome through the same general approach (Sunstein, 2017a).

Should governments nudge?

In 2017, Richard Thaler was awarded the Nobel Prize in Economics, as had long been anticipated but many doubted would ever happen – including the author of this chapter. Along with Daniel Kahneman's award, this solidifies the place of behavioral economics – particularly nudges – in policy discourse at a minimum, yet few have gone so far as to say whether governments *should* use nudges and other behavioral insights in policy.

This changed with a 2017 article in *Psychological Science*, perhaps the most influential journal in psychology. Authored by many of the names cited in this volume, including Thaler himself, nine individuals presented a robust argument on the cost-effectiveness of nudge interventions relative to traditional policy tools (Benartzi et al., 2017). Their conclusion: in certain cases, nudges have shown substantially greater impacts for significantly lower costs, which should encourage governments to invest more in them *alongside traditional approaches*. When presenting their findings, they use many of the same domains categorized in this book – energy, health, education, the workplace – and expand them to include specific aspects such as improved financial stability and reduced threats to physical security. Considering this, they recommend more centralized sharing of data through a repository of effective interventions. They further encourage researchers to assess nudges relative to other approaches, as this will better assist decision-makers in determining whether behavioral approaches are a better option or complementary within a toolkit, rather than seeing them simply as an either/or.

The value of psychology and behavioral economics in public policy

Remember: when it comes to behavioral policy, better often beats perfect. To review all of the material covered in this textbook is to observe that behavioral approaches have the unique perspective of attempting to understand individuals in context. Rather than taking a full population or assuming everyone is *homo economicus*, real circumstances, preferences, and capabilities are considered in behavioral policy.

Given that perspective, one might say that *nudge equals nuance*: to be effective, behavioral interventions have to understand the heterogeneity of a population. The best example of this nuance comes from perhaps *the* defining study of behavioral interventions, at least in environmental behavior: the use of social norms via energy bills (Schultz et al., 2007). While the initial aim of reducing excessive use in some homes was met, the boomerang effect of increased consumption in homes that had previously used less had to be addressed with an injunctive social norm. In this way, it was clear that a single intervention alone would not apply universally, but a nuanced approach that targeted individual behaviors at multiple levels would be far more effective at creating a net positive result. Such aspects apply across behavioral interventions and help us balance between looking at the immediate effect (e.g. positive change in one group) and the ultimate consequences (e.g. negative change in another group) or lack of any sustained effect.

So now that we have brought all of these concepts and cases together, what really is the value of behavioral insights in policy? Does a 3 percent increase in tax payments or an 80 percent reduction in plastic bag consumption make a real difference in the well-being of populations? Sorry to disappoint, but there may not be one simple way to answer that, and it is far too critical to oversimplify such a complex question with a soundbite response. Instead, consider five critical questions:

1 Do they reduce inequalities?
2 Do they improve well-being?

3 Is the sum of all impacts significant considering the costs and challenges in the way?
4 Do they sustain – directly or otherwise?
5 Do they make the lives of individuals and populations better, safer, and more stable?

Think back to the earliest examples in Chapter 4 – how we can perceive the value of money in different ways at different times through our mental accounting. When only a classical approach was used, such as penalties for missing payments, only some parts of a population changed behavior, yet when behaviorally informed approaches were introduced, a much greater impact was visible. In successful instances like this, we can see a clear argument for gains across diverse groups, which translate to positive effects for individuals and populations, even if these are simply one-off outcomes. However, even some effective behavioral policies may not make a substantial impact on the wider issues involved: for example, moderate improvements in energy consumption from individuals will not stem or reroute global warming (Allcott, 2015). Thus, the first level of value of behavioral insights lies not in the measurable difference between control and treatment groups but in the associated value that would not have been achieved otherwise.

But that value can be contained to a short window, and frankly, many nudges simply do not have lasting impacts on behaviors or related outcomes. This may be due to researchers missing out on identifying or addressing the root explanations for the issues (Loewenstein & Chater, 2017). That is perhaps a double-edged sword, though, as this quick and dirty aspect is also an appealing aspect of nudges (Loewenstein & Chater, 2017). As such, the next level is to determine how long other methods might have sustained a change along with how long the benefits are relevant from the first level – being nudged into a retirement plan therefore has long-term implications, even if the behavior is necessary only once. Finally, the cumulative effects of those impacts, their longevity, and their reach are the ultimate level at which it can be determined if, how, and to what extent the use of behavioral insights is valuable to individuals and populations. This is not to say that such approaches should be seen as a replacement for traditional policy tools, but they should be seen as a powerful complement to those that may already be in place (Loewenstein & Chater, 2017).

Conclusion

This chapter – and the entire body of work preceding it – has attempted to present clearly the value of evidence in policy, the potential for psychology and behavioral economics as powerful policy tools, and the opportunities for such tools to impact well-being across entire populations. We opened by presenting the history and features of policy, followed by systematic approaches to development and (later) evaluation. We covered the major topics, people, and theories that led to the widespread interest in behavioral economics in science and beyond. Six chapters presented critical policy domains where behavioral approaches to policy have been evaluated. In each of these, we presented both highly cited and lesser known examples, including those with significant impacts and some yet to be assessed. These examples are intended not only to inform but to catalyze further innovations where appropriate, as they offer incredible value as levers as described in the introduction. To conclude the volume, this chapter discussed what it means for policies to have an impact. We then calibrated what we meant by "impact" to have some clarity about the ultimate outcome to be targeted. While we strongly endorse this to be securing and advancing population well-being, it would not be appropriate to ignore vital aspects such as personal safety and security, as well as various forms of stability, which must be in place for populations to develop and flourish. Without question, these must include political, economic, and environmental.

It is our hope that this work will become a source for the next wave of researchers and policymakers to seek innovative and effective ways to achieve those ends. In doing so, we believe this creates the best opportunity to offer the greatest outcomes for the largest number of people. We strongly acknowledge the pioneers of the field who are referenced throughout the volume and thank them for the spectacular contribution they have made to society, the social sciences, and civic leaders. We do this hoping to both inspire those up-and-coming leaders with visions of making a positive impact through their work, whether in science, industry, or public service. If successful, we hope this volume has made some contribution toward their education, which is perhaps the most powerful tool we have to impact the well-being of populations.

Essay question

1 What are the implications of calibrating all policies to focus on improving well-being as the ultimate outcome?

Postlude

The bulk of the work on this volume was completed prior to the pandemic of 2020–2021. Since then, as the world has gone through a tremendous shift across almost all aspects of life, there has been a constant stream of new outputs produced on behavioral applications to policy. These include both direct testing of behavioral aspects of COVID-19, such as wearing masks, washing hands, or getting the vaccine, or more broadly. While this book focused more on teaching the fundamentals of how psychology and behavioral economics inform policy, we do encourage readers to consider work that captures, where this has (and has not) been impacted by the pandemic. Publications on this topic are only emerging now, but these suggested articles shed some light on those insights.

Note

1 We also note that, with this in mind, we typically avoid use of the term "behavior change." To apply the golden rule is to desire that individuals have outcomes they desire that also align with the best interests of society. It does not focus solely on the change, as change alone is rarely the ultimate goal.

Additional insights and further reading

Ahmed, A., & Jackson, J. (2021). Race, risk, and personal responsibility in the response to COVID-19. *Columbia Law Review*, *121*(3), 47–70.

Allen, J. D., Abuelezam, N. N., Rose, R., & Fontenot, H. B. (2021). Factors associated with the intention to obtain a COVID-19 vaccine among a racially/ethnically diverse sample of women in the USA. *Translational Behavioral Medicine*, *11*(3), 785–792.

Dai, H., Saccardo, S., Han, M., Roh, L., Raja, N., Vangala, S., . . . & Croymans, D. (2021). Behavioral nudges increase COVID-19 vaccinations: Two randomized controlled trials. SSRN 3817832.

Pennycook, G., McPhetres, J., Zhang, Y., Lu, J. G., & Rand, D. G. (2020). Fighting COVID-19 misinformation on social media: Experimental evidence for a scalable accuracy-nudge intervention. *Psychological Science*, *31*(7), 770–780.

Rosenfeld, D. L., Balcetis, E., Bastian, B., Berkman, E. T., Bosson, J. K., Brannon, T. N., . . . & Tomiyama, A. J. (2021). Psychological science in the wake of COVID-19: Social, methodological, and meta-scientific considerations. *Perspectives on Psychological Science.*

Sanders, M., Stockdale, E., Hume, S., & John, P. (2021). Loss aversion fails to replicate in the coronavirus pandemic: Evidence from an online experiment. *Economics Letters*, 199, 109433.

Van Bavel, J. J., Baicker, K., Boggio, P. S., Capraro, V., Cichocka, A., Cikara, M., . . . Willer, R. (2020). Using social and behavioural science to support COVID-19 pandemic response. *Nature Human Behaviour*, *4*(5), 460–471.

Volpp, K. G., Loewenstein, G., & Buttenheim, A. M. (2021). Behaviorally informed strategies for a national COVID-19 vaccine promotion program. *JAMA*, *325*(2), 125–126.

Glossary

Absenteeism. Chronic deficiency in maintaining obligations or attendance associated with established roles, such as students at school or employees at work.

Active choice. When an actor or group must make a decision where no default or automated option is given.

Actors. Participants carrying out a defined role as part of an action, decision, or process.

Adaptive toolbox. A repertoire of simple and efficient rules for decision-making with risk or under uncertainty.

Aims. The defined goals to be achieved as part of an action, behavior, or decision.

Anchoring. A cognitive bias describing the tendency to overly depend on an initial segment of information (the anchor) compared to information received subsequently. (Is sometimes referred to as *left-digit* or *first-digit bias*, though that can be problematic.)

Assessment (policy assessment). A detailed evaluation or judgment of a policy's impact and outcomes guided by various indicators, such as economic, social, contextual, and procedural features.

Assigning responsibility. Delegating task ownership with the specific purpose of sharing duties that may offer a collective benefit, such as improved environmental behaviors.

Attainment gap. The disparity in outcomes between groups that are otherwise equal in ability, typically in the context of education.

Authenticity message. Providing information meant to appeal to intrinsic motivation (as opposed to extrinsic) about a choice or behavior.

Availability heuristic. The tendency to make judgments about an event on the basis of how easily the event and related details or examples come to mind.

Bandwagon effect. The tendency to align one's own beliefs and behaviors to those of the majority.

Behavioral barriers. Obstacles to choices or actions that hinder the ability to attain certain outcomes, even if there are clear benefits associated and individuals might otherwise carry those out if not obstructed.

Behavioral economics. An interdisciplinary field studying the psychosocial factors involved in decision-making, typically where financial aspects are a major feature of the choice and/or its direct outcomes.

Behavioral insights. The salient conclusions derived from studies and applications of behavioral sciences (most commonly from behavioral economics specifically).

Behavioral science. Empirical, data-driven study of decision and behavior processes, as well as their outcomes within and between individuals, groups, and social systems.

Benefit/impact labeling. A strategy to increase the saliency of relevant product features to guide choices, typically using packaging visuals or texts.

Bias. A cognitive process used to make decisions on the basis of immediately available information from prior experiences or beliefs not necessarily applicable in the immediate or all contexts (see **heuristics**).

Big Data. Collated data sets of behavioral footprints (often digital) and other measures acquired at large volume, velocity, and variety, matched from multiple sources with different original purposes for collection.

Blended learning. An educational approach that combines the traditional classroom method with e-learning.

Blind-spot bias. Acknowledgment of how biases influence the judgments of others without recognizing or admitting the impact on one's own judgments.

Boomerang effect. Differential changes in behaviors or choices as the result of a common intervention. Typically, one group has a positive outcome and another has an unintended, inverse change, often resulting in mitigated aggregate impacts as improvements and losses cancel out. This is a form of an unintended consequence, but not a side effect.

Bottlenecks. Features, nodes, or other points in any process or pathway where the number of elements seeking to flow through is greater than the capacity to allow passage. In the policy context, this often refers to a gap between intention and action.

Bounded rationality. A theory proposing that while individuals typically want to have the best opportunity for a successful outcome, when there is uncertainty and risk, choices may often be limited to instinct, intuition, or other emotionally driven responses, as opposed to systematic or fully informed decisions.

Call to action. An exhortation or stimulus that prompts an explicit, defined, and often immediate response.

Centralized model. A placement strategy whereby expertise, administration, or leadership is directly or equally accessible to all departments in an organization.

Checklists. Salient steps of a process produced in guideline form, typically presented in a mandatory, chronological order.

Choice architecture. The features and design of the environment or context in which decisions are made, including the amount of information, influences, preferences, and obstacles related to the decision.

Chunking. Taking a large task and breaking it into smaller, more manageable elements, typically in order to increase the likelihood of someone completing it.

Coat-tailing. When a positive option is paired with a popular option (related or otherwise) in the hope that making it visible in a convenient way will increase the likelihood of people choosing the positive option. The popular option may also be positive, or it can be negative or neutral in the context.

Coercive power. Potential to use punishment or the threat of punishment to influence decision-making.

Cognitive behavioral therapy. Psychosocial treatment to improve mental health with an emphasis on skill building in partnership with a care provider to identify harmful patterns of thoughts and behaviors that result in or exacerbate mental illness.

Coherence bias. Forcing the desire to see a causal link on the basis of how well it fits with or reinforces existing beliefs, even if the link might not exist.

Cohort analysis. Evaluation approach that follows grouped or pooled participants through a process and monitors attrition at various points.

Commitment device. A tool used to engage individuals in making a choice that limits or restricts another choice in the future, typically to avoid an unwanted or impulsive behavior that would harm long-term goals.

Commitment device: contract. A tool that voluntarily binds an individual to carrying out (or not carrying out) a choice or behavior in advance, typically through signing a document or registering to a program.

Common pool resource. A good that benefits a group but is consumed on an individual basis such that it can be at risk if overused by members in a group.

Comparison messaging. A tool to influence behavior by informing people about their behavior compared to others.

Competitive altruism. A phenomenon in which individuals engage in cooperative behavior motivated by the status-enhancing benefits that the behavior creates.

Competitors. Individuals who will support policies or other interventions as long as they result in comparatively better outcomes for themselves.

Completion award. Reward given for achieving or carrying out a certain behavior, irrespective of quality or ranking.

Confidence (self-rated). A projection of uncertainty involving the extent to which an individual anticipates accuracy when predicting an outcome. These outcomes may involve risk or uncertainty, or they may be deterministic in nature.

Confirmation bias. Seeking out or interpreting information that best matches an individual's perception of reality while simultaneously discarding or failing to seek out information that may contradict or otherwise undermine the initial or preferred belief.

Consistency. A tendency to desire to appear stable in choices, sometimes leading individuals to select the choice most characteristic of their personality rather than a better option that may have been presented.

Conspicuous conservation. The willingness of consumers to pay higher prices for green goods to signal their environmental concern to others, thereby increasing their social status.

Constituent policy. Policies that establish organizations or power structures giving an executive authority to have oversight of a domain, such as mental health or fiscal planning.

Convenience. A choice or behavior that becomes more used or preferred on the basis of greater simplicity of access and utilization as well as fewer frictions (such as time or travel) compared to other options, without respect to quality or resource cost.

Crowdsourcing. An approach to procuring data, information, resources, or other input by indiscriminately opening pathways publicly to contribution or engagement, such as using web-based forums, group emails, or social media. This is often done through posing open requests to loosely or unrestricted audiences with requests for input.

Decision-making. The cognitive process of choosing one or more among multiple options, typically where outcomes vary in terms of risk, uncertainty, value, and cost.

Decoy effect. When a preference between given choices changes upon the entrance of a new option (does not apply to the new option, only to the ranking of preference between those in the initial scenario) in a way that may appear irrational.

Default (choice/option/setting). The predetermined choice that is applied unless an individual deliberately selects another option.

Default effect. When a given option is selected more on the basis of it being the preset choice than if it had not been automatically chosen, while the same alternate options remain available.

Defensive policy. An intervention aimed at a near-term approach to reduce either the risk of a known threat or the number of individuals passing the threshold of realizing that threat. This approach seeks better outcomes on the presumption of fewer unwanted outcomes as opposed to deliberately improving the situation in the near term.

Defined-contribution scheme. A retirement savings plan feature based on the agreement made by employer and employee to make contributions to the employee's savings plan on a specified, regular basis.

Descriptive norm. A statement that describes the most common behavior of a certain population in a certain domain, usually including a quantified definition of most common or average.

Diagnosis. Precise identification of an issue. In the policy context, it is a process that draws on cohort analyses, process maps, and bottlenecks identified in the problem definition stage of policymaking.

Diffuse model. A placement strategy whereby expertise is embedded within, and therefore preferentially made available to, certain departments.

Disclosure. Provision of information specifically related to a behavior, often involving previously ambiguous or unknown outcomes. Typically applied on the expectation that being aware of the information would encourage a better choice.

Discouragement (effect). When monitoring goal processes, failing to reach set goals might lead to worsening choices and fear of not reaching them may result in actively avoiding future tracking.

Distributive policy. Interventions aimed at ensuring representative circulation of and access to resources among specific groups within a population.

Diversification bias. The tendency to seek greater variation (or simply overestimate the need) for future actions when making multiple choices in a single moment than if choices were made sequentially, when variability tends to be less.

Drivers of change. Numerous social, economic, environmental, and other contextual factors that are likely to result in behavioral change and therefore are relevant to policy.

Dropout. Leaving education before completion of a program or degree.

Dual process theory. A framework depicting two systems of thinking used for decision-making: (1) the slow, conscious processing system and (2) the fast, automatic processing system.

Ecolabeling. Providing information about the environmental properties and/or impact of a product to encourage a pro-environmental alternative, typically in a salient manner that does not require detailed understanding of energy, consumption, or other environmental factors.

Ecological rationality. A theory of practical rationality where making a particular decision is presumed to depend on the context in which the choice or behavior takes place.

Economic evaluation. An assessment of the effectiveness of a policy, program, or other intervention in terms of its resource use and, often, the sustainability of those effects. May include a conclusion about the worthiness of continuing, translating, or scaling up the intervention, as well as for comparison with other interventions.

Effect size. A statistical calculation of how large the impact is between groups in an analysis, such as differences in or strength of relationships. This typically complements an initial analysis that simply focuses on whether any impact is concluded to exist.

Effectiveness. A measure of the extent to which a given intervention achieved a set goal or progressed in the intended direction.

Efficacy. A theoretical depiction of the extent to which a policy or intervention achieved its intended aims.

Efficiency. A measure of the relationship between achieving a defined outcome and the resources (including time) required to arrive there, typically in comparison with other options.

Effort tax. The cost of procrastination, such as the difference in price between acting immediately and delaying an action or choice.

e-learning. Instruction and study method utilizing online or digital (either partial or in full) platforms for instruction.

Empathy gap. Underestimation of the extent to which emotion (or other subjective, visceral features of a given context or state) can influence observed behaviors. May also describe a decreased ability to appreciate the complexity or impact of features on distal individuals or out-groups compared to proximal individuals from in-groups.

Empowerment. Having the authority to give ownership or increase sovereignty over a situation or choice.

Endowment effect. A form of cognitive bias where individuals appear to give greater value to losing what they already have as opposed to not having it at all.

Engagement. Participation in a group or action eliciting high levels of observed involvement and/or psychological attachment (in the form of elevated cognitive processing).

Enhanced active choice. The process where individuals must make a choice (active choice), but a favored option is evident as the negative costs associated with the discouraged or less preferred alternative are made salient.

Environmental engineering. Changing the physical or procedural context in such a way that desirable choices are more easily accessible, even if options remain the same and no explicit effort is made to intervene in those behaviors or choices.

Eudaimonia. The aspect of well-being associated with positive functioning, performance, and ability.

Evaluation. The assessment of the decisions, costs, processes, and outcomes related to the development and implementation of a policy or other intervention.

Evaluation manager. An individual responsible for coordinating efforts with active stakeholders in leading an evaluation process.

Evaluative (well-being). The aspect of well-being measured by overall subjective assessment (often satisfaction) of a situation, whether past, present, or confined to a range of time.

Evidence. Scientifically supported information or conclusions that are primarily identified through peer-reviewed sources, professional or official documentation, or qualified reporting.

Evidence-based medicine. The intentional, structured, and systematic use of best available scientific evidence for making decisions about the individual care of patients.

Evidence-based policy. A paradigm that incorporates scientific evidence into the process of decision-making regarding population-level interventions, namely, the process of identifying the best method for addressing a defined issue.

Evidence-based practice. An integration of subject-specific expertise, high-impact research findings, and the interests of direct stakeholders for professional application, commonly patients and caregivers in health services.

Ex ante**.** Analyses seeking to predict the costs and consequences of a specific event before it has occurred. Sometimes referred to as *a priori* analyses.

Expected utility theory. A framework to give quantifiable values to rational choice theory, which assumes that, in decision-making situations, individuals assign a hypothetical ranking to the available alternatives on the basis of their perceived utility of each option and then select the optimal choice.

Expectancy value theory. An assumption that an individual's achievement performance, persistence, and decisions are heavily determined by their expectancy for success and subjective task values.

Experimental design. A framework for research conducted explicitly to see if differences or changes will be elicited between conditions, typically comparing the outcomes of at least one group receiving an intervention or treatment, and at least one (control) group that does not.

Ex post**.** An analysis of the real costs and consequences tied to a specific (policy) event after it has occurred.

Extremeness aversion (or sometimes as the **compromise effect**)**.** The tendency to choose an option based on it being moderate in comparison to extreme alternatives, in which the true utility of the moderate choice is likely to be miscalculated or ignored.

Extrinsic motivation. Incentives for choices, behaviors, or preferences that are based on external factors, typically visible to others, such as financial rewards or public recognition.

Fairness. The extent to which every person appears to have standards applied evenly regardless of individual features or group membership.

Fast automatic processing. An automated process used for decision-making that is triggered by the perception of certain cues. These processes create a default response and can be changed, complemented, or substituted with a slow conscious processing response.

Feedback. The process of being provided with information on performance of a task or in a formal role, often includes evaluations of demeanor and problem-solving.

Fidelity. The extent to which a policy or intervention was implemented as planned.

Financial literacy. A combination of awareness, knowledge, skill, attitude, competency, and behavior necessary to make sound financial decisions toward individual financial well-being.

First-generation interventions. Communications between institutions and the people they serve focused on singular behaviors for which nudging the program user to take a specific action qualifies as successful.

Fixed mindset. A tendency to believe that talent is innate, such that nothing can be done to change it, and a belief system that has less emphasis on the role of malleability, development, and practice.

Focus group. A small meeting of individuals discussing a certain topic in an interactive setting meant to elicit feedback, preferences, or general views, but which may not represent a wider population.

Forecasting. Using past and present data to calculate the probabilities and values of risks and outcomes for future events as well as various decisions or behaviors.

Framing/Framing effect. A bias leading to the reordering of preferences on the basis of only how options are presented, such as gains or losses. The objective values and outcomes are constant, but changes in willingness to take risks adjust to how options are presented. This presentation of logically equivalent information in different ways influences perception of the message itself.

Framework. An overarching guideline with principles and features for a process or construct. May or may not be treated as prescriptive for best practice or a general checklist.

Future bias. The tendency to give greater weight to the most proximal options of future events. For example, when two future events occur, greater weight is given to whichever occurs first.

Future discounting/temporal discounting. A cognitive bias in which individuals give greater weight to immediate or present choices, costs, values, or options than those in the future, such that they may prefer a lesser immediate gain over a larger gain at a later time. May also be described as a devaluation of future events, wherein proximal consequences influence behavior more strongly than distal consequences.

Future visualization. Use of mental imagery to create a vision of future events with the intent of producing salient elements of the outcome that improves decisions toward a goal.

Gamification. Presenting information or personal data in interactive formats meant to appear like a competitive game, whether with oneself or with others. This is done instead of static numerical presentation or less engaging formats. Applications may include daily targets, scores, level completion and progression, interactive learning features, or timed aspects.

Gini coefficient. A measure where 0 indicates perfectly equal wealth distribution and 1 completely unequal wealth distribution across a population. Commonly used as a metric for assessing national economic inequality.

Goal progress monitoring. The option for participants of an intervention to check whether they have met targets established previously for a specific date or over a time period.

Green nudges. An indirect technique involving choices and behaviors of individuals or groups for the purposes of encouraging pro-environmental behavior.

Green options/products/alternatives. Products, services, or behaviors that lead to reduced consumption of a nonrenewable resource or increased uptake of a replacement product that is less harmful for the environment.

Gross domestic product (GDP). The total market value of the goods and services produced by a given economy (typically a country) during a specified period of time.

Growth. A term used to describe measurements of change through the evaluation of all markets compared to a previous or recent period, such as the difference from one year-end to the previous year-end or a specific month compared to that month in a prior year.

Growth mindset. A tendency to believe that individuals have the capacity to change their abilities as they may develop over time, experience, and practice.

Gut feeling. The initial belief, reaction, or preference when confronted with information where an opinion, choice, or disposition is required. May result in implicit bias.

Halo effect. A cognitive bias involving the tendency of an impression made of one character or entity (e.g. person, company, brand, product) to influence the impression of another character or entity.

Hawthorne effect (observer effect). A theory that suggests individuals may change their behavior simply as a result of being observed.

Health in All Policies. A strategy requiring all policy initiatives to include specific measures of the impact on health, no matter what general domain they explicitly target.

Health literacy. The ability to seek, access, understand, evaluate, and apply relevant and critical health information.

Health promotion. A policy or intervention approach that focuses on enabling, empowering, informing, or otherwise supporting individuals and populations to improve health, even if no illness is identified or imminent. A unique form of promotion that explicitly does not involve medical care while specifically emphasizing improved health.

Hedonia. The aspect of well-being associated with pleasurable feeling, emotion, and experience.

Heuristic. A cognitive approach relying on efficiency (rules-of-thumb), ostensibly used to make rapid judgments and decisions, though it may increase the possibility of bias or error due to lack of robust input deliberation.

High-risk approach. Interventions that explicitly target vulnerable individuals or groups that face an identifiable risk of certain problems or disease at a higher rate than the total population rather than targeting an entire population; often a form of prevention or treatment.

Homo economicus. The figurative human being characterized by entirely rational decision-making that is grounded in maximizing expected utilities of choices (see rational choice theory). Used as a reference in contemporary theory.

Hyperbolic discounting. An underweighting of future events such that there is a tendency to favor smaller rewards in the present over larger rewards in the future, amplified by how far in the future the reward would be realized.

Ideological policy. A presumed feature of all policies having a philosophical approach to interventions that focuses on achieving a cultural or normative value in itself, such as equality or fairness, rather than a target that is primarily associated with further outcomes.

Impact. The wider value associated with the effects of an intervention, policy, or finding, such as its ability to be applied in additional settings, commercial potential, or measurable link to improved well-being.

Implementation intentions. Specific plans about when and how an individual will carry out an action, typically with the belief that this will increase the likelihood of the intention being realized.

Implicit/explicit bias. When greater value is placed on the superficial or primary information provided than on the implications of what is not stated. This may lead to poor choices that fail to consider the total cost (financial or otherwise) of an option.

Incentive. Objective or subjective value attached to a behavior. Can be used as an explicit reward to increase likelihood of carrying out a desired behavior. May be directly tied to the behavior or used to encourage the behavior.

Incentive: extrinsic. Any reward that is entirely based on external value rather than inherent positive features, such that any gain is primarily about benefits received for the behavior rather than for simply carrying out the behavior itself.

Incentive: financial/cash/short-term monetary. A monetary reward received in honor of completing a behavior or achieving a result desired by the issuer, typically targeting discrete or short-term actions.

Incentive: intrinsic. Any reward that is entirely based on internalized value, such that the gain is primarily about the sake of carrying out the behavior itself, such as fulfilment or joy, rather than any external benefits.

Incentive: non-monetary. Other forms of reward not involving financial elements, such as an increased rating or grade or improved terms of an agreement.

Incentive: verbal. Written or oral rewards for completing a behavior, such as certificates or commendations.

Index for Evidence in Policy (INDEP). A tool to assess how much evidence is available for a given area of study in considering policy applications.

Inequality. The measurable or theoretical difference between those doing the best and those doing the worst in a group or population.

Inertia. The tendency to continue doing what is already being done or has been started instead of changing or halting a behavior or altering a pattern of choices.

Information and communication technology (ICT). Any form of equipment or (electronic) machinery used for the explicit purpose of linking people and information.

Information effect. Providing material with relevant data or insights such that it influences behavior in a way that may not have happened had it not been provided. Strongly associated with disclosure, but material may not necessarily identify optimal choices.

Injunction. A complementary feature or tool within an intervention used for avoiding or reducing the risk of an unwanted outcome, typically to inoculate against unequal outcomes where a previously positive behavior worsens as a result of the intervention, canceling out positive effects in other groups.

Injunctive norm. An intervention applied in a descriptive format to illuminate how a behavior is likely to be perceived (i.e. approved or disapproved), such that it changes the perception of whether to carry out the behavior or not.

Innovation. Constructing novel ideas and approaches to solve a problem or to create more efficient processes, which go beyond mere improvement and include redesign or differentiation from previous approaches.

Intervention. Any action taken or treatment with the aim of making a change from the status quo in process and/or outcomes.

Intrinsic motivation. Incentives for choices, behaviors, or preferences that appeal to internal factors, typically not visible to others, such as personal feelings of accomplishment or the application of values.

Irrational. Choices or behaviors that appear to deviate from what would produce an optimal outcome for an individual or group or to otherwise go against self-interest.

Issue. A specific topic identified as relevant on the basis of specified parameters. The topic can be positive (opportunity), negative (problem), or neutral (no clear ideal or unwanted outcomes).

Keynesian economics. A school of thinking wherein governments lower taxes and increase spending to boost productivity to stimulate, maximize, and generally respond to aggregate market demand.

Key performance indicators (KPIs). The primary features of a program or policy that are most relevant for determining progress, impact, resource use, and/or engagement.

Knowledge-action gap. The difference between the information people have regarding a decision and their awareness of necessary steps to perform the behavior.

Labeling. (1) Classifying something or someone according to a certain category. (2) Placing salient information on a product or option to inform a decision-maker about features in such a way that it may influence preference or choice, often for comparison with proximal alternatives.

Large number bias. The tendency to give smaller value to differences between larger numbers than differences between smaller values. Often featured implicitly in studies involving mental accounting, marginal or relative comparisons, or others involving financial computation.

Law. A rule that is founded on and aims to carry out a specific aspect of governmental legislation regarding actions or behaviors for which violation results in penalty, punishment, or sanction.

Leakage. A policy that reduces one behavior but results in substitution with another, potentially more harmful behavior.

Learning management system (LMS). Software used by teachers to track student progress and provide information, assignments, and course materials to students.

Legacy systems. Outdated or aging information technology networks or platforms that are still being used, resulting in limited functionality.

Legislation. Use of a governmental process of passing laws to regulate various aspects of life, including choices and behaviors, and penalties associated with violations of laws once affirmed.

Legitimate coercion. The authorized authority of governments to exert power.

Lever. The actions (i.e. interventions, policies) that can be taken to induce change (typically focused on improvement) that take into account significant risks, contextual factors, and other drivers of change.

Libertarian paternalism. A form of government influence over choices and behaviors that does not explicitly mandate preferences or actions, but seeks to elicit optimal outcomes while supporting autonomy, often through subtle processes.

Loss aversion. The tendency to prefer certainty of smaller gains over risk of potentially larger gains, inverted when outcomes are losses, and risk to avoid a larger loss is preferred over a certain smaller loss.

Lottery. Use of vouchers for non-guaranteed rewards for completion of a behavior.

Marginal utility. The added value (positive or negative) for each additional unit of a good (bought, sold, or otherwise received).

Mass media. Platforms for communication that are designed to reach the largest possible volume of people through the most accessible, uninhibited, and indiscriminate means.

Massive open online course. An educational offering available online to a large number of people in multiple geographic locations, often without formal registration, prerequisites for attendance, or assessment. Often referred to as a MOOC (pronounced MOO-k).

Mastery goal orientation. The tendency to focus on the achievement and development of peak competence and task proficiency.

Maximization. Seeking to gain the ideal or ultimate outcome through resources available, though with no mandatory expectation of limiting resources. May also be understood as capitalizing on resources to the greatest possible extent, even if a specific outcome is not achieved.

Memory. In the context of behavioral insights, refers to how an individual subjectively stores information that may involve bias, error, or omission (unintentional or selective), which may serve as a lever for interventions to correct. May be seen as a feature, tool, bias, or unmeasured theoretical construct.

Mental accounting. A cognitive process of organizing, evaluating, and keeping track of financial activities and relative values. It is often used to explain why people tend to view costs and gains in oversimplified relation to their temporarily available resources, expectations, and demands, as opposed to their general budget.

Meta-analysis. An evaluation of studies with common questions, treatments, interventions, and/or problems collected through systematic compilation, usually for the purpose of comparing options to identify best practices or general patterns of effectiveness.

Method. In the policy context, the specific use of levers, interventions, and evaluations seeking to elicit and understand the desired outcomes that will influence parameters associated with the specified issue.

Monitoring. The continual process of assessing progress toward goals as policies are implemented.

Motivation crowding theory. Refers to the effect of external incentives (e.g. small monetary rewards) or punishments having a negative effect on intrinsic motivation.

Naming effect. The strategy of addressing an individual by their first name in order to encourage a certain behavior, presumed to occur due to increased engagement through the appearance of familiarity. This is in contrast to generic headings for mass audiences.

Narrative communication. An approach to presenting information through storytelling, often using a form of chronology with intermittent interpretation and dialogue, as opposed to a fixed format of data and analysis.

Neuroeconomics. An interdisciplinary field combining economics and neuroscience to study the neurological and biological bases of decision-making processes.

Noise. Randomly occurring errors in decision-making influenced by unstable situational factors as opposed to bias, irrational choices, or other inherent flaws. Can often be incorrectly interpreted to involve a pattern when none actually exists.

Non-experimental design. Research that does not manipulate the phenomenon observed or introduces external variables to observe naturally occurring relationships between variables.

Normative messages. Information provided for the purpose of indicating a socially desired behavior seen as typical within a group such that it leads to conformity to that behavior within the group.

Novelty effect. The tendency to notice, remember, and/or prefer a piece of information simply because it is unique or new and not because of any inherent qualities or values.

Nudge/Nudging. An indirect technique aimed at influencing the choices and actions of groups and individuals without limiting or forcing a preferred behavior, but instead making subtle adjustments in the choice architecture that might encourage optimal behaviors.

Operational transparency. Revealing the otherwise hidden work that the government performs by making it visible to the public.

Operationalization. Defining terms and constructs specifically and precisely for a given context, particularly in a research or policy setting where multiple disciplines are involved and may use similar concept names with different meanings otherwise.

Optimism bias. A cognitive bias that leads individuals to believe that negative events are less likely to happen to them and positive outcomes are more likely.

Optimization. The act of seeking to attain the best possible results while sacrificing the least or fewest resources.

Optimum/optimal outcome. A targeted goal from a policy or intervention to be achieved with the least expenditure of resources.

Opt in. When a default is set to require an active choice to participate; otherwise, nonparticipation is the presumed, default choice.

Opt out. When a default is set to require an active choice not to participate; otherwise, participation is the presumed, default choice.

Organizational behavior. An area of scientific study focusing on individual and collective interactions within defined institutions, often workplaces, schools, hospitals, athletic teams, or other professional contexts.

Overweighting small probabilities. The tendency to overestimate the likelihood of improbable events, often because the way they are reported when they do occur gives an inflated impression of their frequency. The overestimation is typically in reference to how likely more probable events are compared.

Parameter. A measurable, defined, distinct characteristic of a study, policy, or population.

Participation. Providing individuals and groups the opportunity to take part in different forms of decision-making.

Participation effect. An observable increase in a desired behavior, perception, trust, or valuation on the basis of having individuals actively engage directly with an activity, organization, or policy.

Partnering. Typically refers to the use of a companion system that assigns an individual to directly engage with a targeted person in an intervention, with the aim of improved behaviors, choices, or sustained commitment toward a goal.

Path dependence. The continued use of a process or a product that may no longer be best suited for its current purpose, primarily because the costs of switching are high.

Pedometer. A device used to count the steps taken by an individual, typically on a daily basis.

Personalization. A specialized flow of communication that targets interventions according to specifically measured traits of the individual, whether objective or latent.

Phasing. Breaking down an intervention into different parts and implementing them in different temporal stages. The distinct phases are the critical feature that distinguishes this from the general term *rolling out*.

Planning prompt. A foresight tool used to generate, motivate, and increase the likelihood of an individual carrying out specific behaviors over time by scheduling critical choice benchmarks.

Policy. Population-based intervention established – intentionally or otherwise – to produce an outcome that is determined to be optimal, ideal, or necessary.

Policy analysis. The multidisciplinary process of assessing features of a population intervention in terms of production, implementation, outcomes, and impact on resources.

Policy design. Describing the features of population interventions, particularly including those related to the methods to be applied and how they seek to realize their purpose.

Policy development. The process of designing a population intervention as well as procuring necessary resources and stakeholders for implementation.

Policy effectiveness. The success of an implemented intervention in attaining its intended behavioral outcome or general outcome (or both) within its target population.

Policy evaluation. A systematic assessment of population interventions toward meeting objectives, implementing processes, and integrating relevant evidence and methods. Unlike policy analysis, policy evaluation typically offers a conclusion about overall effectiveness and value.

Policy instruments/tools. Means through which policies attempt to reach their outcomes, traditionally focused on taxation, mandate, and/or subsidy, but increasingly including behavioral insights.

Policy papers. Reports focused on a specific policy issue that provide recommendations for action; may also include analysis or forecasting of impacts.

Policy platform. An interactive compilation of information and evidence gathered through the process of implementing an intervention using relevant measurements for evaluation, such as phasing, sensing, and scaling. All steps useful for the implementation and improvement of policies are also specified.

Policy process. The stages of how policies are catalyzed, formulated, implemented, and assessed for measurable impact on the world.

Policy toolkits. Portfolios of multiple relevant instruments for targeting an objective, often where a single intervention is deemed insufficient and would lack robustness when applied on a population level or across multiple populations. Commonly used to improve policy implementation processes on the basis of lessons learned as well as to increase efficiency and effectiveness.

Policymaking. The development process of policies, which may involve stages of agenda setting, policy formulation, decision-making, evidence review, policy implementation, and the planning of an eventual evaluation. In many cases, will involve formal agencies or institutions with leadership responsibilities for defined communities and populations.

Population. All members of a group as defined by certain parameters. In the policy context, this relates to everyone that the intervention may influence, whether or not it is effective in doing so, and irrespective of which individuals or groups are specifically intended to be impacted.

Population approach. Interventions that aim to improve the average level of all members of the defined group, rather than only those suffering, at risk, or doing well.

Portion size (or volume/container) effect. Changes in the amount of a good consumed based on how much was provided to the consumer as opposed to how much was desired or requested, often in the context of food and beverage.

Positive deviants. Members of a group in a negative circumstance (associated with negative outcomes) identified as outliers or exceptions due to their positive individual outcomes.

Preference framing. A cognitive bias in which one perceives risks and gains differently depending on what information is provided and how, which often narrows the range of additional factors considered in any immediate decision associated with the information.

Present bias. The tendency of people to overweight immediate outcomes relative to outcomes that are further in the future. Strongly associated with temporal and future discounting.

Presenteeism. Attending work while ill or otherwise unable to perform duties such that standards are either put at risk or simply not maintained. Often relates to inefficiency characterized by poor mental health, low motivation, or distraction.

Prevention. Interventions that seek to avoid a problem prior to it materializing through actions that reduce known risks or strengthen any safeguards between risk and realization of unwanted outcomes.

Priming. An exposure to one stimulus influences disposition to subsequent information, often narrowing or underweighting other possible perspectives considered or heightening awareness of specific features of the stimulus.

Proactive policy. Long-term intervention strategy where an opportunity for improvement is being targeted; no specific threat is being addressed.

Process map. A visual aid that depicts all steps of a given process and notes which actors are responsible for which steps.

Pro-environmental behavior. Behavior that consciously seeks to lessen the negative impact of individual actions on the environment (or increase positive effects), often through consumer choice or consumption behaviors.

Pro-environmental values. Concepts or beliefs that the society or community places on desirable behavior or goods to lessen the negative impact (or increase positive impact) on the environment.

Projection bias. The expectation that our preferences or behaviors remain consistent over time. Sometimes used to indicate overconfidence in ability to accurately anticipate future preferences or behaviors.

Promotion. Any policy focused on increasing a group average in a given context (e.g. income, health) across all members of the population, as opposed to targeting only those in one group (e.g. poor, unhealthy). Strongly tied to proactive policies.

Proselves. Individuals who are likely to reject social interventions or policies if there is no benefit to them or if they incur costs.

Prosocials. Individuals who are likely to support policies that are in the interest of the general society, regardless of the personal benefits from the policy (or lack thereof).

Prosocial incentive. Any reward that is provided on the basis of a behavior to the benefit of an individual or a group other than those responsible for that behavior.

Prospect Theory. Behavioral framework seeking to explain how decisions are made between alternatives that involve risk under uncertainty (likelihood of gains or losses) that accounts for deviations from expected utility theory. Suggests that losses are experienced more negatively than equivalent gains are experienced positively; thus, humans are more risk averse as values increase for gains and more risk seeking for losses as they increase. Includes multiple predicted indications of those behaviors, such as the effects of framing and magnitudes.

Prototyping. Designing rough drafts of potential interventions and collecting user feedback to iterate further development and design prior to formal implementation.

Public good. A commodity that is made available by a government, individual, or organization to all members of a group without exclusion, such that it may be freely consumed by all members of the group irrespective of how much others consume.

Randomized controlled trial (RCT). A study design in which individuals are assigned randomly to an intervention or control group specifically for the purpose of seeing if the intervention elicits a significantly different outcome than having no intervention. May include more than two groups.

Rational choice theory. An economic framework for understanding behaviors based on the assumption that individuals will prefer to exchange limited resources for the alternative offering the greatest return and that this general approach should be consistent, attached to a goal, possible to evaluate or reflect on, and benefit self-interest.

Rationality. The assumption that individual behaviors, choices, preferences, and beliefs will be in their own best interests, maximize desired outcomes, and reduce or prevent harm.

Rebound effect. Even though a significant gain is expected from new technologies, a reduction is detected as a consequence of changes in human behaviors. This effect is also known as the take-back effect.

Reciprocity. The assumption that an individual is more likely to offer a contribution to another if they have previously benefited from such a contribution or if such a contribution may be made to them at some point in the future, directly or indirectly related to the initial act.

Redistributive policy. Policy aimed at transferring resources from one group to another.

Reference forecasting. An economic method for making predictions on the basis of analysis of similar ("reference") situations that have occurred previously. Outcomes are forecast on the basis of past outcomes observed, adjusted for real or anticipated changes in context.

Regulation. Specifications within laws on the details that keep features of products, costs, or behaviors within the boundaries and avoid penalties associated with violations.

Regulatory policy. Policy aimed at defining permitted and restricted activities in a defined market.

Reminders. Cues or messages to ensure the critical activities are made salient with respect to when they are meant to be carried out, with the aim to encourage desired behaviors that may not have been completed otherwise.

Removal/display. A strategy to influence consumption choices by making products easier or harder to access based on whether they are the desired option.

Representativeness heuristic. Overestimating the probability of salient or vivid events on the basis of characteristics that appear to apply, yet are not actually indicative of likelihood. Often occurs when similarities are highlighted and differences are not considered.

Retention. An employee or group of employees remaining with an organization, often presented as rates or timelines.

Reward. Use of incentives for a behavior or choice to increase the likelihood of eliciting it.

Risk aversion. The tendency to avoid scenarios in which outcomes are not guaranteed and, where possible, to reduce the uncertainty.

Risk perception. Beliefs about potential harm or the possibility of a loss when facing uncertainty about a choice.

Rose Hypothesis. An argument that the population approach to interventions (as opposed to the high-risk approach) may be more effective at increasing the average level of a population in certain contexts. It stipulates that the conditions necessary to reliably achieve this include identifying within-group variability and matching it to relevant interventions, while also addressing group-specific risk factors and exposures (positive and negative).

Salience. The extent to which the features of a choice are made explicit, comprehensible, and memorable, influencing how easily the information can be accessed.

Saliency bias. Making a decision on the basis of the most easily perceived aspect of a choice context, presumptively abstaining from seeking or utilizing any further information.

Saliency: checklists. Reducing the risk of human error through a simple algorithm that makes information, or a process, more accessible by separating it into discrete, manageable steps. The approach is meant to increase adherence to all steps, particularly those that are likely to be missed if left to memory alone.

Saliency: headlines. Making information visually appealing, engaging, and easily understandable such that it increases access and memorability.

Saliency: labeling. Making information about a product more evident, accessible, comprehensible, and memorable by highlighting key features in a visual, simplified way that requires no expertise to utilize or apply.

Saliency: message weights (implicit/explicit). A key factor leading to implicit and explicit biases, where the information presented initially is made engaging and memorable, such that implications are overshadowed or ignored by novel features, giving less weight to critical information not made salient.

Saliency: pricing. Making the total cost of a product more accessible, typically in visual terms, to increase awareness of costs when making a consumer purchase choice.

Saliency: simplicity. A tool for streamlining key information into discrete or otherwise distinct pieces primarily for the purpose of reducing complexity that may discourage better choices or decrease interest in having robust information for making a decision. Typically requires message weighting proportional to the importance of each distinct piece of information.

Satisficing. The tendency to set an aspiration or goal to be achieved and then choose the first available option that meets the minimum requirements necessary to achieve it.

Scaling. Moving from smaller projects, pilots, early phases, or controlled trials to wider applications, such as regional, national, or international implementation.

Scholarly writing. Specialized writing in a formal language, supported by a body of literature and containing original thoughts or a novel synthesis of findings, typically discipline-specific in tone and format with substantial use of jargon.

Scientific dissemination. The communication of research, whether original theory, findings, or methods, or related editorial or review writing. Commonly done via academic journals with peer review, but also found in institutional reporting and some mainstream sources with specialized content.

Second-generation interventions. Communications focused on processes and routines, which involve more complex behavioral change related to decisions clients may make over time.

Segmentation. Breaking down complex tasks into pieces or phases, such as immediate goals and long-term goals, aimed at increasing task completion of desirable behaviors.

Self-affirmation theory. Proposes that self-integrity can be maintained and preserved from threat or stress by making individuals reflect on their values when making a decision.

Self-determination theory. A broad framework to study human motivation and personality concerning three presumed universal needs: autonomy, competence, and social relatedness.

Self-efficacy. An individual's perception of their own abilities and competencies to realize desired outcomes for defined goals or tasks.

Self-justification. The tendency for an individual to defend their own actions or behaviors – or that of a member or members of an in-group – to a greater extent than if carried out by someone else.

Sense of commitment. The feeling of being obliged to a certain task, situation, opinion, or person, often to sustain an activity or to reduce the effects of temporal discounting related to immediate or future behaviors.

Sense-making. The process of giving meaning to the world around us, enabling individuals to act in it.

Sensing. An informal evaluation of a policy as it is being implemented, often matching data from salient procedural features and feedback from stakeholders.

Sharing duties. Breaking large tasks into smaller phases or roles aimed at improving performance by assigning each to an ideal individual or group (based on the necessary competencies or interests in the task), rather than making one individual responsible for all aspects. May also relate to partnering in social actions, such as setting a group target aimed at controlling behaviors of all members.

Silo. A group of people or functional area of a large organization that is isolated from the rest of the organization or peer groups in other organizations.

Similarity. Utilizing perceptions of closeness in features to others as an intervention tool to establish norms. May include race, gender, attitude, values, beliefs, interests, or personality and may be used to predict influence on future behaviors.

Simplification. A method of saliency aimed at reducing complexity to cover only the most critical or fundamental pieces of information, typically related to a choice or behavior with risky or uncertain outcomes.

Situation modification intervention. An intervention aimed at changing circumstances to foster self-control.

Slow, conscious processing system. A deliberate, explicit thinking process used for decision-making such that individuals consciously work through all possible considerations. These processes can be changed by, for example, education or persuasion.

Social comparison. An individual assessment of choices, beliefs, or values with reference to group norms. It is considered a powerful tool to influence human behavior on the assumption that individuals have a strong tendency to conform to such norms.

Social cues. A set of social behaviors that act as a source of information for judging individuals in terms of status, personality, beliefs, or intellect, such as facial expressions, speech, tone of voice, or general appearance. These features are heavily relied upon in interpreting situations involving human interactions.

Social desirability bias. The tendency for individuals to give a response that appears to meet standards or norms, such as empathy, rationality, or consistency, when a respondent is being observed, such as a survey or interview, even if this response is not indicative of true beliefs, preferences, or eventual behaviors.

Social dilemmas. Decisions where individuals have to weigh personal interests against the wider collective group interest or vice versa, from the perspective of either individuals affected or decision-makers responsible for an influential choice, typically when outcomes may not be even for all individuals or groups.

Social norms. Informal rules and standards that define what is seen as desirable or acceptable behaviors, beliefs, or preferences within a group. Social norms are often defined by what is seen as common or average within a group.

Social status. The relative rank of an individual in a social hierarchy based on several social factors, such as family, personality traits, duties, lifestyle, economic resources, employment or career, group membership, and actions.

Social status competition. The activation of a position someone holds in a society as a mechanism to encourage prosocial behavior on the basis of perceived heightened effectiveness due to that position.

Socioeconomic status (SES). A multifactor, evolving measure of the social standing of an individual or group, largely based on income and equity relative to comparator groups, such as region or demographic feature similarity, along with factors such as education, employment, and household features.

Stated intentions. A specific, communicated plan of when and how an action is to be performed, irrespective of actual behavior later. Often used as a method to increase likelihood of a future desired behavior being realized.

Statistical power. The probability that a given analysis is able to detect a significant finding if one truly exists.

Status quo bias. A preference not to change current behavior, arrangement, or process, based on the idea that changes introduce uncertainty, whereas no change is associated with a sufficient outcome. May also refer to the overuse of examples or archetypes to describe a group or explain a behavior.

Stereotype boost. An increase in performance of an individual when performance-related, positive norms (whether accurate or not) associated with their social group are made salient.

Stereotype threat. The risk of an individual conforming to a negative norm (whether accurate or not) associated with a social group to which they belong such that it results in unwanted behaviors or outcomes that may otherwise not have occurred.

Structural problems. Barriers to optimal outcomes or rational decisions that are the result of inefficient systems, typically physical or administrative, which reduce the availability of desired features in the decision-making process. Often considered when optimal behaviors would have been more likely if not for barriers.

Student facing dashboards. Digital platforms that inform and give feedback to students about their performance relative to others.

Superficial effect. Results of a study or intervention where immediate impacts are not sustained over the long term. May also refer to a high-level finding that appears substantial but is mitigated by variability, skew, outliers, or another underlying confound.

Sustainability (of a policy). The assessment of impact over time, focusing specifically on how long effects continue to occur after policy implementation, usually with reference to resources needed to maintain effects over time.

Systematic review. Extensive, structured compilation of empirical evidence that rigorously collates the research on a certain topic, treatment, or method, ideally toward the convergence of best practice or an ability to make direct comparisons (often meta-analyses) of effects.

Tax compliance. The honest declaration and timely payment of tax money owed to the state, whether voluntary or enforced. Noncompliance includes deliberately paying less in taxes than assigned by either legal (tax avoidance) or illegal methods (tax evasion).

Temporal discounting/future discounting. A cognitive bias in which individuals give greater weight to immediate or present choices, costs, values, or options than those in the future, such that they may prefer a lesser immediate gain over a larger gain at a later time. May also be described as a devaluation of future events, wherein proximal consequences influence behavior more strongly than distal consequences.

Theory of planned behavior. A psychological framework describing how attitudes toward behavior, subjective norms, and perceived behavioral control shape behavioral intentions and therefore behaviors.

Traditional channels. Pathways for communication that predominantly rely on top-down communication and are prevailing methods for dissemination.

Tragedy of the commons. When individuals consume the maximum amount available of a common pool resource, thereby exhausting the supply of the resource on a group level such that only privileged groups will have access.

Transition. Shifting from one major life phase to another, such as graduating from school, beginning a new job, or leaving prison. Involves a significant change in what is considered normative behavior.

Translation. Converting the results of scientific research into conclusive insights aimed at subsequent and consequential applications.

Treatment. Any intervention that focuses specifically on moving an individual or group from beyond the threshold for belonging to a negative category (e.g. illness, injury, poverty, obesity, smoking, underperforming) to a positive, or at least improving, status within that condition.

Trust. The extent to which an individual accepts potential vulnerability on the basis of actions, behaviors, or recommendations of an individual, group, or institution, particularly those whose outcomes involve risk or uncertainty. In behavioral terms, it is the level of probability an individual assigns to the likelihood of accuracy in information received from a source.

User feedback. Responses from individuals or groups who are using or likely to use a product or service or to participate in a program.

Utility value. Assigned worth to a given choice that considers both the objective and subjective outcomes associated with each option.

Value-action gap. The difference between stated beliefs or standards and actual behavior. Typically when an individual considers a certain outcome as desirable, yet does not act on it when presented the opportunity.

Virtual learning environment (VLE). An online platform where content can be shared, students and teachers can communicate, assessments can be completed, and other supplementary classroom resources are available.

Warnings. Salient messages to deter high-risk, high-cost choices.

Web 2.0 services. Internet-based technologies intended to be consumer-centered, allowing users to interact with others and create content rather than passively observe.

Windfall effects. Typically suboptimal behavior considered out of character or irrational that arises out of unexpected, sudden gains.

Windfall gains. Unexpected, sudden increases in resources.

Note: *This glossary is intended as a general reference for common terms from publications from behavioral sciences, primarily in psychology and economics. As it is a multidisciplinary field with considerable overlap in definitions from various terms, some aspects may appear repetitive but not identical. This should normalize as the field grows and more consistency and standards are in place for jargon. All definitions have been written from scratch in an attempt to align those variations; please notify the editor if any appear overtly similar to published versions or, alternatively, contradict available definitions. Also note that all definitions are applied in the behavioral science and policy context. Other definitions may apply to the terms in other contexts.*

Bibliography

Abroms, L. C., Padmanabhan, N., Thaweethai, L., & Phillips, T. (2011). iPhone apps for smoking cessation: A content analysis. *American Journal of Preventive Medicine, 40*(3), 279–285.

Abualrub, R., & Al-Zaru, I. (2008). Job stress, recognition, job performance and intention to stay at work among Jordanian hospital nurses. *Journal of Nursing Management, 16*(3), 227–236. https://doi.org/10.1111/j.1365-2834.2007.00810.x

Ackerman, F. (1997). *Why do we recycle?: Markets, values, and public policy*. Washington, DC: Island Press.

Adams, B., Brockington, D., Dyson, J., & Vira, B. (2001). *Common choices: Policy options for common pool resources*. Retrieved from www-cpr.geog.cam.ac.uk

Adams, B., Brockington, D., Dyson, J., & Vira, B. (2002). *Analytical framework for dialogue on common pool resource management* (Common Pool Resources Policy Paper 1). Retrieved from www-cpr.geog.cam.ac.uk

Adams, P., & Hunt, S. (2013). *Encouraging consumers to claim redress: Evidence from a field trial* (FCA Occasional Paper No. 2). Retrieved from https://ssrn.com/abstract=2885791

Adler, A., & Seligman, M. E. (2016). Using wellbeing for public policy: Theory, measurement, and recommendations. *International Journal of Wellbeing, 6*(1), 1–35.

Adler, M., & Zigbostromlio, E. (1996). *Gazing into the Oracle: The Delphi method and its application to social policy and public health*. London: Jessica Kingsley Publishers.

Adukaite, A., van Zyl, I., Er, Ş., & Cantoni, L. (2017). Teacher perceptions on the use of digital gamified learning in tourism education: The case of South African secondary schools. *Computers and Education, 111*, 172–190. https://doi.org/10.1016/j.compedu.2017.04.008

Advisory, Conciliation and Arbitration Service (ACAS). (2015). *Seeking better solutions: Tackling bullying and ill-treatment in Britain's workplaces*. Policy Discussion Paper.

Agarwal, R., Gupta, A. K., & Kraut, R. (2008). Editorial overview – The interplay between digital and social networks. *Information Systems Research, 19*(3), 243–252.

Agarwal, S., Amromin, G., Ben-David, I., Chomsisengphet, S., & Evanoff, D. D. (2010). Learning to cope: Voluntary financial education and loan performance during a housing crisis. *American Economic Review: Papers & Proceedings, 100*, 495–500.

Agarwal, S., Chomsisengphet, S., Mahoney, N., & Stroebel, J. (2014). Regulating consumer financial products: Evidence from credit cards. *The Quarterly Journal of Economics, 130*(1), 111–164.

Agudo-Peregrina, Á. F., Hernández-García, Á., & Pascual-Miguel, F. J. (2014). Behavioral intention, use behavior and the acceptance of electronic learning systems: Differences between higher education and lifelong learning. *Computers in Human Behavior, 34*, 301–314. https://doi.org/10.1016/j.chb.2013.10.035

Ahmed, K., Shahbaz, M., Qasim, A., & Long, W. (2015). The linkages between deforestation, energy and growth for environmental degradation in Pakistan. *Ecological Indicators, 49*, 95–103.

Ainslie, G. (1975). Specious reward: A behavioral theory of impulsiveness and impulse control. *Psychological Bulletin, 82*(4), 463–496. https://doi.org/10.1037/h0076860

Ajzen, I. (2002a). Perceived behavioral control, self-efficacy, locus of control, and the theory of planned behavior 1. *Journal of Applied Social Psychology, 32*(4), 665–683. https://doi.org/10.1111/j.1559-1816.2002.tb00236.x

Ajzen, I. (2002b). *Constructing a TPB questionnaire: Conceptual and methodological considerations.* Retrieved from http://chuang.epage.au.edu.tw/ezfiles/168/1168/attach/20/pta_41176_7688352_57138.pdf

Aked, J., & Thompson, S. (2011). *Five ways to wellbeing: New applications, new ways of thinking.* London: New Economics Foundation. Retrieved from https://neweconomics.org/uploads/files/d80eba95560c09605d_uzm6b1n6a.pdf

Allais, P. M. (1953). Le comportement de l'homme rationnel devant le risque: Critique des postulats et axiomes de l'école Américaine. *Econometrica, 21*(4), 503–546.

Allcott, H. (2015). Site selection bias in program evaluation. *Quarterly Journal of Economics, 130*(3), 1117–1165.

Allcott, H., & Gentzkow, M. (2017). Social media and fake news in the 2016 election. *Journal of Economic Perspectives, 31*(2), 211–236.

Allcott, H., & Mullainathan, S. (2010). Behavior and energy policy. *Science, 327*(5970), 1204–1205.

Allcott, H., & Rogers, T. (2014). The short-run and long-run effects of behavioral interventions: Experimental evidence from energy conservation. *American Economic Review, 104*(10), 3003–3037.

Allen, J. D., Shelton, R. C., Emmons, K. M., & Linnan, L. (2018). Fidelity and its relationship to implementation effectiveness, adaptation, and dissemination. In R. C. Brownson, G. A. Colditz, & E. K. Proctor (Eds.), *Dissemination and implementation research in health: Translating science to practice* (2nd ed., pp. 267–284). New York: Oxford University Press.

Allin, P., & Hand, D. J. (2017). New statistics for old? Measuring the wellbeing of the UK. *Journal of the Royal Statistical Society: Series A (Statistics in Society), 180*(1), 3–43.

Allingham, M. G., & Sandmo, A. (1972). Income tax evasion: A theoretical analysis. *Journal of Public Economics, 1*, 323–338.

Alm, J., Cherry, T., Jones, M., & McKee, M. (2010). Taxpayer information assistance services and tax compliance behavior. *Journal of Economic Psychology, 31*(4), 577–586. https://doi.org/10.1016/j.joep.2010.03.018

Alpert, M., & Raiffa, H. (1982). A progress report on the training of probability assessors. In D. Kahneman, P. Slovic, & A. Tversky (Eds.), *Judgment under uncertainty: Heuristics and biases* (pp. 294–305). Cambridge: Cambridge University Press.

American Cancer Society. (n.d.). *American Cancer Society guidelines for the early detection of cancer.* Retrieved from www.cancer.org/healthy/find-cancer-early/cancer-screening-guidelines/american-cancer-society-guidelines-for-the-early-detection-of-cancer.html

Anagnostopoulos, D., Lingard, B., & Sellar, S. (2016). Argumentation in educational policy disputes: Competing visions of quality and equity. *Theory into Practice, 55*, 342–351. https://doi.org/10.1080/00405841.2016.1208071

Anagnostopoulou, E., Urbančič, J., Bothos, E., Magoutas, B., Bradesko, L., Schrammel, J., & Mentzas, G. (2018). From mobility patterns to behavioural change: Leveraging travel behaviour and personality profiles to nudge for sustainable transportation. *Journal of Intelligent Information Systems, 54*, 157–178.

Anders, J. (2012). The link between household income, university applications and university attendance. *Fiscal Studies*, *33*(2), 185–210. https://doi.org/10.1111/j.1475-5890.2012.00158.x

Andersen, S. C., & Nielsen, H. S. (2016). Reading intervention with a growth mindset approach improves children's skills. *Proceedings of the National Academy of Sciences*, *113*(43), 12111–12113. https://doi.org/10.1073/pnas.1607946113

Anderson, C. L., & Stamoulis, K. (2007). Applying behavioural economics to international development policy. In G. Mavrotas & A. Shorrocks (Eds.), *Advancing development: Core themes in global economics* (pp. 664–685). Basingstoke: Palgrave Macmillan.

Anderson, J. (2015). "Living in a communal garden" associated with well-being while reducing urban sprawl by 40%: A mixed-methods cross-sectional study. *Frontiers in Public Health*, *3*(173).

Anderson, J., & Baldwin, C. (2017). Building well-being: Neighbourhood flourishing and approaches for participatory urban design intervention. In *Handbook of community well-being research* (pp. 313–337). Dordrecht: Springer Netherlands.

Anderson, J., Ruggeri, K., Steemers, K., & Huppert, F. (2017). Lively social space, well-being activity, and urban design: Findings from a low-cost community-led public space intervention. *Environment and Behavior*, *49*(6), 685–716.

Anderson, S. E., & Togneri, W. (2005). School district-wide reform policies in education. In N. Bascia, A. Cumming, A. Datnow, K. Leithwood, & D. Livingstone (Eds.), *International handbook of educational policy*. Dordrecht: Springer International Handbooks of Education.

Angrist, J. D., Lang, D., & Oreopoulos, P. (2009). Incentives and services for college achievement: Evidence from a randomized trial. *American Economic Journal: Applied Economics*, *1*(1), 136–163. Retrieved from www.jstor.org/stable/25760150

Angrist, J. D., Oreopoulos, P., & Williams, T. (2014). When opportunity knocks, who answers? New evidence on college achievement awards. *Journal of Human Resources*, *49*(3), 572–610. https://doi.org/10.3368/jhr.49.3.572

Ansari, A., & Mela, C. F. (2003). E-customization. *Journal of Marketing Research*, *40*(2), 131–145.

Antonovsky, A. (1979). *Health, stress, and coping*. San Francisco, CA: Jossey-Bass.

Apergis, N., & Payne, J. E. (2009). Energy consumption and economic growth in Central America: Evidence from a panel cointegration and error correction model. *Energy Economics*, *31*(2), 211–216.

Apergis, N., & Payne, J. E. (2010). The emissions, energy consumption, and growth nexus: Evidence from the Commonwealth of Independent States. *Energy Policy*, *38*(1), 650–655.

Aranda-Jan, C. B., Mohutsiwa-Dibe, N., & Loukanova, S. (2014). Systematic review on what works, what does not work and why of implementation of mobile health (mHealth) projects in Africa. *BMC Public Health*, *14*(1), 188.

Ariely, D. (2008). *Predictably irrational: The hidden forces that shape our decisions*. London: Harper Collins.

Ariely, D., Kamenica, E., & Prlec, D. (2008). Man's search for meaning: The case of Legos. *Journal of Economic Behavior & Organization*, *67*(3–4), 671–677.

Ariely, D., & Wertenbroch, K. (2002). Procrastination, deadlines, and performance: Self-control by precommitment. *Psychological Science*, *13*(3), 219–224. https://doi.org/10.1111/1467-9280.00441

Armstrong, R., Doyle, J., Lamb, C., & Waters, E. (2006). Multi-sectoral health promotion and public health: The role of evidence. *Journal of Public Health*, *28*(2), 168–172. https://doi.org/10.1093/pubmed/fdl013

Aronson, J., Fried, C. B., & Good, C. (2002). Reducing the effects of stereotype threat on African American college students by shaping theories of intelligence. *Journal of Experimental Social Psychology, 38*(2), 113–125. https://doi.org/10.1006/jesp.2001.1491

Arriaga, A. F., Bader, A. M., Wong, J. M., Lipsitz, S. R., Berry, W. R., Ziewacz, J. E., . . . & Gawande, A. A. (2013). Simulation-based trial of surgical-crisis checklists. *New England Journal of Medicine, 368*(3), 246–253. https://doi.org/10.1056/NEJMsa1204720

Artino, A. R. (2010). Online or face-to-face learning? Exploring the personal factors that predict students' choice of instructional format. *Internet and Higher Education, 13*(4), 272–276. https://doi.org/10.1016/j.iheduc.2010.07.005

Asensio, O. I., & Delmas, M. A. (2015). Nonprice incentives and energy conservation. *Proceedings of the National Academy of Sciences, 112*(6), E510–E515. https://doi.org/10.1073/pnas.1401880112

Ásgeirsdóttir, T. L., Corman, H., Noonan, K., Ólafsdóttir, Þ., & Reichman, N. E. (2014). Was the economic crisis of 2008 good for Icelanders? Impact on health behaviors. *Economics & Human Biology, 13*, 1–19.

Ashraf, N., Karlan, D., & Yin, W. (2006). Tying Odysseus to the mast: Evidence from a commitment savings product in the Philippines. *The Quarterly Journal of Economics, 121*(2), 635–672.

Åslund, O., & Skans, O. (2012). Do Anonymous job application procedures level the playing field? *ILR Review, 65*(1), 82–107. https://doi.org/10.1177/001979391206500105

Association of Accounting Technicians (AAT). (2015). *Work – in numbers*. Retrieved from www.aat.org.uk/news/article/work-numbers

Atkinson, A., & Messy, F. (2013). *Promoting financial inclusion through financial education: OECD/INFE evidence, policies and practice* (OECD Working Papers on Finance, Insurance and Private Pensions, 34). Paris: OECD Publishing.

Atsma, F., Veldhuizen, I., De Vegt, F., Doggen, C., & De Kort, W. (2011). Cardiovascular and demographic characteristics in whole blood and plasma donors: Results from the Donor InSight study. *Transfusion, 51*(2), 412–420. https://doi.org/10.1111/j.1537-2995.2010.02867.x

Attari, S. Z., DeKay, M. L., Davidson, C. I., & de Bruin, W. B. (2010). Public perceptions of energy consumption and savings. *Proceedings of the National Academy of Sciences, 107*(37), 16054–16059.

Attewell, P., Heil, S., & Reisel, L. (2012). What is academic momentum? And does it matter? *Educational Evaluation and Policy Analysis, 34*(1), 27–44.

Audet, M., Gascon, S., Rahbar, H., & Soliman, M. (2017). *Using behavioural insights to improve government programs and services: The case of Job Match*. Retrieved from https://canadiangovernmentexecutive.ca/using-behavioural-insights-to-improve-government-programs-and-services-the-case-of-job-match

Australian Development Agency (ADA). (2009). *Guidelines for project and programme evaluations*. Retrieved from www.oecd.org/development/evaluation/dcdndep/47069197.pdf

Ayres, I. (2007). *Supercrunchers: How anything can be predicted*. London: Murray.

Azmat, G., & Iriberri, N. (2010). The importance of relative performance feedback information: Evidence from a natural experiment using high school students. *Journal of Public Economics, 94*(7), 435–452. https://doi.org/10.1016/j.jpubeco.2010.04.001

Babcock, H. M., Gemeinhart, N., Jones, M., Dunagan, W. C., & Woeltje, K. F. (2010). Mandatory influenza vaccination of health care workers: Translating policy to practice. *Clinical Infectious Diseases, 50*(4), 459–464.

Bachrach, Y., Kosinski, M., Graepel, T., Kohli, P., & Stillwell, D. (2012). Personality and patterns of Facebook usage. In *Proceedings of the 4th annual ACM web science conference* (pp. 24–32). ACM.

Back, M. D., Stopfer, J. M., Vazire, S., Gaddis, S., Schmukle, S. C., Egloff, B., & Gosling, S. D. (2010). Facebook profiles reflect actual personality, not self-idealization. *Psychological Science, 21*(3), 372–374.

Badilla Quintana, M. G., Vera Sagredo, A., & Lytras, M. D. (2017). Pre-service teachers' skills and perceptions about the use of virtual learning environments to improve teaching and learning. *Behaviour & Information Technology, 3001*(August), 1–14.

Baird, P., Cullinan, D., Landers, P., & Reardon, L. (2016). *Nudges for child support: Applying behavioral insights to increase collections.* Washington, DC: Office of Planning, Research and Evaluation.

Baird, P., Reardon, L., Cullinan, D., McDermott, D., & Landers, P. (2015). *Reminders to pay: Using behavioral economics to increase child support payments.* Retrieved from https://bit.ly/2MAUYLz

Baker, J., & Cameron, M. (1996). The effects of the service environment on affect and consumer perception of waiting time: An integrative review and research propositions. *Academy of Marketing Science, 24*(4), 338.

Balfanz, R., & Byrnes, V. (2013). *Meeting the challenge of combating chronic absenteeism: Impact of the NYC mayor's interagency task force on chronic absenteeism and school attendance and its implications for other cities.* New York: Everyone Graduates Center, Johns Hopkins University School of Education. Retrieved from http://bit.ly/2yuwyJz

Ballantyne, J. C., & Fleisher, L. A. (2010). Ethical issues in opioid prescribing for chronic pain. *Pain, 148*(3), 365–367. https://doi.org/10.1016/j.pain.2009.10.020

Balnaves, M., Donald, S. H., & Shoesmith, B. (2008). *Media theories and approaches: A global perspective.* Basingstoke: Palgrave Macmillan.

Balu, R., Porter, K., & Gunton, B. (2016). *Can informing parents help high school students show up for school: Results from a partnership between new visions for public schools and MDRC.* New York: MDRC. Retrieved from http://bit.ly/2kP2khd

Bardach, E., & Patashnik, E. M. (2015). *A practical guide for policy analysis: The eightfold path to more effective problem solving.* Washington, DC: CQ Press.

Bareket-Bojmel, L., Hochman, G., & Ariely, D. (2017). It's (not) all about the Jacksons: Testing different types of short-term bonuses in the field. *Journal of Management, 43*(2), 534–554.

Barratt, H., Campbell, M., Moore, L., Zwarenstein, M., & Bower, P. (2016). Randomised controlled trials of complex interventions and large-scale transformation of services. *Health Services and Delivery Research, 16*(4), 19–36.

Barrera-Osorio, F., Bertrand, M., Linden, L. L., & Perez-Calle, F. (2011). Improving the design of conditional transfer programs: Evidence from a randomized education experiment in Colombia. *American Economic Journal: Applied Economics, 3*(2), 167–195. Retrieved from www.jstor.org/stable/41288633

Barroso, J. M. D. (2013, May). *Speech by President Barroso on the preparations of the European Council of 22 May.* Retrieved from http://europa.eu/rapid/press-release_SPEECH-13-434_en.htm

Barth, M., Fischer, D., Michelsen, G., Nemnich, C., & Rode, H. (2012). Tackling the knowledge – Action gap in sustainable consumption: Insights from a participatory school programme. *Journal of Education for Sustainable Development, 6*(2), 301–312. https://doi.org/10.1177/0973408212475266

Battisti, G. (2008). Innovations and the economics of new technology spreading within and across users: Gaps and way forward. *Journal of Cleaner Production, 16*, 22–31.
Beach, L. R., & Mitchell, T. R. (1978). A contingency model for the selection of decision strategies. *The Academy of Management Review, 3*(3), 439–449. https://doi.org/10.2307/257535
Beal, D., Rueda-Sabater, E., Yong, S. E., & Heng, S. L. (2016). *The private-sector opportunity to improve well-being*. The Boston Consulting Group.
Beccaria, C. (2004). *On crimes and punishments*. Whitefish, MT: Kessinger.
Becker, M. W., Alzahabi, R., & Hopwood, C. J. (2013). Media multitasking is associated with symptoms of depression and social anxiety. *Cyberpsychology, Behavior, and Social Networking, 16*(2), 132–135. https://doi.org/10.1089/cyber.2012.0291
Behavioural Insights Team. (2011). *Behaviour change and energy use*. London: Cabinet Office. Retrieved from https://bit.ly/2oofqkc
Behavioural Insights Team. (2012). *New BIT trial results: Helping people back into work*. Retrieved from https://bit.ly/2C2hTKT
Behavioural Insights Team. (2013). *Applying behavioural insights to organ donation: Preliminary results from a randomised controlled trial*. London: Behavioural Insights Team, Cabinet Office.
Behavioural Insights Team. (2014). *EAST: Four simple ways to apply behavioural insights*. London: Behavioural Insights. Retrieved from https://bit.ly/2tHU6Zm
Behavioural Insights Team. (2016a). *Behavioral Insights for cities*. London: Behavioural Insights Team, Cabinet Office. Retrieved from https://bit.ly/2eM2G1J
Behavioural Insights Team. (2016b). *Moments of choice*. Behavioural Insights Team Final Report. London: Behavioural Insights Team, Cabinet Office. Retrieved from https://bit.ly/2C2sVzM
Behavioural Insights Team. (2018). *The Behavioural Insights Team annual report 2017–18*. London: The Behavioural Insights Team.
Behavioural Insights Team & Britain, G. (2015). *Update report 2013–2015*. Behavioural Insights Limited. Retrieved from https://bit.ly/1JgDhaT
Bell, S., & Morse, S. (2013). Towards an understanding of how policy making groups use indicators. *Ecological Indicators, 35*, 13–23.
Belot, M., James, J., & Nolen, P. (2016). Incentives and children's dietary choices: A field experiment in primary schools. *Journal of Health Economics, 50*, 213–229.
Benartzi, S., Beshears, J., Milkman, K. L., Sunstein, C. R., Thaler, R. H., Shankar, M., . . . & Galing, S. (2017). Should governments invest more in nudging? *Psychological Science, 28*(8), 1041–1055.
Benartzi, S., & Lehrer, J. (2015). *The smarter screen: Surprising ways to influence and improve online behavior*. New York: Portfolio/Penguin.
Benartzi, S., & Lewin, R. (2012). *Save more tomorrow* (1st ed.). New York: Portfolio/Penguin.
Benhassine, N., Devoto, F., Duflo, E., Dupas, P., & Pouliquen, V. (2015). Turning a shove into a nudge? A "labeled cash transfer" for education. *American Economic Journal: Economic Policy, 7*(3), 86–125. Retrieved from www.nber.org/ papers/w19227
Bennett, G., & Jessani, N. (2011). *Knowledge translation toolkit*. New Delhi: Sage.
Bentley, R. A., O'Brien, M. J., & Brock, W. A. (2014). Mapping collective behavior in the big-data era. *Behavioral and Brain Sciences, 37*(1), 63–76.
Berger, J., & Schwartz, E. M. (2011). What drives immediate and ongoing word of mouth? *Journal of Marketing Research, 48*(5), 869–880.

Bergman, P., & Chan, E. W. (2017). *Leveraging technology to engage parents at scale: Evidence from a randomized controlled trial* (CESifo Working Paper Series, No. 6493). Retrieved from www.columbia.edu/~psb2101/ParentRCT.pdf

Bergman, P., & Chan, E. W. (2019). Leveraging parents through low-cost technology: The impact of high-frequency information on student achievement. *Journal of Human Resources*. https://doi.org/10.3368/jhr.56.1.1118-9837R1.

Bergman, P., Lasky-Fink, J., & Rogers, T. (2019). Simplification and defaults affect adoption and impact of technology, but decision makers do not realize it. *Organizational Behavior and Human Decision Processes, 158*, 66–79.

Bergman, P., & Rogers, T. (2017). *Is this technology useless? How seemingly irrelevant factors affect adoption and efficacy* (HKS Working Paper No. RWP17-021). Cambridge, MA. Retrieved from http://bit.ly/2yu6RKB

Bernhardt, J. M., Mays, D., Eroglu, D., & Daniel, K. L. (2009). New communication channels: Changing the nature of customer engagement. *Social Marketing Quarterly, 15*, 7–15.

Bernhardt, J. M., Mays, D., & Hall, A. K. (2012). Social marketing at the right place and right time with new media. *Journal of Social Marketing, 2*(2), 130–137.

Bernhardt, J. M., Mays, D., & Kreuter, M. W. (2011). Dissemination 2.0: Closing the gap between knowledge and practice with new media and marketing. *Journal of Health Communication, 16*(Suppl. 1), 32–44.

Berry, D. A., Cronin, K. A., Plevritis, S. K., Fryback, D. G., Clarke, L., Zelen, M., . . . & Feuer, E. J. (2005). Effect of screening and adjuvant therapy on mortality from breast cancer. *New England Journal of Medicine, 353*(17), 1784–1792.

Besharat, A., Varki, S., & Craig, A. W. (2015). Keeping consumers in the red: Hedonic debt prioritization within multiple debt accounts. *Journal of Consumer Psychology, 25*(2), 311–316. https://doi.org/10.1016/j.jcps.2014.08.005

Beshears, J., Choi, J., Laibson, D., & Madrian, B. (2006). The importance of default options for retirement savings outcomes: Evidence from the United States. In J. R. Brown, J. B. Liebman, & D. A. Wise (Eds.), *Social security policy in a changing environment*. Chicago, IL: University of Chicago Press. https://doi.org/10.3386/w12009

Beshears, J., & Gino, F. (2015). Leaders as decision architects. *Harvard Business Review, 93*(5), 52–62.

Best, M., & Neuhauser, D. (2006). Walter A Shewhart, 1924, and the Hawthorne factory. *Quality and Safety in Health Care, 15*(2), 142–143.

Betsch, C., Böhm, R., & Chapman, G. B. (2015). Using behavioral insights to increase vaccination policy effectiveness. *Policy Insights from the Behavioral and Brain Sciences, 2*(1), 61–73.

Bettinger, E. P. (2012). Paying to learn: The effect of financial incentives on elementary school test scores. *Review of Economics and Statistics, 94*(3), 686–698. Retrieved from https://bit.ly/2MBRvMO

Bettinger, E. P., Long, B. T., Oreopoulos, P., & Sanbonmatsu, L. (2012). The role of application assistance and information in college decisions: Results from the H&R Block Fafsa experiment. *The Quarterly Journal of Economics, 127*(3), 1205–1242. https://doi.org/10.1093/qje/qjs017

Bettinger, E. P., & Slonim, R. (2007). Patience among children. *Journal of Public Economics, 91*(1), 343–363. https://doi.org/10.1016/j.jpubeco.2006.05.010

Bharadwaj, B. (2016). *Plastic bag ban in Nepal: Enforcement and effectiveness* (Policy Brief 109). Retrieved August 28, 2018 from https://bit.ly/2NCRfd2

Bhargava, S., & Manoli, D. (2015). Psychological frictions and the incomplete take-up of social benefits: Evidence from an IRS field experiment. *American Economic Review, 105*(11), 3489–3529.

Bholat, D., Broughton, N., Parker, A., Ter Meer, J., & Walczak, E. (2018). Enhancing central bank communications with behavioural insights. *SSRN Electronic Journal.* https://doi.org/10.2139/ssrn.3233695

Binelli, C., Loveless, M., & Whitefield, S. (2015). What is social inequality and why does it matter? Evidence from central and eastern Europe. *World Development, 70*, 239–248.

Birch, S. A., & Bloom, P. (2007). The curse of knowledge in reasoning about false beliefs. *Psychological Science, 18*(5), 382–386.

Bitterman, A., Gray, L., & Goldring, R. (2013). *Characteristics of public and private elementary and secondary schools in the United States: Results from the 2011–12 Schools and Staffing Survey. First look* (NCES 2013–312). Washington, DC: National Center for Education Statistics.

Black, C. (2008). *Working for a healthier tomorrow.* London: The Stationery Office.

Blackwell, L. S., Trzesniewski, K. H., & Dweck, C. S. (2007). Implicit theories of intelligence predict achievement across an adolescent transition: A longitudinal study and an intervention. *Child Development, 78*(1), 246–263. https://doi.org/10.1111/j.1467-8624.2007.00995.x

Blake, J. (1999). Overcoming the "value-action gap" in environmental policy: Tensions between national policy and local experience. *Local Environment, 4*(3), 257–278.

Bloom, N., Genakos, C., Martin, R., & Sadun, R. (2010). Modern management: Good for the environment or just hot air? *The Economic Journal, 120*(544), 551–572.

Blundell, R., & Costa Dias, M. (2002). Alternative approaches to evaluation in empirical microeconomics. *Portuguese Economic Journal, 1*, 91–115.

Bogner, H. R., Morales, K. H., de Vries, H. F., & Cappola, A. R. (2012). Integrated management of type 2 diabetes mellitus and depression treatment to improve medication adherence: A randomized controlled trial. *The Annals of Family Medicine, 10*(1), 15–22.

Bolderdijk, J. W., Steg, L., Geller, E. S., Lehman, P. K., & Postmes, T. (2012). Comparing the effectiveness of monetary versus moral motives in environmental campaigning. *Nature Climate Change, 3*, 1–4. https://doi.org/10.1038/nclimate1767

Bonde, M. T., Makransky, G., Wandall, J., Larsen, M. V., Morsing, M., Jarmer, H., & Sommer, M. O. A. (2014). Improving biotech education through gamified laboratory simulations. *Nature Biotechnology, 32*(7), 694–697. https://doi.org/10.1038/nbt.2955

Booher-Jennings, J. (2005). Below the bubble: "Educational triage" and the Texas accountability system. *American Educational Research Journal, 42*(2), 231–268.

Booth, F. W., Roberts, C. K., & Laye, M. J. (2012). Lack of exercise is a major cause of chronic diseases. *Comprehensive Physiology, 2*(2), 1143.

Börner, K. (2012). Visualization: Picturing science. *Nature, 487*(7408), 430–431.

Börner, K., Maltese, A., Balliet, R. N., & Heimlich, J. (2015). Investigating aspects of data visualization literacy using 20 information visualizations and 273 science museum visitors. *Information Visualization, 15*(3), 198–213.

Borsari, B., & Carey, K. B. (2003). Descriptive and injunctive norms in college drinking: A meta-analytic integration. *Journal of Studies on Alcohol, 64*(3), 331–341. https://doi.org/10.15288/jsa.2003.64.331

Bostrom, A., Morgan, M. G., Fischhoff, B., & Read, D. (1994). What do people know about global climate change? 1. Mental models. *Risk Analysis, 14*(6), 959–970.

Bowen, S., & Zwi, A. B. (2005). Pathways to "evidence-informed" policy and practice: A framework for action. *PLoS Medicine*, *2*(7). https://doi.org/10.1371/journal.pmed.0020166

Bowles, S. (2008). Policies designed for self-interested citizens may undermine "the moral sentiments": Evidence from economic experiments. *Science*, *320*, 1605–1609. https://doi.org/10.1126/science.1152110

Bradshaw, J., & Klein, W. C. (2007). Health promotion. In J. A. Blackburn & C. N. Dulmus (Eds.), *Handbook of gerontology: Evidence-based approaches to theory, practice, and policy* (pp. 169–200). San Francisco, CA: John Wiley & Sons.

Brandon, A., List, J. L., Metcalfe, R. D., Price, M. K., & Rundhammer, F. (2018). Testing the crowd out in social nudges: Evidence from a natural field experiment in the market for electricity. *Proceeding of the National Academy of Sciences*, 201802874. https://doi.org/10.1073/pnas.1802874115

Breman, A. (2011). Give more tomorrow: Two field experiments on altruism and intertemporal choice. *Journal of Public Economics*, *95*, 1349–1357.

Brewer, N. T., Chapman, G. B., Rothman, A. J., Leask, J., & Kempe, A. (2017). Increasing vaccination: putting psychological science into action. *Psychological Science in the Public Interest*, *18*(3), 149–207. https://doi.org/10.1177/1529100618760521

Brodie, M., Foehr, U., Rideout, V., Baer, N., Miller, C., Flournoy, R., & Altman, D. (2001). Communicating health information through the entertainment media. *Health Affairs*, *20*(1), 192–199.

Brosius, H. B. (1999). Research note: The influence of exemplars on recipients' judgements: The part played by similarity between exemplar and recipient. *European Journal of Communication*, *14*(2), 213–224.

Brossard, D., & Scheufele, D. A. (2013). Science, new media, and the public. *Science*, *339*(6115), 40–41.

Brown, M. T., & Bussell, J. K. (2011, April). Medication adherence: WHO cares? *Mayo Clinic Proceedings*, *86*(4), 304–314. Amsterdam: Elsevier.

Brown, Z., Johnstone, N., Hascic, I., Vong, L., & Barascud, F. (2012). *Testing the effect of defaults on the thermostat settings of OECD employees* (OECD Environment Working Papers 51). Paris: OECD Publishing. https://doi.org/10.1787/5k8xdh41r8jd-en

Brownson, R. C., Allen, P., Jacob, R. R., Harris, J. K., Duggan, K., Hipp, P. R., & Erwin, P. C. (2015). Understanding mis-implementation in public health practice. *American Journal of Preventive Medicine*, *48*(5), 543–551.

Bruhn, M., Legovini, A., Zia, B., Leão, L. de S., & Marchetti, R. (2014). *The impact of high school financial education: Large-scale experimental evidence from Brazil*. Washington, DC: World Bank Group. Retrieved from http://bit.ly/2xo6T4f

Bruner, J. S. (2009). *Actual minds, possible worlds*. Cambridge, MA: Harvard University Press.

Bryan, G., Karlan, D., & Nelson, S. (2010). Commitment devices. *Annual Review of Economics*, *2*(1), 671–698. https://doi.org/10.1146/annurev.economics.102308.124324

Bryman, A., & Burgess, B. (Eds.). (1994). *Analyzing qualitative data*. London: Routledge.

Buehler, R., Griffin, D., & Ross, M. (1994). Exploring the "planning fallacy": Why people underestimate their task completion times. *Journal of Personality and Social Psychology*, *67*(3), 366–381. https://doi.org/10.1037/0022-3514.67.3.366

Buell, R. W., Porter, E., & Norton, M. I. (2017). *Surfacing the submerged state: Operational transparency increases trust in and engagement with government* (Harvard Business School Working Papers No. 14–034).

Bundesministerium für Finanzen. (2016). *Horizontal monitoring evaluationsbericht.* Berlin: Bundesministerium für Finanzen. Retrieved from http://bit.ly/2wKig9n

Burstein, P. (2003). The impact of public opinion on public policy: A review and an agenda. *Political Research Quarterly, 56*(1), 29–40. https://doi.org/10.2307/321988

Burt, R. (2004). Structural holes and good ideas. *The American Journal of Sociology, 110*(2), 349–399. https://doi.org/10.1086/421787

Burton, A. (2008). Cardiovascular health: Hard data for hard water. *Environmental Health Perspectives, 116*(3), A114.

Busso, M., Dinkelman, T., Martínez, A. C., & Romero, D. (2017). The effects of financial aid and returns information in selective and less selective schools: Experimental evidence from Chile. *Labour Economics, 45*, 79–91. https://doi.org/10.1016/j. labeco.2016.11.001

Cairney, P. (2016). *The politics of evidence-based policy making.* London: Palgrave Springer.

Cairney, P., & Heikkila, T. (2014). A comparison of theories of the policy process. In P. Sabatier & C. M. Weibe (Eds.), *Theories of the policy process* (pp. 363–390). Boulder, CO: Westview Press.

Callan, V. J., Johnston, M. A., & Poulsen, A. L. (2015). How organisations are using blended e-learning to deliver more flexible approaches to trade training. *Journal of Vocational Education & Training, 67*(3), 294–309. https://doi.org/10.1080/13636820.2015.1050445

Callison, K., & Kaestner, R. (2014). Do higher tobacco taxes reduce adult smoking? New evidence of the effect of recent cigarette tax increases on adult smoking. *Economic Inquiry, 52*(1), 155–172.

Camerer, C. F., Dreber, A., Forsell, E., Ho, T. H., Huber, J., Johannesson, M., . . . & Heikensten, E. (2016). Evaluating replicability of laboratory experiments in economics. *Science, 351*(6280), 1433–1436.

Camerer, C. F., Issacharoff, S., Loewenstein, G., O'Donoghue, T., Rabin, M., & Rabint, M. (2003). Regulation for conservatives: Behavioral economics and the case for "asymmetric paternalism". *University of Pennsylvania Law Review, 151*(3), 1211–1254. https://doi.org/10.2307/3312889

Camerer, C. F., & Loewenstein, G. (2004). Behavioral economics: Past, present, future. In C. F. Camerer, G. Loewenstein, & M. Rabin (Eds.), *Advances in behavioral economics.* Princeton and Oxford: Princeton University Press. Retrieved from https://www.researchgate.net/publication/228359684_Behavioral_Economics_Past_Present_Future

Campbell, F., Conti, G., Heckman, J. J., Moon, S. H., Pinto, R., Pungello, E., & Pan, Y. (2014). Early childhood investments substantially boost adult health. *Science, 343*(6178), 1478–1485. https://doi.org/10.1126/science.1248429

Caramel, L. (2014). Besieged by the rising tides of climate change, Kiribati buys land in Fiji. *The Guardian*, 1. Retrieved August 28, 2018 from http://bit.ly/2C1wExl

Cardon, D. (2015). *A quoi rêvent les algorithmes. Nos vies à l'heure des big data.* Paris: Editions de Seuil et La République des Idées.

Carpenter, J., Bowles, S., Gintis, H., & Hwang, S. (2009). Strong reciprocity and team production: Theory and evidence. *Journal of Economic Behavior & Organization, 71*(2), 221–232. https://doi.org/10.1016/j.jebo.2009.03.011

Carrera, M., Royer, H., Stehr, M., & Sydnor, J. (2018). Can financial incentives help people trying to establish new habits? Experimental evidence with new gym members. *Journal of Health Economics, 58*, 202–214. https://doi.org/10.1016/j.jhealeco.2018.02.010

Carroll, A. (2017, November 6). Don't nudge me: The limits of behavioral economics in medicine. *New York Times.*

Carroll, G. D., Choi, J. J., Laibson, D., Madrian, B. C., & Metrick, A. (2009). Optimal defaults and active decisions. *The Quarterly Journal of Economics, 124*(4), 1639–1674.

Carter, T. J., & Gilovich, T. (2010). The relative relativity of material and experiential purchases. *Journal of Personality and Social Psychology, 98*(1), 146–159. https://doi.org/10.1037/a0017145

Cartwright, N. (2007). Are RCTs the gold standard? *BioSocieties, 2*(1), 11–20. https://doi.org/10.1017/S1745855207005029

Cartwright, N. (2009). Evidence-based policy: What's to be done about relevance? *Philosophical Studies, 143*(1), 127–136.

Cartwright, N., Goldfinch, A., & Howick, J. (2010). Evidence-based policy: Where is our theory of evidence? *Journal of Children's Services, 4*(4), 6–14.

Cartwright, N., & Hardie, J. (2012). *Evidence-based policy: A practical guide to doing it better*. Oxford: Oxford University Press.

Cartwright, N., & Stegenga, J. (2011). A theory of evidence for evidence-based policy. In P. Dawid, W. Twining, & D. Vasilaki (Eds.), *Evidence, inference and enquiry*. Oxford: Oxford University Press.

Casini, A., Hubert, C., & Kaelen, R. (2016). Professional recognition as protective factor against burnout. In *Behaviour change: Making an impact on health and health services* (1st ed., p. 673). Aberdeen, Scotland: European Health Psychology Society. Retrieved from www.ehps2016.org/files/EHPS2016_Abstracts_Book_08082016.pdf

Castelo, N., Hardy, E., House, J., Mazar, N., Tsai, C., & Zhao, M. (2015). Moving citizens online: Using salience & message framing to motivate behavior change. *Behavioral Science & Policy, 1*(2), 57–68.

Castilla, E. J. (2012). Gender, race, and the new (merit-based) employment relationship. *Industrial Relations, 51*(Suppl. 1), 528–562. https://doi.org/10.1111/j.1468-232X.2012.00689

Castleman, B. L., & Page, L. C. (2015). Summer nudging: Can personalized text messages and peer mentor outreach increase college going among low-income high school graduates? *Journal of Economic Behavior & Organization, 115*, 144–160. https://doi.org/10.1016/j.jebo.2014.12.008

Caudill, E. M., & Murphy, P. E. (2000). Consumer online privacy: Legal and ethical issues. *Journal of Public Policy & Marketing, 19*(1), 7–19.

Ceballos, G., Ehrlich, P. R., Barnosky, A. D., García, A., Pringle, R. M., & Palmer, T. M. (2015). Accelerated modern human-induced species losses: Entering the sixth mass extinction. *Science Advances, 1*(5). https://doi.org/10.1126/sciadv.1400253

Centers for Disease Control and Prevention. (2011, November 4). *Vital signs: Overdoses of prescription opioid pain relievers – United States, 1999–2008*. Retrieved from www.cdc.gov/mmwr/preview/mmwrhtml/mm6043a4.htm?s_cid=mm6043a4_w

Centers for Disease Control and Prevention. (2013). *Antibiotic resistance threats in the United States*. Retrieved from www.cdc.gov/drugresistance/threat-report-2013/pdf/ar-threats-2013-508.pdf

Centers for Disease Control and Prevention. (2015). *Policy implementation analysis*. Retrieved from www.cdc.gov/program/data/policyanalyses/index.htm

Centola, D. (2018). *How behavior spreads*. Princeton, NJ: Princeton University Press.

Cerutti, E., Claessens, S., & Laeven, L. (2017). The use and effectiveness of macroprudential policies: New evidence. *Journal of Financial Stability, 28*, 203–224. https://doi.org/10.1016/j.jfs.2015.10.004

Cerutti, N. (2017). Social dilemmas in environmental economics and policy considerations: A review. *Ethics in Progress, 8*(1), 156–173. https://doi.org/10.14746/eip.2017.1.10
Chaiyachati, K. H., Hubbard, R. A., Yeager, A., Mugo, B., Shea, J. A., Rosin, R., & Grande, D. (2018). Rideshare-based medical transportation for Medicaid patients and primary care show rates: A difference-in-difference analysis of a pilot program. *Journal of General Internal Medicine, 33*(6), 863–868.
Chaloupka, F. J. (1999). How effective are taxes in reducing tobacco consumption? In C. Jeanrenaud & N. Soguel (Eds.), *Valuing the cost of smoking: Assessment methods, risk perception and policy options* (pp. 205–218). Dordrecht: Springer Netherlands.
Chande, R., Luca, M., Sanders, M., Soon, X., Borcan, O., Barak-Corren, N., . . . & Robinson, S. (2017). *Using text reminders to increase attendance and attainment: Evidence from a field experiment.* Retrieved from http://bit.ly/2weU9vu
Chandola, T., Brunner, E., & Marmot, M. (2006). Chronic stress at work and the metabolic syndrome: Prospective study. *BMJ (Clinical Research Ed.), 332*(7540), 521–525. https://doi.org/10.1136/bmj.38693.435301.80
Chapman, G. B., Li, M., Colby, H., & Yoon, H. (2010). Opting in vs opting out of influenza vaccination. *JAMA, 304*(1), 43–44.
Charness, G., & Gneezy, U. (2009). Incentives to exercise. *Econometrica, 77*(3), 909–931.
Chater, N., & Loewenstein, G. (2016). The under-appreciated drive for sense-making. *Journal of Economic Behavior & Organization, 126*, 137–154.
Chatman, J. (1991). Matching people and organizations: Selection and socialization in public accounting firms. *Administrative Science Quarterly, 36*(3), 459–484. https://doi.org/10.2307/2393204
Cheung, K. K., Mirzaei, M., & Leeder, S. (2010). Health policy analysis: A tool to evaluate in policy documents the alignment between policy statements and intended outcomes. *Australian Health Review, 34*(4), 405–413.
Chevallier, P., Pouyaud, B., Suarez, W., & Condom, T. (2011). Climate change threats to environment in the tropical Andes: Glaciers and water resources. *Regional Environmental Change, 11*(1), 179–187.
Childers, T. L., & Houston, M. J. (1984). Conditions for a picture-superiority effect on consumer memory. *Journal of Consumer Research, 11*(2), 643. https://doi.org/10.1086/209001
Choi, J. J. (2015). Contributions to defined contribution saving plans. *Annual Review of Financial Economics, 7*, 161–178.
Choi, S. J., & Pritchard, A. C. (2003). Behavioral economics and the SEC. *Stanford Law Review*, 1–73. Retrieved from https://repository.law.umich.edu/cgi/viewcontent.cgi?article=2575&context=articles
Chou, W. Y. S., Hunt, Y. M., Beckjord, E. B., Moser, R. P., & Hesse, B. W. (2009). Social media use in the United States: Implications for health communication. *Journal of Medical Internet Research, 11*(4), e48. https://doi.org/10.2196/jmir.1249
Chou, W. Y. S., Prestin, A., Lyons, C., & Wen, K. Y. (2013, January). Web 2.0 for health promotion: Reviewing the current evidence. *American Journal of Public Health, 103*(1), e9–e18. https://doi.org/10.2105/AJPH.2012.301071
Cialdini, R. B. (2003). Crafting normative messages to protect the environment. *Current Directions in Psychological Science, 12*(4), 105–109. https://doi.org/10.1111/1467-8721.01242
Cialdini, R. B., Reno, R. R., & Kallgren, C. A. (1990). A focus theory of normative conduct: Recycling the concept of norms to reduce littering in public places. *Journal of*

Personality and Social Psychology, *58*(6), 1015–1026. https://doi.org/10.1037/0022-3514.58.6.1015

Cialdini, R. B., & Trost, M. R. (1998). Social influence: Social norms, conformity, and compliance. In D. T. Gilbert, S. T. Fiske, & G. Lindzey (Eds.), *The handbook of social psychology* (pp. 151–192). New York: McGraw-Hill. https://doi.org/10.2307/2654253

Cingano, F. (2014). *Trends in income inequality and its. Impact on economic growth* (OECD Social, Employment and Migration Working Papers, No. 163). Paris: OECD Publishing. https://doi.org/10.1787/5jxrjncwxv6j-en

Clayson, D. E. (2005). Performance overconfidence: Metacognitive effects or misplaced student expectations? *Journal of Marketing Education*, *27*(2), 122–129. https://doi.org/10.1177/0273475304273525

Clemes, S. A., O'Connell, S. E., & Edwardson, C. L. (2014). Office workers' objectively measured sedentary behavior and physical activity during and outside working hours. *Journal of Occupational and Environmental Medicine*, *56*(3), 298–303.

Close, K. L., Baxter, L. S., Ravelojaona, V. A., Rakotoarison, H. N., Bruno, E., Herbert, A., . . . & White, M. C. (2017). Overcoming challenges in implementing the WHO Surgical Safety Checklist: Lessons learnt from using a checklist training course to facilitate rapid scale up in Madagascar, *BMJ Global Health*, *2*(4), 2:e00043. https://doi.org/10.1136/bmjgh-2017-000430

Coelho Do Vale, R., Pieters, P., & Zeelenberg, M. (2008). Flying under the radar: Perverse package size effects on consumption self-regulation. *Journal of Consumer Research*, *35*, 380–390. https://doi.org/10.1086/589564

Cohen, G. L., Garcia, J., Apfel, N., & Master, A. (2006). Reducing the racial achievement gap: A social-psychological intervention. *Science*, *313*(5791), 1307–1310. https://doi.org/10.1126/ science.1128317

Cohen, G. L., Garcia, J., Purdie-Vaughns, V., Apfel, N., & Brzustoski, P. (2009). Recursive processes in self-affirmation: Intervening to close the minority achievement gap. *Science*, *324*(5925), 400–403. https://doi.org/10.1126/science.1170769

Cohen, J. (1992). A power primer. *Psychological Bulletin*, *112*(1), 155–159. https://doi.org/10.1037/0033-2909.112.1.155

Commission on the Future of Higher Education. (2006). *A test of leadership: Charting the future of U.S. higher education*. Washington, DC: U.S. Department of Education.

Committee Horizontal Monitoring Tax and Customs Administration. (2012). *Tax supervision – Made to measure*. Retrieved from http://bit.ly/2MFZEj6

Community Tool Box. (n.d.). *Evaluating community programs and initiatives*. Retrieved from http://ctb.ku.edu/en/table-of-contents/evaluate/evaluation/framework-for-evaluation/main

Condron, D. J., Tope, D., Steidl, C. R., & Freeman, K. J. (2013). Racial segregation and the black/white achievement gap, 1992 to 2009. *The Sociological Quarterly*, *54*(1), 130–157. https://doi.org/10.1111/tsq.12010

Conijn, R., Snijders, C., Kleingeld, A., & Matzat, U. (2017). Predicting student performance from LMS data: A comparison of 17 blended courses using moodle LMS. *IEEE Transactions on Learning Technologies*, *10*(1), 17–29. https://doi.org/10.1109/TLT.2016.2616312

Consumer Financial Protection Bureau. (2013). *A review of the impact of the CARD Act on the consumer credit card market*. CARD Act Report. Retrieved from https://files.consumerfinance.gov/f/201309_cfpb_card-act-report.pdf

Convention on Biological Diversity (CBD). (2010). *Drinking water, biodiversity and development: A good practice guide*. Convention on Biological Diversity. Secretariat of the Convention on Biological Diversity. Montreal. Retrieved from http://bit.ly/2wwON09

Convery, F., McDonnell, S., & Ferreira, S. (2007). The most popular tax in Europe? Lessons from the Irish plastic bags levy. *Environmental and Resource Economics, 38*(1), 1–11.

Copps, J. (2011). *'If you treasure it, measure it': The UK Civil Service's response to well-being*. NPC's Well-Being Measure blog. Retrieved from http://bit.ly/2Pkm46G

Cowling, T. G. (1955). The letters of Johann Bernoulli. *Nature, 176*, 1187.

Crompton, P., & Wu, Y. (2005). Energy consumption in China: Past trends and future directions. *Energy Economics, 27*(1), 195–208.

Croy, G., Gerrans, P., & Speelman, C. (2010). Injunctive social norms primacy over descriptive social norms in retirement savings decisions. *The International Journal of Aging and Human Development, 71*(4), 259–282. https://doi.org/10.2190/ag.71.4.a

Dagevos, H., & Voordouw, J. (2013). Sustainability and meat consumption: Is reduction realistic? *Sustainability: Science, Practice and Policy, 9*(2), 60–69.

Dahill-Brown, S. E., Witte, J. F., & Wolfe, B. (2016). Income and access to higher education: Are high quality universities becoming more or less elite? A longitudinal case study of admissions at UW-Madison. *RSF: The Russell Sage Foundation Journal of the Social Sciences, 2*(1), 69–89.

Dahlstrom, M. F. (2010). The role of causality in information acceptance in narratives: An example from science communication. *Communication Research, 37*(6), 857–875.

Dahlstrom, M. F. (2014). Using narratives and storytelling to communicate science with nonexpert audiences. *Proceedings of the National Academy of Sciences, 111*(Suppl. 4), 13614–13620.

Dahlstrom, M. F., & Ho, S. S. (2012). Ethical considerations of using narrative to communicate science. *Science Communication, 34*(5), 592–617.

Dalkey, N. C. (1967). *Delphi*. The RAND Corporation, Santa Monica, CA. Retrieved from www.rand.org/content/dam/rand/pubs/papers/2006/P3704.pdf

Damgaard, M. T., & Nielsen, H. S. (2017). *The use of nudges and other behavioural approaches in education* (EENEE Analytic Report No. 29). Luxembourg: Publications Office of the European Union.

Danaher, K., & Crandall, C. S. (2008). Stereotype threat in applied settings re-examined. *Journal of Applied Social Psychology, 38*(6), 1639–1655. https://doi.org/10.1111/j.1559-1816.2008.00362.x

Danaher, P. J., & Rossiter, J. R. (2011). Comparing perceptions of marketing communication channels. *European Journal of Marketing, 45*(1/2), 6–42.

Davidson, B. (2017). Storytelling and evidence-based policy: Lessons from the grey literature. *Palgrave Communications, 3*.

Davies, S. C. (2014). *Annual report of the Chief Medical Officer 2013: Public mental health priorities – Investing in the evidence*. London: Department of Health and Social Care.

Davies, W. (2015). *The happiness industry: How the government and big business sold us well-being*. New York: Verso Books.

de Beer, L., Pienaar, J., & Rothmann, S. (2015). Work overload, burnout, and psychological ill-health symptoms: A three-wave mediation model of the employee health impairment process. *Anxiety, Stress, & Coping, 29*(4), 387–399. https://doi.org/10.1080/10615806.2015.1061123

de Brey, C., Musu, L., McFarland, J., Wilkinson-Flicker, S., Diliberti, M., Zhang, A., . . . & Wang, X. (2019). *Status and trends in the education of racial and ethnic groups 2018* (NCES 2019-038). National Center for Education Statistics.

de Bruin, W. B., & Bostrom, A. (2013). Assessing what to address in science communication. *Proceedings of the National Academy of Sciences, 110*(Suppl. 3), 14062–14068.

de Castro e Lima Baesse, D., Grisolia, A. M., & de Oliveira, A. E. F. (2016). Pedagogical monitoring as a tool to reduce dropout in distance learning in family health. *BMC Medical Education, 16*(1), 1–8. https://doi.org/10.1186/s12909-016-0735-9

Dechausay, N., & Anzelone, C. (2016). *Cutting through complexity: Using behavioral science to improve Indiana's Child Care Subsidy Program* (OPRE Report 2016–03). Washington, DC: Office of Planning, Research and Evaluation, Administration for Children and Families, U.S. Department of Health and Human Services. Retrieved from www.mdrc.org/sites/default/files/Cutting_through_Complexity_FR.pdf

Dechausay, N., Anzelone, C., & Reardon, L. (2015). *The power of prompts: Using behavioral insights to encourage people to participate*. Washington, DC: Office of Planning, Research & Evaluation.

Deci, E. L., Koestner, R., & Ryan, R. (1999). A meta-analytic review of experiments examining the effects of extrinsic rewards on intrinsic motivation. *Psychological Bulletin, 125*(6), 627–668. https://doi.org/10.1037//0033-2909.125.6.627

Deci, E. L., Koestner, R., & Ryan, R. M. (2001). Extrinsic rewards and intrinsic motivation in education: Reconsidered once again. *Review of Educational Research, 71*(1), 1–27.

Deci, E. L., & Ryan, R. M. (1975). *Intrinsic motivation*. New York: John Wiley & Sons, Inc.

Deci, E. L., & Ryan, R. M. (1980). Self-determination theory: When mind mediates behavior. *The Journal of Mind and Behavior, 1*(1), 33–43.

Deci, E. L., & Ryan, R. M. (1985). *Intrinsic motivation and self-determination in human behavior*. New York: Plenum Publishing Co.

Deci, E. L., Ryan, R. M., & Koestner, R. (1999). A meta-analytic review of experiments examining the effects of extrinsic rewards on intrinsic motivation. *Psychological Bulletin, 125*(6), 627–668.

DeCicca, P., Kenkel, D., & Mathios, A. (2002). Putting out the fires: Will higher taxes reduce the onset of youth smoking? *Journal of Political Economy, 110*(1), 144–169. https://doi.org/10.1086/324386

Dee, T. S. (2015). Social identity and achievement gaps: Evidence from an affirmation intervention. *Journal of Research on Educational Effectiveness, 8*(2), 149–168. https://doi.org/10.1080/19345747.2014.906009

De Grauwe, P. (2012). *Lectures on behavioral macroeconomics*. Princeton, NJ: Princeton University Press.

de Jong, T., Linn, M. C., & Zacharia, Z. C. (2013). Physical and virtual laboratories in science and engineering education. *Science, 340*(6130), 305–308. https://doi.org/10.1126/science.1230579

DeJong, W., Schneider, S. K., Towvim, L. G., Murphy, M. J., Doerr, E. E., Simonsen, N. R., . . . & Scribner, R. A. (2006). A multisite randomized trial of social norms marketing campaigns to reduce college student drinking. *Journal of Studies on Alcohol, 67*(6), 868–879. https://doi.org/10.15288/jsa.2006.67.868

DeJong, W., Schneider, S. K., Towvim, L. G., Murphy, M. J., Doerr, E. E., Simonsen, N. R., . . . & Scribner, R. A. (2009). A multisite randomized trial of social norms marketing campaigns to reduce college student drinking: A replication failure. *Substance Abuse, 30*(2), 127–140. https://doi.org/10.1080/08897070902802059

de Leeuw, A., Valois, P., Ajzen, I., & Schmidt, P. (2015). Using the theory of planned behavior to identify key beliefs underlying pro-environmental behavior in high-school students: Implications for educational interventions. *Journal of Environmental Psychology, 42*, 128–138.

Deluca, P., et al. (2007). Cost-utility analysis. In M. S. Ritsner & A. G. Awad (Eds.), *Quality of life impairment in schizophrenia, mood and anxiety disorders*. Dordrecht: Springer.

Deluca, P., et al. (2012). Identifying emerging trends in recreational drug use: Outcomes from the Psychonaut Web Mapping Project. *Progress in Neuro-Psychopharmacology and Biological Psychiatry, 39*(2), 221–226.

De Martino, B., Kumaran, D., Seymour, B., & Dolan, R. J. (2006). Frames, biases, and rational decision-making in the human brain. *Science, 313*(5787), 684–687.

Demeritt, A. D., & Hoff, K. (2018). *The making of behavioral development economics* (World Bank Policy Research Working Paper No. 8317). Retrieved from SSRN https://ssrn.com/abstract=3109075

de Paola, M., Scoppa, V., & Nisticò, R. (2012). Monetary incentives and student achievement in a depressed labor market: Results from a randomized experiment. *Journal of Human Capital, 6*(1), 56–85. https://doi.org/10.1086/664795

Department of Energy & Climate Change. (2012). *Green deal: Final impact assessment*. Retrieved from www.gov.uk/government/publications/green-deal-impact-assessment

Department for Environment, Food & Rural Affairs. (2016). *Single-use plastic carrier bags charge: Data in England for 2015 to 2016*. Retrieved from www.gov.uk/government/publications/carrier-bag-charge-summary-of-data-in-england/single-use-plastic-carrier-bags-charge-data-in-england-for-2015-to-2016

Department for Environment, Food & Rural Affairs. (2017). *Single-use plastic carrier bags charge: Data in England for 2016 to 2017*. Retrieved from www.gov.uk/government/publications/carrier-bag-charge-summary-of-data-in-england/single-use-plastic-carrier-bags-charge-data-in-england-for-2016-to-2017

Department for Environment, Food & Rural Affairs. (2018). *Single-use plastic carrier bags charge: Data in England for 2017 to 2018*. Retrieved from www.gov.uk/government/publications/carrier-bag-charge-summary-of-data-in-england/single-use-plastic-carrier-bags-charge-data-in-england-for-2017-to-2018

Department for Work and Pensions. (2013). *Automatic enrolment: Qualitative research with large employers*. Gov.uk. Retrieved from www.gov.uk/government/publications/automatic-enrolment-qualitative-research-with-large-employers-rr851

Department of Health and Human Services. (2013). *Prescribers with questionable patterns in Medicare part D*. Office of Inspector General. Retrieved from https://oig.hhs.gov/oei/reports/oei-02-09-00603.pdf

Dernovsek, M. Z., Prevolnik-Rupel, V., & Tavcar, R. (2007). Cost-utility analysis. In M. S. Ritsner & A. G. Awad (Eds.), *Quality of life impairment in schizophrenia, mood and anxiety disorders*. Dordrecht: Springer.

Derous, E., Ryan, A., & Nguyen, H. (2011). Multiple categorization in resume screening: Examining effects on hiring discrimination against Arab applicants in field and lab settings. *Journal of Organizational Behavior, 33*(4), 544–570. https://doi.org/10.1002/job.769

DeSantis, C., Ma, J., Bryan, L., & Jemal, A. (2014). Breast cancer statistics, 2013. *A Cancer Journal for Clinicians, 64*(1), 52–62.

Devoto, F., Dulfo, E., Dupas, P., Parienté, W., & Pons, V. (2012). Happiness on tap: Piped water adoption in urban Morocco. *American Economic Journal: Economic Policy, 4*(4), 68–99.

Diaye, M. A., & Urdanivia, M. W. (2009). Violation of the transitivity axiom may explain why, in empirical studies, a significant number of subjects violate GARP. *Journal of Mathematical Psychology, 53*(6), 586–592.
Diener, E. (2006). Guidelines for national indicators of subjective well-being and ill-being. *Journal of Happiness Studies, 7*(4), 397–404.
Diener, E. (2009). *Well-being for public policy*. New York: Oxford University Press.
Diener, E. (2018). Social well-being: Research and policy recommendations. In Global Happiness Council (Ed.), *Global happiness policy report 2018* (pp. 129–158). Retrieved from www.happinesscouncil.org/
Diener, E., & Seligman, M. E. (2004). Beyond money: Toward an economy of well-being. *Psychological Science in the Public Interest, 5*(1), 1–31.
DiMaggio, P. (1997). Culture and cognition. *Annual Review of Sociology, 23*, 263–287.
Dirks, K. T., & Ferrin, D. L. (2002). Trust in leadership: Meta-analytic findings and implications for research and practice. *Journal of Applied Psychology, 87*, 611–628.
Doctor, J. N., Nguyen, A., Lev, R., Lucas, J., Knight, T., Zhao, H., & Menchine, M. (2018). Opioid prescribing decreases after learning of a patient's fatal overdose. *Science, 361*(6402), 588–590. https://doi.org/10.1126/science.aat4595
Dodge, R., Daly, A. P., Huyton, J., & Sanders, L. D. (2012). The challenge of defining wellbeing. *International Journal of Wellbeing, 2*(3).
Doern, G. B., & Wilson, V. S. (1974). The concept of regulation and regulatory reform. In *Issues in Canadian public policy* (pp. 8–35). Toronto: Macmillan.
Dolan, P., & Galizzi, M. M. (2015). Like ripples on a pond: Behavioral spillovers and their consequences for research and policy. *Journal of Economic Psychology, 47*, 1–16.
Dolan, P., Hallsworth, M., Halpern, D., King, D., Metcalfe, R., & Vlaev, I. (2012). Influencing behaviour: The mindspace way. *Journal of Economic Psychology, 33*(1), 264–277. https://doi.org/10.1016/j.joep.2011.10.009
Doss, C., Fahle, E. M., Loeb, S., & York, B. N. (2017). *Supporting parenting through differentiated and personalized text-messaging: Testing effects on learning during kindergarten* (CEPA Working Paper No. 16–18). Retrieved from Stanford Center for Education Policy Analysis http://cepa.stanford.edu/wp16-18
Doyle, Y. G., Furey, A., & Flowers, J. (2006). Sick individuals and sick populations: 20 years later. *Journal of Epidemiology and Community Health, 60*(5), 396–398. https://doi.org/10.1136/jech.2005.042770
Drechsler, M., Eppink, F. V., & Wätzold, F. (2011). Does proactive biodiversity conservation save costs? *Biodiversity and Conservation, 20*(5), 1045–1055. https://doi.org/10.1007/s10531-011-0013-4
Druckman, J. N. (2001). The implications of framing effects for citizen competence. *Political Behavior, 23*(3), 225–256.
Drummond, M. F., Sculpher, M. J., Claxton, K., Stoddart, G. L., & Torrance, G. W. (2015). *Methods for the economic evaluation of healthcare programmes*. Oxford: Oxford University Press.
Duckworth, A. L., White, R. E., Matteucci, A. J., Shearer, A., & Gross, J. J. (2016). A stitch in time: Strategic self-control in high school and college students. *Journal of Educational Psychology, 108*(3), 329. https://doi.org/10.1037/edu0000062
Dunn, E. W., Aknin, L. B., & Norton, M. I. (2014). Prosocial spending and happiness. *Current Directions in Psychological Science, 23*(1), 41–47. https://doi.org/10.1177/0963721413512503

Dunn, E. W., Gilbert, D. T., & Wilson, T. D. (2011). If money doesn't make you happy, then you probably aren't spending it right. *Journal of Consumer Psychology*, *21*(2), 115–125. https://doi.org/10.1016/j.jcps.2011.02.002

Dweck, C. S. (2006). *Mindset: The new psychology of success*. New York: Ballantine Books.

Easterlin, R. A. (2013). Happiness, growth, and public policy. *Economic Inquiry*, *51*(1), 1–15. https://doi.org/10.1111/j.1465-7295.2012.00505.x

Ebeling, F., & Lotz, S. (2015). Domestic uptake of green energy promoted by opt-out tariffs. *Nature Climate Change*, *5*(9), 868–871. https://doi.org/10.1038/nclimate2681

Eccles, J. S., Adler, T. F., Futterman, R., Goff, S. B., & Kaczala, C. M. (1983). Expectancies, values, and academic behaviors. In J. T. Spence (Ed.), *Achievement and achievement motivation* (pp. 75–146). San Francisco, CA: Freeman.

Eccles, J. S., & Wigfield, A. (2002). Motivational beliefs, values, and goals. *Annual Review of Psychology*, *53*(1), 109–132. Retrieved from https://bit.ly/2Gri6Z8

Economic and Social Research Council (ESRC). (2017). *What is impact*? Retrieved from www.esrc.ac.uk/research/impact-toolkit/what-is-impact

Eddy, D. M. (1982). Probabilistic reasoning in clinical medicine: Problems and opportunities. In D. Kahneman, P. Slovic, & A. Tversky (Eds.), *Judgment under uncertainty: Heuristics and BIASES* (pp. 249–267). Cambridge: Cambridge University Press.

Egebark, J., & Ekström, M. (2016). Can indifference make the world greener? *Journal of Environmental Economics and Management*, *76*, 1–13. https://doi.org/10.1016/j.jeem.2015.11.004

Einhorn, H. J., & Hogarth, R. M. (1978). Confidence in judgment: Persistence of the illusion of validity. *Psychological Review*, *85*(5), 395–416. https://doi.org/10.1037/0033-295X.85.5.395

El Chammay, R. (2017). A policy implementer's perspective. *World Psychiatry*, *16*(1), 43–44. https://doi.org/10.1002/wps.20379

Ellingsen, T., & Johannesson, M. (2005). *Trust as an incentive*. Stockholm School of Economics mimeo. Preliminary version.

Ellsberg, D. (1961). Risk, ambiguity, and the savage axioms. *Quarterly Journal of Economics*, *75*(4), 643–669.

El-Masri, M., & Tarhini, A. (2017). Factors affecting the adoption of e-learning systems in Qatar and USA: Extending the Unified Theory of Acceptance and Use of Technology 2 (UTAUT2). *Educational Technology Research and Development*, 1–21. https://doi.org/10.1007/s11423-016-9508-8

El Nokali, N. E., Bachman, H. J., & Votruba-Drzal, E. (2010). Parent involvement and children's academic and social development in elementary school. *Child Development*, *81*(3), 988–1005. https://doi.org/10.1111/j.1467-8624.2010.01447.x

Elsen, M., van Giesen, R., & Leenheer, J. (2015). *Milan BExpo 2015: A behavioural study on food choices and eating habits*. Brussels: Consumers, Health, Agriculture and Food Executive Agency (CHAFEA). Retrieved from https://bit.ly/2N0LKrm

Employee Benefit Research Institute (EBRI). (2005). *How to increase worker savings? 401(k)s provide ideas*. Washington, DC: EBRI News.

Erbach, G. (2015). *Energy union new impetus for coordination and integration of energy policies in the EU* (Policy Report 1). European Parliament: Members' Research Service PE 551.310.

Ericson, K. M. M., Kingsdale, J., Layton, T., & Sacarny, A. (2017). Nudging leads consumers in Colorado to shop but not switch ACA Marketplace plans. *Health Affairs*, *36*(2), 311–319. https://doi.org/10.1377/hlthaff.2016.0993

Ericsson, K. A., Krampe, R. T., & Tesch-Römer, C. (1993). The role of deliberate practice in the acquisition of expert performance. *Psychological Review, 100*(3), 363–406.

European Commission. (2010). *Questions & answers: New energy labels for televisions, refrigerators, dishwashers and washing machines*. Brussels: European Commission. MEMO/10/451. Retrieved from https://bit.ly/2ooKh0d

European Commission. (2016). *Behavioural insights applied to policies*. Brussels: European Commission. Retrieved from https://bit.ly/2LEiaTO

European Network for Workplace Health Promotion (ENWHP). (1997). *Luxembourg declaration on workplace health promotion in the European Union*. Retrieved from www.enwhp.org

Everett, J. A., Caviola, L., Kahane, G., Savulescu, J., & Faber, N. S. (2015). Doing good by doing nothing? The role of social norms in explaining default effects in altruistic contexts. *European Journal of Social Psychology, 45*(2), 230–241. https://doi.org/10.1002/ejsp.2080

Fabian, H., & Dunlop, A. W. (2007). *Outcomes of good practice in transition processes for children entering primary school* (Working Papers in Early Childhood Development, No. 42). The Hague: Bernard van Leer Foundation.

Falk, A., Becker, A., Dohmen, T., Enke, B., Huffman, D., & Sunde, U. (2018). Global evidence on economic preferences. *The Quarterly Journal of Economics, 133*(4), 1645–1692.

Falkinger, J., Fehr, E., Gächter, S., & Winter-Ember, R. (2000). A simple mechanism for the efficient provision of public goods: Experimental evidence. *American Economic Review, 90*(1), 247–264.

Farrell, M., Smith, J., Reardon, L., & Obara, E. (2016). *Framing the message: Using behavioral economics to engage TANF recipients*. Washington, DC: Office of Planning, Research & Evaluation.

Farrington, C., Aristidou, A., & Ruggeri, K. (2014). mHealth and global mental health: Still waiting for the mH 2 wedding? *Globalization and Health, 10*(1), 17. https://doi.org/10.1186%2F1744-8603-10-17

Farver-Vestergaard, I., & Ruggeri, K. (2017). Setting national policy agendas in light of the Denmark results for well-being. *JAMA Psychiatry, 74*(8), 773–774. https://doi.org/10.1001/jamapsychiatry.2017.1330

Fast, N. J., Sivanathan, N., Mayer, N. D., & Galinsky, A. D. (2012). Power and overconfident decision-making. *Organizational Behavior and Human Decision Processes, 117*(2), 249–260. https://doi.org/0.1016/j.obhdp.2011.11.009

Faulkner, G., Dale, L., & Lau, E. (2019). Examining the use of loyalty point incentives to encourage health and fitness centre participation. *Preventive Medicine Reports, 14*, 100831.

Feldstein, M. (2008). Effects of taxes on economic behavior. *National Tax Journal, 61*(1), 131–139.

Ferguson, E., Bibby, P. A., Leaviss, J., & Weyman, A. (2003). *Effective design of workplace risk communications*. HSE Books.

Fernandes, D., Lynch Jr, J. G., & Netemeyer, R. G. (2014). Financial literacy, financial education, and downstream financial behaviors. *Management Science, 60*(8), 1861–1883. https://doi.org/10.1287

Ferraro, P. J., Miranda, J. J., & Price, M. K. (2011). The persistence of treatment effects with norm-based policy instruments: Evidence from a randomized environmental policy experiment. *American Economic Review, 101*(3), 318–322. https://doi.org/10.1257/aer.101.3.318

Fertman, C. I., & Allensworth, D. D. (2016). *Health promotion programs: From theory to practice.* San Francisco, CA: John Wiley & Sons.
Festinger, L. (1954). A theory of social comparison processes. *Human Relations, 7*(2), 117–140.
Financial Conduct Authority. (2015). *Message received? The impact of annual summaries, text alerts and mobile apps on consumer banking behaviour* (FCA Occasional Papers in Financial Regulation, 10). Retrieved from www.fca.org.uk/static/documents/occasional-papers/occasional-paper-10.pdf
Financial Conduct Authority. (2016). *Our responsibilities: Mutual societies.* Retrieved from www.fca.org.uk/firms/our-responsibilities-mutual-societies
Fischer, A. R. H., Wentholt, M. T. A., Rowe, G., & Frewer, L. J. (2014). Expert involvement in policy development: A systematic review of current practice. *Science and Public Policy, 41*(3), 332–343. https://doi.org/10.1093/scipol/sct062
Flore, P. C., & Wicherts, J. M. (2015). Does stereotype threat influence performance of girls in stereotyped domains? A meta-analysis. *Journal of School Psychology, 53*(1), 25–44.
Flowers, J., Bailey, K., Streather, M., & Wilkinson, J. (2004). *Indications of public health in the English regions.* Stockton: Association of Public Health Observatories.
Foliano, F., Rolfe, H., Buzzeo, J., Runge, J., & Wilkinson, D. (2019). *Changing mindsets: Effectiveness trial.* London: National Institute of Economic and Social Research.
Food and Agriculture Organization of the United Nations (FAO). (2012). *The state of food and agriculture.* Rome: FAO. Retrieved from www.fao.org/docrep/017/i3028e/ i3028e.pdf
Fox, D. M. (2005). Evidence of evidence-based health policy: The politics of systematic reviews in coverage decisions. *Health Affairs, 24*(1), 114–122. https://doi.org/10.1377/hlthaff.24.1.114
Fox, S., & Bernhardt, J. M. (2010). Health communication 2.0: The promise of peer participation. In L. F. Rutten, B. W. Hesse, R. P. Moser, & G. L. Kreps (Eds.), *Building the evidence base in cancer communication* (pp. 257–270). Cresskill, NJ: Hampton Press.
Fox, T., & Fimeche, C. (2013). *Global food: Waste not, want not.* London: Institution of Mechanical Engineers.
Frank, B., & Kirchler, E. (2006). Günter Schmölders and economic psychology: An introduction. In G. Schmölders (Ed.), *The psychology of money and public finance.* New York: Palgrave Macmillan.
Frankel, F., & DePace, A. H. (2012). *Visual strategies: A practical guide to graphics for scientists and engineers.* New Haven, CT: Yale University Press.
Frederick, S., & Loewenstein, G. (1999). Hedonic adaptation. In D. Kahneman, N. Schwarz, & E. Diener (Eds.), *Well-being: The foundations of hedonic psychology* (pp. 302–329). New York: Russell Sage Foundation.
Frederick, S., Loewenstein, G., & O'Donoghue, T. (2002). Time discounting and time preference: A critical review. In G. Loewenstein, D. Read, & R. Baumeister (Eds.), *Time and decision: Economic and psychological perspectives on intertemporal choice* (pp. 13–86). New York: Russell Sage Foundation.
Frederiks, E. R., Stenner, K., & Hobman, E. V. (2015). Household energy use: Applying behavioural economics to understand consumer decision-making and behaviour. *Renewable and Sustainable Energy Reviews, 41*, 1385–1394. https://doi.org/10.1016/j.rser.2014.09.026
Free, C., Knight, R., Robertson, S., Whittaker, R., Edwards, P., Zhou, W., . . . & Roberts, I. (2011). Smoking cessation support delivered via mobile phone text messaging (txt2stop): A single-blind, randomised trial. *The Lancet, 378*, 49–55. https://doi.org/10.1016/S0140-6736(11)60701-0

Frey, B. S., & Goette, L. (1999). *Does pay motivate volunteers?* Zurich: Institute for Empirical Research in Economics, University of Zurich. Retrieved from www.econ.uzh.ch/static/wp_iew/iewwp007.pdf

Frey, B. S., & Oberholzer-Gee, F. (1997). The cost of price incentives: An empirical analysis of motivation crowding-out. *The American Economic Review, 87*(4), 746–755. Retrieved from www.jstor.org/stable/2951373

Fryer Jr, R. G., Levitt, S. D., List, J., & Sadoff, S. (2012). *Enhancing the efficacy of teacher incentives through loss aversion: A field experiment* (No. w18237). National Bureau of Economic Research. Retrieved from https://bit.ly/2BYTrdl

Fuchs, C. (2011). An alternative view of privacy on Facebook. *Information, 2*(1), 140–165. https://doi.org/10.3390/info2010140

Fullwood, J. (2016). *A cat, a hat and a simple measure of gobbledygook: How readable is your writing?* Retrieved from https://bit.ly/2d1519i

Gabriel, D. C., James, J. C., David, L., Madrian, C. B., & Andrew, M. (2009). Optimal defaults and active decisions. *Quarterly Journal of Economics, 124*(4), 1639–1674. https://doi.org/10.1162/qjec.2009.124.4.1639

Galesic, M., & Garcia-Retamero, R. (2010). Statistical numeracy for health: A cross-cultural comparison with probabilistic national samples. *Archives of Internal Medicine, 170*(5), 462–468. https://doi.org/10.1001/archinternmed.2009.481

Galizzi, M. M. (2014). What is really behavioural in behavioural health policies? And, does it work? *Applied Economics Perspectives and Policy, 36*(1), 25–60.

Galizzi, M. M. (2017). Behavioral aspects of policy formulation: Experiments, behavioral insights, nudges. In M. Howlett & I. Mukherjee (Eds.), *Handbook of policy formulation* (Handbooks of Research on Public Policy Series). Cheltenham, UK: Edward Elgar Publishing. ISBN: 9781784719319.

Galizzi, M. M., & Whitmarsh, L. E. (2019). How to measure behavioral spillovers: A methodological review and checklist. *Frontiers in Psychology, 10*, 342. https://doi.org/10.3389/fpsyg.2019.00342

Gallagher, K. M., & Updegraff, J. A. (2012). Health message framing effects on attitudes, intentions, and behavior: A meta-analytic review. *Annals of Behavioral Medicine, 43*(1), 101–116. https://doi.org/10.1007/s12160-011-9308-7

Galton, F. (1907). Vox populi (The wisdom of the crowds). *Nature, 75*, 450–451.

Gangl, K., Hofmann, E., & Kirchler, E. (2015). Tax authorities' interaction with taxpayers: A conception of compliance in social dilemmas by power and trust. *New Ideas in Psychology, 37*, 13–23. https://doi.org/10.1016/j.newideapsych.2014.12.001

Garbers, Y., & Konradt, U. (2013). The effect of financial incentives on performance: A quantitative review of individual and team-based financial incentives. *Journal of Occupational and Organizational Psychology, 87*(1), 102–137. https://doi.org/10.1111/joop.12039

Garfein, R. S., & Doshi, R. P. (2019). Synchronous and asynchronous video observed therapy (VOT) for tuberculosis treatment adherence monitoring and support. *Journal of Clinical Tuberculosis and Other Mycobacterial Diseases, 17*, 100098. https://doi.org/10.1016/j.jctube.2019.100098

Gastwirth, J. L. (1972). The estimation of the Lorenz Curve and Gini Index. *The Review of Economics and Statistics, 54*(3), 306–316.

Gatineau, M., & Dent, M. (2011). *Obesity and mental health.* Oxford: National Obesity Observatory.

GBD 2016 Alcohol Collaborators. (2018). Alcohol use and burden: A systematic analysis from the Global Burden of Disease Study 2016 for 195 countries and territories, 1990–2016. *The Lancet*, *6736*(18), 1–21. https://doi.org/10.1016/S0140-6736(18)31310-2

Gehlbach, H., Brinkworth, M. E., King, A. M., Hsu, L. M., McIntyre, J., & Rogers, T. (2016). Creating birds of similar feathers: Leveraging similarity to improve teacher–student relationships and academic achievement. *Journal of Educational Psychology*, *108*(3), 342–352. https://doi.org/10.1037/edu0000042

Gehlbach, H., & Robinson, C. D. (2018). Mitigating illusory results through preregistration in education. *Journal of Research on Educational Effectiveness*, *11*(2), 296–315. https://doi.org/10.1080/19345747.2017.1387950

Gentile, M., Linciano, N., Lucarelli, C., & Soccorso, S. (2015). *Financial disclosure, risk perception and investment choices: Evidence from a consumer testing exercise* (CONSOB Working Papers No. 82). Rome.

Gershenson, S., Hart, C., Hyman, J., Lindsay, C., & Papageorge, N. W. (2018). *The long-run impacts of same-race teachers* (No. w25254). National Bureau of Economic Research.

Gertler, P. J., Martinez, S., Premand, P., Rawlings, L. B., & Vermeersch, C. M. (2016). *Impact evaluation in practice*. Washington, DC: World Bank Publications.

Giest, S., & Mukherjee, I. (2018). Behavioral instruments in renewable energy and the role of big data: A policy perspective. *Energy Policy*, *123*, 360–366. https://doi.org/10.1016/j.enpol.2018.09.006

Gifford, R., Scannell, L., Kormos, C., Smolova, L., Biel, A., Boncu, S., . . . & Kaiser, F. G. (2009). Temporal pessimism and spatial optimism in environmental assessments: An 18-nation study. *Journal of Environmental Psychology*, *29*(1), 1–12.

Gigerenzer, G. (2008). Why heuristics work. *Perspectives on Psychological Science*, *3*(1), 20–29.

Gigerenzer, G. (2015). *Risk savvy: How to make good decisions*. London: Penguin.

Gigerenzer, G., & Brighton, H. (2009). Homo heuristicus: Why biased minds make better inferences. *Topics in Cognitive Science*, *1*(1), 107–143.

Gigerenzer, G., & Gaissmaier, W. (2011). Heuristic decision-making. *Annual Review of Psychology*, *62*, 451–482.

Gigerenzer, G., & Goldstein, D. G. (1996). Reasoning the fast and frugal way: Models of bounded rationality. *Psychological Review*, *103*(4), 650–669.

Gigerenzer, G., Hoffrage, U., & Kleinbolting, H. (1991). Probabilistic mental models: A Brunswikian theory of confidence. *Psychological Review*, *98*(4), 506–528.

Gigerenzer, G., & Kurzenhauser, S. (2005). Fast and frugal heuristics in medical decision-making. In R. Bibace, J. D. Laird, K. L. Noller, & J. Valsiner (Eds.), *Science and medicine in dialogue: Thinking through particulars and universals* (pp. 3–15). Westport, CT: Praeger.

Gigerenzer, G., & Selten, R. (2002). *Bounded rationality: The adaptive toolbox* (Vol. 1). London: MIT Press.

Gigerenzer, G., Todd, P. M., & The ABC Research Group. (1999). *Simple heuristics that make us smart*. Oxford: Oxford University Press.

Giles, E., Robalino, S., McColl, E., Sniehotta, F., & Adams, J. (2014). The effectiveness of financial incentives for health behaviour change: Systematic review and meta-analysis. *PLoS ONE*, *9*(3). https://doi.org/10.1371/journal.pone.0090347

Gino, F. (2017, October 10). The rise of behavioral economics and its influence on organizations. *Harvard Business Review*.

Glasziou, P. (2004). Assessing the quality of research. *BMJ, 328*(7430), 39–41. https://doi.org/10.1136/bmj.328.7430.39

Glen, A. (2017). *Career pathways: One city working together*. Retrieved from www1.nyc.gov/assets/careerpathways/downloads/pdf/career-pathways-full-report.pdf

Glenn, T., & Monteith, S. (2014). New measures of mental state and behavior based on data collected from sensors, smartphones, and the internet. *Current Psychiatry Reports, 16*, 523. https://doi.org/10.1007/s11920-014-0523-3

Glimcher, P. W., & Fehr, E. (2008). *Neuroeconomics: Decision making and the brain*. London, UK, Waltham, MA, and San Diego, CA: Academic Press. ISBN: 978-0-12-416008-8

Global Fund Advocates Network (GFAN). (n.d.). *Here I am campaign*. Retrieved from www.globalfundadvocatesnetwork.org/campaigns/here-i-am-campaign/#.WeCYKmi0PIU

Gneezy, U., Meier, S., & Rey-Biel, P. (2011). When and why incentives (don't) work to modify behavior. *Journal of Economic Perspectives, 25*(4), 191–210.

Gneezy, U., Niederle, M., & Rustichini, A. (2003). Performance in competitive environments: Gender differences. *The Quarterly Journal of Economics, 118*(3), 1049–1074. https://doi.org/10.1162/00335530360698496

Gneezy, U., & Rustichini, A. (2000). A fine is a price. *The Journal of Legal Studies, 29*(1), 1.

Goh, J., Pfeffer, J., & Zenios, S. A. (2015). Workplace stressors and health outcomes: Health policy for the workplace. *Behavioral Science & Policy, 1*(1), 43–52.

Goldstein, N. J., Cialdini, R. B., & Griskevicius, V. (2008). A room with a viewpoint: Using social norms to motivate environmental conservation in hotels. *Journal of Consumer Research, 35*(3), 472–482.

Gonzalez-Zapata, L. I., Ortiz-Moncada, R., & Alvarez-Dardet, C. (2007). Mapping public policy options responding to obesity: The case of Spain. *Obesity Review, 8*(2), 99–108. https://doi.org/10.1111/j.1467-789X.2007.00365.x

Gornall, J., Betts, R., Burke, E., Clark, R., Camp, J., Willett, K., & Wiltshire, A. (2010). Implications of climate change for agricultural productivity in the early twenty-first century. *Philosophical Transactions of the Royal Society B: Biological Sciences, 365*(1554), 2973–2989.

Gosnell, G., List, J., & Metcalfe, R. (2016). *A new approach to an age-old problem: Solving externalities by incenting workers directly* (GRI Working Papers 262). Grantham Research Institute on Climate Change and the Environment. https://doi.org/10.3386/w22316

Government of Canada. (2016). *Demographic snapshot of Canada's federal public service, 2017*. Retrieved April 4, 2020 from https://bit.ly/3bidalm

Government of Ontario. (2016). *Behavioural Insights pilot project – Organ donor registration*. Retrieved October 11, 2018 from https://bit.ly/2yplt0l

The Government & Public Sector Practice. (2018). *Driving online tax payments in Kenya*. Retrieved from http://sites.wpp.com/govtpractice/reports/our-work-ogilvy-kra/

Green, L., Fry, A. F., & Myerson, J. (1994). Discounting of delayed rewards: A life-span comparison. *Psychological Science, 5*(1), 33–36. https://doi.org/10.1111/j.1467-9280.1994. tb00610.x

Green, L., Myerson, J., & Macaux, E. W. (2005). Temporal discounting when the choice is between two delayed rewards. *Journal of Experimental Psychology: Learning, Memory, and Cognition, 31*(5), 1121–1133.

Green, M. C. (2006). Narratives and cancer communication. *Journal of Communication, 56*(1), S163–S183.

Green, M. C., & Brock, T. C. (2002). In the mind's eye: Transportation-imagery model of narrative persuasion. In M. C. Green, J. J. Strange, & T. C. Brock (Eds.), *Narrative impact: Social and cognitive foundations* (pp. 315–341). Mahwah, NJ: Lawrence Erlbaum.

Greenhalgh, T., & Russell, J. (2006). Reframing evidence synthesis as rhetorical action in the policy making drama. *Healthcare Policy/Politiques De Santé*, *1*(2), 34–42. https://doi.org/10.12927/hcpol.2006.17873

Greening, L. A., Greene, D. L., & Difiglio, C. (2000). Energy efficiency and consumption – The rebound effect – A survey. *Energy Policy*, *28*(6–7), 389–401. https://doi.org/10.1016/S0301-4215(00)0021-5

Gregg, P., & Washbrook, E. (2011). The socio-economic gradient in child outcomes: The role of attitudes, behaviours and beliefs. *Longitudinal and Life Course Studies*, *2*(1), 41–58. https://doi.org/10.14301/llcs.v2i1.142

Gregrich, R. J. (2003). A note to researchers: Communicating science to policy makers and practitioners. *Journal of Substance Abuse Treatment*, *25*(3), 233–237.

Grijalva, C. G., Griffin, M. R., & Page, P. (2013). Antibiotic prescription rates for acute respiratory tract infections in US ambulatory settings. *JAMA*, *302*(7), 758–766. https://doi.org/10.1001/jama.2009.1163

Grimshaw, J. M., Eccles, M. P., Lavis, J. N., Hill, S. J., & Squires, J. E. (2012). Knowledge translation of research findings. *Implementation Science*, *7*(1), 50.

Griskevicius, V., Van den Bergh, B., & Tybur, J. M. (2010). Going green to be seen? Status, reputation and conspicuous conservation. *Journal of Personality and Social Psychology*, *98*, 392–404.

Griswold, M., Fullman, N., Hawley, C., Arian, N., Zimsen, S., & Tymeson, H., et al. (2018). Alcohol use and burden for 195 countries and territories, 1990–2016: A systematic analysis for the Global Burden of Disease Study 2016. *The Lancet*, *392*(10152), 1015–1035.

Groot, B., Sanders, M., Rogers, T., & Bloomenthal, E. (2017). *I get by with a little help from my friends: Two field experiments on social support and attendance in further education colleges in the UK*. London: Behavioural Insights Team, Cabinet Office. Retrieved from http://bit.ly/2iEPb93

Grossman, R. S. (2013). *Wrong: Nine economic policy disasters and what we can learn from them*. Oxford: Oxford University Press.

Grüne-Yanoff, T., & Hertwig, R. (2015). Nudge versus boost: How coherent are policy and theory? *Minds and Machines*, *26*(1–2), 149–183.

Gu, F., & Widén-Wulff, G. (2011). Scholarly communication and possible changes in the context of social media: A Finnish case study. *The Electronic Library*, *29*(6), 762–776.

Gudmundsdottir, D. G. (2013). The impact of economic crisis on happiness. *Social Indicators Research*, *110*(3), 1083–1101.

Guilbeault, D., Becker, J., & Centola, D. (2018). Social learning and partisan bias in the interpretation of climate trends. *Proceedings of the National Academy of the Sciences*, *115*(39), 9714–9719.

Gunningham, N., & Sinclair, D. (1999). Regulatory pluralism: Designing policy mixes for environmental protection. *Law & Policy*, *21*(1), 49–76.

Guyatt, G., Rennie, D., Meade, M., & Cook, D. (Eds.). (2002). *Users' guides to the medical literature: A manual for evidence-based clinical practice* (Vol. 20). Chicago, IL: JAMA Press.

Hafner, M., Pollard, J., & van Stolk, C. (2018). *Incentives and physical activity: An assessment of the association between Vitality's Active Rewards with Apple Watch benefit and sustained physical activity improvements*. The RAND Corporation, Santa Monica, California. Retrieved from https://bit.ly/34NF3Q0

Hagman, W., Andersson, D., Västfjäll, D., & Tinghög, G. (2015). Public views on policies involving nudges. *Review of Philosophy and Psychology*, *6*, 439–453. https://doi.org/10.1007/s13164-015-0263-2

Haisley, E., Mostafa, R., & Loewenstein, G. (2008). Subjective relative income and lottery ticket purchases. *Journal of Behavioral Decision Making*, *21*(3), 283–295. https://doi.org/10.1002/bdm.588

Hall, C. C., Galvez, M. M., & Sederbaum, I. M. (2014). Assumptions about behavior and choice in response to public assistance: A behavioral decision analysis. *Policy Insights from the Behavioral and Brain Sciences*, *1*(1), 137–143.

Hallahan, K., Holtzhausen, D. R., van Ruler, B., Verčič, D., & Sriramesh, K. (2007). Defining strategic communication. *International Journal of Strategic Communication*, *1*(1), 3–35. https://doi.org/10.1080/15531180701285244

Hallsworth, M. (2016). Seven ways of applying behavioral science to health policy. In I. G. Cohen, H. F. Lynch, & C. R. Sunstein (Eds.), *Nudging health: Health law and behavioral economics* (pp. 40–48). Baltimore, MA: Johns Hopkins University Press.

Hallsworth, M., & Burd, H. (2018). *Green means go: How to help patients make informed choices about their healthcare*. Retrieved March 23, 2020 from www.bi.team/blogs/green-means-go-how-to-help-patients-make-informed-choices-about-their-healthcare/

Hallsworth, M., List, J. A., Metcalfe, R. D., & Vlaev, I. (2014). *The behavioralist as tax collector: Using natural field experiments to enhance tax compliance* (National Bureau of Economic Research Working Paper 20007). Retrieved from www.nber.org/papers/w20007

Hanks, A. S., Just, D. R., Smith, L. E., & Wansink, B. (2012). Healthy convenience: Nudging students toward healthier choices in the lunchroom. *Journal of Public Health*, *34*(3), 370–376. https://doi.org/10.1093/pubmed/fds003

Hannan, M. T., Pólos, L., & Carroll, G. R. (2007). *Logics of organization theory: Audiences, codes, and ecologies*. Princeton, NJ: Princeton University Press.

Hannon, P. A., Fernandez, M. E., Williams, R., Mullen, P. D., Escoffery, C., Kreuter, M. W., . . ., & Bowen, D. J. (2010). Cancer control planners' perceptions and use of evidence-based programs. *Journal of Public Health Management and Practice*, *16*, E1–E8. https://doi.org/10.1097/PHH.0b013e3181b3a3b1

Hanselman, P., Rozek, C. S., Grigg, J., & Borman, G. D. (2016). New evidence on self-affirmation effects and theorized sources of heterogeneity from large-scale replications. *Journal of Educational Psychology*, *109*(3), 405–424. https://doi.org/10.1037/edu0000141

Hansen, H., Bourgois, P., & Drucker, E. (2014). Pathologizing poverty: New forms of diagnosis, disability, and structural stigma under welfare reform. *Social Science & Medicine*, *103*, 76–83. https://doi.org/10.1016/j.socscimed.2013.06.033

Hansson, S. O. (1994). *Decision theory: A brief introduction*. Stockholm: Department of Philosophy and the History of Technology. Royal Institute of Technology. Retrieved from https://people.kth.se/~soh/decisiontheory.pdf

Harackiewicz, J. M., Rozek, C. S., Hulleman, C. S., & Hyde, J. S. (2012). Helping parents to motivate adolescents in mathematics and science: An experimental test of a utility-value intervention. *Psychological Science*, *23*(8), 899–906. https://doi.org/10.1177/0956797611435530

Harding, M. E. (1920). Discussion on the value of alcohol as a therapeutic agent. *Proceedings of the Royal Society of Medicine*, *13*, 56–57. Retrieved from https://bit.ly/2MDuzfX

Hardy, C. L., & Van Vugt, M. (2006). Nice guys finish first: The competitive altruism hypothesis. *Personality and Social Psychology Bulletin, 32*(10), 1402–1413. https://doi.org/10.1177/0146167206291006

Harkin, B., Webb, T. L., Chang, B. P., Prestwich, A., Conner, M., Kellar, I., . . . & Sheeran, P. (2016). Does monitoring goal progress promote goal attainment? A meta-analysis of the experimental evidence. *Psychological Bulletin, 142*(2), 198–229. https://doi.org/10.1037/bul0000025

Hattie, J., & Timperley, H. (2007). The power of feedback. *Review of Educational Research, 77*(1), 81–112. https://doi.org/10.3102/003465430298487

Hawe, P., & Potvin, L. (2009). What is population health intervention research? *Canadian Journal of Public Health/Revue Canadienne De Santé Publique, 100*(1) (Suppl. I), 8–14. https://doi.org/10.17269/cjph.100.1748

Hawton, K., Bergen, H., Simkin, S., Dodd, S., Pocock, P., Bernal, W., . . . & Kapur, N. (2013). Long term effect of reduced pack sizes of paracetamol on poisoning deaths and liver transplant activity in England and Wales: Interrupted time series analyses. *BMJ, 346*, f403. https://doi.org/10.1136/bmj.f403

Hawton, K., Fagg, J., Simkin, S., Bale, E., & Bond, A. (1997). Trends in deliberate self-harm in Oxford, 1985–1995: Implications for clinical services and the prevention of suicide. *The British Journal of Psychiatry, 171*(6), 556–560. https://doi.org/10.1192/bjp.171.6.556

Hawton, K., Harriss, L., Hall, S., Simkin, S., Bale, E., & Bond, A. (2003). Deliberate self-harm in Oxford, 1990–2000: A time of change in patient characteristics. *Psychological Medicine, 33*(6), 987–995. https://doi.org/10.1017/S0033291703007943

Haynes, A. B., Weiser, T. G., Berry, W. R., Lipsitz, S. R., Breizat, A. H. S., Dellinger, E. P., . . . & Merry, A. F. (2009). A surgical safety checklist to reduce morbidity and mortality in a global population. *New England Journal of Medicine, 360*(5), 491–499. https://doi.org/10.1056/NEJMsa0810119

Haynes, R., McDonald, H., & Garg, A. (2002). Helping patients follow prescribed treatment. *JAMA, 288*(22), 2880–2883. https://doi.org/10.1001/jama.288.22.2880

Head, B. W. (2008). Three lenses of evidence-based policy. *Australian Journal of Public Administration, 67*(1), 1–11. https://doi.org/10.1111/j.1467-8500.2007.00564.x

Head, B. W. (2015). Toward more "evidence-informed" policy making? *Public Administration Review, 76*(3), 472–484. https://doi.org/10.1111/puar.12475

Health Resources and Services Administration (HRSA). (2018, August 25). *Organ procurement and transplantation network*. Richmond, VA: U.S. Department of Health & Human Services. Retrieved from https://optn.transplant.hrsa.gov

Health and Safety Executive (HSE). (2017). *Health and safety at work: Summary statistics for Great Britain 2017*. Retrieved from www.hse.gov.uk/statistics/overall/hssh1617.pdf

Heard, K., O'Toole, E., Naimpally, R., & Bressler, L. (2017). *Real-world challenges to randomization and their solutions*. J-PAL. Retrieved from https://bit.ly/2RIXpw2

Heckman, J. J. (2008). Schools, skills, and synapses. *Economic Inquiry, 46*(3), 289–324. https://doi.org/10.1111/j.1465-7295.2008.00163.x

Heilbronner, S. R. (2017). Modeling risky decision-making in nonhuman animals: Shared core features. *Current Opinion in Behavioral Sciences, 16*, 23–29.

Heilman, M. E. (2012). Gender stereotypes and workplace bias. *Research in Organizational Behavior, 32*, 113–135. https://doi.org/10.1016/j.riob.2012.11.003

Heinzle, S. L., & Wüstenhagen, R. (2012). Dynamic adjustment of eco-labeling schemes and consumer choice – The revision of the EU energy label as a missed opportunity? *Business Strategy and the Environment, 21*(1), 60–70. https://doi.org/10.1002/bse.722

Henrich, J., Boyd, R., Bowles, S., Camerer, C., Fehr, E., Gintis, H., & McElreath, R. (2001). In search of homo economicus: Behavioral experiments in 15 small-scale societies. *American Economic Review, 91*(2), 73–78. Retrieved from https://bit.ly/2BX1mrD

Herring, C. (2009). Does diversity pay?: Race, gender, and the business case for diversity. *American Sociological Review, 74*(2), 208–224. https://doi.org/10.1177/000312240907400203

Hertwig, R., & Grüne-Yanoff, T. (2017). Nudging and boosting: Steering or empowering good decisions. *Perspectives on Psychological Science, 12*(6), 973–986.

Higgins, S. T., Heil, S. H., Solomon, L. J., Bernstein, I. M., Plebani Lussier, J., Abel, R. L., . . . & Badger, G. J. (2004). A pilot study on voucher-based incentives to promote abstinence from cigarette smoking during pregnancy and postpartum. *Nicotine and Tobacco Research, 6*(6), 1015–1020.

Hill, C. J., Corbett, C., & St Rose, A. (2010). *Why so few? Women in science, technology, engineering, and mathematics*. Washington, DC: American Association of University Women.

Hill, G., & Howell, R. T. (2014). Moderators and mediators of pro-social spending and well-being: The influence of values and psychological need satisfaction. *Personality and Individual Differences, 69*, 69–74. https://doi.org/10.1016/j.paid.2014.05.013

Hirsh, J. B., Kang, S. K., & Bodenhausen, G. V. (2012). Personalized persuasion: Tailoring persuasive appeals to recipients' personality traits. *Psychological Science, 23*(6), 578–581. https://doi.org/10.1177/0956797611436349

H.M.S. Treasury. (2013). *Spending round 2013*. Retrieved from https://bit.ly/2orlNmJ

Ho, A. D. (2008). The problem with "proficiency": Limitations of statistics and policy under No Child Left Behind. *Educational Researcher, 37*(6), 351–360.

Hodson, D., & Maher, I. (2001). The open method as a new mode of governance: The case of soft economic policy co-ordination. *Journal of Common Market Studies, 39*(4), 719–746. https://doi.org/10.1111/1468-5965.00328

Hoff, K., & Stiglitz, J. E. (2016). Striving for balance in economics: Towards a theory of the social determination of behavior. *Journal of Economic Behavior & Organization, 126*, 25–57.

Hoffman, A. J. (2011). Talking past each other? Cultural framing of skeptical and convinced logics in the climate change debate. *Organization & Environment, 24*(1), 3–33. https://doi.org/10.1177/1086026611404336

Hoffrage, U., Lindsey, S., Hertwig, R., & Gigerenzer, G. (2000). Communicating statistical information. *Science, 290*(5500), 2261–2262. https://doi.org/10.1126/science.290.5500.2261

Holt, C. A., & Roth, A. E. (2004). The Nash equilibrium: A perspective. *Proceedings of the National Academy of Sciences, 101*(12), 3999–4002.

Hong, T., Yan, D., D'Oca, S., & Chen, C. F. (2017). Ten questions concerning occupant behavior in buildings: The big picture. *Building and Environment, 114*, 518–530. https://doi.org/10.1016/j.buildenv.2016.12.006

Hornsey, M. J., Harris, E. A., Bain, P. G., & Fielding, K. S. (2016). Meta-analyses of the determinants and outcomes of belief in climate change. *Nature Climate Change, 6*(6), 622–626. https://doi.org/10.1038/NCLIMATE2943

Horrigan, J. B. (2010). *Broadband adoption and use in America*. Washington, DC: Federal Communications Commission.

Horst, M. (2011). Taking our own medicine: On an experiment in science communication. *Science and Engineering Ethics, 17*(4), 801–815. https://doi.org/10.1007/s11948-011-9306-y

Hospido, L., Villanueva, E., & Zamarro, G. (2015). Finance for all: The impact of financial literacy training in compulsory secondary education in Spain. *SSRN Electronic Journal*. https://doi.org/10.2139/ssrn.2559642

Hossain, T., & List, J. A. (2012). The behavioralist visits the factory: Increasing productivity using simple framing manipulations. *Management Science, 58*(12), 2151–2167.

Hourani, L., Williams, T., & Kress, A. (2006). Stress, mental health, and job performance among active duty military personnel. *Military Medicine, 171*(9), 849–856.

Howell, R. T., & Hill, G. (2009). The mediators of experiential purchases: Determining the impact of psychological needs satisfaction and social comparison. *The Journal of Positive Psychology, 4*(6), 511–522. https://doi.org/10.1080/17439760903270993

Howlett, M., McConnell, A., & Perl, A. (2017). Moving policy theory forward: Connecting multiple stream and advocacy coalition frameworks to policy cycle models of analysis. *Australian Journal of Public Administration, 76*, 65–79. https://doi.org/10.1111/1467-8500.12191

Howlett, M., & Mukherjee, I. (2017). Policy design: From tools to patches. *Canadian Public Administration, 60*(1), 140–144. https://doi.org/10.1111/capa.12209

Howlett, M., Mukherjee, I., & Woo, J. J. (2015). From tools to toolkits in policy design studies: The new design orientation towards policy formulation research. *Policy & Politics, 43*(2), 291–311.

Howlett, M., & Rayner, J. (2013). Patching vs packaging in policy formulation: Assessing policy portfolio design. *Politics and Governance, 1*(2), 170–182.

Hoxby, C., & Turner, S. (2013). *Expanding college opportunities for high-achieving, low income students* (Stanford Institute for Economic Policy Research Discussion Paper 12–014). Retrieved from http://bit.ly/2kTr2wA

Hsee, C. K., & Rottenstreich, Y. (2004). Music, pandas, and muggers: On the affective psychology of value. *Journal of Experimental Psychology: General, 133*(1), 23–30. https://doi.org/10.1037/h0054346

Hughes, J. R., Keely, J., & Naud, S. (2004). Shape of the relapse curve and long-term abstinence among untreated smokers. *Addiction, 99*(1), 29–38. https://doi.org/j.1360-0443.2004.00540.x

Hulleman, C. S., Godes, O., Hendricks, B. L., & Harackiewicz, J. M. (2010). Enhancing interest and performance with a utility value intervention. *Journal of Educational Psychology, 102*(4), 880.

Hulleman, C. S., & Harackiewicz, J. M. (2009). Promoting interest and performance in high school science classes. *Science, 326*, 1410–1412. https://doi.org/10.1126/science.1177067

Huppert, F. A. (2009). A new approach to reducing disorder and improving well-being. *Perspectives on Psychological Science, 4*(1), 108–111.

Huppert, F. A. (2014). *The state of wellbeing science*. London: John Wiley & Sons.

Huppert, F. A., Baylis, N., & Keverne, B. (Eds.). (2005). *The science of well-being*. New York: Oxford University Press.

Huppert, F., & Ruggeri, K. (2018). 15. Policy challenges: Well-being as a priority in public mental health. In D. Bhugra, K. Bhui, S. Y. S. Wong, & S. E. Gilman (Eds.), *Oxford textbook of public mental health*. Oxford: Oxford University Press.

Huppert, F. A., & Ruggeri, K. (2019). Controversies in well-being: Confronting and resolving the challenges. In D. Bhugra, K. Bhul, S. Wong, & S. Gillman (Eds.), *Oxford textbook of public mental health* (pp. 131–140). Oxford: Oxford University Press.

Huppert, F. A., & So, T. T. (2013). Flourishing across Europe: Application of a new conceptual framework for defining well-being. *Social Indicators Research, 110*(3), 837–861.

Hurlstone, M. J., Lewandowsky, S., Newell, B. R., & Sewell, B. (2014). The effect of framing and normative messages in building support for climate policies. *PLoS ONE, 9*(12).

Hyder, A. A., Corluka, A., Winch, P. J., El-Shinnawy, A., Ghassany, H., Malekafzali, H., . . . & Ghaffar, A. (2010). National policymakers speak out: Are researchers giving them what they need? *Health Policy and Planning, 26*(1), 73–82.

Insel, T. R. (2009). Translating scientific opportunity into public health impact: A strategic plan for research on mental illness. *Archives of General Psychiatry, 66*(2), 128–133.

International Energy Agency. (2009). *World energy outlook*. Retrieved from https://bit.ly/2C2htEj

Internet Live Stats. (2017). *Internet users*. Retrieved from https://bit.ly/RdZ6QH

Irlenbusch, B., & Ruchala, G. (2008). Relative rewards within team-based compensation. *Labour Economics, 15*(2), 141–167. https://doi.org/10.1016/j.labeco.2007.02.003

Ising, H., & Kruppa, B. (2004). Health effects caused by noise: Evidence in the literature from the past 25 years. *Noise and Health, 6*(22), 5.

Ittner, C., Larcker, F., & Pizzini, M. (2007). Performance-based compensation in member-owned firms: An examination of medical group practices. *Journal of Accounting and Economics, 44*(3), 300–327.

Jachimowicz, J., Duncan, S., Weber, E., & Johnson, E. (2018). When and why defaults influence decisions: A meta-analysis of default effects. *SSRN Electronic Journal*. https://doi.org/10.2139/ssrn.2727301

Jachimowicz, J., Hauser, O. P., O'Brien, J. D., Sherman, E., & Galinsky, A. D. (2018). The critical role of second-order normative beliefs in predicting energy conservation. *Nature Human Behaviour, 2*(10), 757–764. https://doi.org/10.1038/s41592-018-0434-0

Jachimowicz, J., Matz, S., & Polonski, V. (2017). *The Behavioral Scientist's ethics checklist*. Behavioral Scientist. Retrieved from https://bit.ly/2PiJWr6

Jalava, N., Joensen, J. S., & Pellas, E. (2015). Grades and rank: Impacts of non-financial incentives on test performance. *Journal of Economic Behavior & Organization, 115*, 161–196. https://doi.org/10.1016/j.jebo.2014.12.004

Jambeck, J. R., Geyer, R., Wilcox, C., Siegler, T. R., Perryman, M., Andrady, A., . . . & Law, K. L. (2015). Plastic waste inputs from land into the ocean. *Science, 347*(6223), 768–771.

Jamieson, D., & Giraldez, J. (2017). *Behavioral insight brief: Overview of behavioral insights*. Ottawa: Policy Horizons Canada.

Jencks, C., & Phillips, M. (1998). *The black-white test score gap*. Washington, DC: Brookings Institution Press.

Jensen, J. D. (2008). Scientific uncertainty in news coverage of cancer research: Effects of hedging on scientists' and journalists' credibility. *Human Communication Research, 34*(3), 347–369.

Jensen, R. T., & Miller, N. H. (2011). Do consumer price subsidies really improve nutrition? *The Review of Economics and Statistics, 93*(4), 1205–1223.

Jewell, C. J., & Bero, L. A. (2008). "Developing good taste in evidence": Facilitators of and hindrances to evidence-informed health policymaking in state government. *The Milbank Quarterly, 86*(2), 177–208.

Jiao, B., Zafar, Z., Will, B., Ruggeri, K., Li, S., & Muennig, P. (2017). The cost-effectiveness of lowering permissible noise levels around US airports. *International Journal of Environmental Research and Public Health, 14*(1497), 1–10.

Jin, X., Wah, B. W., Cheng, X., & Wang, Y. (2015). Significance and challenges of big data research. *Big Data Research*, *2*(2), 59–64.

Jogelkar, A. (2012, November 26). The perils of translational research. *Scientific American*. Retrieved from https://bit.ly/2PPoATn

John, P., MacDonald, E., & Sanders, M. (2015). Targeting voter registration with incentives: A randomized controlled trial of a lottery in a London borough. *Electoral Studies*, *40*, 170–175.

Johns, G. (2007). Absenteeism. In G. Ritzer (Ed.), *The Blackwell encyclopedia of sociology*. (pp. 4–7). Malden, MA: Blackwell Publishing.

Johnson, E. J., & Goldstein, D. (2003). Do defaults save lives? *Science*, *5649*(302), 1338–1339. https://doi.org/10.1126/science.1091721

Johnson, E. J., Hassin, R., Baker, T., Bajger, A. T., & Treuer, G. (2013). Can consumers make affordable care affordable? The value of choice architecture. *PLoS ONE*, *8*(12), e81521.

Johnson, E. J., Shu, S. B., Dellaert, B. G. C., Fox, C., Goldstein, D. G., Häubl, G., . . . & Weber, E. U. (2012). Beyond nudges: Tools of a choice architecture. *Marketing Letters*, *23*(2), 487–504.

Johnson, R. B., & Onwuegbuzie, A. J. (2004). Mixed methods research: A research paradigm whose time has come. *Educational Researcher*, *33*(7), 14–26.

Jolls, C., & Sunstein, C. R. (2006). The law of implicit bias. *California Law Review*, 969–996.

Jones, M. A., & Higgs, J. (2000). Will evidence-based practice take the reasoning out of practice? In J. Higgs & M. A. Jones (Eds.), *Clinical reasoning in the health professionals* (2nd ed., pp. 307–315). Oxford: Butterworth-Heinemann.

Jones, N. R. V., Conklin, A. I., Suhrcke, M., & Monsivais, P. (2014). The growing price gap between more and less healthy foods: Analysis of a Novel Longitudinal UK Dataset. *PLoS ONE*, *9*(10), e109343. https://doi.org/10.1371/journal.pone.0109343

Jost, A. (2017). *Is monetary policy too complex for the public?: Evidence from the UK* (Swiss National Bank Working Papers. No. 15/2017). Retrieved from https://bit.ly/2MFA0eE

Jukes, M. C., Jere, C. M., & Pridmore, P. (2014). Evaluating the provision of flexible learning for children at risk of primary school dropout in Malawi. *International Journal of Educational Development*, *39*, 181–192. https://doi.org/10.1016/j.ijedudev.2014.07.006

Jung, J. Y., & Mellers, B. A. (2016). American attitudes toward nudges. *Judgment & Decision Making*, *11*(1), 62–74.

Kácha, O., & Ruggeri, K. (2018). Nudging intrinsic motivation in environmental risk and social policy. *Journal of Risk Research*, 1–12. https://doi.org/10.1080/13669877.2018.1459799

Kahneman, D. (2003a). A perspective on judgment and choice: Mapping bounded rationality. *The American Psychologist*, *58*(9), 697–720. https://doi.org/10.1037/0003-066X.58.9.697

Kahneman, D. (2003b). Maps of bounded rationality: Psychology for behavioral economics. *American Economic Review*, *93*(5), 1449–1475.

Kahneman, D. (2011). *Thinking, fast and slow*. New York: Farrar, Straus and Giroux.

Kahneman, D., & Deaton, A. (2010). High income improves evaluation of life but not emotional well-being. *Proceedings of the National Academy of Sciences*, *107*(38), 16489–16493. https://doi.org/10.1073/pnas.1011492107

Kahneman, D., Knetsch, J. L., & Thaler, R. H. (1991). Anomalies: The endowment effect, loss aversion, and status quo bias. *The Journal of Economic Perspectives*, *5*(1), 193–206. https://doi.org/10.1257/jep.5.1.193

Kahneman, D., Sibony, O., & Sunstein, C. (2021). *Noise: A flaw in human judgement*. New York: Little, Brown Spark.
Kahneman, D., & Tversky, A. (1972). Subjective probability: A judgment of representativeness. *Cognitive Psychology*, *3*(3), 430–454. https://doi.org/10.1016/0010-0285(72)90016-3
Kahneman, D., & Tversky, A. (1979). Prospect theory: An analysis of decision under risk. *Econometrica: Journal of the Econometric Society*, *47*(3), 263–291. https://doi.org/10.1111/j.1536-7150.2011.00774.x
Kahneman, D., & Tversky, A. (1984). Choices, values, and frames. *American Psychologist*, *39*(4), 341–350. https://doi.org/10.1037/0003-066X.39.4.341
Kalev, A., Dobbin, F., & Kelly, E. (2006). Best practices or best guesses? Assessing the efficacy of corporate affirmative action and diversity policies. *American Sociological Review*, *71*(4), 589–617. https://doi.org/10.1177/000312240607100404
Kalousova, L. (2015). Curing over-use by prescribing fees: an evaluation of the effect of user fees' implementation on healthcare use in the Czech Republic. *Health Policy and Planning*, *30*(4), 423–431.
Kamdar, N. (1997). Corporate income tax compliance: A time series analysis. *Atlantic Economic Journal*, *25*(1), 37–49. https://doi.org/10.1007/BF02298475
Kangovi, S., & Asch, D. A. (2018). Behavioral phenotyping in health promotion: Embracing or avoiding failure. *JAMA*, *19104*, 6–7. https://doi.org/10.1001/JAMA.2018.2921
Karlan, D., McConnell, M., Mullainathan, S., & Zinman, J. (2016). Getting to the top of mind: How reminders increase savings. *Management Science*, *62*(12), 3393–3411. https://doi.org/10.1287/mnsc.2015.2296
Katz, E., & Lazarsfeld, P. F. (1957). *Personal influence*. New York: Free Press.
Katz, Y. (2013). Against storytelling of scientific results. *Nature Methods*, *10*(11), 1045.
Keller, P. A., Harlam, B., Loewenstein, G., & Volpp, K. G. (2011). Enhanced active choice: A new method to motivate behavior change. *Journal of Consumer Psychology*, *21*(4), 376–383. https://doi.org/10.1016/j.jcps.2011.06.003
Kennedy, E. H., Beckley, T. M., McFarlane, B. L., & Nadeau, S. (2009). Why we don't "walk the talk": Understanding the environmental values/behaviour gap in Canada. *Human Ecology Review*, *16*(2), 151–160.
Kenrick, D. T., Griskevicius, V., Sundie, J. M., Li, N. P., Li, Y. J., & Neuberg, S. L. (2009). Deep rationality: The evolutionary economics of decision making. *Social Cognition*, *27*(5), 764–785. https://doi.org/10.1521/soco.2009.27.5.764
Kerlikowske, K., Grady, D., Rubin, S. M., Sandrock, C., & Ernster, V. L. (1995). Efficacy of screening mammography: A meta-analysis. *The Journal of the American Medical Association*, *273*(2), 149–154. https://doi.org/10.1001/jama.1995.03520260071035
Kersbergen, I., Oldham, M., Jones, A., Field, M., Angus, C., & Robinson, E. (2018). Reducing the standard serving size of alcoholic beverages prompts reductions in alcohol consumption. *Addiction*, *113*, 1598–1608. https://doi.org/10.1111/add.14228
Keynes, J. M. (1937). The general theory of employment. *The Quarterly Journal of Economics*, *51*(2), 209–223. https://doi.org/10.2307/1882087
Khan, I., & Pardo, A. (2016). Data2U: Scalable real time student feedback in active learning environments. In *Proceedings of the international conference on learning analytics and knowledge* (pp. 249–253). Edinburgh, Scotland: ACM. https://doi.org/10.1145/2883851.2883911
Kiefer, A. K., & Sekaquaptewa, D. (2007). Implicit stereotypes and women's math performance: How implicit gender-math stereotypes influence women's susceptibility

to stereotype threat. *Journal of Experimental Social Psychology*, *43*, 825–832. https://doi.org/10.1016/j.jesp.2006.08.004

Kilburn, K., Handa, S., Angeles, G., Mvula, P., & Tsoka, M. (2017). Short-term impacts of an unconditional cash transfer program on child schooling: Experimental evidence from Malawi. *Economics of Education Review*, *59*, 63–80. https://doi.org/10.1016/j.econedurev.2017.06.002

Kim, B. S., & Kim, J. H. (2007). *Increasing trust in government through more participatory and transparent government*. Presidential Committee on Government Innovation & Decentralization, Republic of Korea. Vienna: UNDESA/DPADM. Retrieved from https://bit.ly/2wAzPGB

Kim, H. L., & Hyun, S. S. (2020). The anchoring effect of aviation green tax for sustainable tourism, based on the nudge theory. *Journal of Sustainable Tourism*, 1–16. https://doi.org/10.1080/09669582.2020.1820017

Kim, H. S., Bigman, C. A., Leader, A. E., Lerman, C., & Cappella, J. N. (2012). Narrative health communication and behavior change: The influence of exemplars in the news on intention to quit smoking. *Journal of Communication*, *62*(3), 473–492. https://doi.org/10.1111/j.1460-2466.2012.01644.x

Klenk, N. L., & Hickey, G. M. (2011). A virtual and anonymous, deliberative and analytic participation process for planning and evaluation: The Concept Mapping Policy Delphi. *International Journal of Forecasting*, *27*(1), 152–165. https://doi.org/10.1016/j.ijforecast.2010.05.002

Knapp, M., McDaid, D., & Parsonage, M. (2011). *Mental health promotion and prevention: The economic case*. London: Department of Health.

Knight, F. H. (1921). *Risk, uncertainty and profit*. New York: Hart, Schaffner and Marx.

Koch, A., Nafziger, J., & Nielsen, H. S. (2015). Behavioral economics of education. *Journal of Economic Behavior & Organization*, *115*, 3–17. https://doi.org/10.1016/j.jebo.2014.09.005

Kogan, M., & Henkel, M. (1983). *Government and research: The Rothschild experiment in a government department*. London: Heinemann Educational Books.

Koivusalo, M. (2010). The state of Health in All policies (HiAP) in the European Union: Potential and pitfalls. *Journal of Epidemiology & Community Health*, *64*(6), 500–503. https://doi.org/10.1136/jech.2009.102020

Kollmuss, A., & Agyeman, J. (2002). Mind the gap: Why do people act environmentally and what are the barriers to pro-environmental behavior? *Environmental Education Research*, *8*(3), 239–260. https://doi.org/10.1080/13504620220145401

Kosinski, M., Stillwell, D., & Graepel, T. (2013). Private traits and attributes are predictable from digital records of human behavior. *Proceedings of the National Academy of Sciences*, *110*(15), 5802–5805. https://doi.org/10.1073/pnas.1218772110

Kosinski, M., Wang, Y., Lakkaraju, H., & Leskovec, J. (2016). Mining Big Data to extract patterns and predict real-life outcomes. *Psychological Methods*, *21*(4), 493. https://doi.org/10.1037/met0000105

Kotchen, M. J. (2005). Impure public goods and the comparative statics of environmentally friendly consumption. *Journal of Environmental Economics and Management*, *49*(2), 281–300. https://doi.org/10.1016/j.jeem.2004.05.003

Kraft, M. A. (2019). *Interpreting effect sizes of education interventions* (EdWorkingPaper: 19–10). Retrieved from Annenberg Institute at Brown University https://doi.org/10.26300/8pjp-2z74

Kraft, M. A., & Rogers, T. (2015). The underutilized potential of teacher-to-parent communication: Evidence from a field experiment. *Economics of Education Review, 47*, 49–63. https://doi.org/10.1016/j.econedurev.2015.04.001
Kramer, L. A., & Weber, J. M. (2011). This is your portfolio on winter: Seasonal affective disorder and risk aversion in financial decision-making. *Social Psychological and Personality Science, 3*(2), 193–199. https://doi.org/10.1177/1948550611415694
Kremer, M., Miguel, E., & Thornton, R. (2009). Incentives to learn. *The Review of Economics and Statistics, 91*(3), 437–456. https://doi.org/10.1162/rest.91.3.437
Kreuter, M. W., Green, M. C., Cappella, J. N., Slater, M. D., Wise, M. E., Storey, D., . . . & Woolley, S. (2007). Narrative communication in cancer prevention and control: A framework to guide research and application. *Annals of Behavioral Medicine, 33*(3), 221–235. https://doi.org/10.1007/BF02879904
Kühberger, A. (1998). The influence of framing on risky decisions: A meta-analysis. *Organizational Behavior and Human Decision Processes, 75*(1), 23–55. https://doi.org/10.1006/obhd.1998.2781
Lacetera, N., Macis, M., & Slonim, R. (2012). Will there be blood? Incentives and displacement effects in pro-social behaviour. *American Economic Journal: Economic Policy, 4*(1), 186–223.
Lacetera, N., Pope, D. G., & Sydnor, J. R. (2012). Heuristic thinking and limited attention in the car market. *The American Economic Review, 102*(5), 2206–2236. https://doi.org/10.3386/w17030
Laibson, D. (1997). Golden eggs and hyperbolic discounting. *The Quarterly Journal of Economics, 112*(2), 443–478. https://doi.org/10.1162/003355397555253
Lambiotte, R., & Kosinski, M. (2014). Tracking the digital footprints of personality. *Proceedings of the IEEE, 102*(12), 1934–1939. https://doi.org/10.1109/JPROC.2014.2359054
Lamborn, A. C. (1998). Foreign policy crises: Case studies and theory building. *International Studies Review, 42*(2), 346–351. https://doi.org/10.1111/1521-9488.1251998125
Landy, F. (1997). Early influences on the development of industrial and organizational psychology. *Journal of Applied Psychology, 82*(4), 467–477. https://doi.org/10.1037/0021-9010.82.4.467
Larrick, R. P., & Soll, J. B. (2008). The MPG illusion. *Science, 320*, 1593–1594.
Lasswell, H. D. (1955). Current studies of the decision process: Automation versus creativity. *Western Political Quarterly, 8*(3), 381–399.
Lauver, D. R., Settersten, L., Kane, J. H., & Henriques, J. B. (2003). Tailored messages, external barriers, and women's utilization of professional breast cancer screening over time. *Cancer, 97*(11), 2724–2735. https://doi.org/10.1002/cncr.11397
Layard, R. (2003). *Happiness: Has social science a clue? Lecture 2: Income and happiness: Rethinking economic policy*. Lionel Robbins Memorial Lecture series, 03–05 Mar 2003. London: London School of Economics.
Layard, R. (2016). *Wellbeing measurement and cost-effectiveness analysis* (Discussion Paper 1). London: London School of Economics.
Leaman, A., & Bordass, B. (1999). Productivity in buildings: The "killer" variables. *Building Research & Information, 27*(1), 4–19. https://doi.org/10.1080/096132199369615
Ledyard, J. O. (1995). Public goods: A survey of experimental research. In *The handbook of experimental economics*. Princeton, NJ: Princeton University Press. Retrieved from https://www.degruyter.com/document/doi/10.1515/9780691213255-004/html

Lee, J. K., Grace, K. A., & Taylor, A. J. (2006). Effect of a pharmacy care program on medication adherence and persistence, blood pressure, and low-density lipoprotein cholesterol: A randomized controlled trial. *JAMA, 296*(21), 2563–2571.

Leipnitz, S., de Vries, M., Clement, M., & Mazar, N. (2018). Providing health checks as incentives to retain blood donors – Evidence from two field experiments. *International Journal of Research in Marketing, 35*(4), 628–640. https://doi.org/10.1016/j.ijresmar.2018.08.004

Leiserowitz, A., Maibach, E. W., Roser-Renouf, C., Feinberg, G., & Howe, P. (2013). *Climate change in the American mind: Americans' global warming beliefs and attitudes in April 2013*. Available at SSRN 2298705.

Lerís, D., Sein-Echaluce, M. L., Hernández, M., & Bueno, C. (2017). Validation of indicators for implementing an adaptive platform for MOOCs. *Computers in Human Behavior, 72*, 783–795. https://doi.org/10.1016/j.chb.2016.07.054

Lerman, A. E., Sadin, M. L., & Trachtman, S. (2017). Policy uptake as political behavior: Evidence from the Affordable Care Act. *American Political Science Review, 111*(4), 755–770. https://doi.org/10.1017/S0003055417000272

Leung, P. T., Macdonald, E. M., Stanbrook, M. B., Dhalla, I. A., & Juurlink, D. N. (2017). A 1980 letter on the risk of opioid addiction. *New England Journal of Medicine, 376*(22), 2194–2195. https://doi.org/10.1056/NEJMc1700150

Leuven, E., Oosterbeek, H., & van der Klaauw, B. (2010). The effect of financial rewards on students' achievement: Evidence from a randomized experiment. *Journal of the European Economic Association, 8*(6), 1243–1265. https://doi.org/10.1111/j.1542-4774.2010.tb00554.x

Levi, M. (1998). A state of trust. In V. Braithwaite & M. Levi (Eds.), *Trust and governance* (pp. 77–101). New York: Rusell Sage Found. https://doi.org/10.1.1.452.7186

Levitt, S. D., List, J. A., Neckermann, S., & Sadoff, S. (2016). The behavioralist goes to school: Leveraging behavioral economics to improve educational performance. *American Economic Journal: Economic Policy, 8*(4), 183–219. Retrieved from http://home.uchicago.edu/jlist/papers/bgs.pdf

Lewandowsky, S., & Oberauer, K. (2016). Motivated rejection of science. *Current Directions in Psychological Science, 25*(4), 217–222. https://doi.org/10.1177/0963721416654436

Lewis, M. (2016). *The undoing project*. New York: W.W. Norton & Company. ISBN: 978-0-393-25459-4

Li, Y. M., & Yeh, Y. S. (2010). Increasing trust in mobile commerce through design aesthetics. *Computers in Human Behavior, 26*(4), 673–684. https://doi.org/10.1016/j.chb.2010.01.004

Liberman, V., Samuels, S. M., & Ross, L. (2004). The name of the game: Predictive power of reputations versus situational labels in determining prisoner's dilemma game moves. *Personality and Social Psychology Bulletin, 30*(9), 1175–1185. https://doi.org/10.1177/0146167204264004

Lichtenstein, S., Fischhoff, B., & Phillips, L. D. (1982). Calibration of probabilities: The state of the art to 1980. In D. Kahneman, P. Slovic, & A. Tversky (Eds.), *Judgment under uncertainty: Heuristics and biases*. Cambridge: Cambridge University Press.

Lilleker, D. G., & Jackson, N. A. (2010). Towards a more participatory style of election campaigning: The impact of Web 2.0 on the UK 2010 general election. *Policy & Internet, 2*(3), 69–98. https://doi.org/10.2202/1944-2866.1064

Lin, V., & Gibson, B. (2003). *Evidence-based health policy: Problems and possibilities*. Oxford: Oxford University Press.

Lindblom, C. E. (1959). The science of "muddling through". *Public Administration Review, 19*(2), 79–88. https://doi.org/10.2307/973677
Linder, N., Lindahl, T., & Borgström, S. (2018). Using Behavioural insights to promote food waste recycling in urban households – Evidence from a longitudinal field experiment. *Frontiers in Psychology, 9*, 352. https://doi.org/10.3389/fpsyg.2018.00352
Linder, S., & Peters, B. (1989). Instruments of government: Perceptions and contexts. *Journal of Public Policy, 9*(1), 35–58. https://doi.org/10.1017/S0143814X00007960
Linos, E., Reinhard, J., & Ruda, S. (2017). Levelling the playing field in police recruitment: Evidence from a field experiment on test performance. *Public Administration, 95*(4), 943–956. https://doi.org/10.1111/padm.12344
Lisi, G. (2012). Testing the slippery slope framework. *Economics Bulletin, 32*(2), 1369–1377. https://doi.org/10.1007/s13398-014-0173-7.2
Littlejohn, A., Hood, N., Milligan, C., & Mustain, P. (2016). Learning in MOOCs: Motivations and self-regulated learning in MOOCs. *Internet and Higher Education, 29*, 40–48. https://doi.org/10.1016/j.iheduc.2015.12.003
Liu, J., Daily, G. C., Ehrlich, P. R., & Luck, G. W. (2003). Effects of household dynamics on resource consumption and biodiversity. *Nature, 421*, 530–533.
Local Government Association. (2013, October). *Changing behaviours in public health: To nudge or to shove?* London: Local Government Association.
Lochner, B., Conrad, R. M., & Graham, E. (2015). Secondary teachers' concerns in adopting learning management systems: A US perspective. *TechTrends, 59*(5), 62–70. https://doi.org/10.1007/s11528-015-0892-4
Lochner, L. (2011). *Non-production benefits of education: Crime, health, and good citizenship* (Working Paper Number 16722). National Bureau of Economic Research. Retrieved from http://bit.ly/2ggjzCO
Locke, E. A., & Latham, G. P. (2002). Building a practically useful theory of goal setting and task motivation: A 35-year odyssey. *American Psychologist, 57*(9), 705–717.
Locke, E. A., Shaw, K. N., Saari, L. M., & Latham, G. P. (1981). Goal setting and task performance: 1969–1980. *Psychological Bulletin, 90*(1), 125–152.
Loewenstein, G., & Chater, N. (2017). Putting nudges in perspective. *Behavioural Public Policy, 1*(1), 26–53. https://doi.org/10.1017/bpp.2016.7
Lonn, S., Aguilar, S. J., & Teasley, S. D. (2015). Investigating student motivation in the context of a learning analytics intervention during a summer bridge program. *Computers in Human Behavior, 47*, 90–97.
Lourenço, J. S., Ciriolo, E., Almeida, S. R., & Troussard, X. (2016). *Behavioural Insights applied to policy: European report 2016*. Brussels: European Commission.
Lowi, T. J. (1966). Distribution, regulation, redistribution: The functions of government. In R. B. Ripley (Ed.), *Public policies and their politics: Techniques of government control* (pp. 27–40). New York: W. W. Norton & Company.
Lowi, T. J. (1972). Four systems of policy, politics, and choice. *Public Administration Review, 32*(4), 298. https://doi.org/10.2307/974990
Lowi, T. J. (1985). The state in politics: The relation between policy and administration. In R. G. Noll (Ed.), *Regulatory policy and the social sciences* (pp. 67–105). Berkeley, CA: University of California Press.
Lu, J. G., Akinola, M., & Mason, M. F. (2017). "Switching on" creativity: Task switching can increase creativity by reducing cognitive fixation. *Organizational Behavior and Human Decision Processes, 139*, 63–75. https://doi.org/10.1016/j.obhdp.2017.01.005

Lunn, P. (2014). *Regulatory policy and behavioural economics*. OECD Publishing. http://doi.org/10.1787/9789264207851-en

Lupia, A. (2013). Communicating science in politicized environments. *Proceedings of the National Academy of Sciences, 110*(Suppl. 3), 14048–14054.

Luyben, P. D. (1982). Prompting thermostat setting behavior: Public response to a presidential appeal for conservation. *Environment and Behavior, 14*(1), 113–128.

Ly, K., Mazar, N., Zhao, M., & Soman, D. (2013). *A practitioner's guide to nudging*. Toronto: University of Toronto.

Macfadyen, L. P., & Dawson, S. (2010). Mining LMS data to develop an "early warning system" for educators: A proof of concept. *Computers and Education, 54*(2), 588–599. https://doi.org/10.1016/j.compedu.2009.09.008

Mackenbach, J. P., Karanikolos, M., & McKee, M. (2013). The unequal health of Europeans: Successes and failures of policies. *The Lancet, 381*(9872), 1125–1134.

Macleod, I. (1965, December 3). 70 m.p.h. *The Spectator*, 11.

Macnamara, J. (2010). *The 21st century media (r)evolution: Emergent communication practices*. New York: Peter Lang.

Madrian, B. C. (2014). *Applying insights from behavioral economics to policy design*. NBER Working Paper Series, 20318. Retrieved from http://www.nber.org/papers/w20318

Madrian, B. C., & Shea, D. F. (2001). The power of suggestion: Inertia in 401(k) participation and savings behavior. *The Quarterly Journal of Economics, 116*(4), 1149–1187.

Maes, T., Barry, J., Leslie, H. A., Vethaak, A. D., Nicolaus, E. E. M., Law, R. J., . . . & Thain, J. E. (2018). Below the surface: Twenty-five years of seafloor litter monitoring in coastal seas of North West Europe (1992–2017). *Science of the Total Environment, 630*, 790–798.

Major, J. M., Zhou, E. H., Wong, H. L., Trinidad, J. P., Pham, T. M., Mehta, H., . . . & Willy, M. E. (2016). Trends in rates of acetaminophen-related adverse events in the United States. *Pharmacoepidemiology and Drug Safety, 25*(5), 590–598. https://doi.org/10.1002/pds.3906

Malik, P. (2006). The axiom of rose. *Canadian Journal of Cardiology, 22*(9), 735. https://doi.org/10.1016/S0828-282X(06)70297-5

Maltese, A. V., & Tai, R. H. (2011). Pipeline persistence: Examining the association of educational experiences with earned degrees in STEM among US students. *Science Education, 95*(5), 877–907.

Markussen, S., Røed, K., & Schreiner, R. (2017). Can compulsory dialogues nudge sick-listed workers back to work? *The Economic Journal, 128*(610), 1276–1303. https://doi.org/10.1111/ecoj.12468

Marques, L. M., & Fuinhas, J. A. (2016). On the global energy consumption and economic growth nexus: A long time span analysis. *International Energy Journal, 15*(4), 143–150.

Marston, G., & Watts, R. (2003). Tampering with the evidence: A critical appraisal of evidence-based policy-making. *The Drawing Board: An Australian Review of Public Affairs, 3*(3), 143–163.

Marteau, T. M., Hollands, J. H., Shemilt, I., & Jebb, S. A. (2015). Downsizing: Policy options to reduce portion sizes to help tackle obesity. *British Medical Journal, 5863*, 1–5. https://doi.org/10.1136/bmj.h5863

Marteau, T. M., Ogilvie, D., Roland, M., & Kelly, M. P. (2011). Judging nudging: Can nudging improve population health? *British Medical Journal, 342*(7791).

Marzilli Ericson, K. M., Kingsdale, J., Layton, T., & Sacarny, A. (2017). Nudging leads consumers in Colorado to shop but not switch ACA marketplace plans. *Health Affairs*, *36*(2), 311–319.

Maslow, A. H. (1943). A theory of human motivation. *Psychological Review*, *50*(4), 370–396.

Mastrandrea, M. D., Field, C. B., Stocker, T. F., Edenhofer, O., Ebi, K. L., Frame, D. J., . . . & Zwiers, F. W. (2010). *Guidance note for lead authors of the IPCC fifth assessment report on consistent treatment of uncertainties*. Retrieved from www.ipcc.ch/pdf/supporting-material/uncertainty-guidance-note.pdf

Matjasko, J. L., Cawley, J. H., Baker-Goering, M. M., & Yokum, D. V. (2016). Applying behavioral economics to public health policy: Illustrative examples and promising directions. *American Journal of Preventive Medicine*, *50*(5), 13–19.

Matz, S. C., Gladstone, J. J., & Stillwell, D. (2016). Money buys happiness when spending fits our personality. *Psychological Science*, *27*(5), 715–725. https://doi.org/10.1177/0956797616635200

Matz, S. C., Gladstone, J. J., & Stillwell, D. (2017a). In a world of Big Data, small effects can still matter: A reply to Boyce, Daly, Hounkpatin, and Wood (2017). *Psychological Science*, *28*(4), 547–550.

Matz, S. C., Kosinski, M., Nave, G., & Stillwell, D. J. (2017b). Psychological targeting as an effective approach to digital mass persuasion. *Proceedings of the National Academy of Sciences*, *114*(48) 12714–12719.

Mayer, A., Cullinan, D., Calmeyer, E., & Patterson, K. (2015). *Engaging providers and clients: Using behavioral economics to increase on-time child care subsidy renewals*. Retrieved from www.acf.hhs.gov/sites/default/files/opre/bias_ok_2015_report_acf_b508.pdf

Maynard, M. (2007, July 4). Say "hybrid" and many people will hear "Prius". *The New York Times*. Retrieved on August 28, 2018 from www.nytimes.com/2007/07/04/business/04hybrid.html

McBride, T. D. (2015). Behavioral economics: "Nudging" underserved populations to be screened for cancer. *Preventing Chronic Disease*, *12*, E06.

McBride, T. D., Coburn, A., MacKinney, C., Mueller, K., Slifkin, R., & Wakefield, M. (2008). Bridging health research and policy: Effective dissemination strategies. *Journal of Public Health Management and Practice*, *14*(2), 150–154.

McCrae, R. R., & John, O. P. (1992). An introduction to the five-factor model and its applications. *Journal of Personality*, *60*(2), 175–215.

McCrone, P. R., Dhanasiri, S., Patel, A., Knapp, M., & Lawton-Smith, S. (2008). *Paying the price: The cost of mental health care in England to 2026*. London: King's Fund.

McCurry, J. (2018, August 8). Tokyo medical school admits changing results to exclude women. *The Guardian*. Retrieved from https://bit.ly/2nlVJt2

McDaid, D., King, D., & Parsonage, M. (2011). Workspace screening for depression and anxiety disorders. In M. Knapp, D. McDaid, & M. Parsonage (Eds.), *Mental health promotion and prevention: The economic case* (pp. 20–21). London: Department of Health.

McFarland, J., Hussar, B., Zhang, J., Wang, X., Wang, K., Hein, S., . . . & Barmer, A. (2019). *The condition of education 2019* (NCES 2019–144). National Center for Education Statistics.

McGarr, O. (2009). The development of ICT across the curriculum in Irish schools: A historical perspective. *British Journal of Educational Technology*, *40*(6), 1094–1108. https://doi.org/10.1111/j.1467-8535.2008.00903.x

McGuire, M., & Iuga, A. O. (2014). Adherence and health care costs. *Risk Management and Healthcare Policy, 7*, 35–44. https://doi.org/10.2147/rmhp.s19801

McInerny, G. J., Chen, M., Freeman, R., Gavaghan, D., Meyer, M., Rowland, F., . . . & Hortal, J. (2014). Information visualisation for science and policy: Engaging users and avoiding bias. *Trends in Ecology & Evolution, 29*(3), 148–157.

McKenzie, C. R., Liersch, M. J., & Finkelstein, S. R. (2006). Recommendations implicit in policy defaults. *Psychological Science, 17*(5), 414–420. https://doi.org/10.1111/j.1467-9280.2006.01721.x

The Medicines (Sale or Supply) (Miscellaneous Provisions) Amendment (No. 2) Regulations 1997 (SI 1997/2045). (1997). Retrieved from https://bit.ly/2wucEhR

Meeker, D., Linder, J. A., Fox, C. R., Friedberg, M. W., Persell, S. D., Goldstein, N. J., . . . Doctor, J. N. (2016). Effect of behavioral interventions on inappropriate antibiotic prescribing among primary care practices a randomized clinical trial. *JAMA – Journal of the American Medical Association, 315*(6), 562–570. https://doi.org/10.1001/jama.2016.0275

Menon, S., Karl, J., & Wignaraja, K. (2009). *Handbook on planning, monitoring and evaluating for development results*. New York: UNDP Evaluation Office.

Milkman, K. L., Beshears, J., Choi, J. J., Laibson, D., & Madrian, B. C. (2011). Using implementation intentions prompts to enhance influenza vaccination rates. *Proceedings of the National Academy of Sciences, 108*(26), 10415–10420.

Milkman, K. L., Minson, J., & Volpp, K. (2014). Holding the hunger games hostage at the gym: An evaluation of temptation bundling. *Management Science, 60*(2), 283–299.

Miller, M., Reichelstein, J., Salas, C., & Zia, B. (2015). Can you help someone become financially capable? A meta-analysis of the literature. *The World Bank Research Observer, 30*(2), 220–246. https://doi.org/10.1093/wbro/lkv009

Min Kim, H., & Kachersky, L. (2006). Dimensions of price salience: A conceptual framework for perceptions of multi-dimensional prices. *Journal of Product & Brand Management, 15*(2), 139–147.

Ministry of the Environment Government of Japan. (2005). *The ministerial conference on the 3R initiative: Chair's summary, April 28–30, 2005, Japan, Tokyo*. Retrieved August 8, 2018 from www.env.go.jp/recycle/3r/en/info/summary.pdf

Ministry of Foreign Affairs. (2009). *Evaluation policy and guidelines for evaluation*. London: Ministry of Foreign Affairs. Retrieved from www.oecd.org/dac/evaluation/iob-evaluation-policy-and-guidelines-for-evaluations.pdf

Mokdad, A. H., Marks, J. S., Stroup, D. F., & Gerberding, J. L. (2004). Actual causes of death in the United States, 2000. *JAMA, 291*(10), 1238–1245.

Moleni, C. M. (2008). *Factors influencing access and retention in primary schooling for children and young people affected by HIV and AIDS: Case studies from Rural Malawi*. London: Department for International Development. Retrieved from http://sofie.ioe.ac.uk/publications/MalawiCaseStudyReport.pdf

Mongin, P. (2019). The Allais paradox: what it became, what it really was, what it now suggests to us. *Economics & Philosophy*, 35(3), 423–459.

Moore, D. A., & Healy, P. J. (2008). The trouble with overconfidence. *Psychological Review, 115*(2), 502–517. https://doi.org/10.1037/0033-295X.115.2.502

Morewedge, C. K., Holtzman, L., & Epley, N. (2007). Unfixed resources: Perceived costs, consumption, and the accessible account effect. *Journal of Consumer Research, 34*, 459–467.

Mostofsky, E., Mukamal, K. J., Giovannucci, E. L., Stampfer, M. J., & Rimm, E. B. (2016). Key findings on alcohol consumption and a variety of health outcomes from the nurses' health study. *American Journal of Public Health, 106*(9), 1586–1591. https://doi.org/10.2105/AJPH.2016.303336

Mourshed, M., Farrell, D., & Barton, D. (2013). *Education to employment: Designing a system that works.* London: McKinsey & Company. Retrieved from https://mck.co/2Pmy0oy

Muchinsky, P. M. (2005). The historical background of I/O psychology. In P. M. Muchinsky (Eds.), *Psychology applied to work* (pp. 1–22). Belmont, CA: Thomson Higher Education.

Mullainathan, S., & Shafir, E. (2013). *Scarcity: Why having too little means so much.* New York: Times Books.

Munafò, M., Smith, R., & Davey, G. (2018). Robust research needs many lines of evidence. *Nature, 553*(7689), 399–401. https://doi.org/10.1038/d41586-018-01023-3

Musser, M. P. (2011). *Taking attendance seriously: How school absences undermine student and school performance in New York City.* New York: Campaign the Fiscal Equity.

Nakamura, R., Suhrcke, M., Pechey, R., Morciano, M., Roland, M., & Marteau, T. M. (2014). Impact on alcohol purchasing of a ban on multi-buy promotions: A quasi-experimental evaluation comparing Scotland with England and Wales. *Addiction, 109*(4), 558–567. https://doi.org/10.1111/add.12419

Nardo, M., Saisana, M., Saltelli, A., Tarantola, S., Hoffman, A., & Giovannini, E. (2005). *Handbook on constructing composite indicators.* Paris: OECD Publishing.

Nash, J. F. (1950). Equilibrium points in n-person games. *PNAS, 36*(1), 48–49. https://doi.org/10.1073/pnas.36.1.48

Nash, N., Whitmarsh, L. E., Capstick, S., Hargreaves, T., Poortinga, W., & Thomas, G. (2017). Climate-relevant behavioural spillover and the potential contribution of social practice theory. *WIREs Climate Change, 8*, e481.

National Audit Office. (2016). *Green deal and energy company obligation.* Department of Energy & Climate Change. London: National Audit Office Publishing. Retrieved from https://bit.ly/2jv5nVN

National Center for Education Statistics. (2017). *Digest of education statistics.* Retrieved from https://bit.ly/2NafL8p

National Center for Health Statistics. (2017). *Health, United States, 2016: With chartbook on long-term trends in health.* Washington, DC: Government Printing Office.

National Foundation for Educational Research (NFER). (2011). *Exploring young people's views on science education.* London: Wellcome Trust. Retrieved from https://bit.ly/2wxDmVY

National Science Foundation. (2009a). *Characteristics of doctoral scientists and engineers in the United States: 2006.* Arlington, VA: National Science Foundation.

National Science Foundation. (2009b). *Women, minorities, and persons with disabilities in science and engineering.* Arlington, VA: National Science Foundation. Retrieved from https://bit.ly/2PmpKEY

National Science Foundation. (2016). *Women, minorities, and persons with disabilities in science and engineering.* Arlington, VA: National Science Foundation. Retrieved from www.nsf.gov/statistics/2017/nsf17310/data.cfm

Nauer, K., White, A., & Yerneni, R. (2008). *Strengthening schools by strengthening families: Community strategies to reverse chronic absenteeism in the early grades and improve supports for children and families.* New York: Center for New York City Affairs. Retrieved from https://bit.ly/2LGwBGX

Ne Gagné, M., & Deci, E. L. (2005). Self-determination theory and work motivation. *Journal of Organizational Behavior, 26*, 331–362. https://doi.org/10.1002/job.322

Nelson, L. D., & Meyvis, T. (2008). Interrupted consumption: Disrupting adaptation to hedonic experiences. *Journal of Marketing Research, 45*(6), 654–664. https://doi.org/10.1509/jmkr.45.6.654

Nelson, S. K., Della Porta, M. D., Jacobs Bao, K., Lee, H. C., Choi, I., & Lyubomirsky, S. (2015). "It's up to you": Experimentally manipulated autonomy support for prosocial behavior improves well-being in two cultures over six weeks. *The Journal of Positive Psychology, 10*(5), 1–14.

Ng, J. Y. Y., Ntoumanis, N., Thøgersen-Ntoumani, C., Deci, E. L., Ryan, R. M., Duda, J. L., & Williams, G. C. (2012). Self-determination theory applied to health contexts: A meta-analysis. *Perspectives on Psychological Science: A Journal of the Association for Psychological Science, 7*(4), 325–340.

NHS Blood and Transplant. (2017). *NHS blood and transplant annual report and accounts 2016/17*. Retrieved from https://bit.ly/3a974m0

Nielsen. (2015). *Global trust in advertising*. Retrieved from https://bit.ly/1Plj03A

Nisa, C. F., Bélanger, J. J., Schumpe, B. M., & Faller, D. G. (2019). Meta-analysis of randomised controlled trials testing behavioural interventions to promote household action on climate change. *Nature Communications, 10*(1), 1–13.

Nisa, C., Varum, C., & Botelho, A. (2017). Promoting sustainable hotel guest behavior: A systematic review and meta-analysis. *Cornell Hospitality Quarterly, 58*(4), 354–363.

Nisbet, M. C. (Ed.). (2018). *The Oxford encyclopedia of climate change communication*. Oxford: Oxford University Press.

Nisbet, M. C., & Scheufele, D. A. (2009). What's next for science communication? Promising directions and lingering distractions. *American Journal of Botany, 96*(10), 1767–1778.

Nisbett, R. E., & Wilson, T. D. (1977). The halo effect: Evidence for unconscious alteration of judgments. *Journal of Personality and Social Psychology, 35*(4), 250–256.

Nolan, J. M., Schultz, P. W., Cialdini, R. B., Goldstein, N. J., & Griskevicius, V. (2008). Normative social influence is underdetected. *Personality and Social Psychology Bulletin, 34*(7), 913–923.

NSW Premier & Cabinet Behavioural Insights Unit, NSW Government Education, & Allianz. (2016). *Applying Behavioural Insights to return to work*. Retrieved from https://bit.ly/2CdLr8D

Nurse, J., Dorey, S., Yao, L., Sigfrid, L., Yfantopolous, P., McDaid, D., . . . & Moreno, J. M. (2014). *The case for investing in public health: A public health summary report for EPHO 8*. Geneva: World Health Organization.

Nutley, S., Davies, H., & Walter, I. (2002). *Evidence based policy and practice: Cross sector lessons from the UK*. Keynote paper for the Social Policy Research and Evaluation Conference, Wellington, New Zealand, 2–3 July.

Nyhan, B., & Reifler, J. (2010). When corrections fail: The persistence of political misperceptions. *Political Behavior, 32*, 303–330.

Nyhan, B., Reifler, J., Richey, S., & Freed, G. L. (2014). Effective messages in vaccine promotion: A randomized trial. *Pediatrics, 133*(4), e835–e842.

O'Connor, A. (2015, August 9). Coca-Cola funds scientists who shift blame for obesity away from bad diets. *New York Times*. Retrieved from https://nyti.ms/2MC9DWJ

O'Donnell, C. L. (2008). Defining, conceptualizing, and measuring fidelity of implementation and its relationship to outcomes in K-12 curriculum intervention research. *Review of Educational Research, 78*(1), 33–84. https://doi.org/10.3102/0034654307313793

O'Donoghue, T., & Rabin, M. (1999). Doing it now or later. *American Economic Review, 89*(1), 103–124. Retrieved from www.jstor.org/stable/116981
OECD. (2008a). *Study into the role of tax intermediaries*. Paris: OECD Publishing.
OECD. (2008b). *OECD environmental outlook to 2030*. Paris: OECD Publishing. Retrieved from https://bit.ly/2ojlHxJ.
OECD. (2009). *Financial education and the crisis*. Paris: OECD Publishing.
OECD. (2010). *Making reform happen lessons from OECD countries: Lessons from OECD countries*. Paris: OECD Publishing. https://doi.org/10.1787/9789264086296-en
OECD. (2013). *Co-operative compliance: A framework*. Paris: OECD Publishing.
OECD. (2014a). *What is impact assessment*. Paris: OECD Publishing. Retrieved from www.oecd.org/sti/inno/What-is-impact-assessment-OECDImpact.pdf
OECD. (2014b). *OECD framework for regulatory policy evaluation*. Paris: OECD Publishing. https://doi.org/10.1787/9789264214453-en
OECD. (2014c). *Regulatory policy and behavioural economics*. Paris: OECD Publishing.
OECD. (2015a). *OECD regulatory policy outlook 2015*. Paris: OECD Publishing. https://doi.org/10.1787/9789264238770-en
OECD. (2015b). *Education policy outlook 2015: Making reforms happen*. Paris: OECD Publishing. https://doi.org/10.1787/9789264225442-en
OECD. (2016a). *Protecting consumers through behavioural insights: Regulating the communications market in Colombia*. Paris: OECD Publishing.
OECD. (2016b). Policy responses to financial education needs in Europe. In *Financial education in Europe: Trends and recent developments*. Paris: OECD Publishing. https://doi.org/10.1787/9789264254855-en
OECD. (2016c). *Survey of adult financial literacy competencies*. Paris: OECD Publishing.
OECD. (2016d). Behavioral insights applications to environmentally relevant policies. In *Insights for environmentally relevant policies: Review of experiences from OECD countries and beyond*. Paris: OECD Publishing. Retrieved from http://bit.ly/2wt0WTG
OECD. (2017a). *Behavioural insights and public policy: Lessons from around the world*. Paris: OECD Publishing. https://doi.org/10.1787/9789264270480-en
OECD. (2017b). *Behavioural insights in public policy: Key messages and summary from OECD international events, May 2017*. Paris: OECD Publishing. Retrieved from http://bit.ly/2wujNi1
OECD. (2017c). *Impact update: What happened next? Protecting consumers through Behavioural Insights: Regulating the communications market in Colombia*. Paris: OECD Publishing.
OECD. (2017d). *Creating a culture of independence: Practical guidance against undue influence*. Paris: OECD Publishing.
OECD. (2017e). Behavioural Insights case studies: Financial products. In *Behavioral Insights and public policy: Lessons from around the world*. Paris: OECD Publishing. https://doi.org/10.1787/9789264270480-en
OECD. (2017f). Behavioural Insights case studies: Tax. In *Behavioral Insights and public policy: Lessons from around the world*. Paris: OECD Publishing. https://doi.org/10.1787/9789264270480-en
OECD. (2017g). Behavioural Insights case studies: Health and safety. In *Behavioral Insights and public policy: Lessons from around the world*. Paris: OECD Publishing. https://doi.org/10.1787/9789264270480-en
OECD. (2017h). *Obesity update*. Paris: OECD Publishing. Retrieved from http://bit.ly/2PRdhdd

OECD. (2017i). Behavioural insights case studies: Energy. In *Behavioral Insights and public policy: Lessons from around the world*. Paris: OECD Publishing. https://doi.org/10.1787/9789264270480-en

OECD. (2017j). Behavioural Insights case studies: Labour market (matching jobs and job-seekers (2) & helping job seekers find employment). In *Behavioral Insights and public policy: Lessons from around the world*. Paris: OECD Publishing. https://doi.org/10.1787/9789264270480-en

OECD. (2019a). *Delivering better policies through behavioural insights: New approaches*. Paris: OECD Publishing. https://doi.org/10.1787/6c9291e2-en

OECD. (2019b). *Tools and ethics for applied behavioural insights: The BASIC toolkit*. Paris: OECD Publishing. https://doi.org/10.1787/9ea76a8f-en

OECD/Korea Development Institute. (2017). *Improving regulatory governance: Trends, practices and the way forward*. Paris: OECD Publishing. https://doi.org/10.1787/9789264280366-en

Oishi, S., Kesebir, S., & Diener, E. (2011). Income inequality and happiness. *Psychological Science, 22*(9), 1095–1100.

Olander, F., & Thøgersen, J. (2014). Informing versus nudging in environmental policy. *Journal of Consumer Policy, 37*(3), 341–356.

Oliver, A. (Ed.). (2013). *Behavioural public policy*. Cambridge, MA: Cambridge University Press.

Oliver, K., Innvar, S., Lorenc, T., Woodman, J., & Thomas, J. (2014a). A systematic review of barriers to and facilitators of the use of evidence by policymakers. *BMC Health Services Research, 14*(2).

Oliver, K., Lorenc, T., & Innvær, S. (2014b). New directions in evidence-based policy research: A critical analysis of the literature. *Health Research Policy and Systems, 12*(34). https://doi.org/10.1186/1478-4505-12-34

O'Reilly, T. (2005). *What is WEB 2.0 – design patterns and business models for the next generation of software*. Retrieved from http://bit.ly/2N4npkp

O'Rourke, E., Haimovitz, K., Ballweber, C., Dweck, C., & Popović, Z. (2014). Brain points: A growth mindset incentive structure boosts persistence in an educational game. In *Proceedings of the SIGCHI conference on human factors in computing systems* (pp. 3339–3348). New York: ACM.

O'Rourke, E., Peach, E., Dweck, C. S., & Popovic, Z. (2016, April). Brain points: A deeper look at a growth mindset incentive structure for an educational game. In *Proceedings of the third (2016) ACM conference on Learning@ Scale* (pp. 41–50). New York: ACM.

Østby, G., & Urdal, H. (2011). *Education and civil conflict: A review of the quantitative, empirical literature*. Background paper prepared for the Education for All global monitoring report.

Ostrom, E. (1990). *Governing the commons: The evolution of institutions for collective action*. Cambridge: Cambridge University Press.

Ostrom, E., Gardner, R., & Walker, J. (1994). *Rules, games, and common-pool resources*. Ann Arbor, MI: The University of Michigan Press.

Ostry, J. D., & Berg, A. (2011). *Inequality and unsustainable growth: Two sides of the same coin*? Washington, DC: International Monetary Fund.

Page, L. C., & Gehlbach, H. (2017). How an artificially intelligent virtual assistant helps students navigate the road to college. *SSRN*. Retrieved from http://bit.ly/2noh4Bd

Page, L. C., & Scott-Clayton, J. (2016). Improving college access in the United States: Barriers and policy responses. *Economics of Education Review, 51*, 4–22.

Page, S. (2007). *The difference – How the power of diversity creates better groups, firms, schools, and societies*. Princeton, NJ: Princeton University Press.

Palinkas, L. A., & Rhoades Cooper, B. (2017). Chapter 20 – Mixed methods evaluation in dissemination and implementation science. In R. C. Brownson, G. A. Colditz, & E. K. Proctor (Eds.), *Dissemination and implementation research in health: Translating science to practice*. Oxford: Oxford University Press.

Pallier, G., Wilkinson, R., Danthiir, V., Kleitman, S., Knezevic, G., Stankov, L., & Roberts, R. D. (2002). The role of individual differences in the accuracy of confidence judgments. *The Journal of General Psychology, 129*(3), 257–299. https://doi.org/10.1080/00221300209602099

Paluck, E. L., & Shepherd, H. (2012). The salience of social referents: A field experiment on collective norms and harassment behavior in a school social network. *Journal of Personality and Social Psychology, 103*(6), 899.

Pang, J., Franklin, M., Young, S., Gibson, M., & Charlile, T. (2017). *The future of common-pool resource management*. Cambridge: The Wilberforce Society. Retrieved from http://bit.ly/2PLz9XH

Papadakis, S. (2016). Creativity and innovation in European education. Ten years eTwinning. Past, present and the future. *International Journal of Technology Enhanced Learning, 8*(3–4). https://doi.org/10.1504/IJTEL.2016.082315

Parkhurst, J. (2017). *The politics of evidence: From evidence-based policy to the good governance of evidence* (Routledge Studies in Governance and Public Policy Series). Abingdon: Routledge.

Parks, C. D. (1994). The predictive ability of social values in resource dilemmas and public goods games. *Personality and Social Psychology Bulletin, 20*(4), 431–438.

Parks, C. D. (2014). Determinants of cooperation in social dilemmas. In D. A. Schroeder & W. G. Graziano (Eds.), *The Oxford handbook of prosocial behavior*. Oxford: Oxford University Press.

Parks, C. D., Joireman, J., & Van Lange, P. A. (2013). Cooperation, trust, and antagonism: How public goods are promoted. *Psychological Science in the Public Interest, 14*(3), 119–165.

Patz, J. A., Frumkin, H., Holloway, T., Vimont, D. J., & Haines, A. (2014). Climate change: Challenges and opportunities for global health. *Jama, 312*(15), 1565–1580.

Paul-Ebhohimhen, V., & Avenell, A. (2008). Systematic review of the use of financial incentives in treatments for obesity and overweight. *Obesity Reviews, 9*(4), 355–367. https://doi.org/10.1111/j.1467-789x.2007.00409.x

Paunesku, D., Walton, G. M., Romero, C., Smith, E. N., Yeager, D. S., & Dweck, C. S. (2015). Mind-set interventions are a scalable treatment for academic underachievement. *Psychological Science, 26*(6), 784–793. https://doi.org/10.1177/0956797615571017

Pawson, R. (2006). *Evidence-based policy: A realist perspective*. London: Sage.

Payne, B. K., Brown-Iannuzzi, J. L., & Hannay, J. W. (2017). Economic inequality increases risk taking. *Proceedings of the National Academy of Sciences, 114*(18), 4643–4648.

Payne, J. W., Bettman, J. R., & Johnson, E. J. (1988). Adaptive strategy selection in decision making. *Journal of Experimental Psychology: Learning, Memory, and Cognition, 14*(3), 534–552. https://doi.org/10.1037/0278-7393.14.3.534

Payne, K. (2017). *The broken ladder: How inequality affects the way we think, live, and die*. New York: Penguin.

Payzan-LeNestour, E., & Bossaerts, P. (2011). Risk, unexpected uncertainty, and estimation uncertainty: Bayesian learning in unstable settings. *PLoS Computational Biology, 7*(1). https://doi.org/10.1371/journal.pcbi.1001048

Pearson, J. M., Watson, K. K., & Platt, M. L. (2014). Decision making: The neuroethological turn. *Neuron, 82*(5), 950–965.

Pellerano, J. A., Price, M. K., Puller, S. L., & Sánchez, G. E. (2017). Do extrinsic incentives undermine social norms? Evidence from a field experiment in energy conservation. *Environmental and Resource Economics, 67*(3), 413–428. https://doi.org/10.1007/s10650-016-0094-3

Pentland, A. (2012). The new science of building great teams. *Harvard Business Review, 90*(4), 60–69.

Perk, J., De Backer, G., Gohlke, H., Graham, I., Reiner, Ž., Verschuren, M., . . . & Wolpert, C. (2012). European guidelines on cardiovascular disease prevention in clinical practice (version 2012). *European Heart Journal, 33*(13), 1635–1701. https://doi.org/10.1093/eurheartj/ehs092

Perry, Y., & Bennett-Levy, J. (2014). Delivering the "H" in NHMRC: The case for implementation research in mental health. *Australian and New Zealand Journal of Public Health, 38*(5), 411–413.

Pettifor, H., Wilson, C., & Chryssochoidis, G. (2015). The appeal of the green deal: Empirical evidence for the influence of energy efficiency policy on renovating homeowners. *Energy Policy, 79*, 161–176.

Pew Charitable Trusts and MacArthur Foundation. (2017). *How states engage in evidence-based policymaking: A national assessment*. Philadelphia and Washington, DC: Pew-MacArthur Results First Initiative. Retrieved from https://bit.ly/2jEbQh7

Pew Research Center. (2008). *Audience segments in a changing news environment: Key News audiences now blend online and traditional sources*. Washington, DC: Pew Research Center. Retrieved from http://people-press.org/reports/pdf/ 444.pdf

Pew Research Center. (2014). *Thirteen years of the public's top priorities*. Washington, DC: Pew Research Center. Retrieved August 29, 2017 from www.people-press. org/interactive/top-priorities/

Pew Research Center. (2015). *Facebook top source for political news among millennials*. Retrieved from www.journalism.org/2015/06/01/facebook-top-source-for-political-news-among-millennials

Pew Research Center. (2018). *Public's policy priorities for 2018*. Retrieved from www.people-press.org/2018/01/25/economic-issues-decline-among-publics-policy-priorities/012518_2/

Phillips, D. L., & Clancy, K. J. (1972). Some effects of "social desirability" in survey studies. *American Journal of Sociology, 77*(5), 921–940.

Pianta, R. C., Kraft-Sayre, M., Rimm-Kaufman, S., Gercke, N., & Higgins, T. (2001). Collaboration in building partnerships between families and schools: The National Center for Early Development and Learning's Kindergarten Transition Intervention. *Early Childhood Research Quarterly, 16*(1), 117–132.

Pichert, D., & Katsikopoulos, K. V. (2008). Green defaults: Information presentation and pro-environmental behaviour. *Journal of Environmental Psychology, 28*(1), 63–73.

Pickett, K. E., & Wilkinson, R. G. (2015). Income inequality and health: A causal review. *Social Science & Medicine, 128*, 316–326.

Pieters, R., & Wedel, M. (2004). Attention capture and transfer in advertising: Brand, pictorial, and text-size effects. *Journal of Marketing, 68*(2), 36–50.

Piketty, T. (2000). Theories of persistent inequality and intergenerational mobility. In A. B. Atkinson & F. Bourguignon (Eds.), *Handbook of income distribution* (Vol. 1, pp. 429–476). Amsterdam: Elsevier.

Piketty, T. (2014). *Capital in the twenty-first century*. Cambridge, MA: The Belknap Press of Harvard University Press.

Piketty, T., & Saez, E. (2014). Inequality in the long run. *Science, 344*(6186), 838–843.

Policy Research Group. (2016). *Insights for impact* (Vol. 1, K. Ruggeri, Ed.). Cambridge: Cambridge University Press.

Pollitt, C. (2013). *Context in public policy and management: The missing link?* Cheltenham: Edward Elgar.

Pollitt, M. G., & Shaorshadze, I. (2011). *The role of behavioural economics in energy and climate policy* (Cambridge Working Paper in Economics). Cambridge University. https://doi.org/10.17863/CAM.1140

Powell, B. J., et al. (2015). A refined compilation of implementation strategies: Results from the Expert Recommendations for Implementing Change (ERIC) project. *Implementation Science, 10*(1), 21.

Prabhakar, R. (2017). Why do people opt-out or not opt-out of automatic enrolment? A focus group study of automatic enrolment into a workplace pension in the United Kingdom. *Journal of European Social Policy, 27*(5), 447–457.

Prasad, R. V. (2014). *Scoping paper: Modern and Rational tax administration system for Papua New Guinea*. Symposium paper presented at the PNG Taxation Research and Review Symposium.

Pridmore, P., & Jere, C. M. (2011). Disrupting patterns of educational inequality and disadvantage in Malawi. *Journal of Comparative and International Education, 41*(4), 513–531. https://doi.org/10.1080/03057925.2011.581518

Prieger, J. E., & Hu, W. M. (2008). The broadband digital divide and the nexus of race, competition, and quality. *Information Economics and Policy, 20*(2), 150–167.

Pronk, N., Katz, A., Lowry, M., & Payfer, J. (2012). Reducing occupational sitting time and improving worker health: The take-a-stand project, 2011. *Preventing Chronic Disease, 9*. https://doi.org/10.5888/pcd9.110323

Pronovost, P., Needham, D., Berenholtz, S., Sinopoli, D., Chu, H., Cosgrove, S., & Goeschel, C. (2006). An intervention to decrease catheter-related bloodstream infections in the ICU. *New England Journal of Medicine, 355*(26), 2725–2732.

Public Health England. (2018). Improving people's health: applying behavioural and social sciences to improve population health and wellbeing in England. *Public Health England Publications* 2018478.

Purnhagen, K. P., & van Herpen, E. (2017). Can bonus packs mislead consumers? A demonstration of how behavioural consumer research can inform unfair commercial practices law on the example of the ECJ's Mars judgement. *Journal of Consumer Policy, 40*(2), 217–234. https://doi.org/10.1007/s10603-017-9345-0

Puska, P. (2002). Successful prevention of non-communicable diseases: 25 year experiences with North Karelia Project in Finland. *Public Health Medicine, 4*(1), 5–7.

Rama, A. (2019). *Policy research perspectives: National Health Expenditures, 2017: The slowdown in spending growth continues*. American Medical Association. Retrieved from www.ama-assn.org/system/files/2019-04/prp-annual-spending-2017.pdf

Ramaprasad, A. (1983). On the definition of feedback. *Systems Research and Behavioral Science, 28*, 4–13. https://doi.org/10.1002/bs.3830280103

Ranck, J. (2011). *Health information and health care: The role of technology in unlocking data and wellness – A discussion paper*. Washington, DC: United Nations Foundation & Vodafone Foundation Technology Partnership.

Reinhard, M., Schindler, S., Raabe, V., Stahlberg, D., & Messner, M. (2014). Less is sometimes more: How repetition of an antismoking advertisement affects attitudes toward smoking and source credibility. *Social Influence*, *9*, 116–132. https://doi.org/10.1080/15534510.2013.790839

Reisch, L., & Sunstein, C. (2016). Do Europeans like nudges? *Judgment & Decision Making*, *11*(4), 310–325.

Reiss, P. C., & White, M. W. (2008). What changes energy consumption? Prices and public pressures. *The RAND Journal of Economics*, *39*(3), 636–663.

Reiter, P., McRee, A., Pepper, J., & Brewer, N. (2012). Default policies and parents' consent for school-located HPV vaccination. *Journal of Behavioral Medicine*, *35*(6), 651–657. https://doi.org/10.1007/s10865-012-9397-1

Resnik, D. B., & Elliott, K. C. (2016). The ethical challenges of socially responsible science. *Accountability in Research*, *23*(1), 31–46. https://doi.org/10.1080/08989621.2014.1002608

Reuters Institute. (2016). *Reuters institute digital news report 2016*. Retrieved from http://reutersinstitute.politics.ox.ac.uk/sites/default/files/Digital%20News%20Report%202016.pdf

Richburg-Hayes, L., Anzelone, C., & Dechausay, N. (2017). *Nudging change in human services*. Final Report of the Behavioral Interventions to Advance Self-Sufficiency (BIAS) Project.

Rishika, R., Kumar, A., Janakiraman, R., & Bezawada, R. (2013). The effect of customers' social media participation on customer visit frequency and profitability: An empirical investigation. *Information Systems Research*, *24*(1), 108–127. https://doi.org/10.1287/isre.1120.0460

Roberto, C. A., Lawman, H. G., Levasseur, M. T., Mitra, N., Peterhans, A., Herring, B., & Bleich, S. N. (2019). Association of a beverage tax on sugar-sweetened and artificially sweetened beverages with changes in beverage prices and sales at chain retailers in a large urban setting. *JAMA*, *321*(18), 1799–1810. https://doi.org/10.1001/jama.2019.4249

Robertson, T., Darling, M., Leifer, J., & Footer, O. (2017). *Behavioral design teams: The next frontier in clinical delivery innovation?* New York: The Commonwealth Fund. Retrieved from https://bit.ly/2LFm8vw

Robinson, B. H. (2009). E-waste: An assessment of global production and environmental impacts. *Science of the Total Environment*, *408*(2), 183–191. https://doi.org/10.1016/j.scitotenv.2009.09.044

Robinson, C. D., Gallus, J., Lee, M. G., & Rogers, T. (2019). The demotivating effect (and unintended message) of awards. *Organizational Behavior and Human Decision Processes*, *164*(4).

Robinson, C. D., Lee, M. G., Dearing, E., & Rogers, T. (2017). *Reducing student absenteeism in the early grades by targeting parental beliefs* (HKS Working Paper No. RWP17-011). https://doi.org/10.2139/ssrn.2929600

Robinson, C. D., Lee, M. G., Dearing, E., & Rogers, T. (2018a). Reducing student absenteeism in the early grades by targeting parental beliefs. *American Educational Research Journal*, *55*(6), 1163–1192. https://doi.org/10.3102/0002831218772274

Robinson, C. D., Lee, M. G., Dearing, E., & Rogers, T. (2018b). Reducing student absenteeism in the early grades by targeting parental beliefs. *American Educational Research Journal*, Online first, 1–30. https://doi.org/10.3102/0002831218772274

Robinson, C. D., Pons, G. A., Duckworth, A. L., & Rogers, T. (2018c). Some middle school students want behavior commitment devices (but take-up does not affect their behavior). *Frontiers in Psychology*, *9*, 206. https://doi.org/10.3389/fpsyg.2018.00206

Robinson, K. (2006). *Ken Robinson: Do schools kill creativity*? [Video file]. Retrieved from www.ted.com/talks/ken_robinson_says_schools_kill_creativity

Robinson, M., Geue, C., Lewsey, J., Mackay, D., Mccartney, G., Curnock, E., & Beeston, C. (2014). Evaluating the impact of the alcohol act on off-trade alcohol sales: A natural experiment in Scotland. *Addiction*, *109*(12), 2035–2043. https://doi.org/10.1111/add.12701

Rodríguez Estrada, F. C., & Davis, L. S. (2015). Improving visual communication of science through the incorporation of graphic design theories and practices into science communication. *Science Communication*, *37*(1), 140–148. https://doi.org/10.1177/1075547014562914

Roethlisberger, F. J., & Dickson, W. J. (1939). *Management and the worker*. Cambridge, MA: Harvard University Press.

Rogers, P. J. (2014). *Overview of impact evaluation*. Florence: UNICEF Office of Research-Innocenti.

Rogers, T., & Feller, A. (2016). *Intervening through influential third parties: Reducing student absences at scale via parents* (Working paper). Cambridge, MA: Harvard University. Retrieved from http://bit.ly/2ky1rJu

Rogers, T., & Feller, A. (2018). Reducing student absences at scale by targeting parents' misbeliefs. *Nature Human Behaviour*, *2*(5), 335–342. https://doi.org/10.1038/s41562-018-0328-1

Rogers, T., Milkman, K. L., John, L. K., & Norton, M. I. (2015). Beyond good intentions: Prompting people to make plans improves follow through on important tasks. *Behavioral Science & Policy*, *1*(2), 41–51.

Rogers, T., Milkman, K. L., & Volpp, K. G. (2014). Commitment devices: Using initiatives to change behavior. *JAMA*, *311*(20), 2065–2066. https://doi.org/10.1001/jama.2014.3485

Roorda, D. L., Koomen, H. M., Spilt, J. L., & Oort, F. J. (2011). The influence of affective teacher–student relationships on students' school engagement and achievement: A meta-analytic approach. *Review of Educational Research*, *81*(4), 493–529.

Roscigno, V. J. (2007). *The face of discrimination: How race and gender impact work and home lives*. Lanham, MD: Rowman and Littlefield Publishers.

Rose, G. (1985). Sick individuals and sick populations. *International Journal of Epidemiology*, *14*(1), 32–38. https://doi.org/10.1093/ije/14.1.32

Rose, G. (2001). Sick individuals and sick populations (reiteration). *International Journal of Epidemiology*, *30*(3), 427–432.

Roth, A. E., & Peranson, E. (1999). The redesign of the matching market for American physicians: Some engineering aspects of economic design. *American Economic Review*, *89*(4), 748–780.

Rowe, G. (1998), The use of structured groups to improve judgmental forecasting. In P. Goodwin & G. Wright (Eds.), *Forecasting with judgement* (pp. 201–235). Chichester: Wiley.

Rowe, G., & Wright, G. (2001). Expert opinions in forecasting. Role of the Delphi technique. In J. S. Armstrong (Ed.), *Principles of forecasting: A handbook of researchers and practitioners*. Boston, MA: Kluwer Academic Publishers.

Rozenberg, J., & Hallegatte, S. (2015). *The impacts of climate change on poverty in 2030 and the potential from rapid, inclusive, and climate-informed development* (Policy Research

Working Paper 7483). Washington, DC: World Bank. Retrieved from https://bit.ly/2C34G4o

Rözer, J., & Kraaykamp, G. (2013). Income inequality and subjective well-being: A cross-national study on the conditional effects of individual and national characteristics. *Social Indicators Research, 113*(3), 1009–1023. https://doi.org/10.1007/s11205-012-0124-7

Ruggeri, K. (2014). Disseminating health research in sub-Saharan Africa through journal partnerships. *The Lancet Global Health, 2*(4), e193–e194. https://doi.org/10.1016/S2214-109X(13)70158-X

Ruggeri, K. (Ed.). (2016). *Insights for Impact*. Cambridge: University of Cambridge.

Ruggeri, K. (2017a). Editorial: Psychology and policy. *Frontiers in Psychology, 8*(497). https://doi.org/10.3389/fpsyg.2017.00497

Ruggeri, K. (2017b). Forward teaching: Recommendations for improving statistical literacy in psychological and behavioral sciences. *PeerJ PrePrints*. https://doi.org/10.7287/peerj.preprints.3265v1

Ruggeri, K. (2019). *Behavioral insights for public policy: Cases and concepts*. New York: Routledge.

Ruggeri, K., & Folke, T. (2021). Unstandard deviation: The untapped value of positive deviance for reducing inequalities. *Perspectives on Psychological Science*.

Ruggeri, K., Folke, T., Benzerga, A., Verra, S., Büttner, C., Steinbeck, V., . . . & Chaiyachati, K. (2020a). Nudging New York: Adaptive models and the limits of behavioral interventions to reduce no-shows and health inequalities. *BMC Health Services Research, 20*(1), 363.

Ruggeri, K., Garcia-Garzon, E., Maguire, Á., Matz, S., & Huppert, F. A. (2020b). Well-being is more than happiness and life satisfaction: a multidimensional analysis of 21 countries. *Health and Quality of Life Outcomes, 18*(1), 1–6.

Ruggeri, K., Maguire, Á., & Cook, G. (2016). The "next big thing" in treatment for relapsed or refractory multiple myeloma may be held back by design – between the lines. *JAMA Oncology, 2*(11), 1405–1406. https://doi.org/10.1001/jamaoncol.2016.1782

Ruggeri, K., Yoon, H., Kácha, O., van der Linden, S., & Muennig, P. (2017). Policy and population behavior in the age of Big Data. *Current Opinion in Behavioral Sciences, 18*, 1–6. https://doi.org/10.1016/j.cobeha.2017.05.010

Ryan, R., & Deci, E. L. (2000). Self-determination theory and the facilitation of intrinsic motivation, social development, and well-being. *The American Psychologist, 55*(1), 68–78.

Rycroft-Malone, J., Seers, K., Titchen, A., Harvey, G., Kitson, A., & McCormack, B. (2004). What counts as evidence in evidence-based practice? *Journal of Advanced Nursing, 47*(1), 81–90. https://doi.org/10.1111/j.1365-2648.2004.03068.x

Sacarny, A., Barnett, M. L., Le, J., Tetkoski, F., Yokum, D., & Agrawal, S. (2018a). Effect of peer comparison letters for high-volume primary care prescribers of quetiapine in older and disabled adults: A randomized clinical trial. *JAMA Psychiatry, 75*(10), 1003–1011. https://doi.org/10.1001/jamapsychiatry.2018.1867

Sacarny, A., Barnett, M. L., Le, J., Tetkoski, F., Yokum, D., & Agrawal, S. (2018b). Effect of peer comparison letters for high-volume primary care prescribers of quetiapine in older and disabled adults: A randomized clinical trial. *JAMA Psychiatry*, E1–E9, https://doi.org/10.1001/jamapsychiatry.2018.1867

Sacarny, A., Yokum, D., Finkelstein, A., & Agrawal, S. (2016). Medicare letters to curb overprescribing of controlled substances had no detectable effect on providers. *Health Affairs, 35*(3), 471–479. https://doi.org/10.1377/hlthaff.2015.1025

Sadana, R., & Harper, S. (2011). Data systems linking social determinants of health with health outcomes: Advancing public goods to support research and evidence-based policy and programs. *Public Health Reports*, *126*(3), 6–13.

Sagiroglu, S., & Sinanc, D. (2013). Big data: A review. In *2013 international conference on Collaboration Technologies and Systems (CTS)* (pp. 42–47). New York: IEEE.

Salamon, L. M. (1981). Rethinking public management: Third-party government and the changing forms of government action. *Public Policy*, *29*(3), 255–275.

Samuelson, W., & Zeckhauser, R. (1988). Status quo bias in decision making. *Journal of Risk and Uncertainty*, *1*(1), 7–59.

Sanders, M., Chande, R., & Selley, E. (2017). *Encouraging people into university*. Retrieved from http://bit.ly/2wl6RK1

Santos, J. M., & van der Linden, S. (2016). Environmental reviews and case studies: Changing norms by changing behavior: The Princeton Drink Local Program. *Environmental Practice*, *18*(2), 116–122.

Saqr, M., Fors, U., & Tedre, M. (2017). How learning analytics can early predict under-achieving students in a blended medical education course. *Medical Teacher*, *39*(7), 757–767. https://doi.org/10.1080/0142159X.2017.1309376

Sashi, C. M. (2012). Customer engagement, buyer-seller relationships, and social media. *Management Decision*, *50*(2), 253–272.

Schacter, D. L. (2012). Adaptive constructive processes and the future of memory. *American Psychologist*, *67*(8), 603.

Schank, R. C., & Abelson, R. P. (1995). Knowledge and memory: The real story. In R. S. Wyer, Jr. (Ed.), *Advances in social cognition* (Vol. 8, pp. 1–85). Hillsdale, NJ: Erlbaum.

Schintler, L. A., & Kulkarni, R. (2014). Big data for policy analysis: The good, the bad, and the ugly. *Review of Policy Research*, *31*(4), 343–348.

Schmidt, H. (2008). Bonuses as incentives and rewards for health responsibility: A good thing? *Journal of Medicine and Philosophy*, *33*(3), 198–220. https://doi.org/10.1093/jmp/jhn007

Schneider, A., & Ingram, H. (1990). Behavioral assumptions of policy tools. *The Journal of Politics*, *52*(2), 510–529. https://doi.org/10.2307/2131904

Schneider, B. (1987). The people make the place. *Personnel Psychology*, *40*(3), 437–453. https://doi.org/10.1097/00006247-199305000-00001

Schneider, F., & Klinglmair, R. (2004, March). *Shadow economies around the world: What do we know?* (IZA Discussion Paper No. 1043; CESifo Working Paper Series No. 1167). Retrieved from https://ssrn.com/abstract=518526

Schooler, J. W. (2014). Metascience could rescue the "replication crisis". *Nature*, *515*(7525), 9.

Schubert, C. (2017). Green nudges: Do they work? Are they ethical? *Ecological Economics*, *132*, 329–342.

Schultz, P. W., Bator, R. J., Large, L. B., Bruni, C. M., & Tabanico, J. J. (2013). Littering in context: Personal and environmental predictors of littering behavior. *Environment and Behavior*, *45*(1), 35–59.

Schultz, P. W., Nolan, J. M., Cialdini, R. B., Goldstein, N. J., & Griskevicius, V. (2007). The constructive, destructive, and reconstructive power of social norms. *Psychological Science*, *18*(5), 429–434.

Schwartz, D., Bruine de Bruin, W., Fischhoff, B., & Lave, L. (2015). Advertising energy saving programs: The potential environmental cost of emphasizing monetary savings. *Journal of Experimental Psychology: Applied*, *21*(2), 158–166.

Scottish Parliament. (2010). *Alcohol etc. (Scotland) Act 2010*. Retrieved from www.legislation.gov.uk/asp/2010/18/pdfs/asp_20100018_en.pdf

Scotto di Carlo, G. (2014). The role of proximity in online popularizations: The case of TED talks. *Discourse Studies, 16*(5), 591–606.

Selinger, E., & Whyte, K. (2012). What counts as a nudge? *The American Journal of Bioethics, 12*(2), 11–12. https://doi.org/10.1080/15265161.2011.634485

Sent, E.-M. (2004). Behavioral economics: How psychology made its (limited) way back into economics. *History of Political Economy, 36*(December), 735–760.

Service, O., Hallsworth, M., Halpern, D., Algate, F., Gallagher, R., & Nguyen, S., . . . & Sanders, M. (2014). *EAST: Four simple ways to apply behavioural insights* (1st ed.). London: Behavioural Insights Team, Cabinet Office. Retrieved from https://bit.ly/1eufWFP

Seth, P., Scholl, L., Rudd, R. A., & Bacon, S. (2018). Overdose deaths involving opioids, cocaine, and psychostimulants – United States, 2015–2016. *American Journal of Transplantation, 18*(6), 1556–1568. https://doi.org/10.1111/ajt.14905

Sexton, S. E., & Sexton, A. L. (2014). Conspicuous conservation: The Prius halo and willingness to pay for environmental bona fides. *Journal of Environmental Economics and Management, 67*(3), 303–317.

Shafir, E., & Leboeuf, R. A. (2002). Rationality. *Annual Review of Psychology, 53*, 491–517.

Shah, A. K., & Oppenheimer, D. M. (2008). Heuristics made easy: An effort-reduction framework. *Psychological Bulletin, 134*(2), 207–222.

Shaxson, L. (2005). Is your evidence robust enough? Questions for policy makers and practitioners. *Evidence and Policy: A Journal of Research, Debate and Practice, 1*(1), 101–111.

Shelby, A., & Ernst, K. (2013). Story and science: How providers and parents can utilize storytelling to combat anti-vaccine misinformation. *Human Vaccines & Immunotherapeutics, 9*(8), 1795–1801.

Shelton, B. E., Hung, J.-L., & Lowenthal, P. R. (2017). Predicting student success by modeling student interaction in asynchronous online courses. *Distance Education, 38*(1), 59–69. https://doi.org/10.1080/01587919.2017.1299562

Shelton, R. C., Cooper, B. R., & Stirman, W. S. (2018). Sustainability of evidence-based interventions in public health and healthcare. *Annual Reviews of Public Health, 39*, 55–76. https://doi.org/10.1146/annurev-publhealth-040617-014731

Shema, H., Bar-Ilan, J., & Thelwall, M. (2012). Research blogs and the discussion of scholarly information. *PLoS ONE, 7*(5). https://doi.org/10.1371/journal.pone.0035869

Sherif, M. (1936). *The psychology of social norms*. Oxford: Harper.

Shi, J., Visschers, V. H., Siegrist, M., & Arvai, J. (2016). Knowledge as a driver of public perceptions about climate change reassessed. *Nature Climate Change, 6*(8), 759–763. https://doi.org/10.1038/NCLIMATE2997

Shih, M. J., Pittinsky, T. L., & Ho, G. C. (2011). Stereotype boost: Positive outcomes from the activation of positive stereotypes. In M. Inzlicht & T. Schmader (Eds.), *Stereotype threat: Theory, process, and application* (pp. 141–158). Oxford: Oxford University Press, Inc. ISBN 978-0-19-973244-9. https://doi.org/10.1093/acprof:oso/9780199732449.001.0001

Siau, K., & Shen, Z. (2003). Building customer trust in mobile commerce. *Communications of the ACM, 46*(4), 91–94.

Simon, H. (1955). A behavioral model of rational choice. *The Quarterly Journal of Economics, 69*(1), 99–118. https://doi.org/10.2307/1884852
Simon, H. (1957a). A behavioral model of rational choice. In *Models of man, social and rational: Mathematical essays on rational human behavior in a social setting* (p. 287). New York: John Wiley and Sons.
Simon, H. (1957b). *Models of man: Social and rational.* New York: John Wiley and Sons.
Simon, H. (1978). Rational decision-making in business organizations. *The American Economic Review, 69*(4), 493–513.
Simon, H. (1991). *Models of my life.* New York: Basic Books.
Smart, L. (2016). *Full disclosure: A round-up of FCA experimental research into giving information* (Financial Conduct Authority (FCA), Occasional Paper 23). Retrieved from www.fca.org.uk/publication/occasional-papers/op16-23.pdf
Smetana, L. K., & Bell, R. L. (2012). Computer simulations to support science instruction and learning: A critical review of the literature. *International Journal of Science Education, 34*(9), 1337–1370. https://doi.org/10.1080/09500693.2011.605182
Smets, K. (2018, July 24). There is more to behavioral economics than biases and fallacies. *Behavioral Scientist.*
Smith, A. (1776). *An inquiry into the nature and causes of the wealth of nations.* London: W. Strahan and T. Cadell.
Smith, S. M., Fahey, T., Smucny, J., & Becker, L. A. (2014). Antibiotics for acute bronchitis. *Cochrane Database of Systematic Reviews, 3,* 1465–1858. https://doi.org/10.1002/14651858.cd000245.pub3
Smith, K. E., & Joyce, K. E. (2012). Capturing complex realities: Understanding efforts to achieve evidence-based policy and practice in public health. *Evidence & Policy: A Journal of Research, Debate and Practice, 8*(1), 57–78.
Social and Behavioral Sciences Team. (2015). *Social and behavioral sciences team: Annual report.* Washington, DC: Office of Science and Technology Policy. Retrieved from https://bit.ly/2Pfb2iM
Soenens, B., Vansteenkiste, M., Lens, W., Luyckx, K., Goossens, L., Beyers, W., & Ryan, R. M. (2007). Conceptualizing parental autonomy support: Adolescent perceptions of promotion of independence versus promotion of volitional functioning. *Developmental Psychology, 43*(3), 633–646.
Sohl, S. J., & Moyer, A. (2007). Tailored interventions to promote mammography screening: A meta-analytic review. *Preventive Medicine, 45*(4), 252–261. https://doi.org/10.1016/j.ypmed.2007.06.009
Soll, J. B., & Klayman, J. (2004). Overconfidence in interval estimates. *Journal of Experimental Psychology: Learning, Memory and Cognition, 30*(2), 299–314.
Sørensen, K., Van den Broucke, S., Fullam, J., Doyle, G., Pelikan, J., Slonska, Z., & Brand, H. (2012). Health literacy and public health: A systematic review and integration of definitions and models. *BMC Public Health, 12*(1), 80. https://doi.org/10.1186/1471-2458-12-80
Sorian, R., & Baugh, T. (2002). Power of information: Closing the gap between research and policy. *Health Affairs, 21*(2), 264–273. https://doi.org/10.1377/hlthaff.21.2.264
Sovacool, B. K. (2014). Energy studies need social science. *Nature, 511*(7511), 529–530. Retrieved from https://bit.ly/2okUcns

Spencer, L., Ritchie, J., Lewis, J., & Dillon, J. (2003). *Quality in qualitative evaluation: A framework for assessing research evidence*. London: Government Chief Social Researcher's Office.

Spencer, S. J., Logel, C., & Davies, P. G. (2016). Stereotype threat. *Annual Review of Psychology, 67*, 415–437. https://doi.org/10.1146/annurev-psych-073115-103235

Spencer, S. J., Steele, C. M., & Quinn, D. M. (1999). Stereotype threat and women's math performance. *Journal of Experimental Social Psychology, 35*(1), 4–28. https://doi.org/10.1006/jesp.1998.1373

Spiegelhalter, D., Pearson, M., & Short, I. (2011). Visualizing uncertainty about the future. *Science, 333*(6048), 1393–1400.

Spreitzer, G., Garrett, L., & Bacevice, P. (2015). Should your company embrace coworking? *MIT Sloan Management Review, 57*(1), 27–29.

Staats, H. J., Wit, A. P., & Midden, C. Y. H. (1996). Communicating the greenhouse effect to the public: Evaluation of a mass media campaign from a social dilemma perspective. *Journal of Environmental Management, 46*(2), 189–203.

Stamatakis, K. A., McBride, T. D., & Brownson, R. C. (2010). Communicating prevention messages to policy makers: The role of stories in promoting physical activity. *Journal of Physical Activity and Health, 7*(Suppl. 1), S99–S107.

Statcounter Global Stats. (2016). *Mobile and tablet internet usage exceeds desktop for first time worldwide*. Retrieved from https://bit.ly/2dYq5PI

Statistics Canada. (2011). *Immigration and ethnocultural diversity in Canada*. Retrieved October 11, 2018 from www12.statcan.gc.ca/nhs-enm/2011/as-sa/99-010-x/99-010-x2011001-eng.cfm

Statistisches Bundesamt. (2017). *Time use survey 2012/2013*. Wiesbaden: Statistisches Bundesamt. Retrieved from www.destatis.de/EN

Statman, M., Fisher, K. L., & Anginer, D. (2008). Affect in a behavioral asset-pricing model. *Financial Analysts Journal, 64*(2), 20–29.

Steele, C. M., & Aronson, J. (1995). Stereotype threat and the intellectual test performance of African Americans. *Journal of Personality and Social Psychology, 69*(5), 797–811. https://doi.org/10.1037/0022-3514.69.5.797

Steg, L., Bolderdijk, J. W., Keizer, K., & Perlaviciute, G. (2014). An integrated framework for encouraging pro-environmental behaviour: The role of values, situational factors and goals. *Journal of Environmental Psychology, 38*, 104–115.

Stegenga, J. (2011). Is meta-analysis the platinum standard of evidence? *Studies in History and Philosophy of Science Part C: Studies in History and Philosophy of Biological and Biomedical Sciences, 42*(4), 497–507.

Steinberg, P. L., Wason, S., Stern, J. M., Deters, L., Kowal, B., & Seigne, J. (2010). YouTube as source of prostate cancer information. *Urology, 75*(3), 619–622.

Stern, P. C., Dietz, T., Abel, T., Guagnano, G. A., & Kalof, L. (1999). A value-belief-norm theory of support for social movements: The case of environmentalism. *Human Ecology Review, 6*(2), 81–97.

Stewart-Brown, S., Middleton, J., & Ashton, J. (2015). Responses to the Chief Medical Officer's report 2013. *The Lancet, 385*(9987), 2576.

Stiefel, L., Schwartz, A. E., & Rotenberg, A. (2011). What do AEFA members say? Summary of results of an education finance and policy survey. *Education Finance and Policy, 6*(2), 267–292.

Stiglitz, J. E. (2012). *The price of inequality: How today's divided society endangers our future*. New York: W W Norton & Company.

Stricker, L. J., & Ward, W. C. (2004). Stereotype threat, inquiring about test takers' ethnicity and gender, and standardized test performance. *Journal of Applied Social Psychology, 34*(4), 665–693. https://doi.org/10.1111/j.1559-1816.2004.tb02564.x

Sunstein, C. R. (2014). Nudging: A very short guide. *Journal of Consumer Policy, 37*(4), 583–588.

Sunstein, C. R. (2015). On interesting policymakers. *Perspectives on Psychological Science, 10*(6), 764–767. https://doi.org/10.1177/1745691615614257

Sunstein, C. R. (2017a). Nudges that fail. *Behavioural Public Policy, 1*(1), 4–25.

Sunstein, C. R. (2017b, September 6). Misconceptions about nudges. *SSRN Electronic Journal*. Retrieved from https://bit.ly/2MB8tuN

Sunstein, C. R., & Reisch, L. A. (2014). Automatically green: Behavioral economics and environmental protection. *Harvard Environmental Law Review, 127*. http://dx.doi.org/10.2139/ssrn.2245657

Sunstein, C. R., Reisch, L. A., & Rauber, J. (2017, January). A world-wide consensus on nudging? Not quite, but almost. *SSRN Electronic Journal*.

Sussman, A. B., & Alter, A. L. (2012). The exception is the rule: Underestimating and overspending on exceptional expenses. *Journal of Consumer Research, 39*(4), 800–814. https://doi.org/10.1086/665833

Sussman, A. B., & O'Brien, R. L. (2016). Knowing when to spend: Unintended financial consequences of earmarking to encourage savings. *Journal of Marketing Research, 53*(5), 790–803.

Sustainable Energy Authority of Ireland [SEAI]. (2018). *Changing energy behaviour – What works?* Retrieved from https://bit.ly/2LzWtEj

Sutherland, W. J., Spiegelhalter, D., & Burgman, M. A. (2013). Twenty tips for interpreting scientific claims. *Nature, 503*(7476), 335–337.

Svenson, O. (1981). Are we all less risky and more skillful than our fellow driver? *Acta Psychologica, 47*(2), 143–148.

Sydney, J., & Fox, S. (2009). Generations online in 2009. *Pew Internet & American Life Project*. Washington, DC: Pew Research Centre.

Taber, C. S., & Lodge, M. (2006). Motivated skepticism in the evaluation of political beliefs. *American Journal of Political Science, 50*(3), 755–769.

Tax and Customs Administration.(2016). *Guide horizontal monitoring tax service providers*. Retrieved from https://bit.ly/2K9xd9I

Taylor, L. C., Clayton, J. D., & Rowley, S. J. (2004). Academic socialization: Understanding parental influences on children's school-related development in the early years. *Review of General Psychology, 8*(3), 163–178.

Taylor, L. C., & Schroeder, R. (2015). Is bigger better? The emergence of Big Data as a tool for international development policy. *GeoJournal, 80*(4), 503–518. https://doi.org/10.1007/s10708-014-9603-5

Taylor, R. L. (2019). Bag leakage: The effect of disposable carryout bag regulations on unregulated bags. *Journal of Environmental Economics and Management, 93*, 254–271.

Teasley, S. D. (2017). Student facing dashboards: One size fits all? *Technology, Knowledge and Learning, 22*(3), 377–384. https://doi.org/10.1007/s10758-017-9314-3

Teng, M. J., Wu, S. Y., & Chou, S. J. H. (2014). Environmental commitment and economic performance – Short-term pain for long-term gain. *Environmental Policy and Governance, 24*(1), 16–27. https://doi.org/10.1002/eet.1634

Tesser, A., & Campbell, J. (1980). Self-definition: The impact of the relative performance and similarity of others. *Social Psychology Quarterly, 43*(3), 341–347.

Tetlock, P. E. (1994). Political psychology or politicized psychology: Is the road to scientific hell paved with good moral intentions? *Political Psychology*, *15*(3), 509–529.
Thackeray, R., Neiger, B. L., Hanson, C. L., & McKenzie, J. F. (2008). Enhancing promotional strategies within social marketing programs: Use of Web 2.0 social media. *Health Promotion Practice*, *9*(4), 338–343. https://doi.org/10.1177/1524839908325335
Thaler, R. H. (1985). Mental accounting and consumer choice. *Marketing Science*, *4*(3), 199–214.
Thaler, R. H. (1999). Mental accounting matters. *Choices, Values, and Frames*, *206*, 241–268.
Thaler, R. H. (2011, September 8). *"Mandate-Schmandate," Rick Perry and the HPV vaccine* [Blog post]. Retrieved from https://bit.ly/2N1qOAx
Thaler, R. H. (2015). *Misbehaving: The making of behavioural economics*. New York: W W Norton & Company.
Thaler, R. H., & Benartzi, S. (2004). Save more tomorrow™: Using behavioral economics to increase employee saving. *Journal of Political Economy*, *112*(S1), S164–S187. https://doi.org/10.1086/380085
Thaler, R. H., & Sunstein, C. R. (2003). Libertarian paternalism. *The American Economic Review*, *93*(2), 175–179. https://doi.org/10.1257/000282803321947001
Thaler, R. H., & Sunstein, C. R. (2008). *Nudge: Improving decisions about health, wealth, and happiness*. London: Penguin Books.
Thaler, R. H., Sunstein, C. R., & Balz, J. P. (2013). Choice architecture. In E. Shafir (Ed.), *The behavioral foundations of public policy*. Princeton, NJ: Princeton University Press.
Thangaratinam, S., & Redman, C. W. (2005), The Delphi technique. *The Obstetrician & Gynaecologist*, *7*, 120–125. https://doi.org/10.1576/toag.7.2.120.27071
Thisgaard, M., & Makransky, G. (2017). Virtual learning simulations in high school: Effects on cognitive and non-cognitive outcomes and implications on the development of STEM academic and career choice. *Frontiers in Psychology*, *8*, 1–13. https://doi.org/10.3389/fpsyg.2017.00805
Thistlethwaite, J., Davies, H., Dornan, T., Greenhalgh, T., Hammick, M., & Scalese, R. (2012). What is evidence? Reflections on the AMEE symposium, Vienna, August 2011. *Medical Teacher*, *34*(6), 454–457.
Thøgersen, J., Jørgensen, A. K., & Sandager, S. (2012). Consumer decision making regarding a "green" everyday product. *Psychology & Marketing*, *29*(4), 187–197. https://doi.org/10.1002/mar.20514
Thomas, L., & Williams, M. (2006). Promoting physical activity in the workplace: Using pedometers to increase daily activity levels. *Health Promotion Journal Of Australia*, *17*(2), 97–102. https://doi.org/10.1071/he06097
Thompson, C. A., & Prottas, D. J. (2006). Relationships among organizational family support, job autonomy, perceived control, and employee well-being. *Journal of Occupational Health Psychology*, *11*(1), 100–118. https://doi.org/10.1037/1076-8998.10.4.100
Thornton, R. L. (2008). The demand for, and impact of, learning HIV status. *The American Economic Review*, *98*(5), 1829–1863. https://doi.org/10.1257/aer.98.5.1829
Thyne, C. L. (2006). ABC's, 123's, and the Golden Rule: The pacifying effect of education on civil war, 1980–1999. *International Studies Quarterly*, *50*(4), 733–754. https://doi.org/10.1111/j.1468-2478.2006.00423.x
Tobler, P. N., Christopoulos, G. I., O'Doherty, J. P., Dolan, R. J., & Schultz, W. (2008). Neuronal distortions of reward probability without choice. *The Journal of Neuroscience*, *28*(45), 11703–11711.

Tod, E., Grant, I., Grant, W., Mesalles-Naranjo, O., Stockton, D., Robinson, M., . . . & Craig, N. (2018). *Hospital admissions, deaths and overall burden of disease attributable to alcohol consumption in Scotland*. Edinburgh: NHS Scotland. Retrieved from https://bit.ly/2MEHWgd

Todd, P. M., & Gigerenzer, G. (2007). Environments that make us smart. *Current Directions in Psychological Science, 16*(3), 167–172.

Torjman, S. (2005). *What is policy*? Ottawa: Caledon Institute of Social Policy.

Tovey, M. (2017). *IEA discussion paper no.80*. Obesity and the Public Purse: Weighting up the True Cost to the Taxpayer. London: Institute of Economic Affairs.

Townsend, T., & Kunimoto, B. (2009). *Capacity, collaboration, and culture: The future of the policy research function in the government of Canada*. Retrieved October 11, 2018 from https://bit.ly/2ynKclx

Trochim, W. M. K. (2009). Evaluation policy and evaluation practice. In W. M. K. Trochim, M. M. Mark, & L. J. Cooksy (Eds.), *Evaluation policy and evaluation practice: New directions for evaluation* (pp. 13–32). New York: John Wiley & Sons.

Trope, Y., & Liberman, N. (2003). Temporal construal. *Psychological Review, 110*(3), 403.

Truelove, H. B., Carrico, A. R., Weber, E. U., Raimi, K. T., & Vandenbergh, M. P. (2014). Positive and negative spillover of pro-environmental behavior: An integrative review and theoretical framework. *Global Environmental Change, 29*, 127–138.

Tucker, C. E. (2014). Social networks, personalized advertising, and privacy controls. *Journal of Marketing Research, 51*(5), 546–562. https://doi.org/10.1509/jmr.10.0355

Turner, V. (1980). Social dramas and stories about them. *Critical Inquiry, 7*(1), 141–168. https://doi.org/10.1086/448092

Turoff, M. (2002). The policy Delphi. In M. Turoff & H. A. Linstone (Eds.), *The Delphi method: Techniques and applications*. Boston, TX: Addison-Wesley Educational Publishers. Retrieved from http://is.njit.edu/pubs/delphibook

Tversky, A., & Kahneman, D. (1973). Availability: A heuristic for judging frequency and probability. *Cognitive Psychology, 5*(2), 207–232.

Tversky, A., & Kahneman, D. (1974). Judgment under uncertainty: Heuristics and biases. *Science, 185*(4157), 1124–1131.

Tversky, A., & Kahneman, D. (1981). The framing of decisions and the psychology of choice. *Science, 211*(4481), 453–458.

Tversky, A., & Kahneman, D. (1985). The framing of decisions and the psychology of choice. In V. T. Covello, J. L. Mumpower, P. J. M. Stallen, & V. R. R. Uppuluri (Eds.), *Environmental impact assessment, technology assessment, and risk analysis: Contributions from the psychological and decision sciences* (pp. 107–129). Berlin: Springer.

Tversky, A., & Kahneman, D. (1986). Rational choice and the framing of decisions. *The Journal of Business, 59*(4), S251–S278. Retrieved May 28, 2021, from http://www.jstor.org/stable/2352759

Tversky, A., & Kahneman, D. (1991). Loss aversion in riskless choice: A reference-dependent model. *The Quarterly Journal of Economics, 106*(4), 1039–1061.

Tversky, A., & Kahneman, D. (1992). Advances in prospect theory – Cumulative representation of uncertainty. *Journal of Risk and Uncertainty, 5*(4), 297–323.

UCAS. (2016). *End of cycle report*. Retrieved from http://bit.ly/2f3f4eC

UNAIDS. (2018). *Global HIV & AIDS statistics – 2018 fact sheet*. Retrieved from https://bit.ly/2aP0STz

UNEG. (2016). *Norms and standards for evaluation*. Retrieved from https://bit.ly/2aiJqZQ

UNESCO. (2011). *Education counts: Toward the millennium development goals*. Paris: UNESCO.
UNESCO. (2014). *Medium-term strategy, 2014–2021*. Paris: UNESCO. Retrieved from https://bit.ly/2Pl9GmF
UNESCO. (2017). *Supporting teachers with mobile technology*. Paris: UNESCO. Retrieved from https://bit.ly/2v0TbG0
UNESCO Institute for Statistics. (2006). *Teachers and educational quality: Monitoring global needs for 2015* (Vol. 253). UNESCO Inst for Statistics.
UNESCO Institute for Statistics. (2018). *School enrollment, tertiary (% gross)*. Retrieved from https://bit.ly/2MXkmdS
UNFPA. (2011). *State of world population report, people and possibilities in a world of 7 billion*. New York: UNFPA.
United Nations. (2018). *World environment day 5 June*. Retrieved from https://bit.ly/2ol8STk
United Nations Development Programme. (2016). *Human development report 2016: Human development for everyone*. Retrieved October 11, 2018 from http://hdr.undp.org/sites/default/files/2016_human_development_report.pdf
United States Department of Justice. (2016). *Advancing diversity in law enforcement*. Retrieved from https://bit.ly/2dJPEjT
United States Environmental Protection Agency. (2012). Agriculture. In *Global anthropogenic non-CO2 greenhouse gas emissions: 1990–2030*. Retrieved on August 28, 2018 from https://bit.ly/2PQJyRG
United States Environmental Protection Agency. (2016). *WaterSense: Types of facilities*. Retrieved from https://bit.ly/2o30MQy
United States Environmental Protection Agency. (2017). *Comparing industry sectors in the 2015 TRI national analysis*. Retrieved from https://bit.ly/2wumQa1
ur Rehman, T. (2016). Historical context of behavioral economics. *Intellectual Economics*, *10*(2), 128–132. https://doi.org/10.1016/j.intele.2017.03.006
U.S. Department of Education. (2019). *Chronic absenteeism in the nation's schools*. Retrieved from www2.ed.gov/datastory/chronicabsenteeism.html#four
Vallgårda, S., Holm, L., & Jensen, J. D. (2015). The Danish tax on saturated fat: Why it did not survive. *European Journal of Clinical Nutrition*, *69*(2), 223–226. https://doi.org/10.1038/ejcn.2014.224
Van Bavel, J. J., Baicker, K., Boggio, P. S., Capraro, V., Cichocka, A., Cikara, M., . . . Willer, R. (2020). Using social and behavioural science to support COVID-19 pandemic response. *Nature Human Behaviour*, *4*(5), 460–471.
Van Boven, L., & Gilovich, T. (2003). To do or to have? That is the question. *Journal of Personality and Social Psychology*, *85*, 1193–1202. https://doi.org/10.1037/0022-3514.85.6.1193
Vandenbroele, J., Slabbinck, H., Van Kerckhove, A., & Vermeir, I. (2019). Mock meat in the butchery: Nudging consumers toward meat substitutes. *Organizational Behavior and Human Decision Processes*. https://doi.org/10.1016/j.obhdp.2019.09.004
van der Berg, S. (2008). How effective are poor schools? Poverty and educational outcomes in South Africa. *Studies in Educational Evaluation*, *34*(3), 145–154. https://doi.org/10.1016/j.stueduc.2008.07.005
van der Linden, S. (2015a). Intrinsic motivation and pro-environmental behaviour. *Nature Climate Change*, *5*(7), 612–613.
van der Linden, S. (2015b). Exploring beliefs about bottled water and intentions to reduce consumption: The dual-effect of social norm activation and persuasive information. *Environment and Behavior*, *47*(5), 526–550.

van der Linden, S. (2017). Determinants and measurement of climate change risk perception, worry, and concern. In M. C. Nisbet (Ed.), *Oxford encyclopedia of climate change communication*. Oxford: Oxford University Press. https://doi.org/10.1093/acrefore/9780190228620.013.318

van der Linden, S. (2018). Warm-glow is associated with low but not high-cost sustainable behaviour. *Nature Sustainability, 1*, 28–30.

van der Linden, S., Leiserowitz, A., Feinberg, G., & Maibach, E. (2014). How to communicate the scientific consensus on climate change: Plain facts, pie charts or metaphors? *Climatic Change, 126*(1–2), 255–262.

van der Linden, S., Maibach, E., & Leiserowitz, A. (2015). Improving public engagement with climate change: Five "best practice" insights from psychological science. *Perspectives on Psychological Science, 10*(6), 758–763.

van der Sluis, M. E., Reezigt, G. J., & Borghans, L. (2017). Implementing new public management in educational policy. *Educational Policy, 31*, 303–329. https://doi.org/10.1177/0895904815598393

van Kamp, I., Leidelmeijer, K., Marsman, G., & de Hollander, A. (2003). Urban environmental quality and human well-being: Towards a conceptual framework and demarcation of concepts: A literature study. *Landscape and Urban Planning, 65*(1), 5–18.

van Klei, W. A., Hoff, R. G., Van Aarnhem, E. E. H. L., Simmermacher, R. K. J., Regli, L. P. E., Kappen, T. H., . . . Peelen, L. M. (2012). Effects of the introduction of the WHO "surgical safety checklist" on in-hospital mortality: A cohort study. *Annals of Surgery, 255*(1), 44–49. https://doi.org/10.1097/SLA.0b013e31823779ae

van Teijlingen, E. R., & Hundley, V. (2001). The importance of pilot studies. *Social Research Update, 35*(35), 1–4.

Venema, T., Kroese, F., & de Ridder, D. (2017). I'm still standing: A longitudinal study on the effect of a default nudge. *Psychology & Health, 33*(5), 669–681. https://doi.org/10.1080/08870446.2017.1385786

Verbič, M., Čok, M., & Sinkovec, D. (2014). Some evidence for implementing an enhanced relationship in Slovenia. *Financial Theory and Practice, 38*(1), 61–80. https://doi.org/10.3326/fintp.38.1.3

Volpp, K. G., Gurmankin Levy, A., Asch, D. A., Berlin, J. A., Murphy, J. J., Gomez, A., . . . & Lerman, C. (2006). A randomized controlled trial of financial incentives for smoking cessation. *Cancer Epidemiology, Biomarkers & Prevention, 15*(1), 12–18.

Volpp, K. G., John, L. K., Troxel, A. B., Norton, L., Fassbender, J., & Loewenstein, G. (2008). Financial incentive-based approaches for weight loss: A randomized trial. *JAMA, 300*(22), 2631–2637. https://doi.org/10.1001/jama.2008.804

Volpp, K. G., Troxel, A., Pauly, M., Glick, H., Puig, A., Asch, D., . . . & Audrain-McGovern, J. (2009). A randomized controlled trial of financial incentives for smoking cessation. *Journal of Vascular Surgery, 49*(5), 1358–1359.

von Neumann, J., & Morgenstern, O. (2007). *Theory of games and economic behavior*. Princeton, NJ: Princeton University Press. (Original work published 1944)

von Winterfeldt, D. (2013). Bridging the gap between science and decision making. *Proceedings of the National Academy of Sciences, 110*(Suppl. 3), 14055–14061.

Vugt, M., Griskevicius, V., & Schultz, P. (2014). Naturally green: Harnessing stone age psychological biases to foster environmental behavior. *Social Issues and Policy Review, 8*(1), 1–32.

Vugts, A., van den Hoven, M., de Vet, E., & Verweij, M. (2018). How autonomy is understood in discussion on the ethics of nudging. *Behavioural Public Policy*, 1–16. https://doi.org/10.1017/bpp.2018.5

Waarden, F. (1992). Dimensions and types of policy networks. *European Journal of Political Research, 21*(1–2), 29–52. https://doi.org/10.1111/j.1475-6765.1992.tb00287.x
Walker, I., & Zhu, Y. (2013). *The impact of university degrees on the lifecycle of earnings: Some further analysis.* London: Department for Business, Innovation & Skills. Retrieved from http://bit.ly/2sszMcB
Wallstedt, H., & Maeurer, M. (2015). The history of tuberculosis management in Sweden. *International Journal of Infectious Diseases, 32*, 179–182. https://doi.org/10.1016/j.ijid.2015.01.018
Walther, J. B., DeAndrea, D., Kim, J., & Anthony, J. C. (2010). The influence of online comments on perceptions of antimarijuana public service announcements on YouTube. *Human Communication Research, 36*(4), 469–492. https://doi.org/10.1111/j.1468-2958.2010.01384.x
Waterman, R. W., & Wood, B. D. (1993). Policy monitoring and policy analysis. *Journal of Policy Analysis and Management, 12*(4), 685–699.
Webb, T. L., Chang, B. P. I., & Benn, Y. (2013). "The ostrich problem": Motivated avoidance or rejection of information about goal progress. *Social and Personality Psychology Compass, 7*(11), 794–807. https://doi.org/10.1111/spc3.12071
Weber, E. U. (2013). Doing the right thing willingly: Behavioral decision theory and environmental policy. In E. Shafir (Ed.), *The behavioral foundations of policy* (pp. 380–397). Princeton, NJ: Princeton University Press.
Weber, E. U. (2015). Climate change demands behavioral change: What are the challenges? *Social Research: An International Quarterly, 82*(3), 561–580.
Wehrens, R., Bekker, M., & Bal, R. (2011). Coordination of research, policy and practice: A case study of collaboration in the field of public health. *Science and Public Policy, 38*(10), 755–766. https://doi.org/10.1093/spp/38.10.755
Weisbach, D., & Sunstein, C. R. (2008). Climate change and discounting the future: A guide for the perplexed. *Yale Law & Policy Review, 27*, 433. https://doi.org/10.2139/ssrn.1223448
Welsh Government. (2016, 6 October). *Single-use carrier bags.* Retrieved from https://bit.ly/2wyz4hd
Wentzel, K. R., Russell, S., & Baker, S. (2016). Emotional support and expectations from parents, teachers, and peers predict adolescent competence at school. *Journal of Educational Psychology, 108*(2), 242–255. https://doi.org/10.1037/edu0000049
Werner-Seidler, A., Perry, Y., & Christensen, H. (2016). An Australian example of translating psychological research into practice and policy: Where we are and where we need to go. *Frontiers in Psychology, 7*(200). https://doi.org/10.3389/fpsyg.2016.00200
Whillans, A. V., Dunn, E. W., Smeets, P., Bekkers, R., & Norton, M. I. (2017). Buying time promotes happiness. *Proceedings of the National Academy of Sciences, 114*(32), 8523–8527. https://doi.org/10.1073/pnas.1706541114
White, T. B., Zahay, D. L., Thorbjørnsen, H., & Shavitt, S. (2008). Getting too personal: Reactance to highly personalized email solicitations. *Marketing Letters, 19*(1), 39–50. https://doi.org/10.1007/s11002-007-9027-9
Whitehead, M., Jones, R., Howell, R., Lilley, R., & Pykett, J. (2014). *Nudging all over the world.* ESRC Report, Swindon and Edinburgh: Economic and Social Research Council.
Whitmarsh, L. (2011). Scepticism and uncertainty about climate change: Dimensions, determinants and change over time. *Global Environmental Change, 21*(2), 690–700. https://doi.org/10.1016/j.gloenvcha.2011.01.016

Whitty, C. J. M. (2015). What makes an academic paper useful for health policy? *BMC Medicine, 13*(1), 301. https://doi.org/10.1186/s12916-015-0544-8
Wigfield, A., & Cambria, J. (2010). Expectancy-value theory: Retrospective and prospective. In *The decade ahead: Theoretical perspectives on motivation and achievement* (pp. 35–70). Bingley: Emerald Group Publishing Limited.
Wikipedia Contributors. (2019, August 31). Phase-out of light plastic bags use. In *Wikipedia, the free encyclopedia*. Retrieved 15:54, August 31, 2019 from https://en.wikipedia.org/wiki/Phase-out_of_lightweight_plastic_bags
Wilcoxen, S., & Tregebov, S. (2018). *Encouraging retirement planning through behavioural insight*. The Behavioural Insights team. Retrieved from https://bit.ly/2Ol7iMq
Wilkinson, L., & Task Force on Statistical Inference. (1999). Statistical methods in psychology journals: Guidelines and explanations. *American Psychologist, 54*(8), 594–604. https://doi.org/10.1037/0003-066X.54.8.594
Wilks, S., Mortimer, M., & Nylén, P. (2006). The introduction of sit – Stand worktables; aspects of attitudes, compliance and satisfaction. *Applied Ergonomics, 37*(3), 359–365. https://doi.org/10.1016/j.apergo.2005.06.007
Wing, C., Simon, K., & Bello-Gomez, R. A. (2018). Designing difference in difference studies: Best practices for public health policy research. *Annual Review of Public Health, 39*(1), 453–469. https://doi.org/10.1146/annurev-publhealth-040617-013507
Wolch, J. R., Byrne, J., & Newell, J. P. (2014). Urban green space, public health, and environmental justice: The challenge of making cities "just green enough". *Landscape and Urban Planning, 125*, 234–244. https://doi.org/10.1016/j.landurbplan.2014.01.017
Woolf, S. H., Purnell, J. Q., Simon, S. M., Zimmerman, E. B., Camberos, G. J., Haley, A., & Fields, R. P. (2015). Translating evidence into population health improvement: Strategies and barriers. *Annual Review of Public Health, 36*, 463–482. https://doi.org/10.1146/annurev-publhealth-082214-110901
World Bank. (2017). *Energy and environment*. Retrieved from https://bit.ly/2Nv6wwb
World Bank Group. (2015). *World development report 2015: Mind, society and behavior*.
World Economic Forum. (2017). *The global risks report*. Retrieved from www.weforum.org/reports/the-global-risks-report-2011
World Health Organization (WHO). (2001). *The world health report 2001, mental health: New understanding, new hope*. Geneva: World Health Organization.
World Health Organization (WHO). (2003a). *Diet, nutrition and the prevention of chronic diseases*. Geneva: World Health Organization. Retrieved from https://bit.ly/2N5qHUu
World Health Organization (WHO). (2003b). *Adherence to long-term therapies: Evidence for action*. Geneva: World Health Organization. Retrieved from https://bit.ly/2ElL9IH
World Health Organization (WHO). (2005). The Bangkok Charter for health promotion in a globalized world. *Health Promotion Journal of Australia, 16*(3), 168.
World Health Organization (WHO). (2006). *The global need for safe blood*. Retrieved from: https://www.who.int/worldblooddonorday/campaignkit/WBDD_GlobalNeed_English.pdf
World Health Organization (WHO). (2007). *Monitoring and evaluation of mental health policies and plans*. Geneva: World Health Organization, Mental Health Policies and Service Guidance Package.
World Health Organization (WHO). (2009). *Global health risks: Mortality and burden of disease attributable to selected major risks*. Geneva: World Health Organization.
World Health Organization (WHO). (2010). *Global recommendations on physical activity for health*. Geneva: World Health Organization.

World Health Organization (WHO). (2013). *Global vaccine action plan 2011–2020*. Geneva: World Health Organization.
World Health Organization (WHO). (2014a). *Health in all policies: Helsinki statement. Framework for country action*. Geneva: World Health Organization.
World Health Organization (WHO). (2014b). *Disseminating the research findings*. Geneva: WHO Document Production Services.
World Health Organization (WHO). (2016). *Children: Reducing mortality*. Retrieved from www.who.int/news-room/fact-sheets/detail/children-reducing-mortality
World Health Organization (WHO). (2017a). *Health promotion and disease prevention through population-based interventions, including action to address social determinants and health inequity*. Geneva: World Health Organization. Retrieved from https://bit.ly/2dL2nXM
World Health Organization (WHO). (2017b). *Obesity and overweight*. Geneva: World Health Organization. Retrieved from www.who.int/mediacentre/factsheets/fs311/en
World Health Organization (WHO). (2017c). *Global tuberculosis report 2017*. Geneva, Switzerland: WHO. Retrieved from https://bit.ly/2PRdBbV
World Health Organization (WHO). (2017d). *Prevalence of obesity among adults*. Geneva: World Health Organization. Retrieved from https://bit.ly/2RINy9B
Wyer, R. S. (2004). *Social comprehension and judgment: The role of situation models, narratives, and implicit theories*. Mahwah, NJ: Lawrence Erlbaum Associates.
Xanthos, D., & Walker, T. R. (2017). International policies to reduce plastic marine pollution from single plastics (plastic bags and microbeads): A review. *Marine Pollution Bulletin, 118*(1–2), 17–26. https://doi.org/10.1016/j.marpolbul.2017.02.048
Xu, L., & Zia, B. (2012). Financial literacy around the world: An overview of the evidence with practical suggestions for the way forward. *Policy Research Working Paper, 6107*, 1–56. https://doi.org/10.3102/00346543067001043
Ybarra, M. L., Jiang, Y., Free, C., Abroms, L. C., & Whittaker, R. (2016). Participant-level meta-analysis of mobile phone-based interventions for smoking cessation across different countries. *Preventive Medicine, 89*, 90–97. https://doi.org/10.1016/j.ypmed.2016.05.002
Ybema, J., Smulders, P., & Bongers, P. (2010). Antecedents and consequences of employee absenteeism: A longitudinal perspective on the role of job satisfaction and burnout. *European Journal of Work and Organizational Psychology, 19*(1), 102–124. https://doi.org/10.1080/13594320902793691
Yeager, D. S., & Walton, G. M. (2011). Social-psychological interventions in education: They're not magic. *Review of Educational Research, 81*(2), 267–301. https://doi.org/10.3102/0034654311405999
Yeomans, M., & Reich, J. (2017). Planning prompts increase and forecast course completion in massive open online courses. *Proceedings of the Seventh International Learning Analytics & Knowledge Conference*, 464–473. https://doi.org/10.1145/3027385.3027416
Yoeli, E., Hoffman, M., Rand, D. G., & Nowak, M. A. (2013). Powering up with indirect reciprocity in a large-scale field experiment. *Proceedings of the National Academy of Sciences, 110*, 10424–10429. https://doi.org/10.1073/pnas.1301210110
Yoon, E., Babar, A., Choudhary, M., Kutner, M., & Pyrsopoulos, N. (2016). Review article acetaminophen-induced hepatotoxicity: A comprehensive update. *Journal of Clinical and Translational Hepatology, 4*, 131–142. https://doi.org/10.14218/JCTH.2015.00052

York, B. N., Loeb, S., & Doss, C. (2018). One step at a time: The effects of an early literacy text messaging program for parents of preschoolers. *The Journal of Human Resources*, 0517–8756R. https://doi.org/10.3368/jhr.54.3.0517-8756R

Young, S. (2014, November). Behavioral insights on big data: Using social media for predicting biomedical outcomes. *Trends in Microbiology*, *22*(11), 601–602.

Yuenyongchaiwat, K. (2016). Effects of 10,000 steps a day on physical and mental health in overweight participants in a community setting: A preliminary study. *Brazilian Journal of Physical Therapy*, *20*(4), 367–373. https://doi.org/10.1590/bjpt-rbf.2014.0160

Zabrucky, K. M., & Moore, D. (1999). Influence of text genre on adults' monitoring of understanding and recall. *Educational Gerontology*, *25*(8), 691–710. https://doi.org/10.1080/036012799267440

Zarcadoolas, C. (2010). The simplicity complex: Exploring simplified health messages in a complex world. *Health Promotion International*, *26*(3), 338–350. https://doi.org/10.1093/heapro/daq075

Zhu, S. H., Melcer, T., Sun, J., Rosbrook, B., & Pierce, J. P. (2000). Smoking cessation with and without assistance: A population-based analysis. *American Journal of Preventive Medicine*, *18*(4), 305–311. https://doi.org/10.1016/S0749-3797(00)00124-0

Zillmann, D. (2006). Exemplification effects in the promotion of safety and health. *Journal of Communication*, *56*(s1), 221–237. https://doi.org/10.1111/j.1460-2466.2006.00291.x

Zuiderwijk, A., & Janssen, M. (2014). Open data policies, their implementation and impact: A framework for comparison. *Government Information Quarterly*, *31*(1), 17–29. https://doi.org/10.1016/j.giq.2013.04.003

Zupan, Z., Evans, A., Couturier, D. L., & Marteau, T. M. (2017). Wine glass size in England from 1700 to 2017: A measure of our time. *BMJ (Online)*, *359*, 1–5. https://doi.org/10.1136/bmj.j5623

Zurovac, D., Talisuna, A. O., & Snow, R. W. (2012). Mobile phone text messaging: Tool for malaria control in Africa. *PLoS Medicine*, *9*(2), e1001176. https://doi.org/10.1371/journal.pmed.10011

Index

Page numbers in *italic* indicate a figure and page numbers in **bold** indicate a table on the corresponding page.